AF262966

PLENTY FOR ALL

The Art of Rick Fröberg

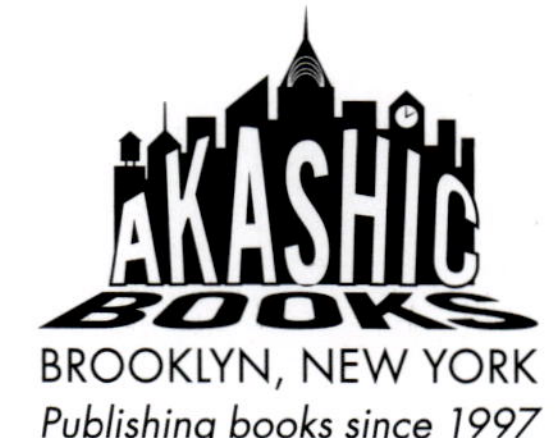

BROOKLYN, NEW YORK
Publishing books since 1997

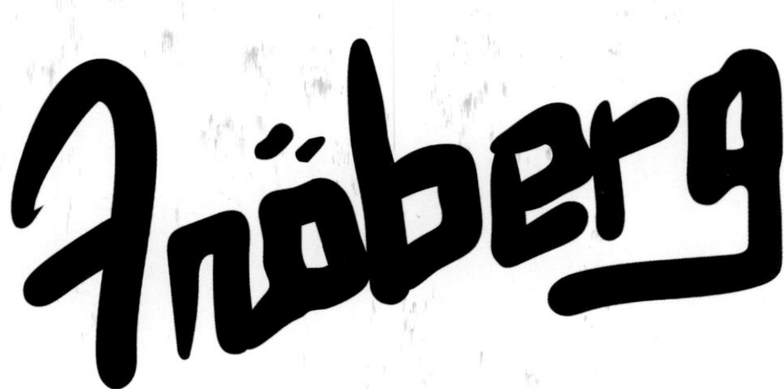

Some readers might notice that the specs for Rick's artwork—dimensions, titles, mediums, etc.—are not included here. Because the images were sourced from a variety of people and places, there was a great deal of missing information, so we opted for omission rather than providing incomplete information.

Published by Akashic Books
Art ©2025 Estate of Eric Farr
Introduction ©2025 Rich Jacobs
Afterword ©2025 Sohrab Habibion

Art Direction & Curation: Rich Jacobs
Layout & Design: Sohrab Habibion

Archival & Editing Assistance: Britton Neubacher
Administrative & Archival Assistance: Gabriel Voiles
Layout & Technical Assistance: Nick Sewell
Photography & Layout Assistance: Alexis Fleisig
Technical & Archival Assistance: Ryan Corey
Archival Assistance: Rob Crow & Pall Jenkins

ISBN: 978-1-63614-267-8
Library of Congress Control Number: 2025941268

First Printing
Printed in China

EU Authorized Representative Details:
Easy Access System Europe
Mustamäe tee 50, 10621 Tallinn, Estonia
gpsr.request@easproject.com

Akashic Books
Instagram, X, Facebook: AkashicBooks
info@akashicbooks.com
www.akashicbooks.com

Table of Contents

Introduction

Rick Fröberg was an extraordinary and busy human for fifty-five years; a creative giant who made art and music with equal devotion. He spent decades as a front man and guitarist in several well-respected and iconic bands while pushing out equally vital, urgent, and gripping expression through his visual art—graphics and illustrations that grace album covers and promotional materials—but he did not stop there. Starting when he was old enough to use a pencil, Rick built up a formidable archive of visual art spanning various eras, mediums, and moods. Many people know him in this context, but not enough. It is the hope that this book will expand that influence and show that he had a very large impact, igniting visual inspiration in much the same way as his music did—music often made with partner in crime John Reis.

Rick Fröberg was born in Southern California and lived in San Diego for much of his early life, where he became an artist, musician, and leading member of a fertile creative community. Rick saw that things could be different—less violent and more interesting—and that he and his friends could and should be heard. Luckily for all of us, he was right. He left California to live in New York for the second half of his creative life. He wasted little time establishing his efforts there, exploring new tools such as computers and digital means to expand his work. He enjoyed a stint at the Funny Garbage design studio, learning Flash animation in the early-adoption stages, and getting to work with artist Gary Panter. Rick's designs would gain recognition in circles outside of his own, prompting many of the bands he would meet on tour to hire him for their album covers, shirts, and logo designs. As his web of output greatly expanded all over the globe, he was invited to do illustrations for several books and publications, including the *New Yorker* and the *New York Times*. This helped spread his reputation and gave people more access to his work.

During lulls in musical activity, Rick had a couple of solo shows and participated in group exhibitions. He was prolific in his production, but like many other artists, he didn't focus a lot of his energy worrying about the "art world"; he focused on making great work and always trying to improve it. He led with sincerity and maintained an incredible curiosity that drove him to keep learning, allowing others to clearly see what he was experiencing and doing through his vivid line work—which was a progression in and of itself. We hope you can see the growth, maturity, and sophistication of his line development through time. It is an important element in his art practice.

Rick sat in on college art courses, visited libraries, went to the zoo to draw animals and to museums to practice the classics. His curiosity and hunger led him to take etching classes, to learn how to blow glass and carve wood and garden, and to teach himself Spanish. He had an infectious passion for knowledge and learning. I would like to express my gratitude to him . . . for his friendship, example, and inspiration. This is something he likely had with many people—I am not unique that way. He loved his friends all over the world and did not like it when people tried to limit his fun or control him. Who does?

I worked with Rick during his early San Diego period by asking him to be in art shows I was hosting in Los Angeles, often at New Image Art in West Hollywood—run by Marsea Goldberg. These early shows were during a time when he needed some help getting his work out into the world, and I feel so honored and humbled to have played a small role in that. We had quite a few shows together, and that continued when we both moved to New York. He and I would go see exhibitions, draw, and have Thanksgiving together. He attended my wedding. As fellow artists and friends, we pushed each other to try harder and do more stuff.

I loved Rick's humor, sarcasm, and wit. He was sharp, funny, and . . . complex. Visually, there were lots of eras and we tried to capture that here with the different sections in the book. Sometimes these overlapped, just like they did with his music. There was a lot happening—at all times. The way Rick worked changed over time, including his use of computers. He was such an excellent drawer from nearly the outset, and that is what attracted me to his work. With this monograph, I want others to be able to see what I did as a young curator and now as the art director for this volume.

This is a labor of beyond just love; it's one also of respect, appreciation, and the desire for you all to see what he saw and felt while processing his life circumstances. It feels massive. He struck a very interesting balance that few can achieve, equally pouring his heart and guts into visual art and music—his chosen forms of self-expression. Even if you're already familiar with his music and his art, I hope you further explore them both. Together they tell the complete story.

There is so much love, generosity, sincere kindness, and heartfelt emotion in Rick's world. We hope you can draw upon the spirit of this and carry it forward in your lives . . . make more of it in your own way. There is absolutely no doubt that this is what he would be doing if he were here still. In honor of Rick, let's all take the time to do just that.

—Rich Jacobs

I, Rick Fröberg, was born in Santa Monica, California, on the nineteenth of January, 1968. I've been drawing since I could hold a pencil and still do. I've always considered myself an illustrator and not an artist—a day's work for a day's pay and all that. I've held many art-related jobs which I will not bore you (or myself) with here, and I've had illustrations in many books and publications, some well known, some not.

I found a place for my work in the 1980s drawing and designing flyers, advertisements, posters, and packaging for various punk rock/rock 'n' roll–related events and products, much of which took place or were generated in San Diego. Later, I moved to New York City and continued working in the same vein. I did other, more serious work there as well.

I am also something of a musician. I was a member of Crash Worship, Pitchfork, Drive Like Jehu, Hot Snakes, and Obits. You may have heard of some of them. If not, no big deal, but it does help explain my chosen genre.

Much of the artwork I'm associated with was part of a Great Movement in the Arts and in Culture here in San Diego beginning in the late '80s. Those who were there know of what I speak. Those who were not were either too young or not sufficiently blessed with the vision and passion that we were. That's okay. We aren't looking down our noses at you or sneering at you. Our Transcendent Spirit of Grace and Inclusion knows no bounds. You are in a safe space. Feel free to buy something.

You may notice that some of these pieces are somewhat cruddy. Also okay. That was, and is, the intention of the artist. We were not looking for professionalism and the art reflects that. Direct strokes, not masterstrokes. I prefer Keith Richards to Kenny Wayne Shepherd and Charles E. Burchfield to William-Adolphe Bouguereau. I also like instant gratification or the nearest thing available. I am not alone in this sentiment and this gives me great comfort.

Thank you in advance for your praise and patronage.

Yours (for a price),
Rick Fröberg

[Rick wrote this "quick-biography" to accompany his 2022 exhibit Rick Fröberg—Let My People Go, *at Melody Jean Moulton's Trash Lamb Gallery in San Diego. It has been lightly edited.]*

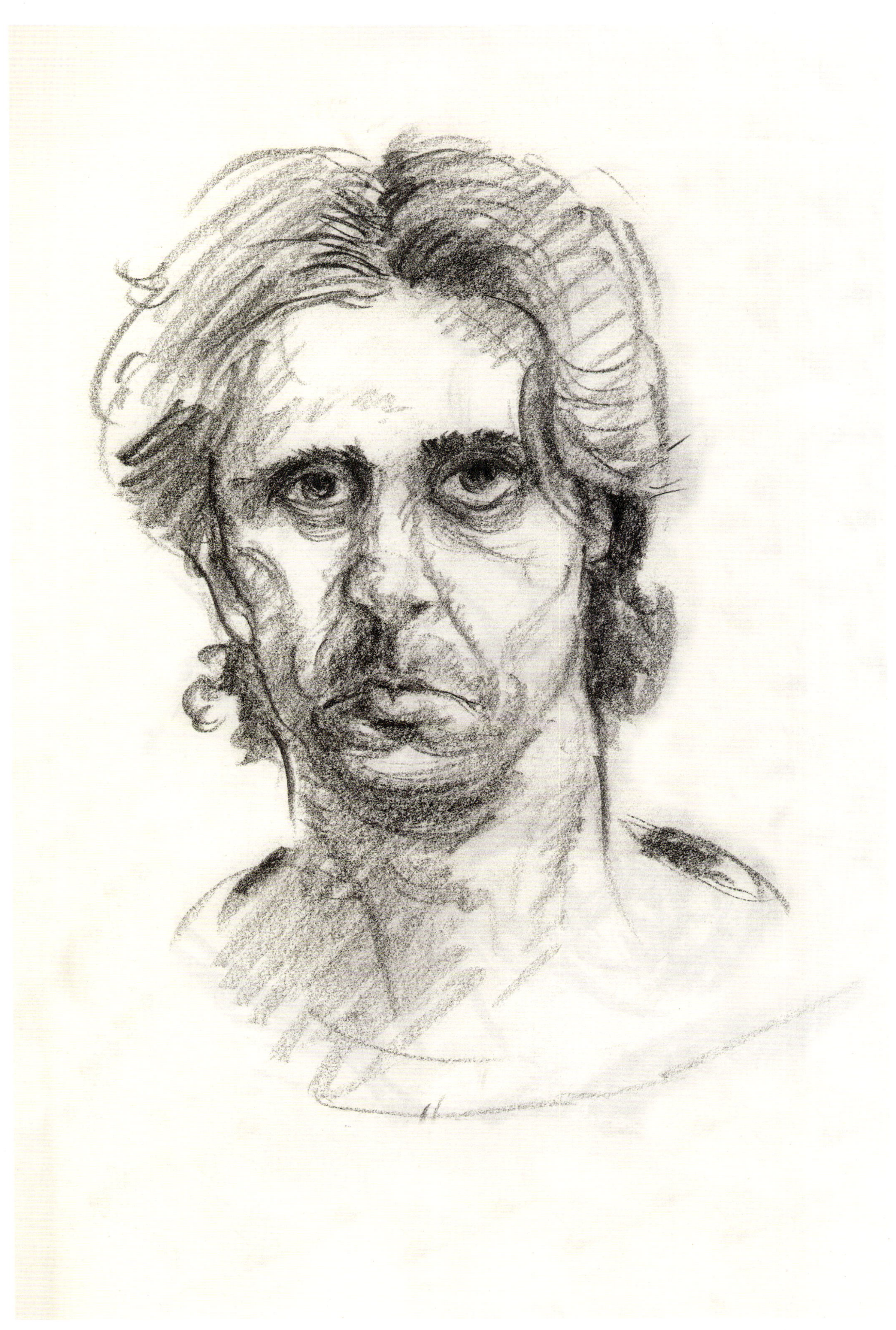

ONE

Pencils, Pens, and Brushes

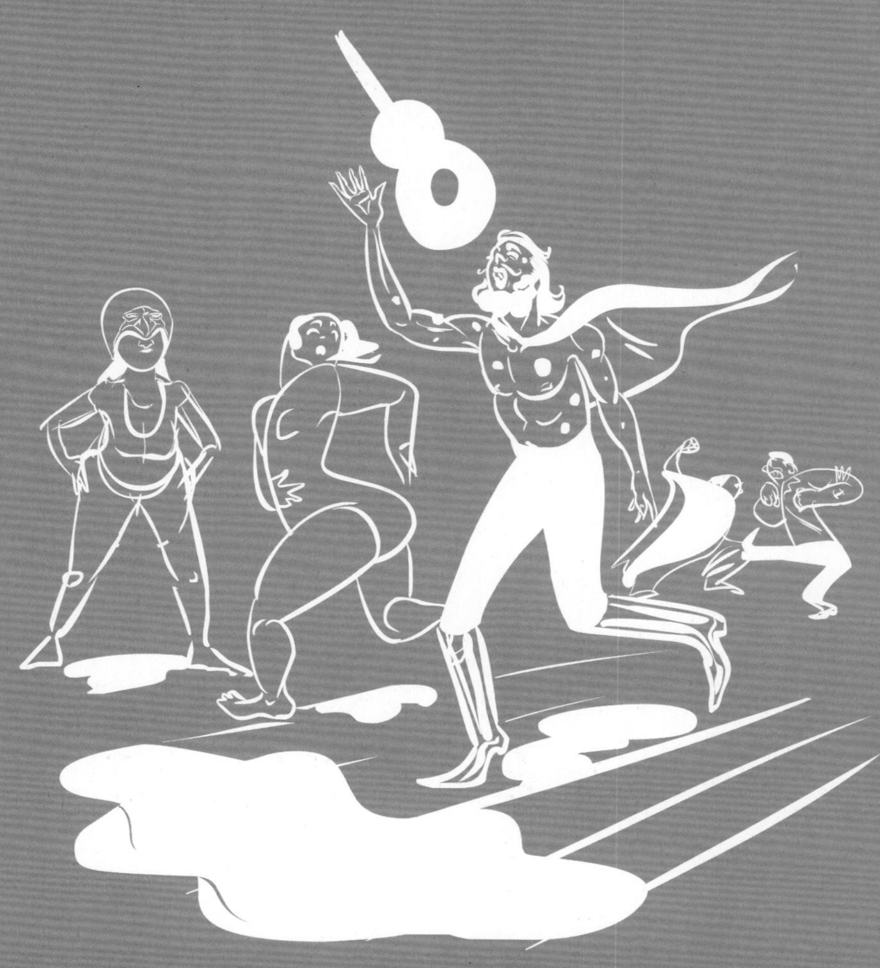

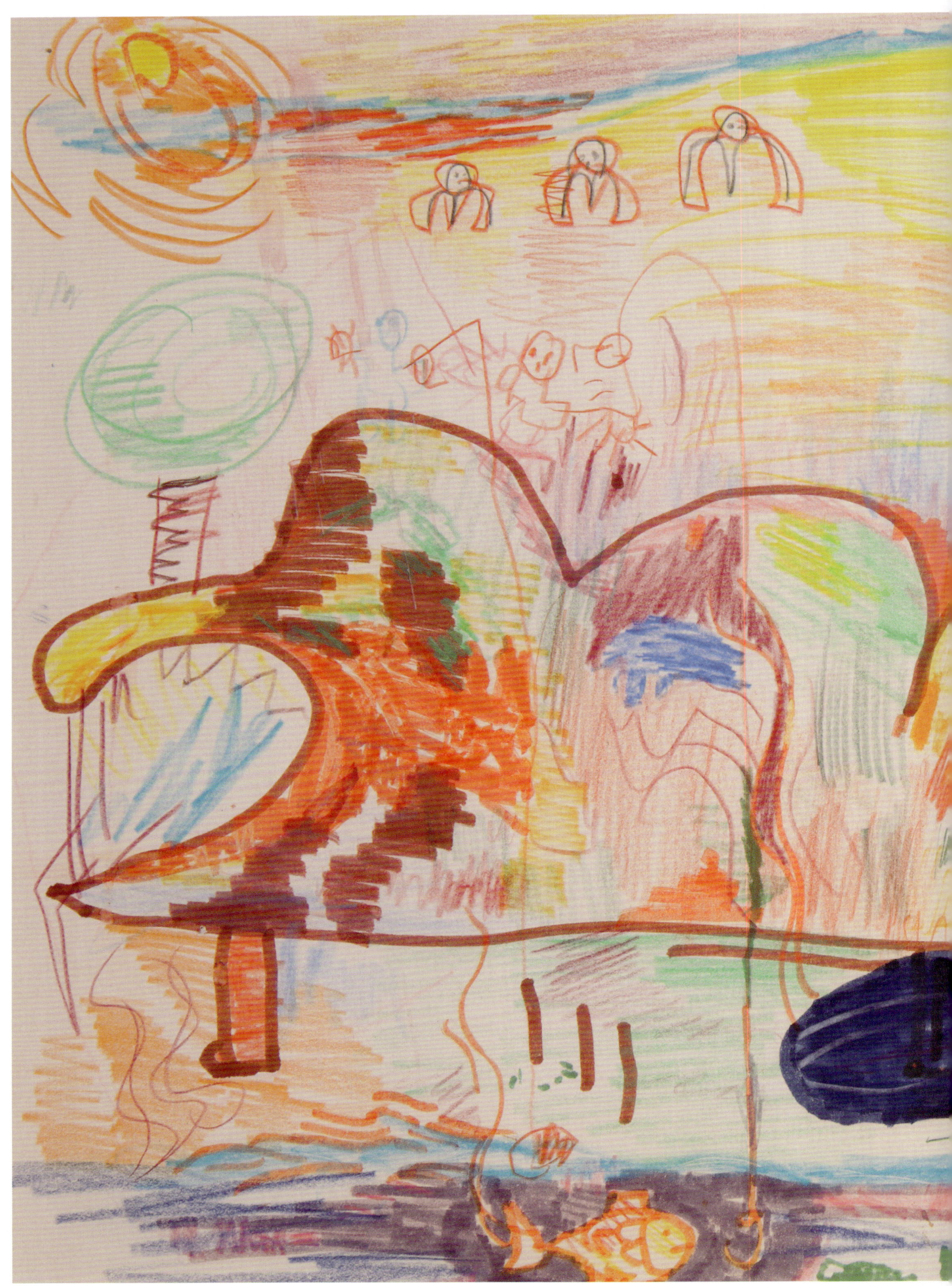

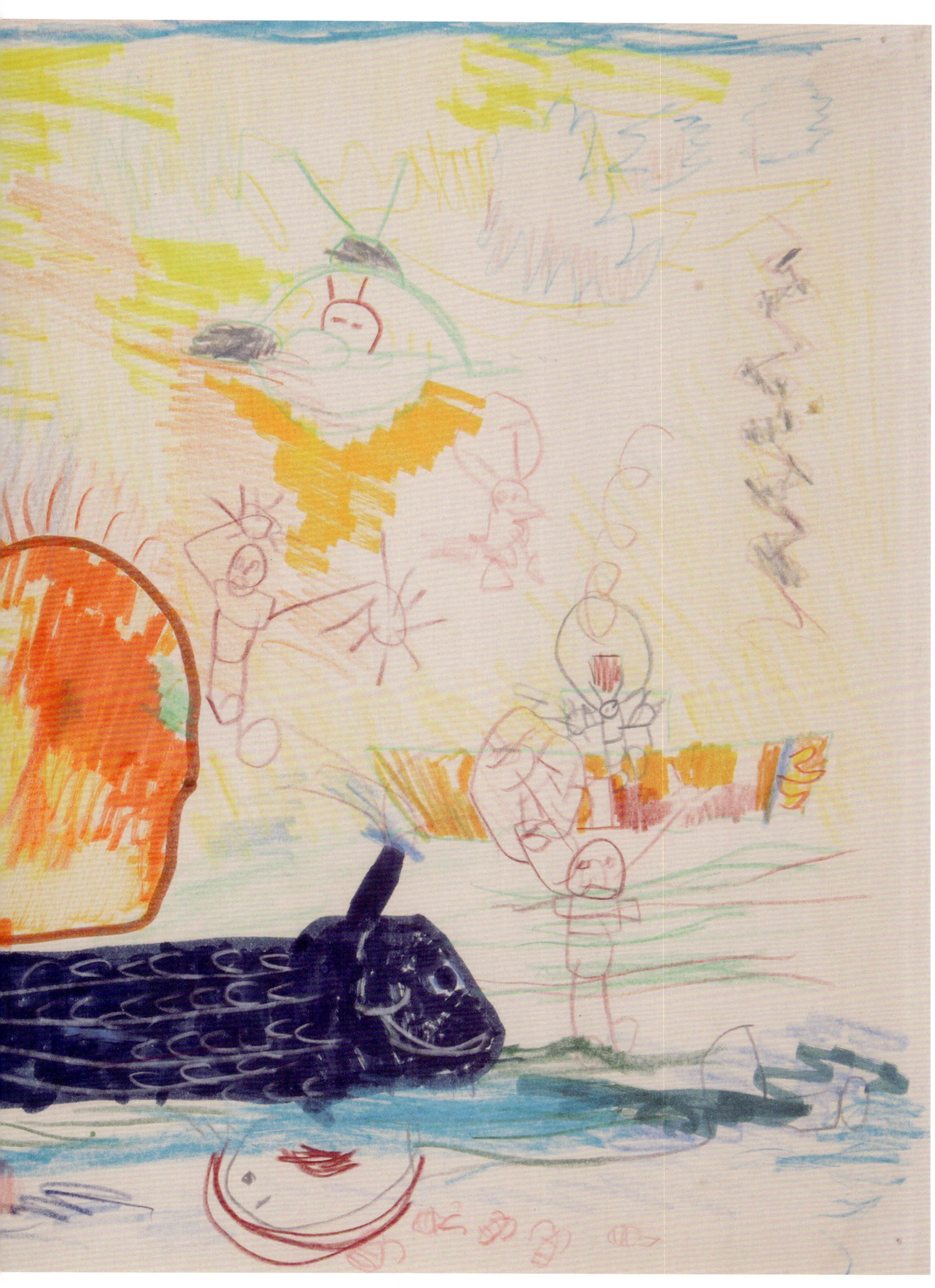

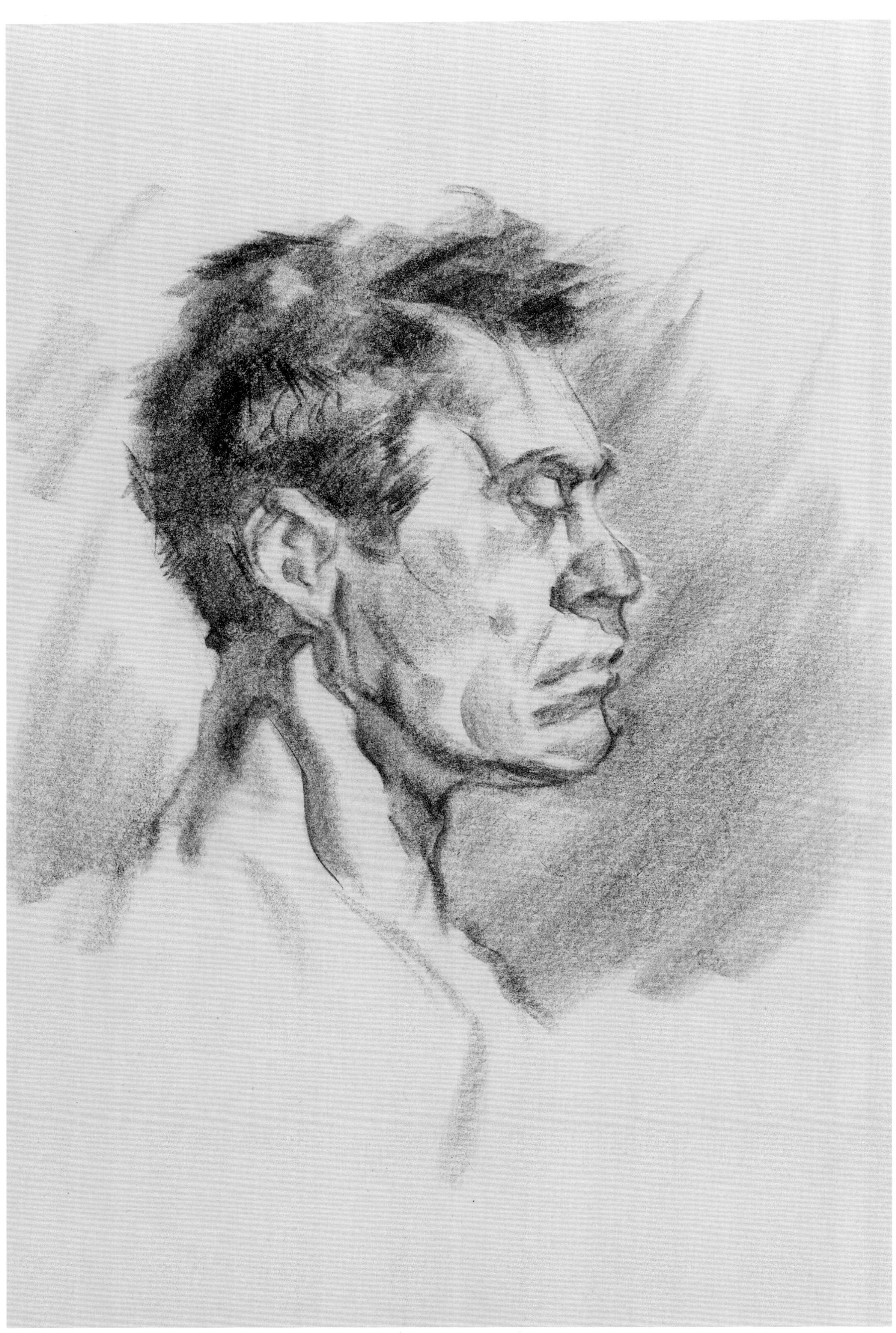

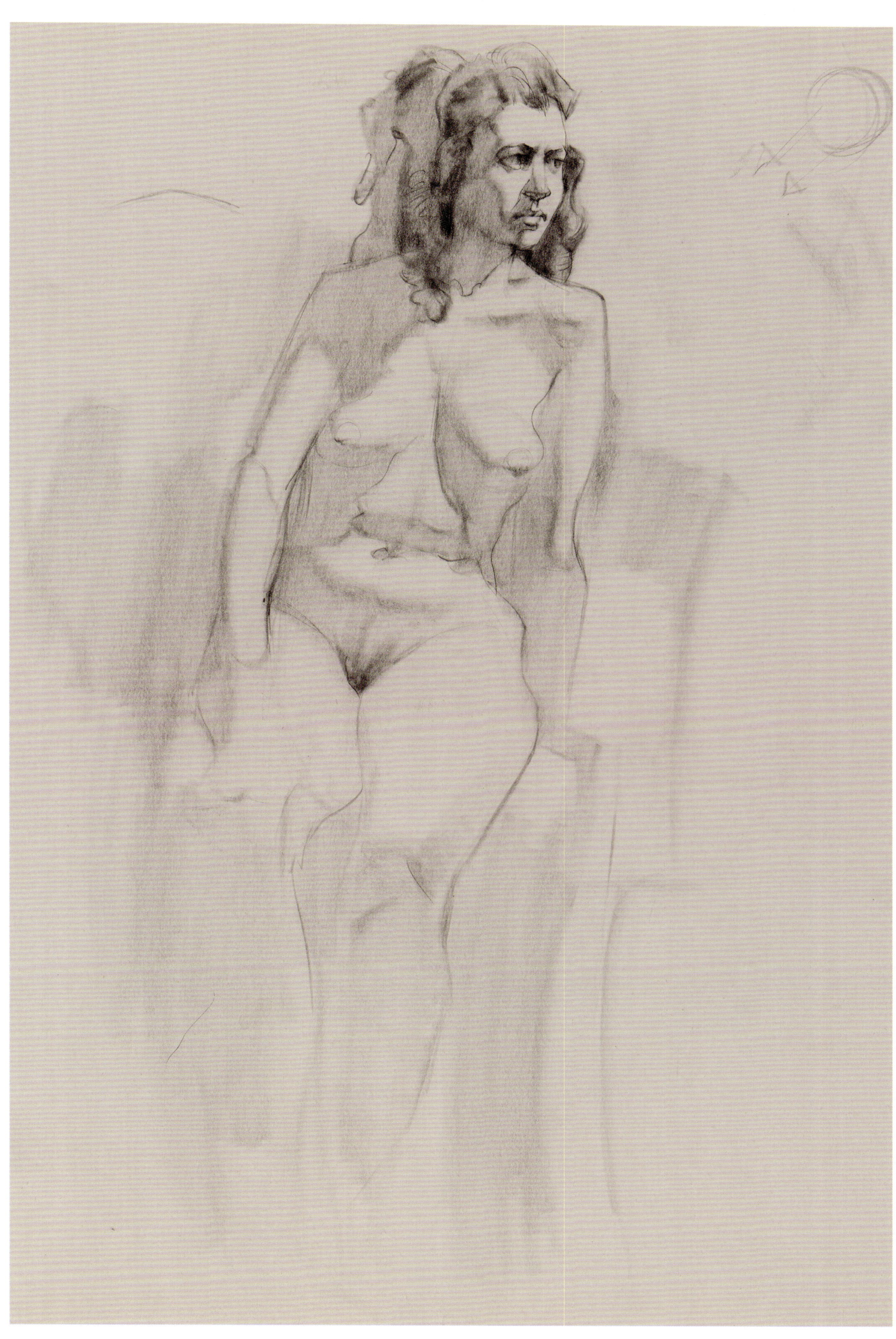

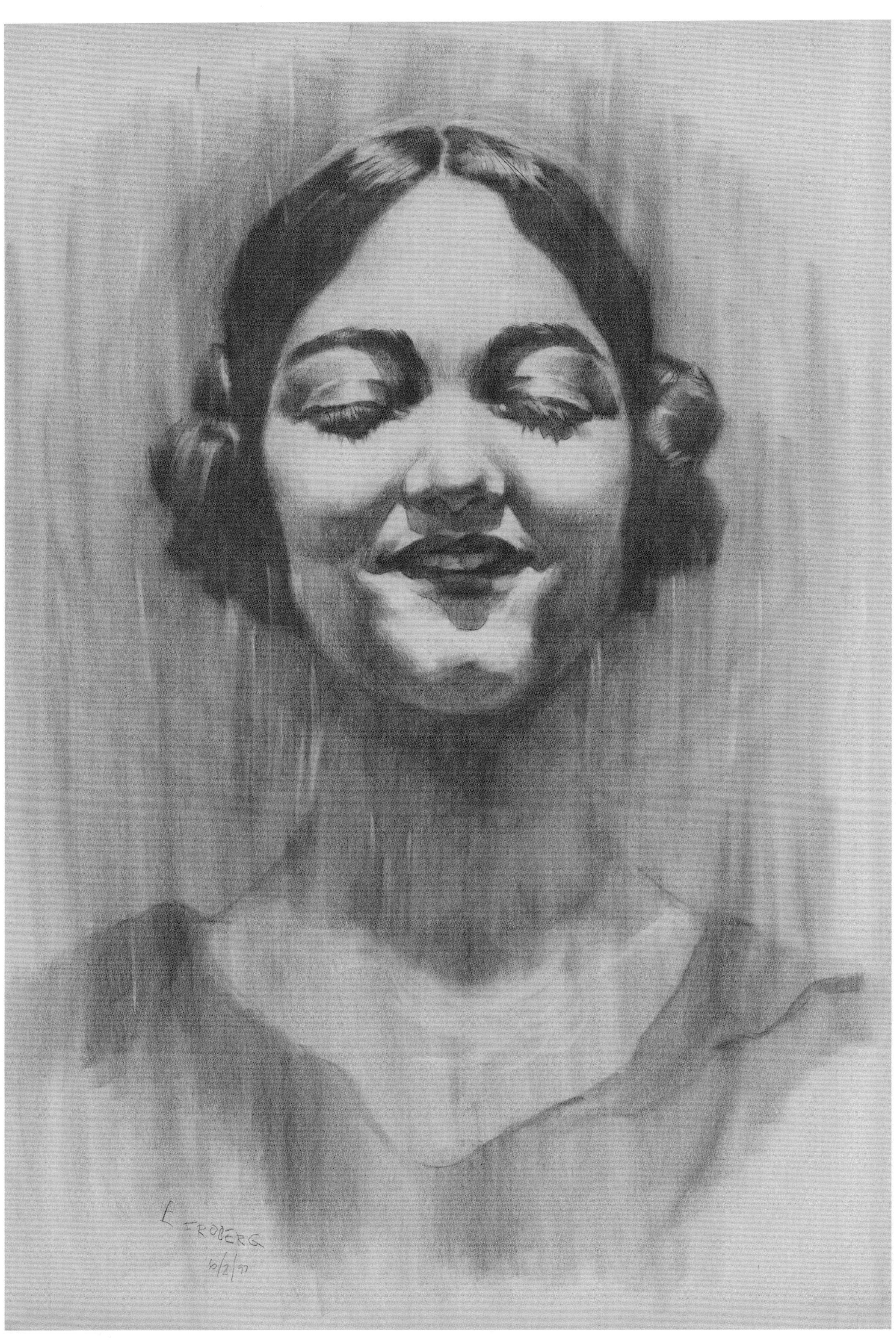
E. FROBERG
10/2/97

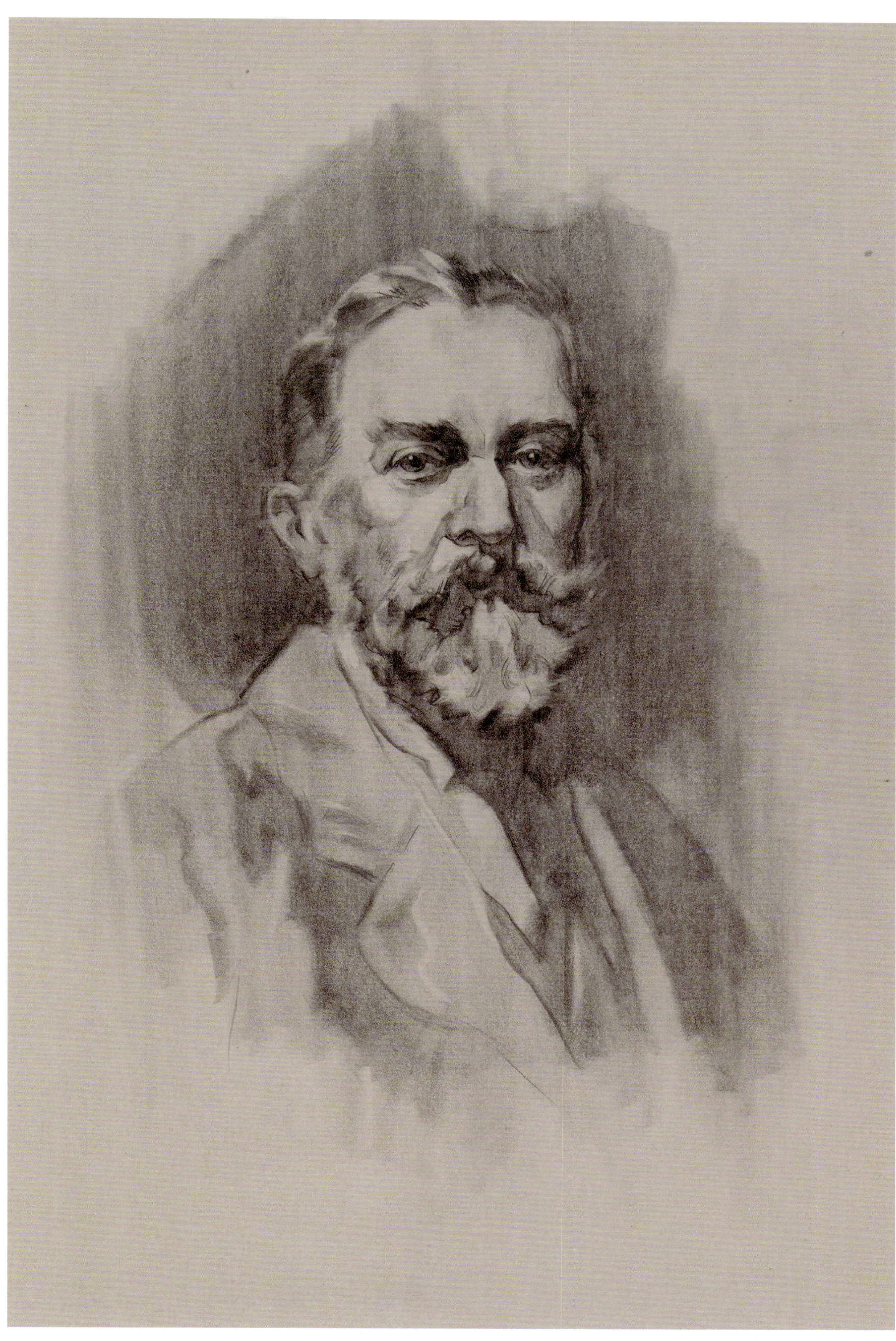

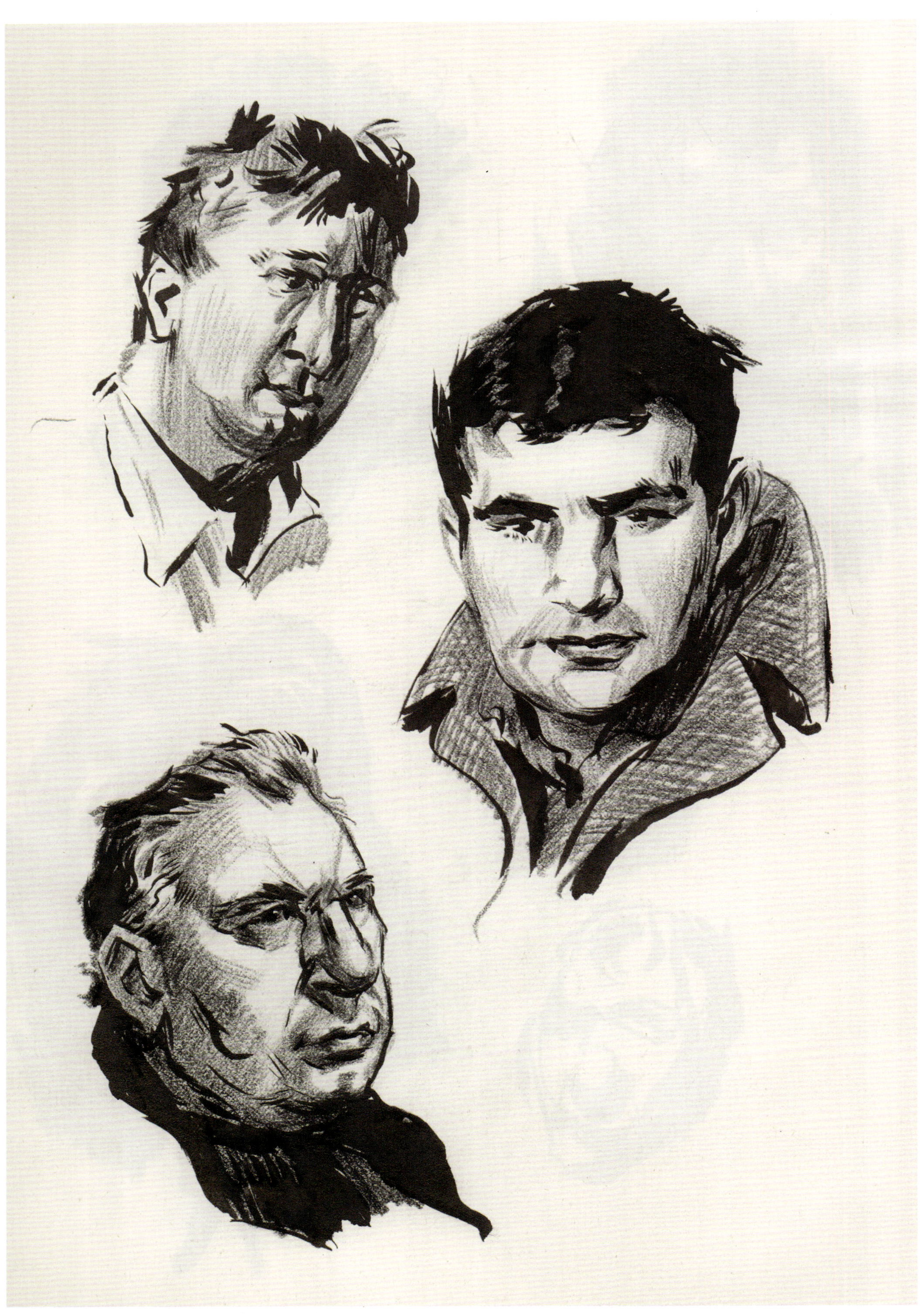

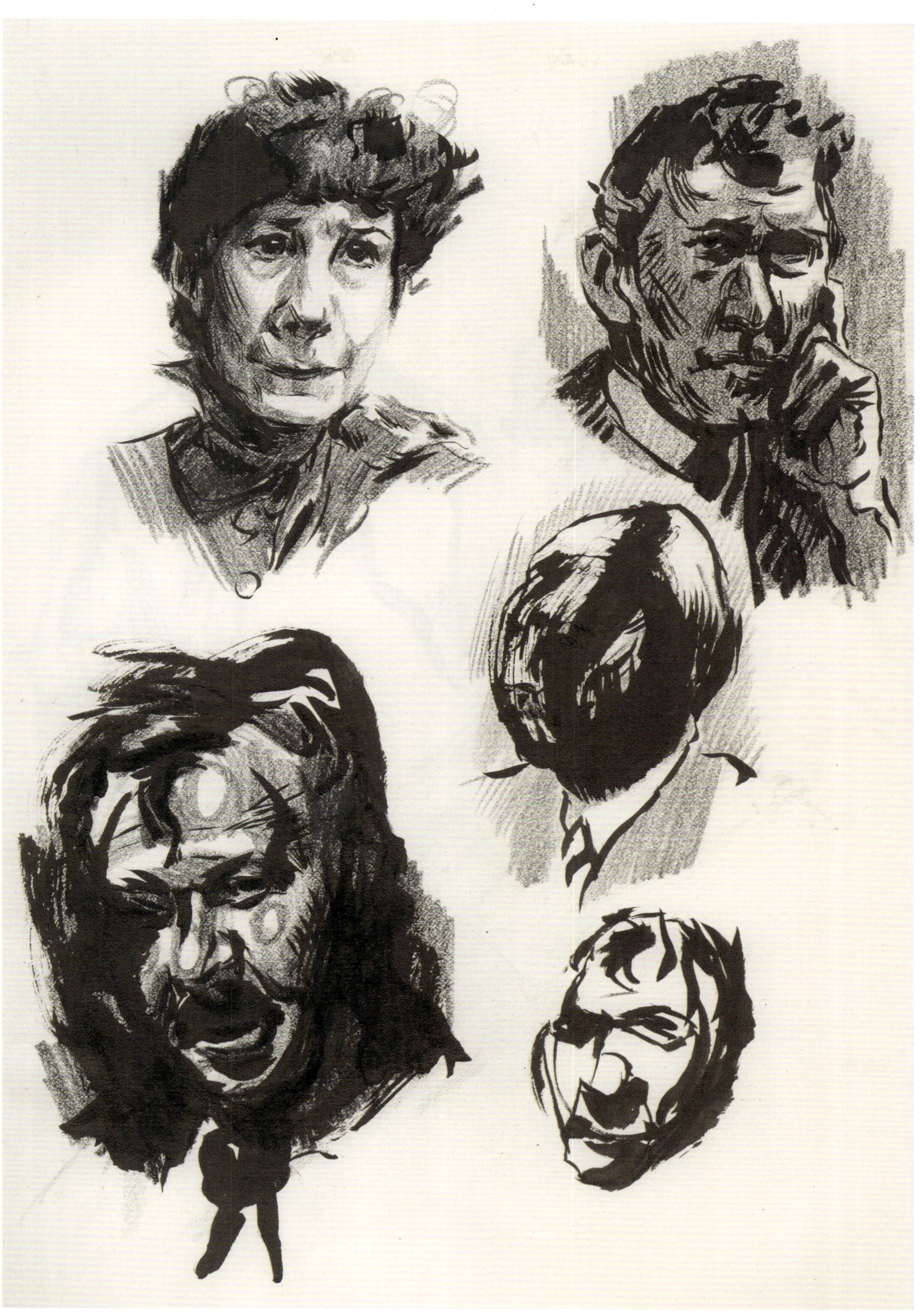

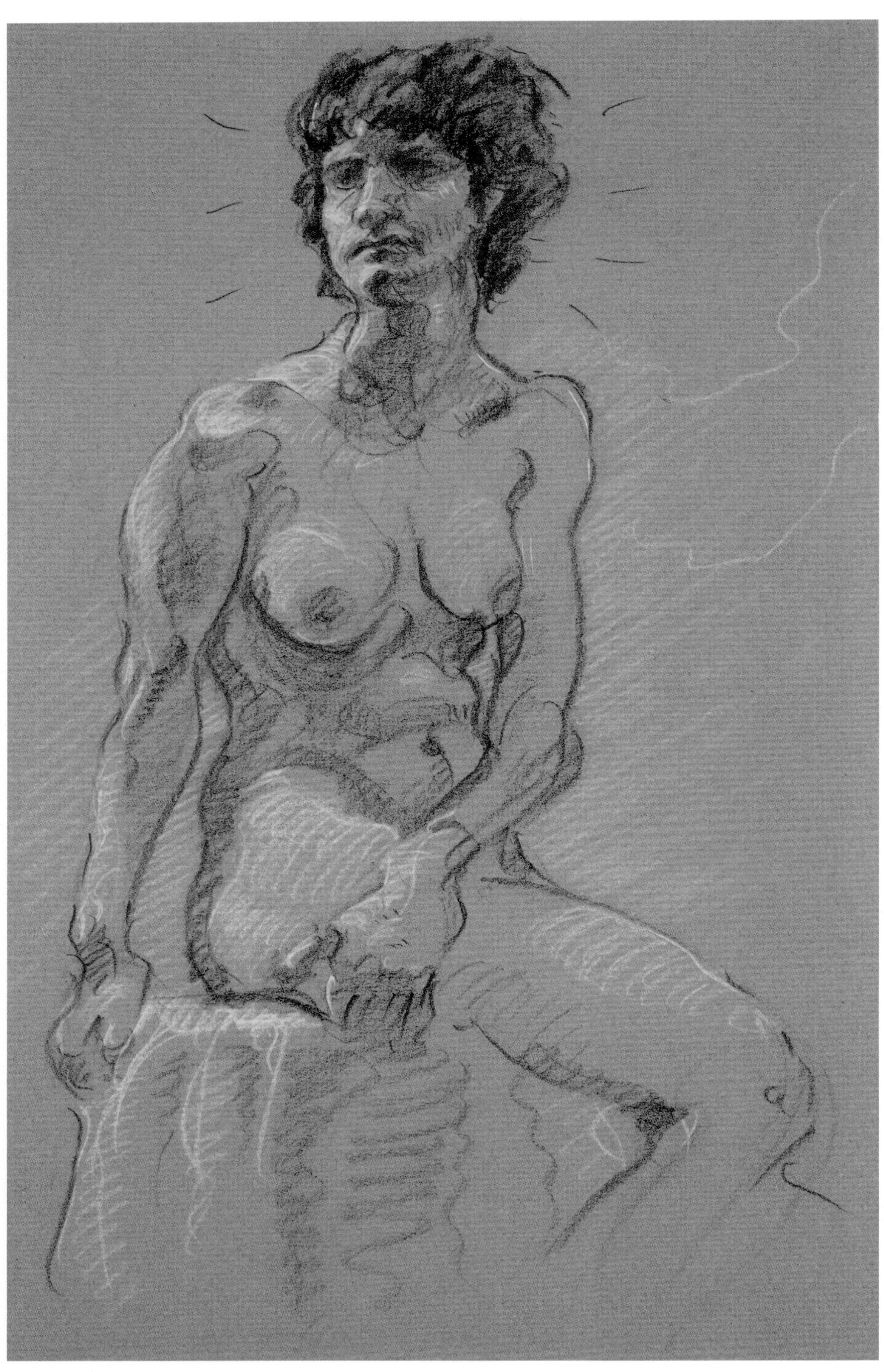

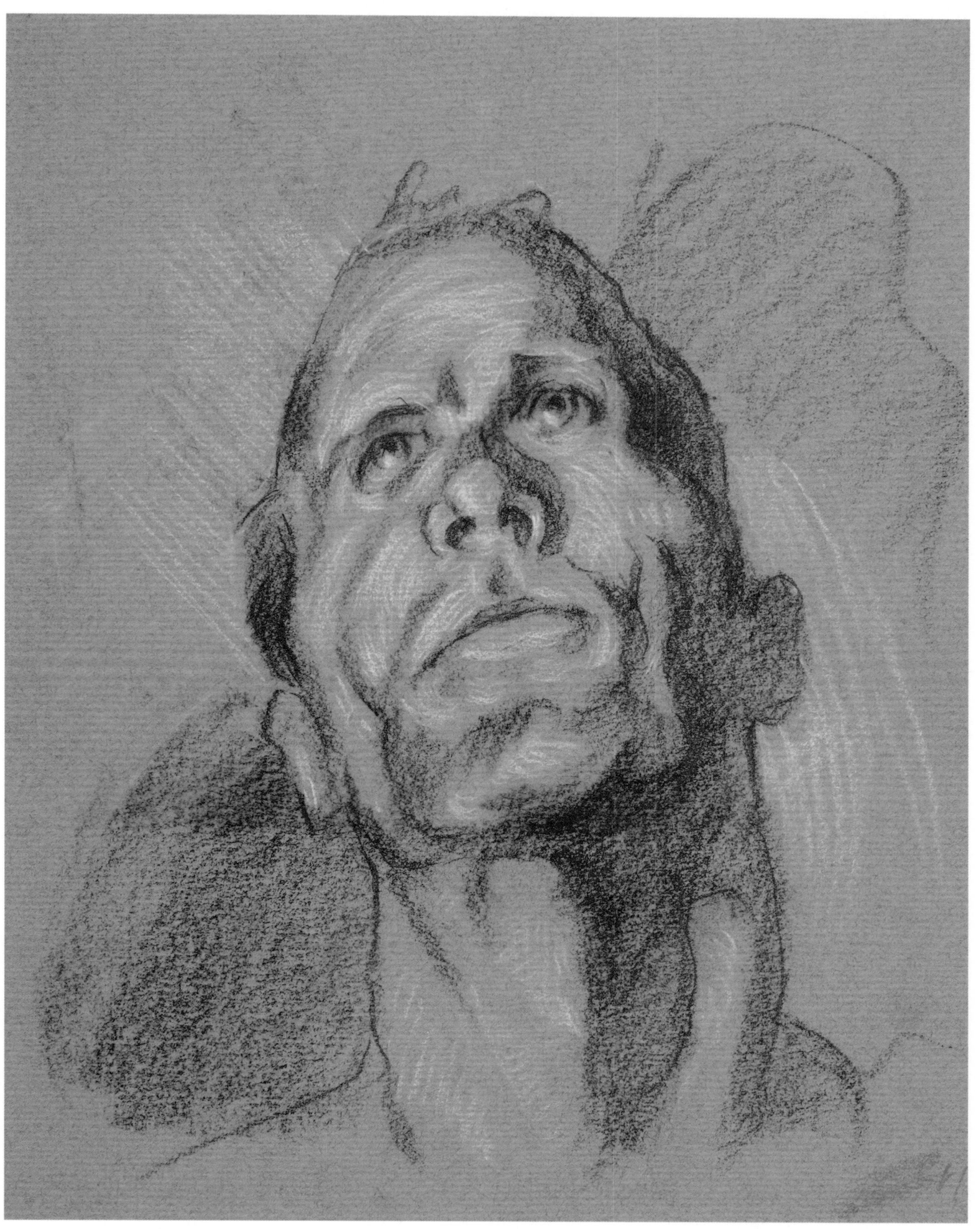

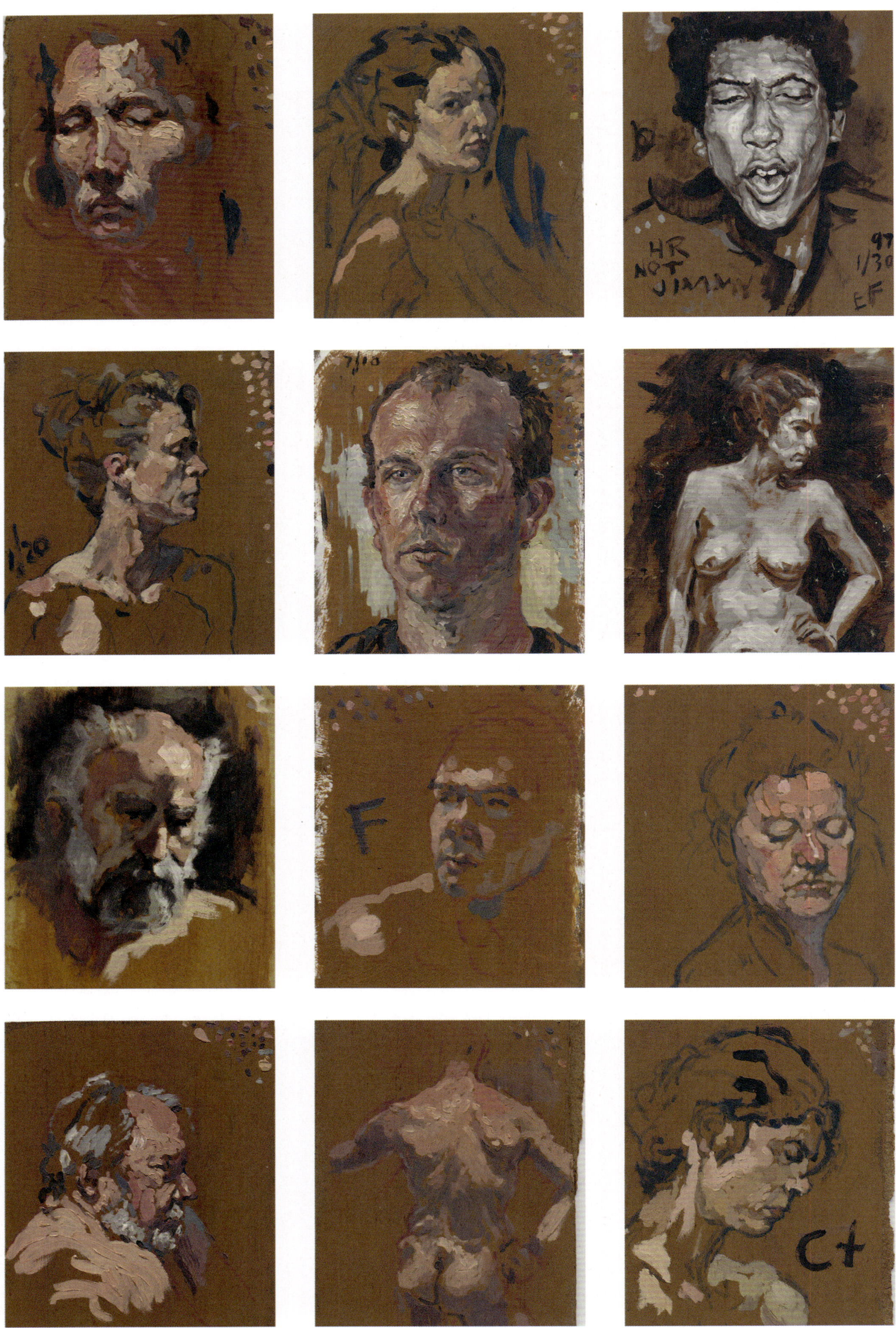

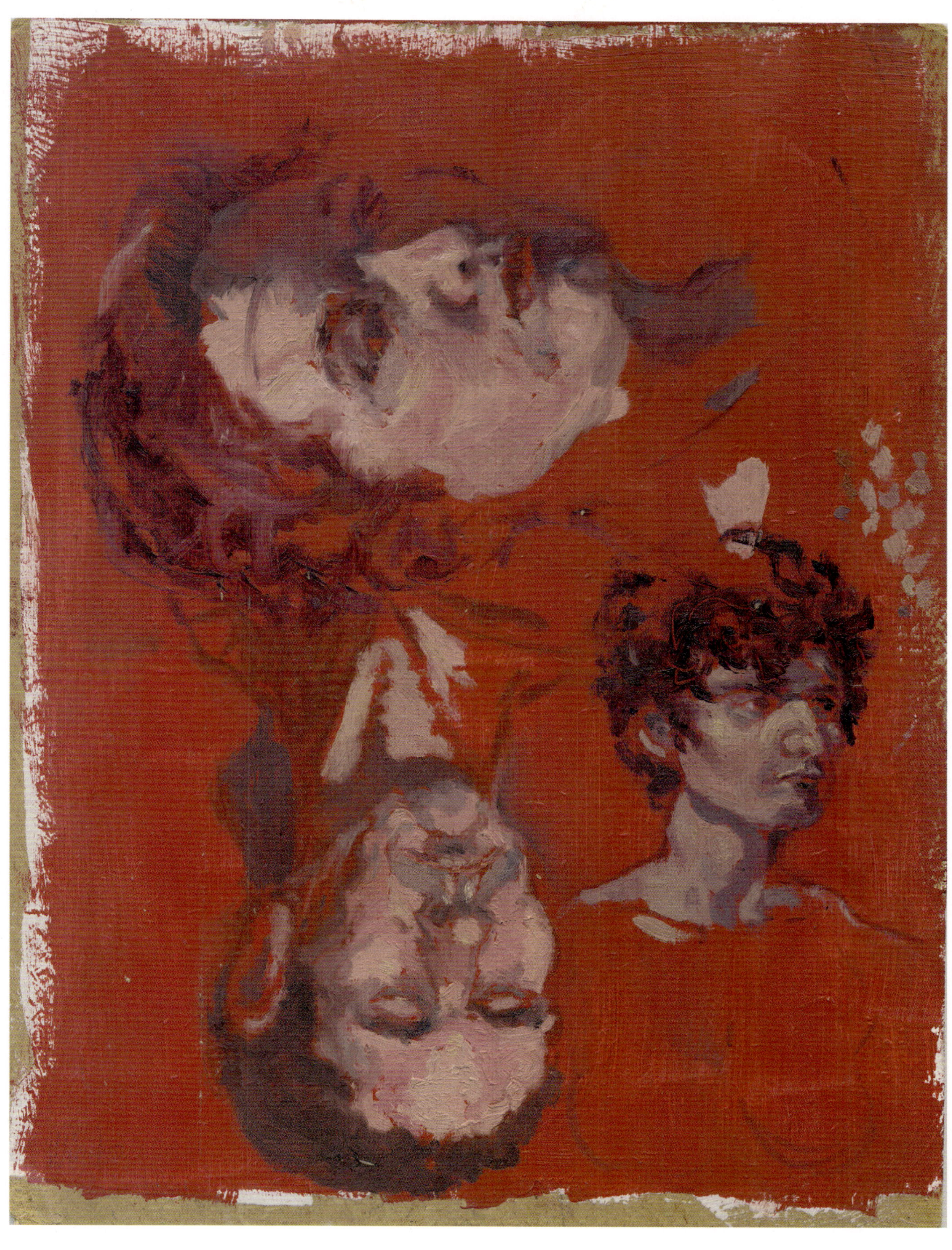

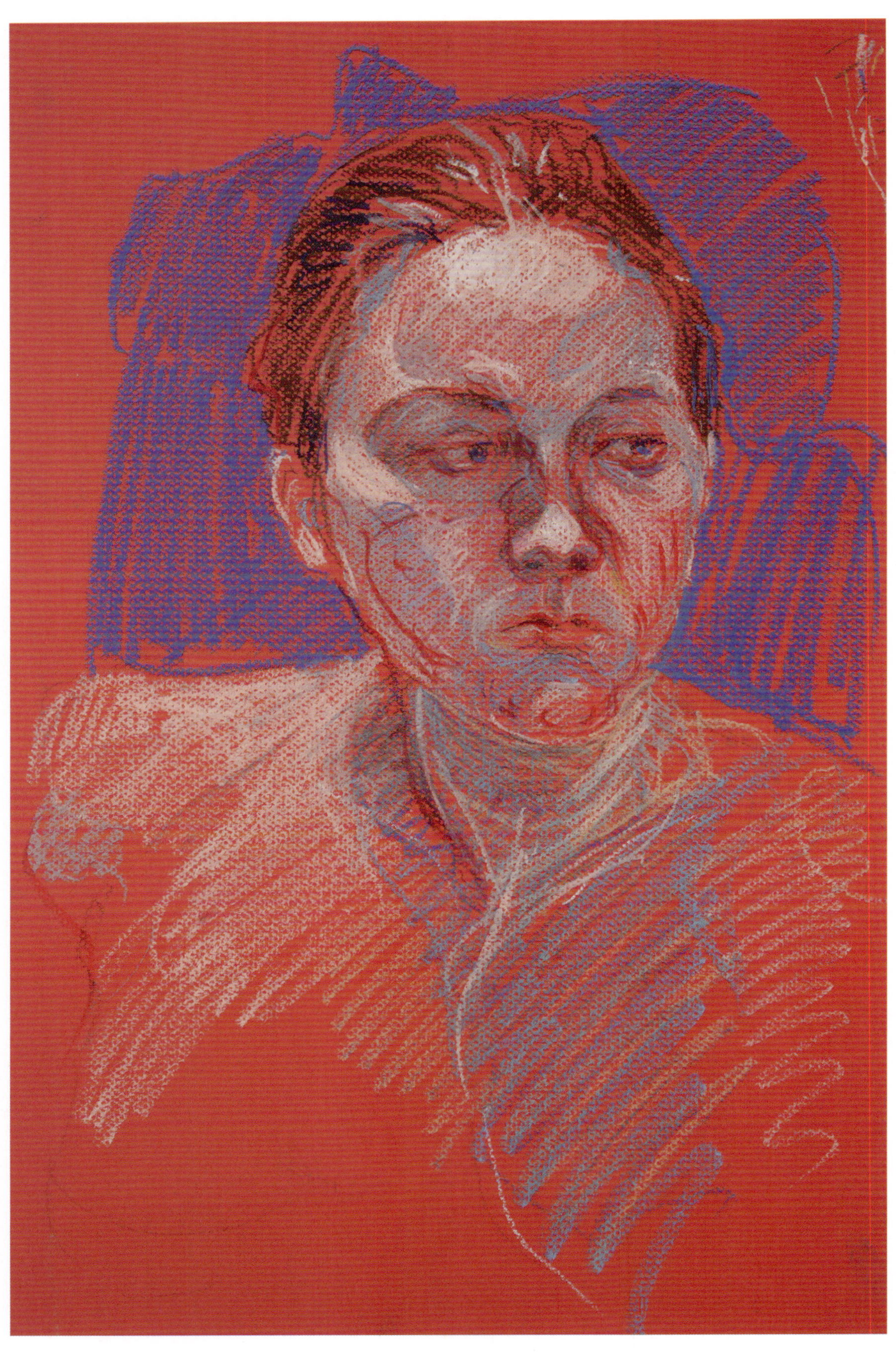

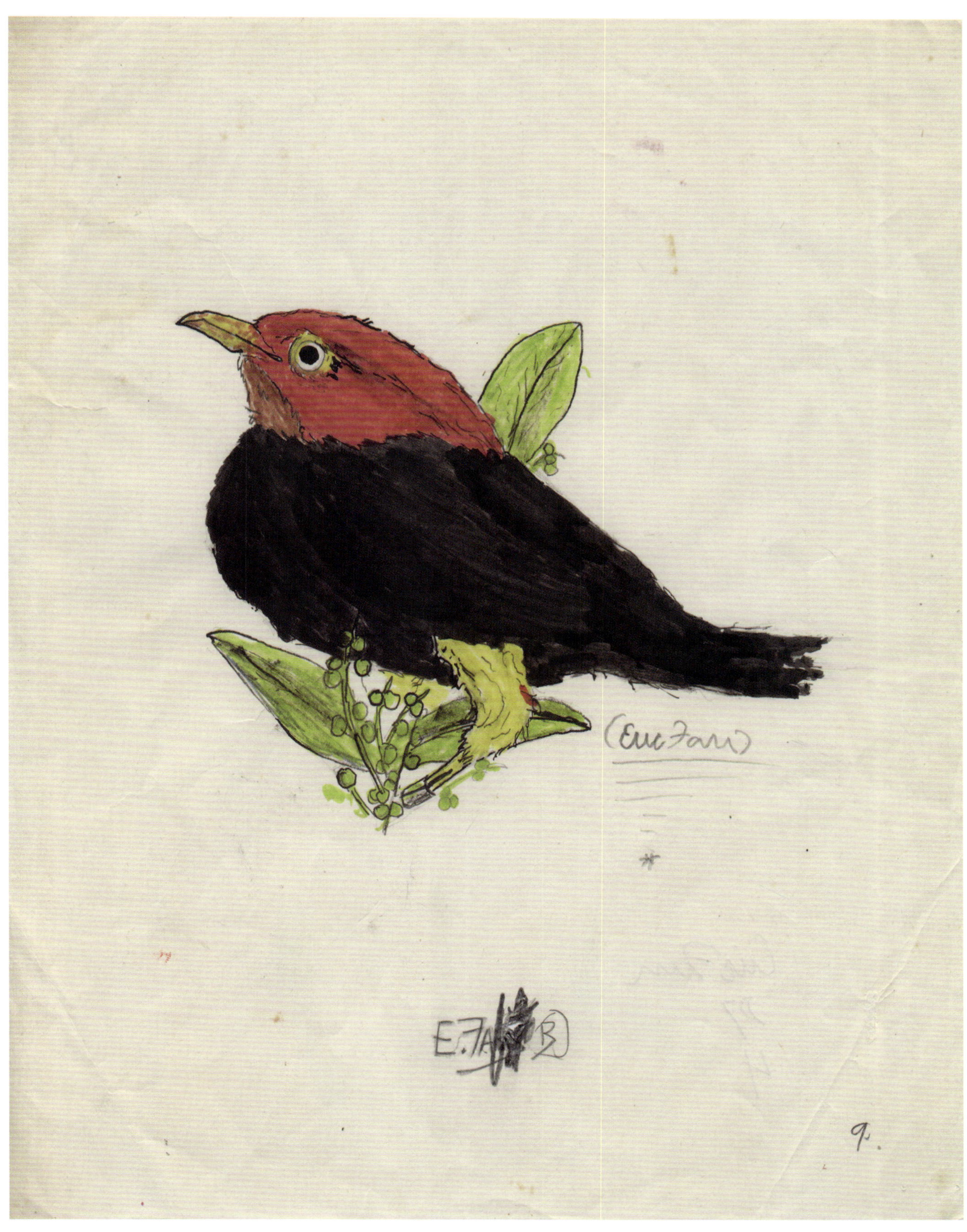

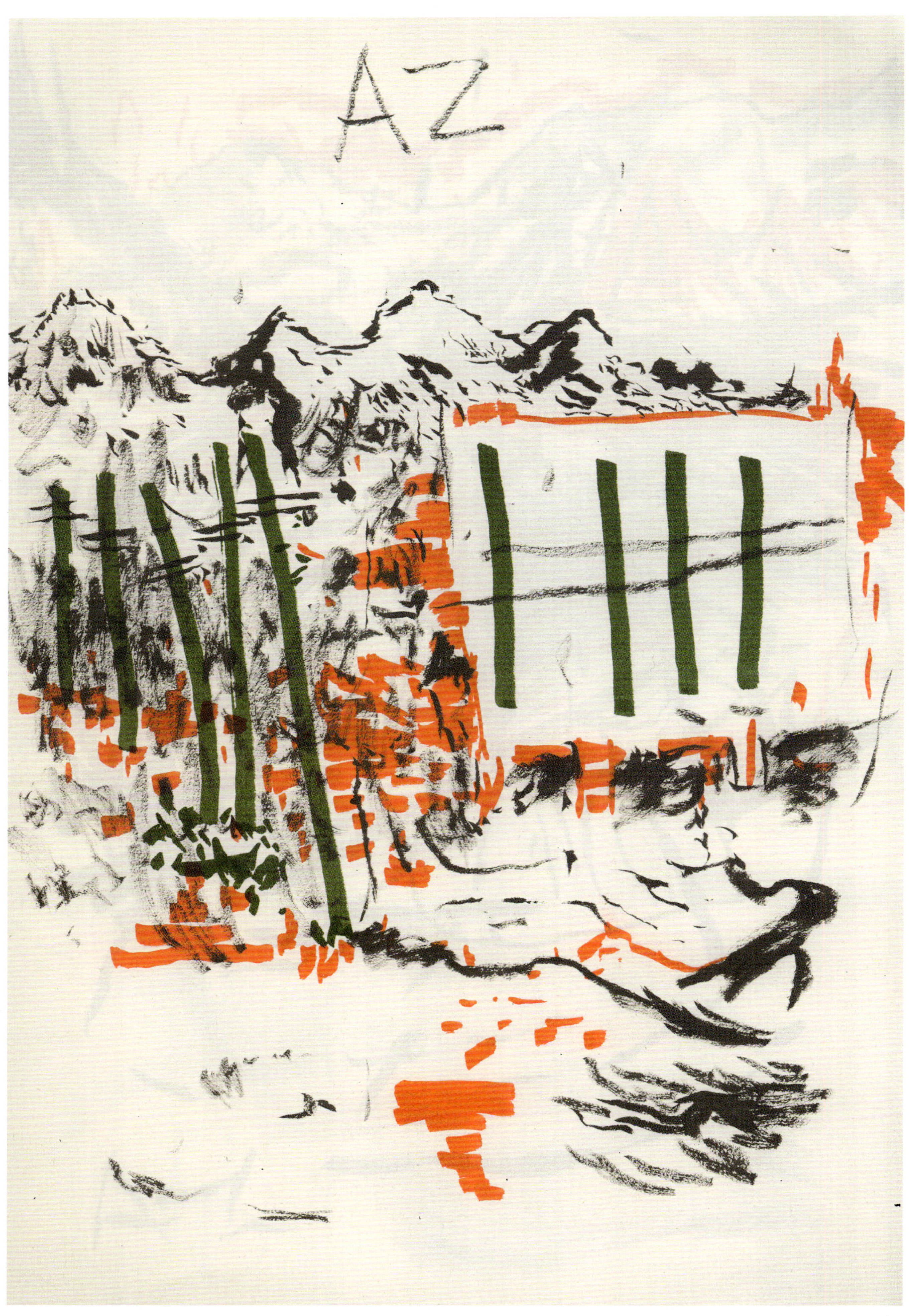

AZ

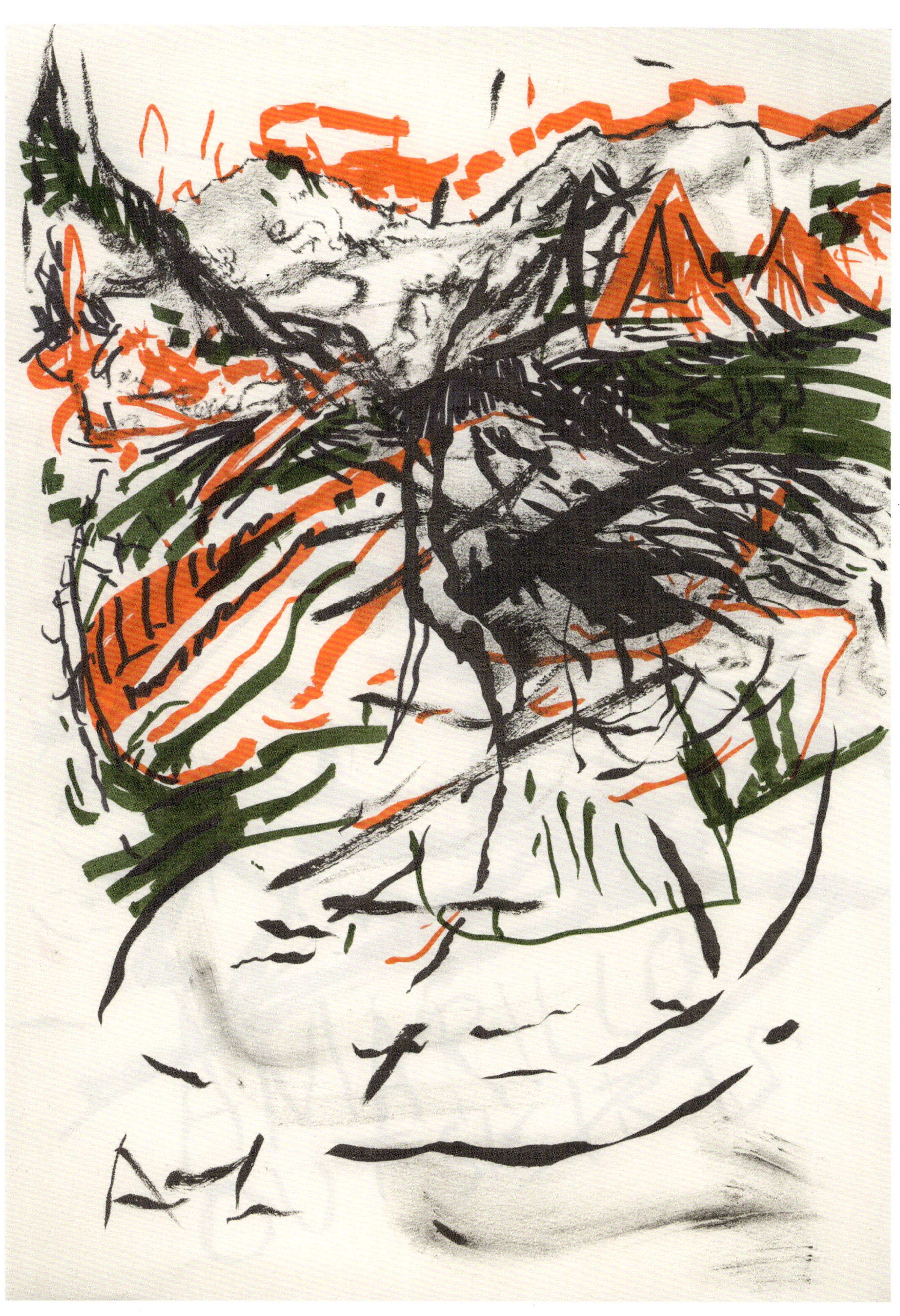

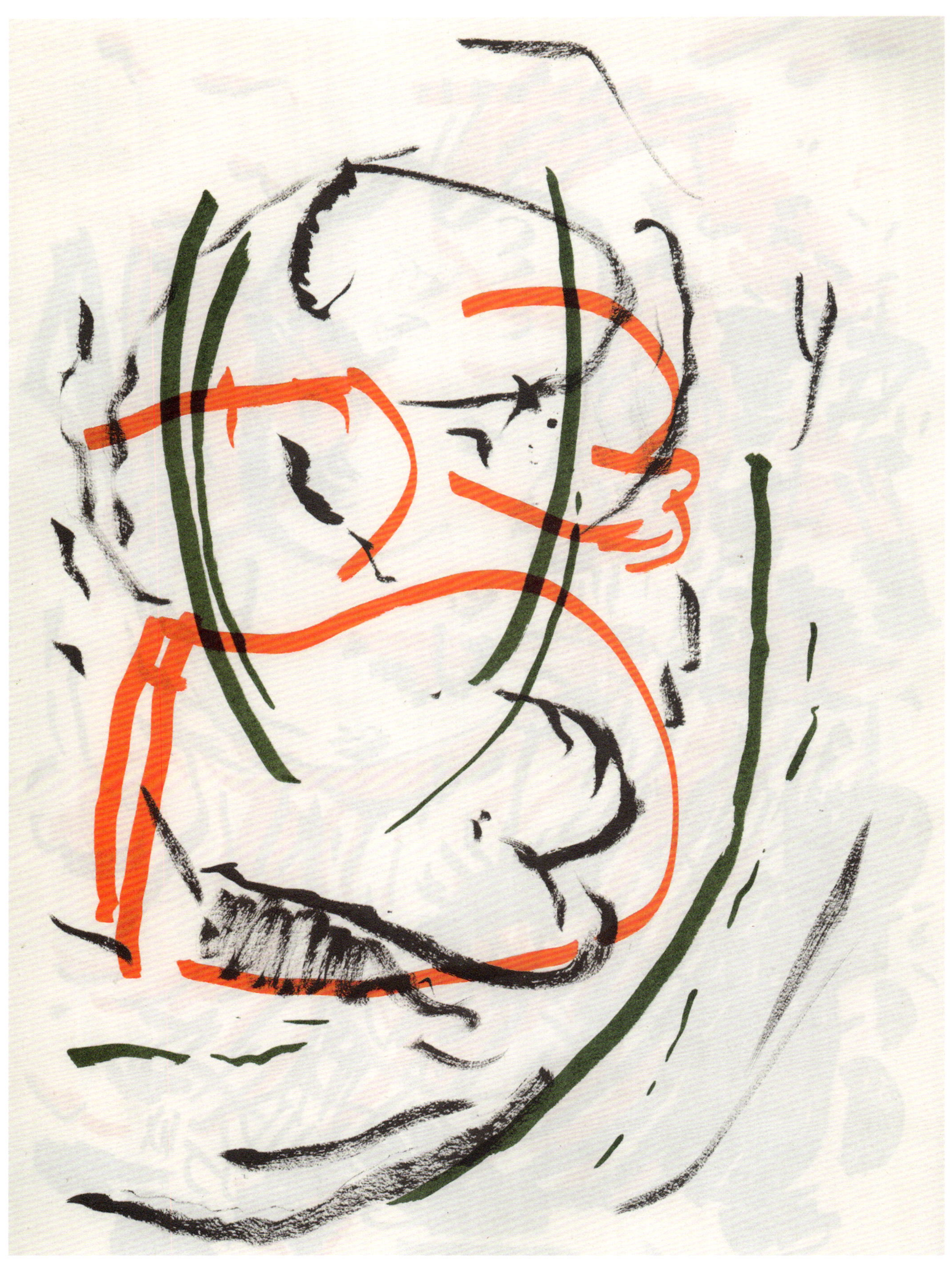

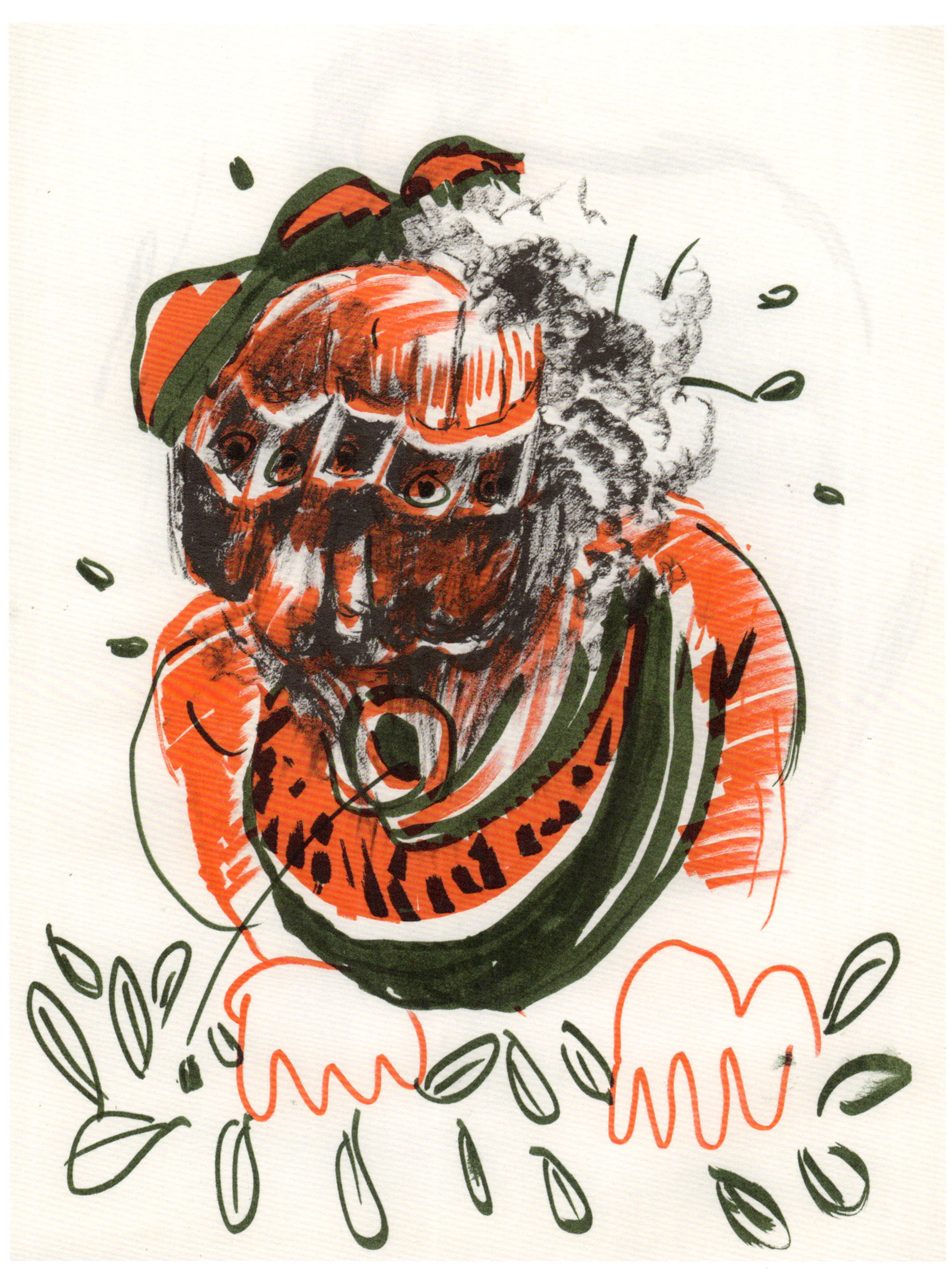

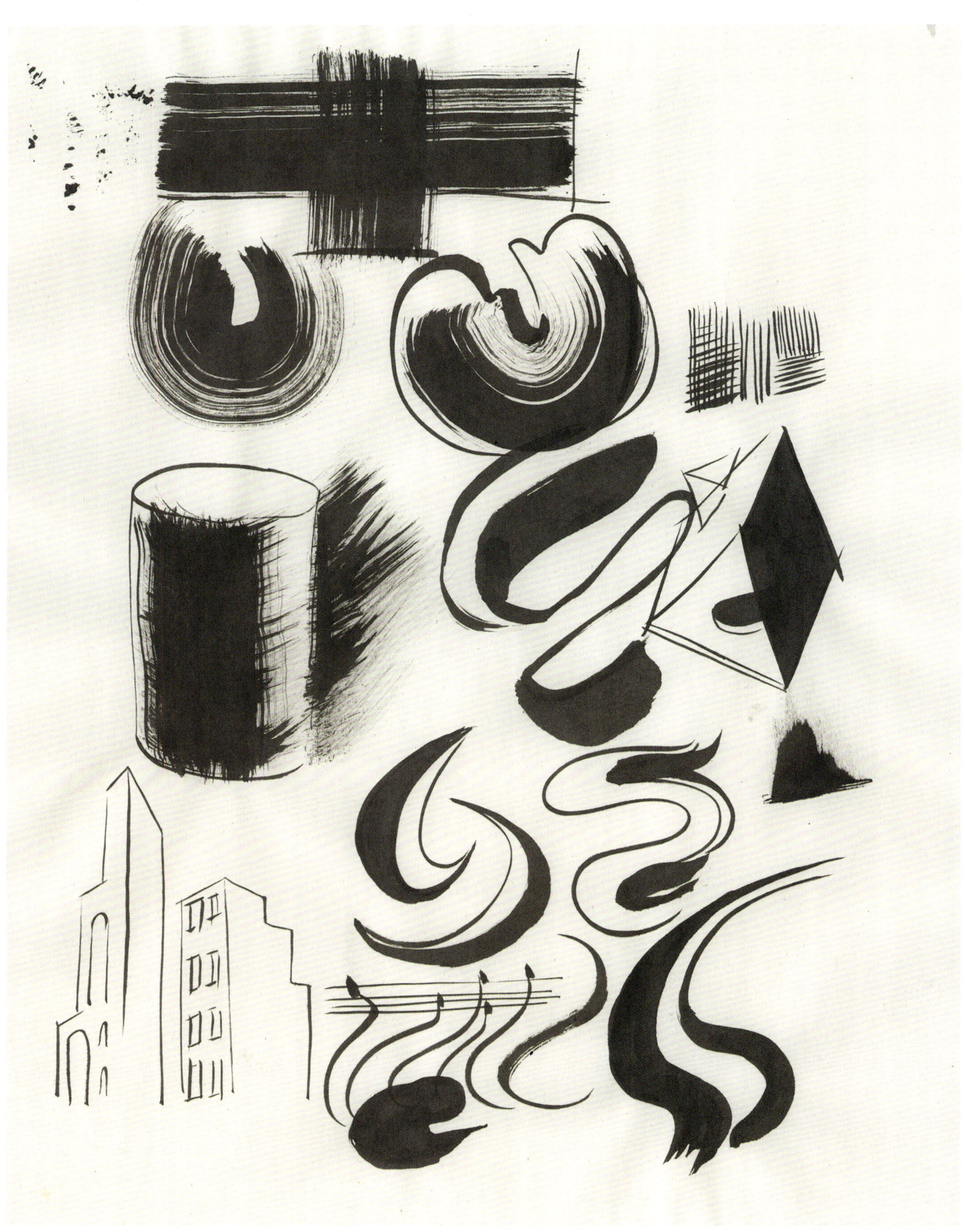

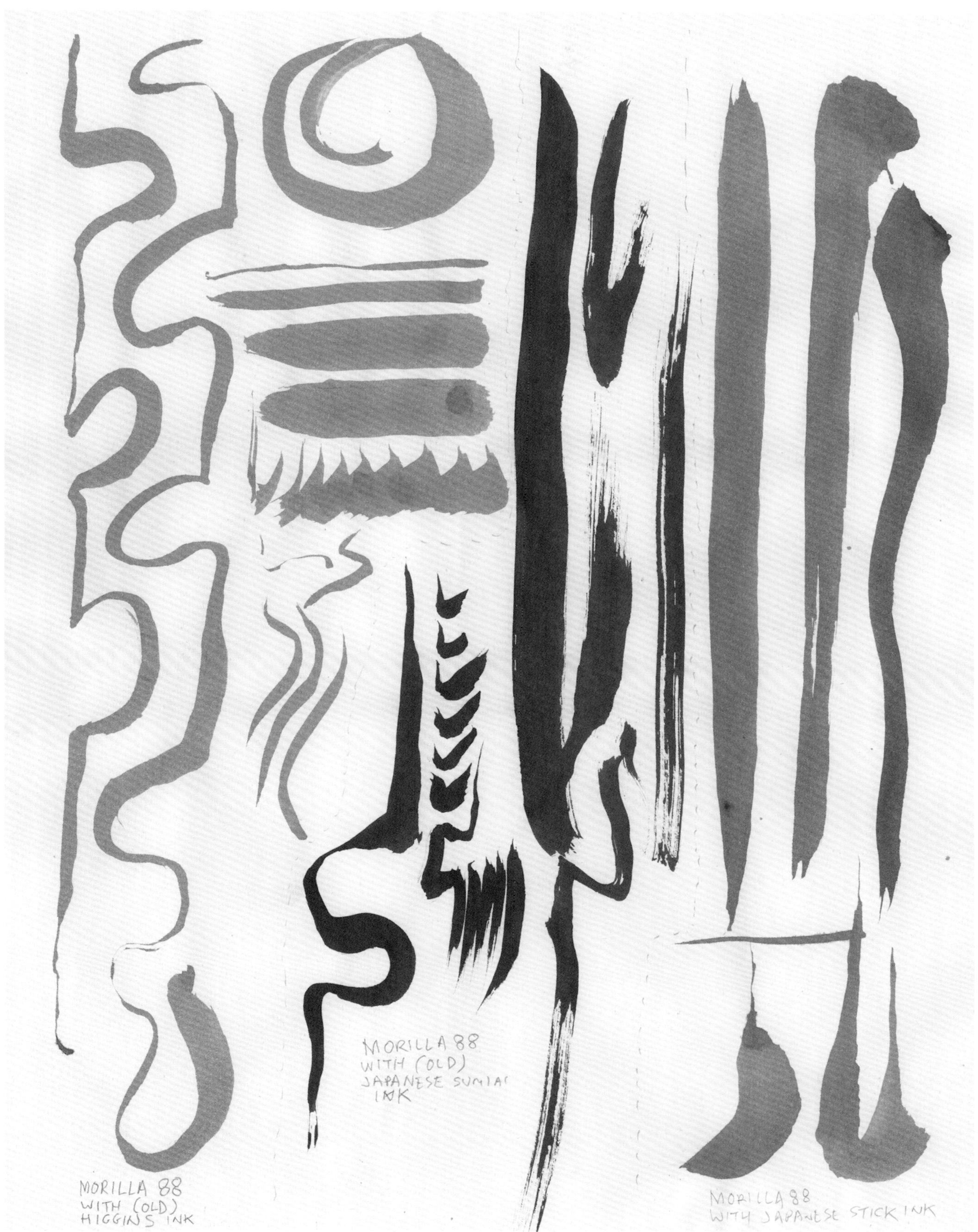

MORILLA 88
WITH (OLD)
JAPANESE SUMI
INK
MORILLA 88
WITH (OLD)
HIGGINS INK
MORILLA 88
WITH JAPANESE STICK INK

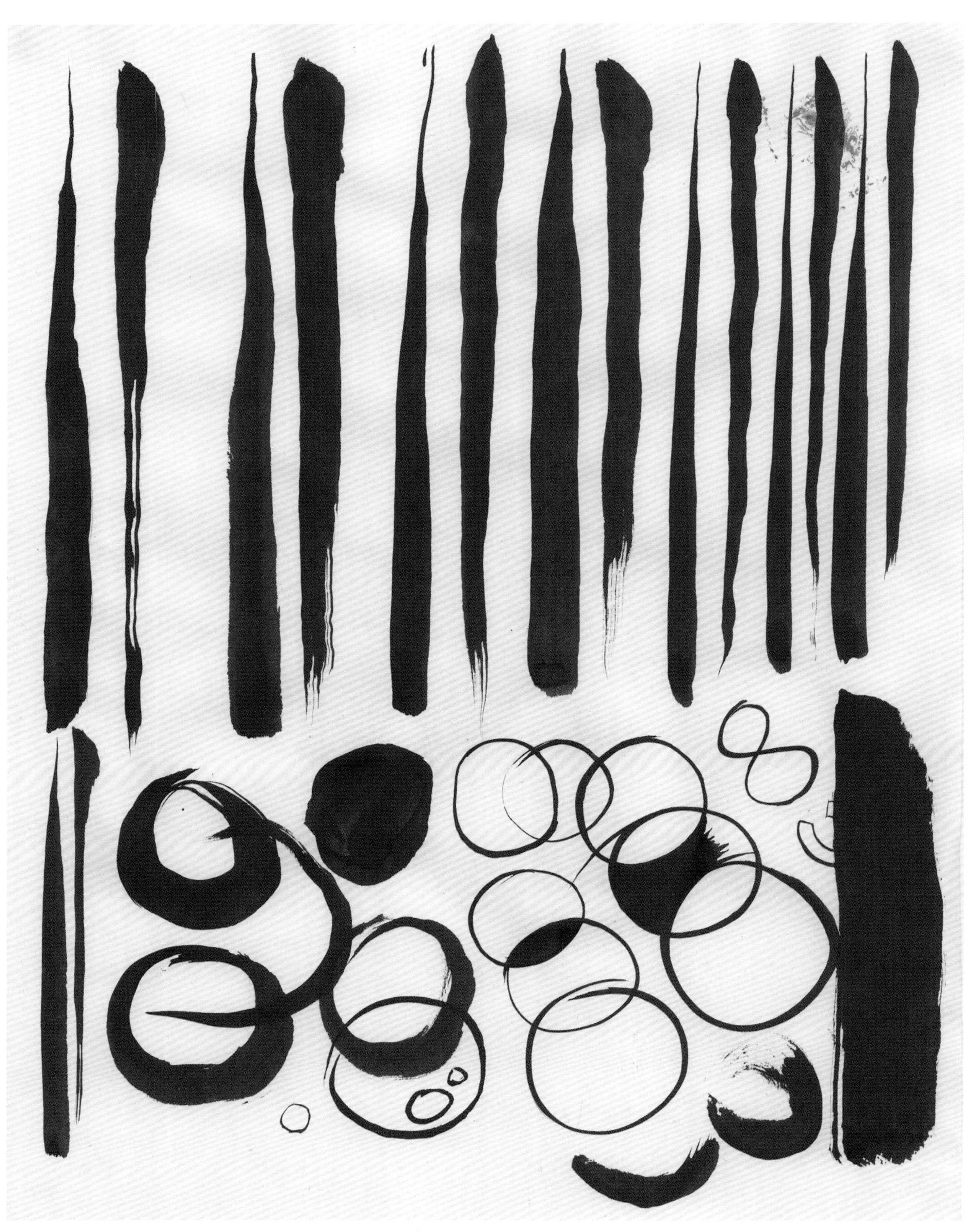

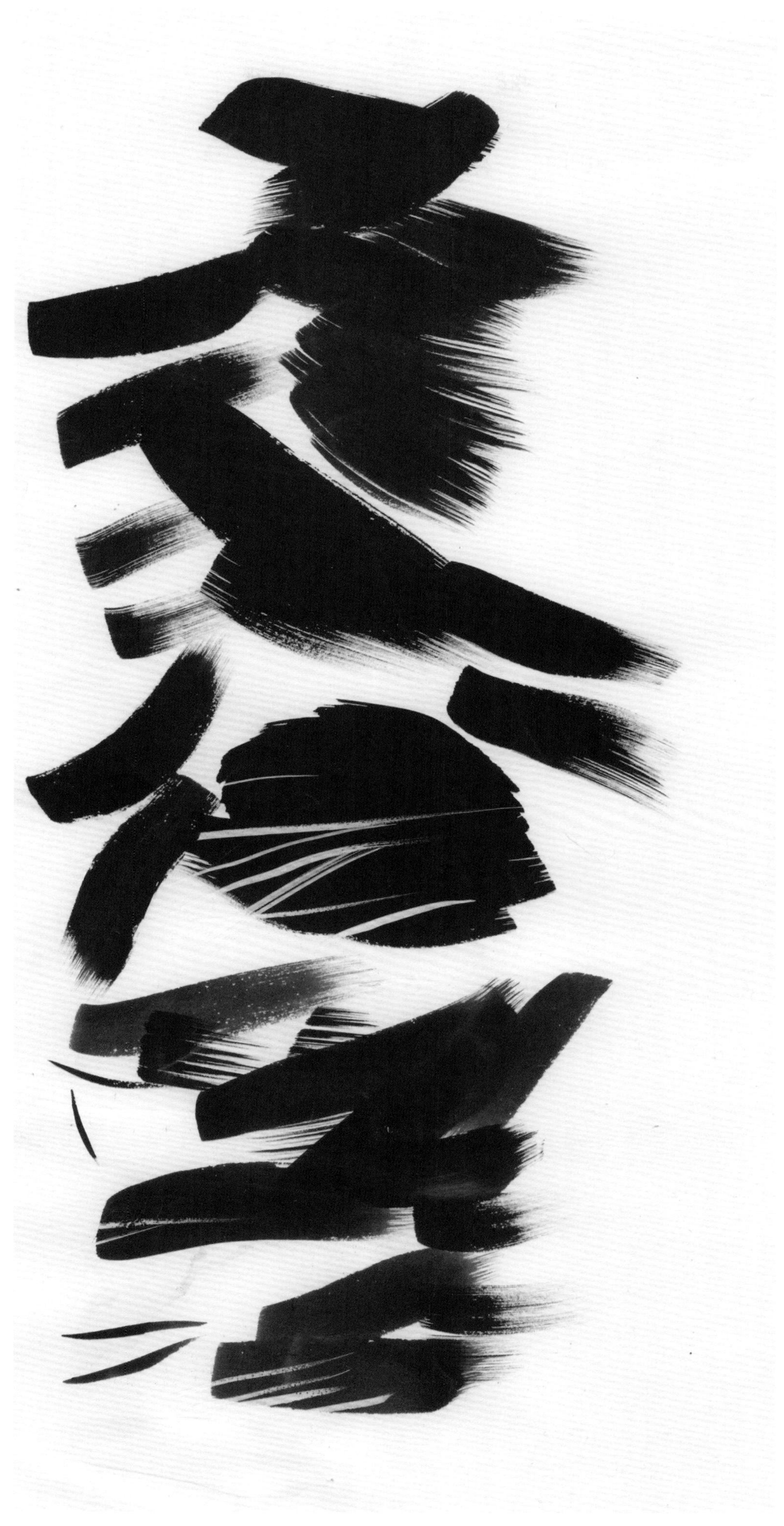

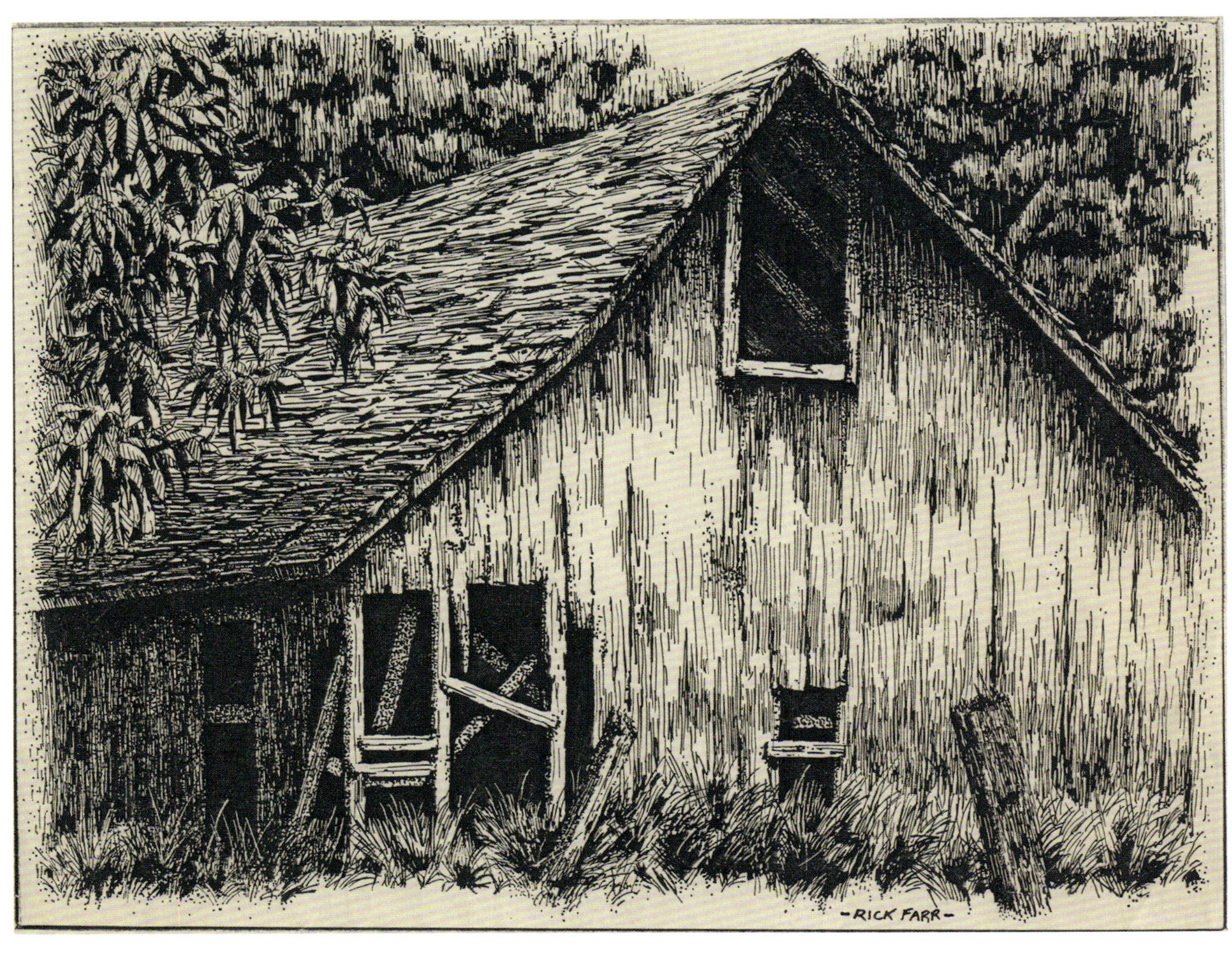

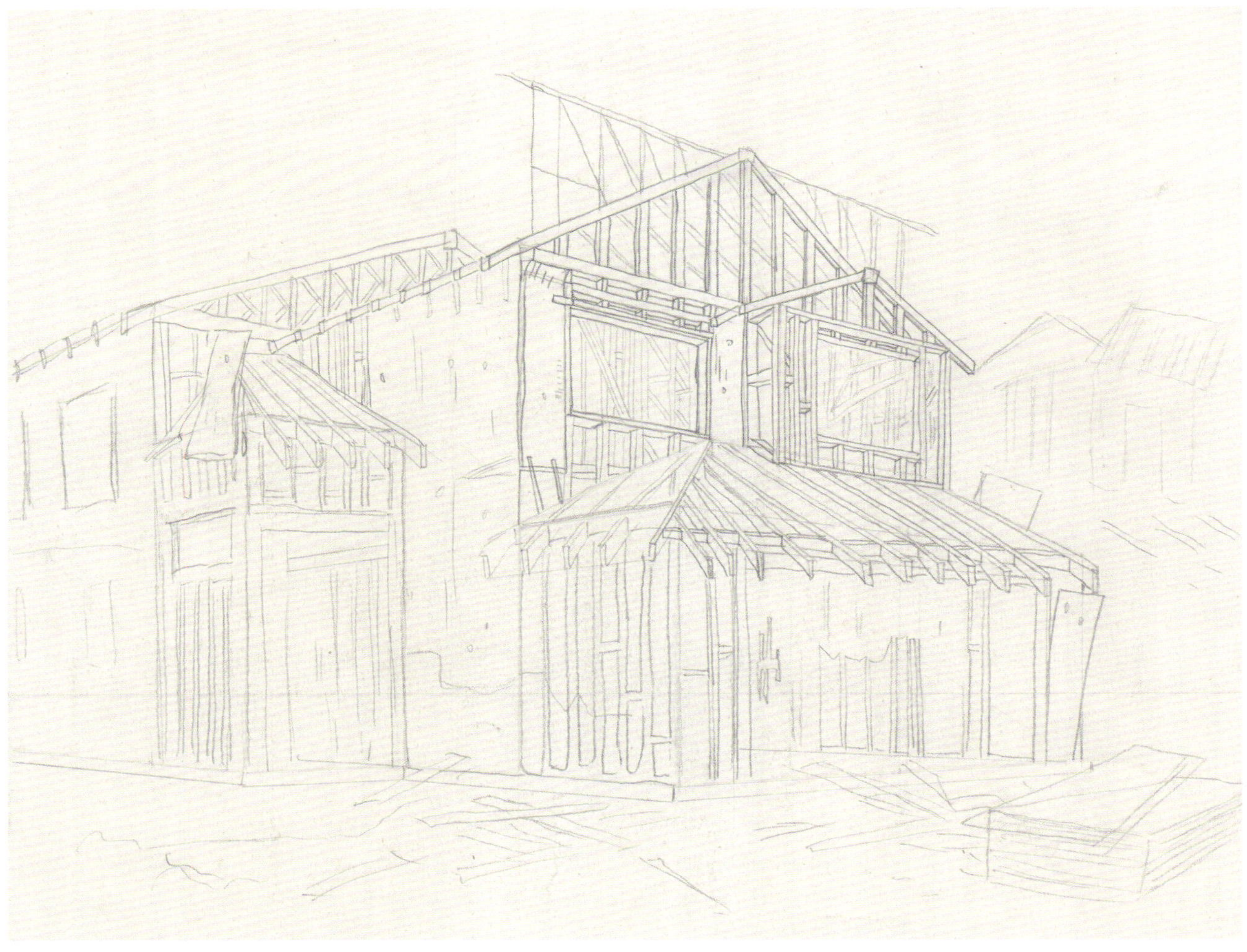

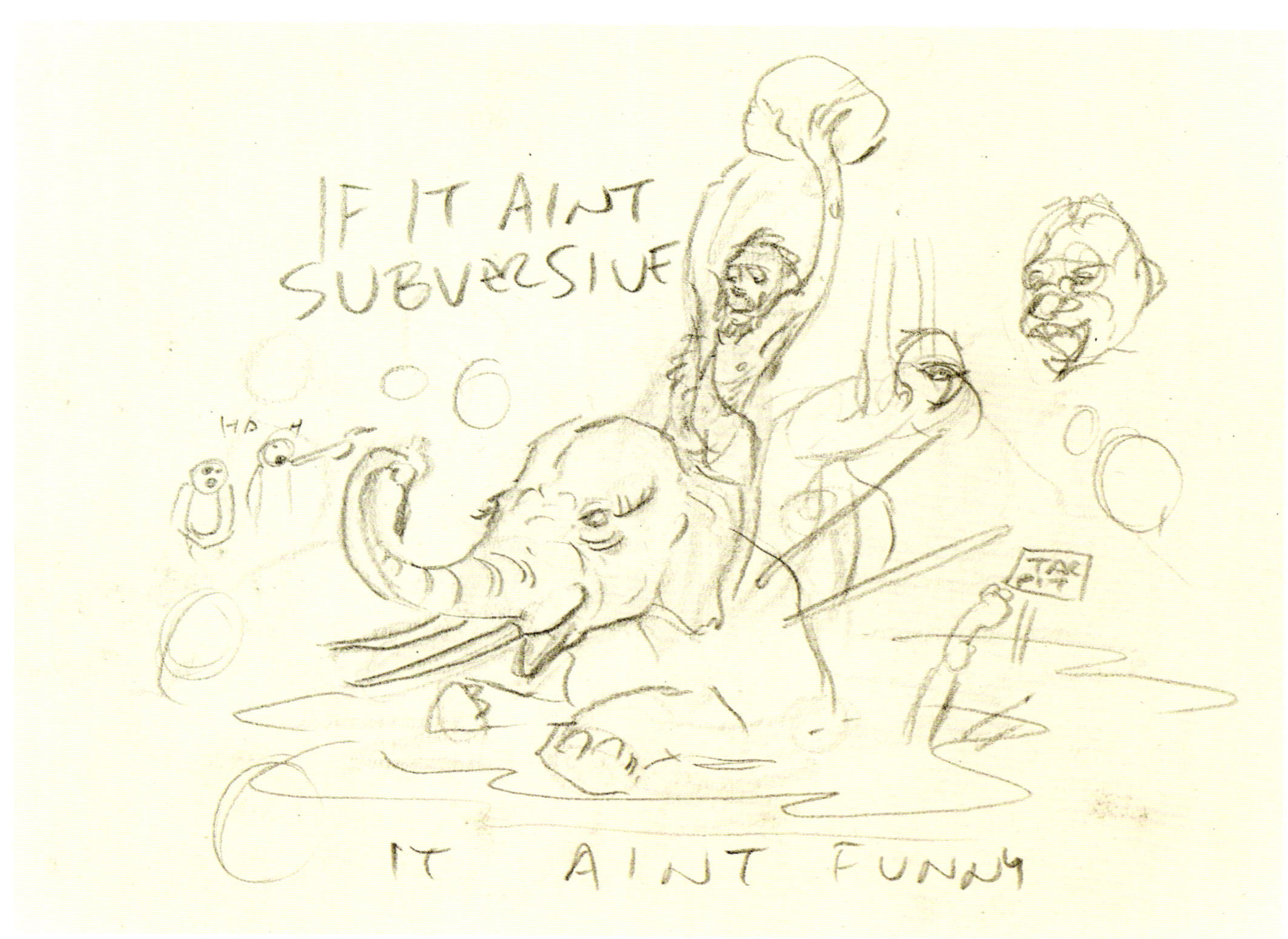

IF IT AINT
SUBVERSIVE
IT AINT FUNNY

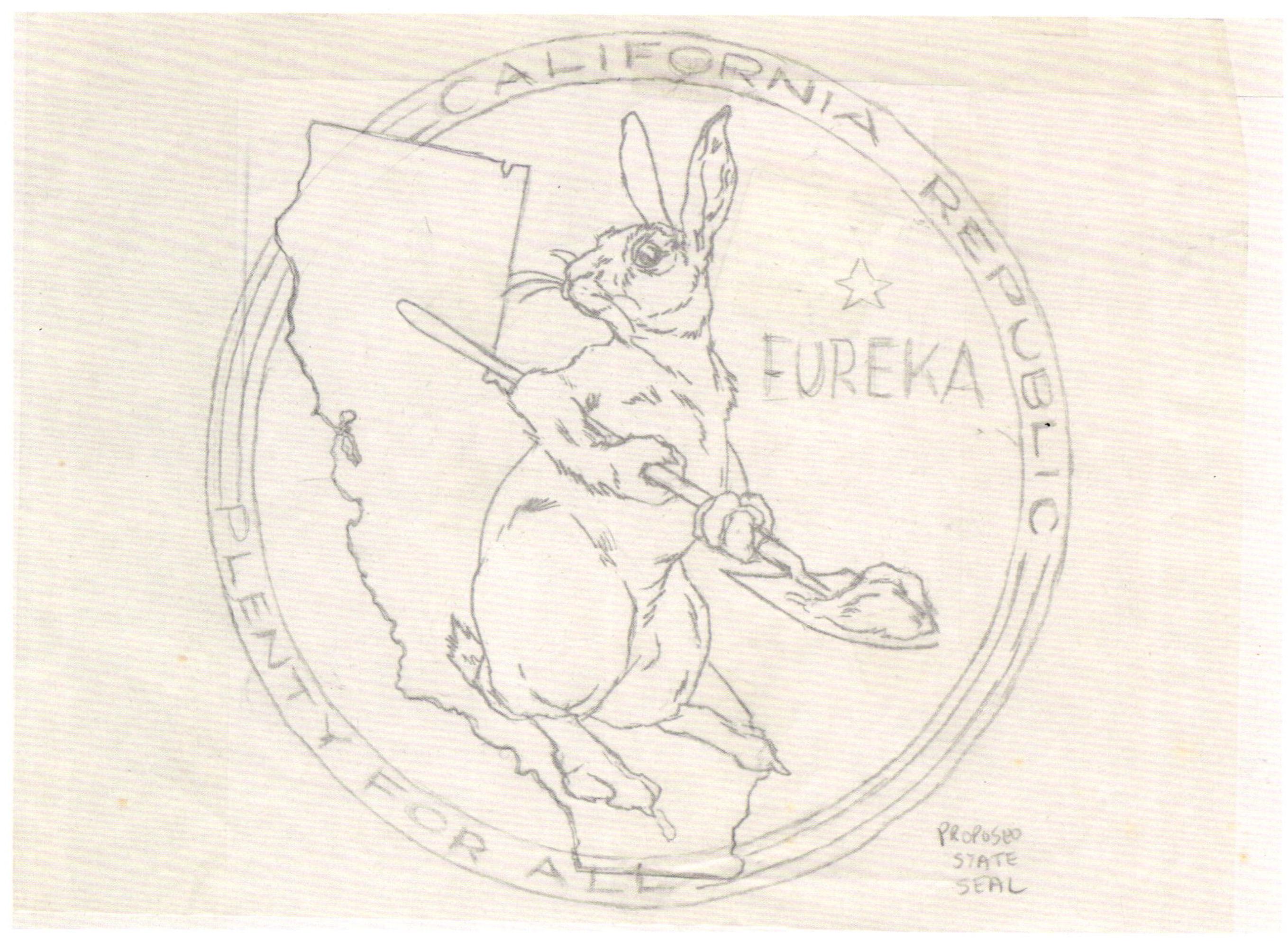

CALIFORNIA REPUBLIC
EUREKA
PLENTY FOR ALL
PROPOSED
STATE
SEAL

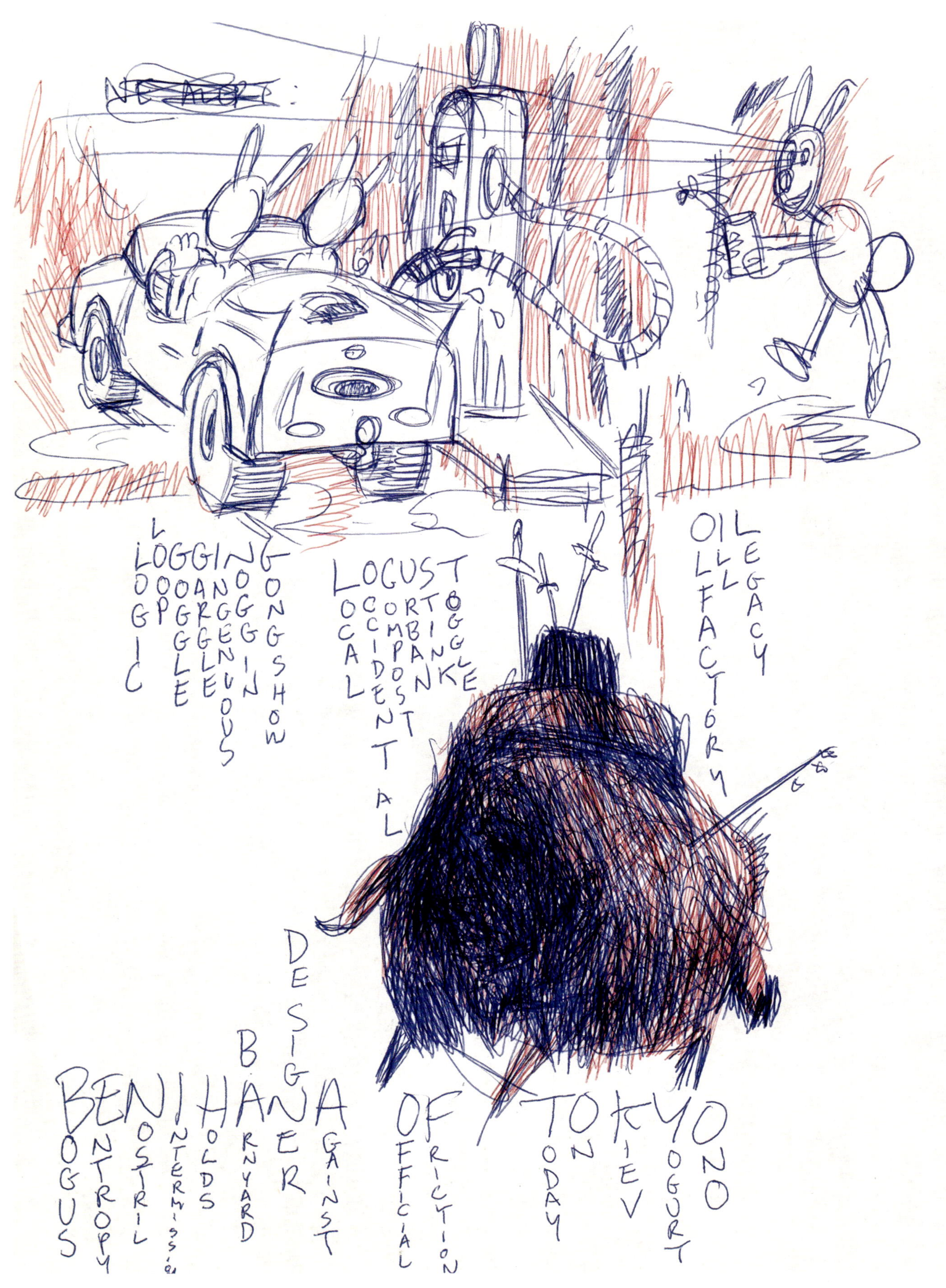

LOGGING
LOGICAL
LONGSHOW
CONTINUOUS
LOCUST
OCCIDENTAL
COMBIG
OIL
LEGACY
FACTORY
BENIHANA
BOGUS
ENTROPY
NOSTRIL
INTERMISSION
BARNYARD
DESIGNER
AGAINST
OF
OFFICIAL
FRICTION
TOKYO
TODAY
KIEV
YOGURT
ONO

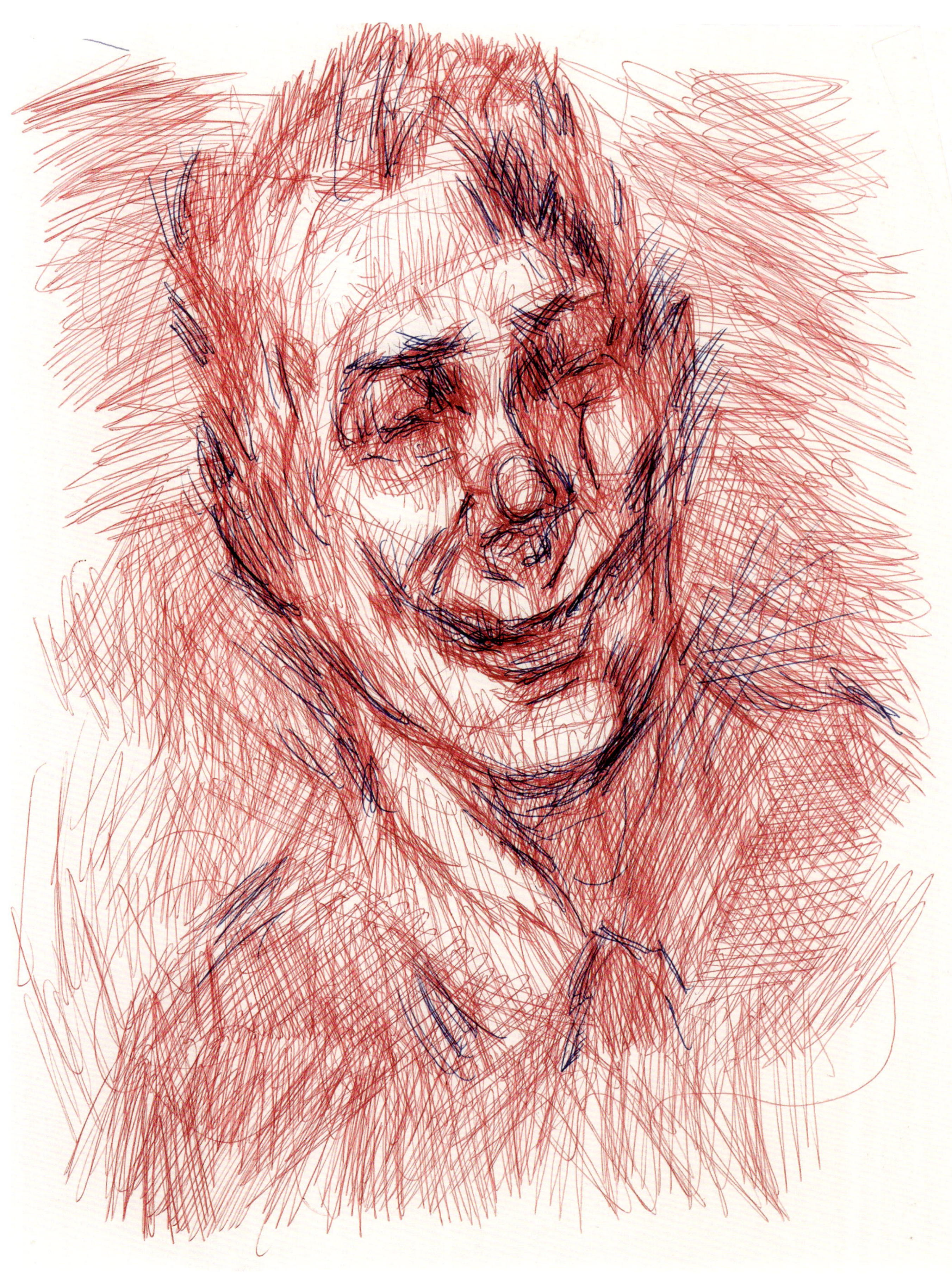

TWO

Etchings, Linocuts, Woodcuts, and Prints

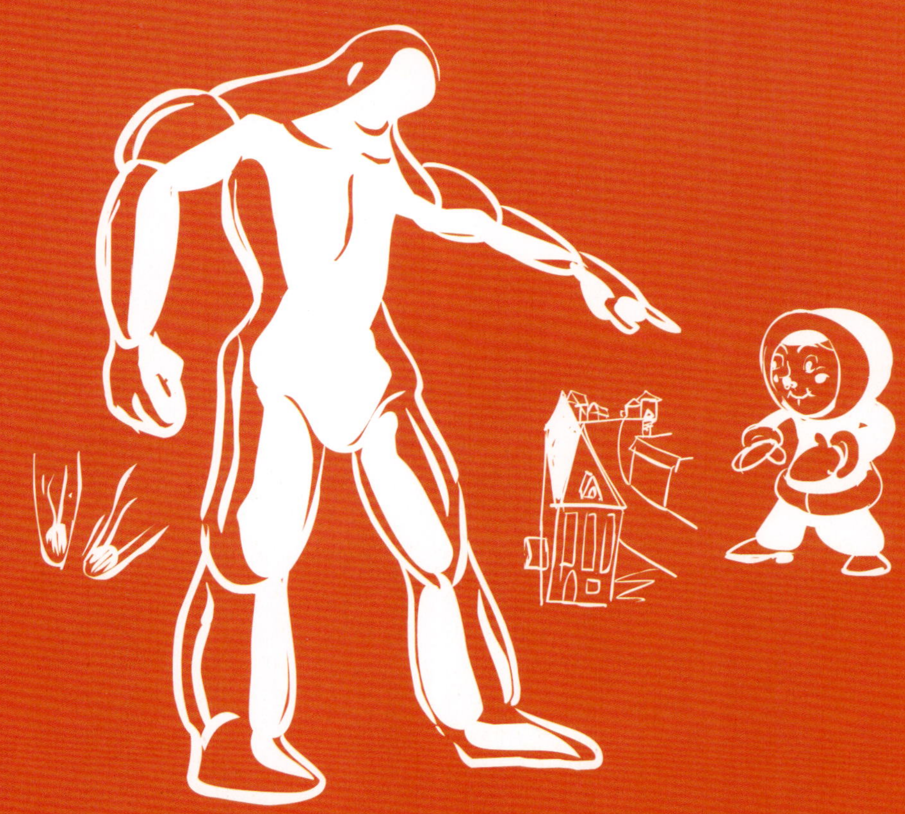

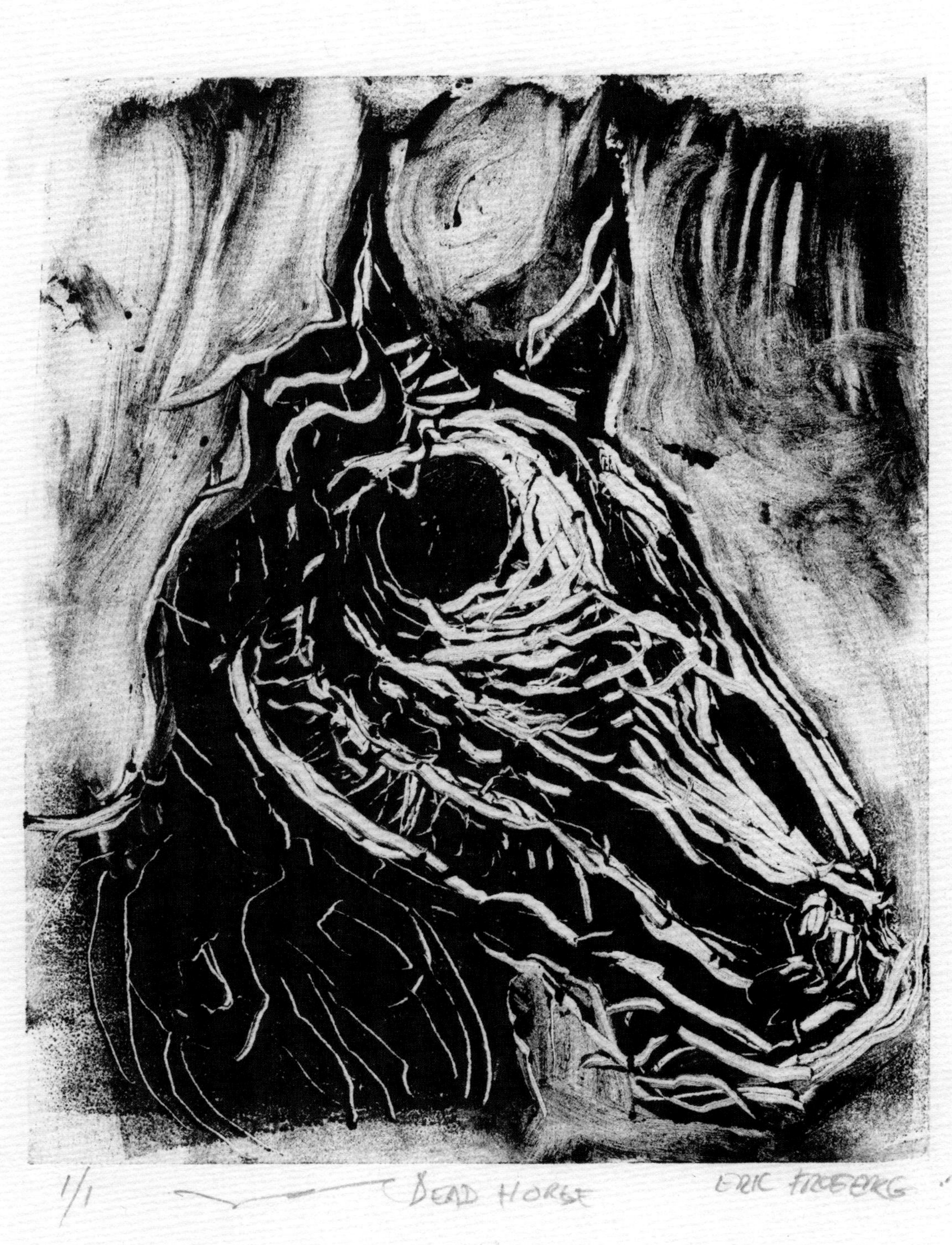

1/1
DEAD HORSE
ERIC FROBERG

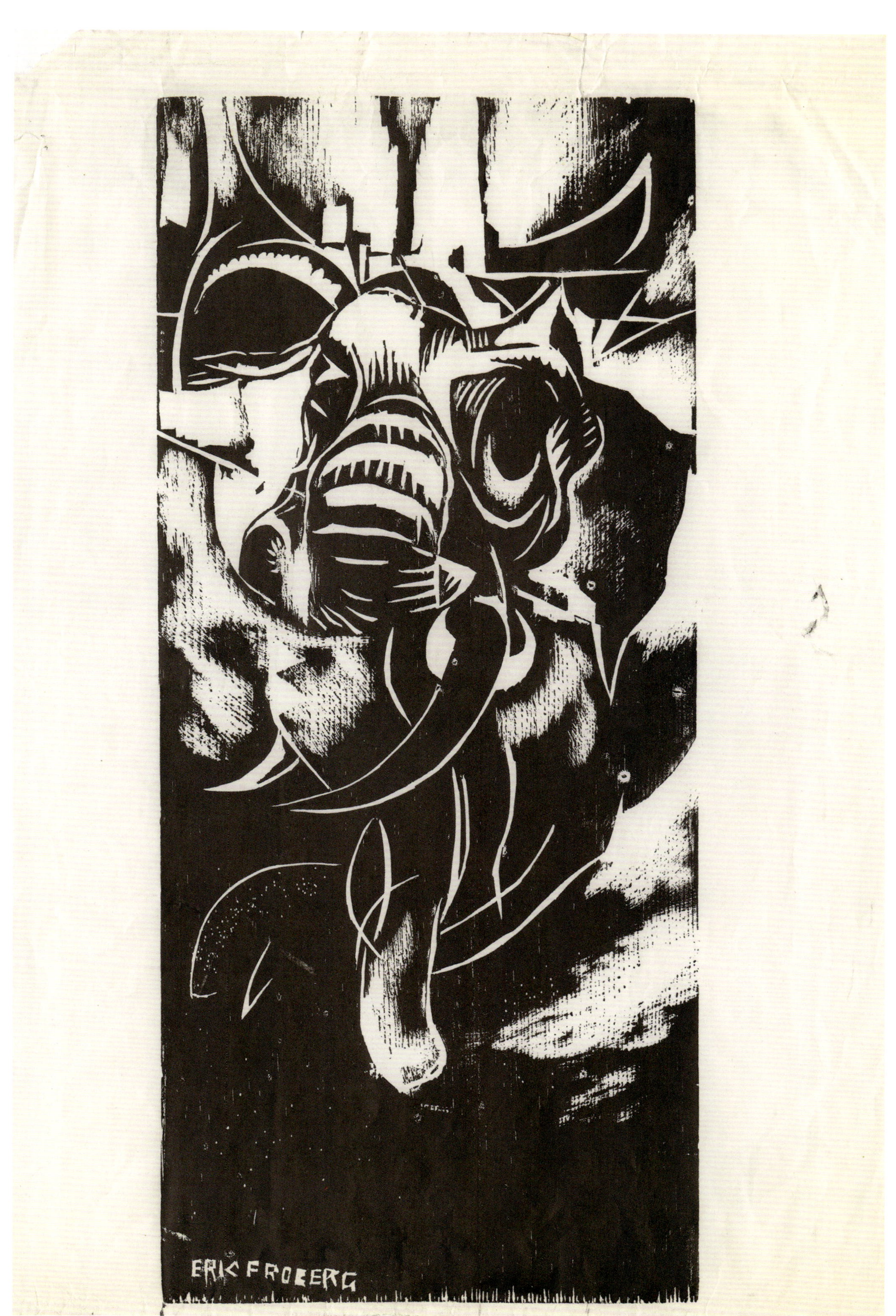

ERIC FROBERG

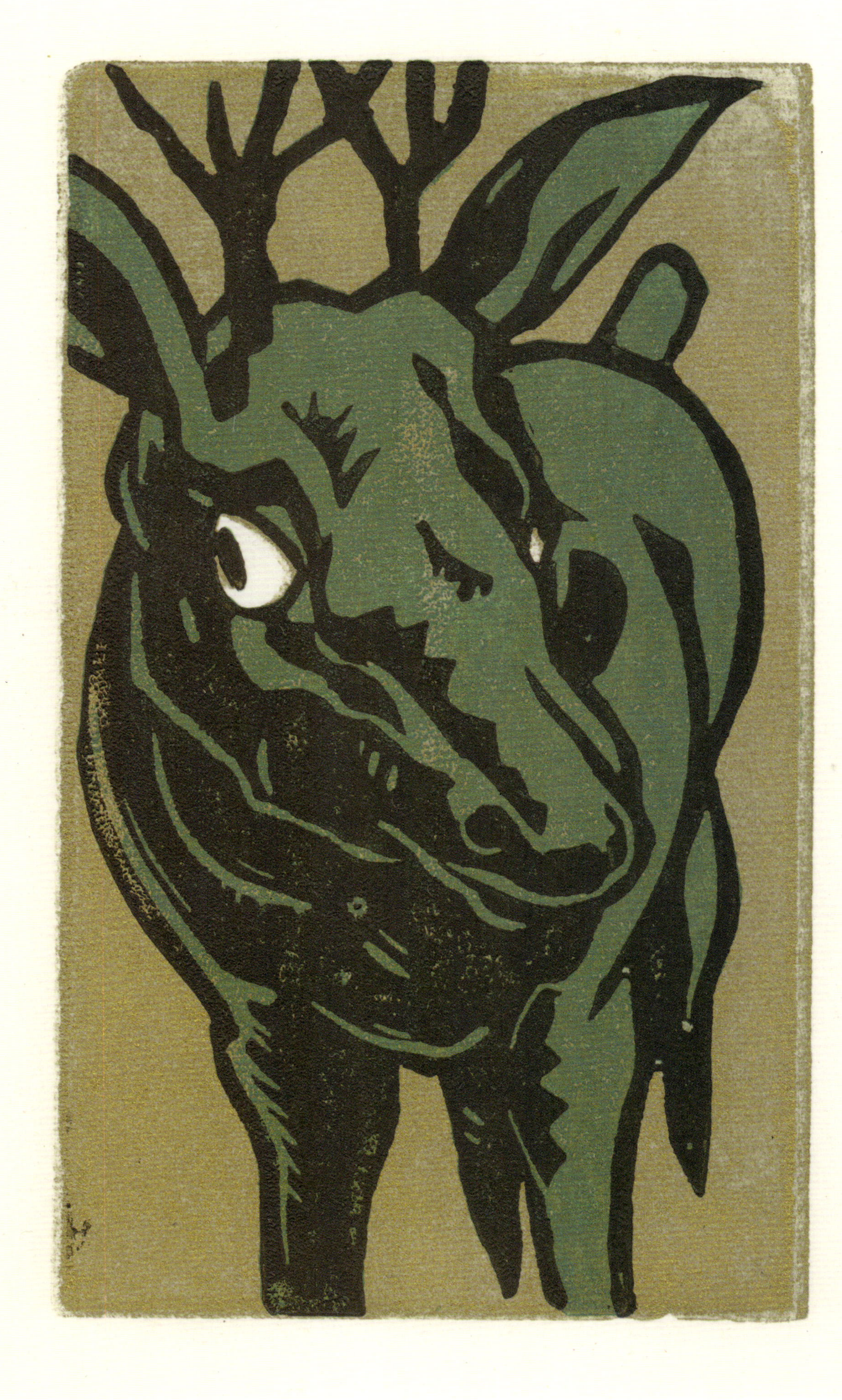

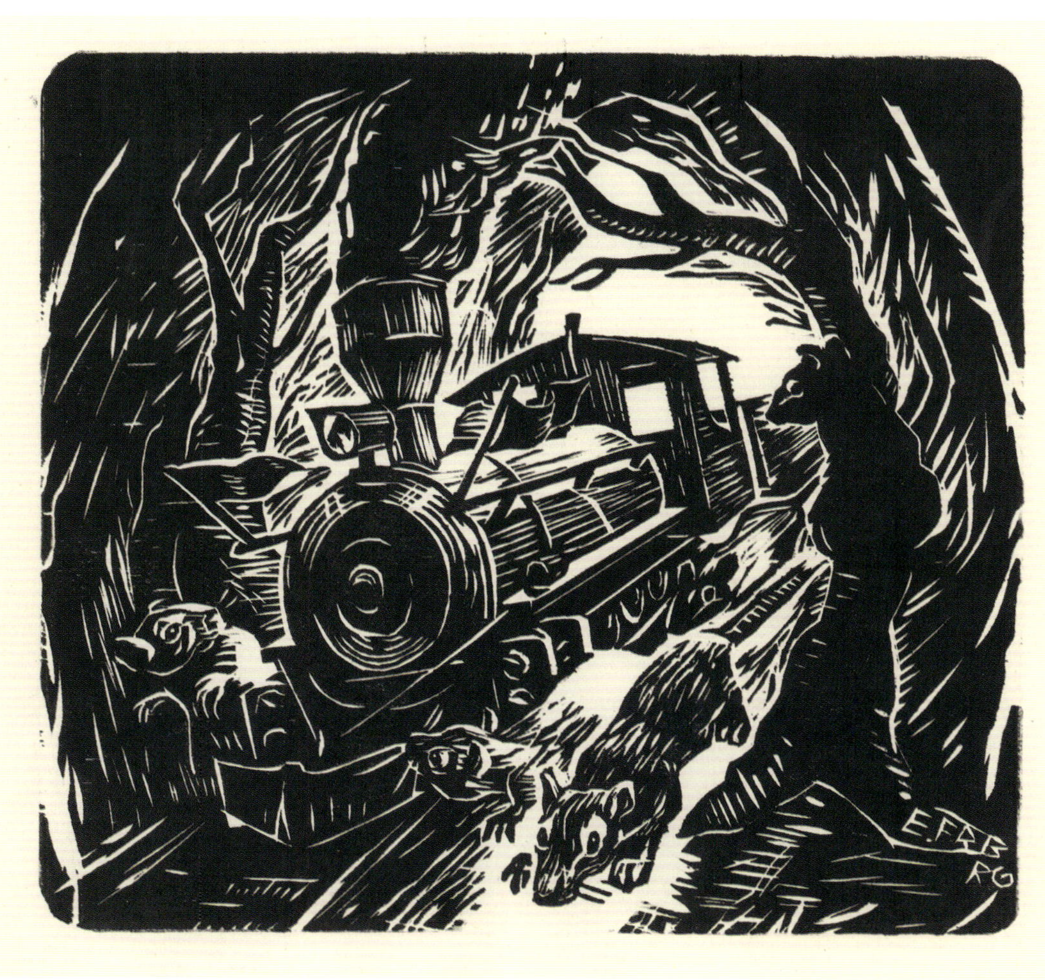

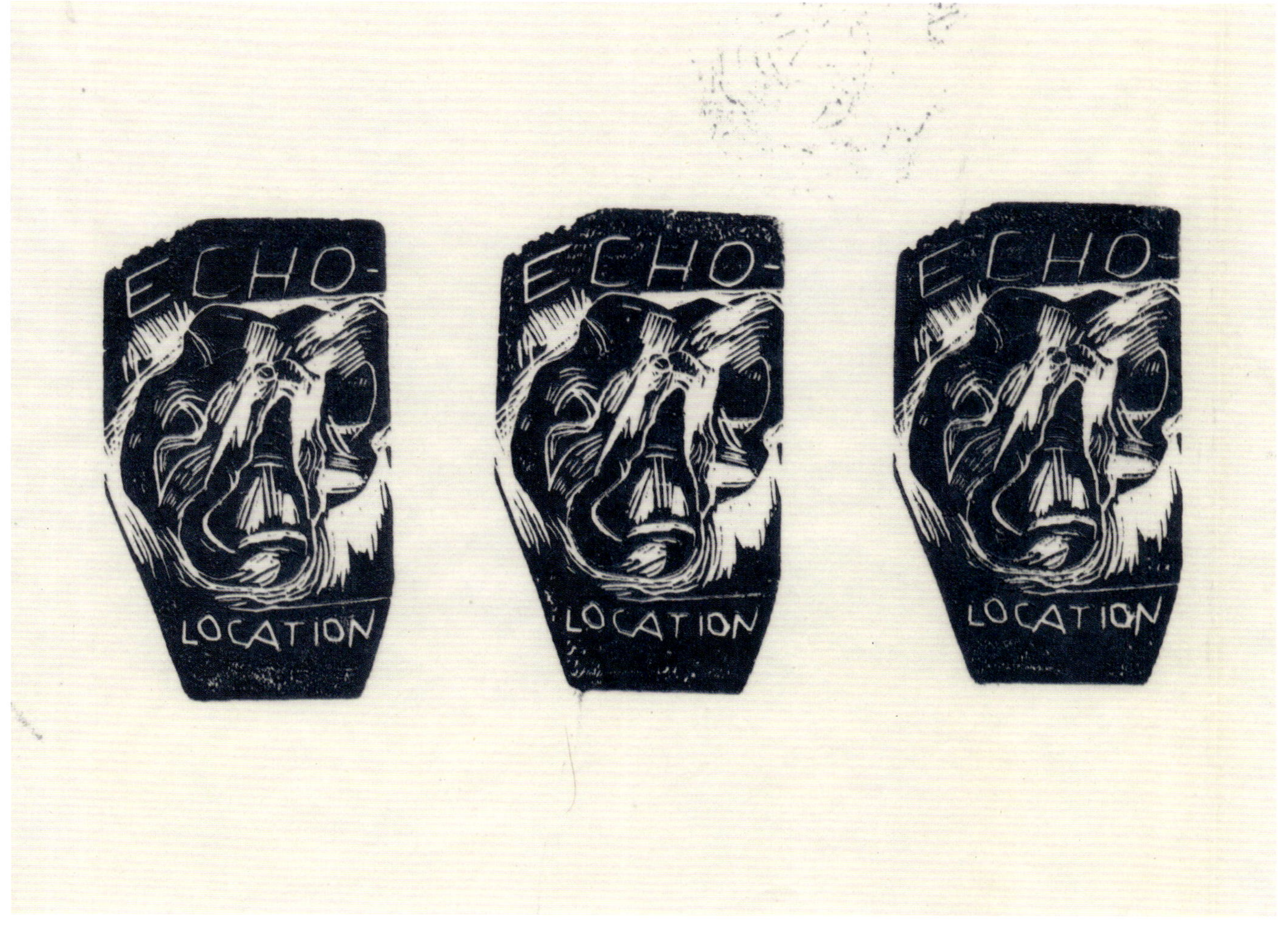
ECHO
LOCATION

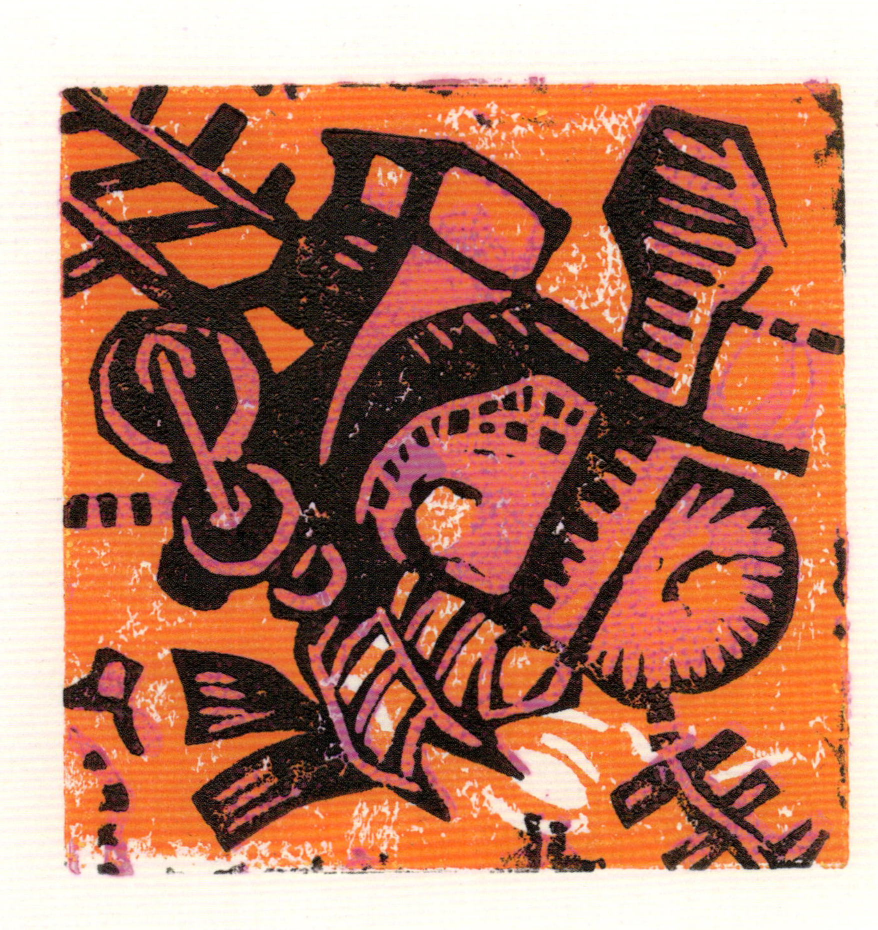

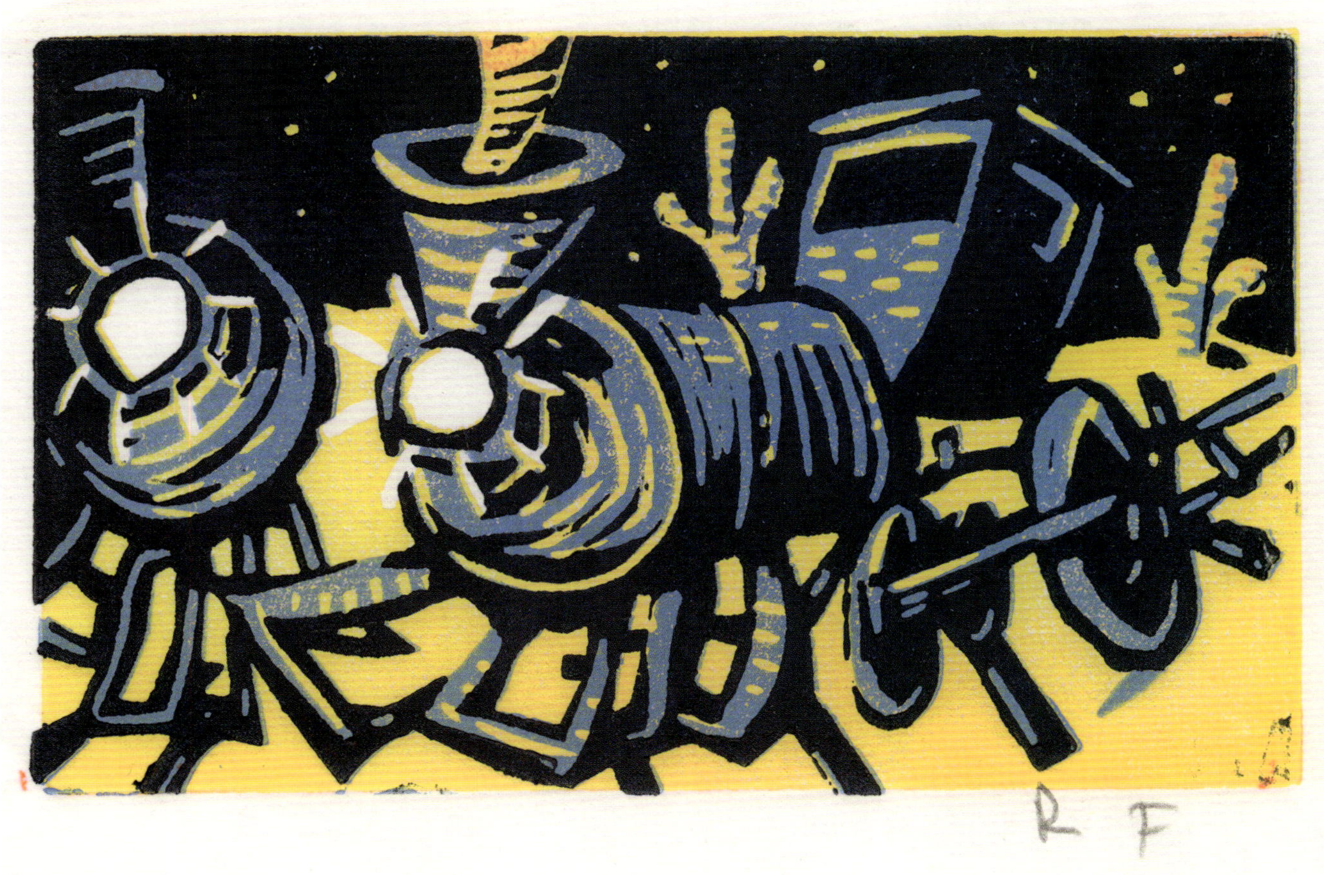
R F

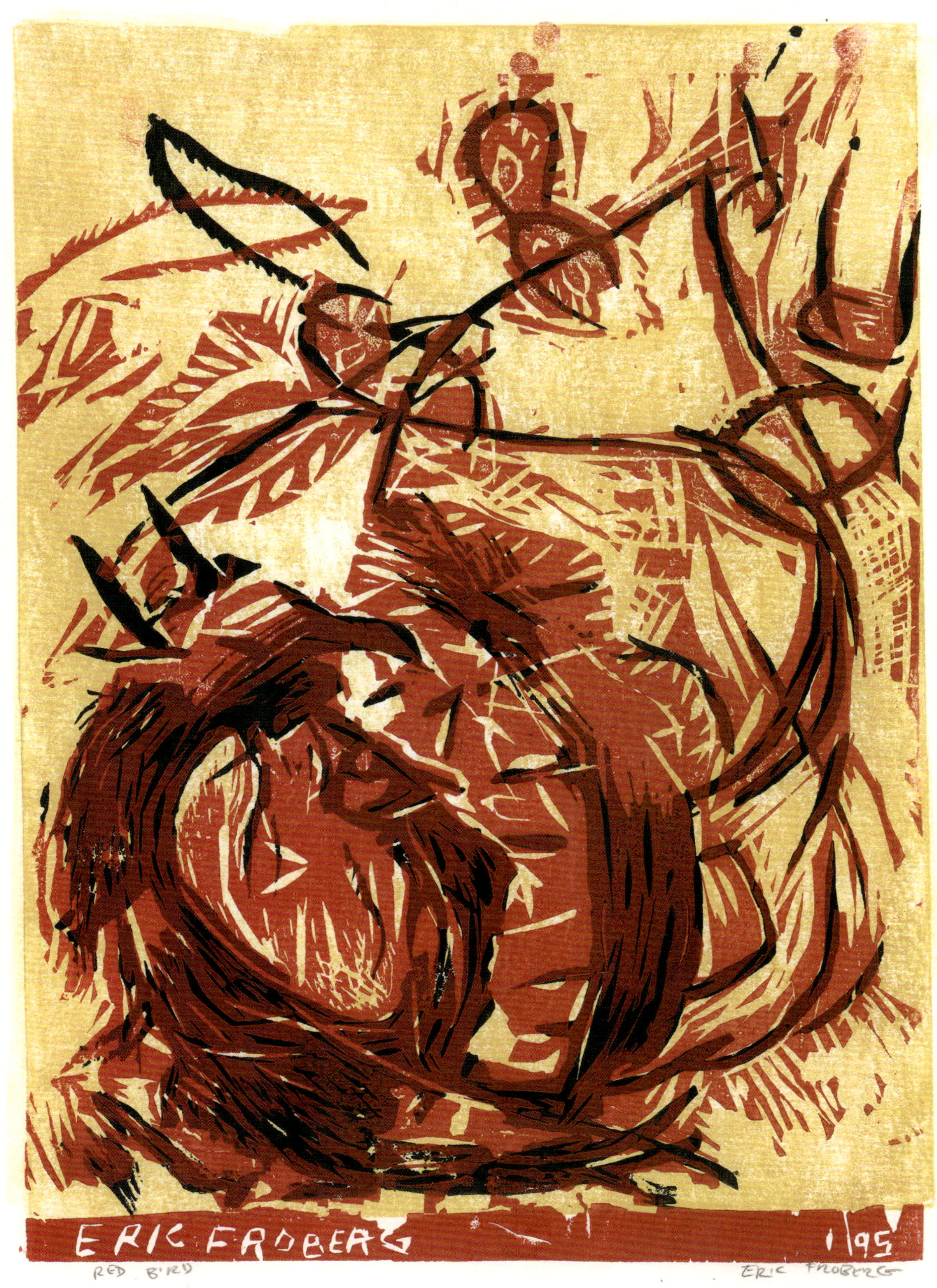

RED BIRD   Eric Froberg

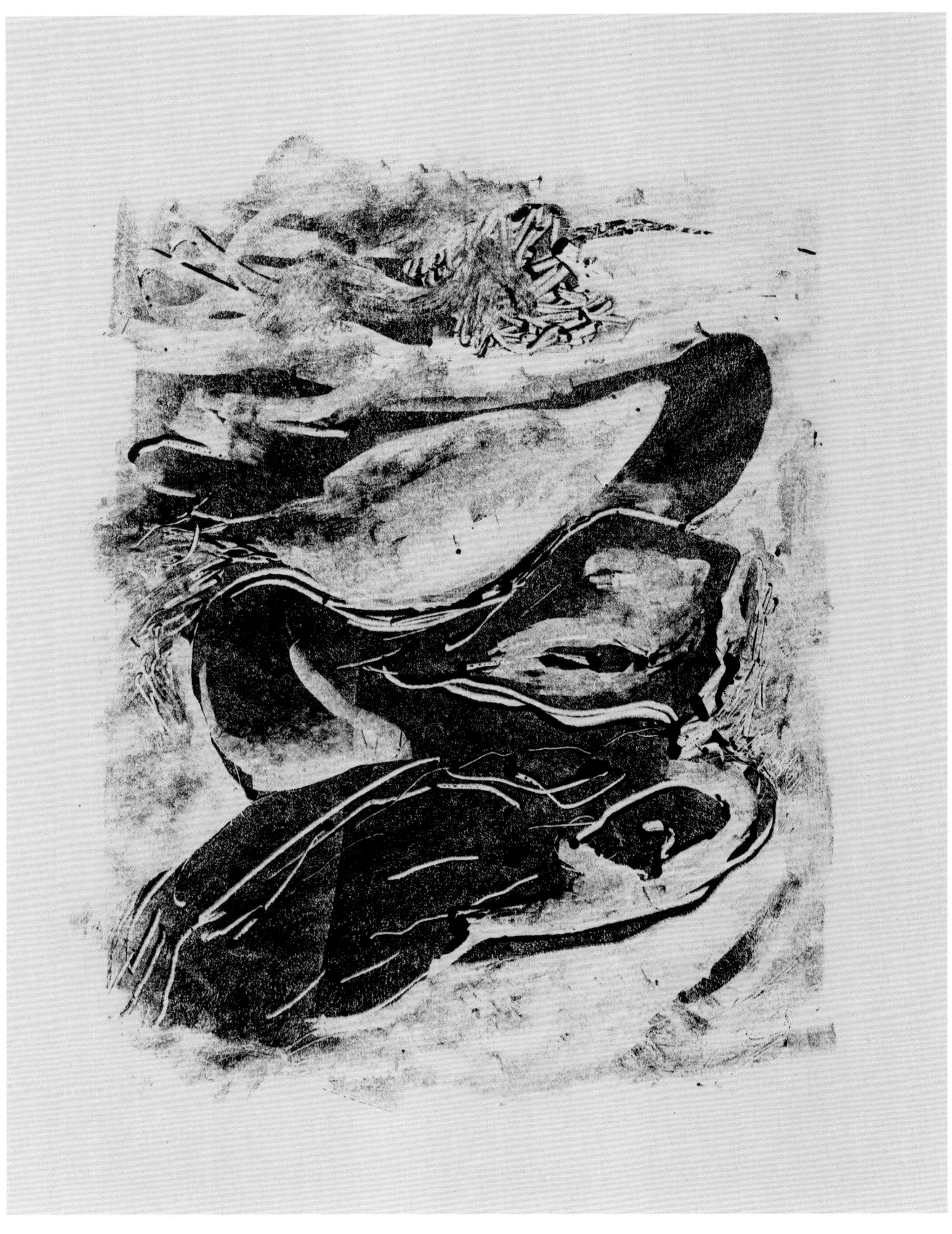

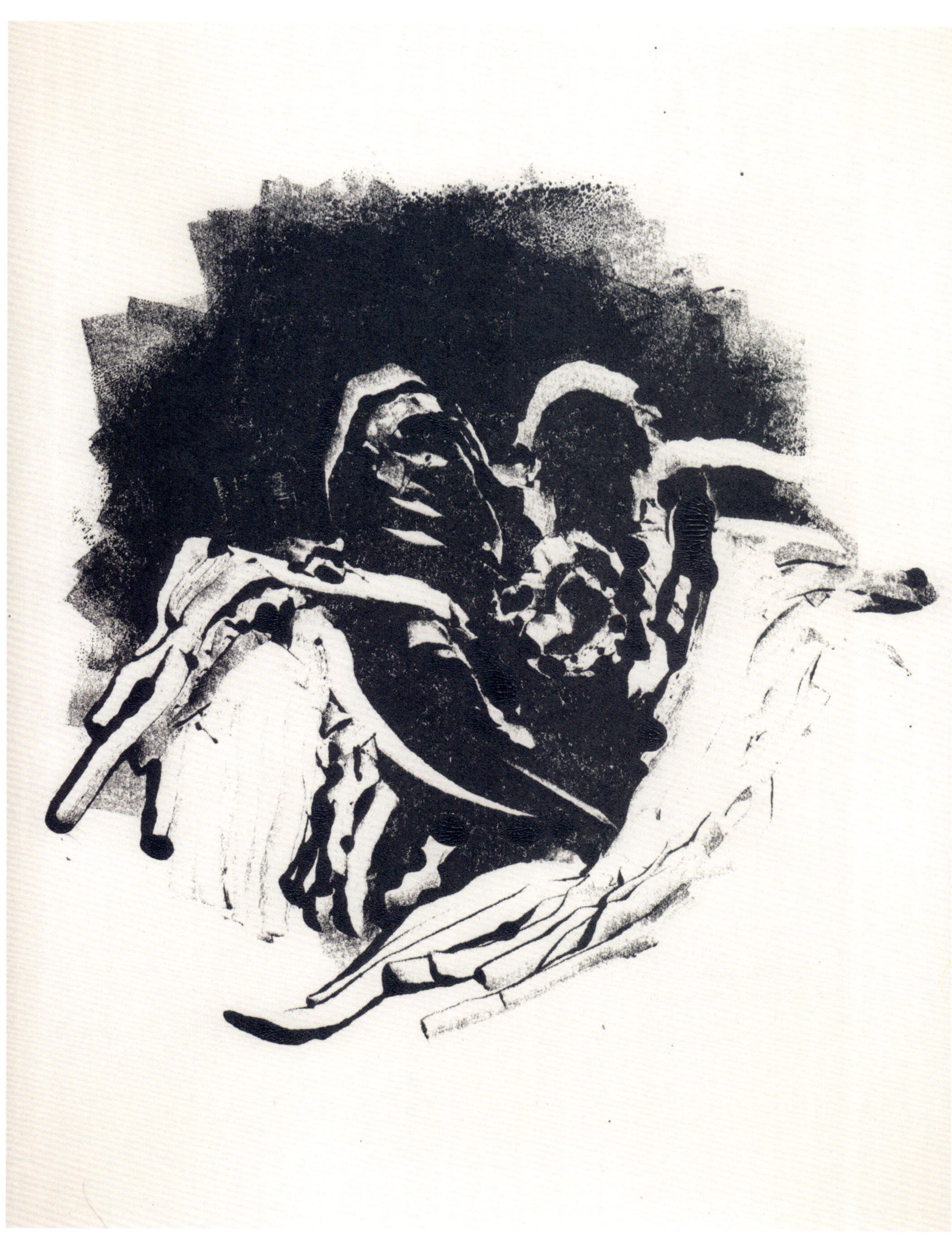

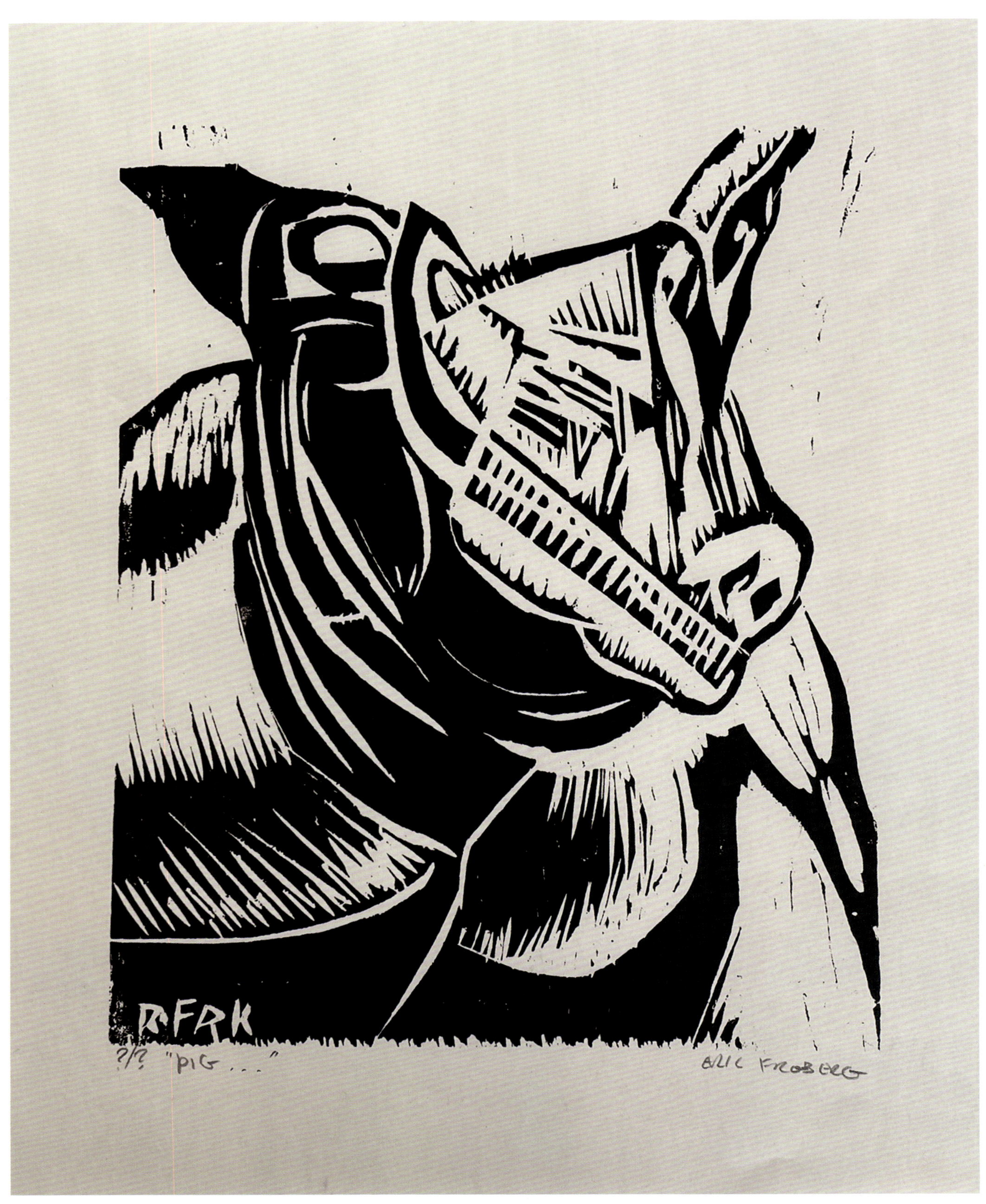
RFRK
?/? "PIG..."
ERIC FROBERG

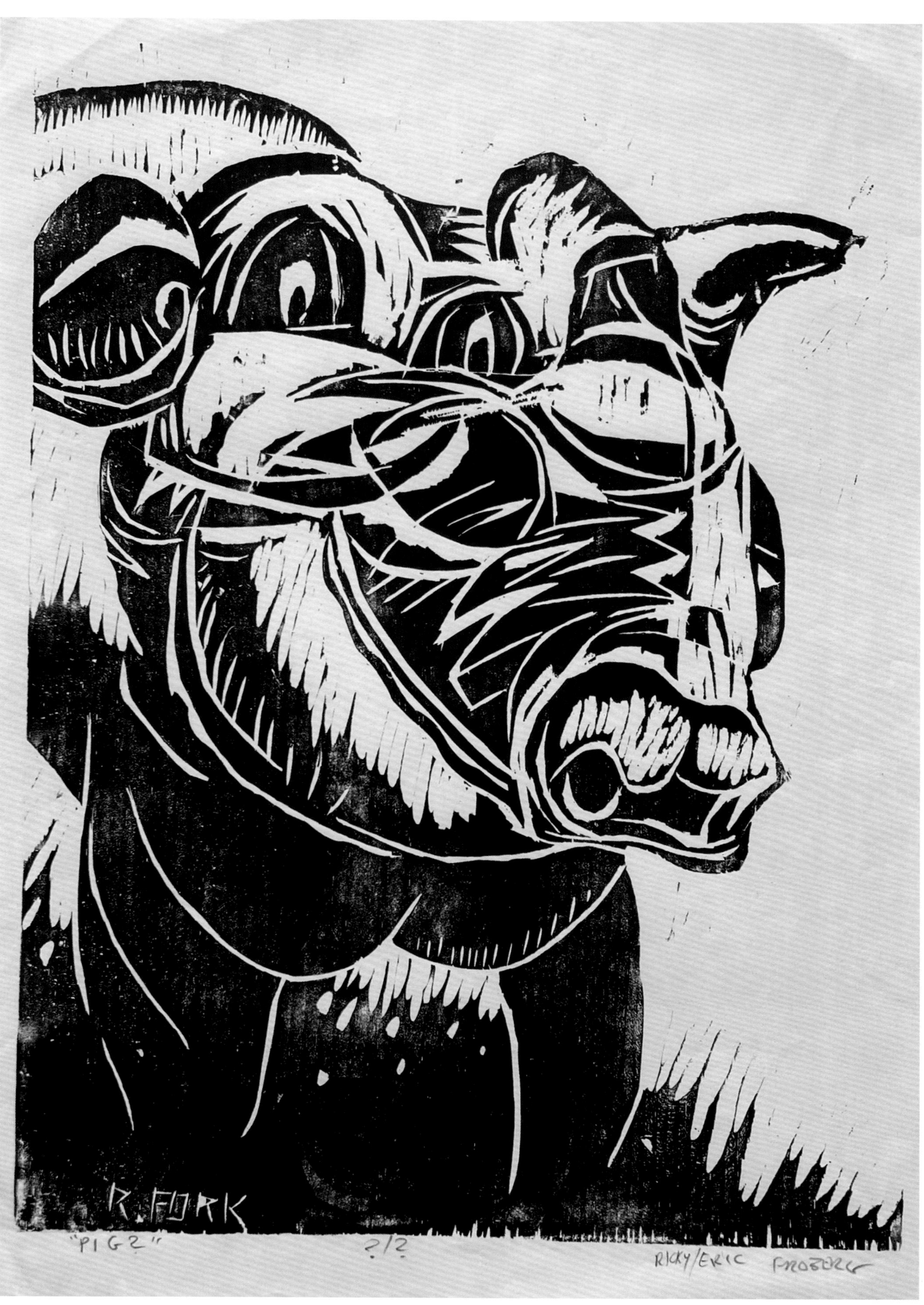

R. FORK
"PIG 2"
2/2
RICKY/ERIC FROBERG

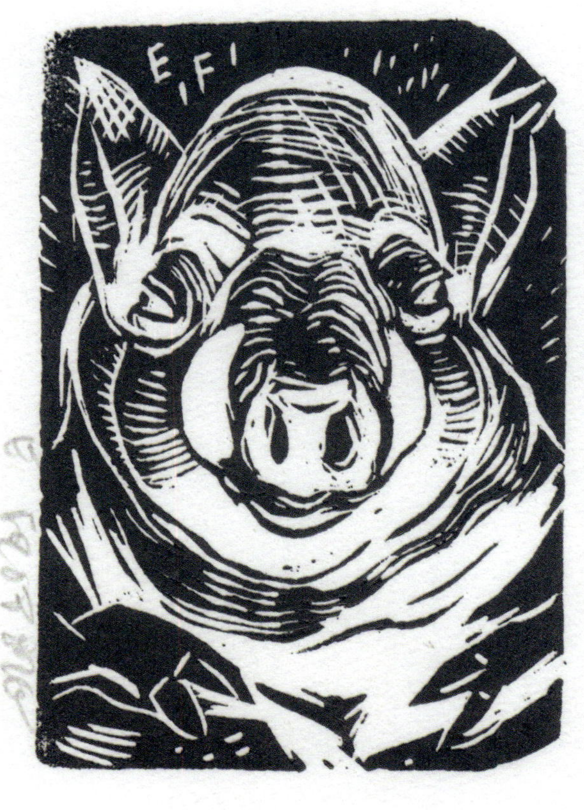

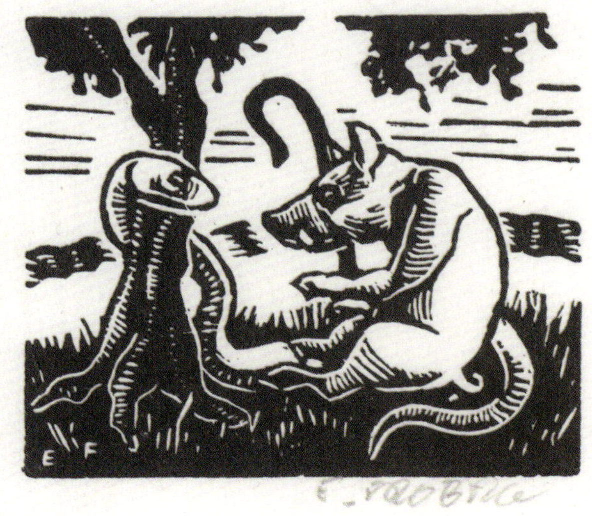

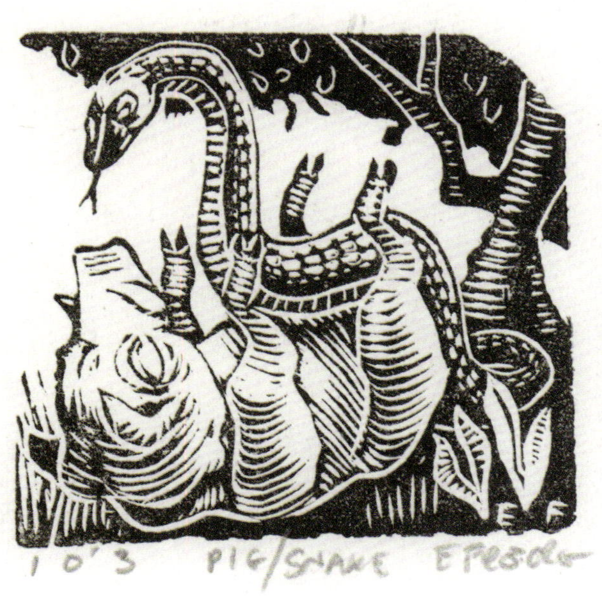

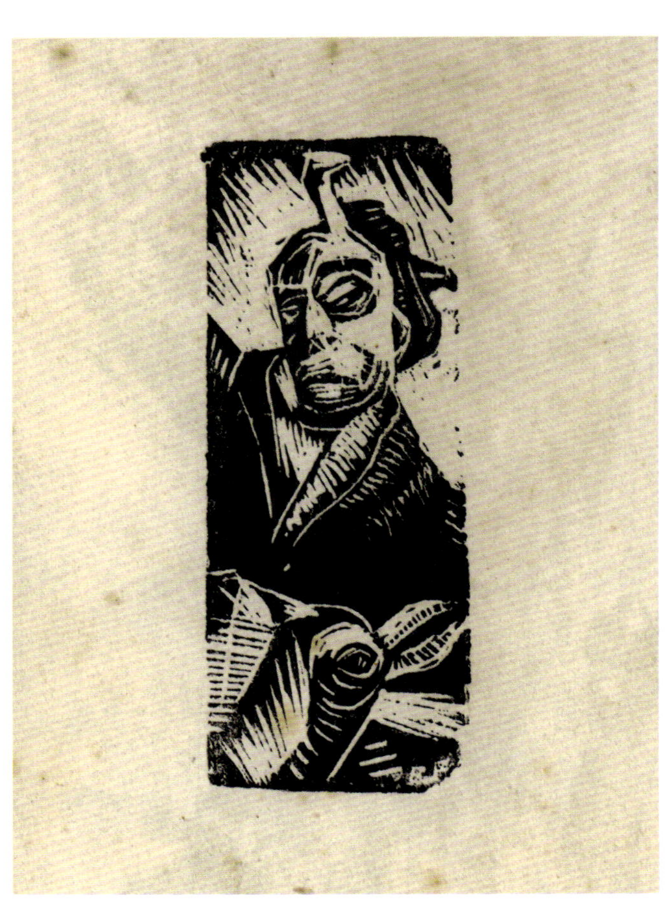

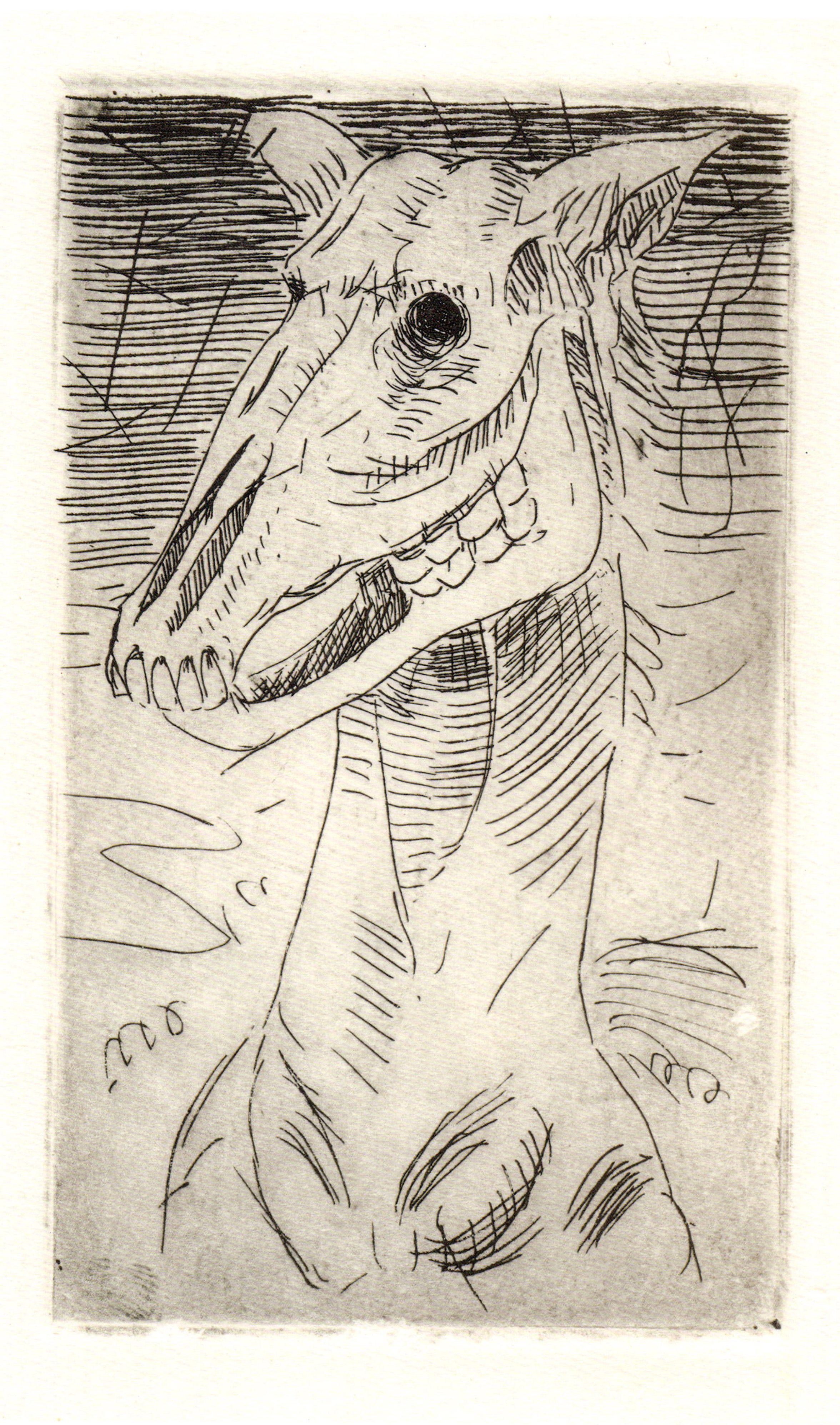

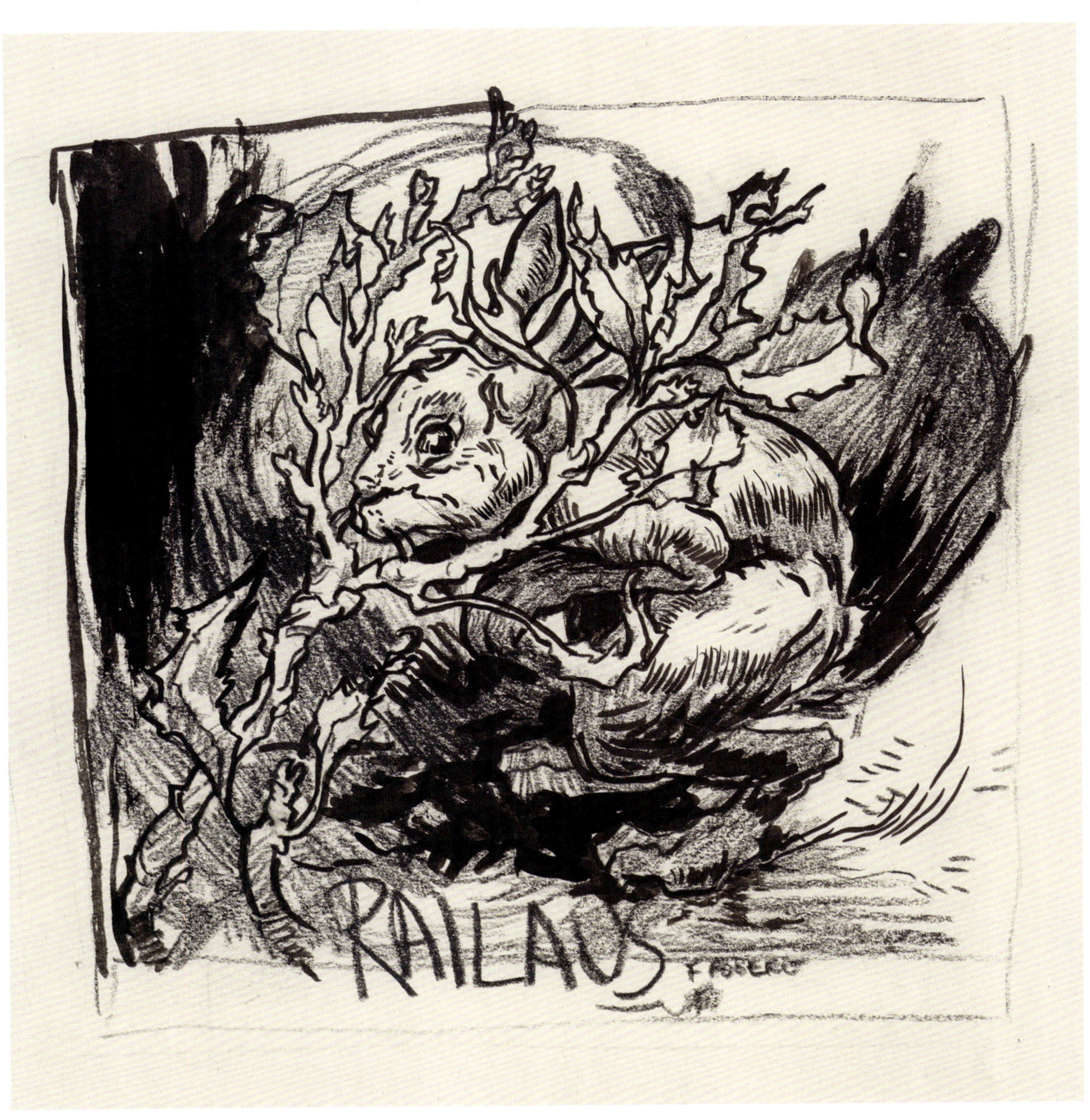
RAILAUS

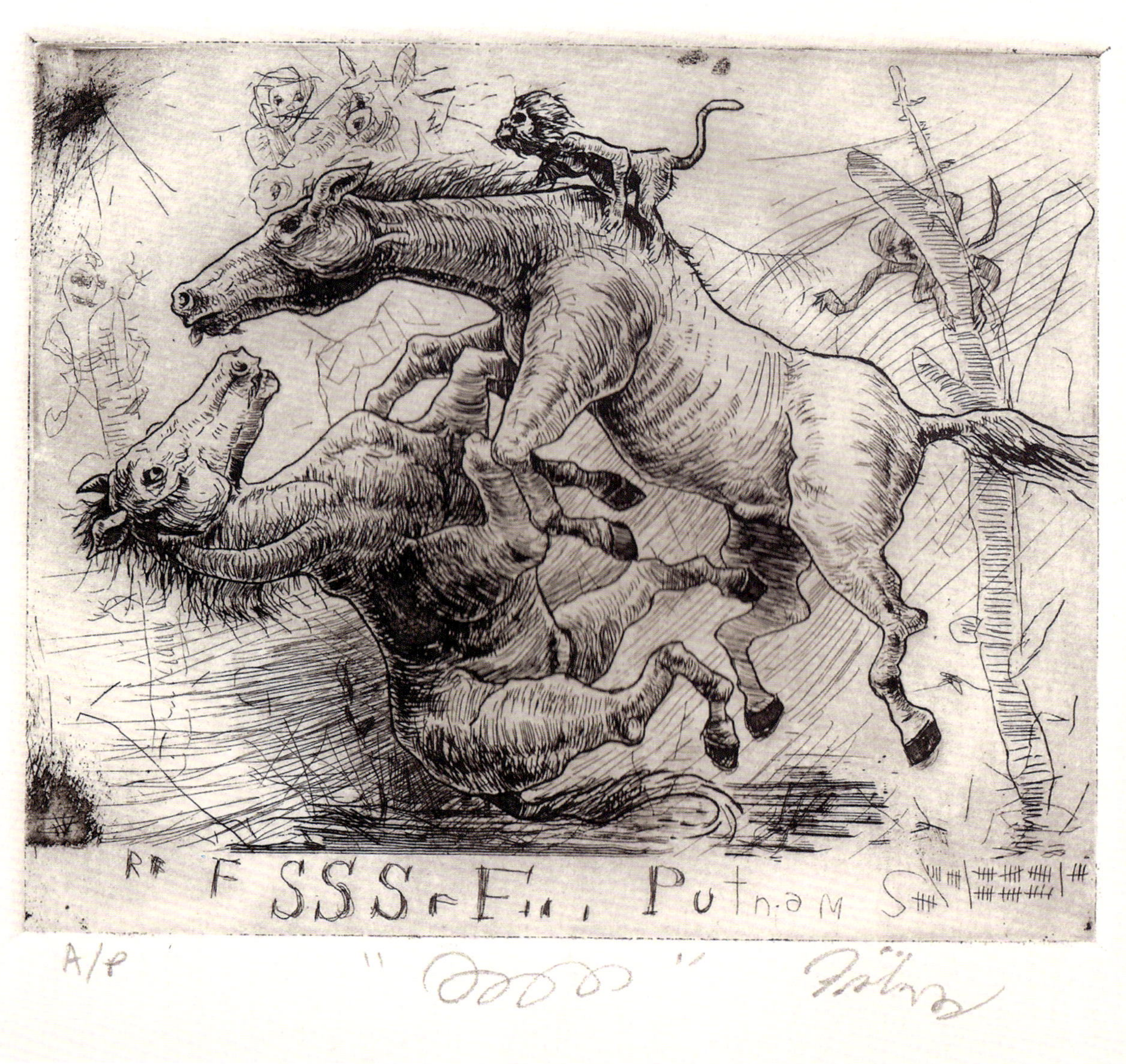
R F SSS F... Putnam S
A/P   "   "

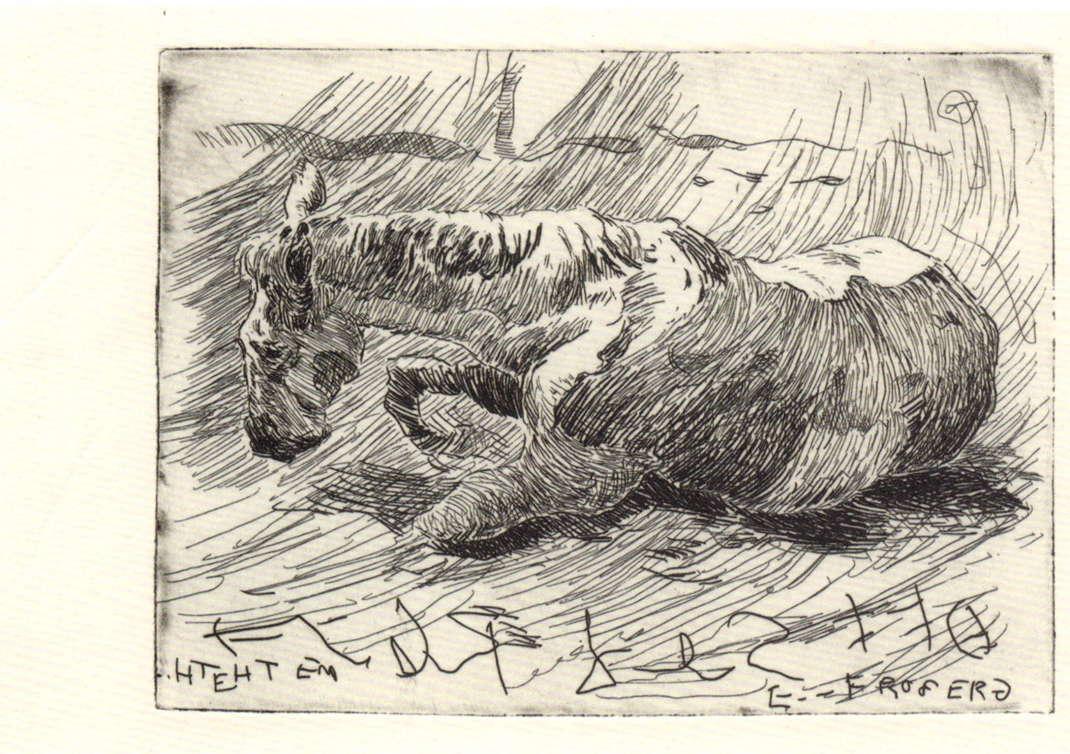
HTEHT EM

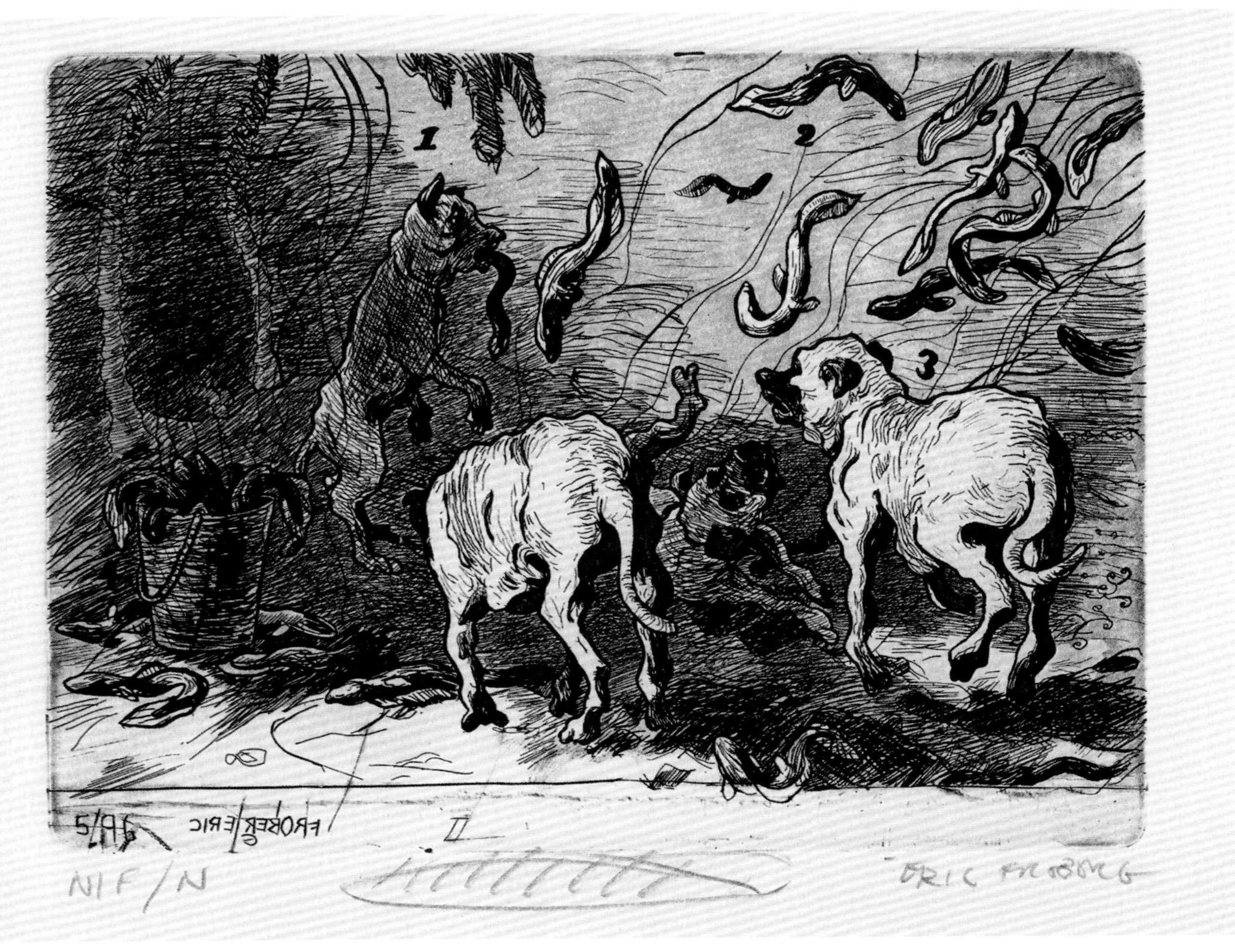
1
2
3
5/A5
FRÖBERG/ERIC
NIF/N
II
ERIC FROBERG

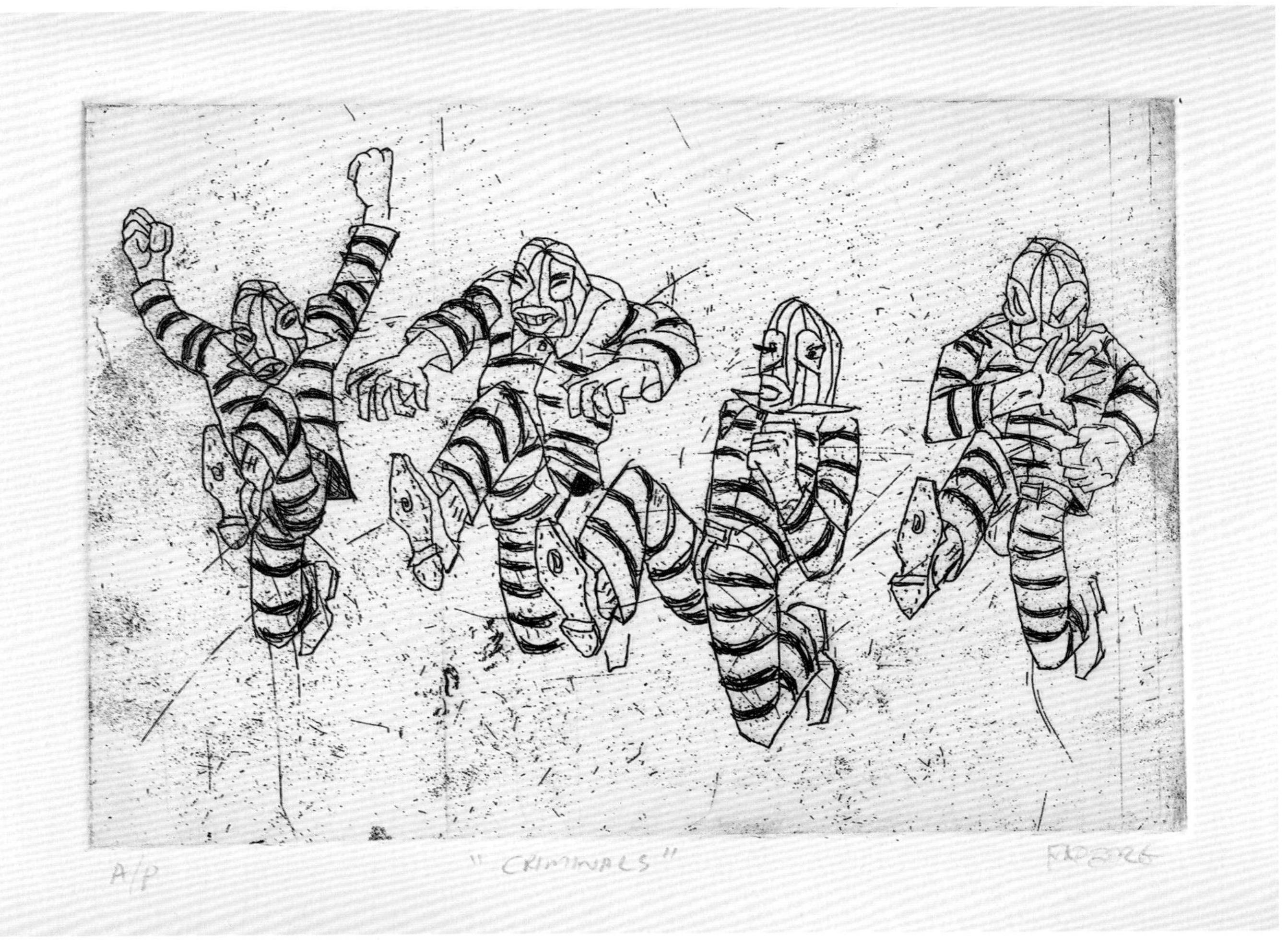
A/P
"CRIMINALS"
FROBERG

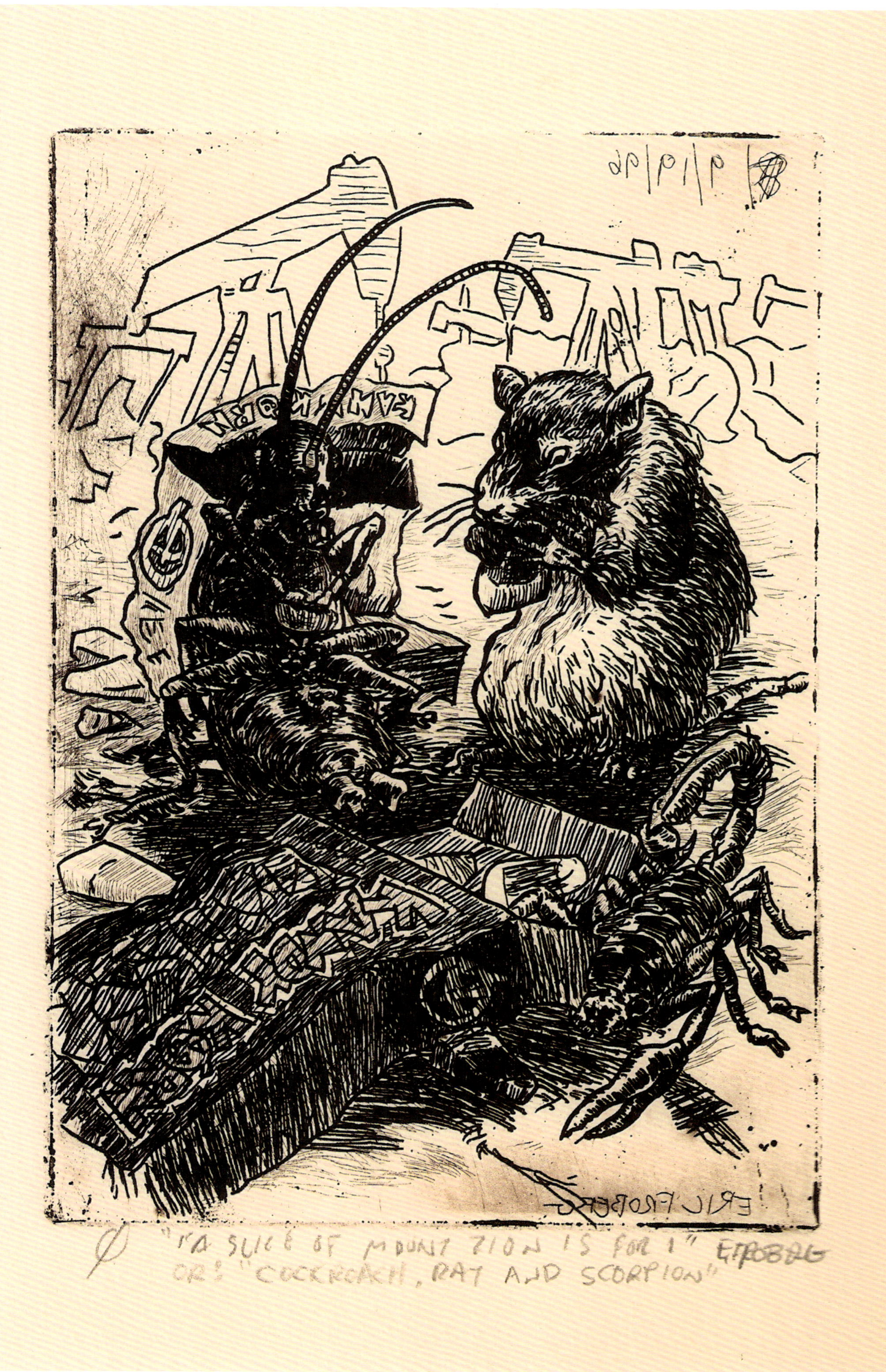

"A SLICE OF MOUNT ZION IS FOR I"
OR: "COCKROACH, RAT AND SCORPION"

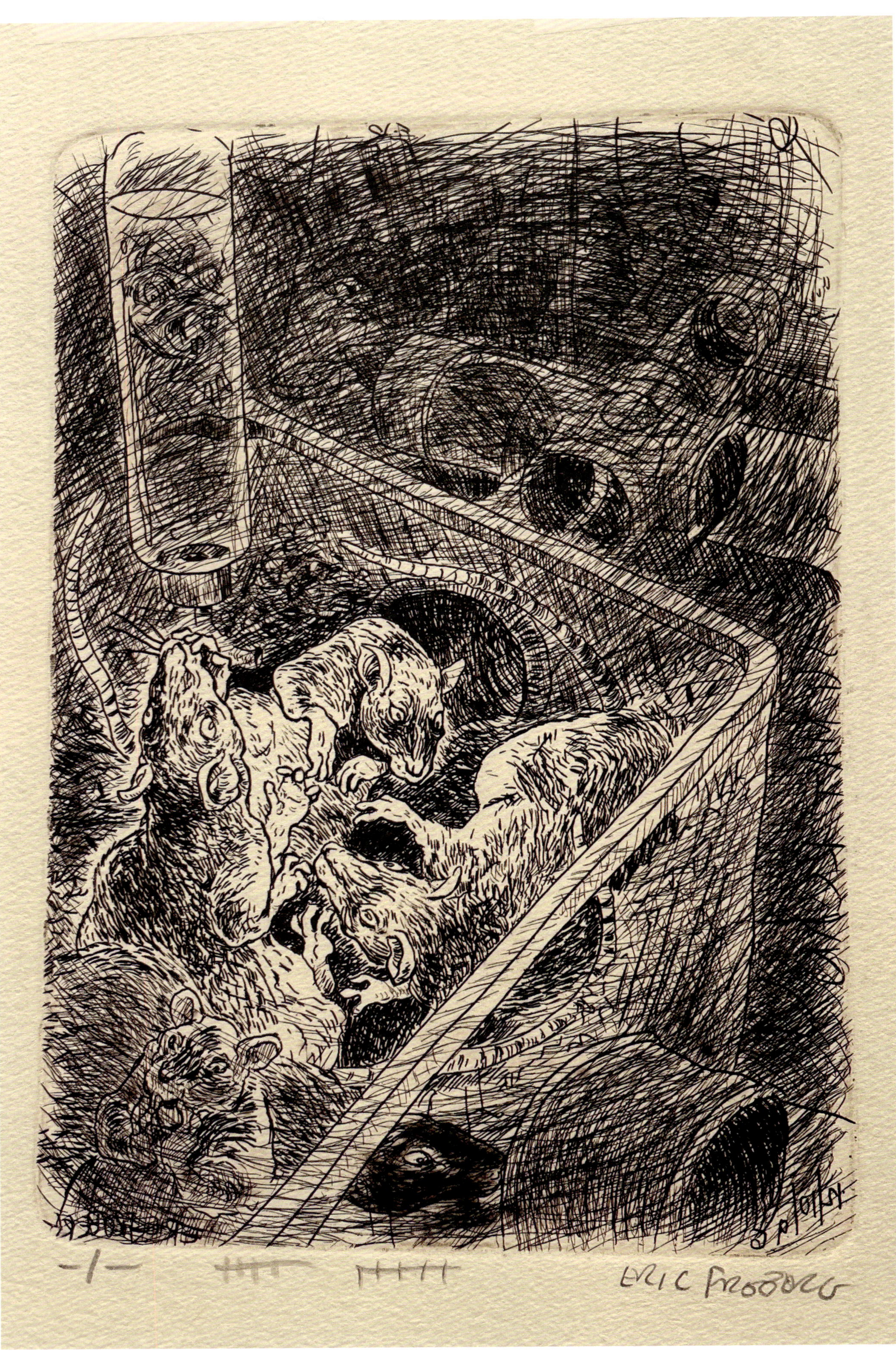
ERIC PROBORG

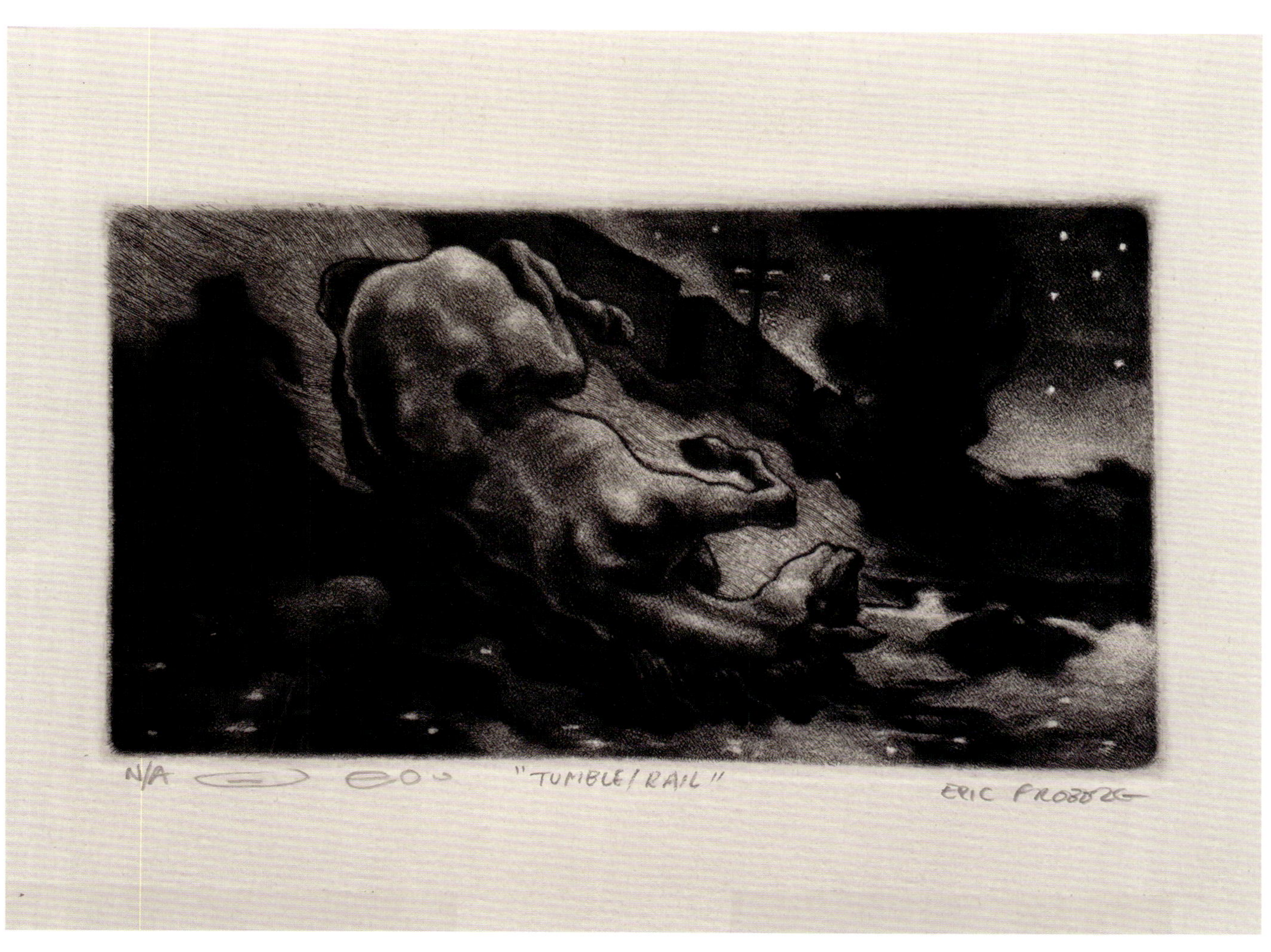
N/A   "TUMBLE/RAIL"   ERIC FROBERG

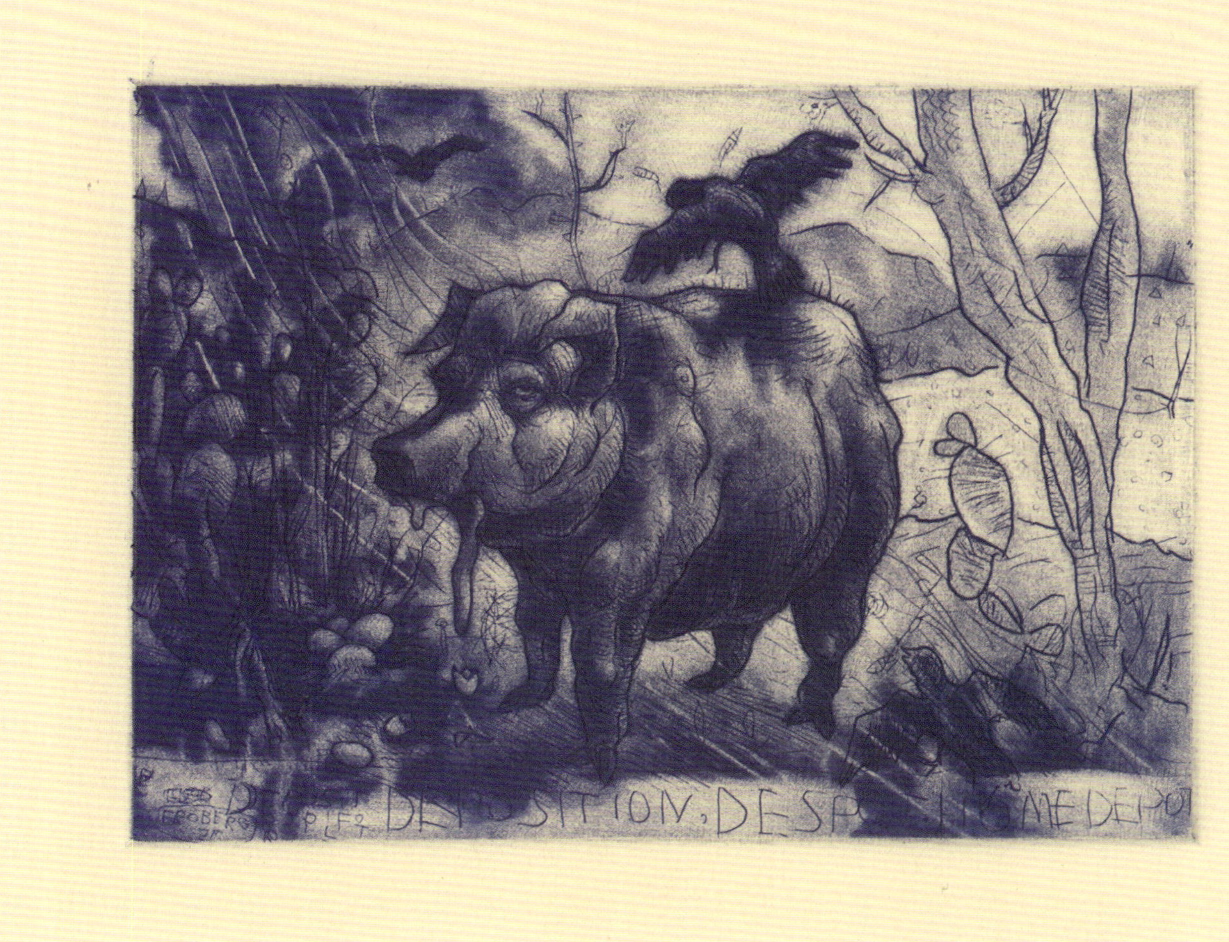

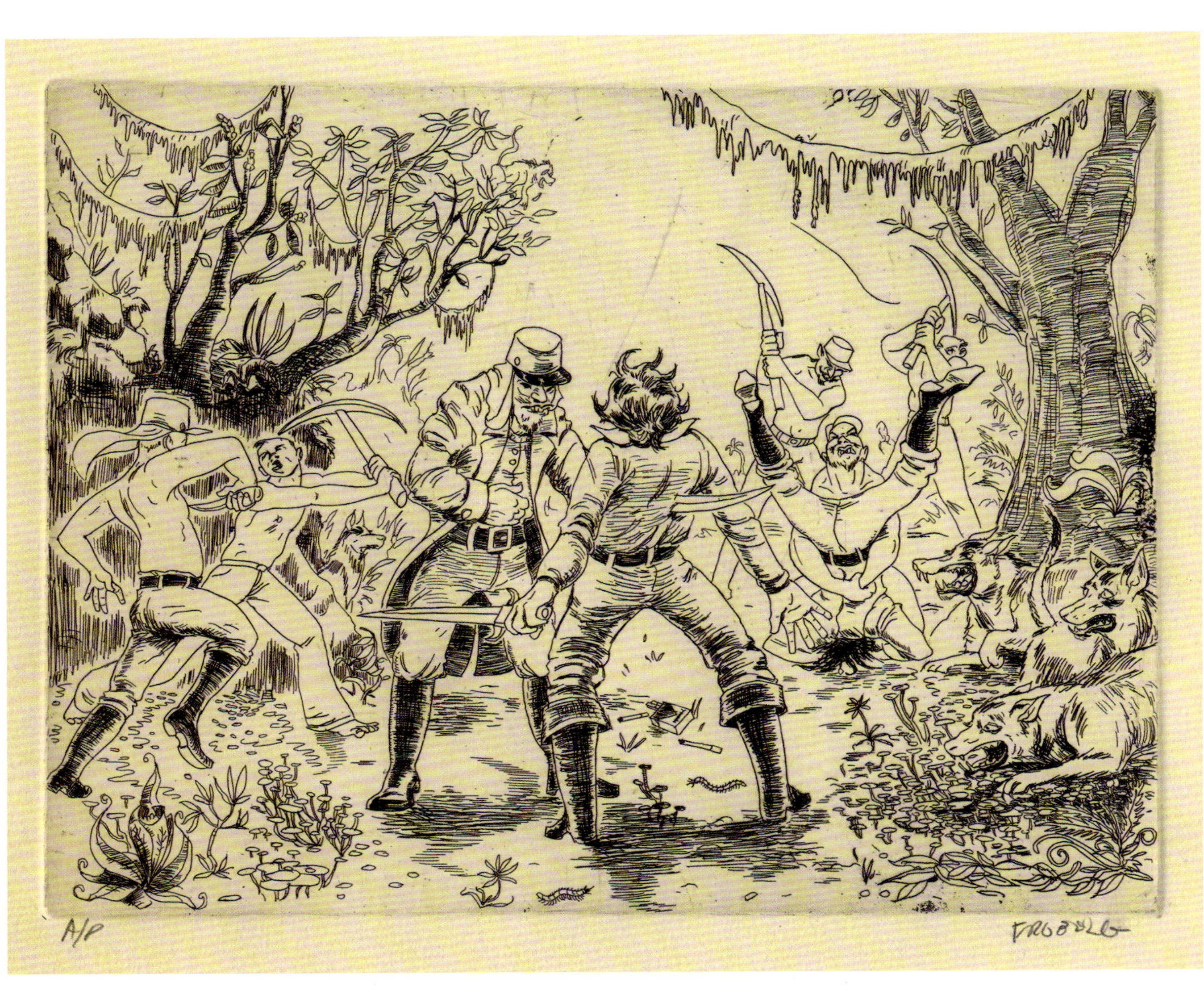
A/P

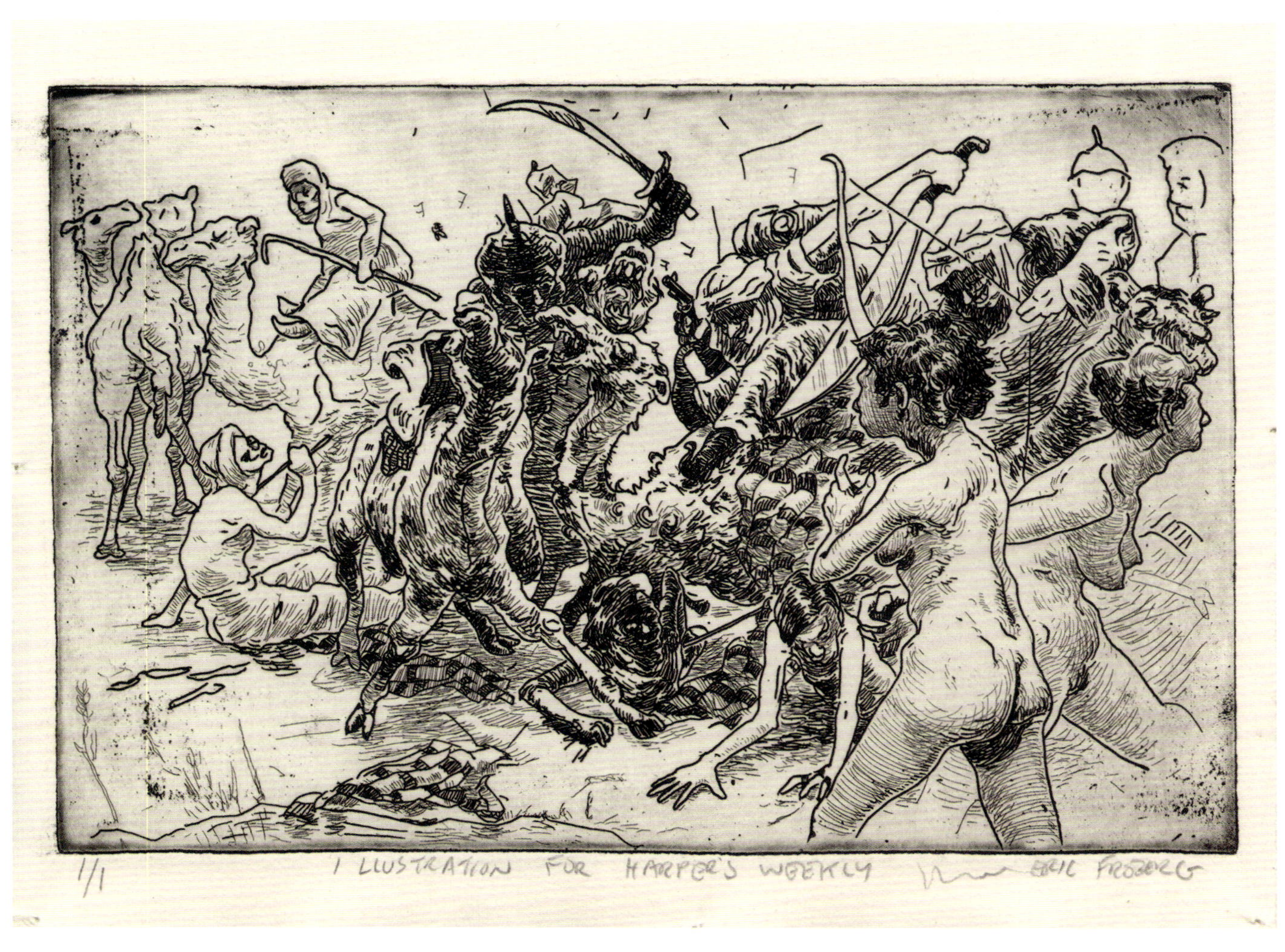

1/1   ILLUSTRATION FOR HARPER'S WEEKLY   ERIC FROBERG

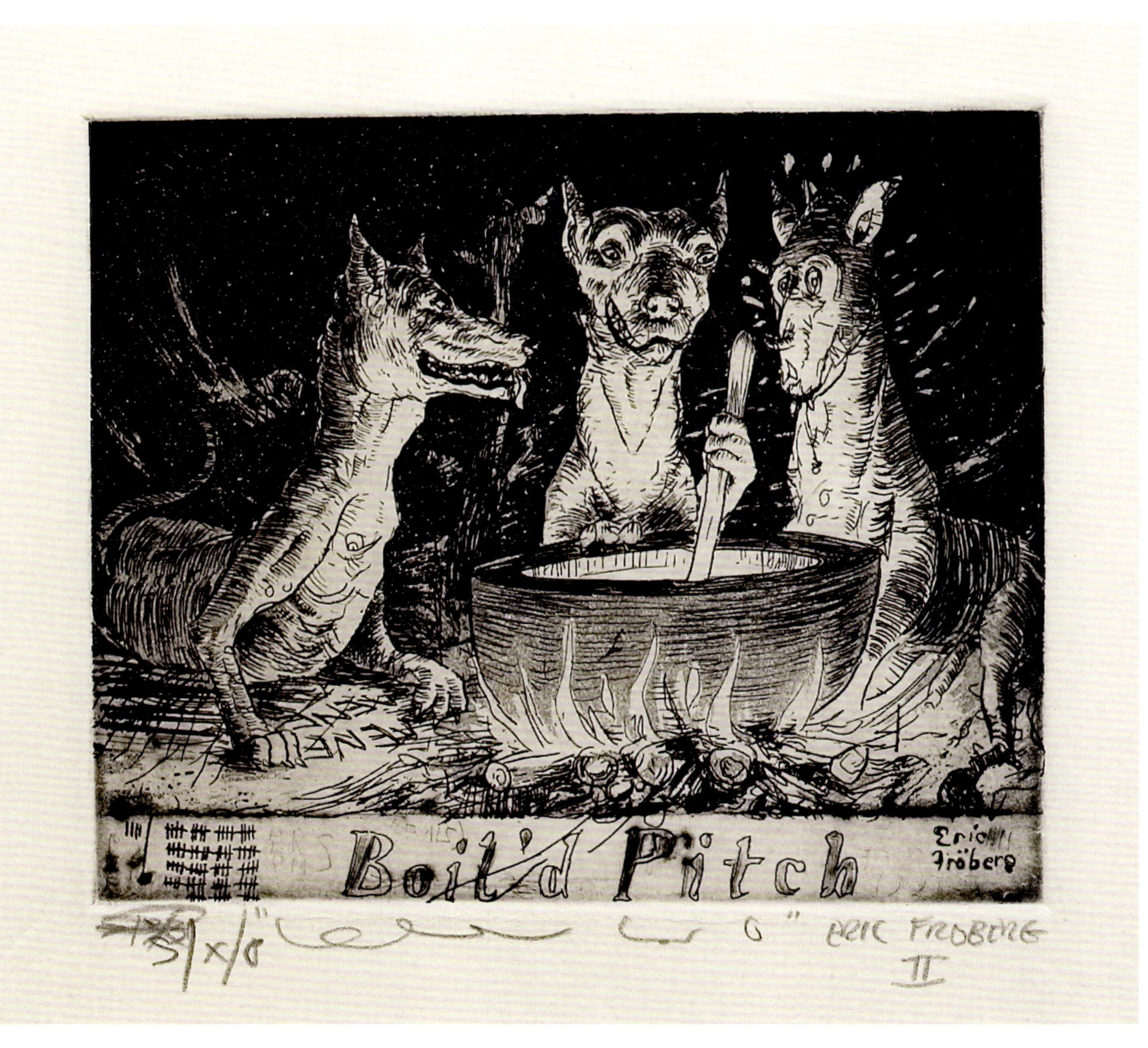

Boil'd Pitch
Eric Fröberg
ERIC FROBERG
II

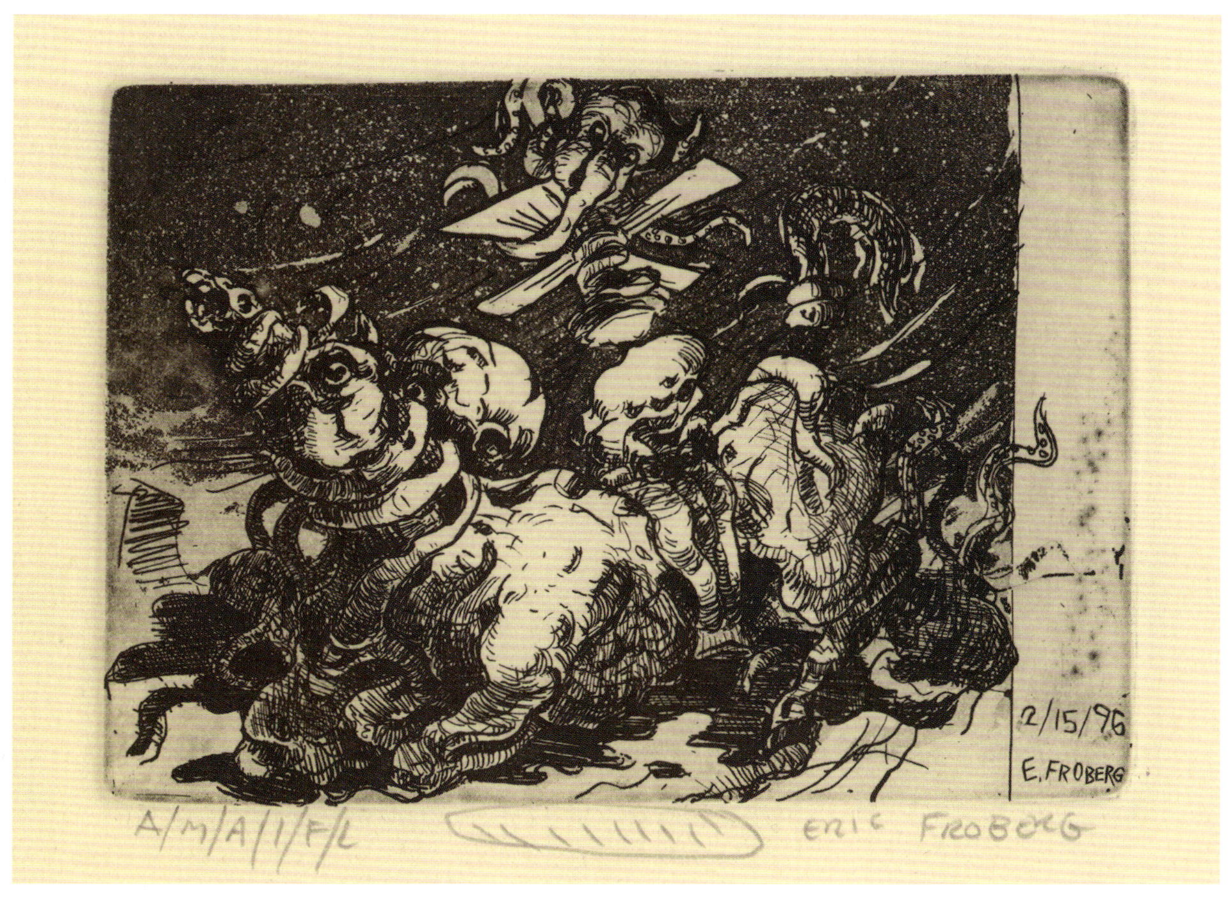

2/15/96
E. FROBERG
A/M/A/I/F/L
ERIC FROBERG

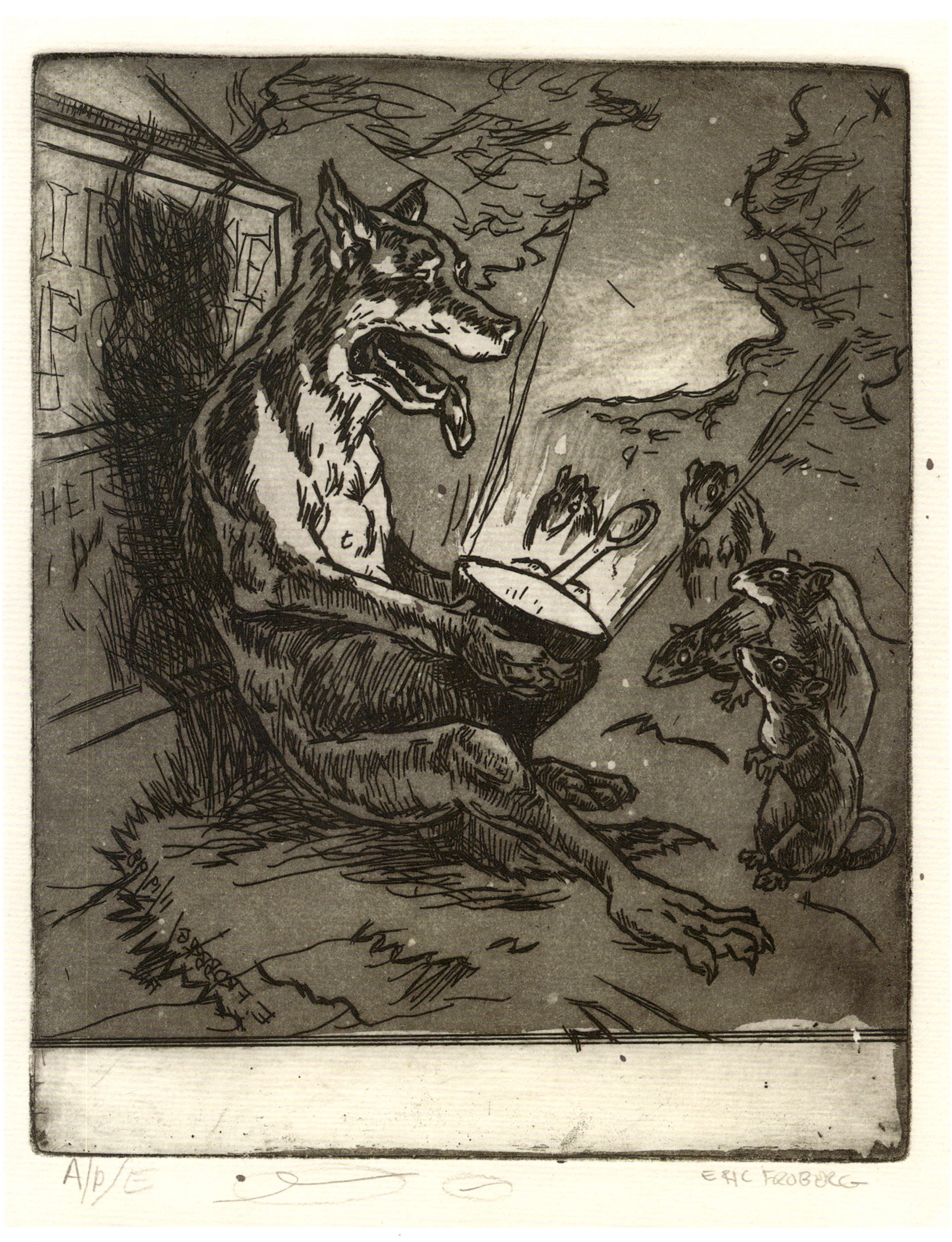

A/P/E   Eric Froberg

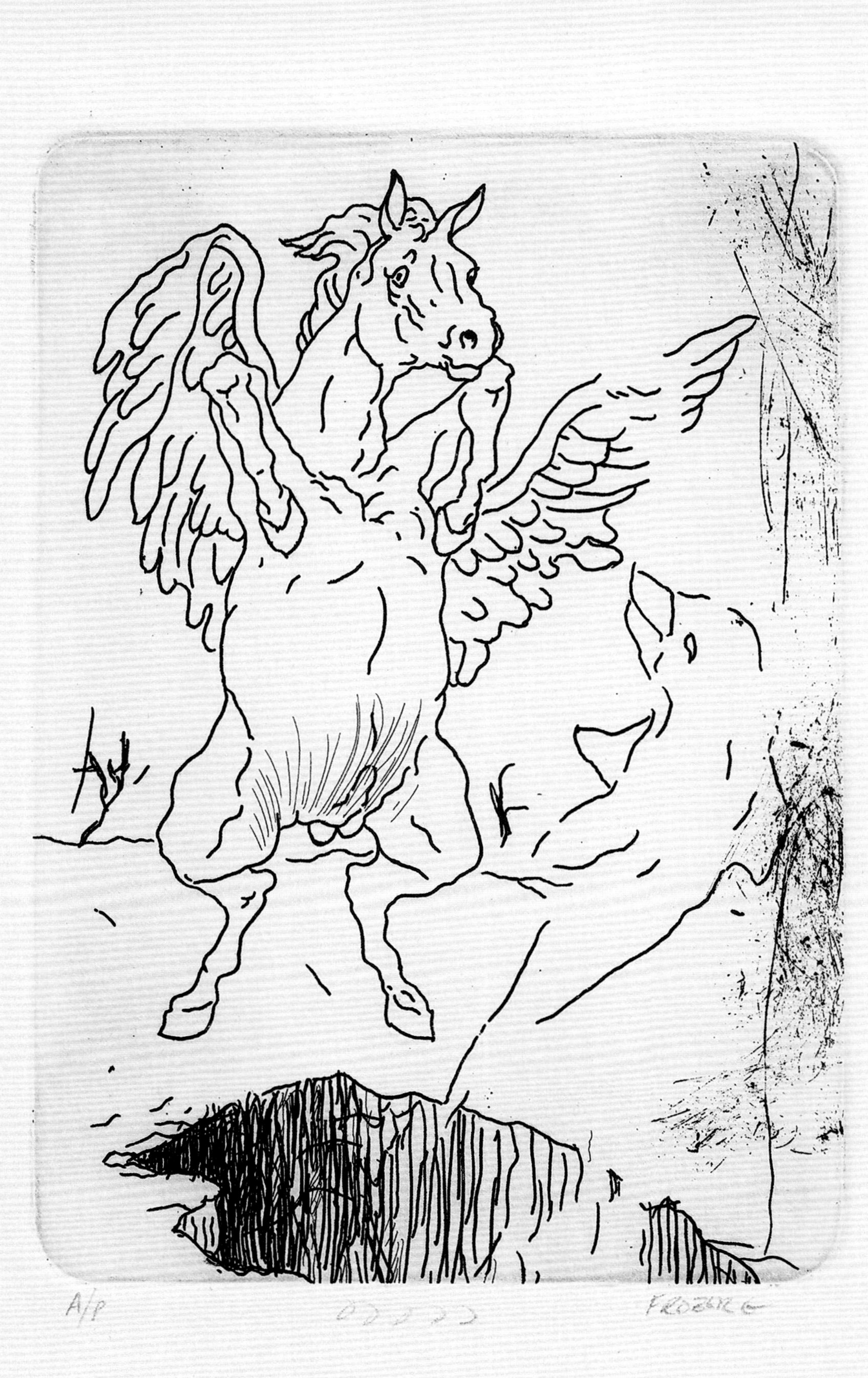

A/P
FROBERG

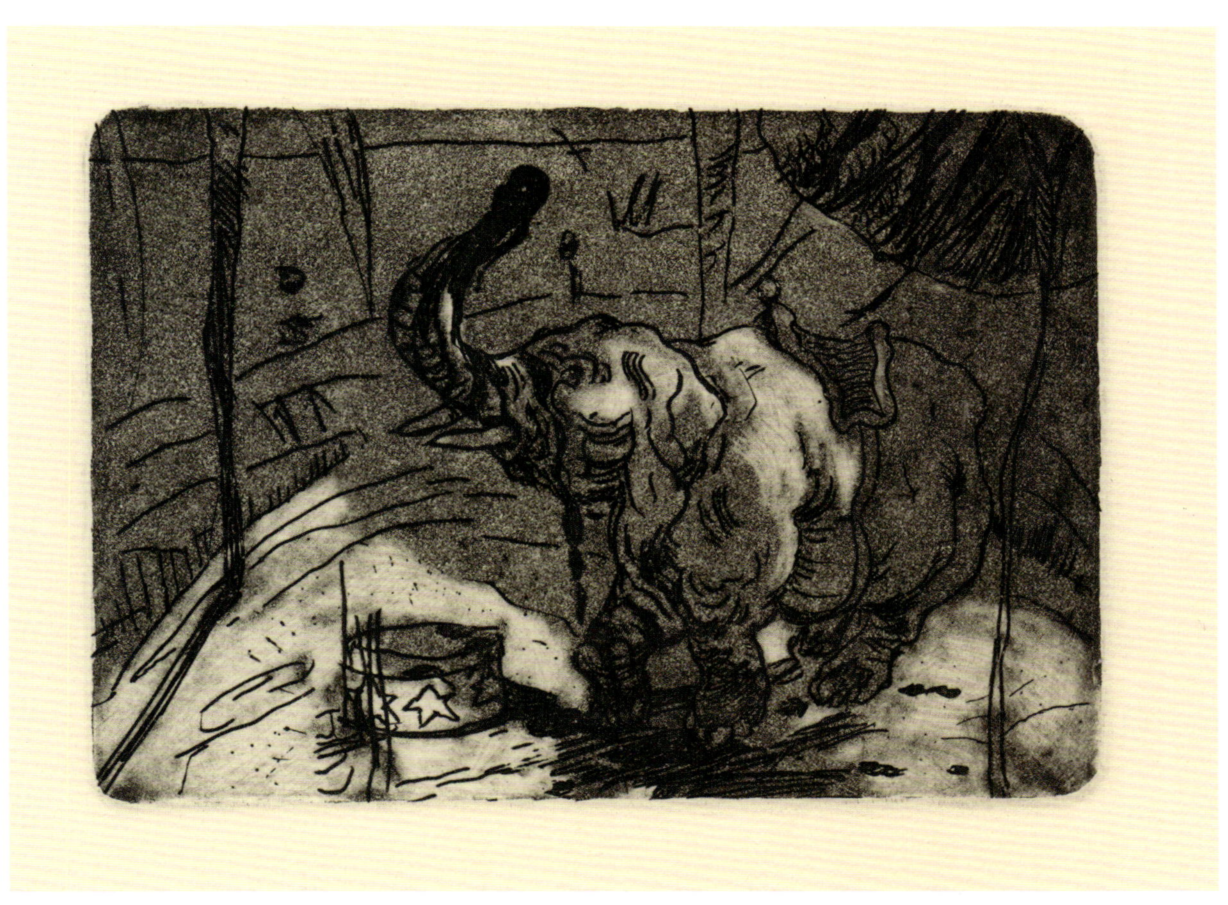

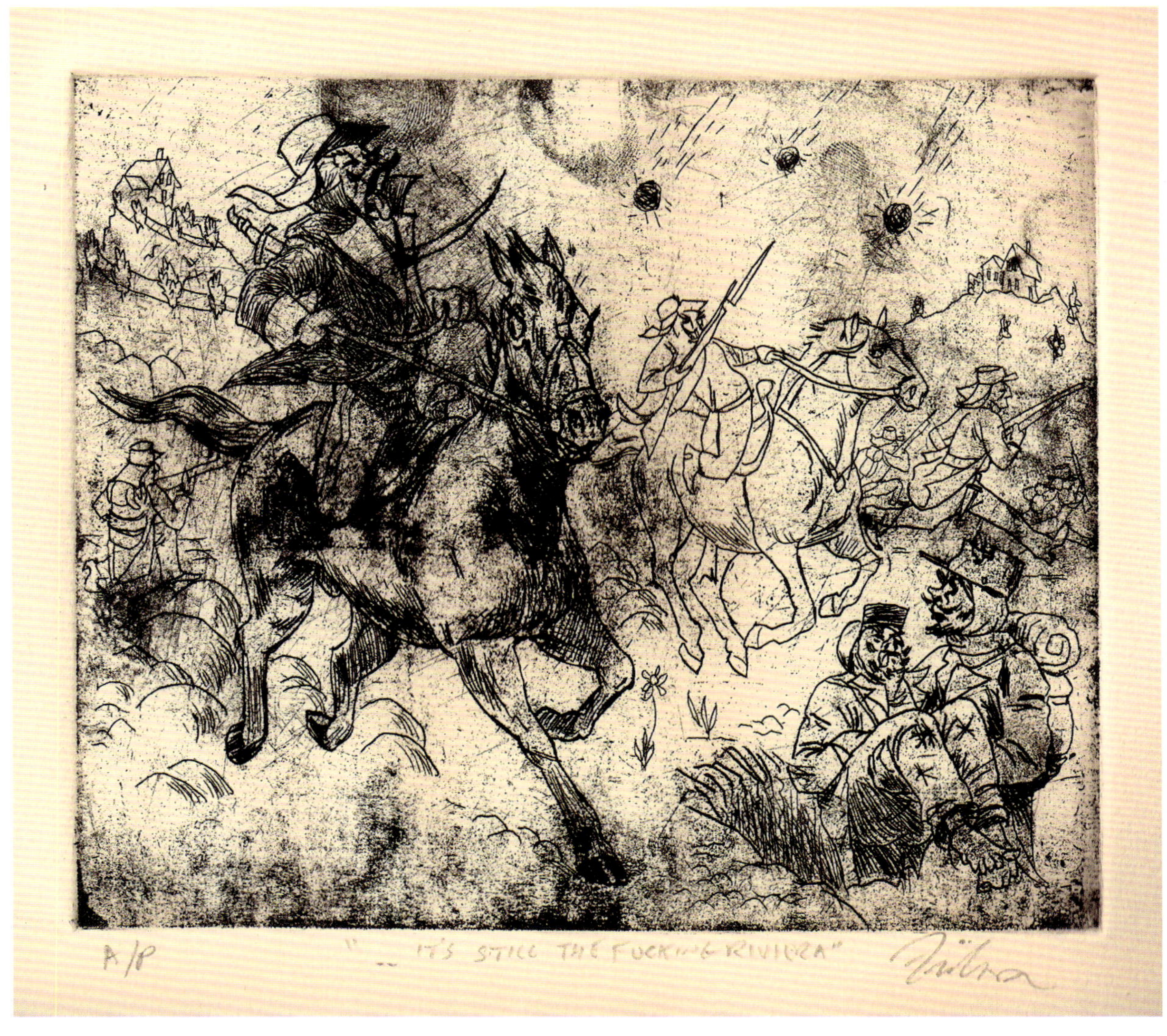

A/P   ".. IT'S STILL THE FUCKING RIVIERA"

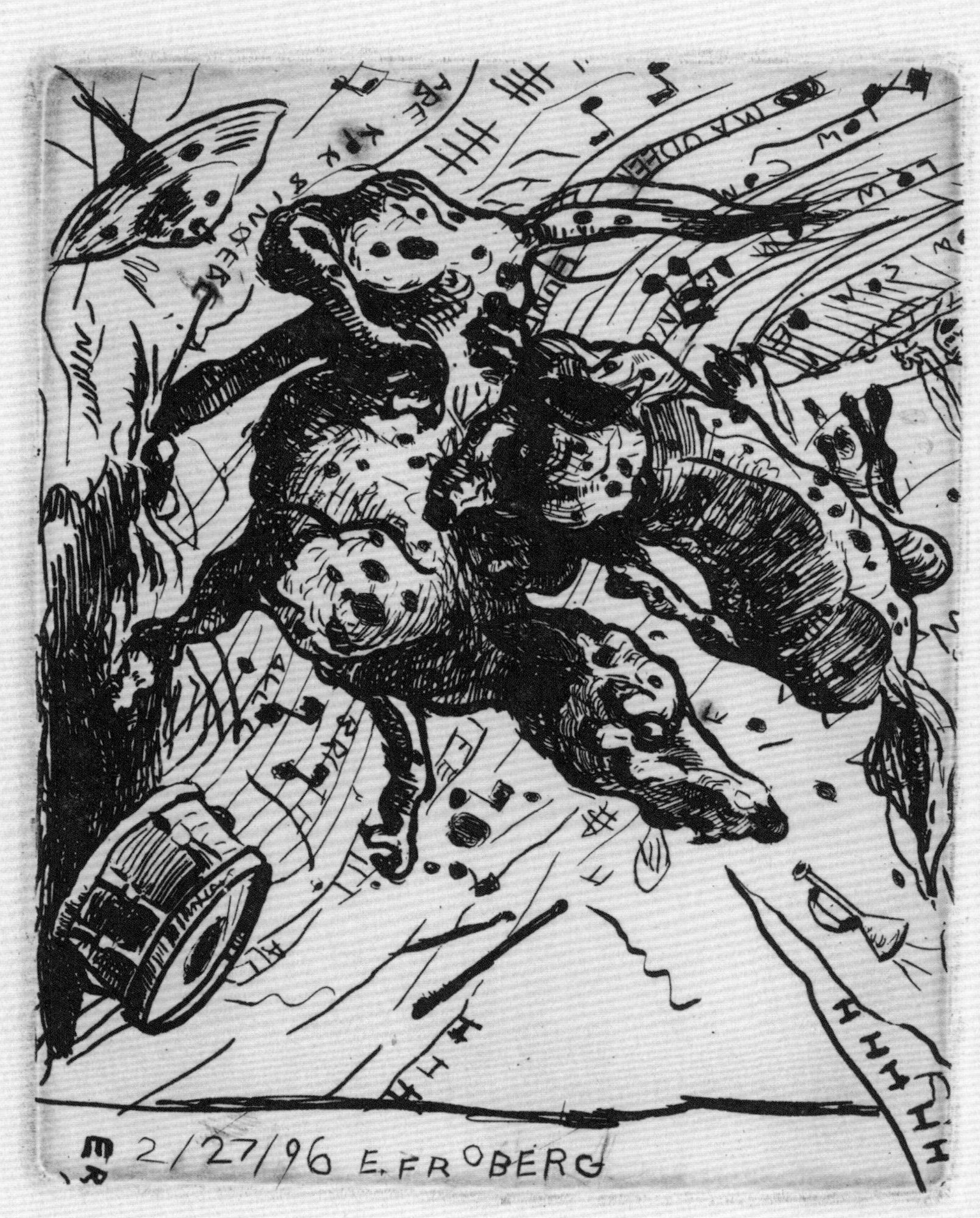
2/27/96 E. FROBERG

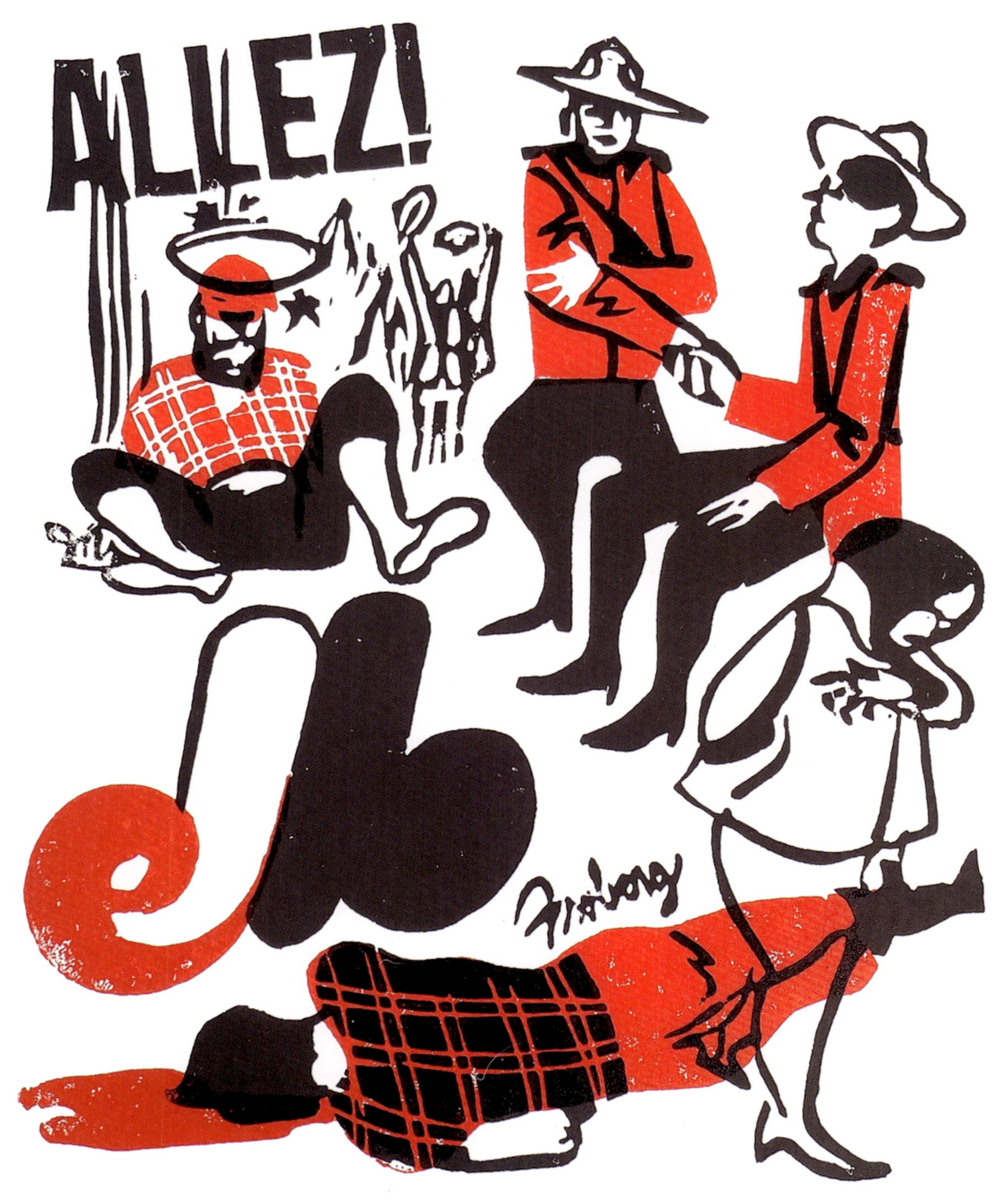

A/P   "ALLEZ!"   Fröberg

THREE

Brush, Ink, and Band-Related Art

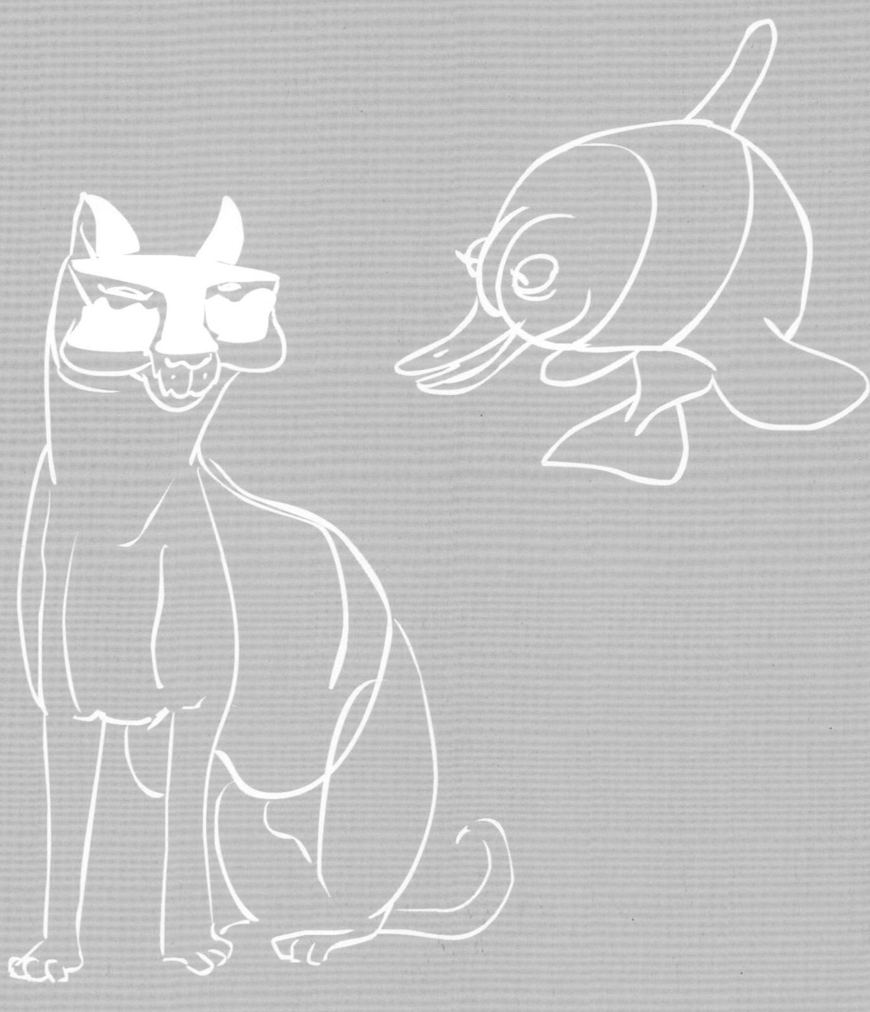

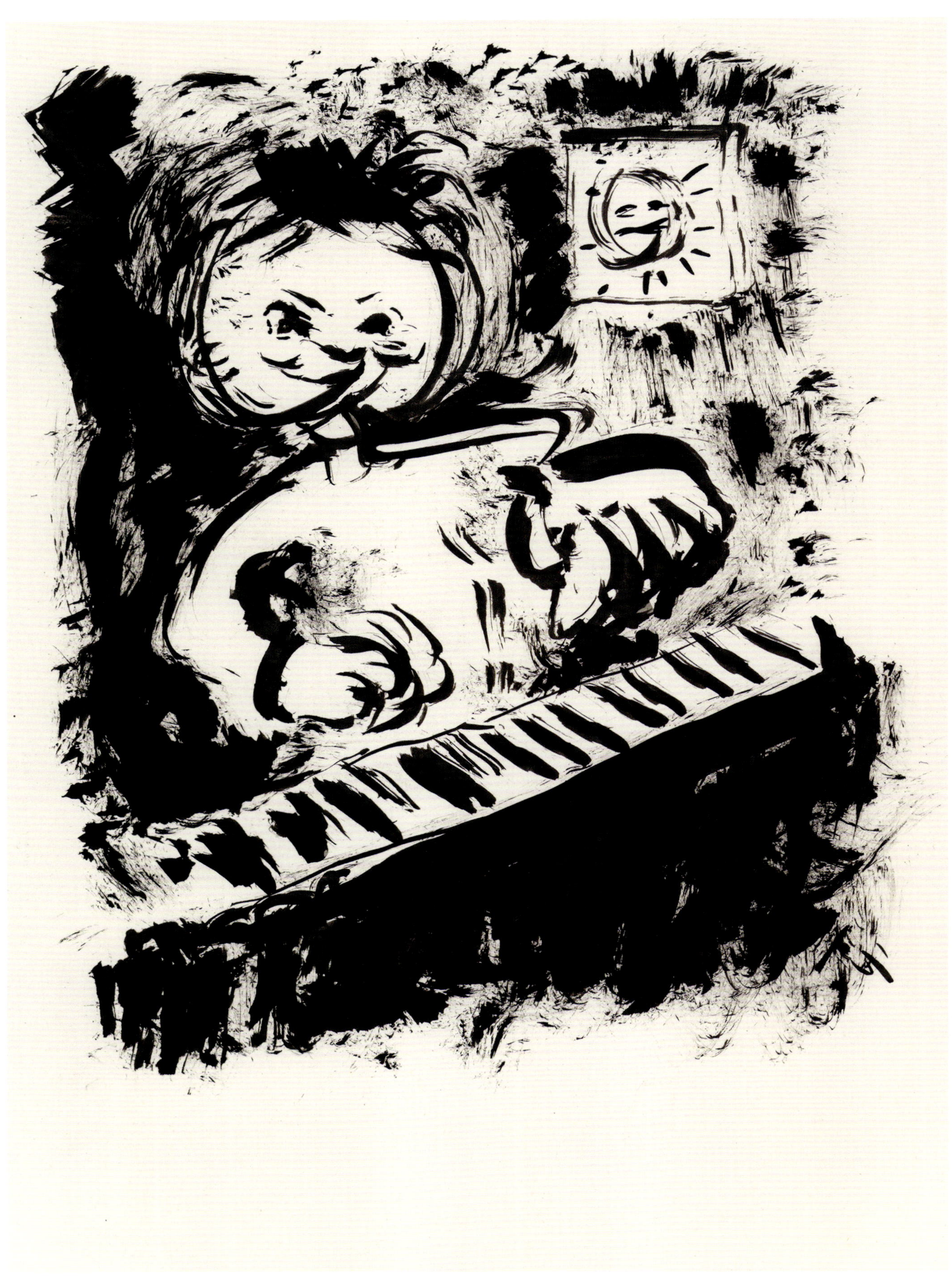

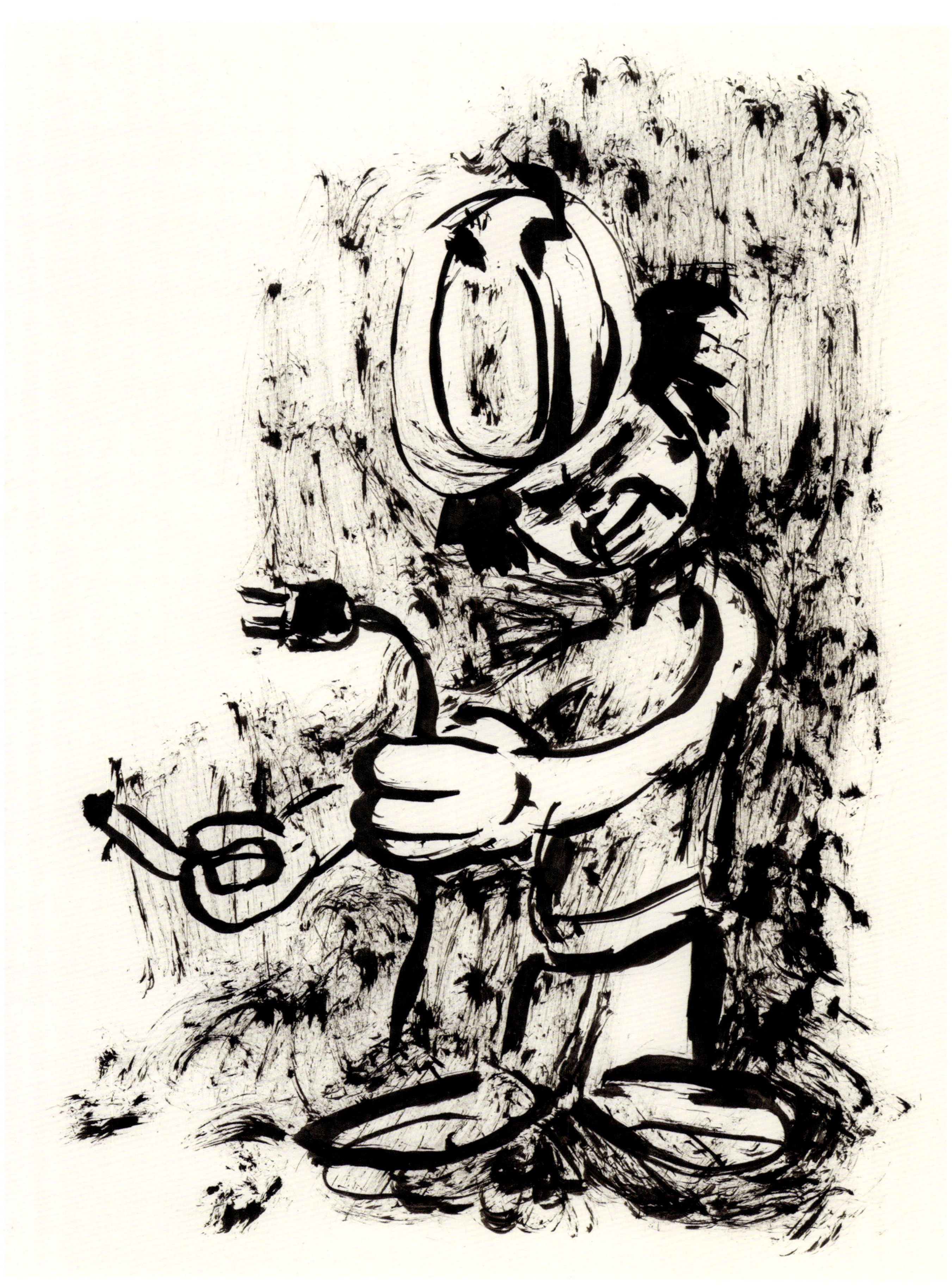

SINEW

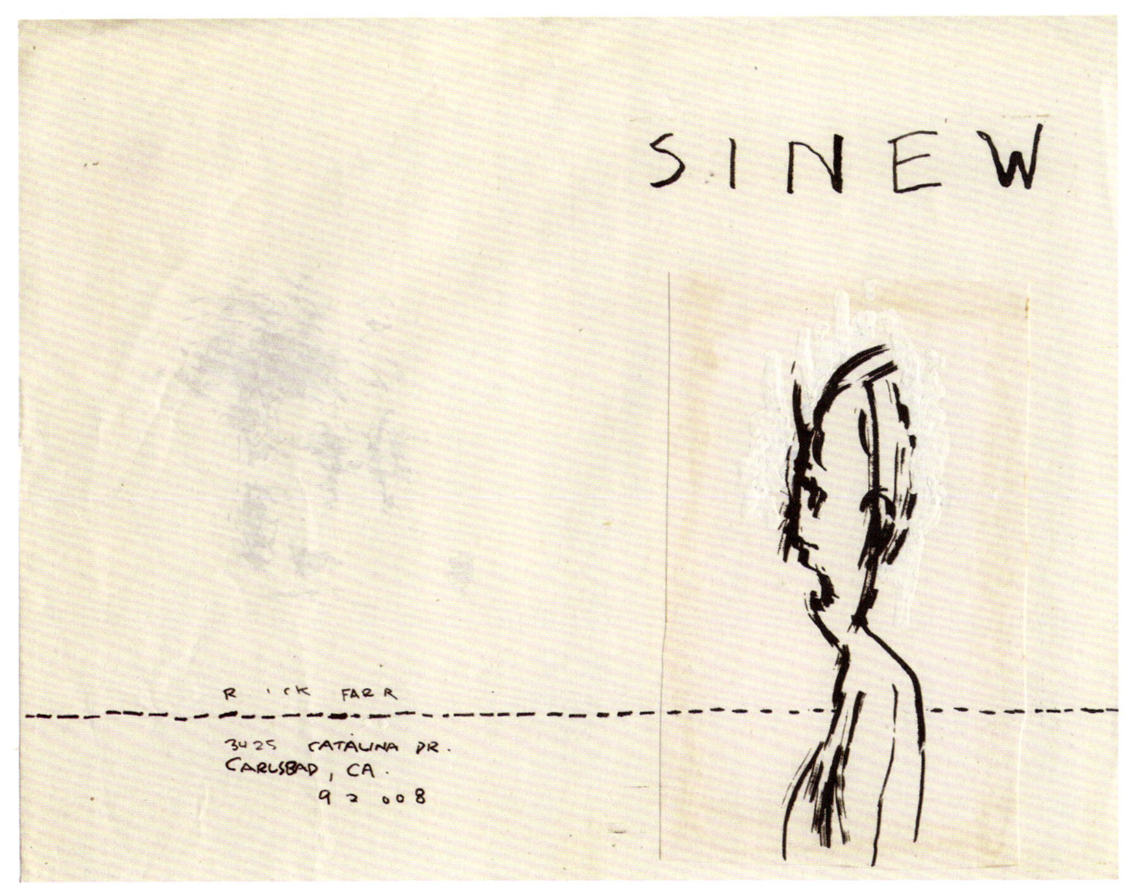

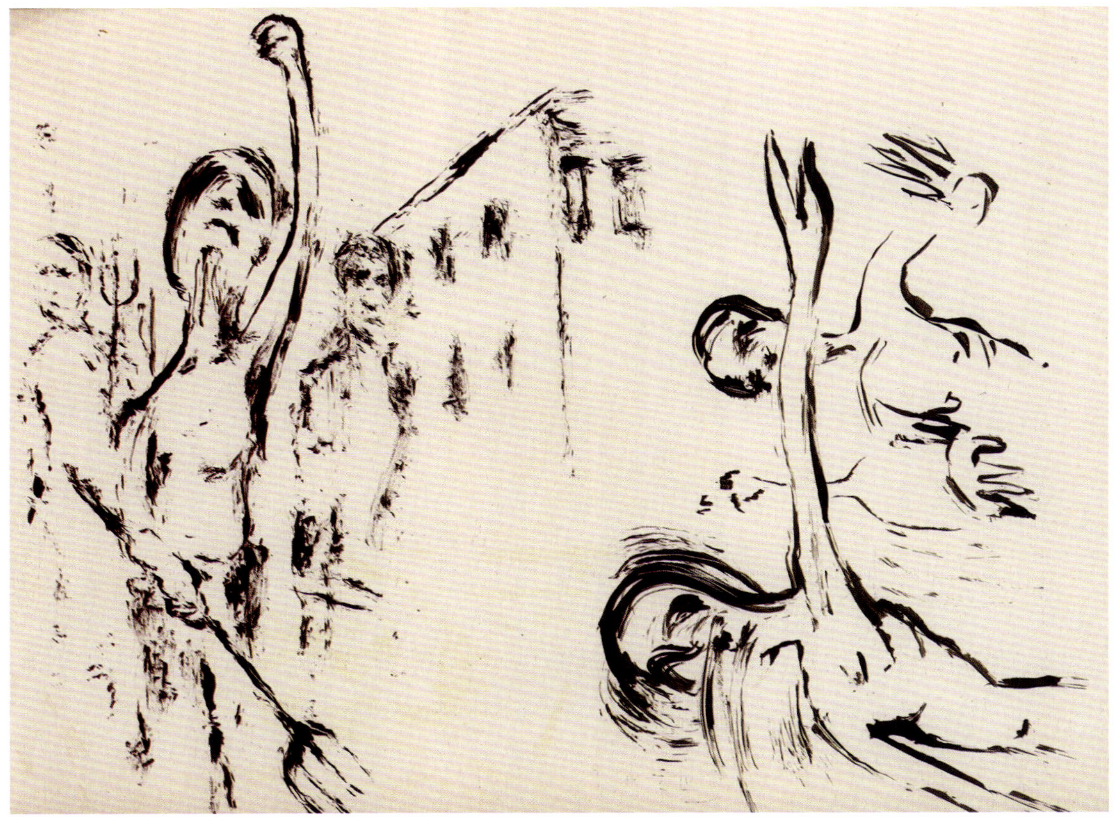

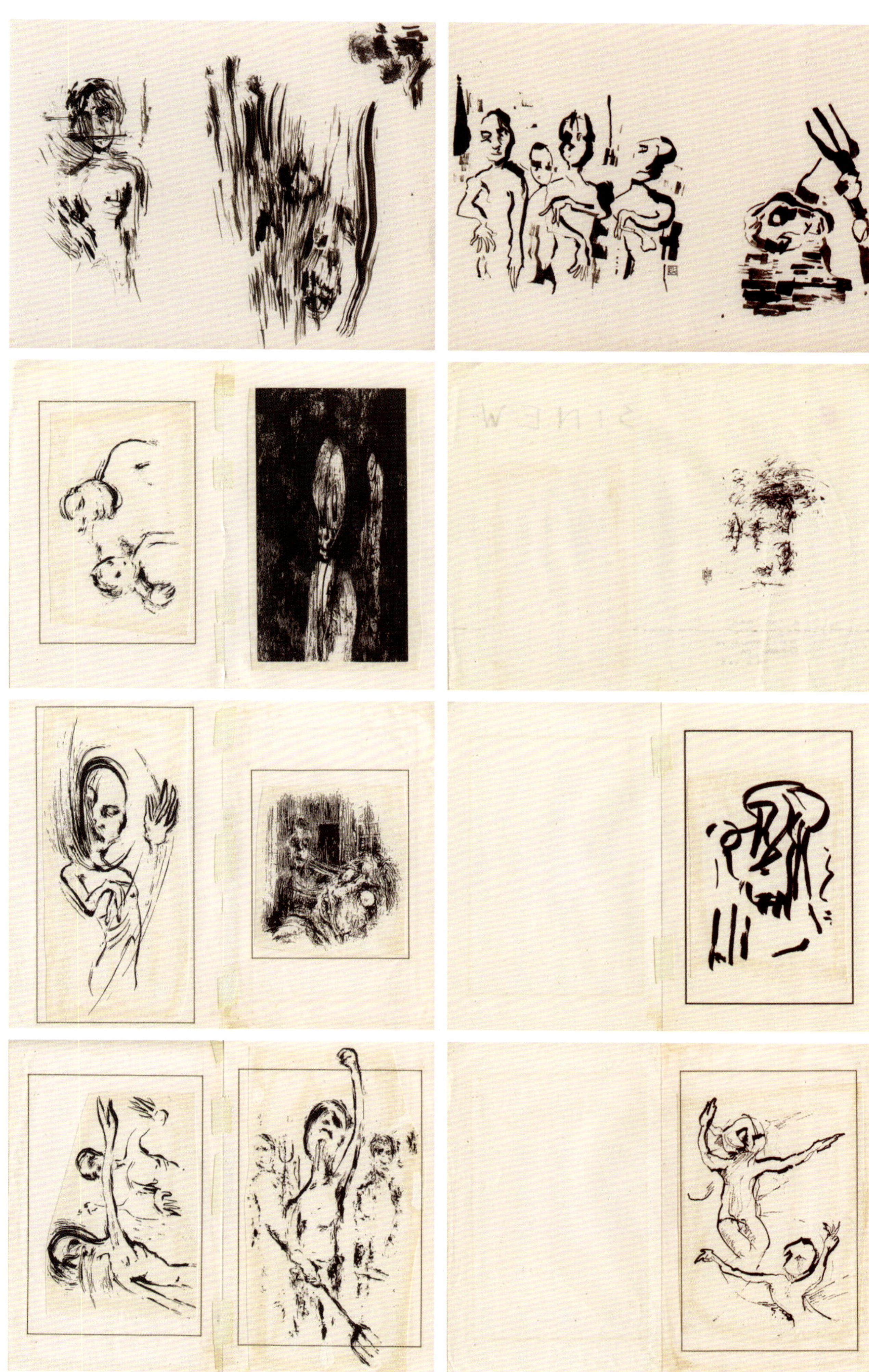

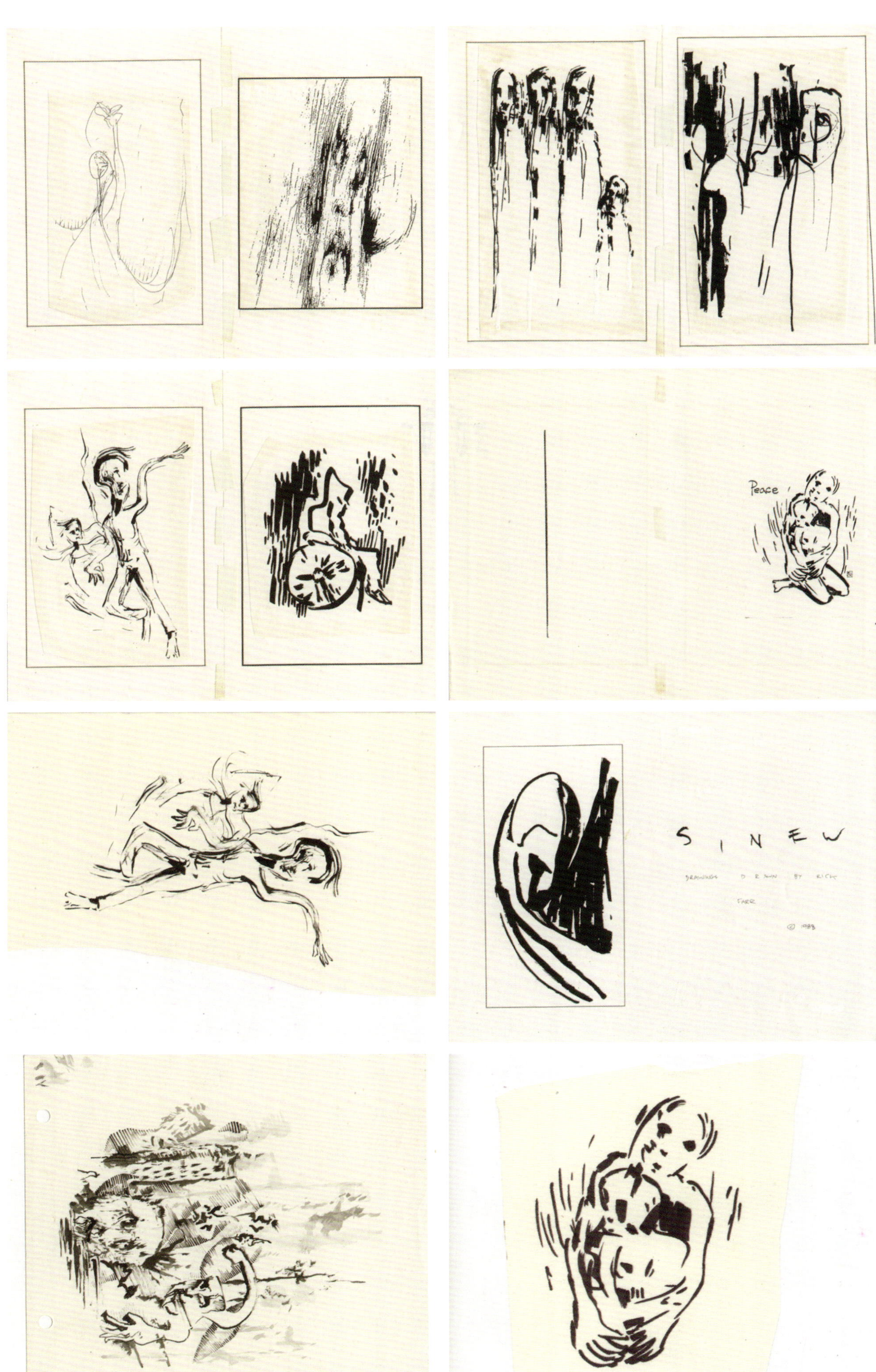

Peace
S I N E W
DRAWINGS DRAWN BY RICK
FARR
© 1988

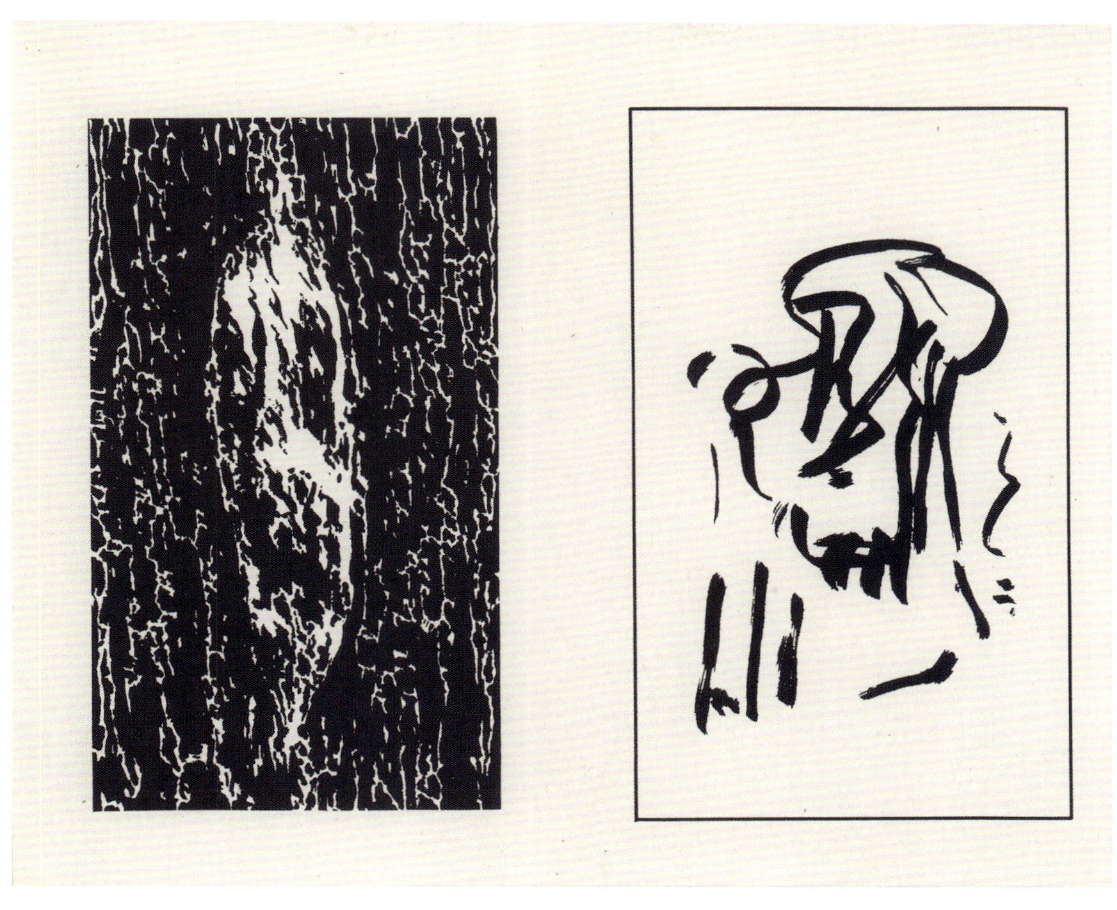

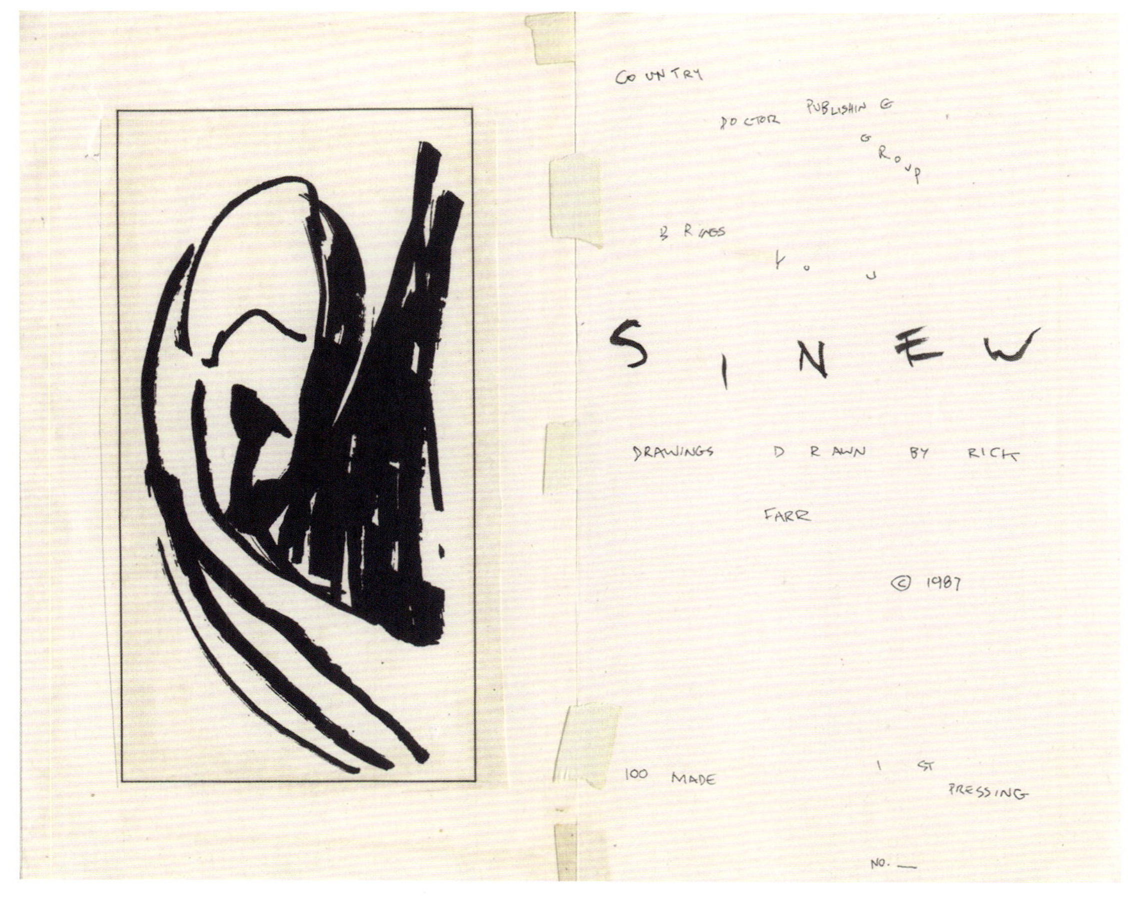

COUNTRY
DOCTOR PUBLISHING
GROUP
BRINGS
YOU
SINEW
DRAWINGS DRAWN BY RICK
FARR
© 1987
100 MADE 1 ST PRESSING
NO. __

sucked in, spit out

so content to shit on each other.
there is no upper hand, no value in
higher...
(ch:) more to me than #1, more to
we than #1, try to consider us as
one. but i can't. because i get
sucked in and spit out

orchestra

what was once an orchestra, now screams
out of tune; confusion is so loud... can't
hear my instruments...
(ch:) decisions shouldn't be made

acoustic

who knows? who cares? not me, not you
... then who? open the door. come
on inside, let your emotions flow...
resonate my soul
(ch:) acoustic emotions, resonate my
body, through my soul, im a believer

soak it in

your excuses bead on my forehead; my
sweat washes them away. seeing
is believing...i haven't seen anything
yet. time to wake the sleeping dog.
(ch:) face the facts and you will see.
we all walk with the enemy. time
to let it all soak in

freedumb

7-11, an institution, supplies my daily
need. who gives a fuck about libya,
im busy being free...
(ch:) freedumb
beat the kids, rape the wife, keep
everything in line. u.s. free-
dom: #1, it's treating me just fine

caretaker

stand. below me. i got the things you
wanna hear ...you don't need a quarter
to put a coin in this machine...
(ch:) i got your soul and a whole lot
more, looks like we made another
border to die over. who said there's
nothing in a name. it's falling down,
smashed down to hell

mind over matter

i never mind you, because you don't
seem to matter ...to me

in my shadow

competition built out of nothing
i condemn these pressures i've created...
(ch:) you are in my shadow, and you die
when i turn out the lights

it's a nice day

the sun is shining, but the moon's still
there... a flag waves... your ass
good bye
(ch:) it's a nice day, to die for me

blazing saddles

it's a sing-a-long, folks

darshana

the truth can't be seen, in knowing
reason... in knowing reason.
(ch:) a fear of failure and rejection is
a fear of knowing your self...
break down the walls of your
fastening tread. things are going downhill,
but im looking up.... it doesn't
seem to connect. in a common plea
we must say... we're not
the same

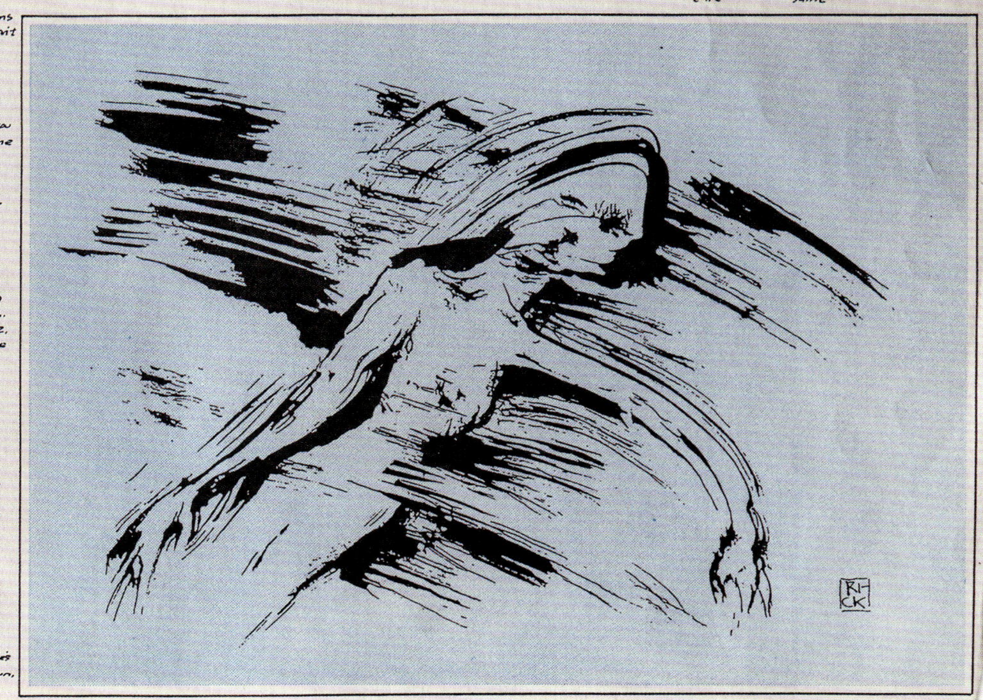

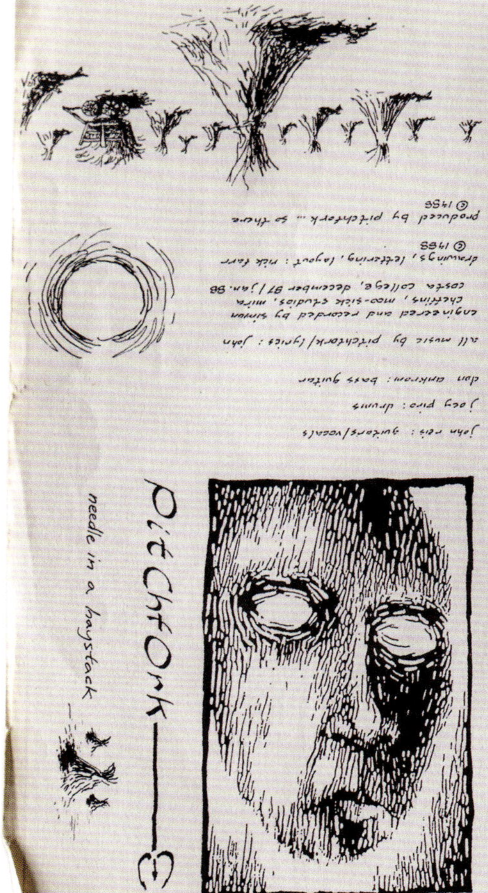
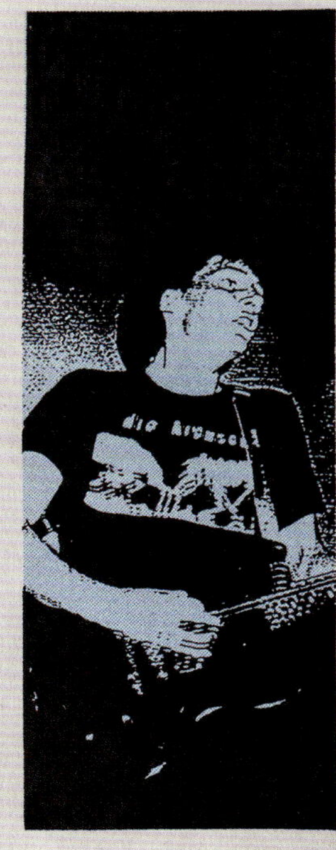
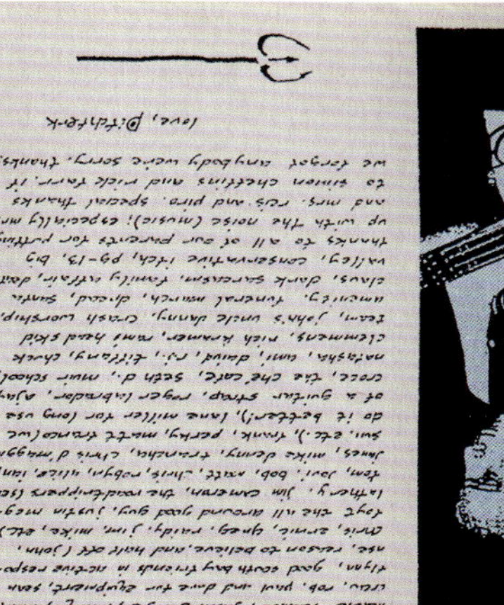
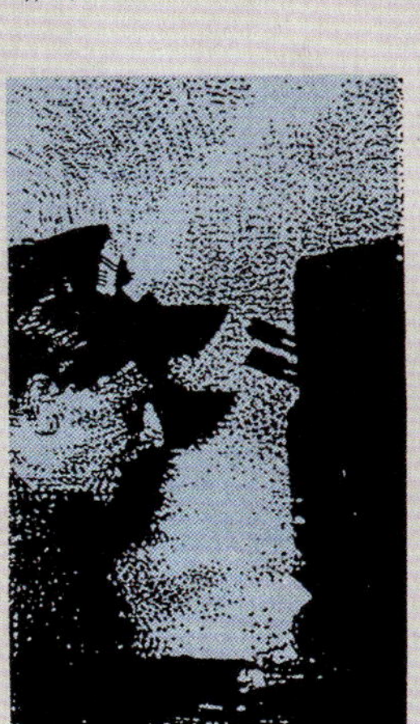
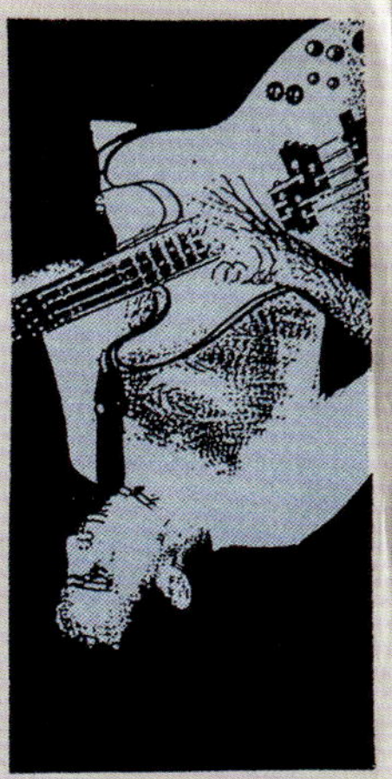
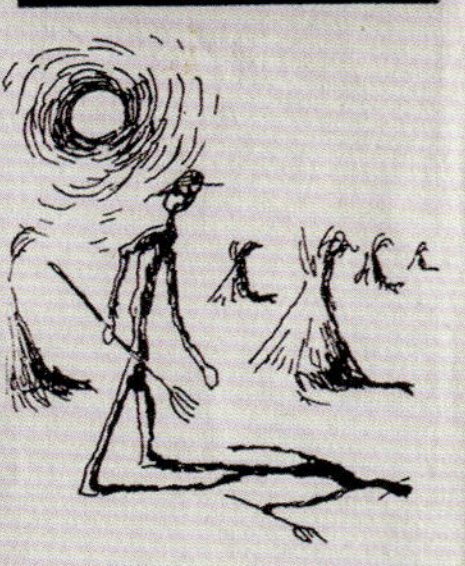

PitchFork
needle in a haystack

john reis: guitars/vocals
joey piro: drums
don ankrom: bass guitar

all music by pitchfork/lyrics: john
engineered and recorded by simon
cheffins, moo-sick studios, mira
costa college, december 87/jan. 88

drawings, lettering, layout: rick farr
© 1988

produced by pitchfork ... so there
© 1988

side 1
sucked in, spit out/caretaker
orchestra
cut and dry
acoustic
it's a nice day/soak it in

side 2
freedumb
mind over matter
darshana
blazing saddles

thank you: p.b. youth, george and the daily impulse, heather swallow, jason traeger, monique, chula crew, rob, paul and dave for equipment, sean flynn, good south bay friends in active response, reason to believe, and half off (john, chris, ernie, greg, raidy, jim, mike, etc), fayt the all around good guy, justin meglathery. jim cameron, the roadtrippers (seth tom, javi, bob, matt, chris, robyn, alice, ian, james, mike denny, trancha, chris d'maggio, sui, etc.), frank, perky, matt franco (we do it better!), lane miller for long use of a guitar strap, roger labrador, ajay croce, the ché cafe, seth d., muir school, natasha, ami, david, r.j., tiffany, chuck clemmens, rich kramer, rams head skid team, john's uncle danny, crash worship, amenity. funeral march, dread, santa claus, dark sarcasm, family affair, death valley, conservative itch, pg-13, big thanks to all of our parents for putting up with the noise (music); especially mr. and mrs. reis and piro. special thanks to simon cheffins and rick farr. if we forgot anybody we're sorry. thanks!

love, pitchfork

for pitchfork information, tapes, propaganda, and other such completely useless things ... write.

pitchfork, c/o john reis
2076 reed avenue,
san diego, california,
92109, in the good ol' u.s.a.

"it's a nice day... to write to me"... john reis

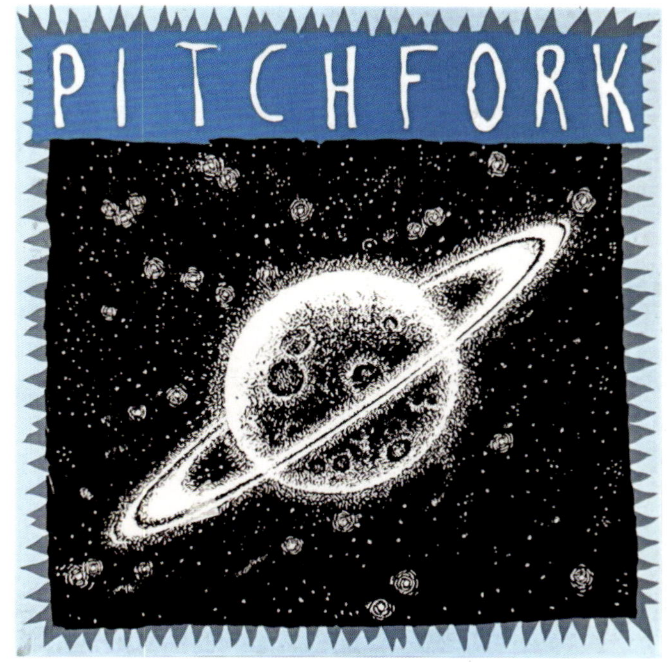
PITCHFORK

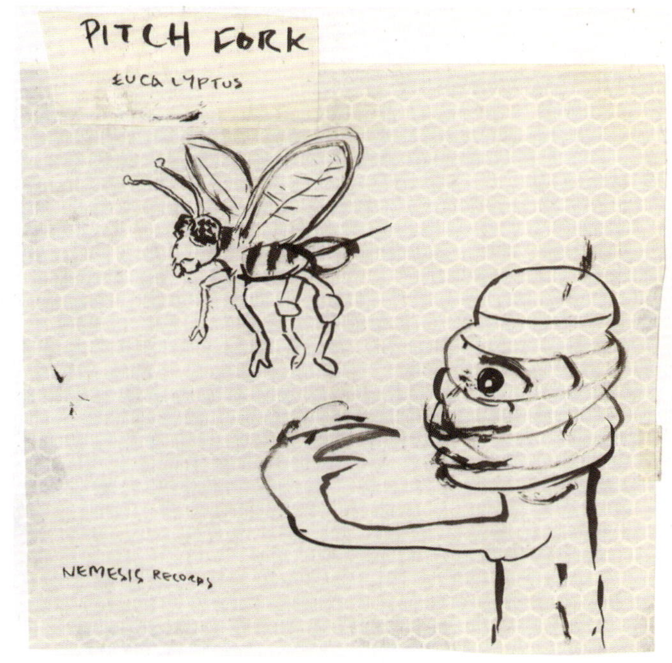
PITCH FORK
EUCALYPTUS
NEMESIS RECORDS

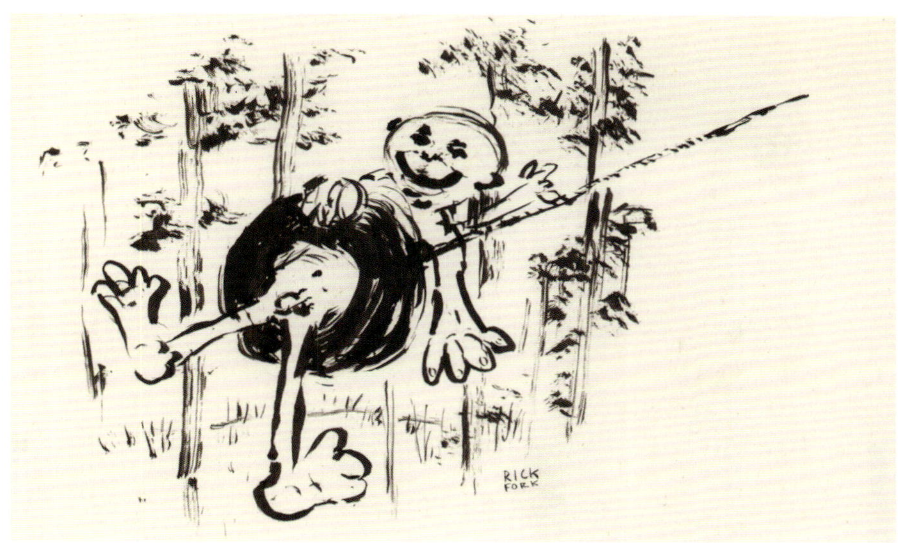
RICK
FORK

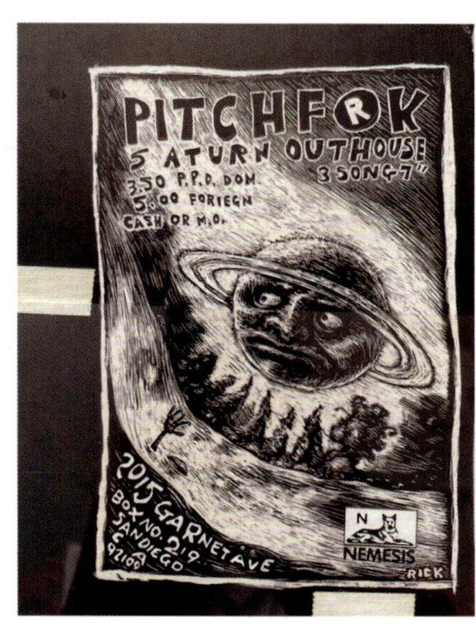
PITCHFORK
SATURN OUTHOUSE
3 SONGS 7"
3.50 P.P.D. DOM
5.00 FORIEGN
CASH OR M.O.
2015 GARNET AVE
BOX NO. 219
SAN DIEGO
92109
NEMESIS
RICK

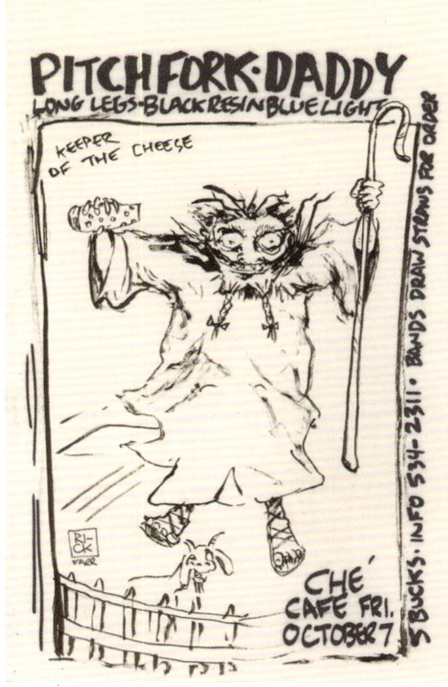
PITCHFORK DADDY
LONG LEGS · BLACK RESIN BLUE LIGHT
KEEPER OF THE CHEESE
5 BUCKS · INFO 534-2311 · BANDS DRAW STRAWS FOR ORDER
CHE' CAFE FRI. OCTOBER 7

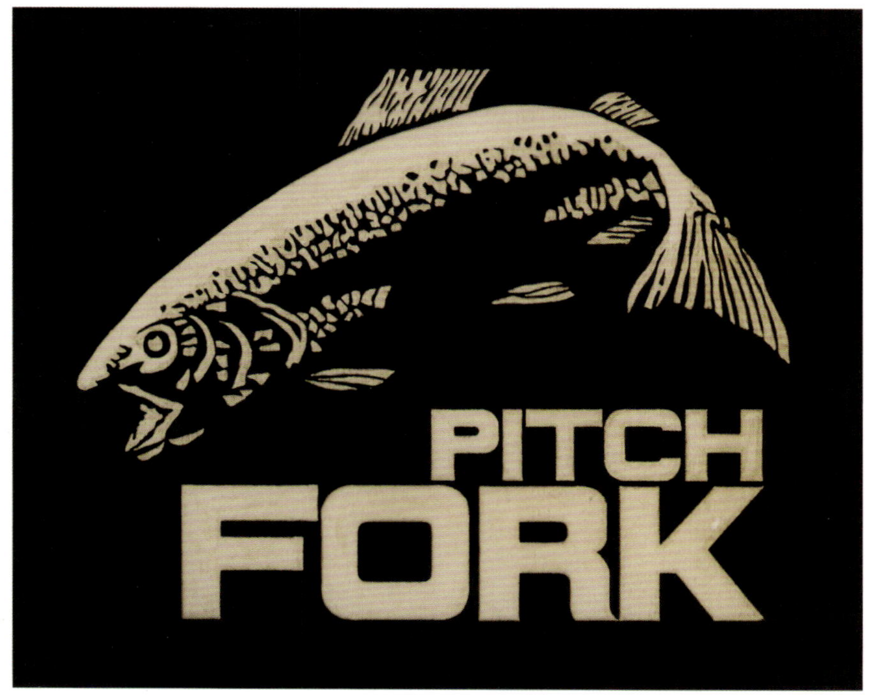
PITCH FORK

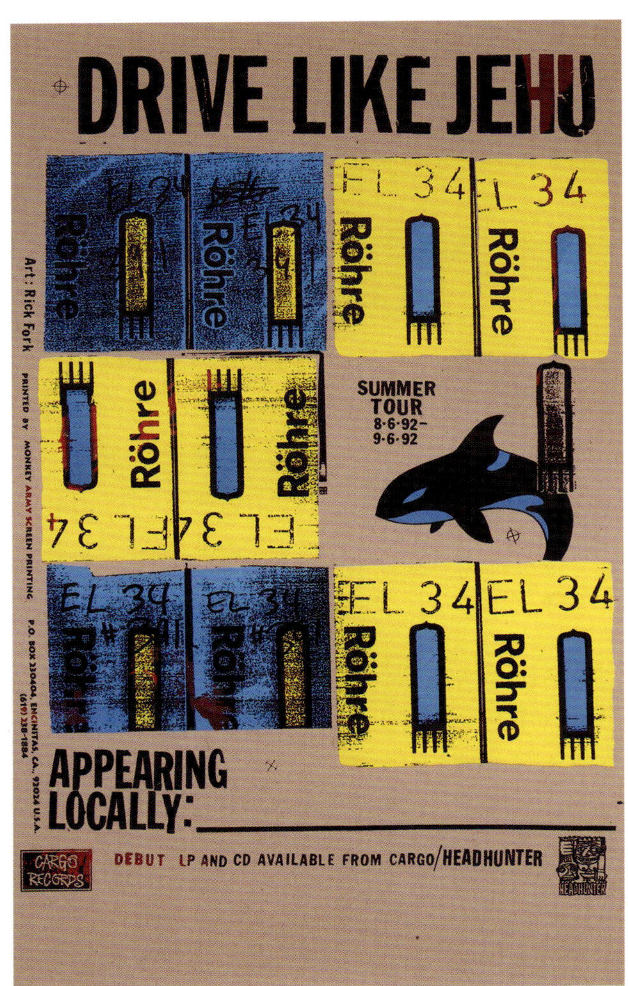

DRIVE LIKE JEHU
EL 34
Röhre
SUMMER TOUR
8·6·92–
9·6·92
APPEARING LOCALLY:
Art: Rick Fork
PRINTED BY MONKEY ARMY SCREEN PRINTING
P.O. BOX 230424, ENCINITAS, CA. 92024 U.S.A.
(619) 287-1864
CARGO RECORDS
DEBUT LP AND CD AVAILABLE FROM CARGO/HEADHUNTER
HEADHUNTER

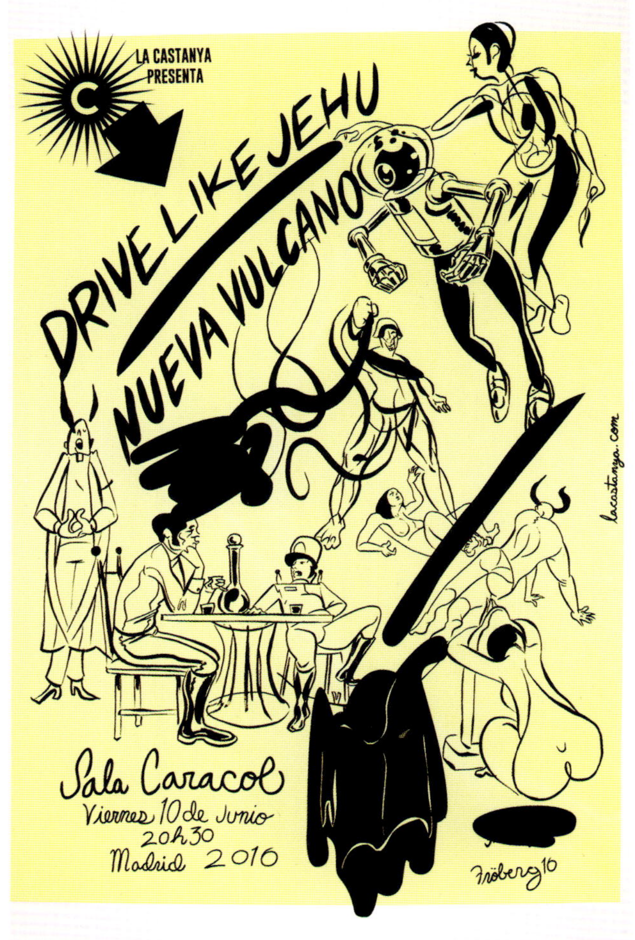

LA CASTANYA PRESENTA
DRIVE LIKE JEHU
NUEVA VULCANO
Sala Caracol
Viernes 10 de Junio
20h30
Madrid 2010
lacastanya.com
Fröberg 10

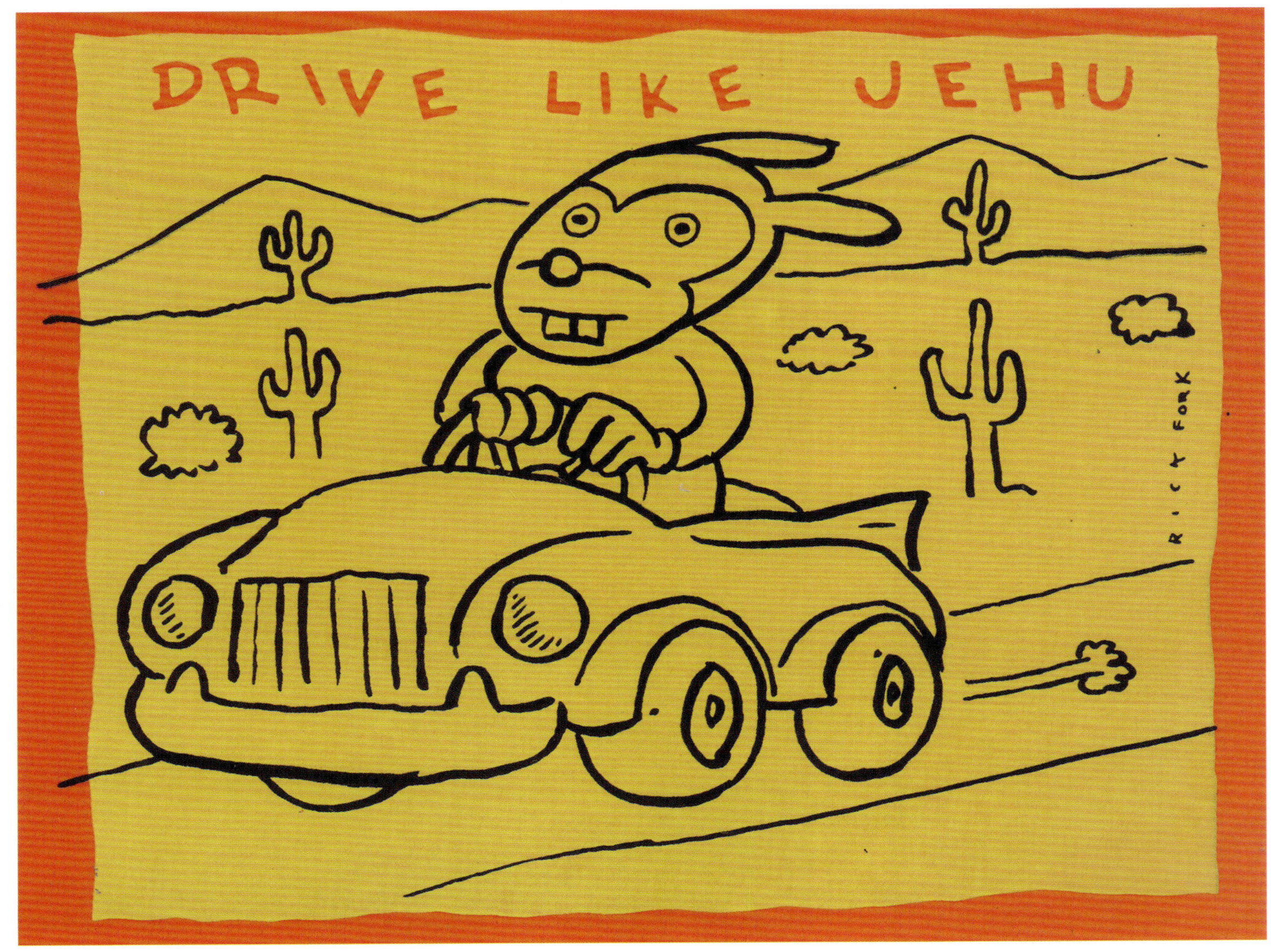

DRIVE LIKE JEHU
Rick Fork

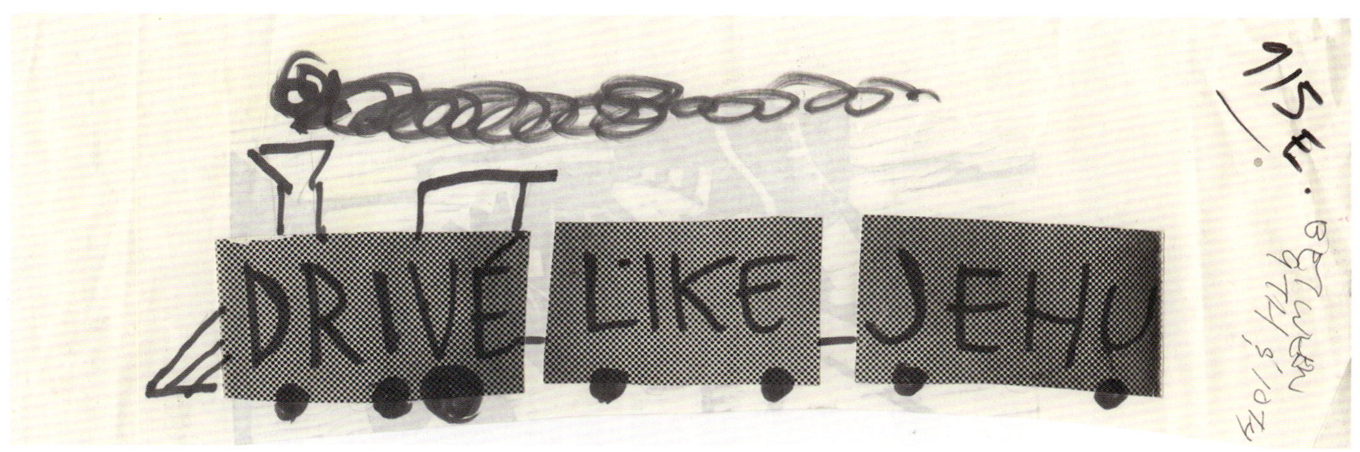
DRIVE LIKE JEHU

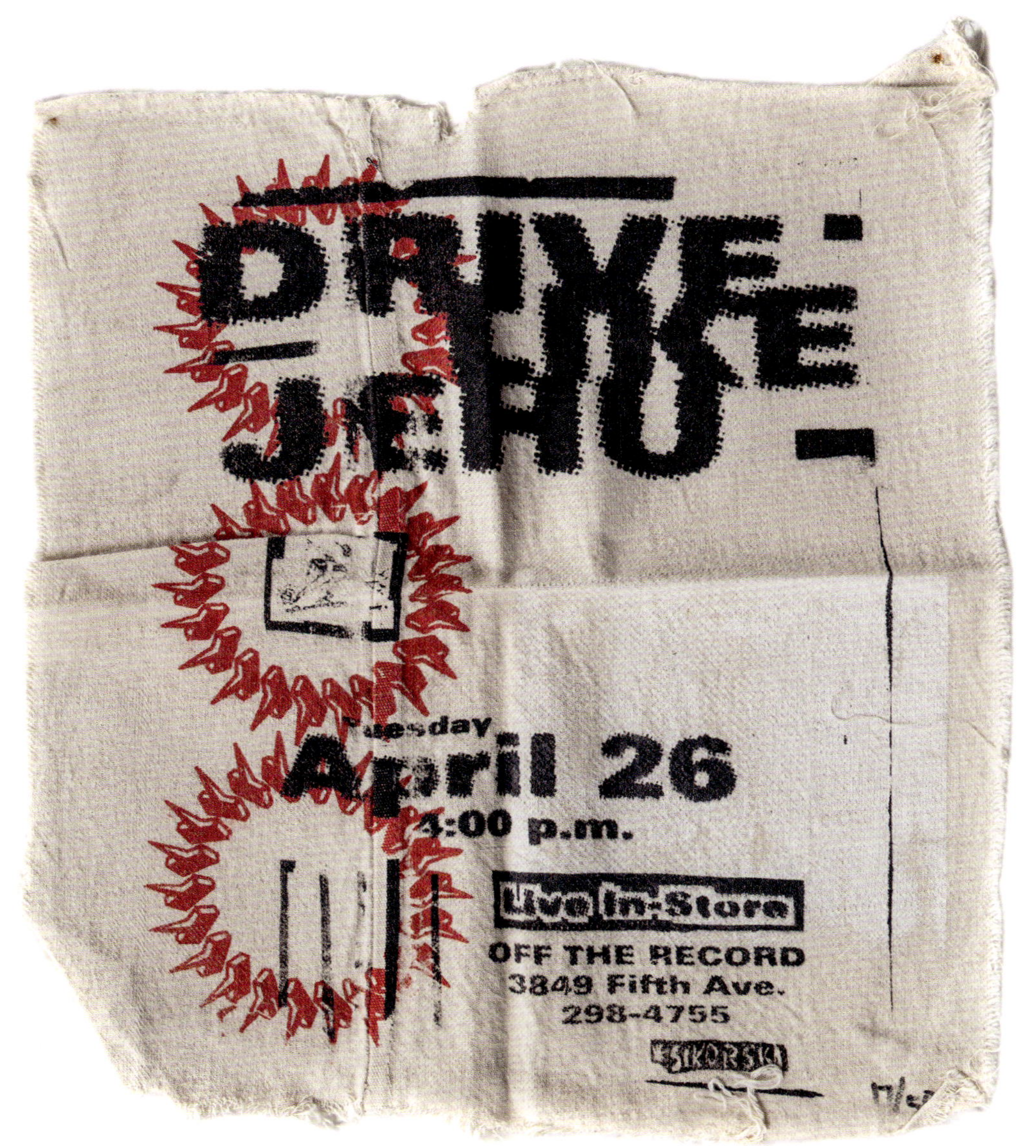
DRIVE
JEHU
Tuesday
April 26
4:00 p.m.
Live In-Store
OFF THE RECORD
3849 Fifth Ave.
298-4755
SIKORSKI

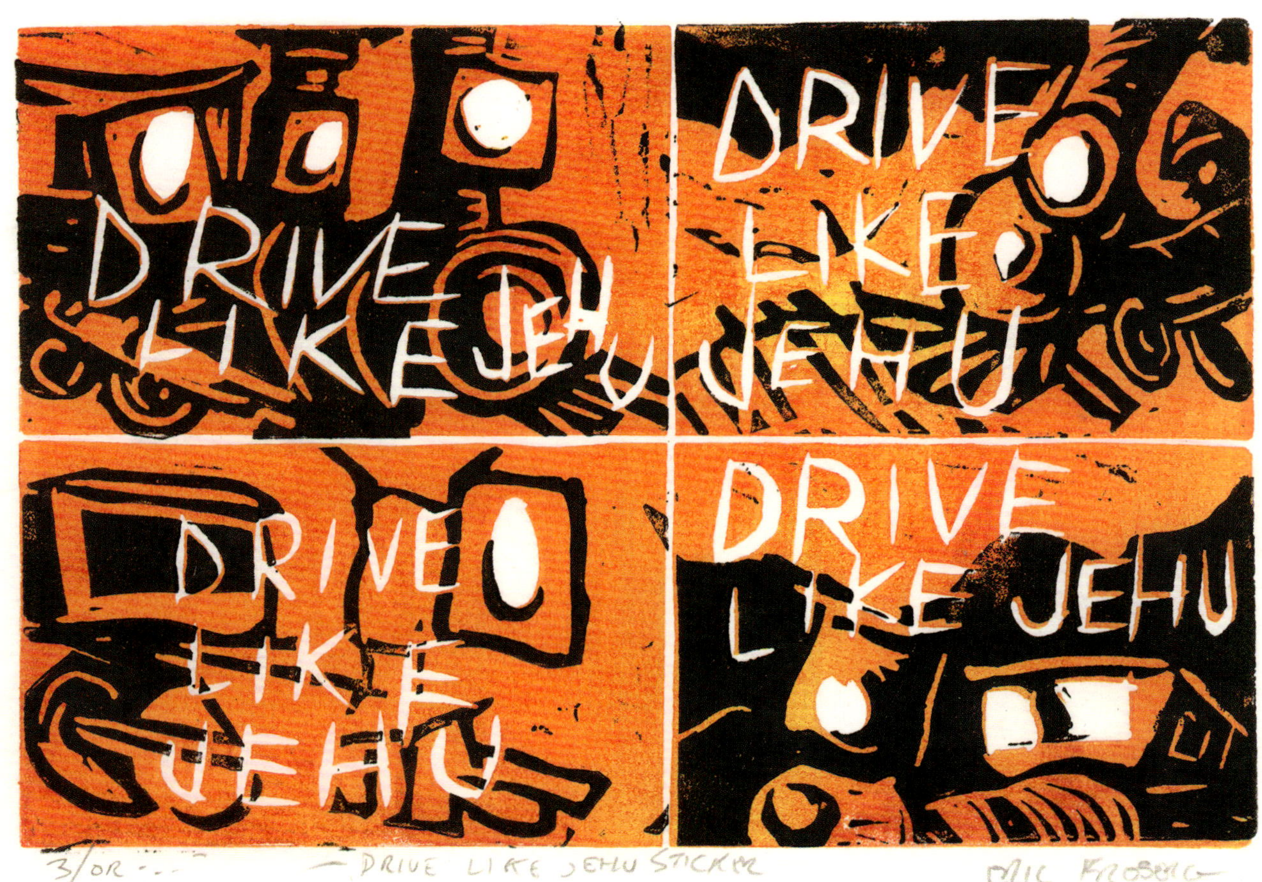
DRIVE LIKE JEHU
DRIVE LIKE JEHU
DRIVE LIKE JEHU
DRIVE LIKE JEHU
3/OR
DRIVE LIKE JEHU STICKER
ERIC KROGBERG

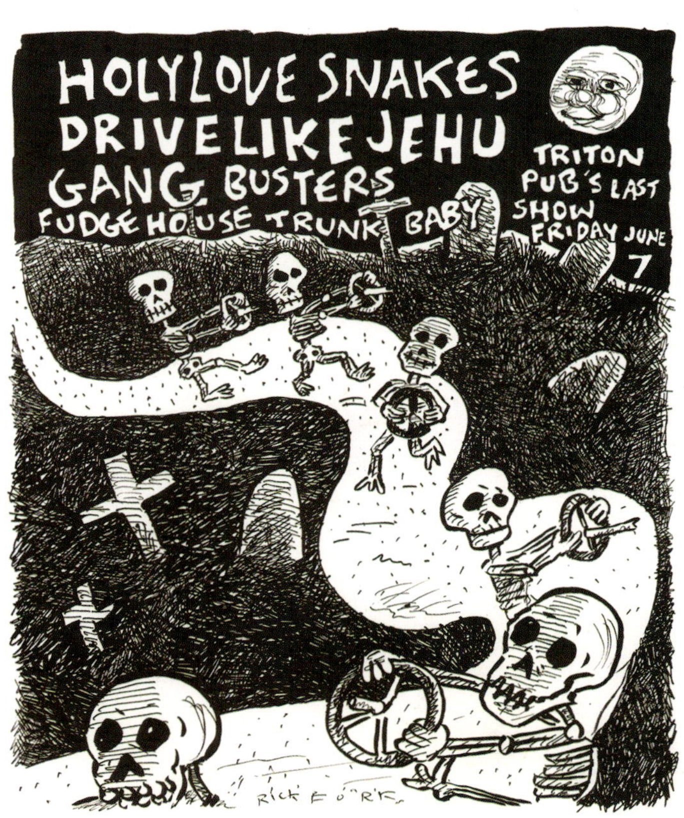
HOLYLOVE SNAKES
DRIVELIKEJEHU
GANG BUSTERS
FUDGE HOUSE TRUNK BABY
TRITON
PUB'S LAST
SHOW
FRIDAY JUNE
7
RICK FORK

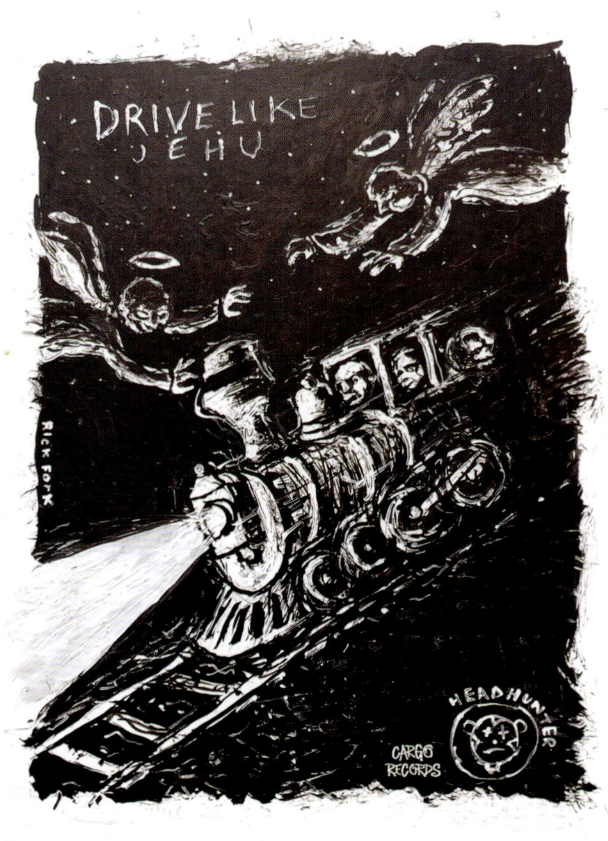
DRIVE LIKE
JEHU
RICK FORK
CARGO
RECORDS
HEADHUNTER

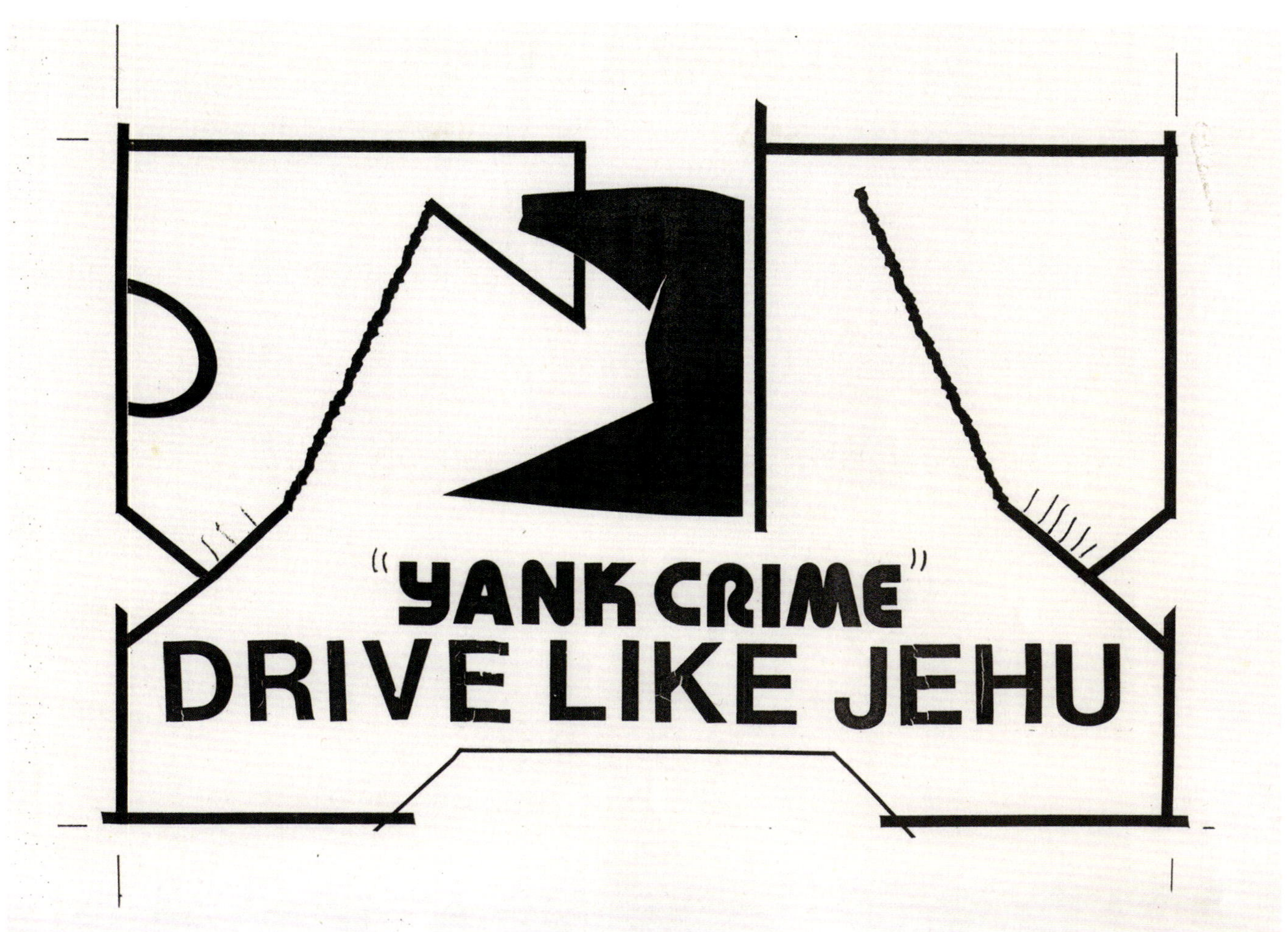
"YANK CRIME"
DRIVE LIKE JEHU

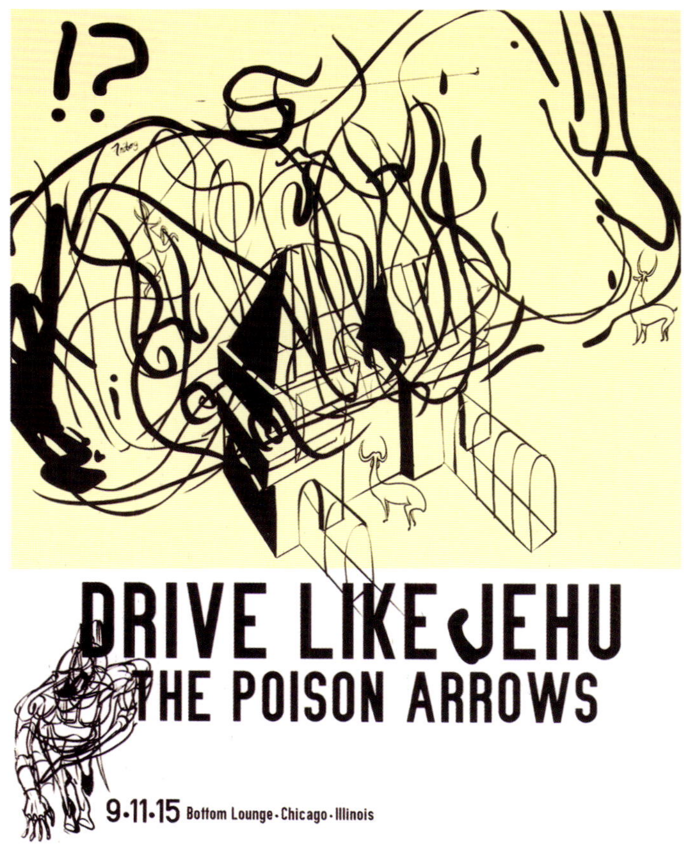
!?
DRIVE LIKE JEHU
THE POISON ARROWS
9-11-15 Bottom Lounge - Chicago - Illinois

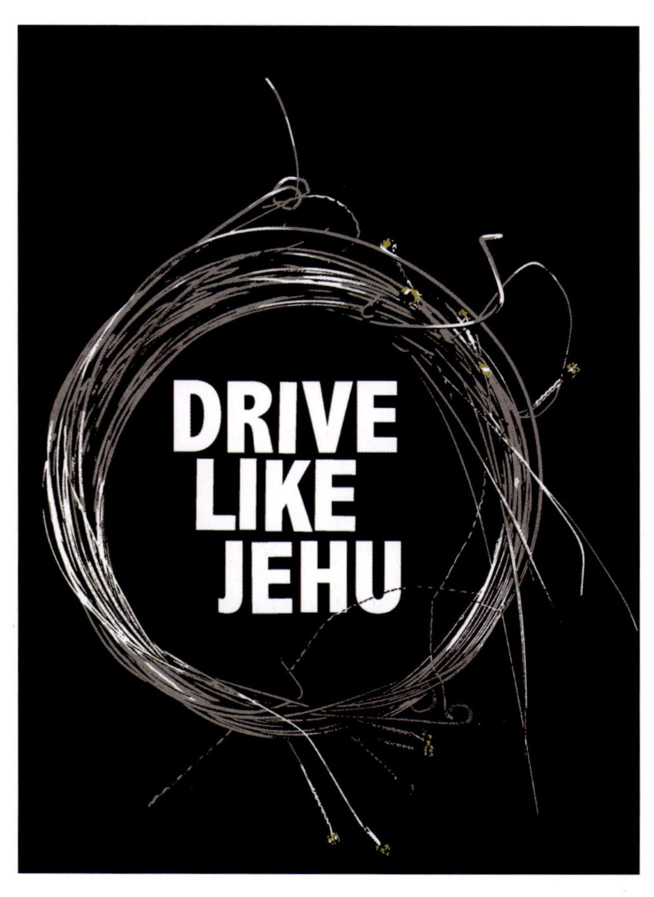
DRIVE
LIKE
JEHU

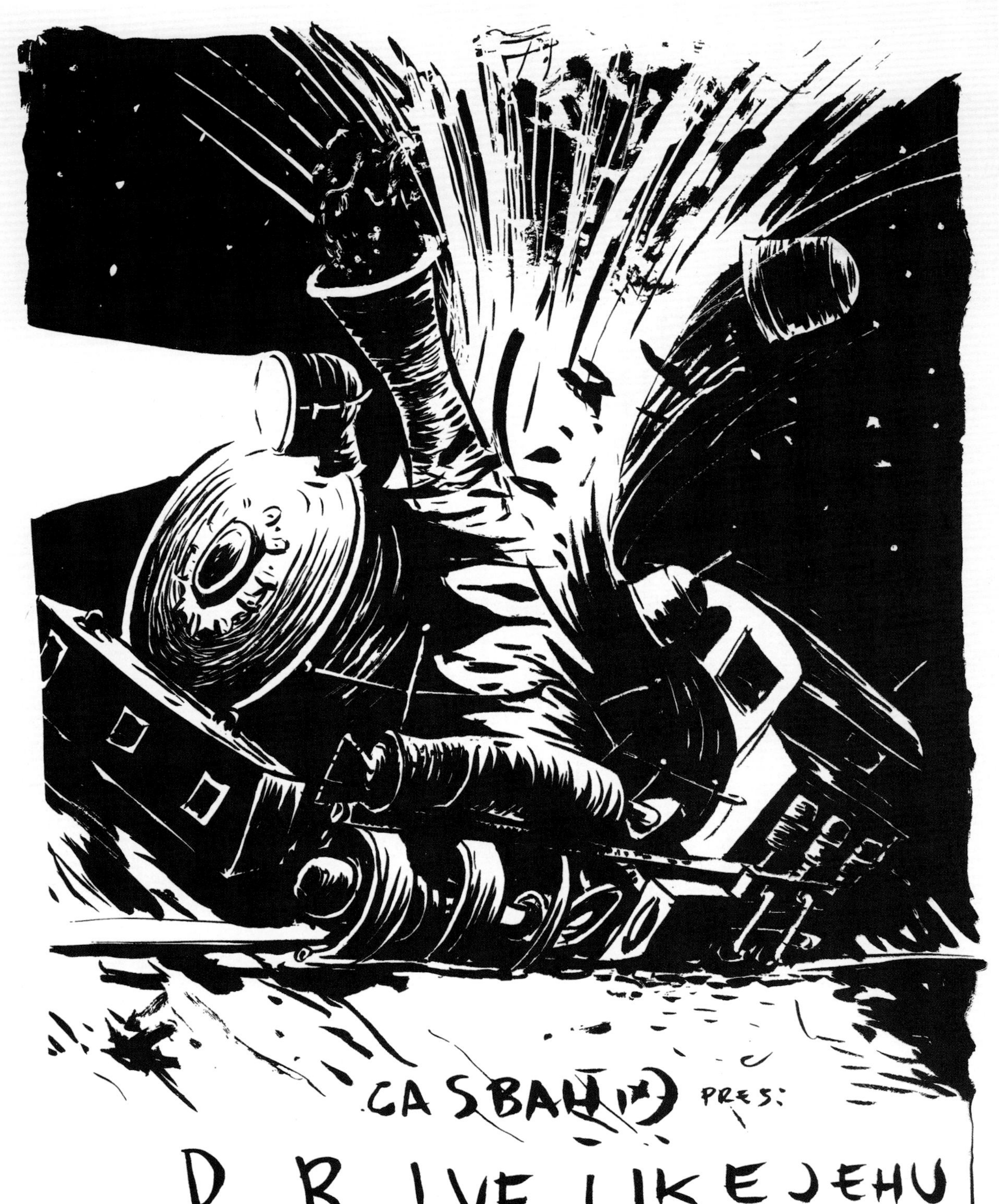
CASBAH (*) PRES:
D R IVE LIKE JEHU
THREE MILE PILOT
CANDY APPLES
FRIDAY 8/20/93
@ SAN DIEGO WOMENS CLUB
3RD & MAPLE IN HILCREST
ALL AGES . TICKETS AT OFF THE RECORD
CASBAH, LOUS, ETC .   POSTER: RICK FOCK

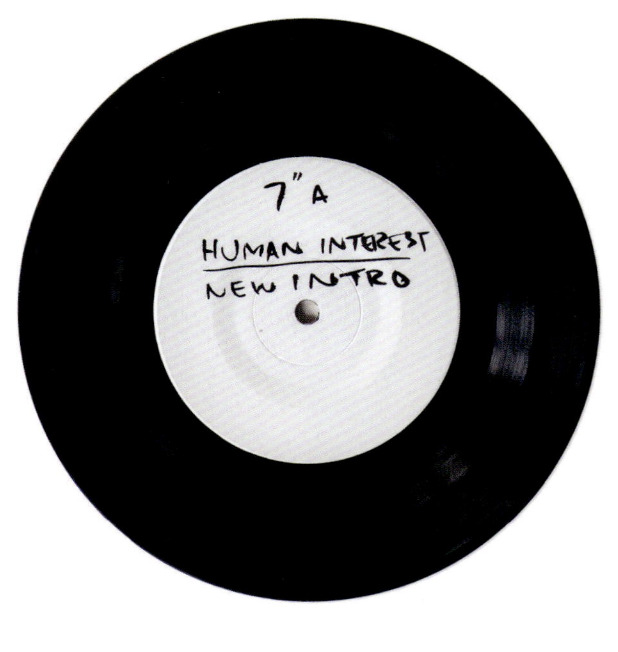
7" A
HUMAN INTEREST
NEW INTRO

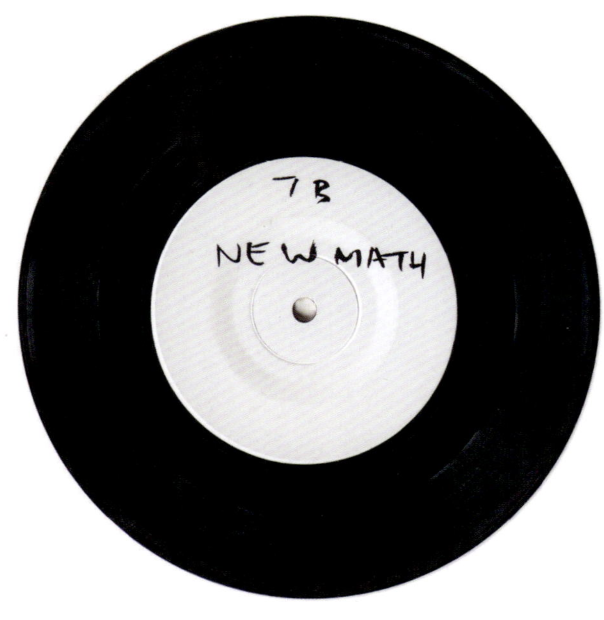
7 B
NEW MATH

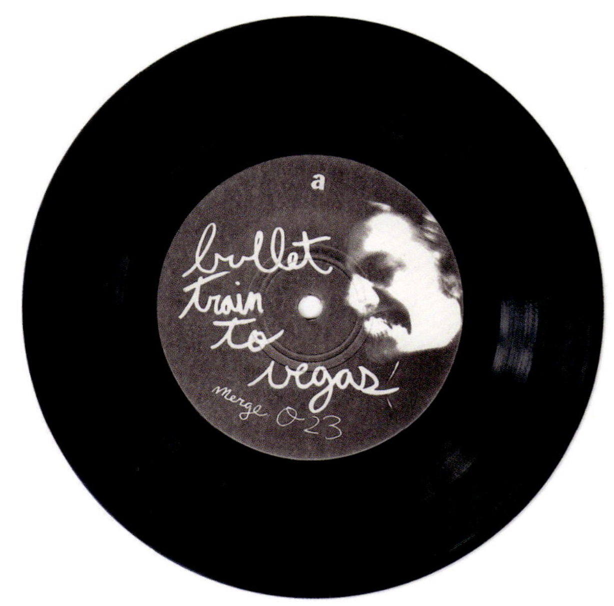
a
bullet
train
to
vegas!
merge 023

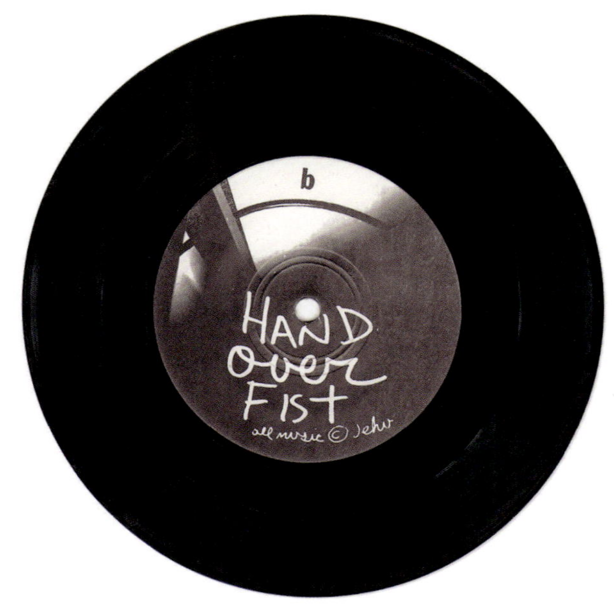
b
HAND
over
FIST
all music © jehu

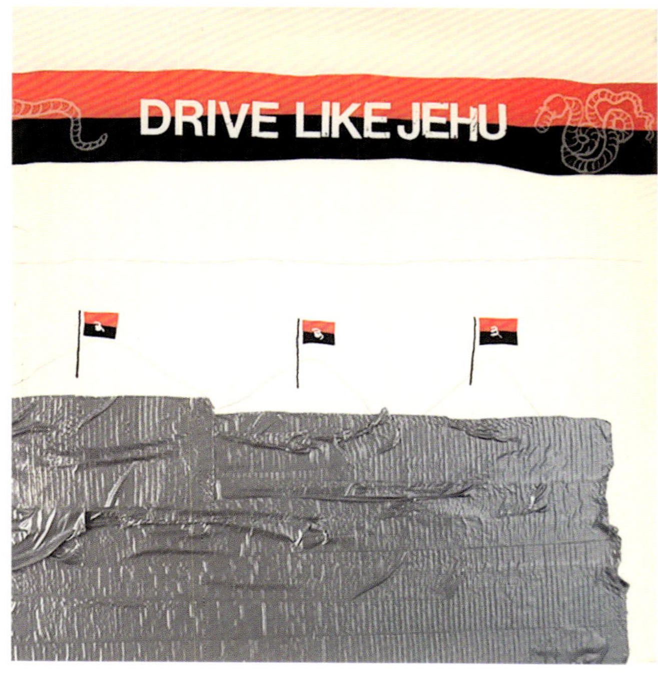
DRIVE LIKE JEHU

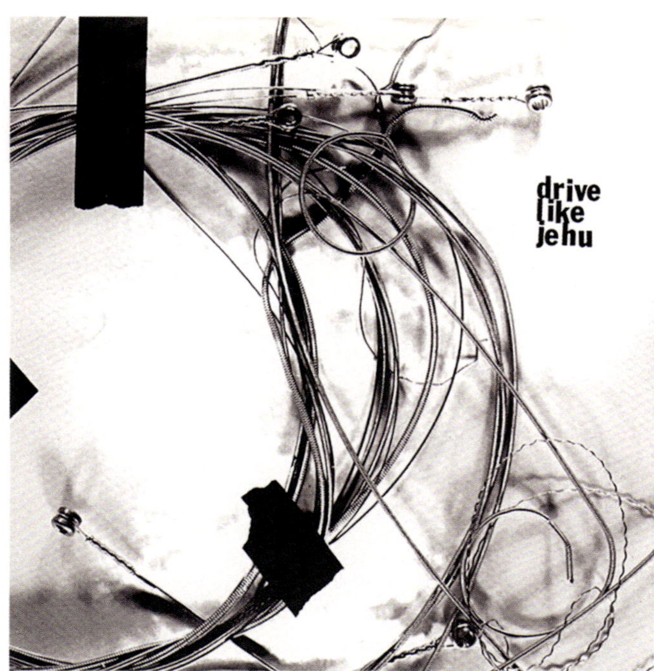
drive
like
jehu

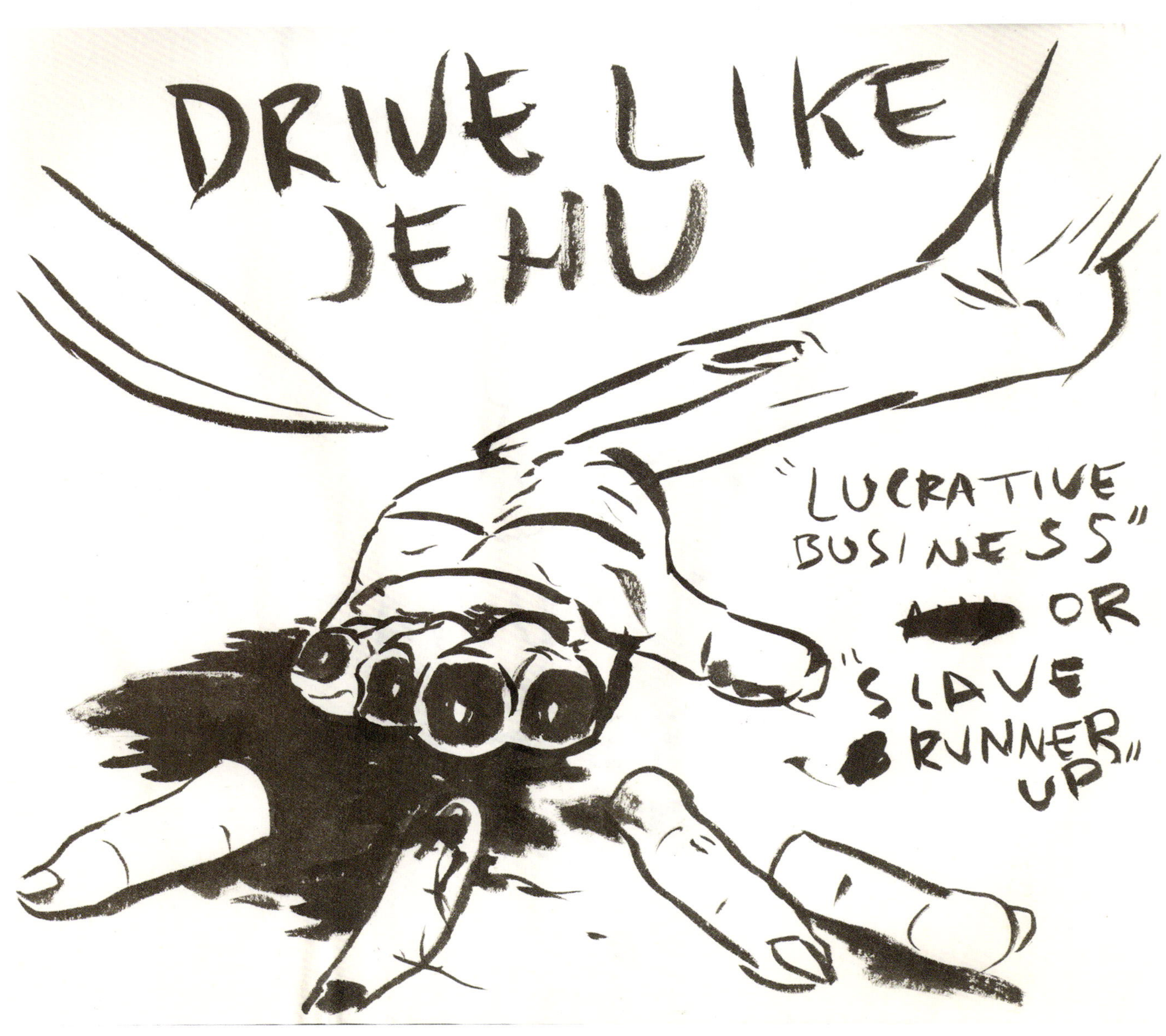
DRIVE LIKE
JEHU
"LUCRATIVE
BUSINESS"
OR
"SLAVE
RUNNER
UP"

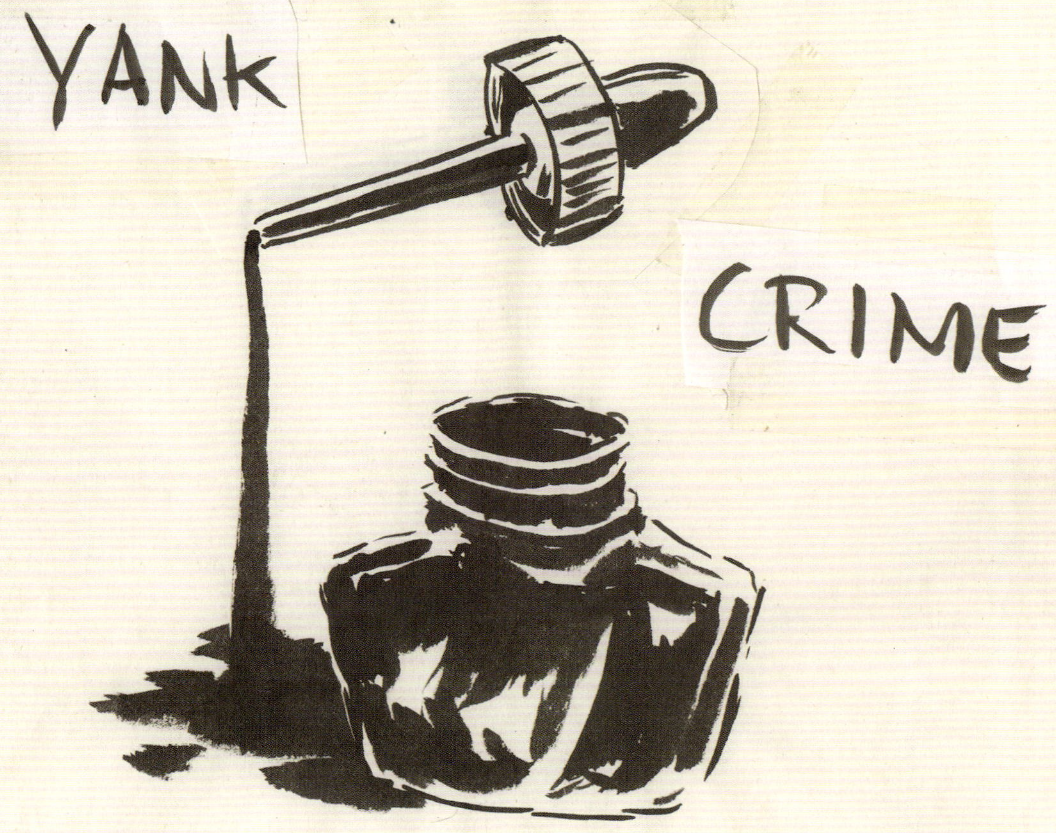
DRIVE LIKE JEHU
YANK
CRIME

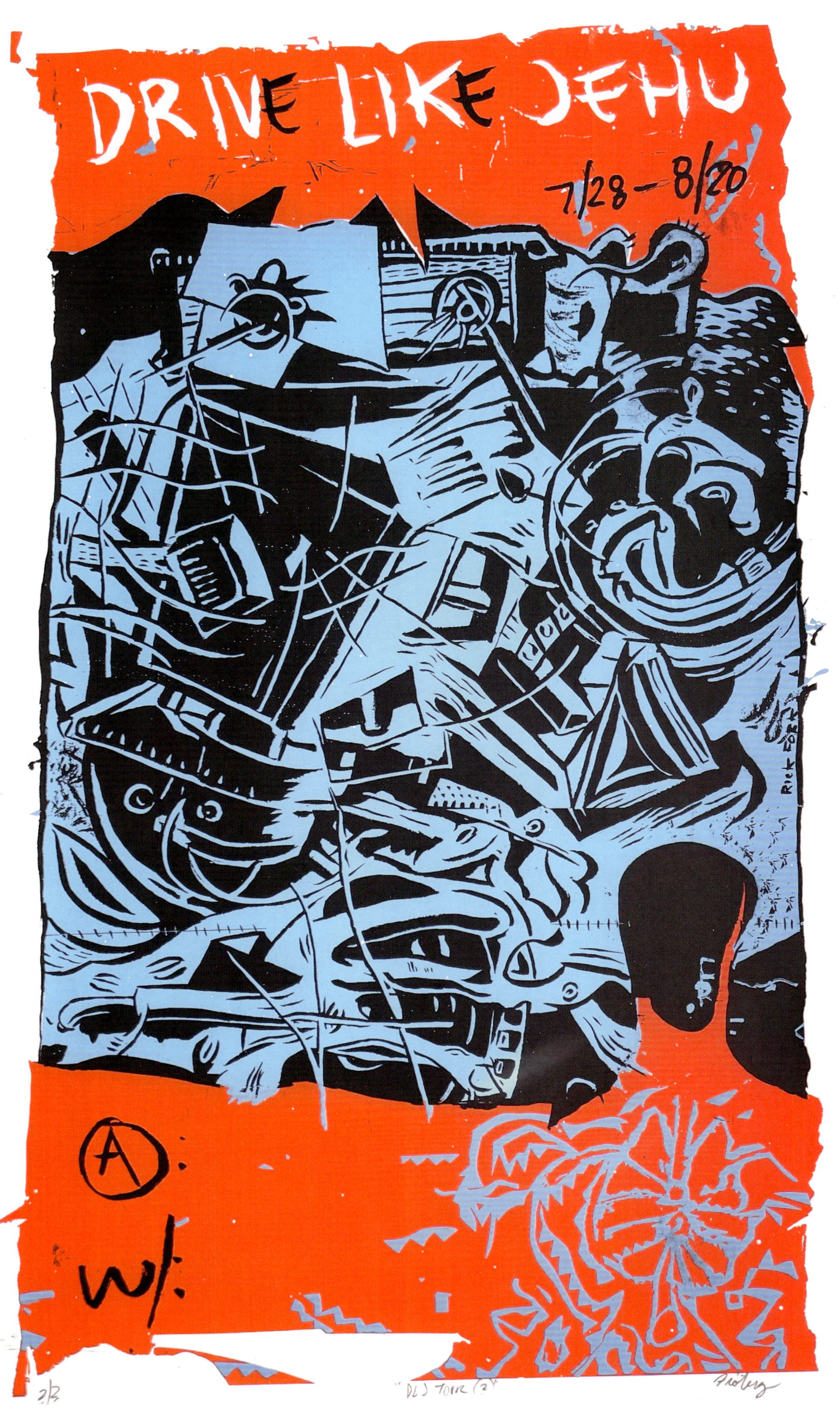

DRIVE LIKE JEHU
7/28 - 8/20
A:
W/.

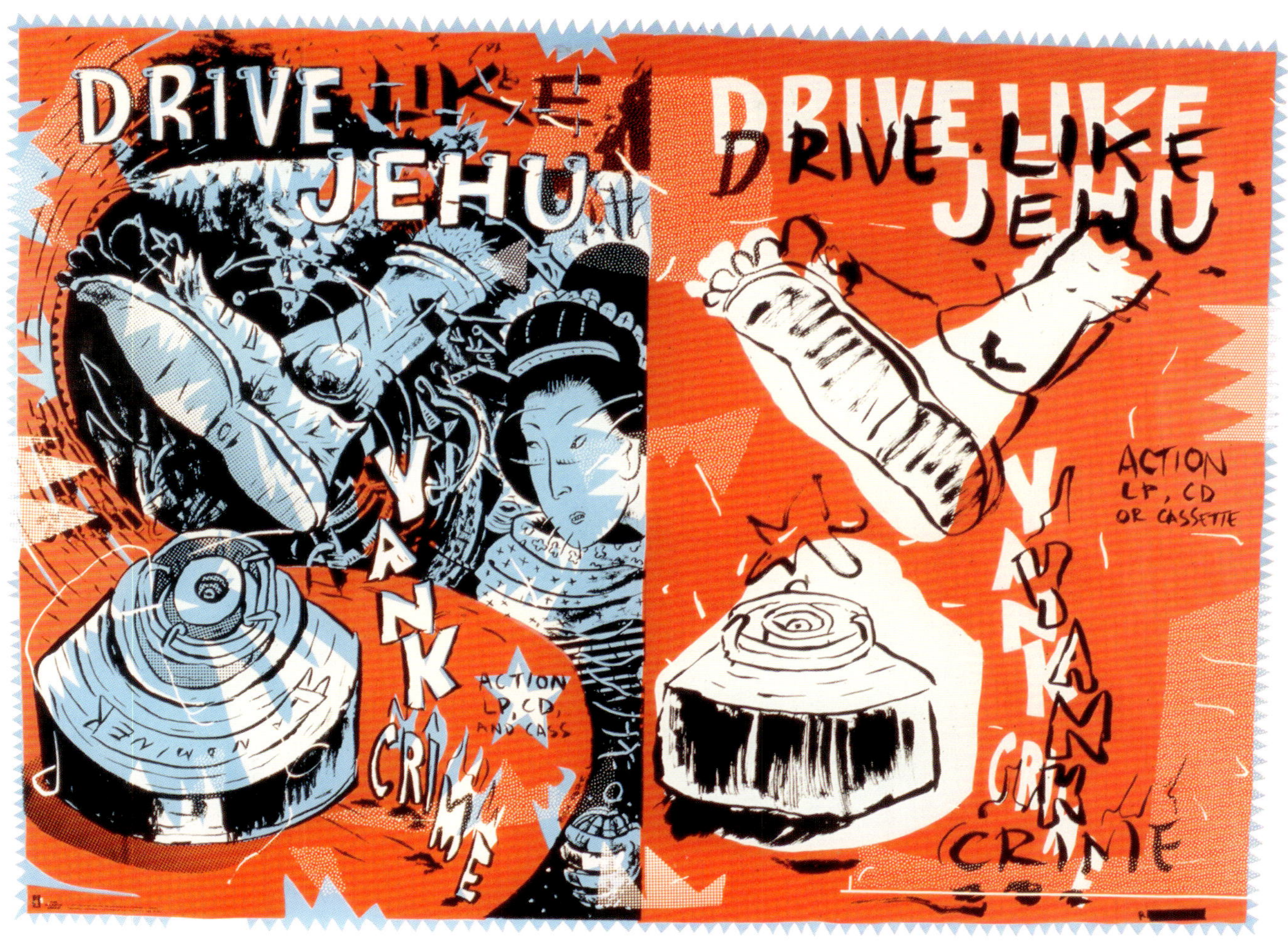

DRIVE LIKE
JEHU
YANK
CRIME
ACTION
LP, CD,
AND CASS
DRIVE LIKE
JEHU
ACTION
LP, CD
OR CASSETTE
YANK
CRIME

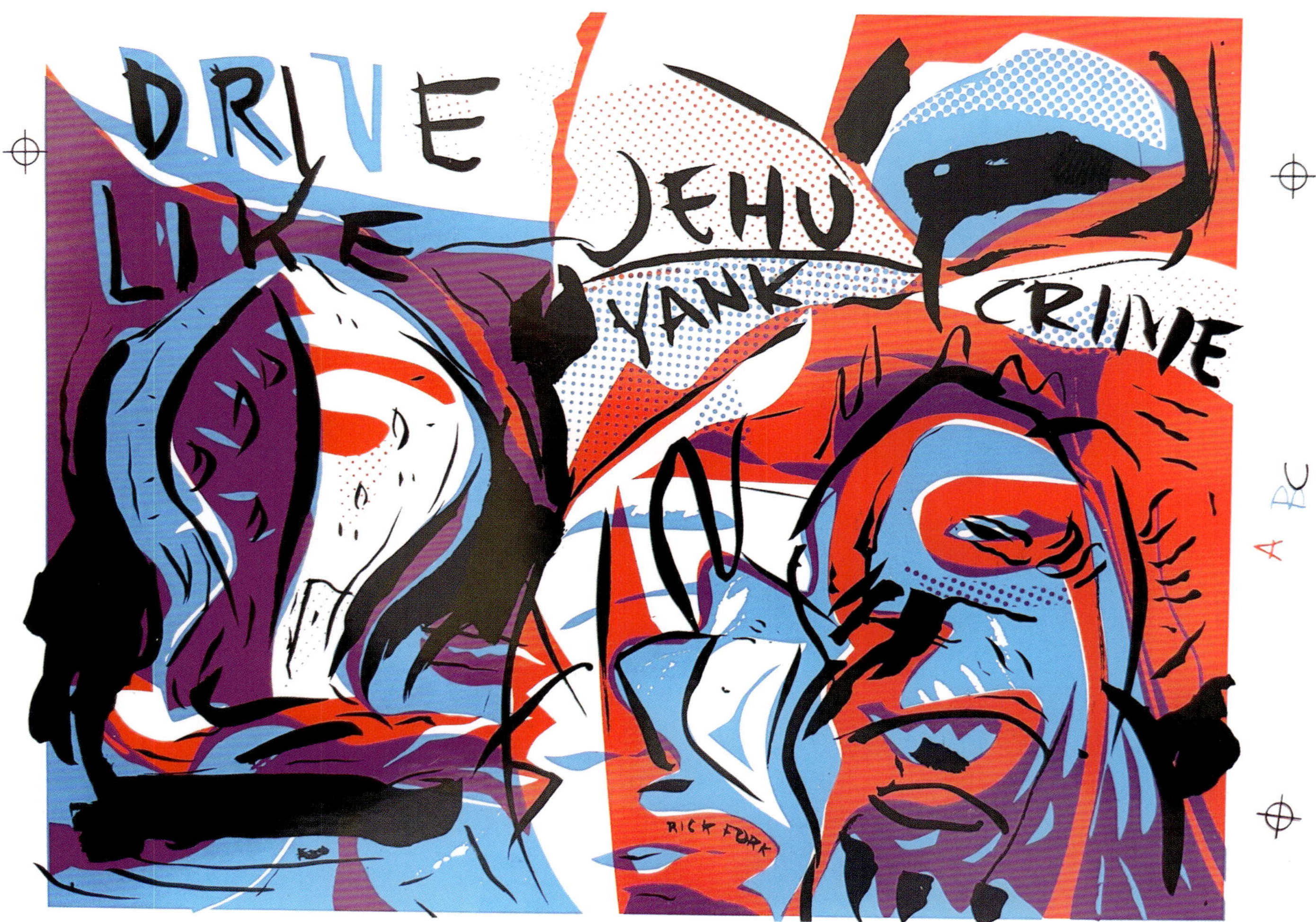

DRIVE
LIKE
JEHU
YANK
CRIME
RICK FORK

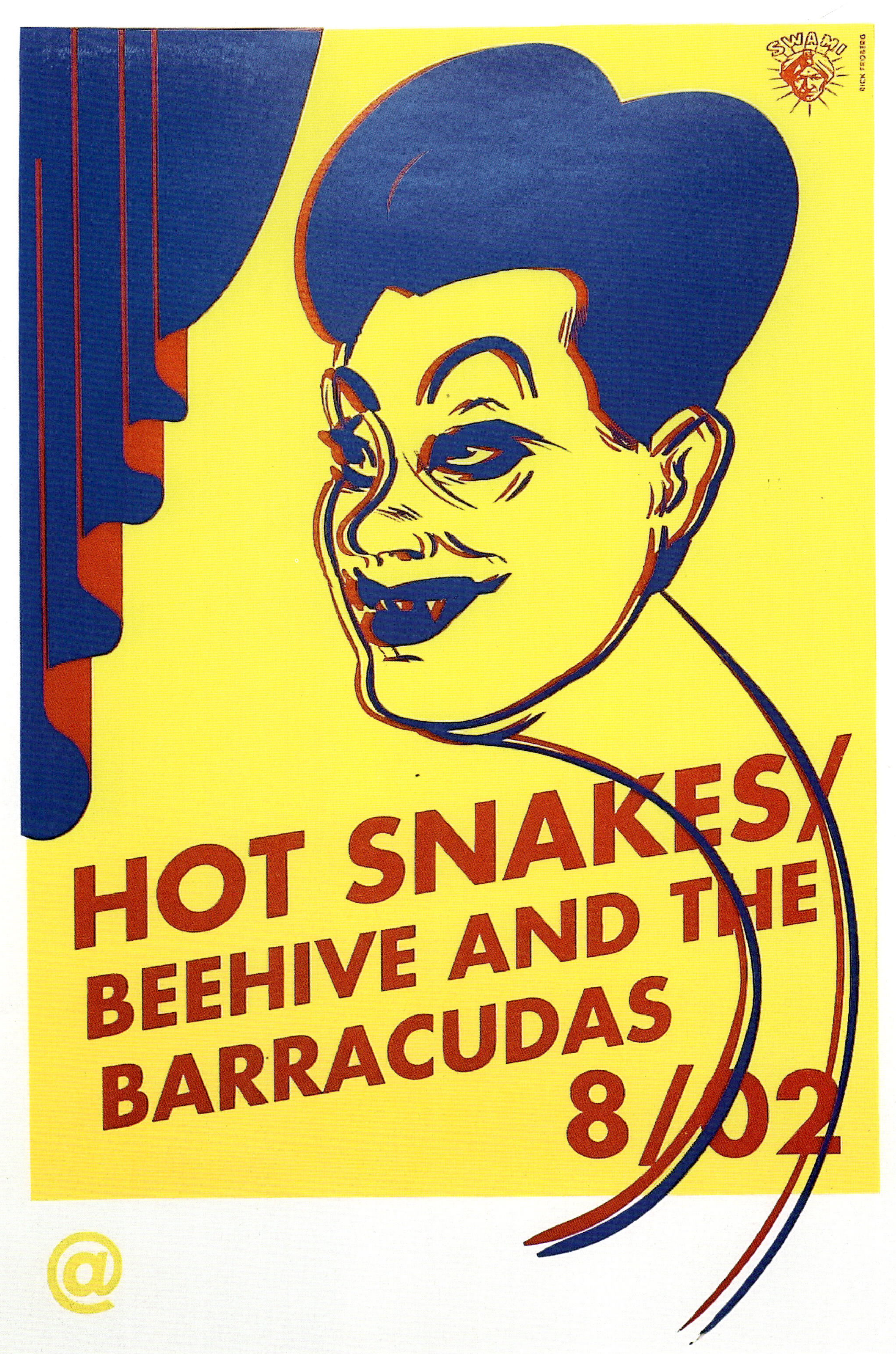

SWAMI
RICK FROBERG
HOT SNAKES/
BEEHIVE AND THE
BARRACUDAS
8/02
@

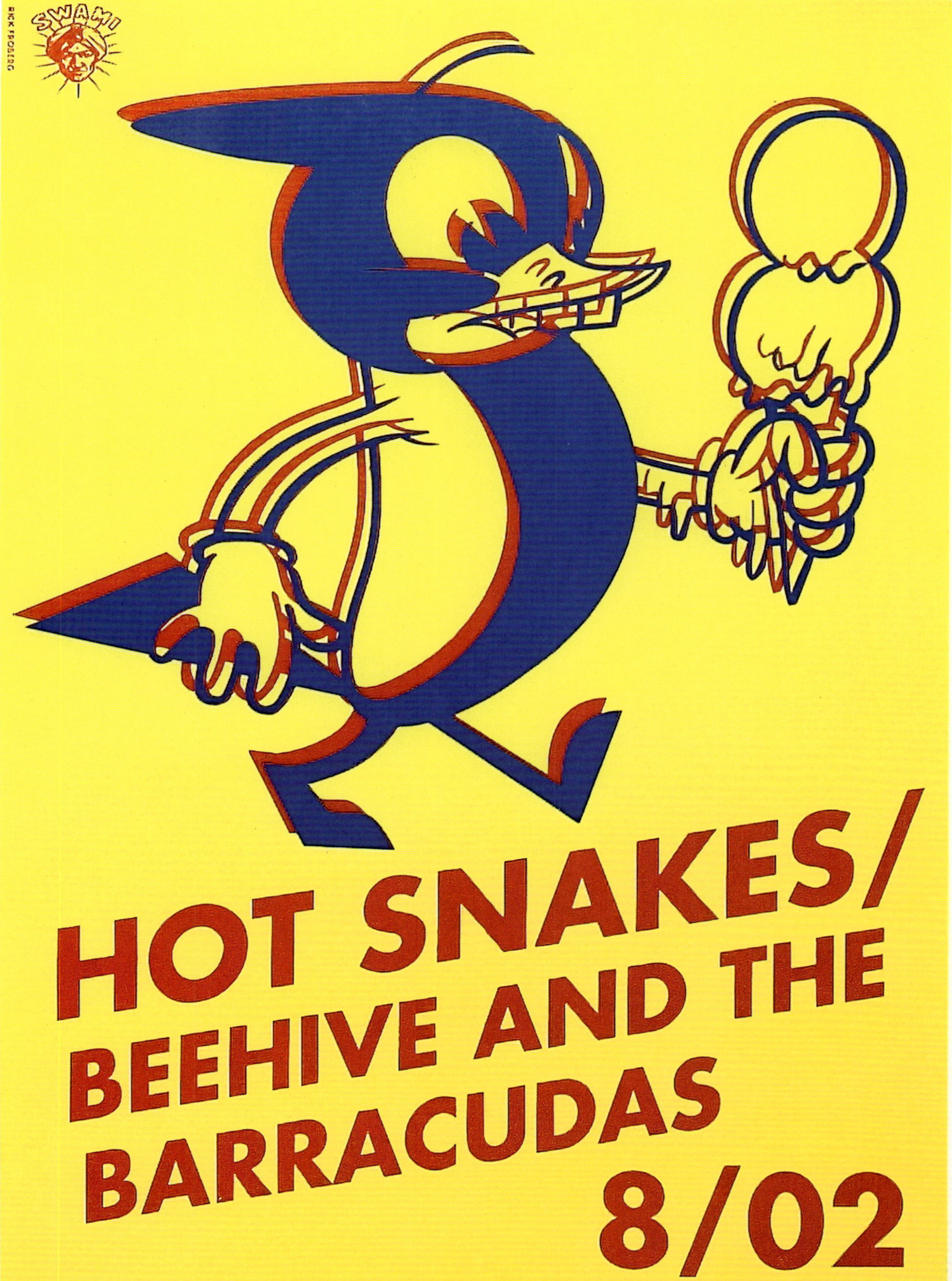

SWAMI
RICK FRODERG
HOT SNAKES/
BEEHIVE AND THE
BARRACUDAS
8/02

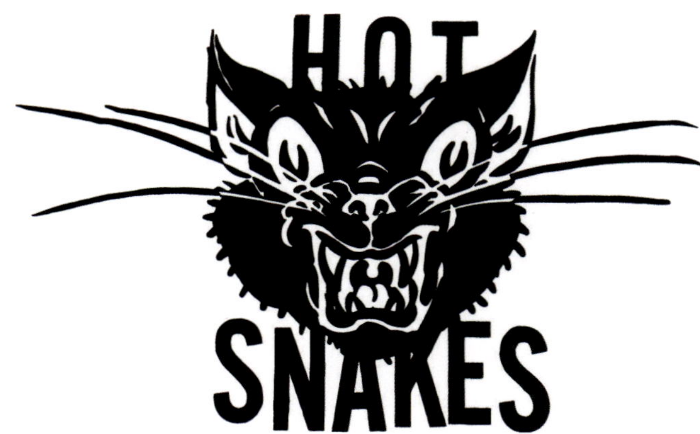
HOT
SNAKES

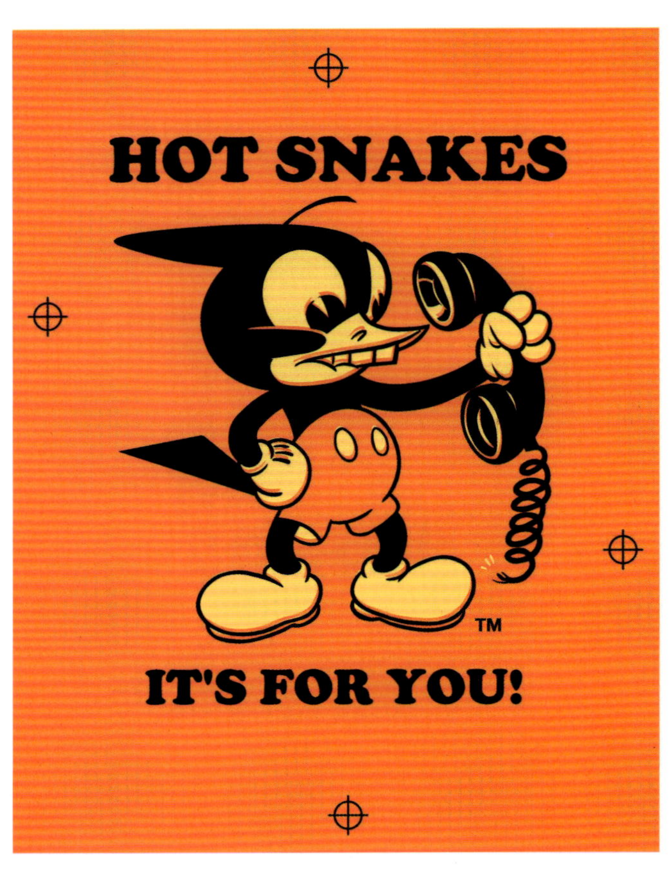
HOT SNAKES
IT'S FOR YOU!

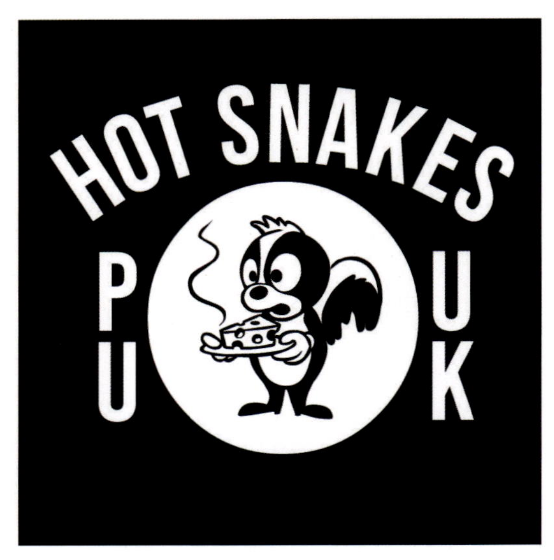
HOT SNAKES
P U U K

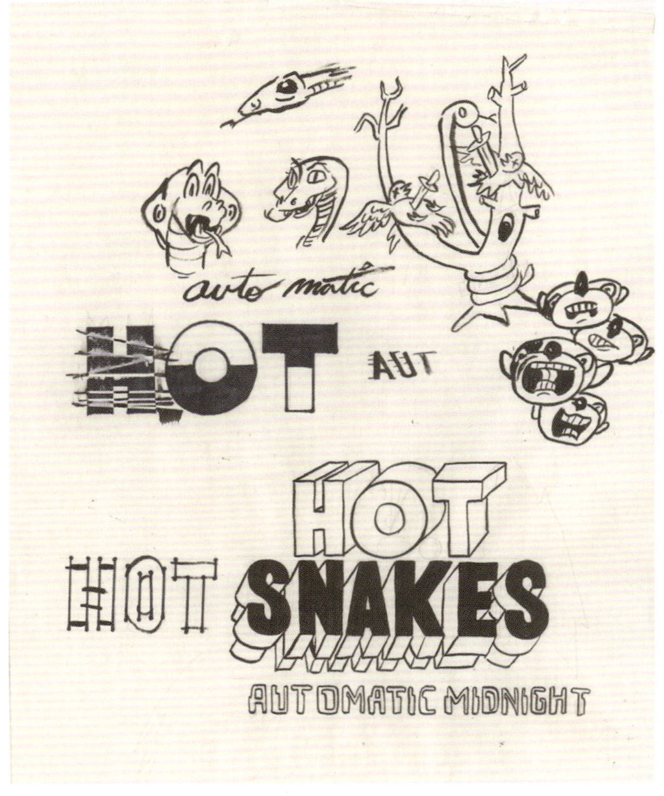
auto matic
HOT
AUT
HOT
HOT SNAKES
AUTOMATIC MIDNIGHT

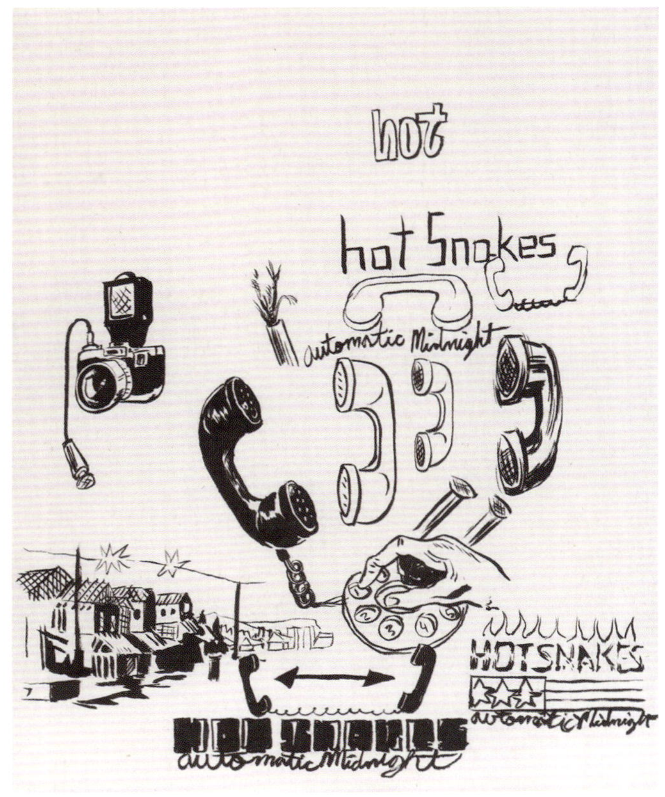
hot
hot Snakes
automatic midnight
HOT SNAKES
automatic Midnight
HOTSNAKES

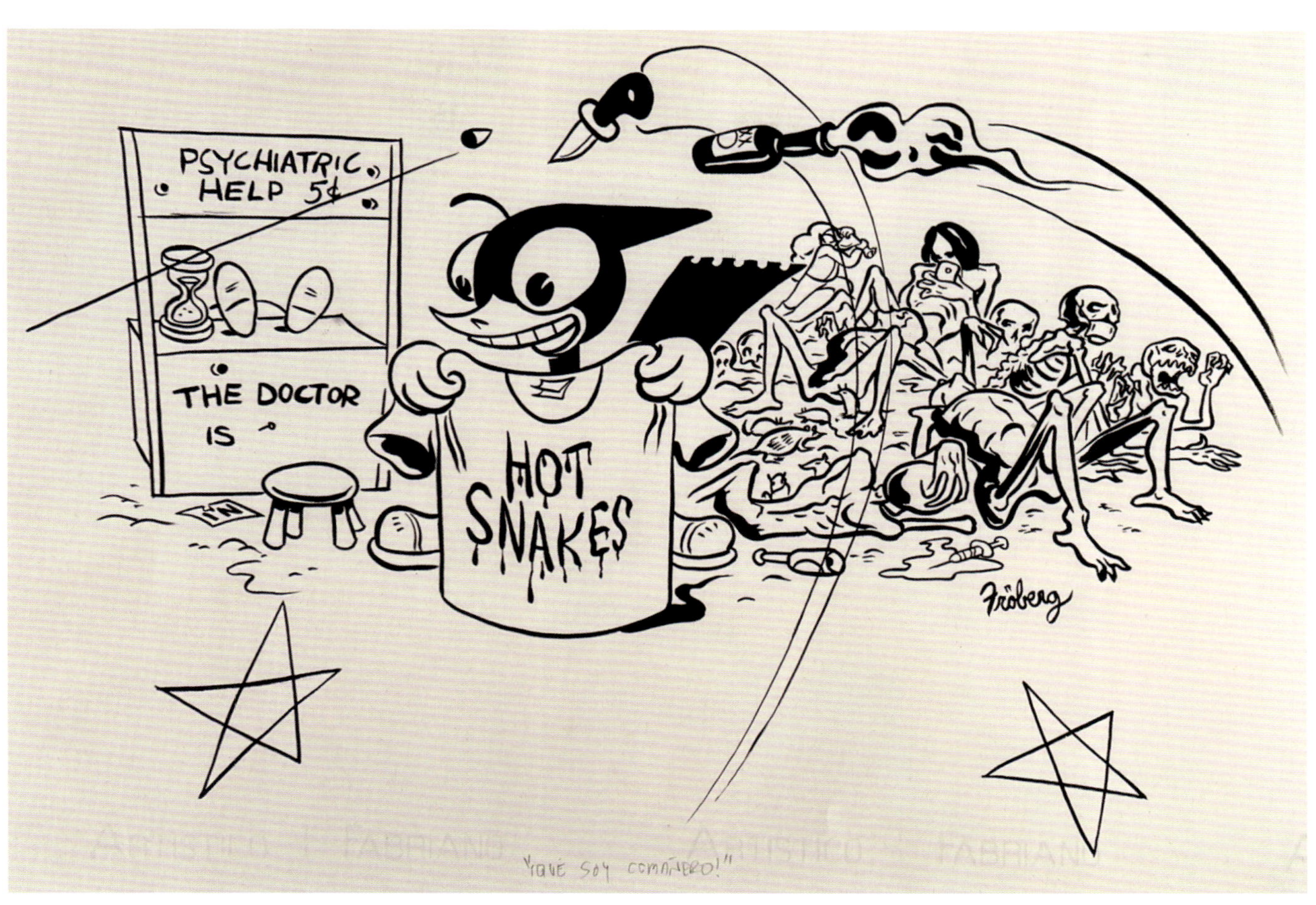

PSYCHIATRIC HELP 5¢
THE DOCTOR IS
IN
HOT SNAKES
Fröberg
"¡QUE SOY COMPAÑERO!"

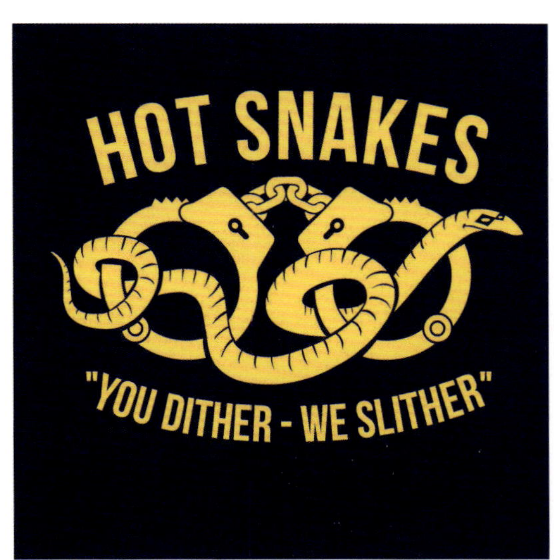

HOT SNAKES
"YOU DITHER - WE SLITHER"

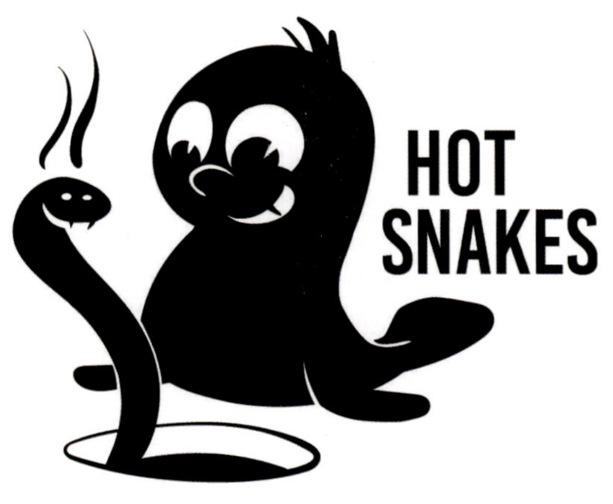

HOT SNAKES

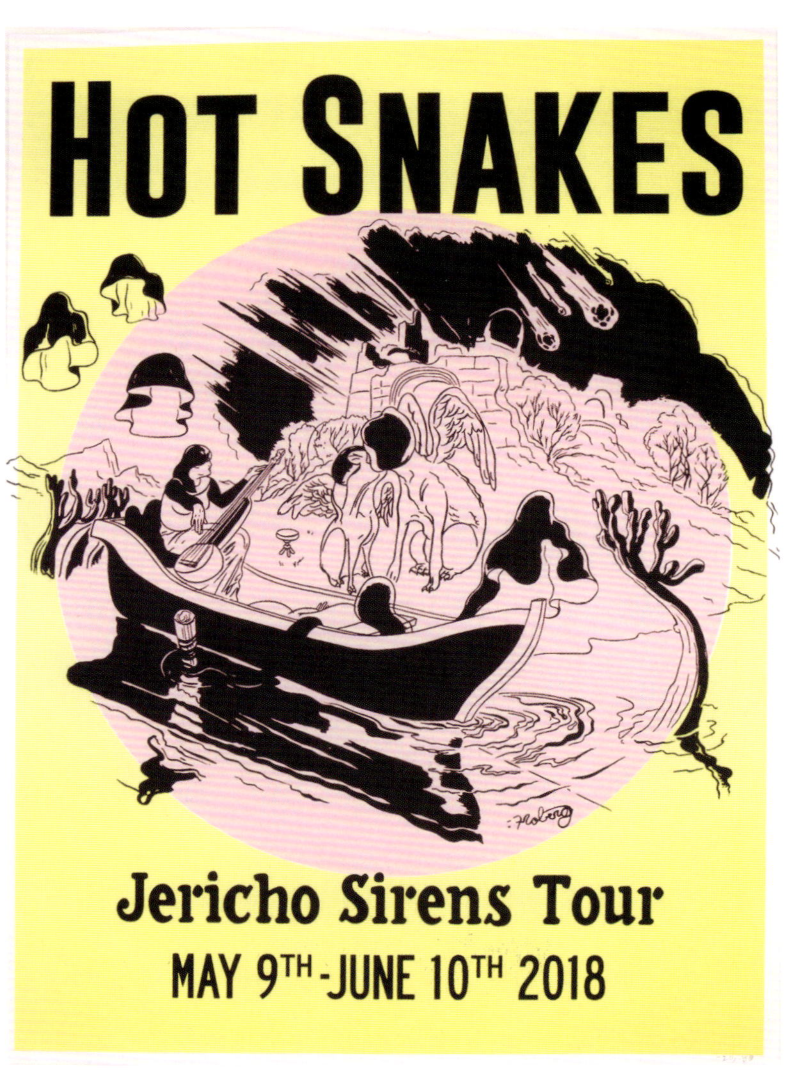

HOT SNAKES
Jericho Sirens Tour
MAY 9TH - JUNE 10TH 2018

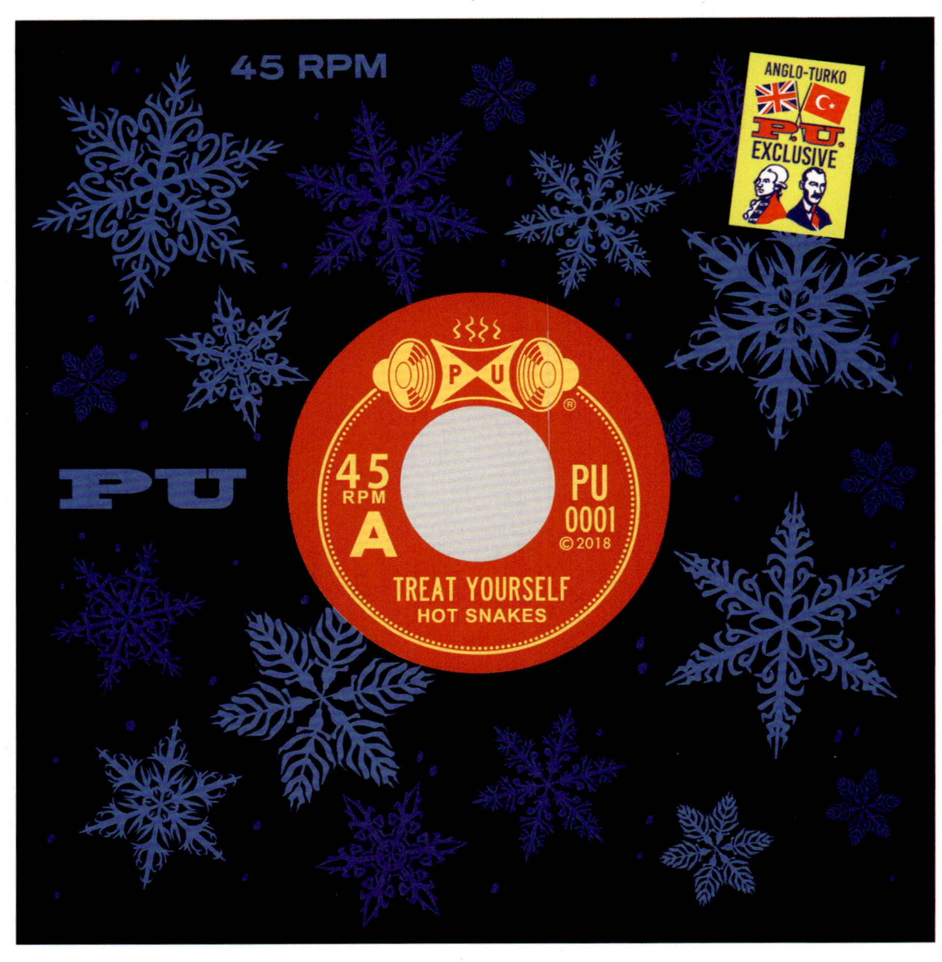
45 RPM
ANGLO-TURKO
P.U.
EXCLUSIVE
PU
45 RPM
A
PU
0001
© 2018
TREAT YOURSELF
HOT SNAKES

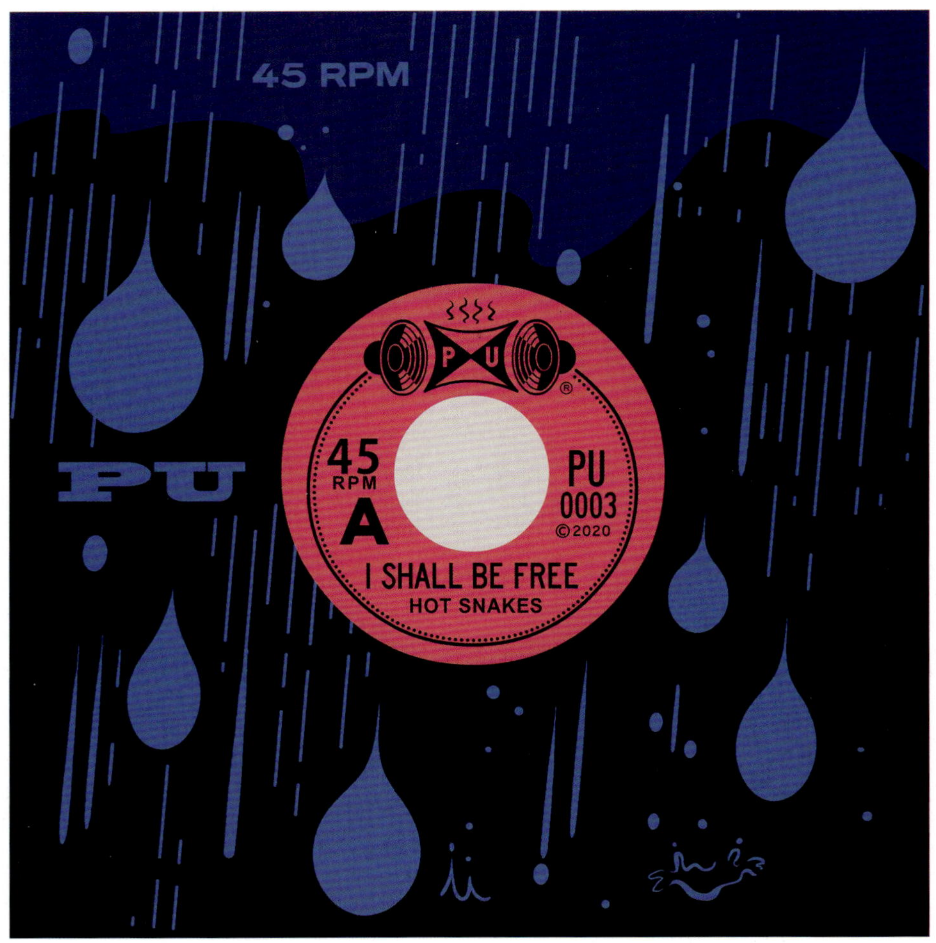
45 RPM
PU
45 RPM
A
PU
0003
© 2020
I SHALL BE FREE
HOT SNAKES

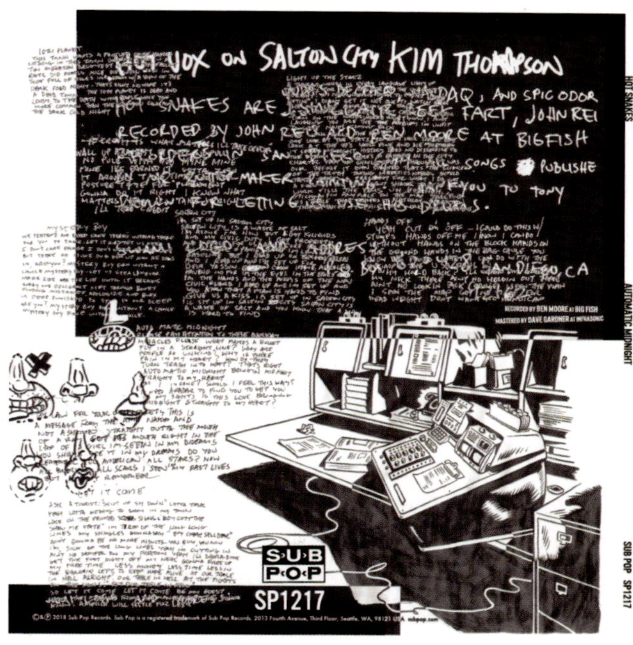

HOT VOX ON SALTON CITY KIM THOMPSON
HOT SNAKES ARE
RECORDED BY JOHN REIS AND BEN MOORE AT BIG FISH
SUB POP
SP1217

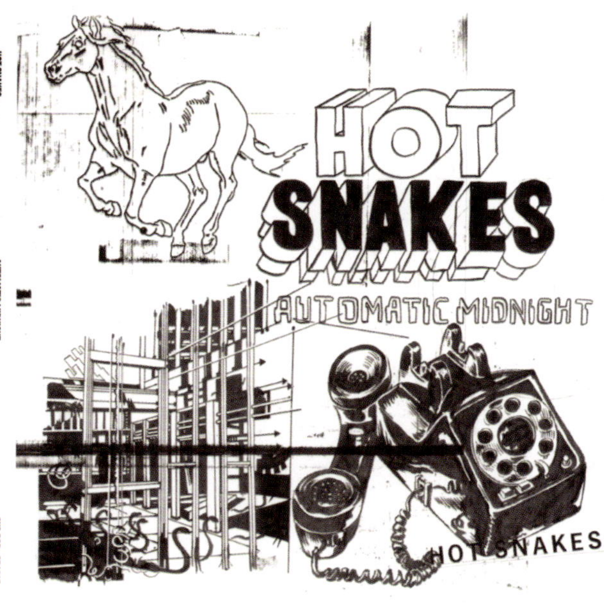

HOT SNAKES
AUTOMATIC MIDNIGHT
HOT SNAKES
SUB POP SP1217

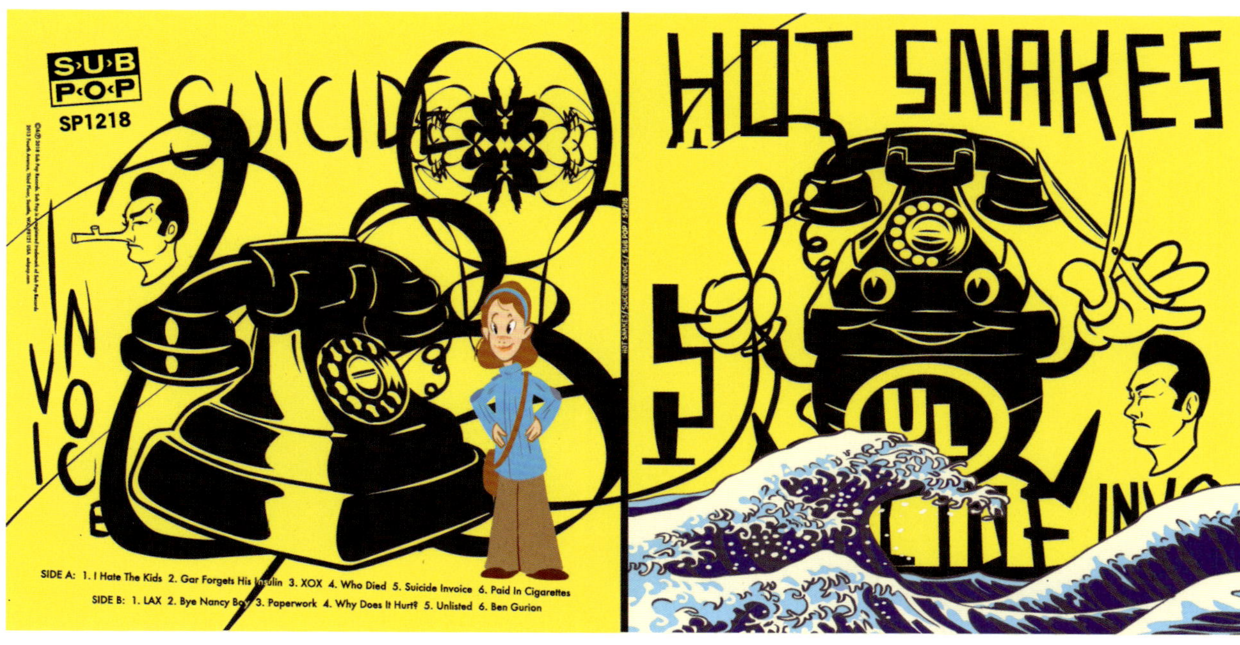

SUB POP
SP1218
SUICIDE INVOICE
HOT SNAKES
SIDE A: 1. I Hate The Kids 2. Gar Forgets His Insulin 3. XOX 4. Who Died 5. Suicide Invoice 6. Paid In Cigarettes
SIDE B: 1. LAX 2. Bye Nancy Boy 3. Paperwork 4. Why Does It Hurt? 5. Unlisted 6. Ben Gurion

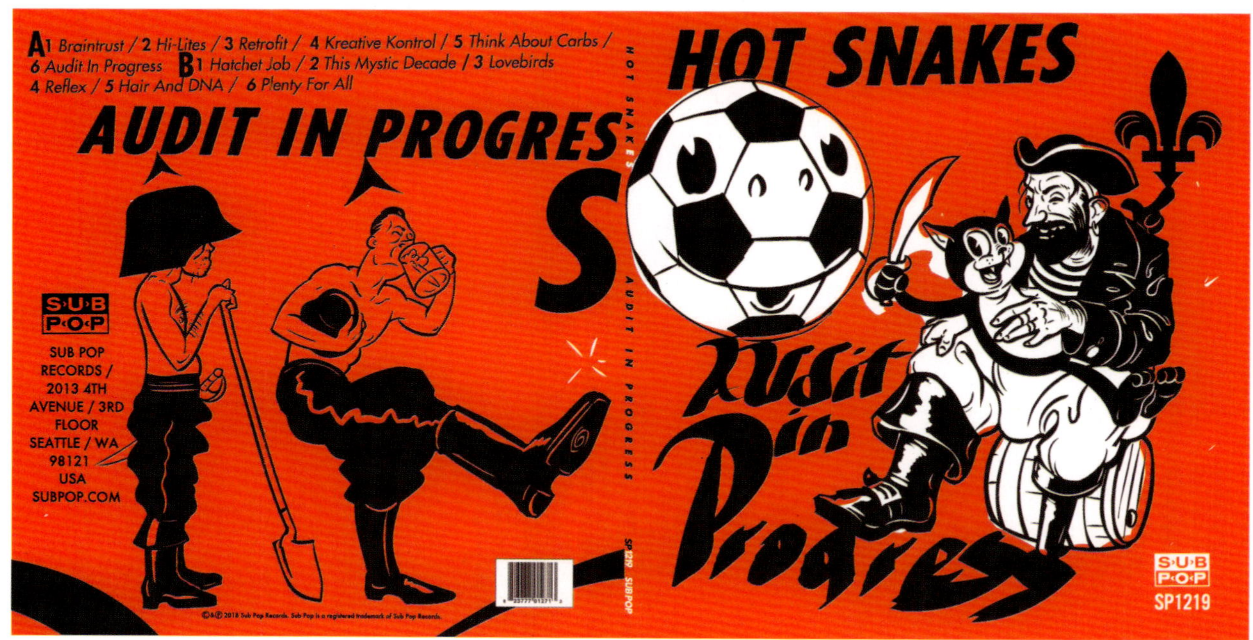

A1 Braintrust / 2 Hi-Lites / 3 Retrofit / 4 Kreative Kontrol / 5 Think About Carbs /
6 Audit In Progress B1 Hatchet Job / 2 This Mystic Decade / 3 Lovebirds
4 Reflex / 5 Hair And DNA / 6 Plenty For All
HOT SNAKES
AUDIT IN PROGRESS
SUB POP
RECORDS /
2013 4TH
AVENUE / 3RD
FLOOR
SEATTLE / WA
98121
USA
SUBPOP.COM
Audit in Progress
SUB POP
SP1219

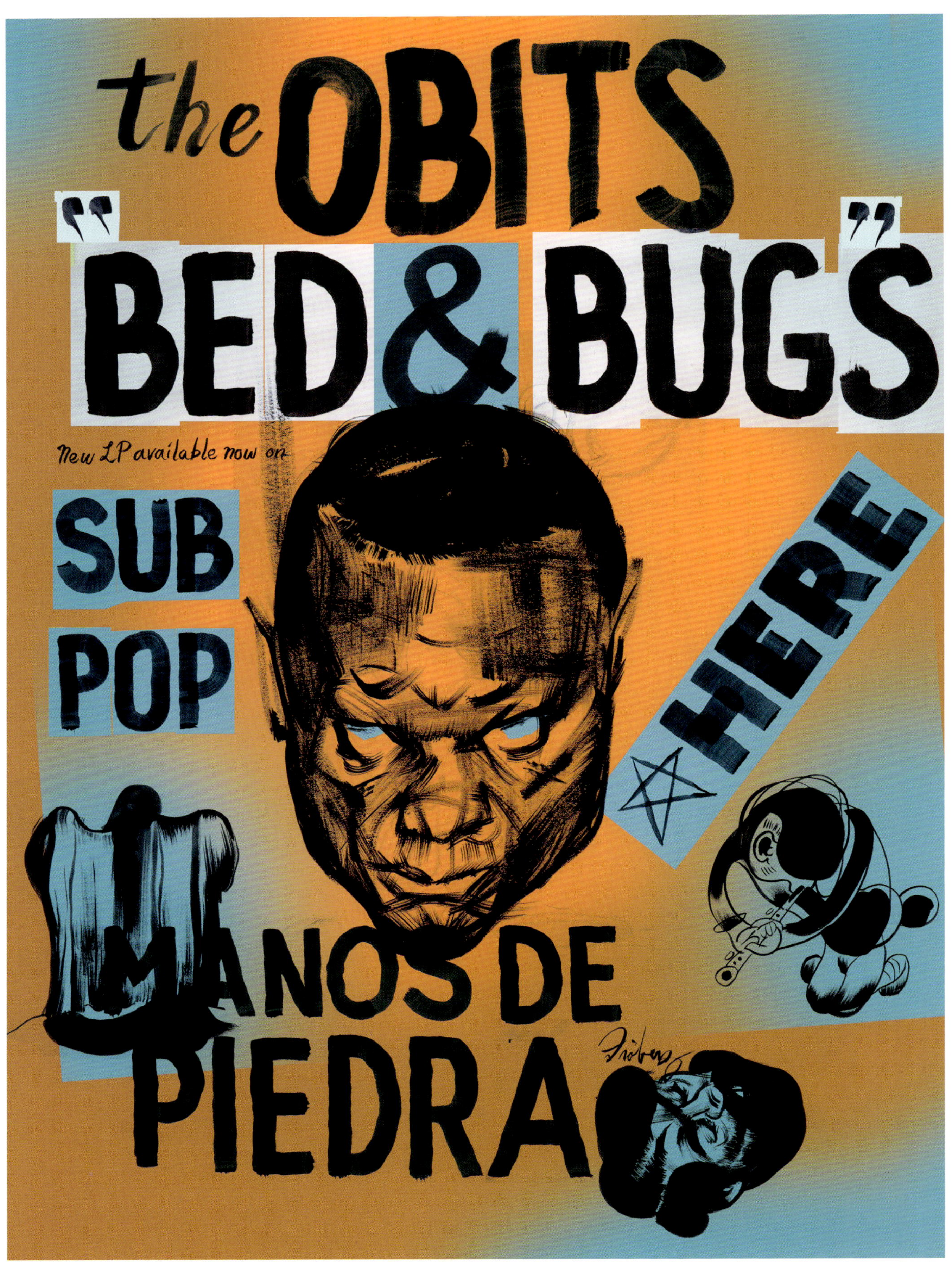

the OBITS
"BED & BUGS"
New LP available now on
SUB POP
HERE
MANOS DE PIEDRA

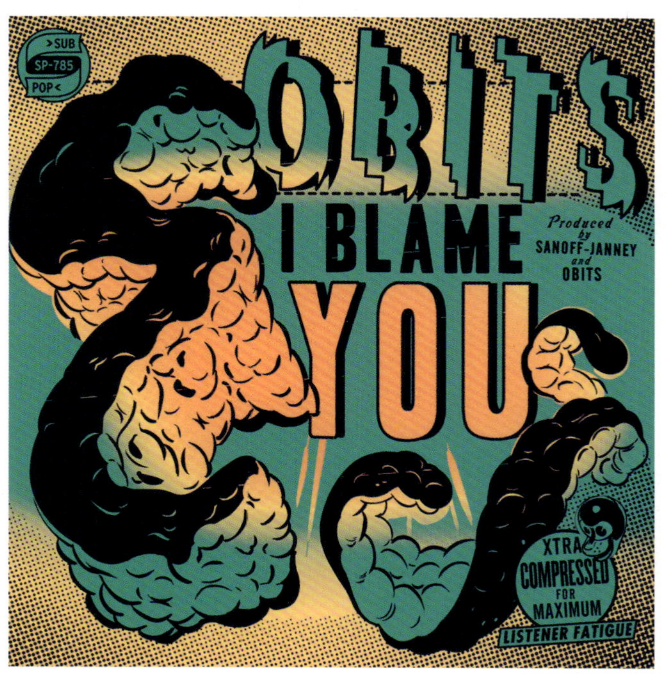
SUB
SP-785
POP
OBITS
I BLAME YOU
Produced by SANOFF-JANNEY and OBITS
XTRA COMPRESSED FOR MAXIMUM LISTENER FATIGUE

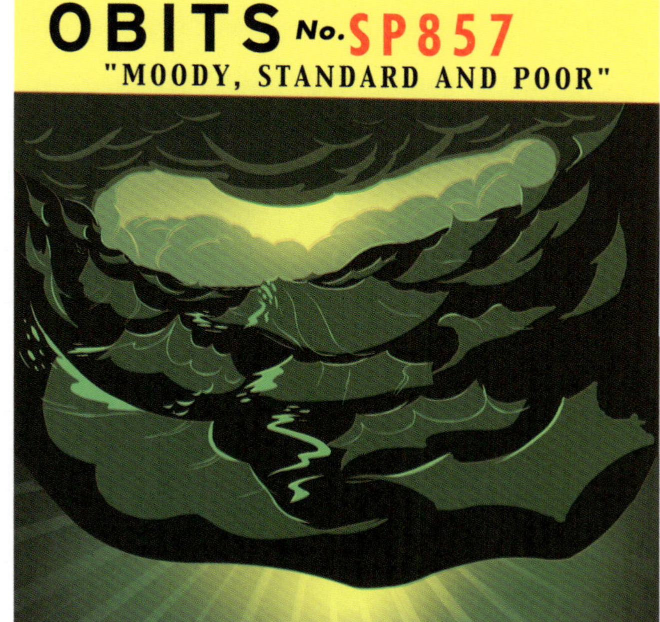
OBITS No. SP857
"MOODY, STANDARD AND POOR"

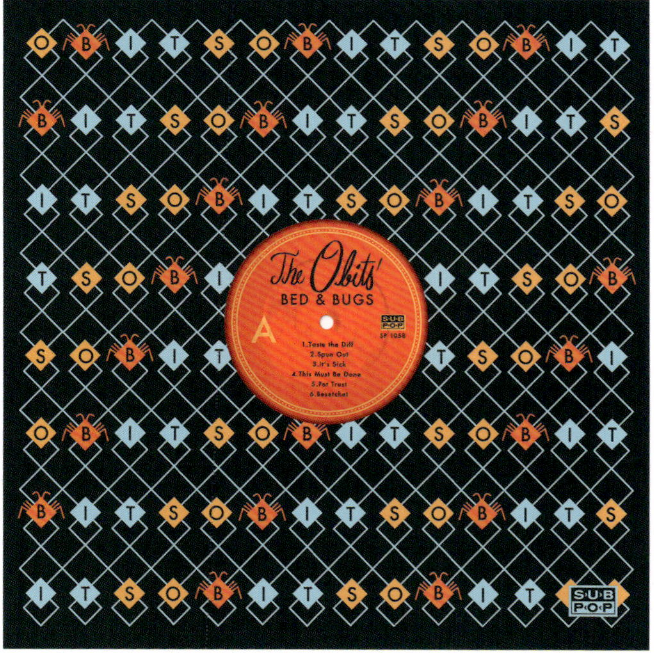
The Obits'
BED & BUGS
A
SUB POP
SP 1036
1. Taste the Diff
2. Spin Out
3. It's Sick
4. This Must Be Done
5. Pet Trash
6. Southchat
SUB POP

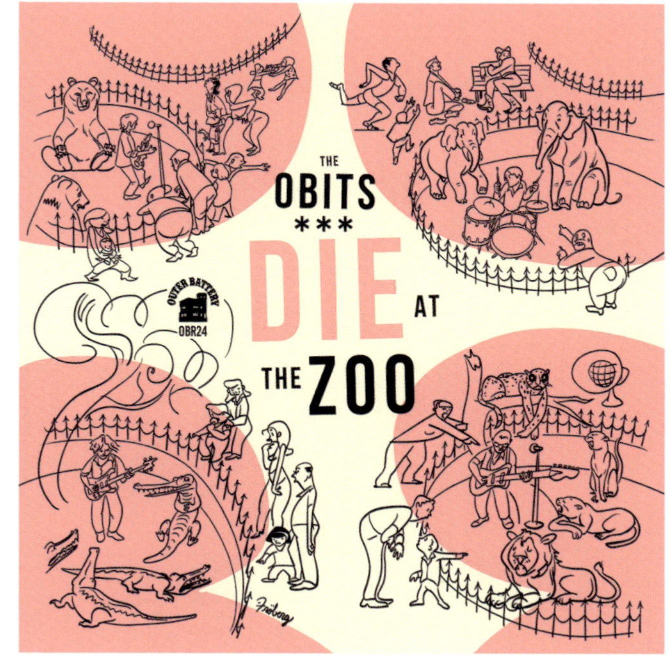
THE OBITS
***
DIE AT THE ZOO
OUTER BATTERY
OBR24

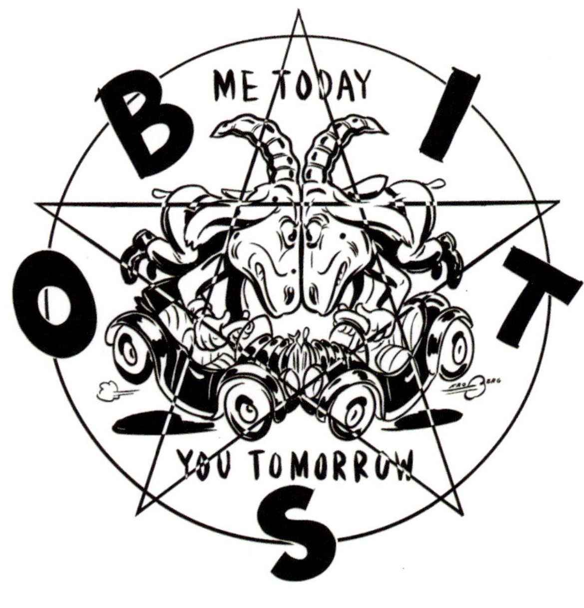
OBITS
ME TODAY
YOU TOMORROW

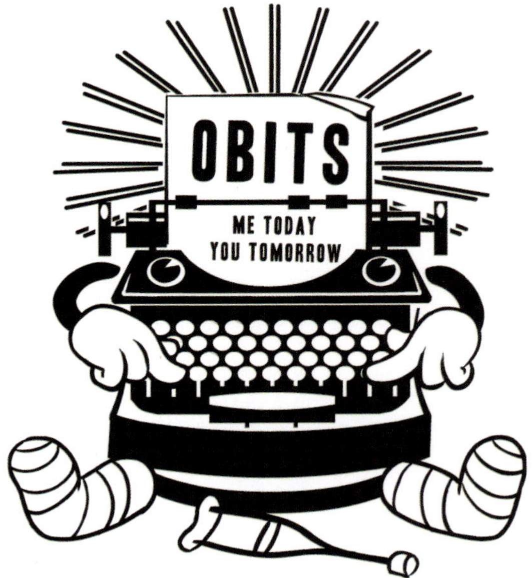
OBITS
ME TODAY
YOU TOMORROW

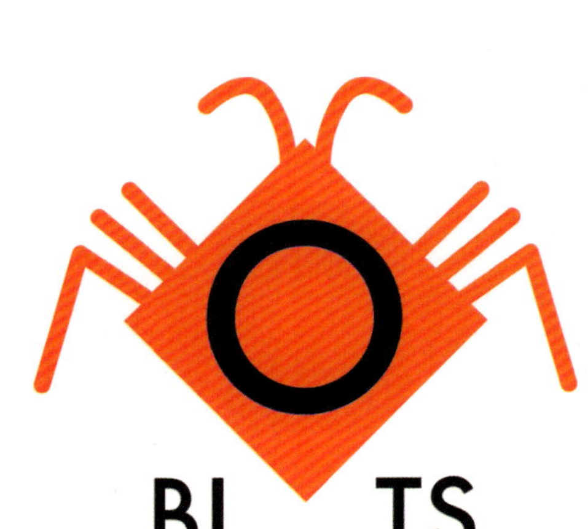
OBITS

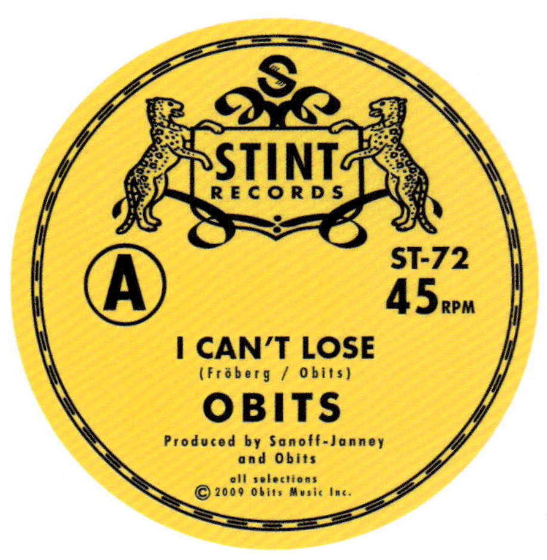
STINT
RECORDS
A
ST-72
45 RPM
I CAN'T LOSE
(Fröberg / Obits)
OBITS
Produced by Sanoff-Janney
and Obits
all selections
© 2009 Obits Music Inc.

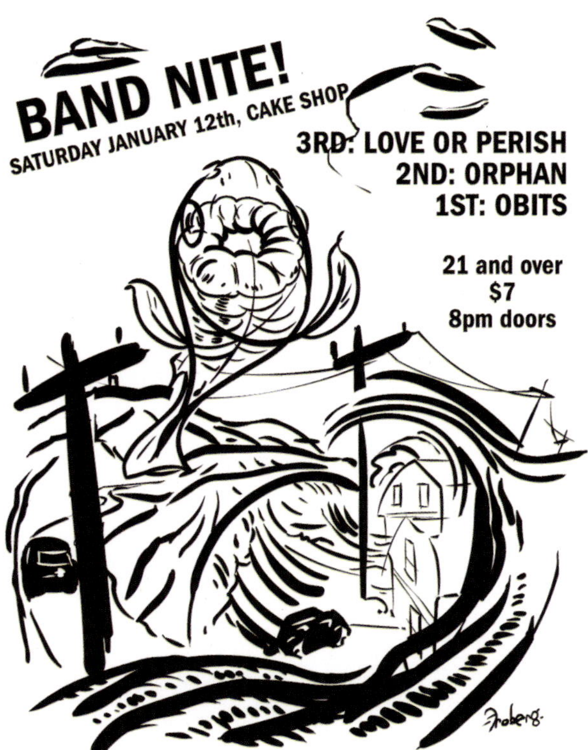
BAND NITE!
SATURDAY JANUARY 12th, CAKE SHOP
3RD: LOVE OR PERISH
2ND: ORPHAN
1ST: OBITS
21 and over
$7
8pm doors
CAKE SHOP: 152 Ludlow btw Stanton and Rivington

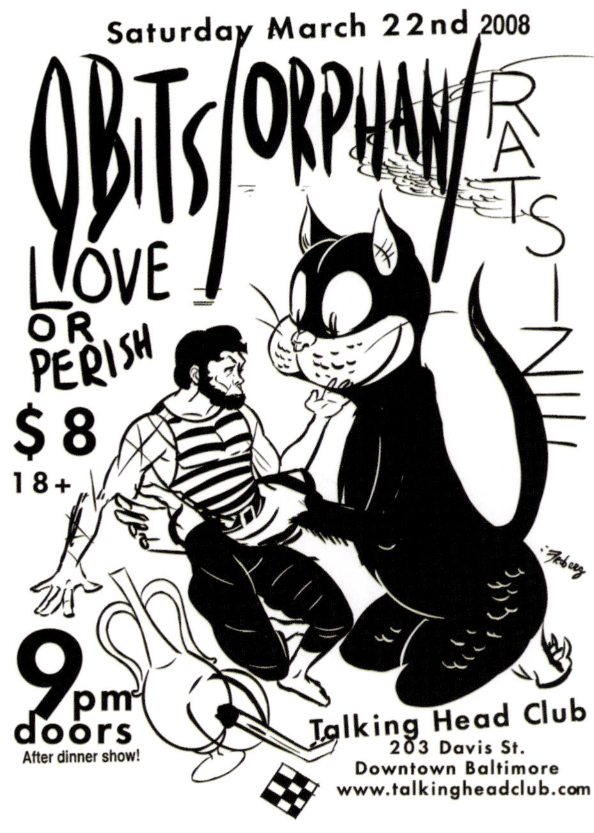
Saturday March 22nd 2008
OBITS / ORPHAN / RATS IN THE WALL
LOVE OR PERISH
$8
18+
9pm doors
After dinner show!
Talking Head Club
203 Davis St.
Downtown Baltimore
www.talkingheadclub.com

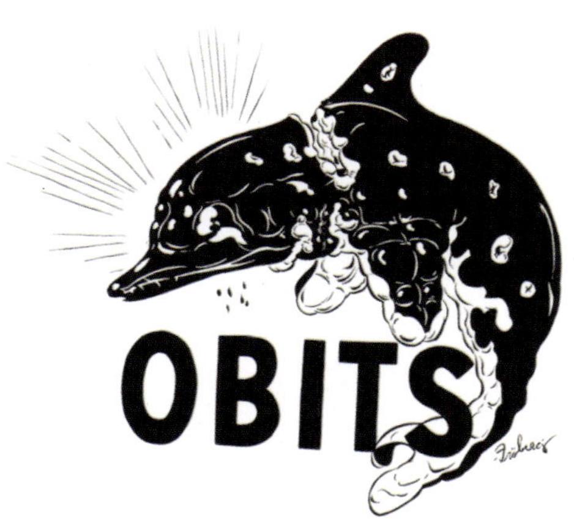
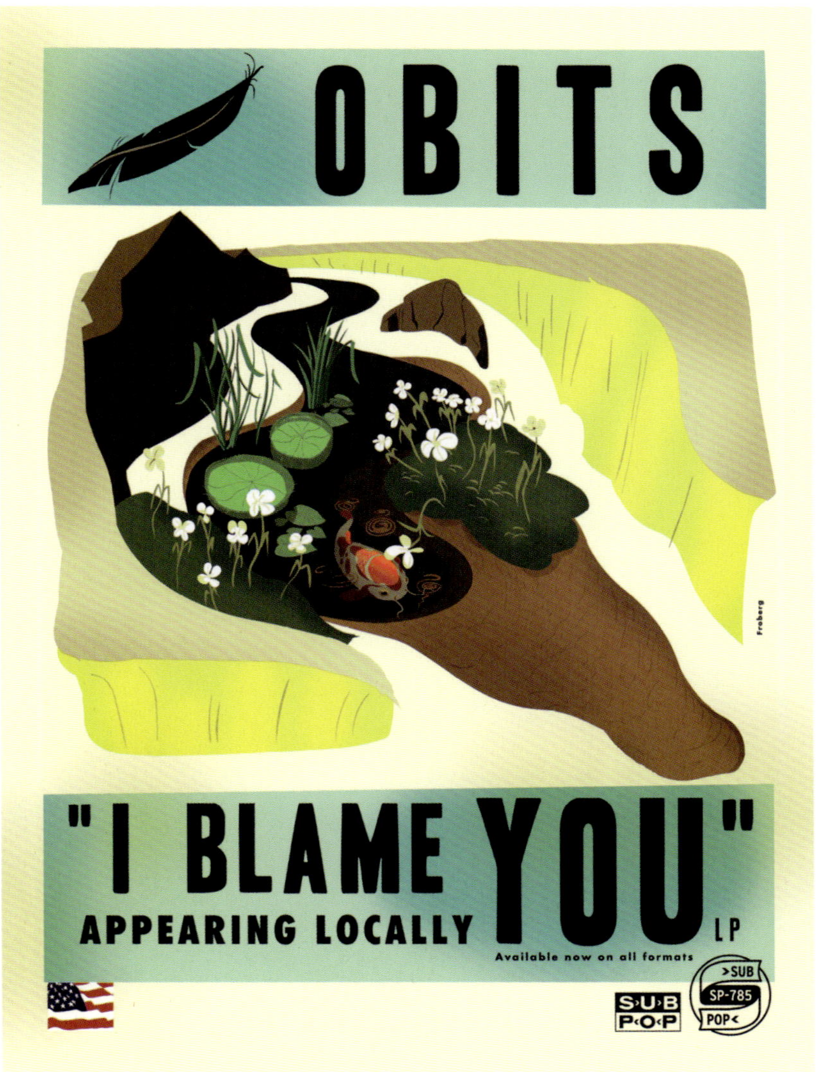
OBITS
"I BLAME YOU"
APPEARING LOCALLY LP
Available now on all formats
SUB POP
SUB SP-785 POP

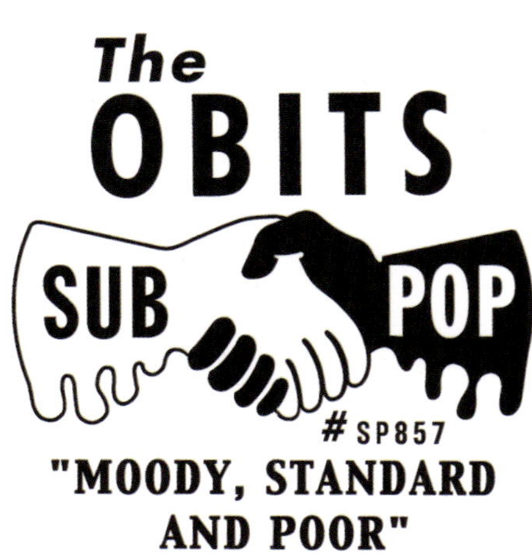
The OBITS
SUB POP
SP857
"MOODY, STANDARD
AND POOR"

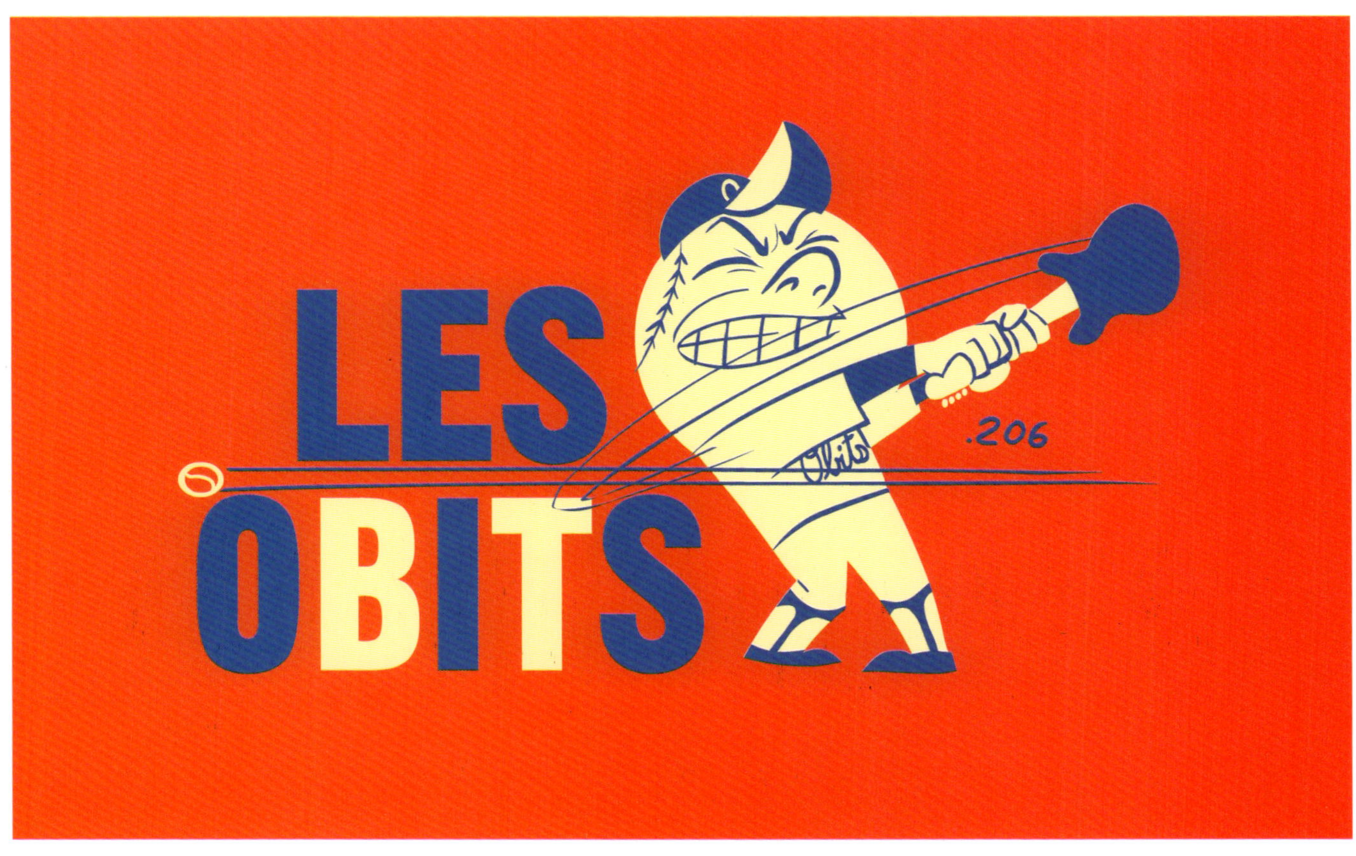
LES OBITS
.206

FOUR

Graphic Design, Illustration, and Commercial Work

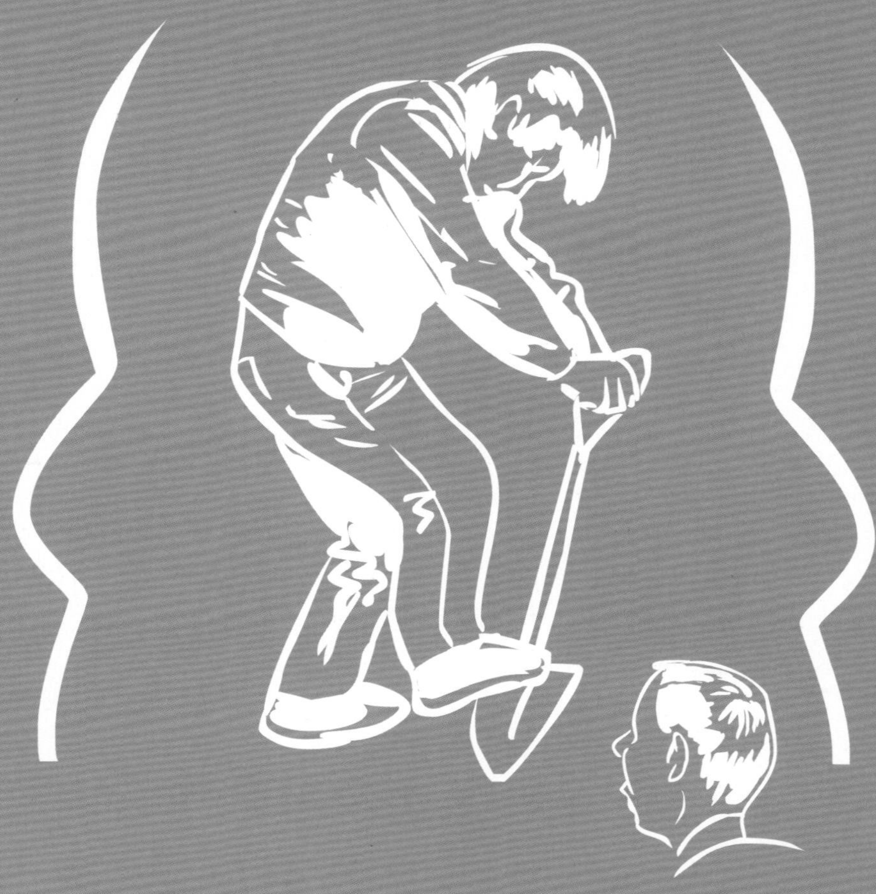

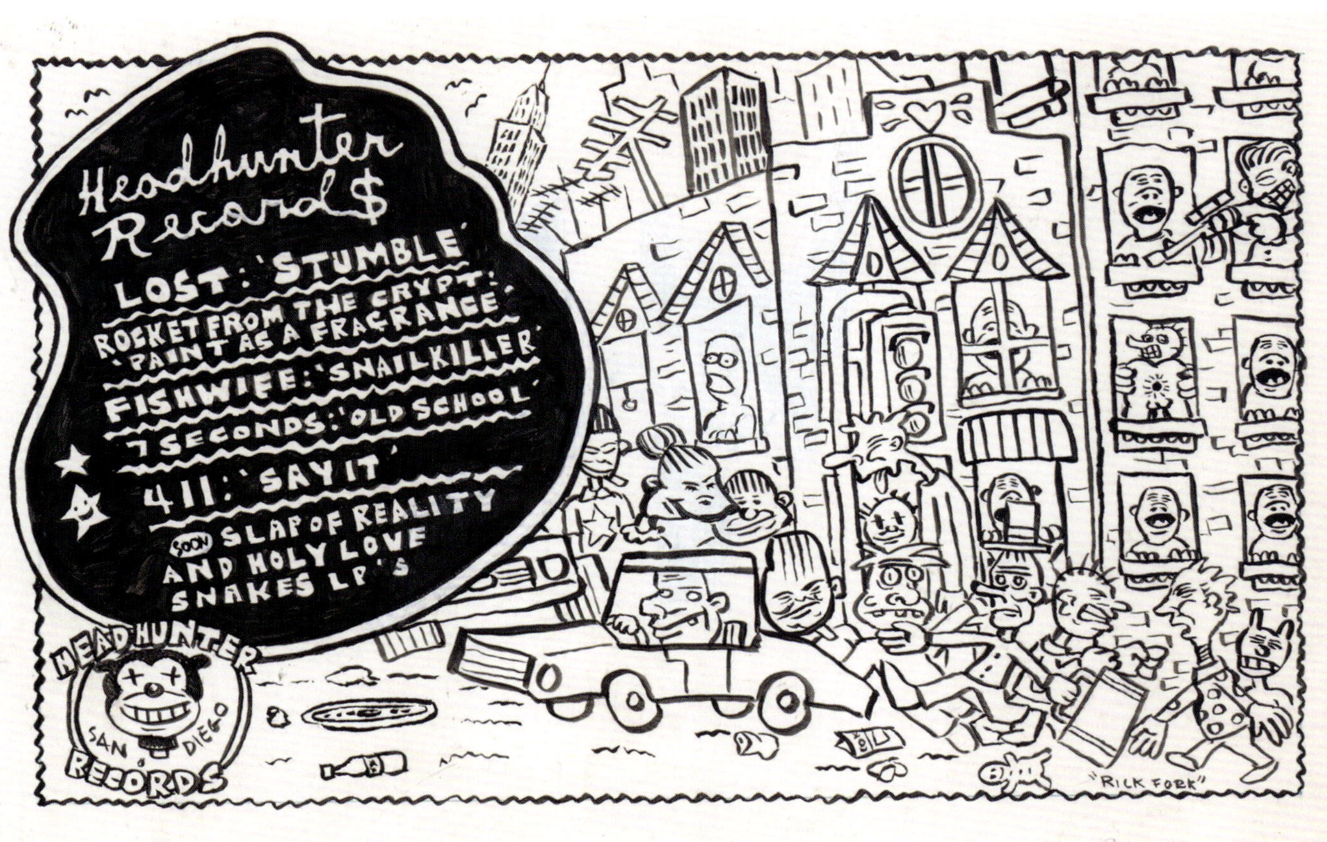

Headhunter
Record$
LOST: 'STUMBLE'
ROCKET FROM THE CRYPT:
'PAINT AS A FRAGRANCE'
FISHWIFE: 'SNAIL KILLER'
7 SECONDS: 'OLD SCHOOL'
411: 'SAY IT'
SOON SLAP OF REALITY
AND HOLY LOVE
SNAKES LP'S
HEADHUNTER
SAN DIEGO
RECORDS
"RICK FORK"

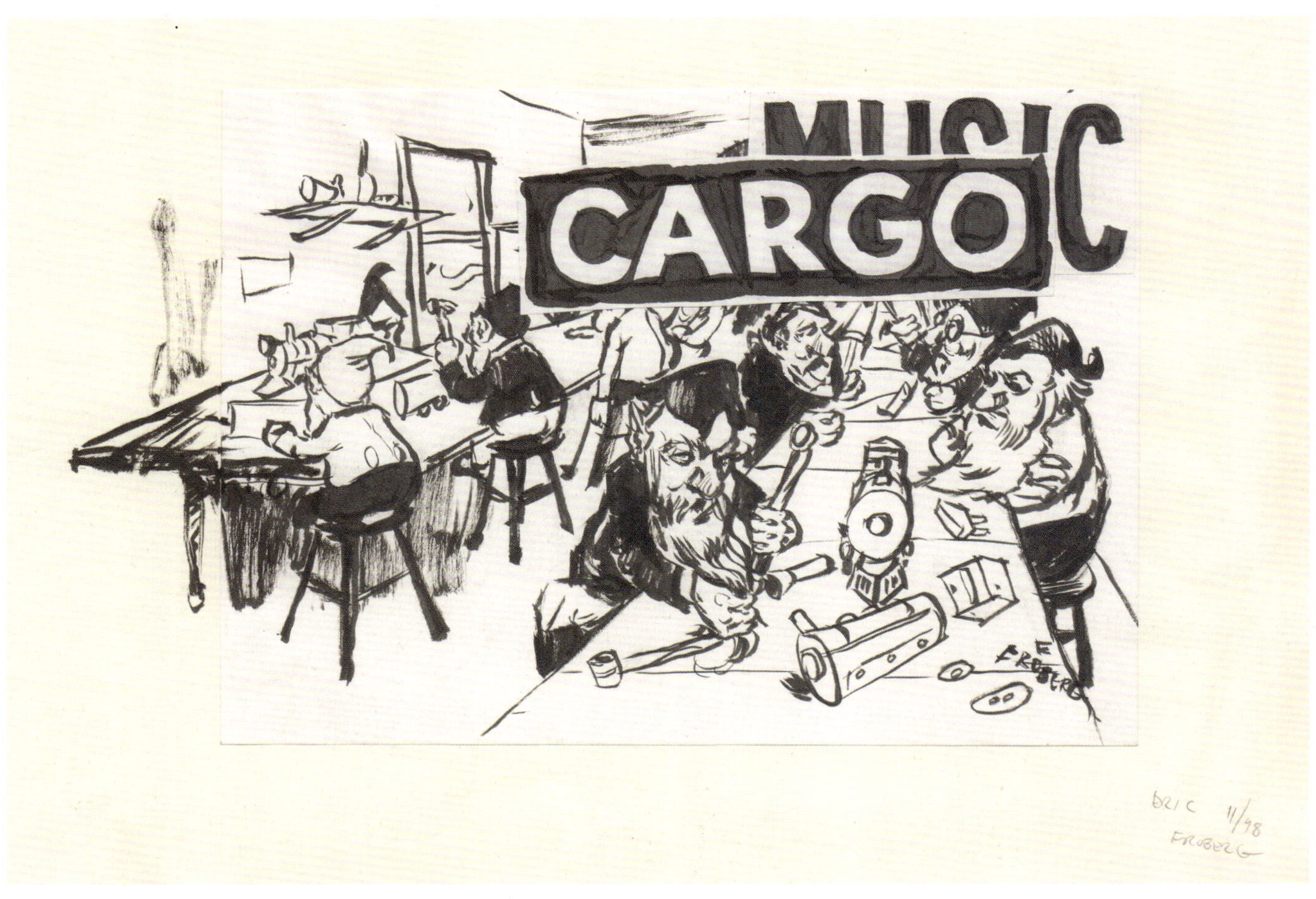

MUSIC
CARGO
FROBERG
eric 11/98
FROBERG

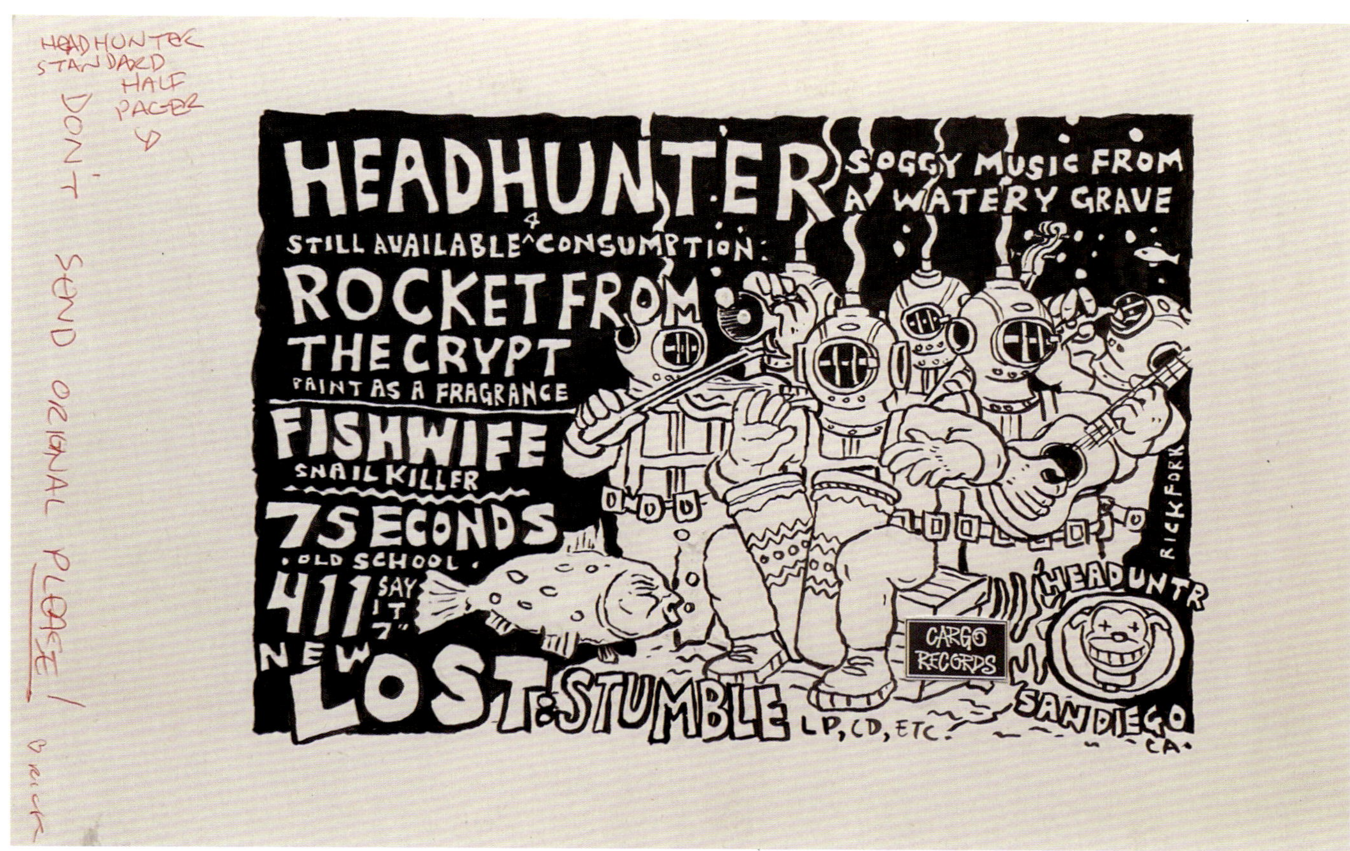

HEADHUNTER
SOGGY MUSIC FROM A WATERY GRAVE
STILL AVAILABLE FOR CONSUMPTION:
ROCKET FROM THE CRYPT
PAINT AS A FRAGRANCE
FISHWIFE
SNAIL KILLER
7 SECONDS
OLD SCHOOL
411 SAY IT 7"
NEW LOST : STUMBLE
LP, CD, ETC.
CARGO RECORDS
HEADHUNTR
SAN DIEGO CA.
RICK FORK

HEADHUNTER
STANDARD
HALF PAGER
DON'T SEND ORIGINAL PLEASE!
B/W

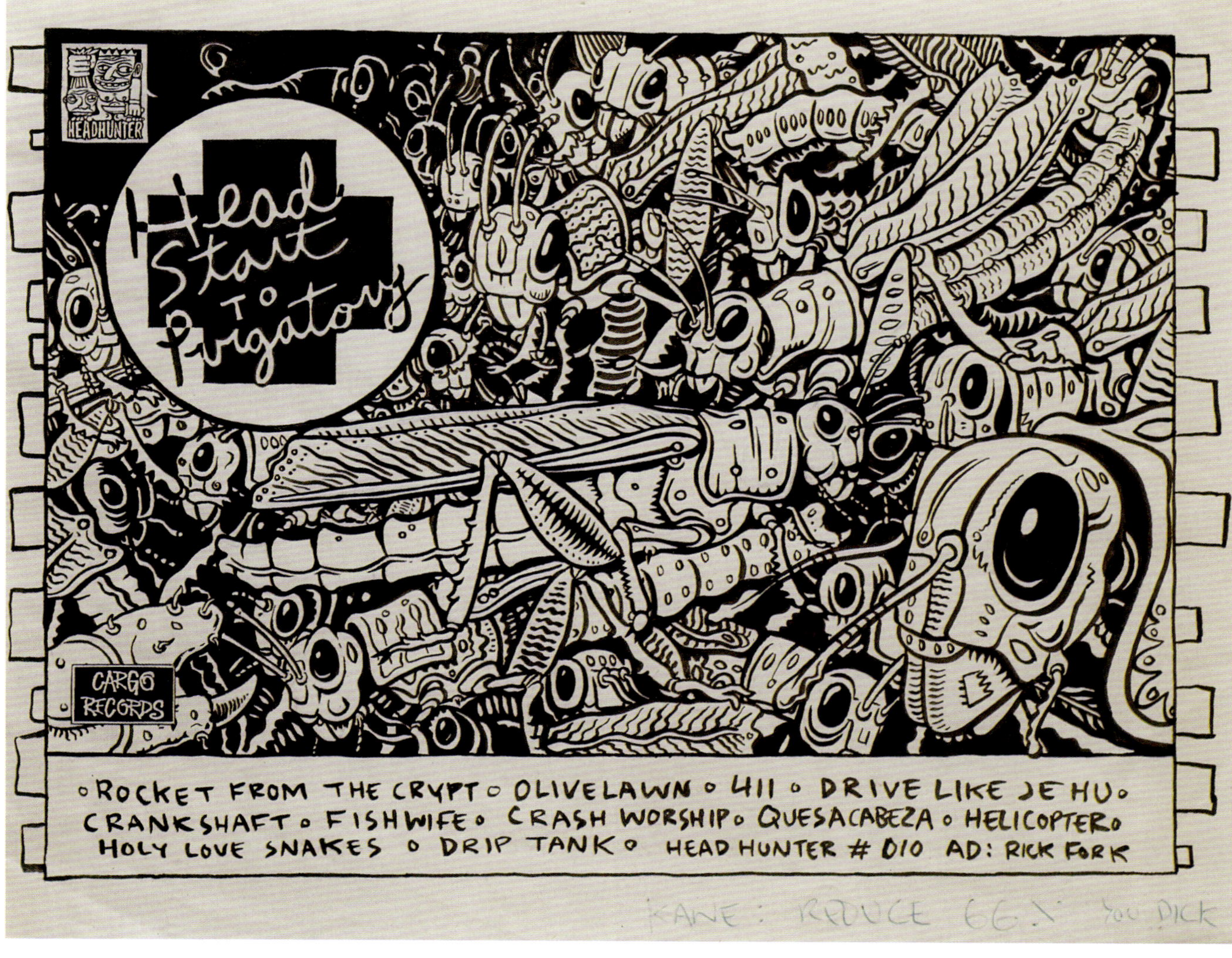

HEADHUNTER
Head Start to Purgatory
CARGO RECORDS
ROCKET FROM THE CRYPT o OLIVELAWN o 411 o DRIVE LIKE JEHU o
CRANKSHAFT o FISHWIFE o CRASH WORSHIP o QUESACABEZA o HELICOPTER o
HOLY LOVE SNAKES o DRIP TANK o HEAD HUNTER # 010 AD: RICK FORK

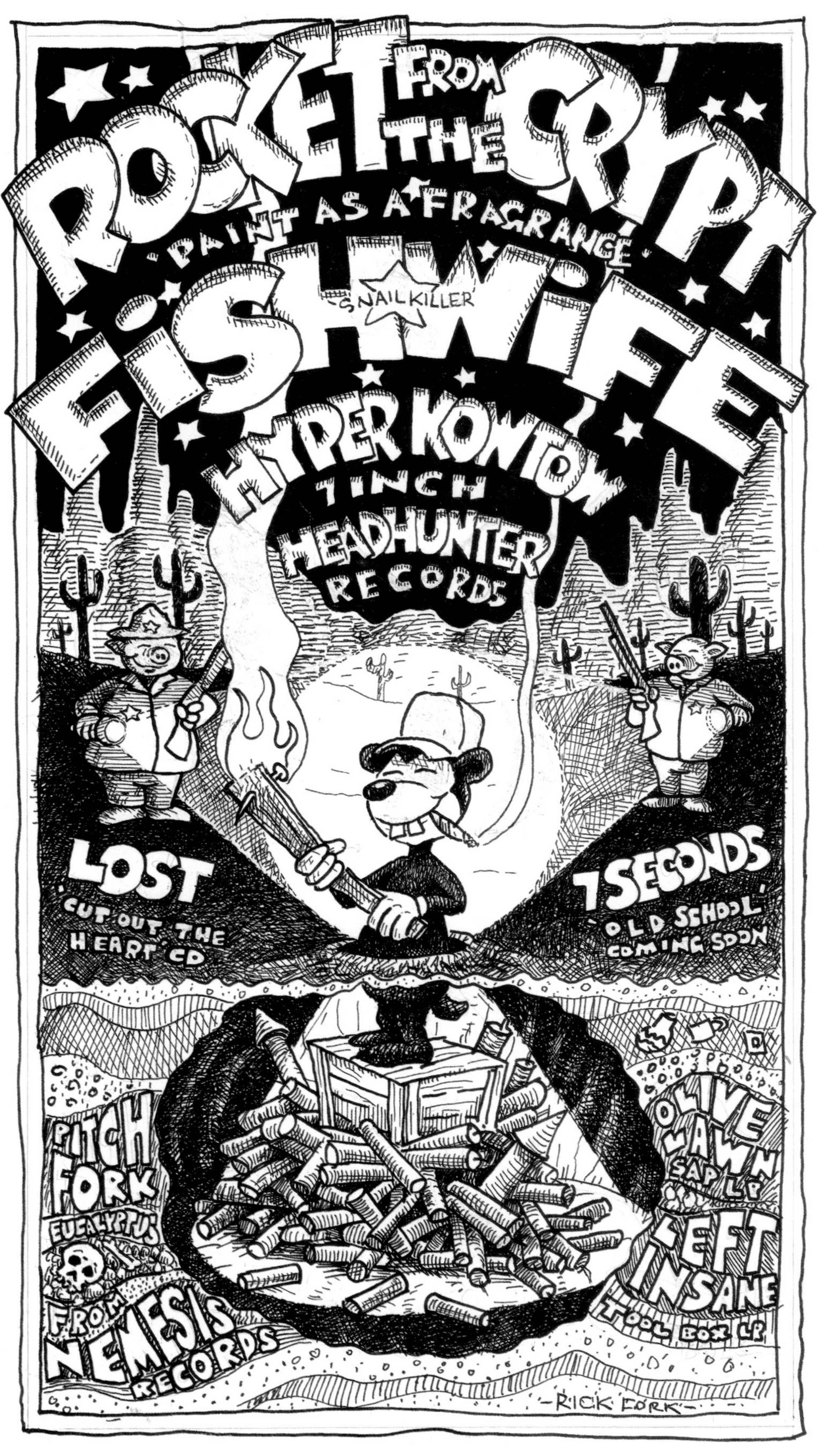

ROCKET FROM THE CRYPT
'PAINT AS A FRAGRANCE'
'SNAIL KILLER'
FISHWIFE
HYPER KONTON
7 INCH
HEADHUNTER
RECORDS
LOST
'CUT OUT THE HEART' CD
7 SECONDS
'OLD SCHOOL'
COMING SOON
PITCH FORK
'EUCALYPTUS'
'FROM HERE'
NEMESIS RECORDS
OLIVE LAWN
'SAP' LP
LEFT INSANE
'TOOL BOX' LP
-RICK FORK-

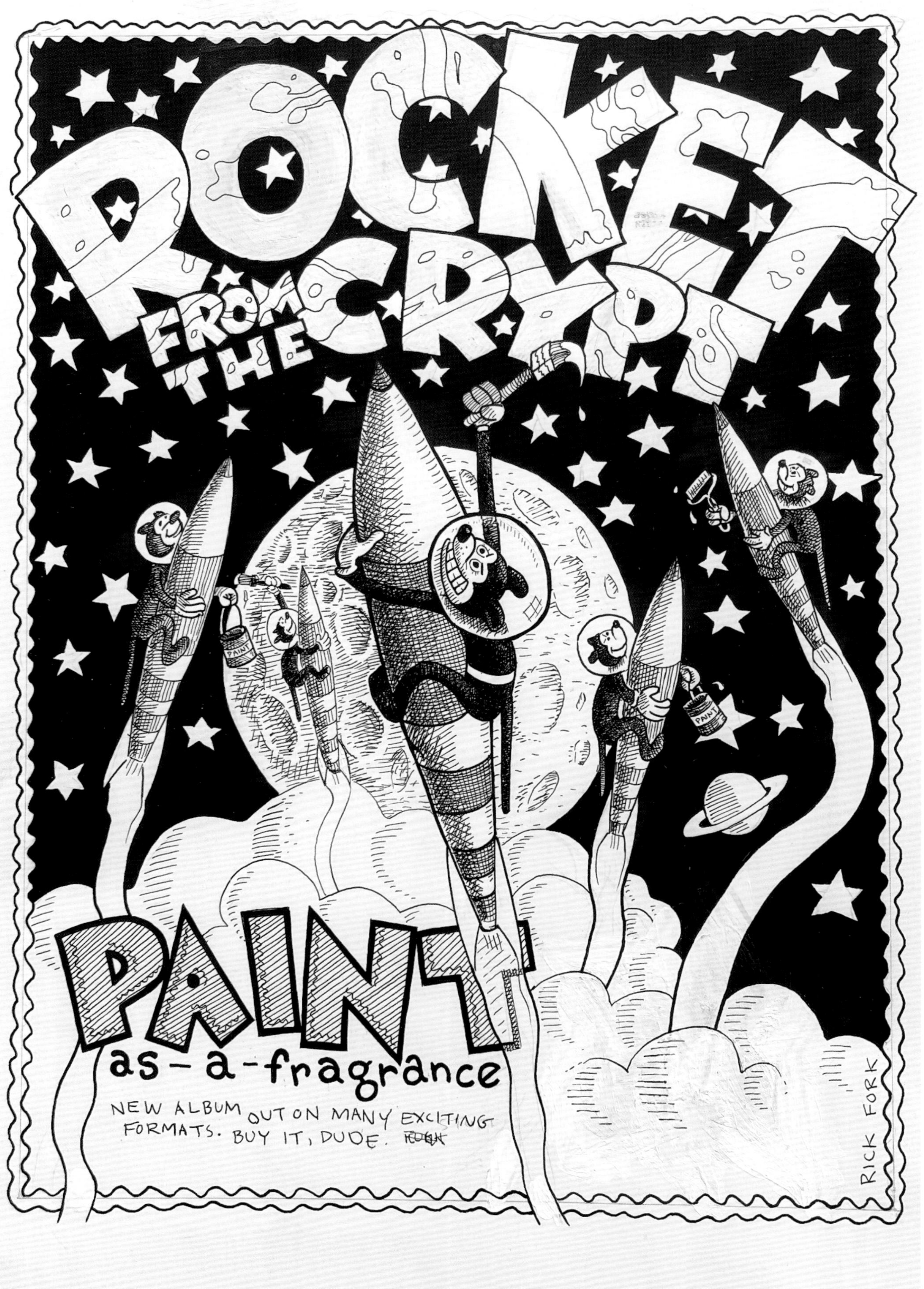

ROCKET
FROM THE CRYPT
PAINT
as-a-fragrance
NEW ALBUM OUT ON MANY EXCITING
FORMATS. BUY IT, DUDE.
PAINT
RICK FORK

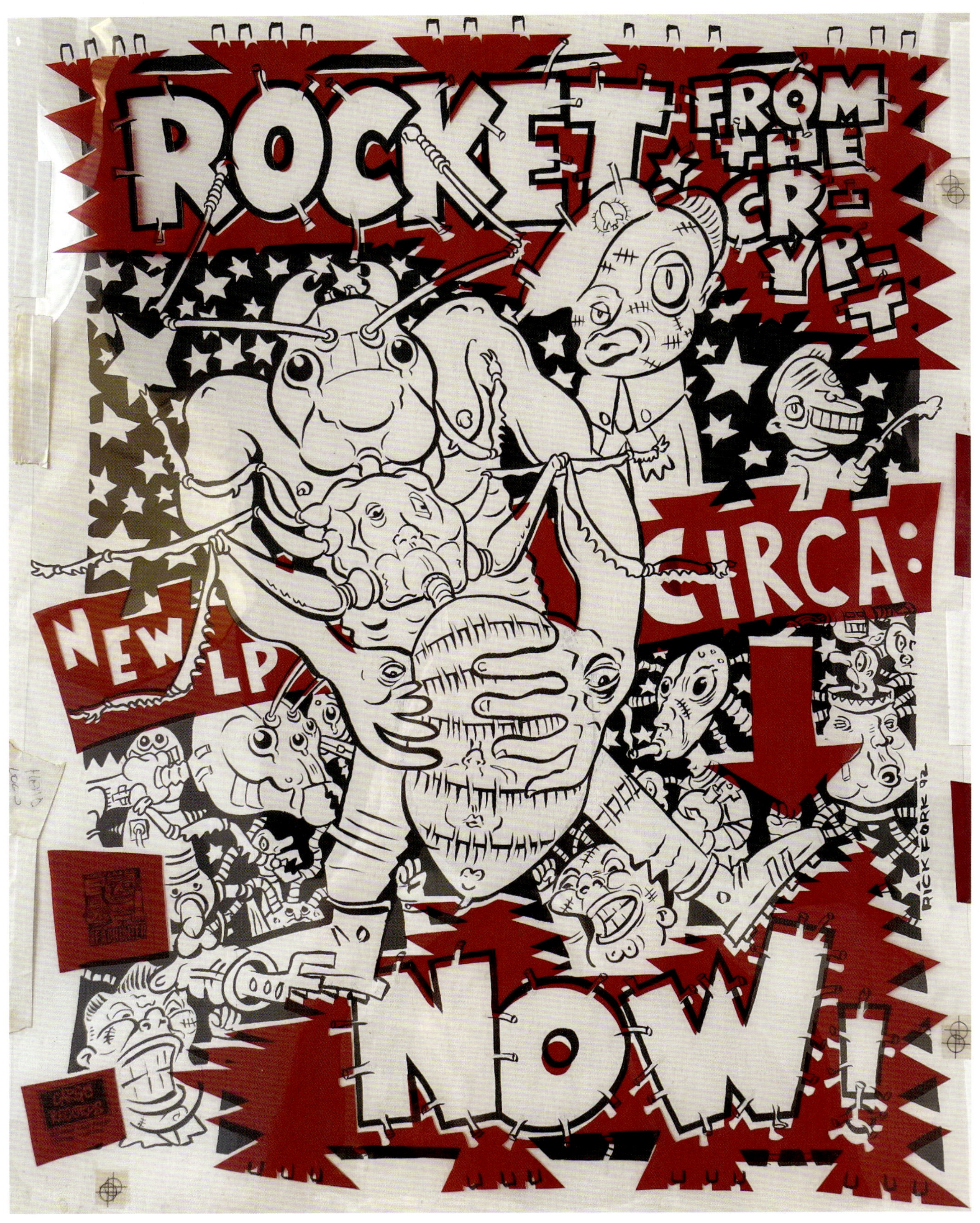

ROCKET
FROM THE CRYPT
NEW LP
CIRCA:
NOW!
RICK FORK 92

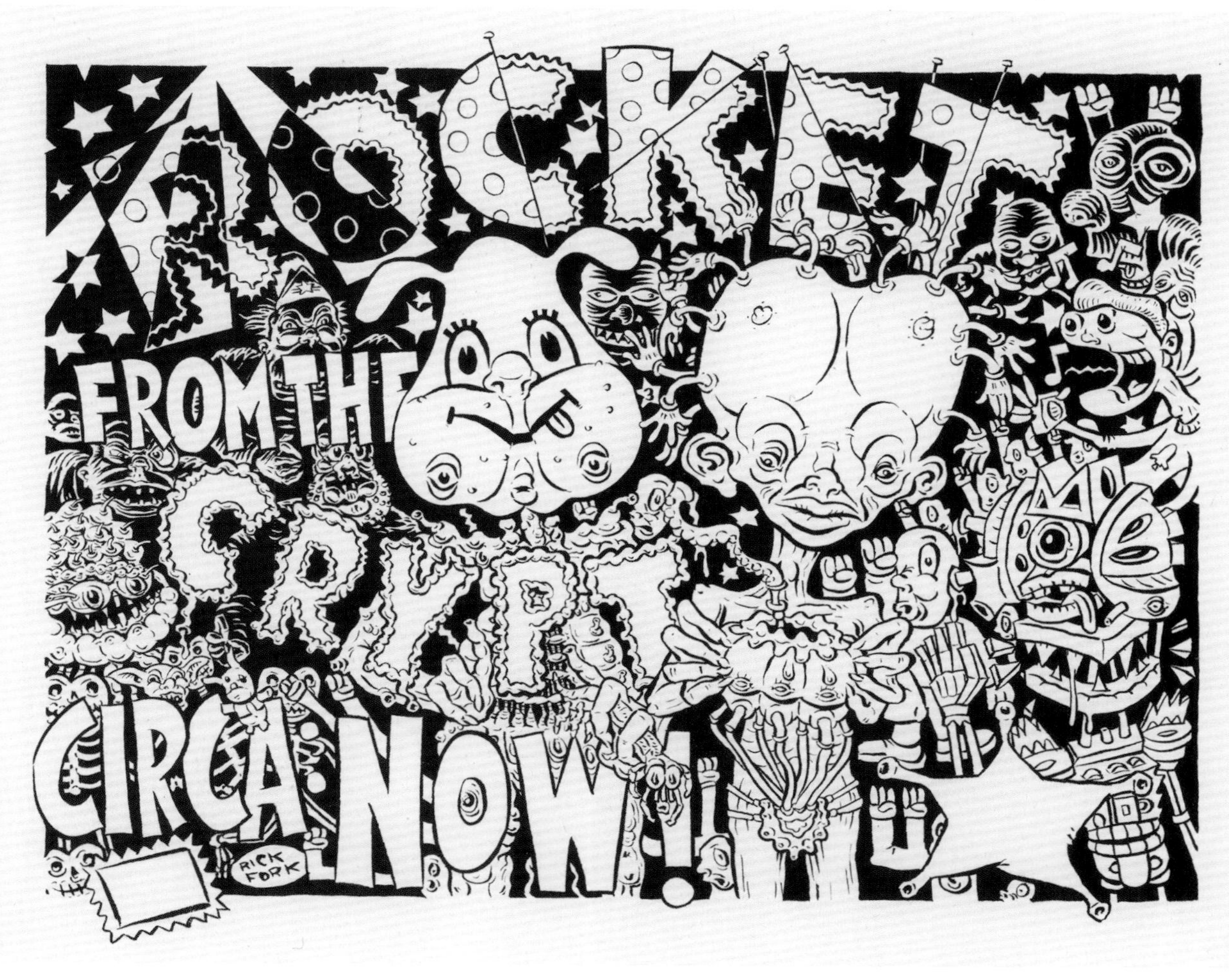

ROCKET
FROM THE
CRYPT
CIRCA NOW!
RICK FORK

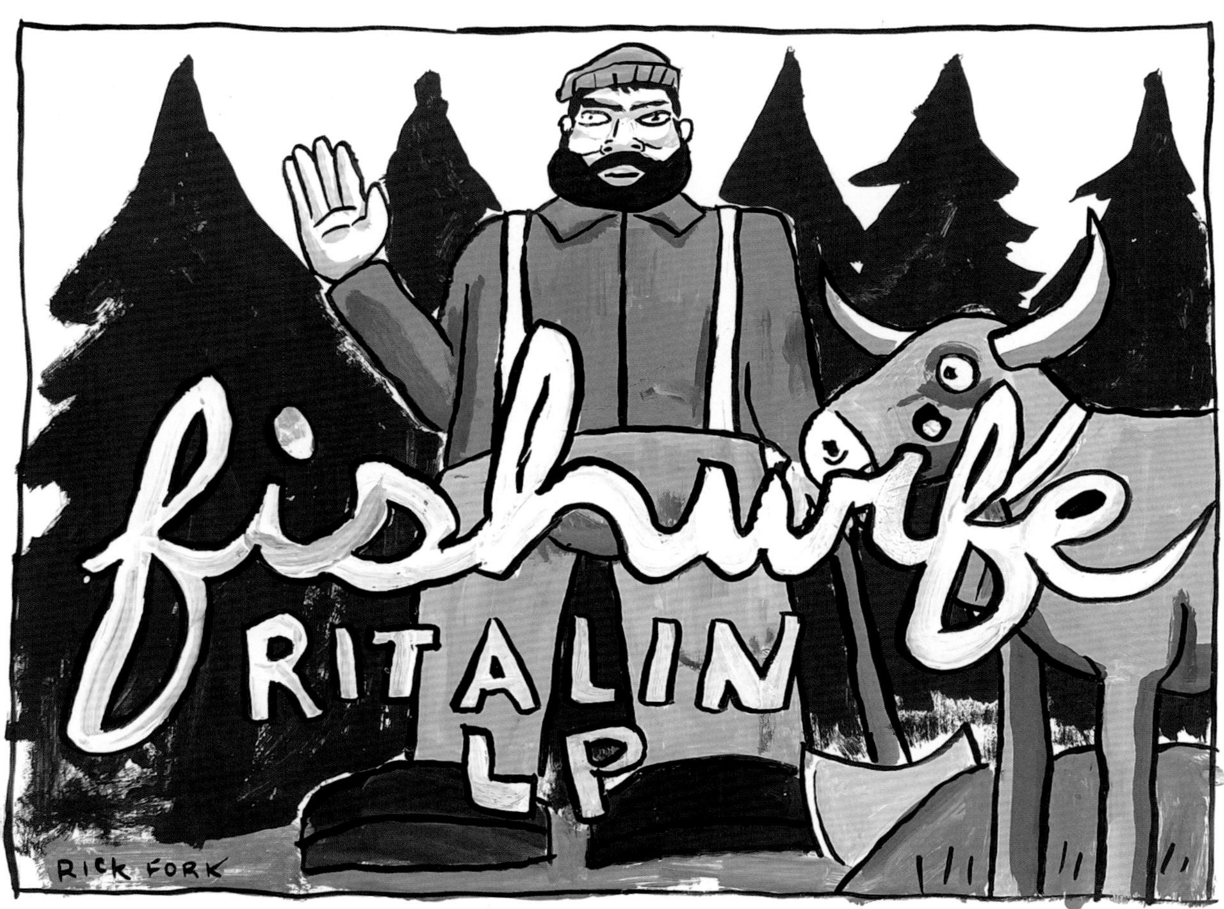

fishwife
RITALIN
LP
RICK FORK

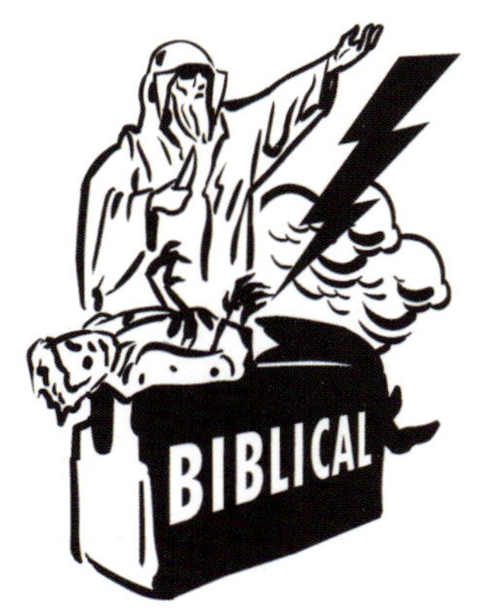

BIBLICAL

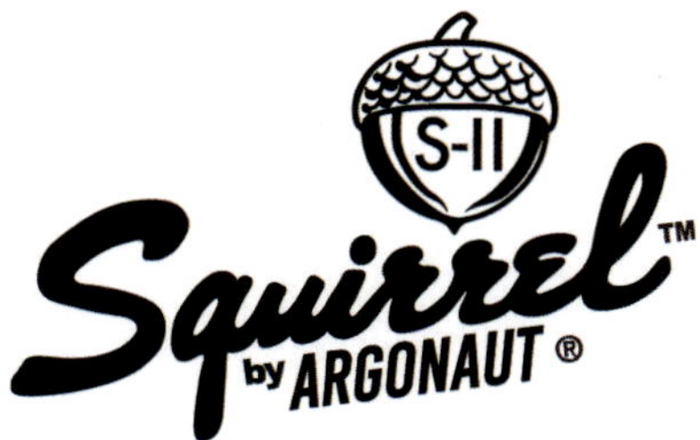

S-II
Squirrel™
by ARGONAUT®

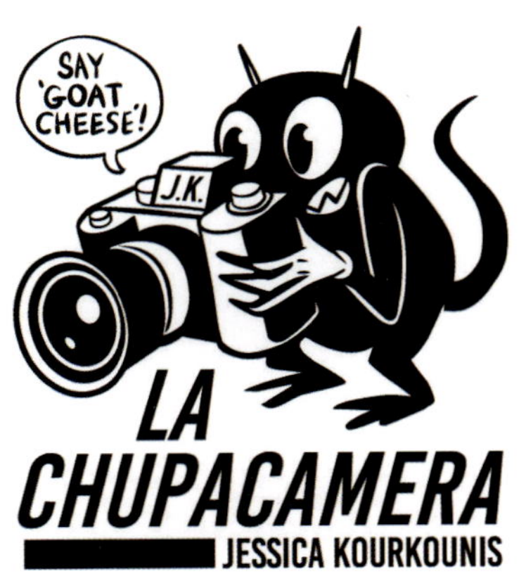

SAY 'GOAT CHEESE'!
J.K.
LA CHUPACAMERA
JESSICA KOURKOUNIS

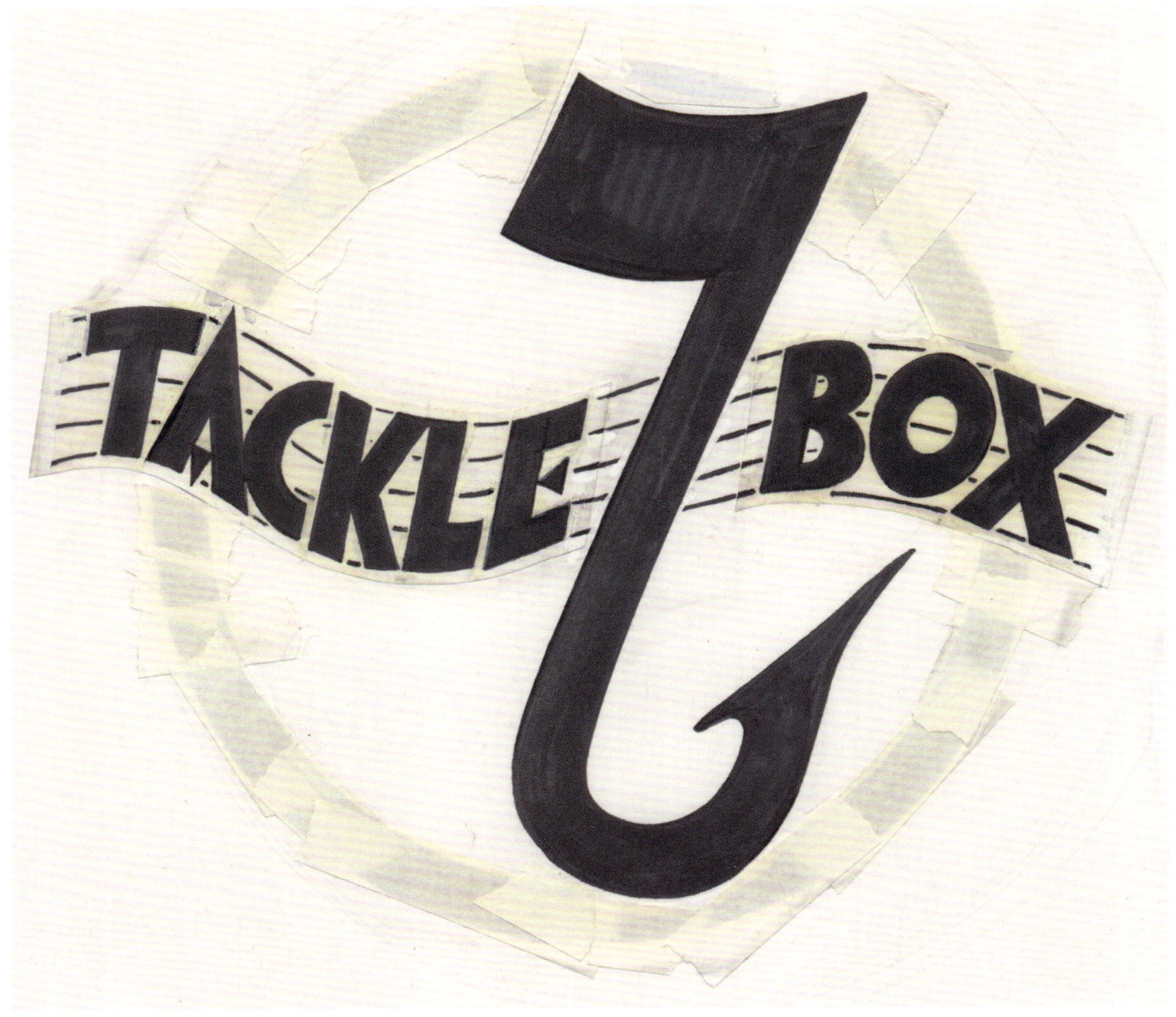

TACKLE BOX

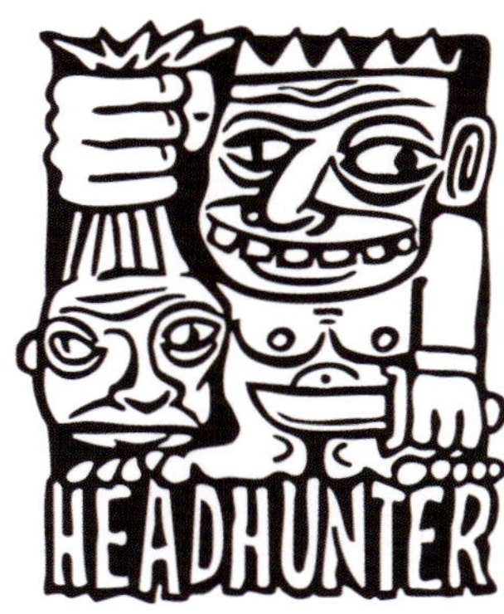

HEADHUNTER

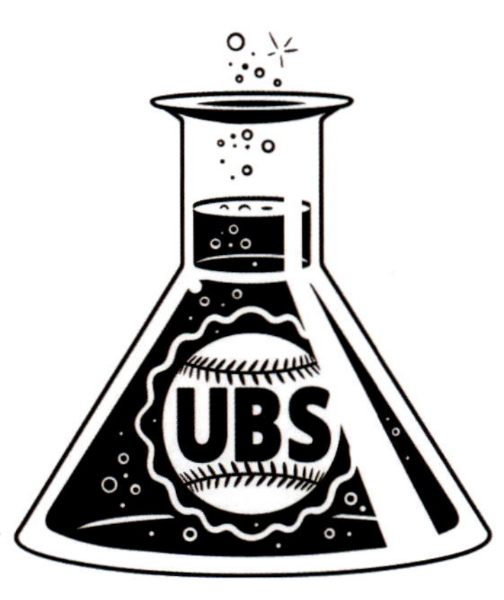

UBS

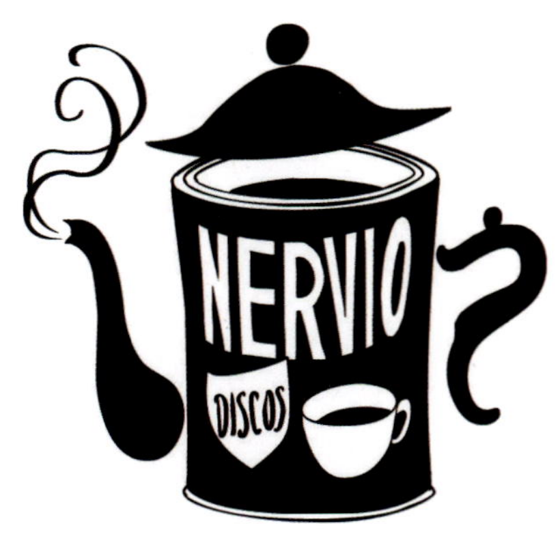

NERVIO
DISCOS

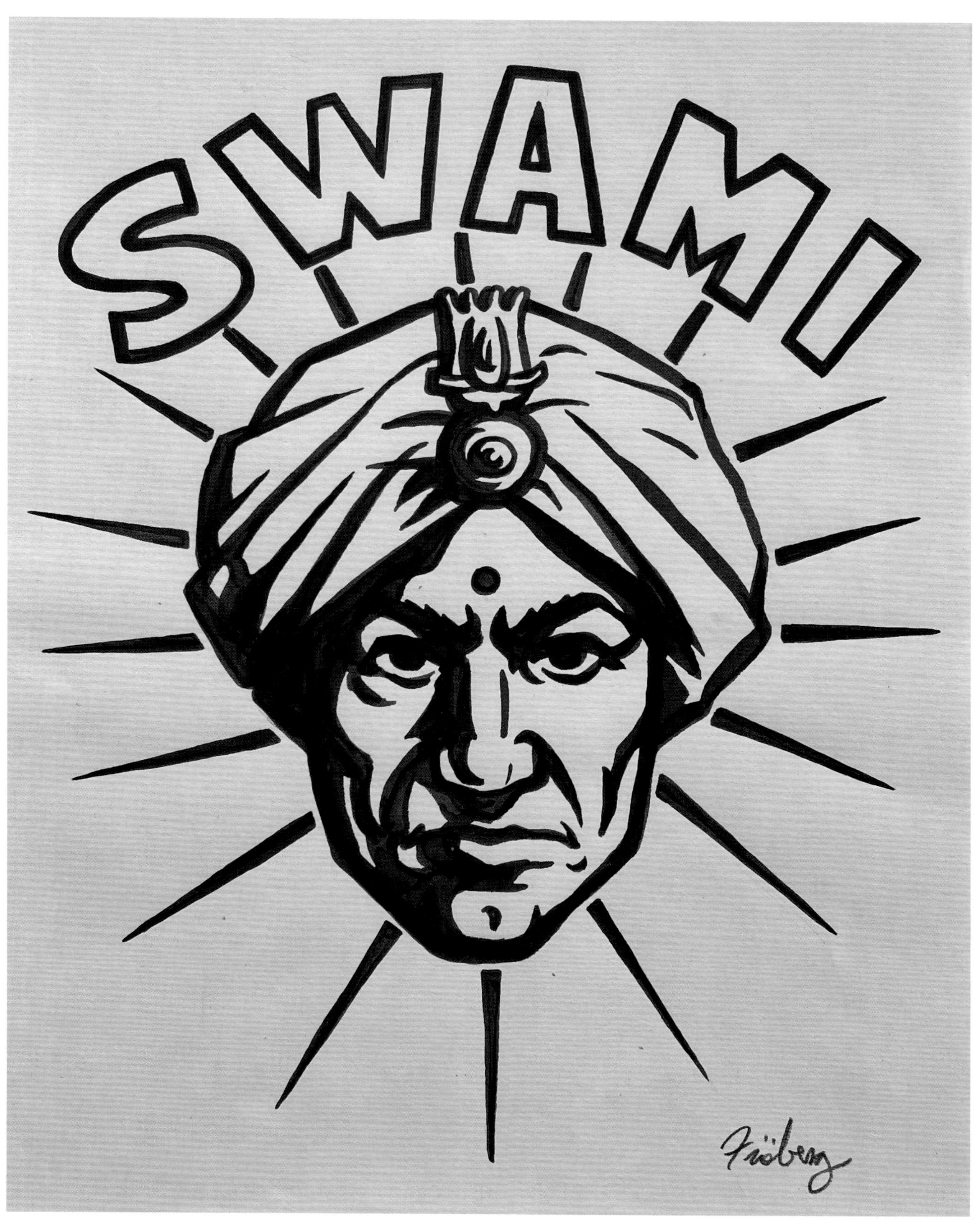

SWAMI

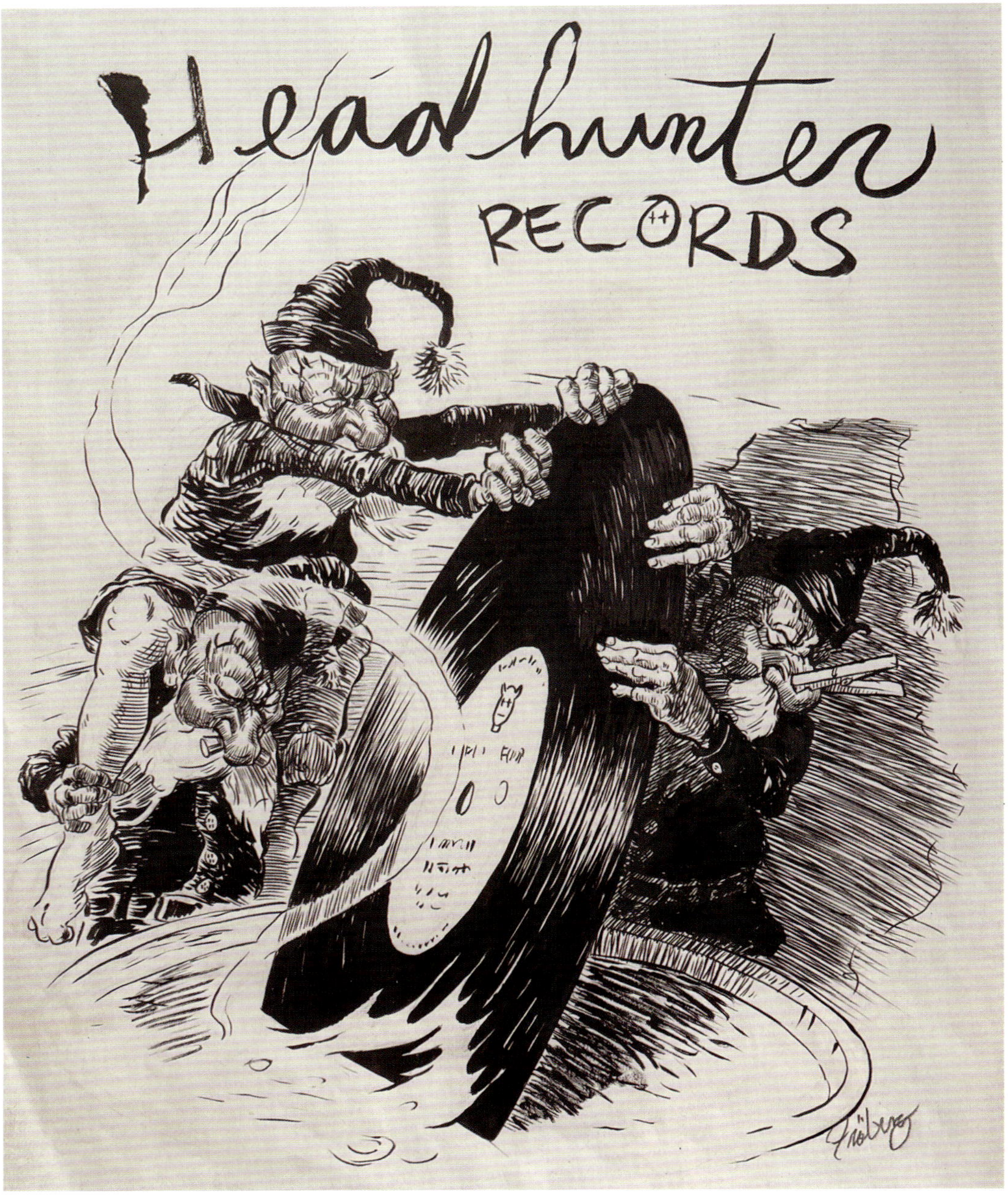

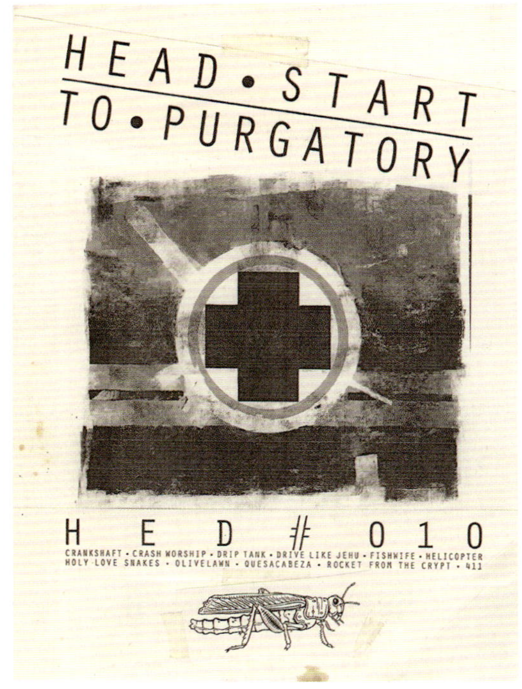

HEAD • START
TO • PURGATORY
HED # 010
CRANKSHAFT • CRASH WORSHIP • DRIP TANK • DRIVE LIKE JEHU • FISHWIFE • HELICOPTER
HOLY LOVE SNAKES • OLIVELAWN • QUESACABEZA • ROCKET FROM THE CRYPT • 411

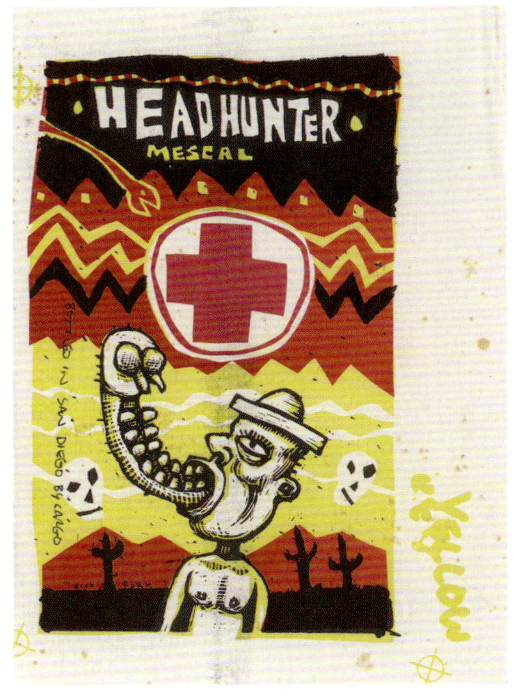

HEADHUNTER
MESCAL
BOTTLED IN SAN DIEGO BY CARGO
yellow

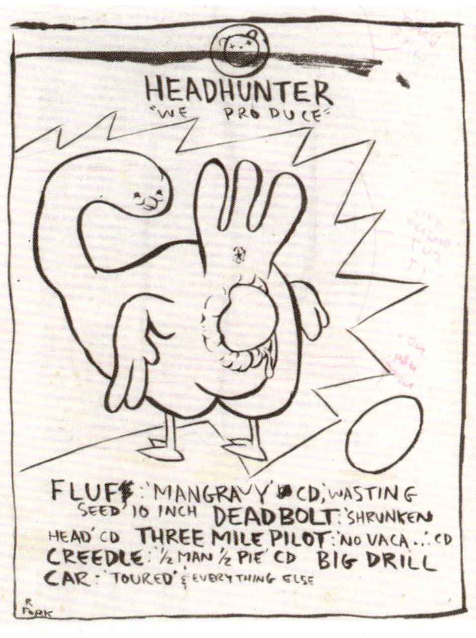

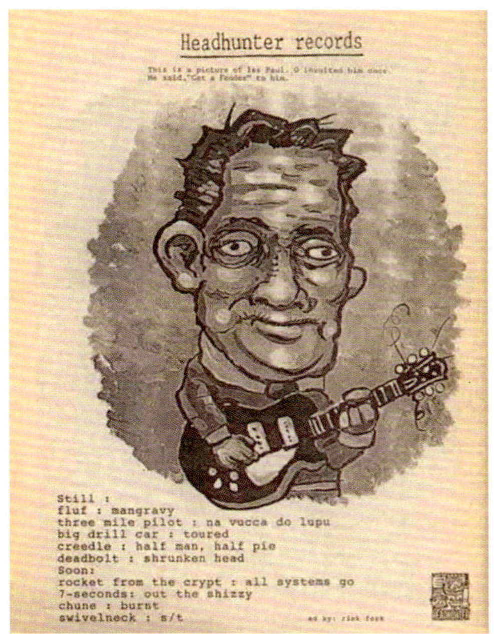
Headhunter records

This is a picture of Les Paul. I insulted him once.
He said, "Get a Fender" to him.

Still :
fluf : mangravy
three mile pilot : na vucca do lupu
big drill car : toured
creedle : half man, half pie
deadbolt : shrunken head
Soon:
rocket from the crypt : all systems go
7-seconds: out the shizzy
chune : burnt
swivelneck : s/t

ad by: rick fork

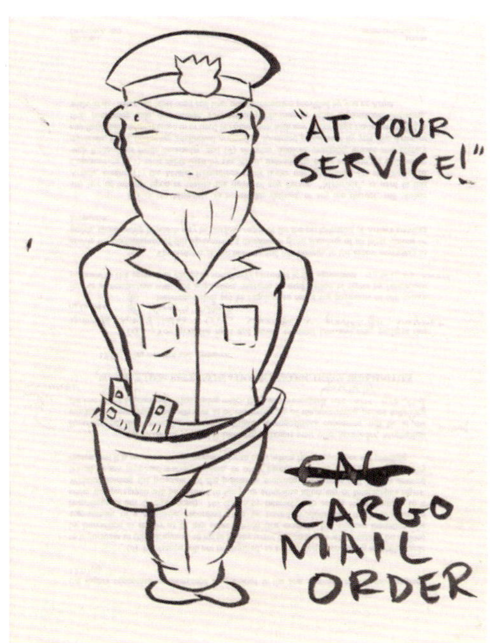

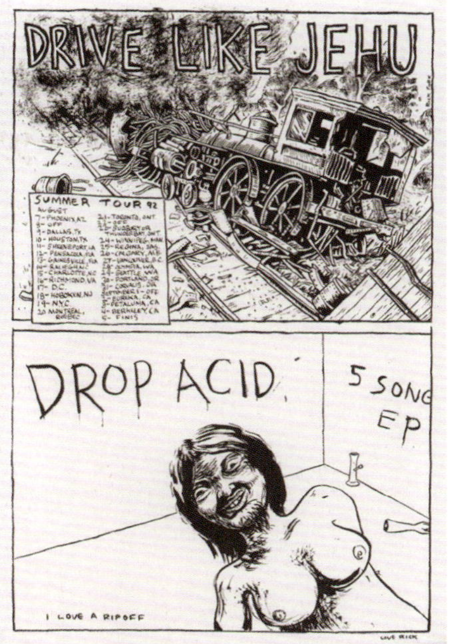

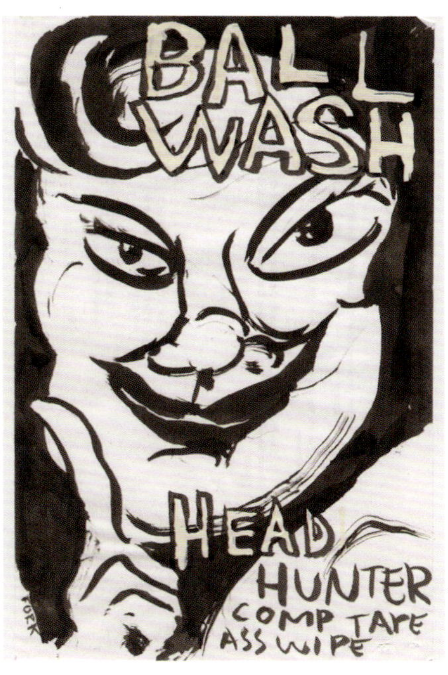

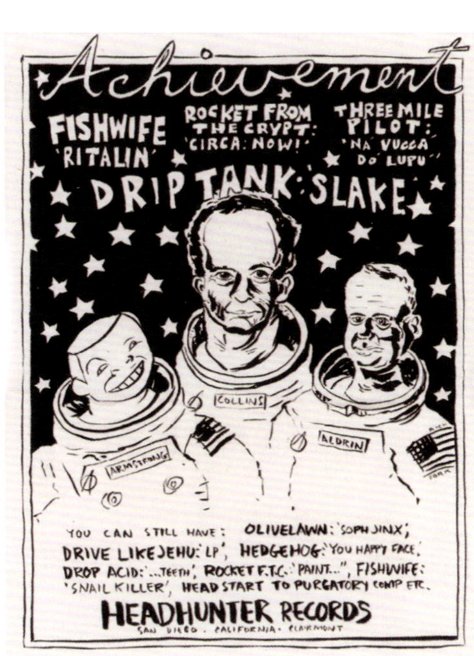

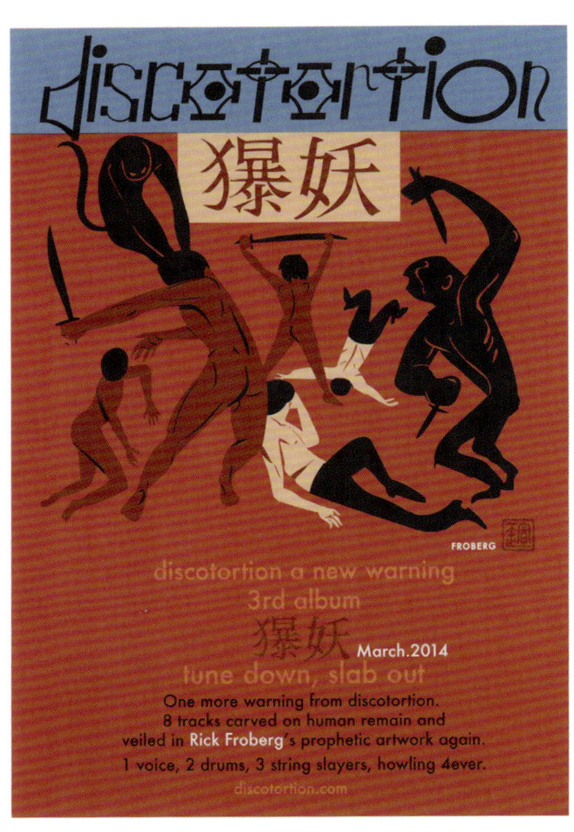
discotortion
爆妖
FROBERG
discotortion a new warning
3rd album
爆妖 March.2014
tune down, slab out
One more warning from discotortion.
8 tracks carved on human remain and
veiled in Rick Froberg's prophetic artwork again.
1 voice, 2 drums, 3 string slayers, howling 4ever.
discotortion.com

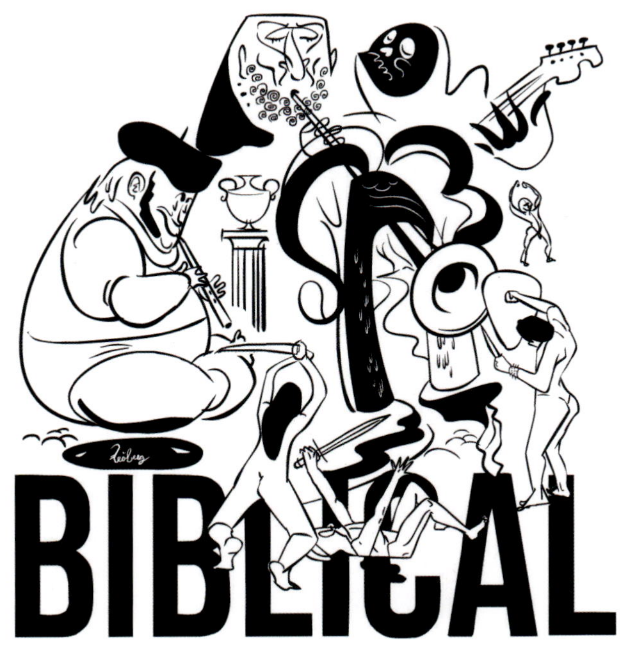
BIBLICAL

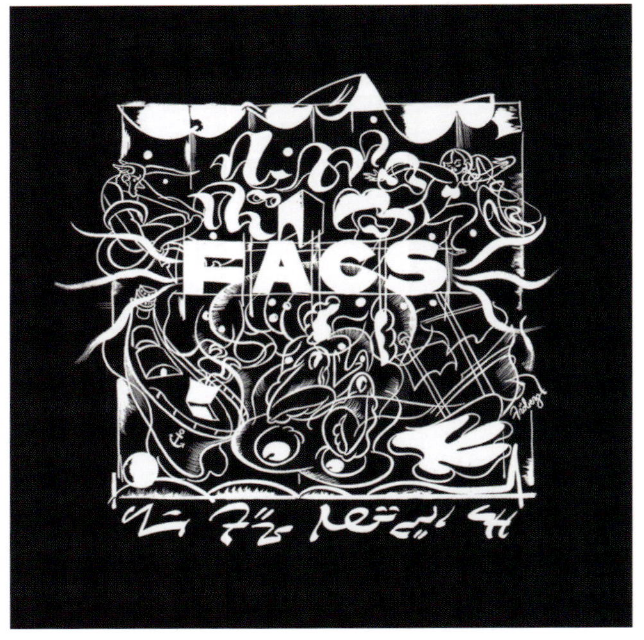
FACS

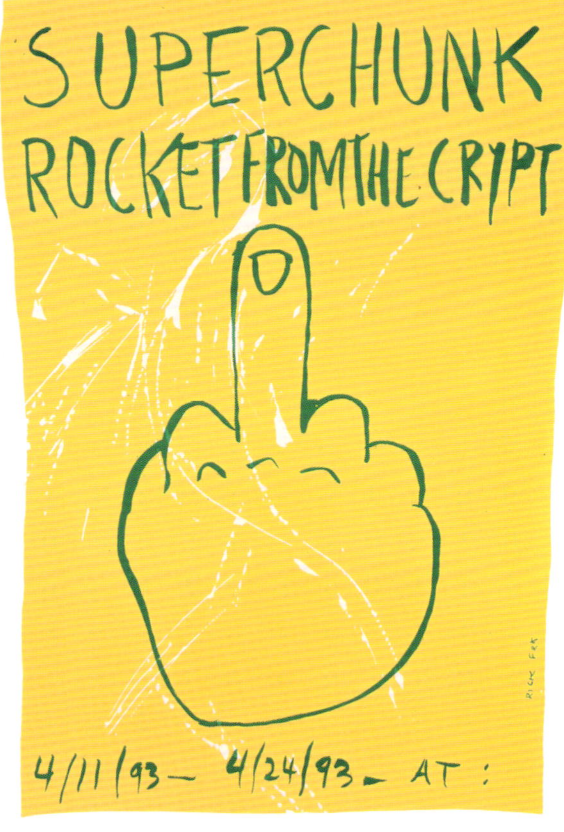
SUPERCHUNK
ROCKET FROM THE CRYPT
4/11/93 — 4/24/93 — AT:

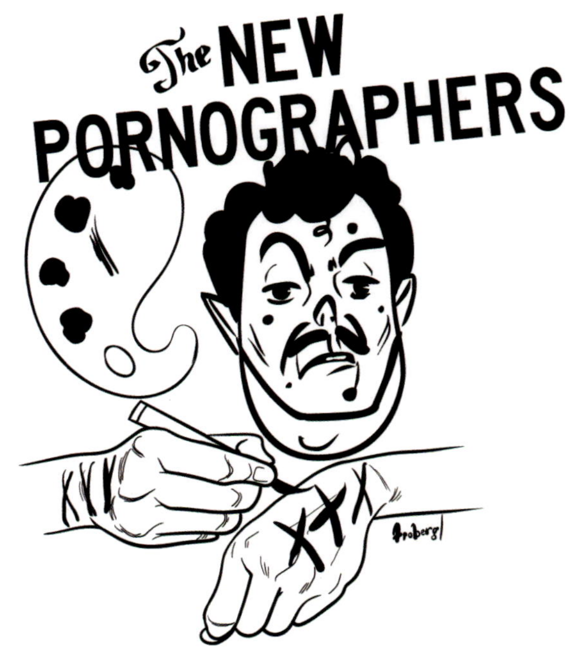
The NEW
PORNOGRAPHERS
XT
Froberg

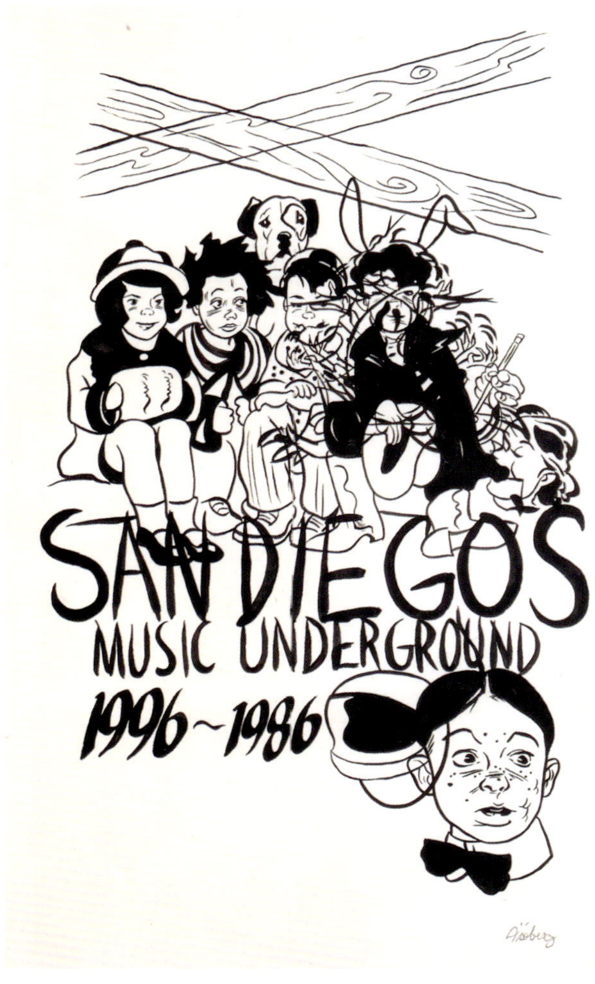
SAN DIEGOS
MUSIC UNDERGROUND
1996~1986

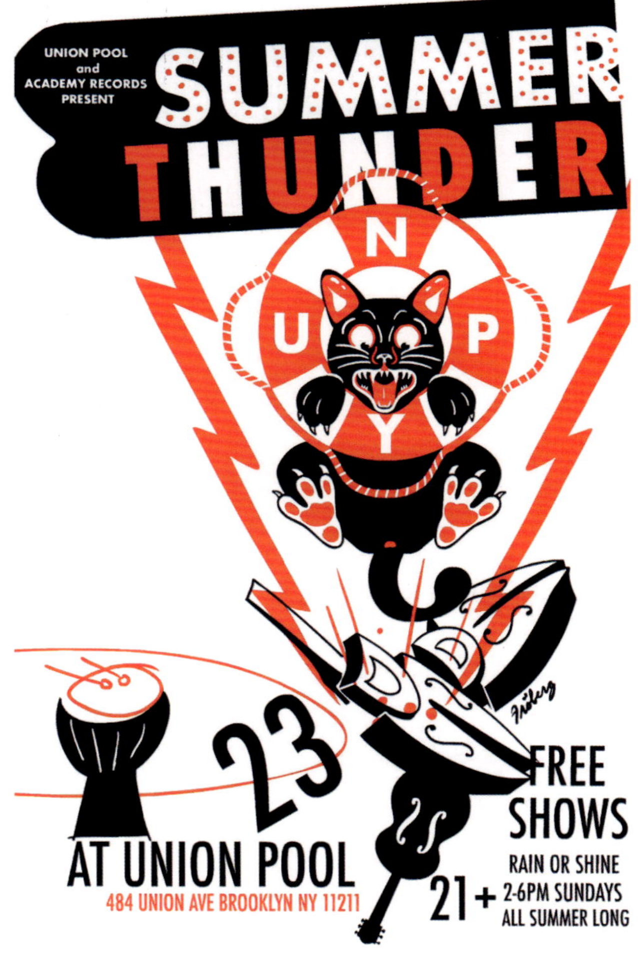
UNION POOL
and
ACADEMY RECORDS
PRESENT
SUMMER
THUNDER
NUP NY
23
AT UNION POOL
484 UNION AVE BROOKLYN NY 11211
FREE
SHOWS
RAIN OR SHINE
21+ 2-6PM SUNDAYS
ALL SUMMER LONG

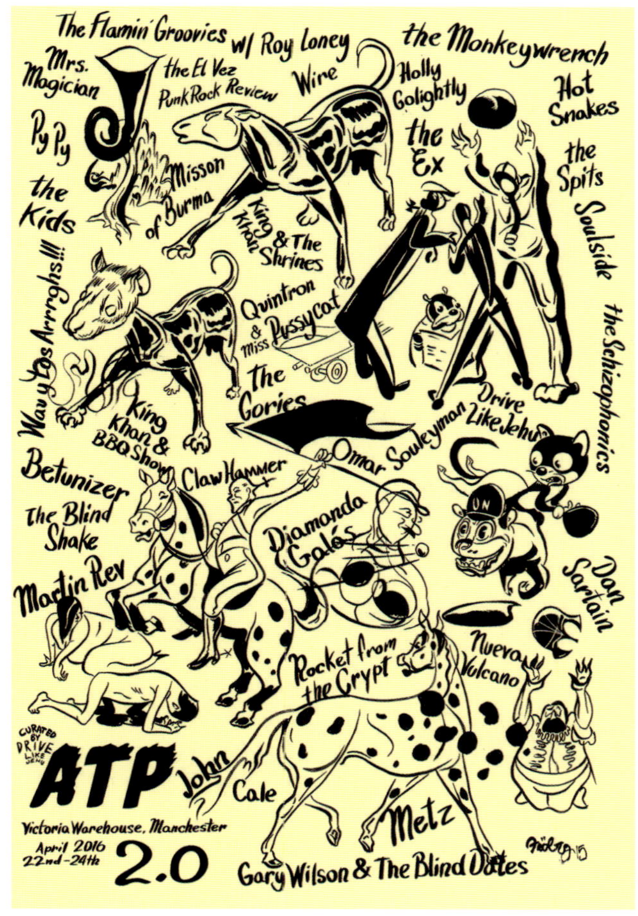
The Flamin' Groovies w/ Roy Loney
Mrs. Magician
the El Vez Punk Rock Review
Wire
the Monkeywrench
Holly Golightly
Hot Snakes
Py Py
the Kids
Misson of Burma
King Khan & The Shrines
the Ex
the Spits
Soulside
Quintron & Miss Pussycat
the Schizophonics
Wau y Los Arrrghs!!!
The Gories
Omar Souleyman
Drive Like Jehu
King Khan & BBQ Show
Betunizer
Claw Hammer
Diamonda Galás
Dan Sartain
The Blind Shake
Martin Rev
Rocket from the Crypt
Nueva Vulcano
ATP
John Cale
Metz
Gary Wilson & The Blind Dates
CURATED BY DRIVE LIKE JEHU
Victoria Warehouse, Manchester
April 2016
22nd-24th
2.0

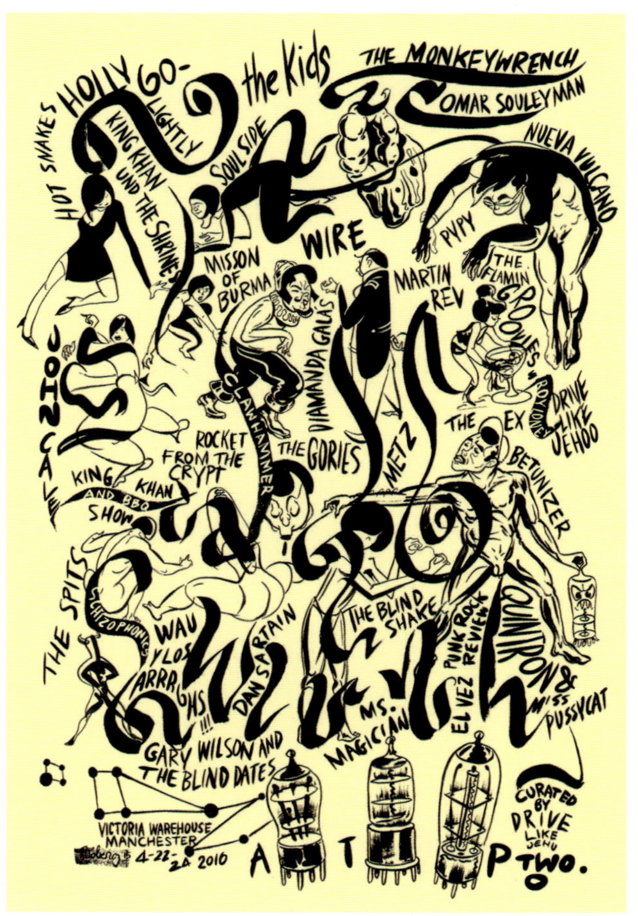
HOT SNAKES
HOLLY GO-LIGHTLY
the Kids
THE MONKEYWRENCH
OMAR SOULEYMAN
KING KHAN AND THE SHRINES
SOULSIDE
NUEVA VULCANO
PYPY
MISSON OF BURMA
WIRE
MARTIN REV
THE FLAMIN GROOVIES
DRIVE LIKE JEHOO
ROCKET FROM THE CRYPT
CLAWHAMMER
THE GORIES
METZ
THE EX
BETUNIZER
KING KHAN AND BBQ SHOW
DIAMANDA GALAS
THE SPITS
SCHIZOPHONICS
WAU Y LOS ARRRGHS!!!
DAN SARTAIN
THE BLIND SHAKE
PUNK ROCK REVIEW
EL VEZ
QUINTRON & MISS PUSSYCAT
MS. MAGICIAN
GARY WILSON AND THE BLIND DATES
VICTORIA WAREHOUSE MANCHESTER
4-23 25 2010
ATP TWO.
CURATED BY DRIVE LIKE JEHU

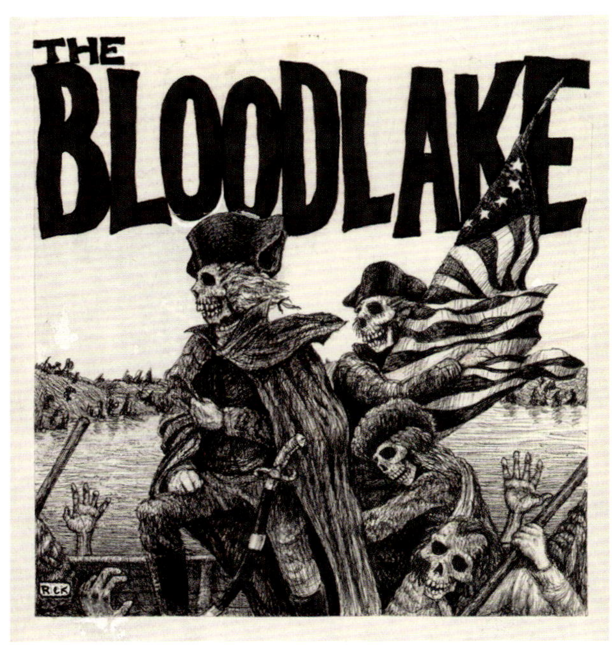
THE
BLOODLAKE

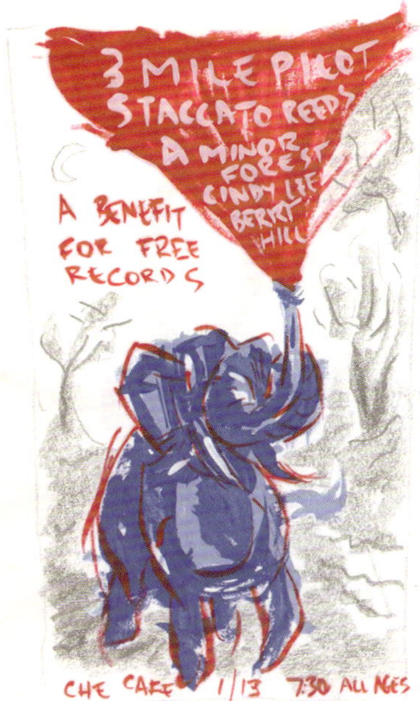
3 MILE PILOT
STACCATO REEDS
A MINOR
FOREST
CINDY LEE
BERRY HILL
A BENEFIT
FOR FREE
RECORDS
CHE CAFE 1/13 7:30 ALL AGES

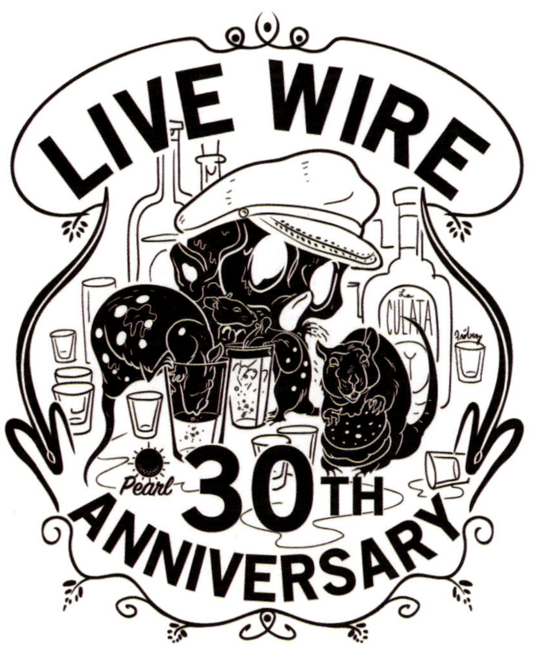
LIVE WIRE
Pearl
30TH
ANNIVERSARY

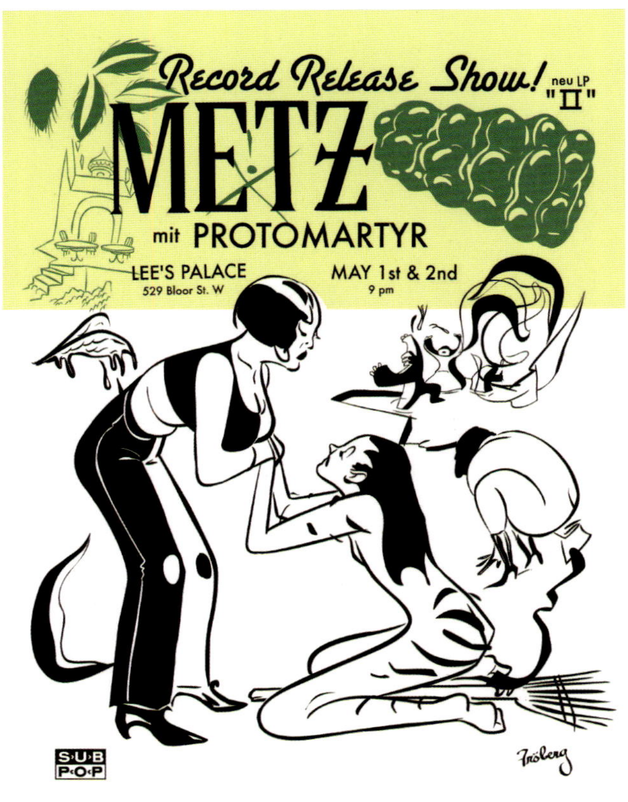
Record Release Show! neu LP "II"
METZ
mit PROTOMARTYR
LEE'S PALACE
529 Bloor St. W
MAY 1st & 2nd
9 pm
SUB POP
Fröberg

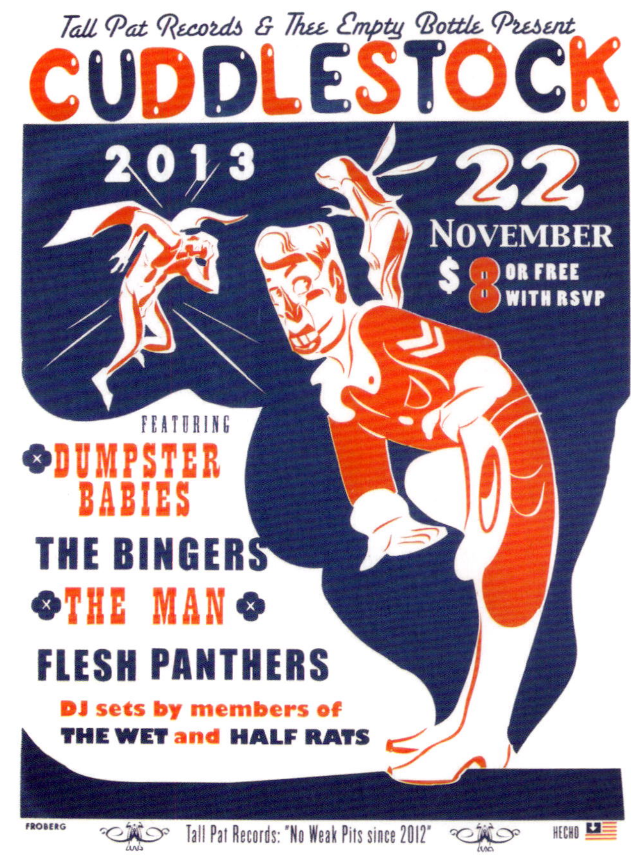
Tall Pat Records & Thee Empty Bottle Present
CUDDLESTOCK
2013
22
NOVEMBER
$8 OR FREE WITH RSVP
FEATURING
DUMPSTER BABIES
THE BINGERS
THE MAN
FLESH PANTHERS
DJ sets by members of
THE WET and HALF RATS
FROBERG
Tall Pat Records: "No Weak Pits since 2012"
HECHO

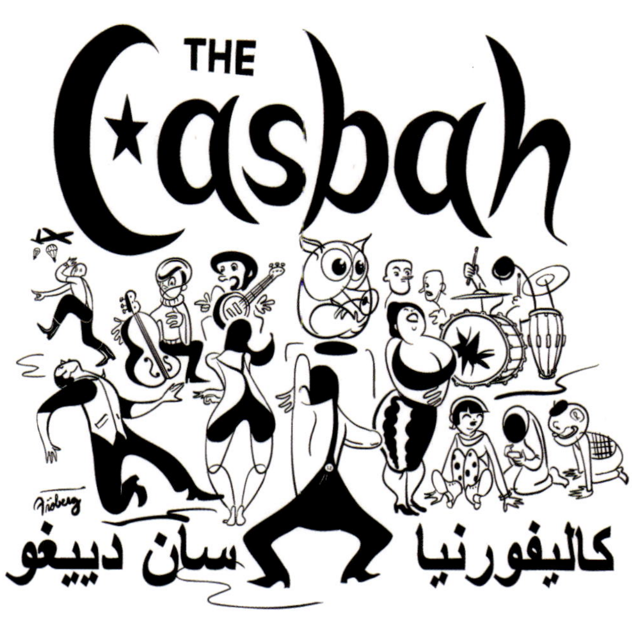

THE
Casbah
كاليفورنيا سان دييغو

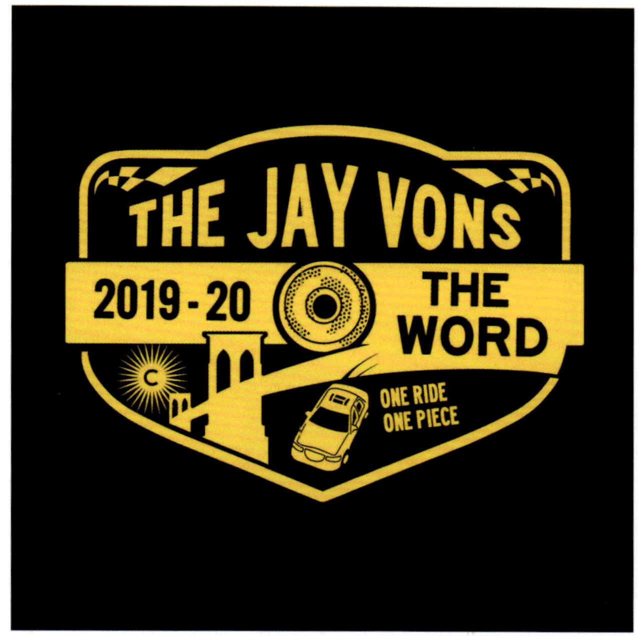

THE JAY VONS
2019 - 20
THE WORD
ONE RIDE
ONE PIECE

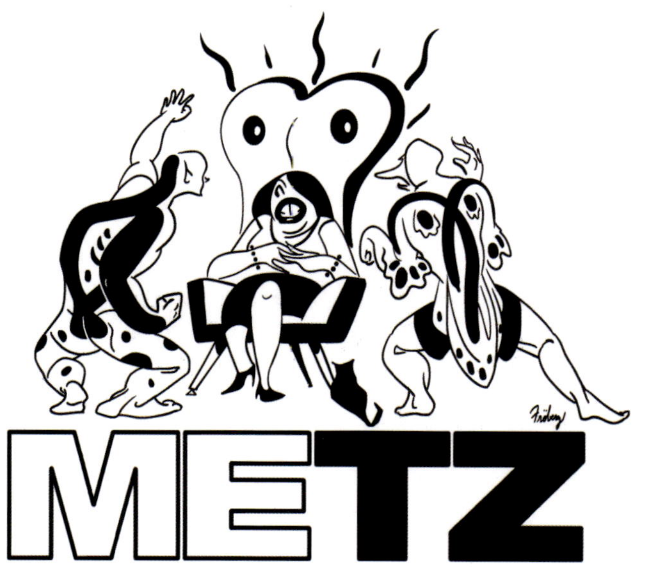

METZ

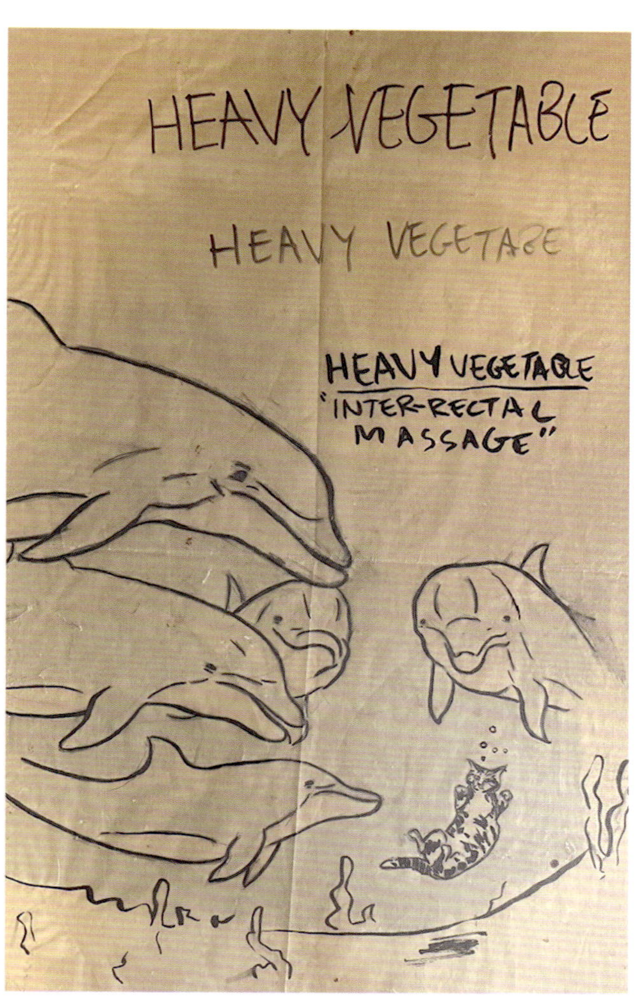

HEAVY VEGETABLE
HEAVY VEGETABE
HEAVY VEGETABE
"INTER-RECTAL
MASSAGE"

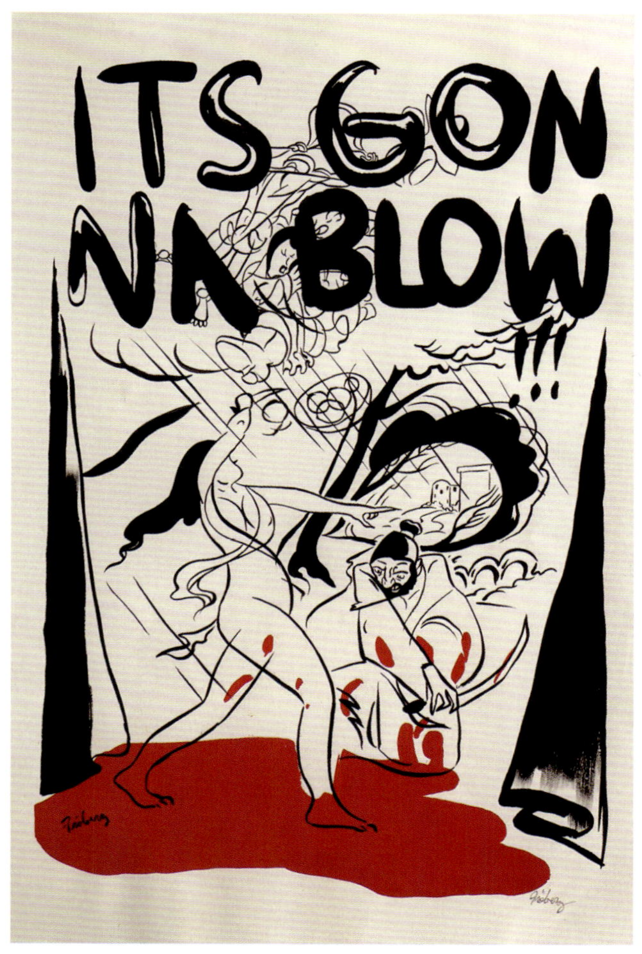

ITS GON
NA BLOW
!!!

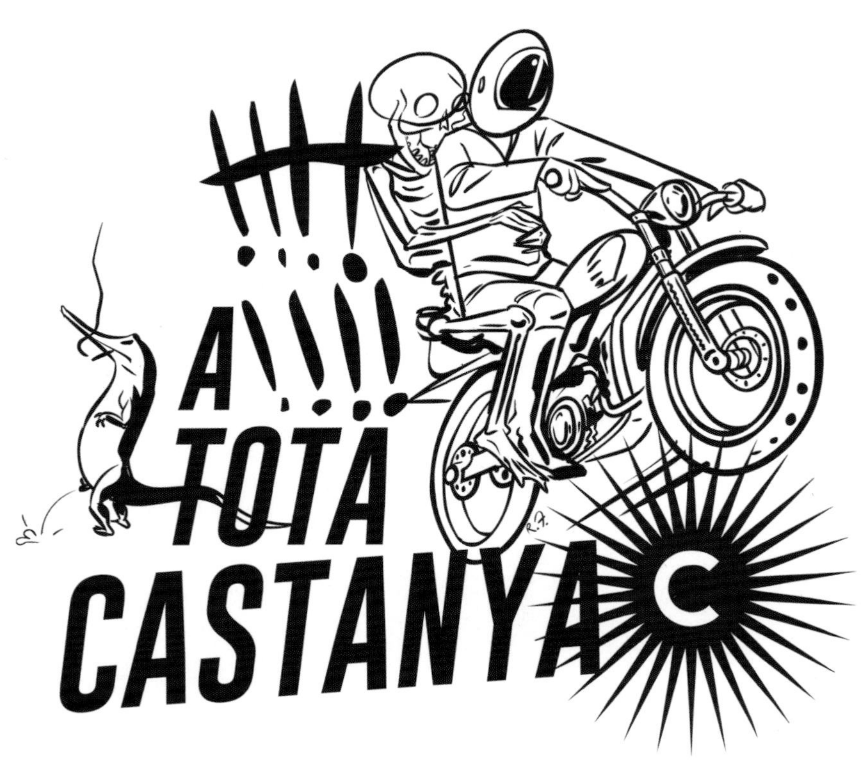
A
TOTA
CASTANYA

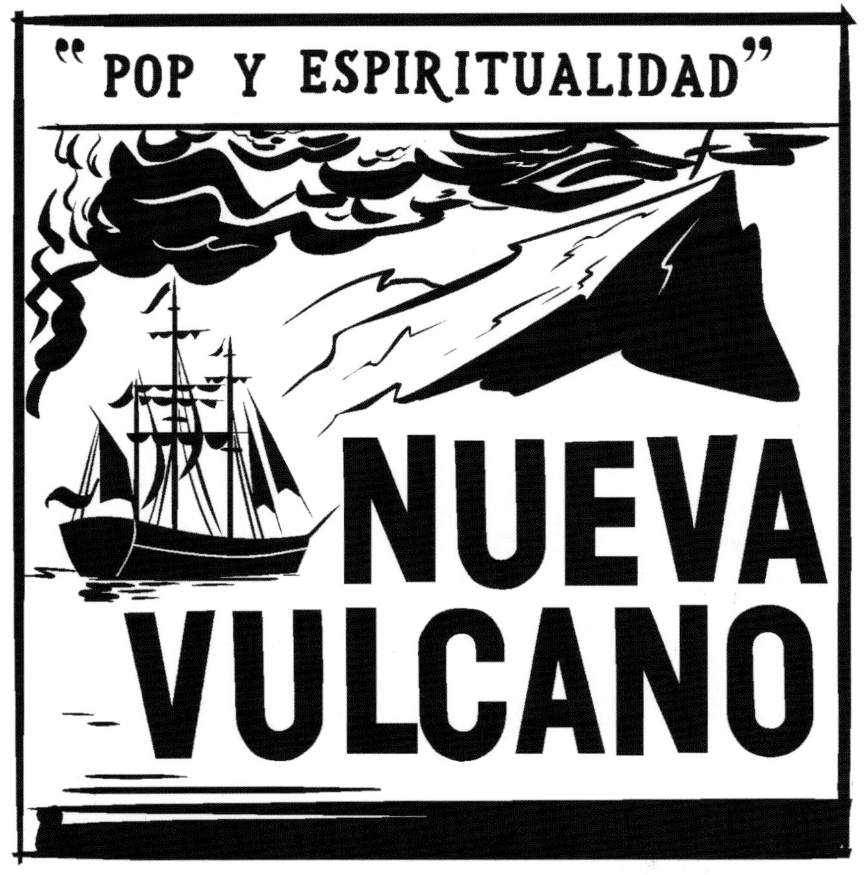
"POP Y ESPIRITUALIDAD"
NUEVA
VULCANO

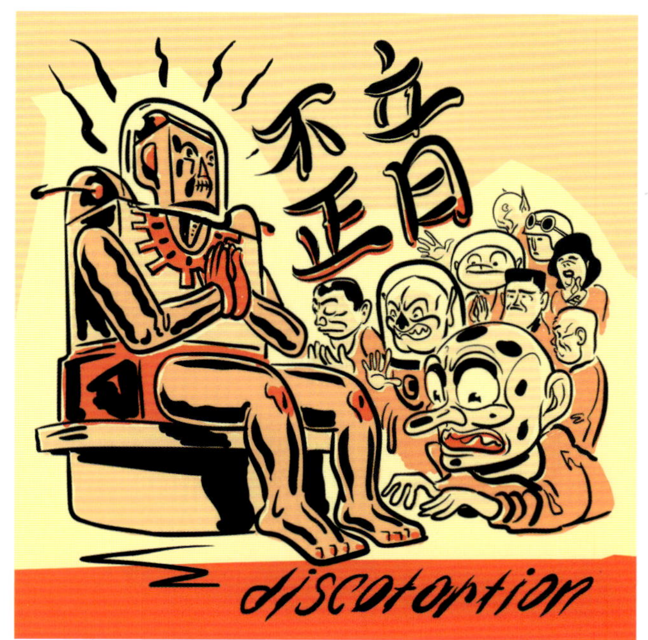

discotortion

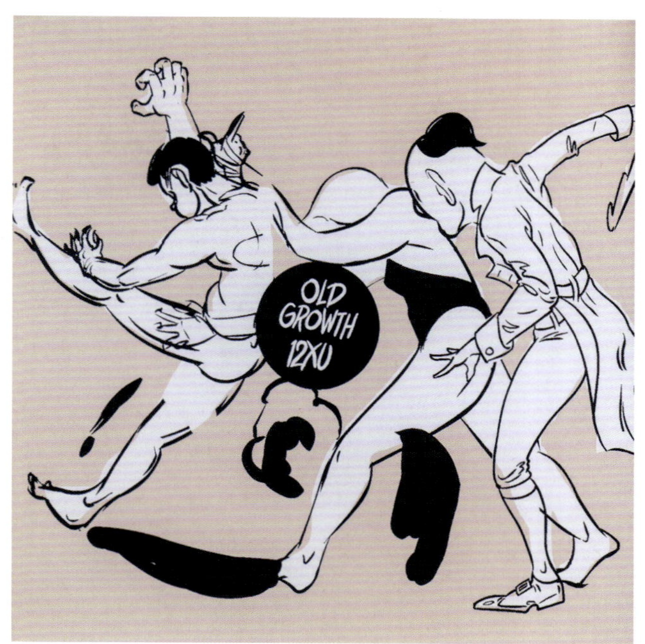

OLD
GROWTH
12XU

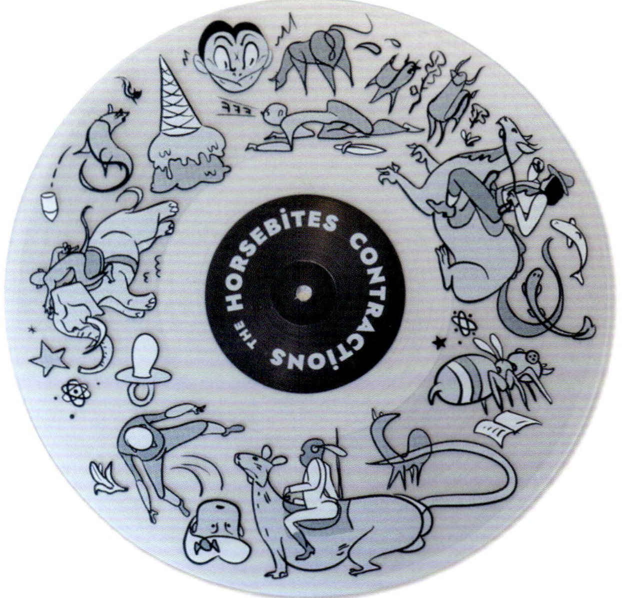

THE HORSEBiTES CONTRACTIONS

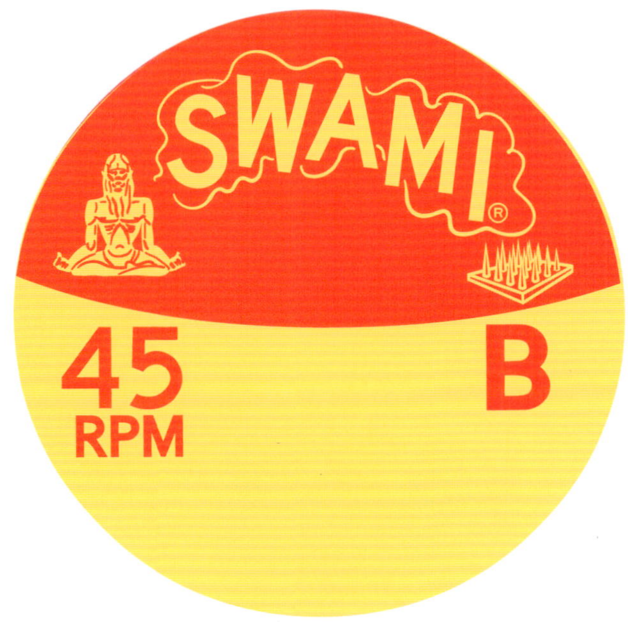

SWAMI
45
RPM
B

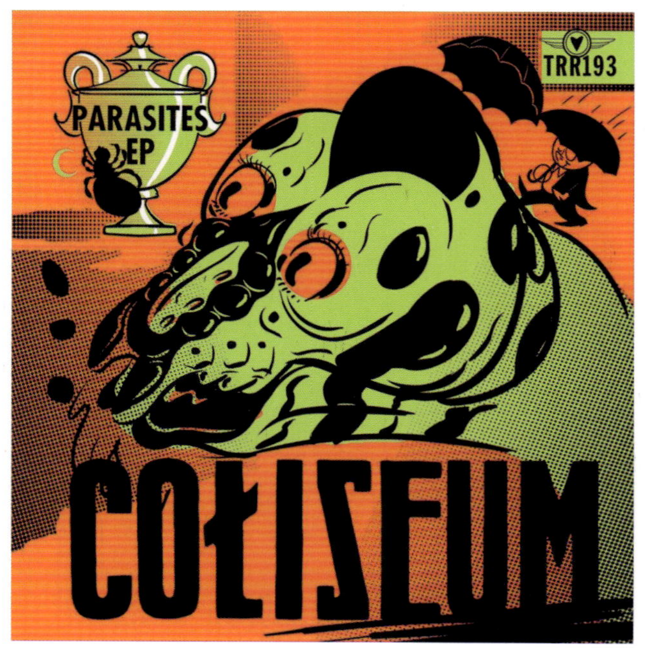

PARASITES EP
TRR193
COLISEUM

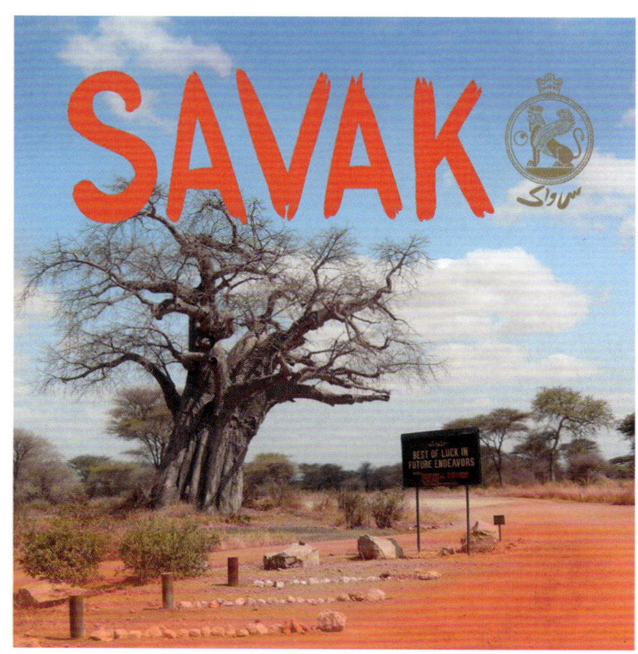

SAVAK
BEST OF LUCK IN
FUTURE ENDEAVORS

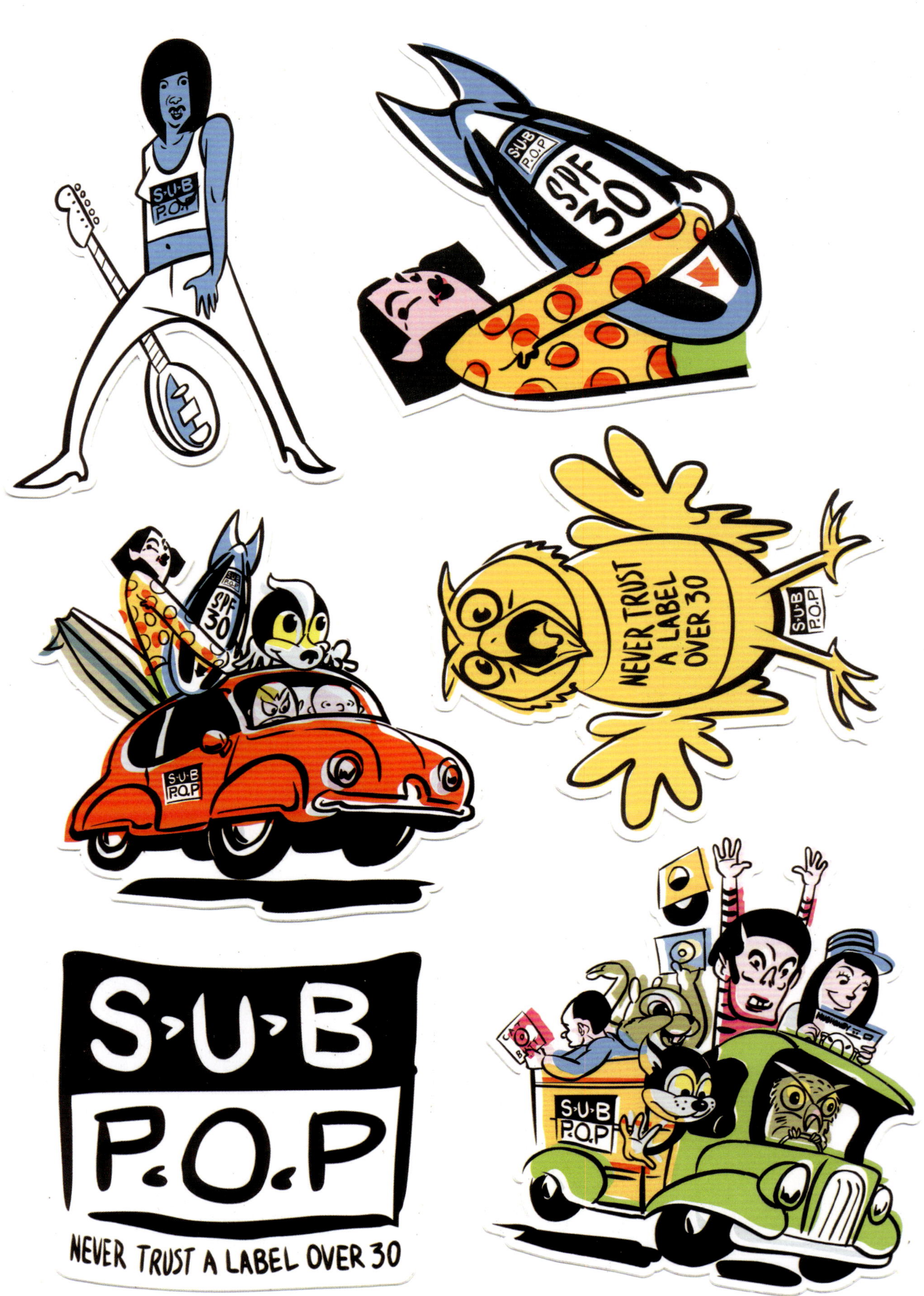
S·U·B P.O.P
SPF 30
NEVER TRUST A LABEL OVER 30
S·U·B P.O.P
S·U·B P.O.P
NEVER TRUST A LABEL OVER 30

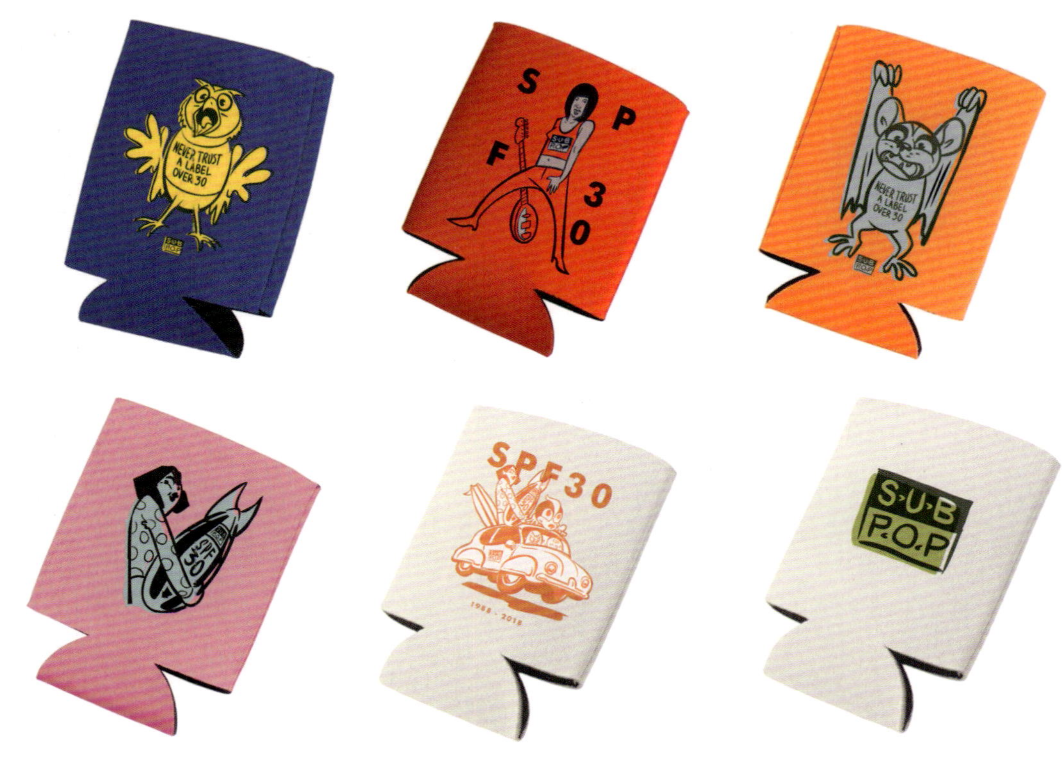

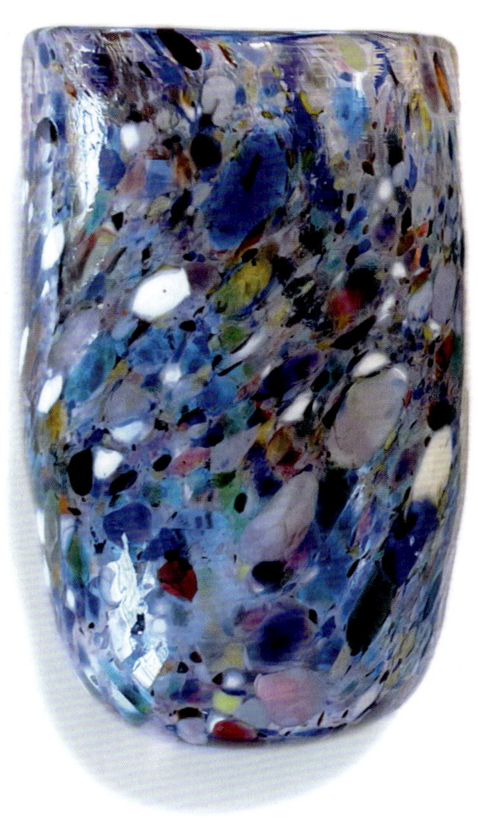

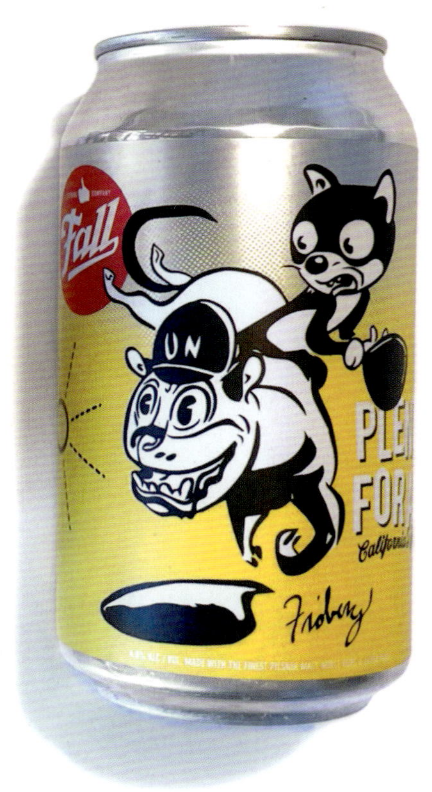

FIVE
Paintings

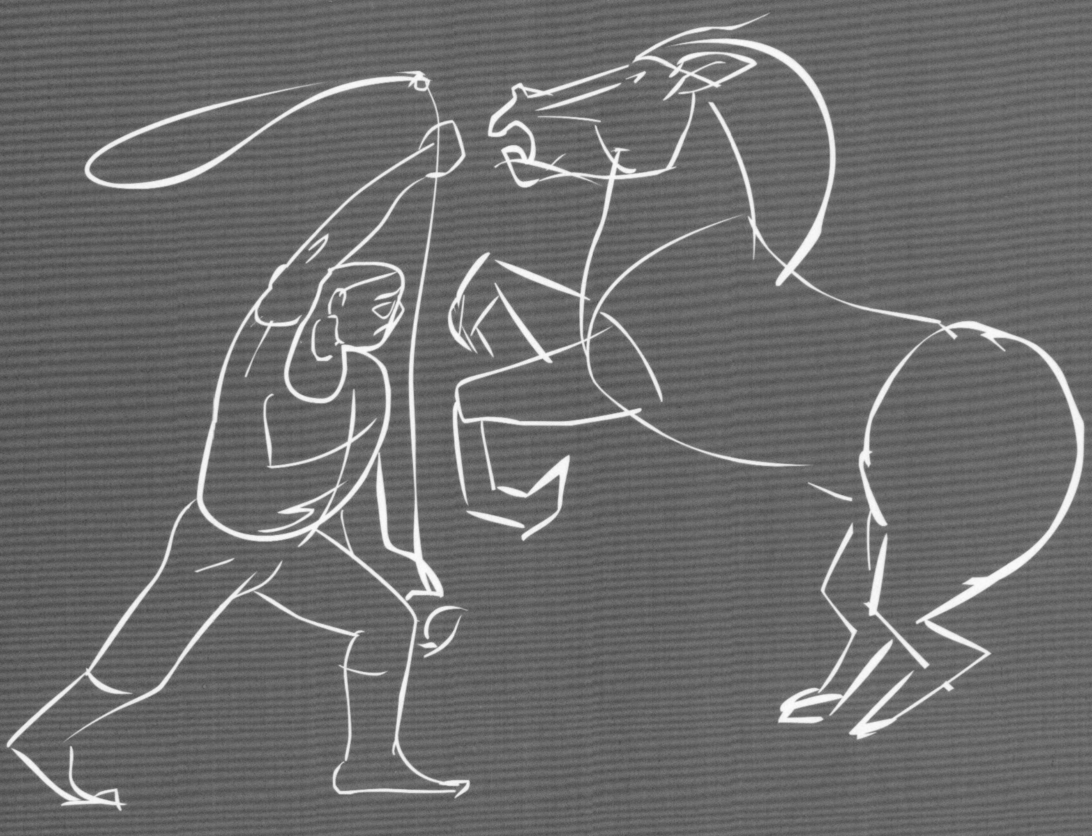

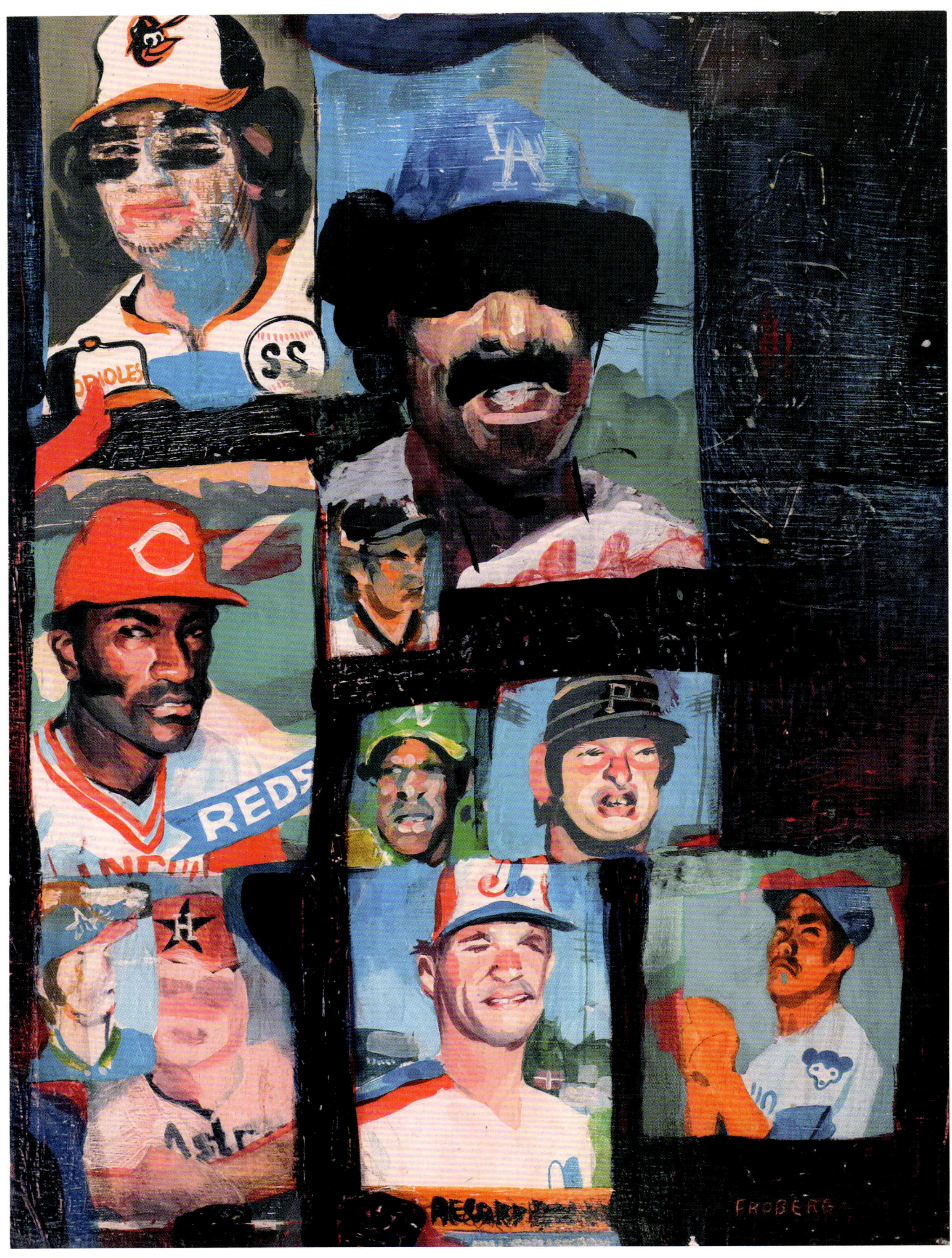

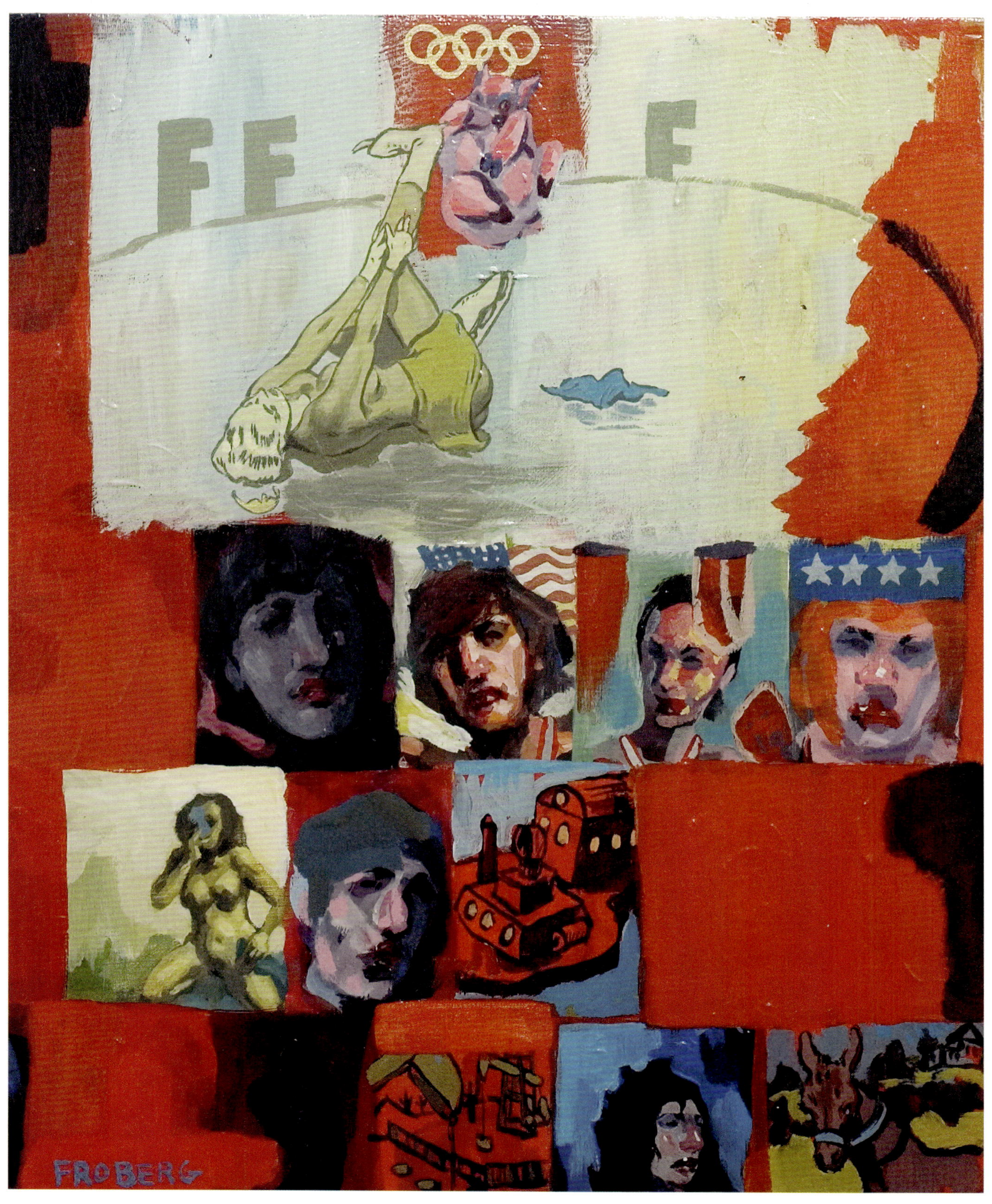

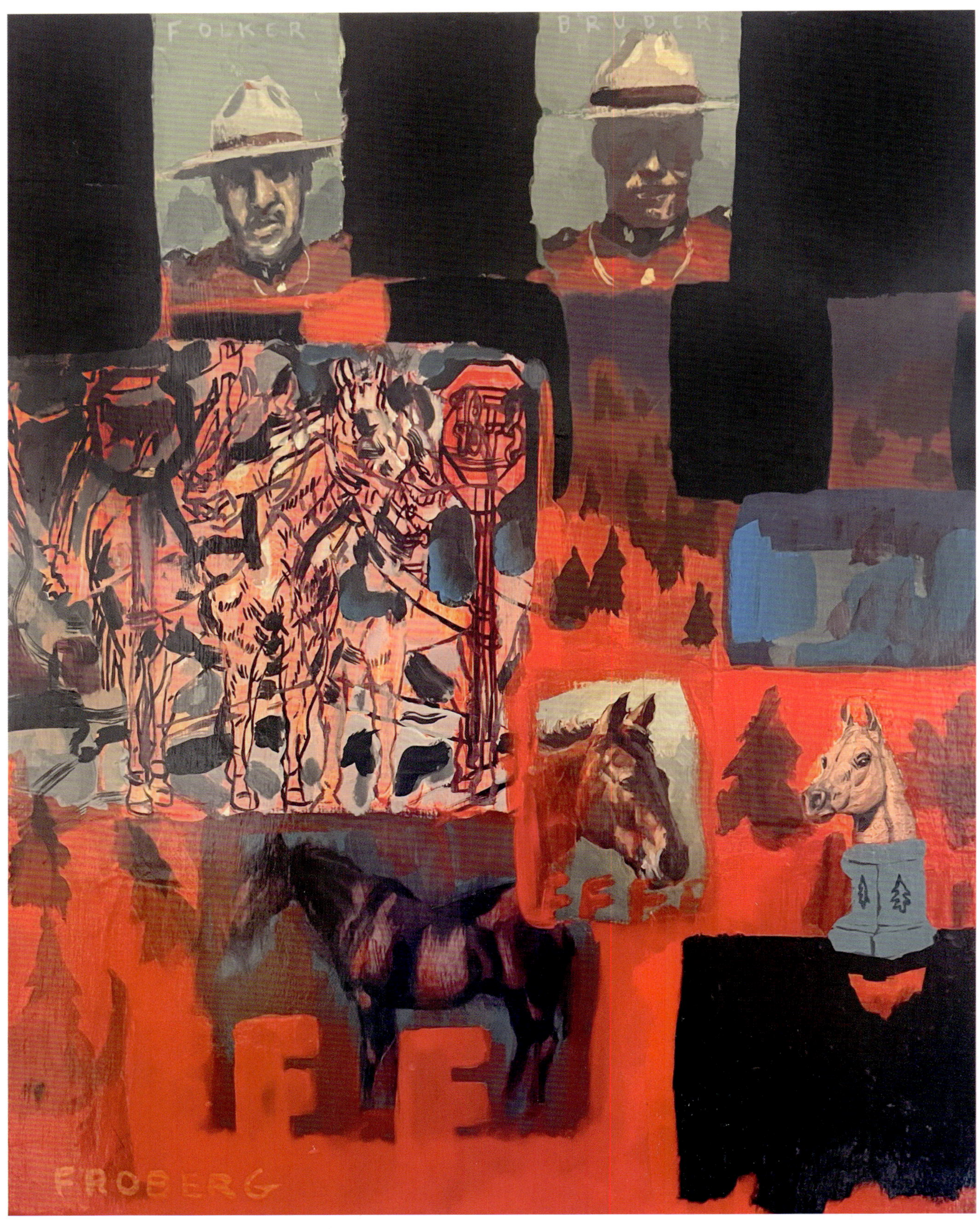
FOLKER
BRUDER
FROBERG

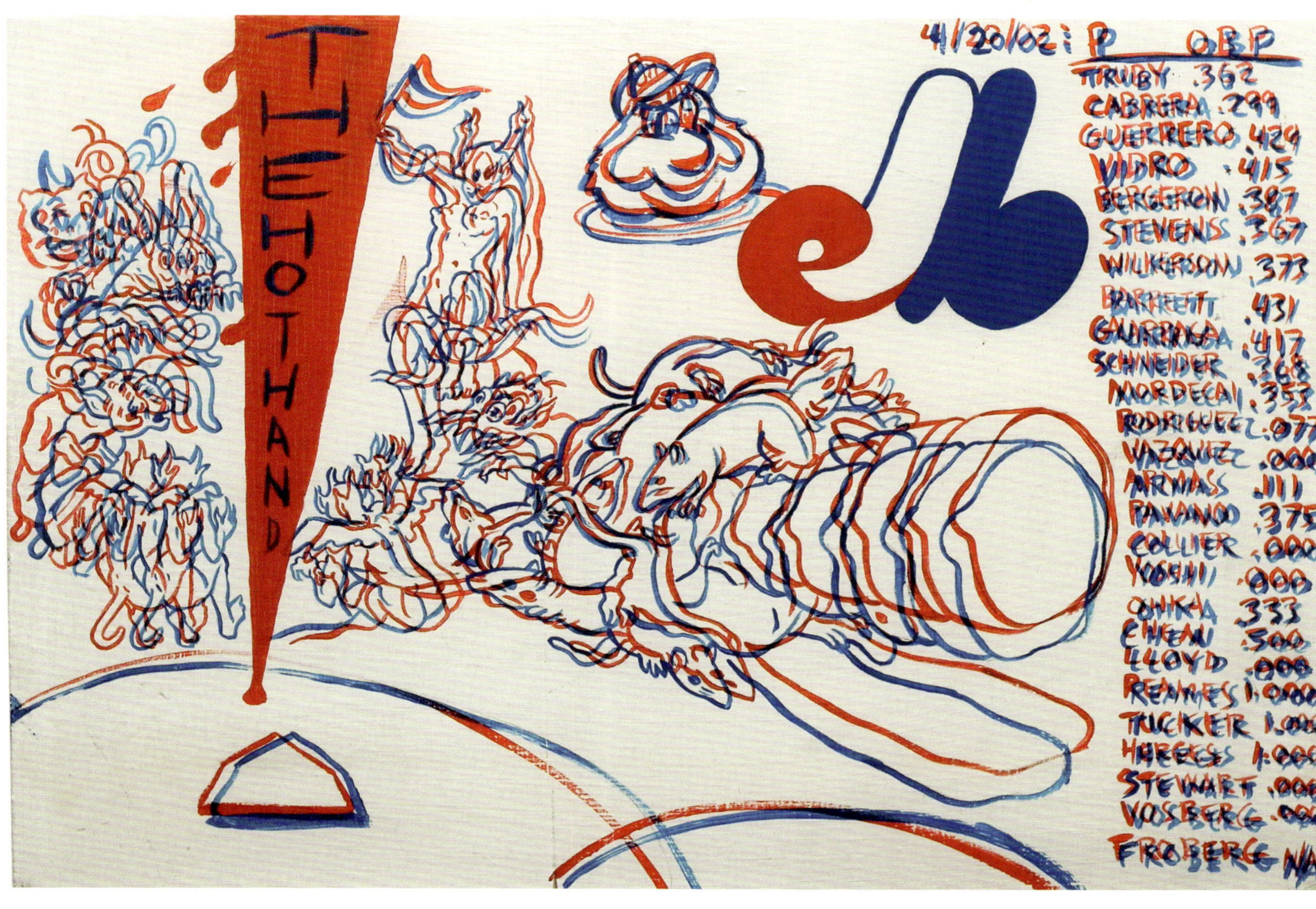

THE HOT HAND
4/20/02 P   OBP
TRUBY .362
CABRERA .299
GUERRERO .429
VIDRO .415
BERGERON .387
STEVENS .367
WILKERSON .373
BARRETT .431
GALARRAGA .417
SCHNEIDER .368
MORDECAI .353
RODRIGUEZ .077
VAZQUEZ .000
ARMAS .111
PAVANO .375
COLLIER .000
YOSHII .000
OHKA .333
CHEAN .500
LLOYD .000
REAMES 1.000
TUCKER 1.000
HERGES 1.000
STEWART .000
VOSBERG .000
FROBERG N/A

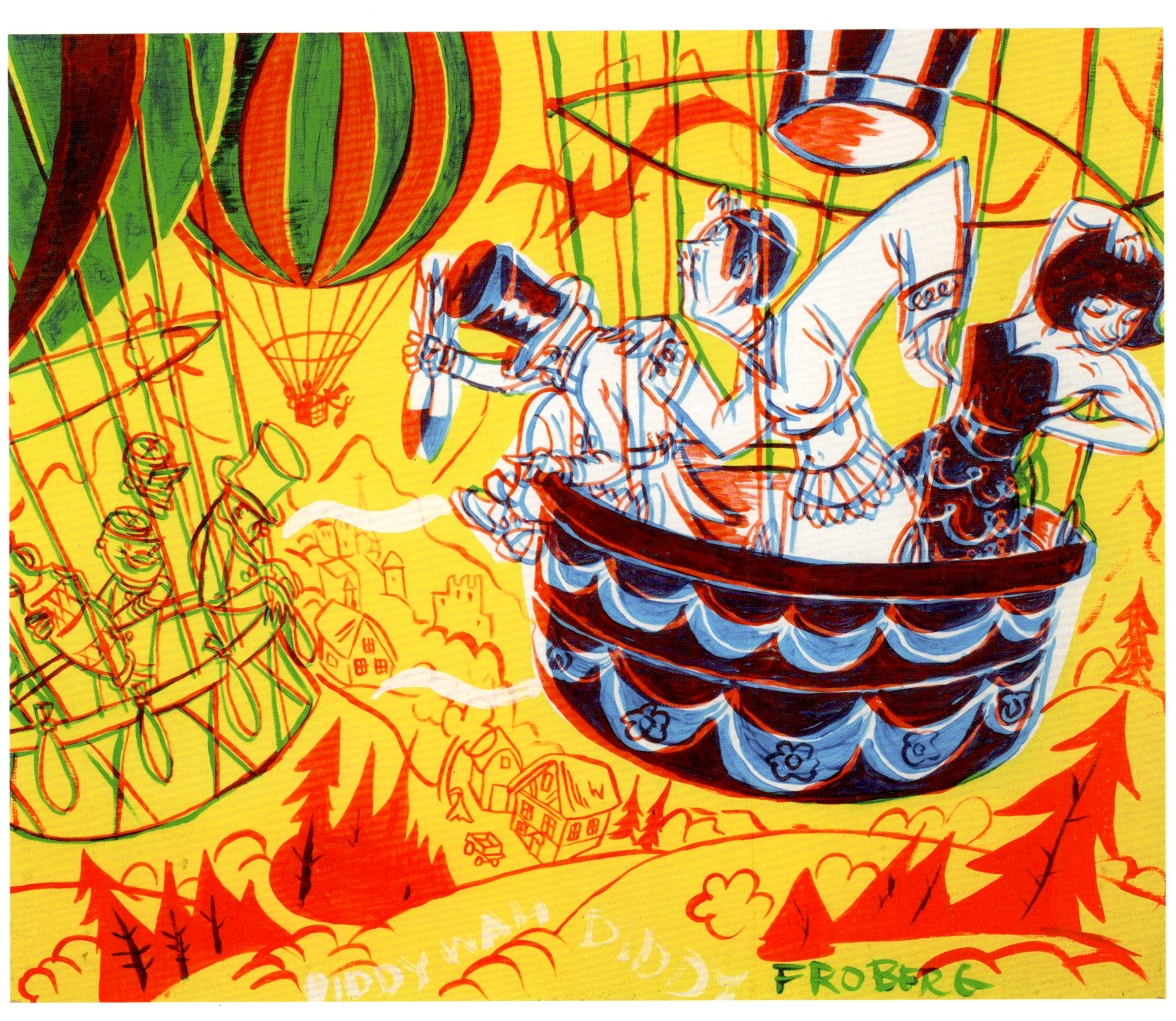
DIDDY WAH DIDDY
FROBERG

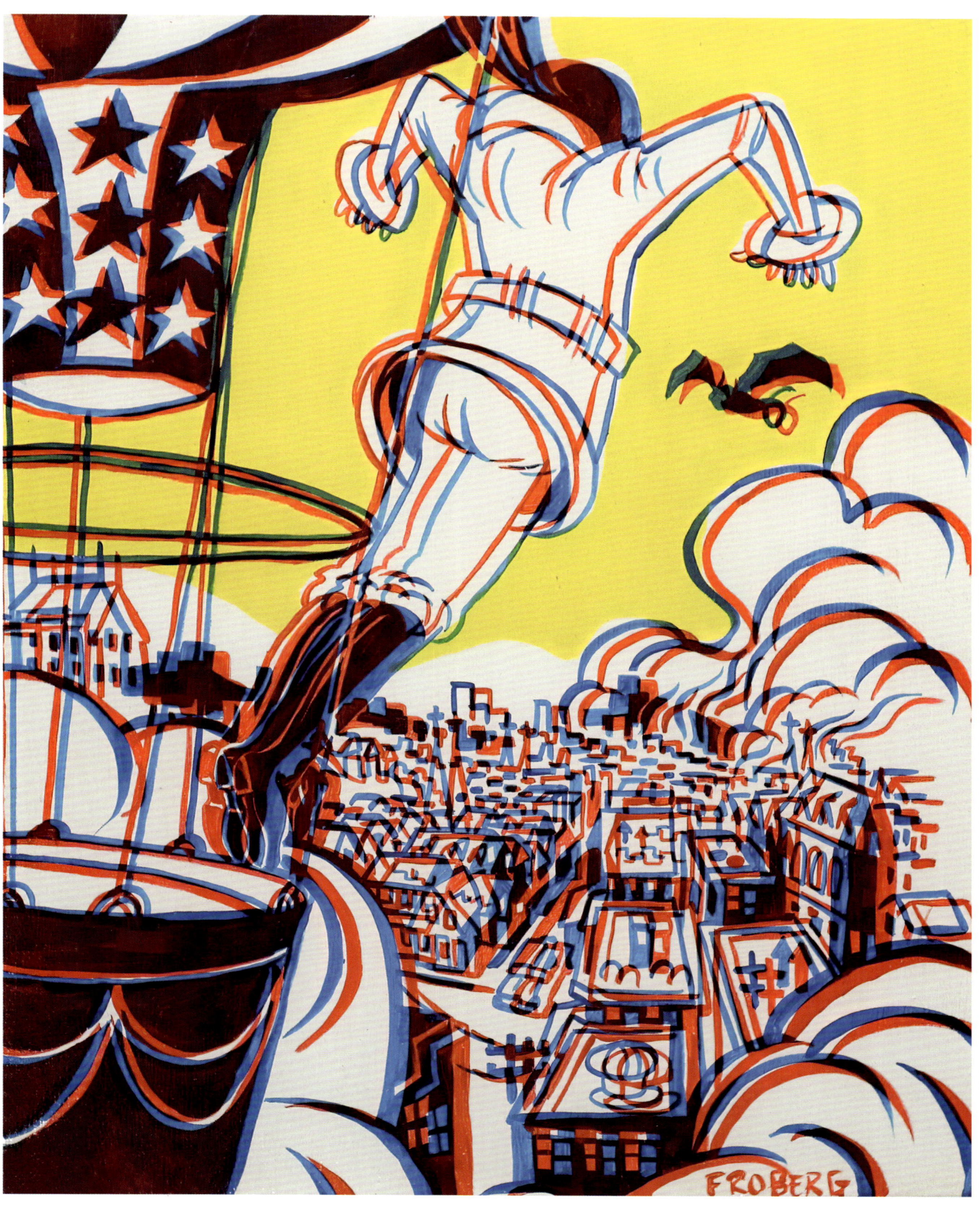
FROBERG

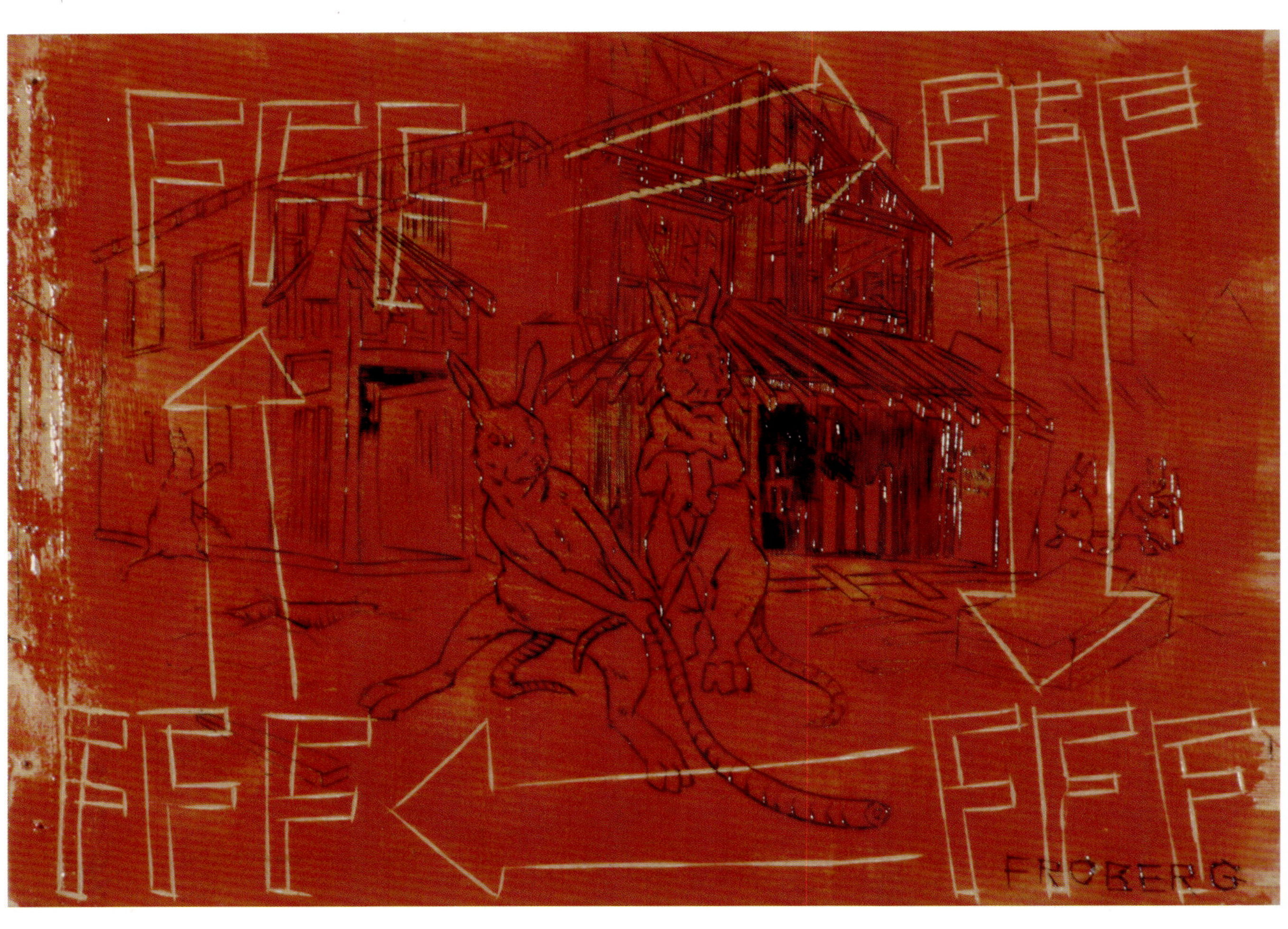

FFF
FFF
FFF
FFF
FROBERG

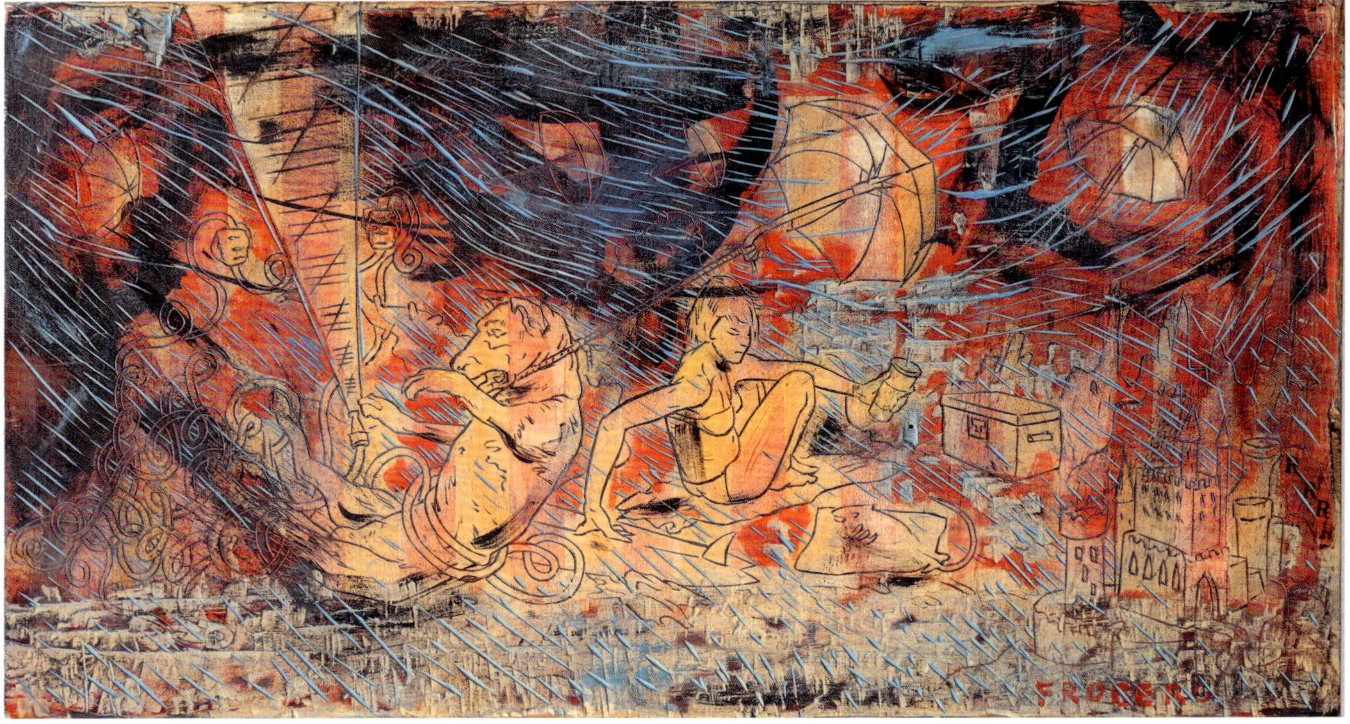

FROBERG

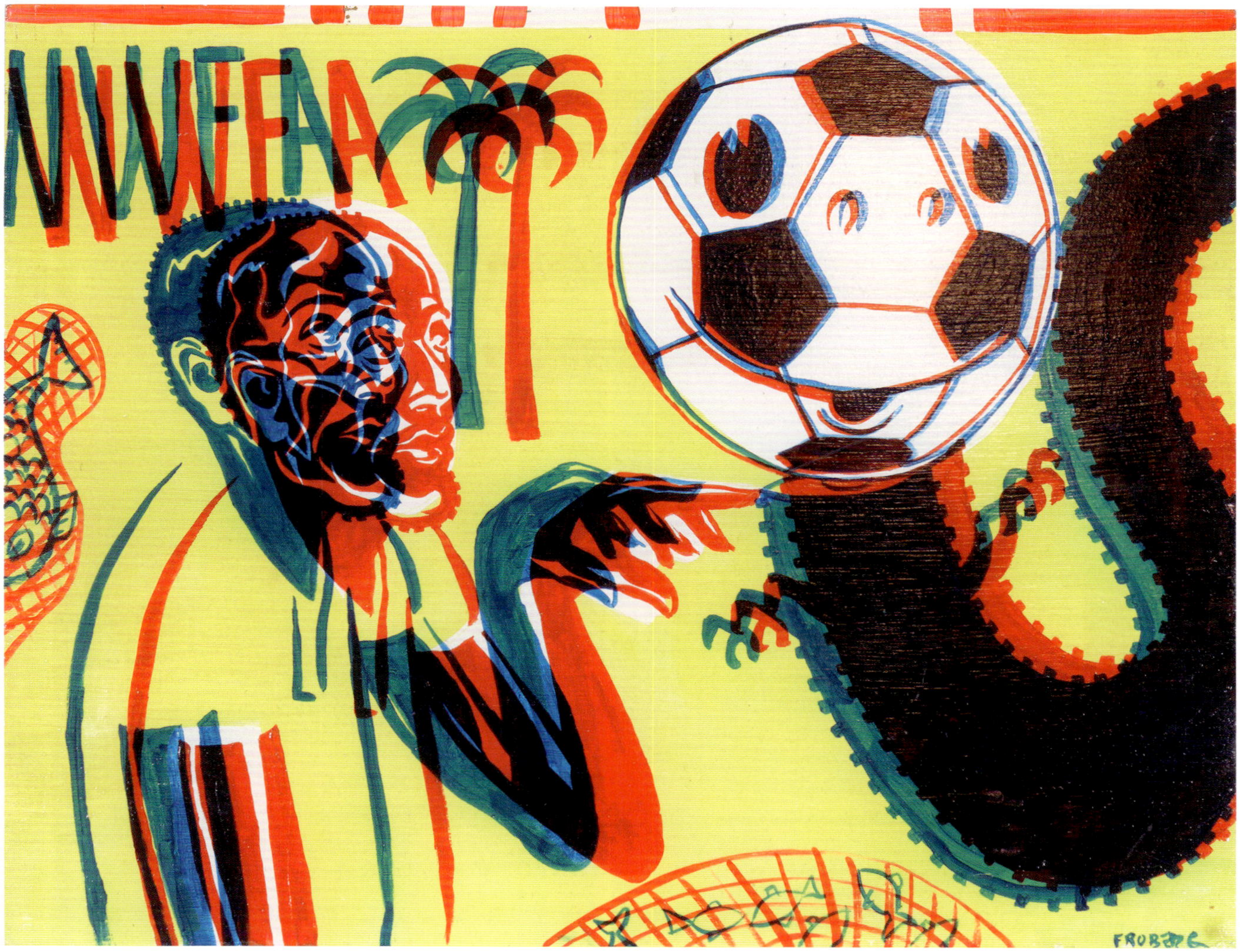

WWFFAA
FROBERG

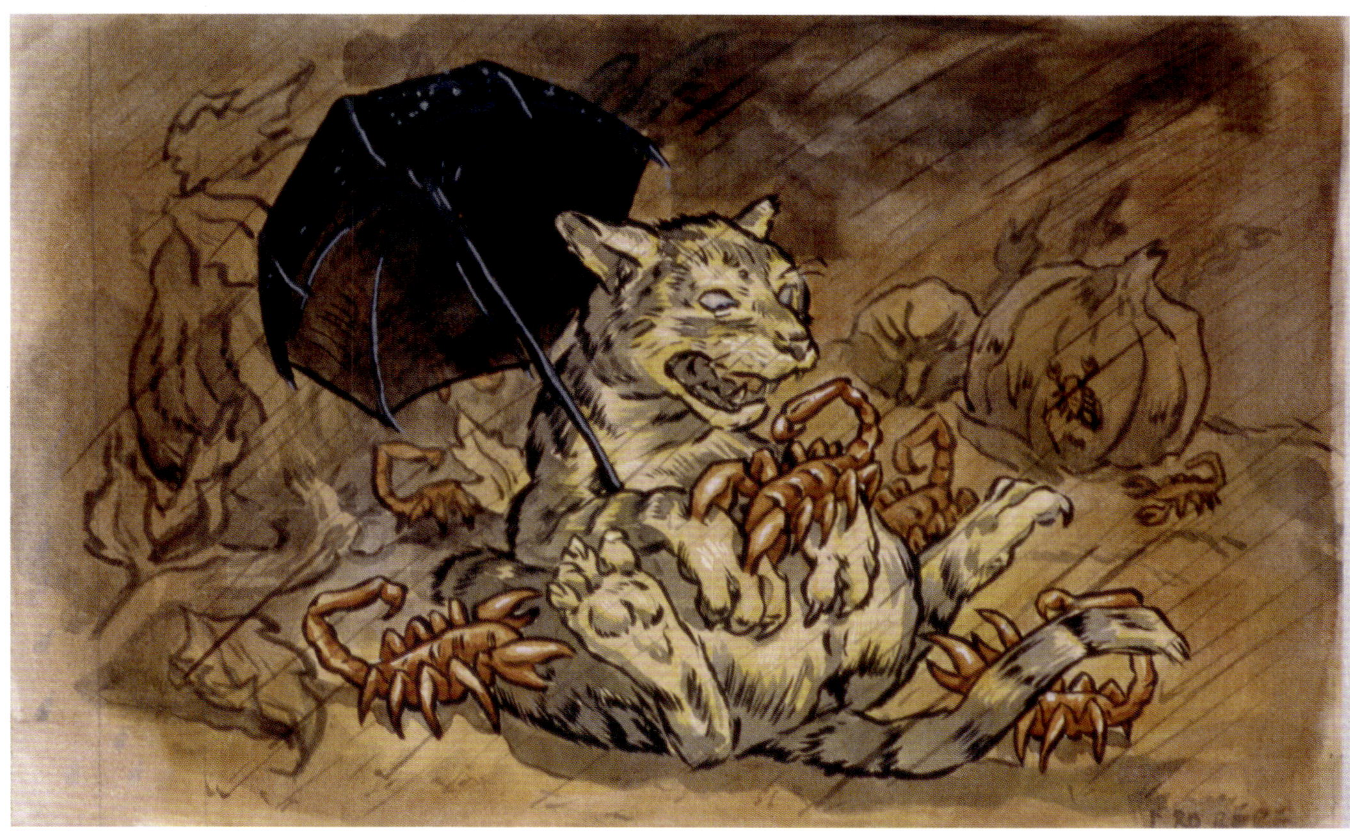

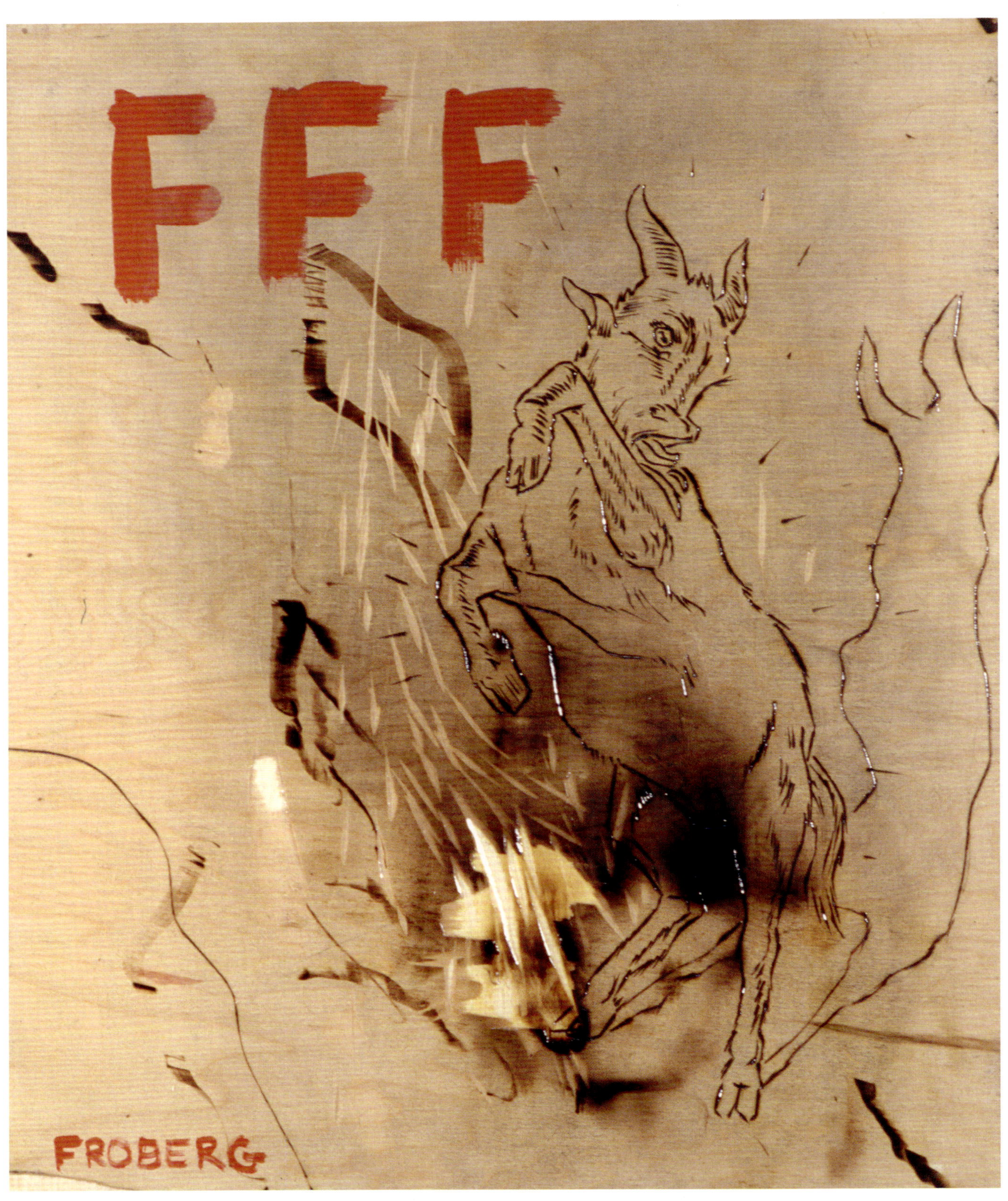

F F F
FROBERG

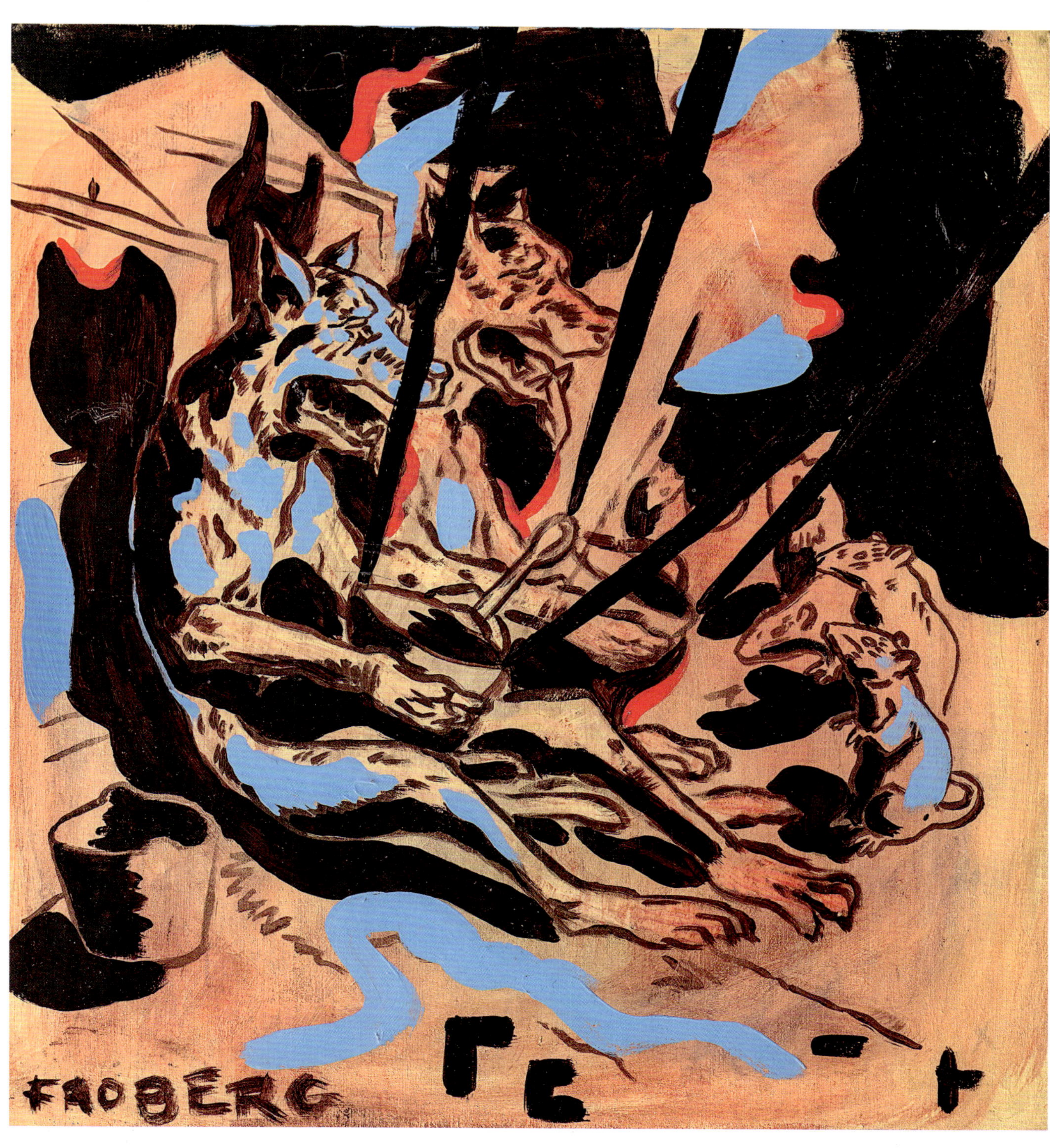
FABERG

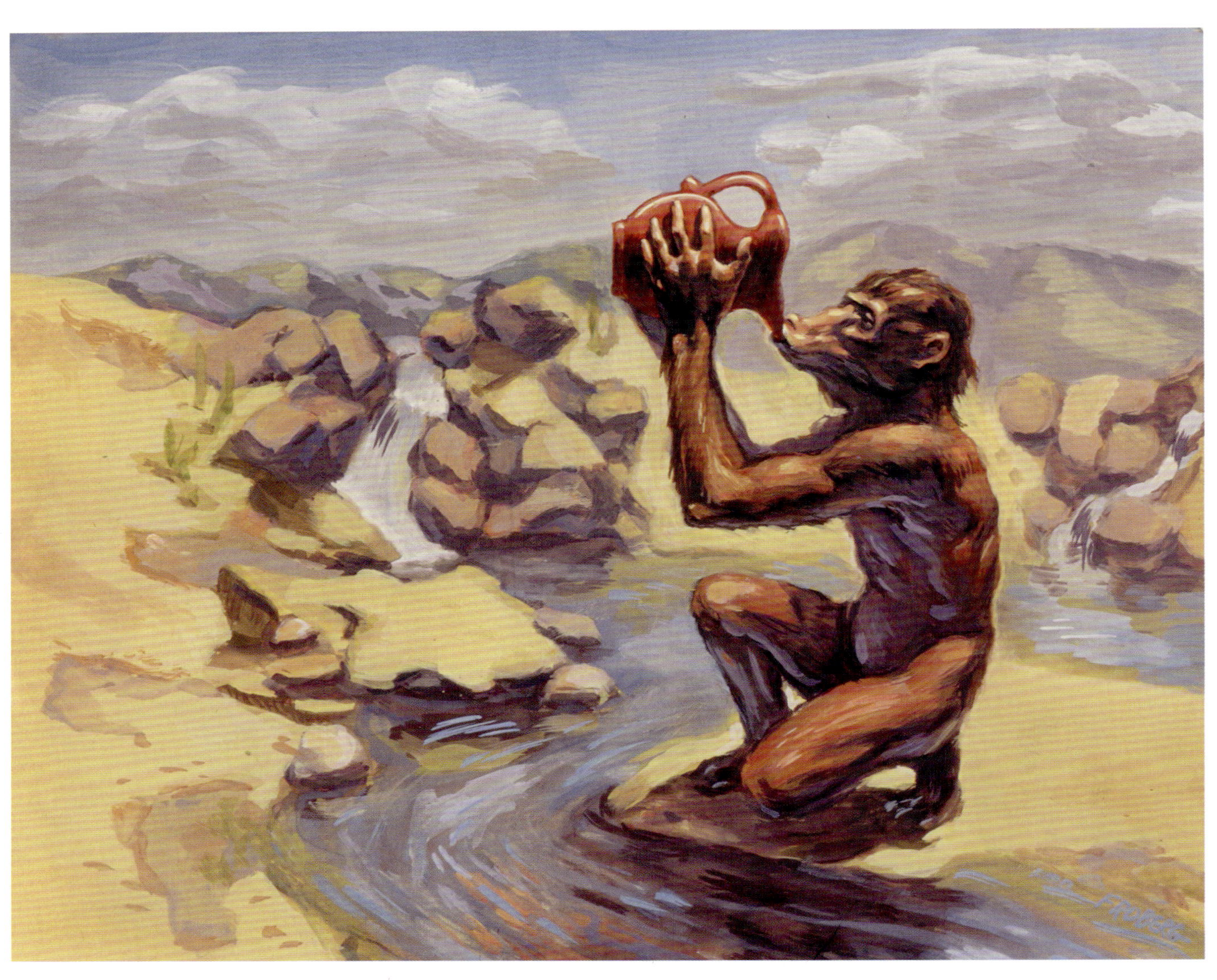

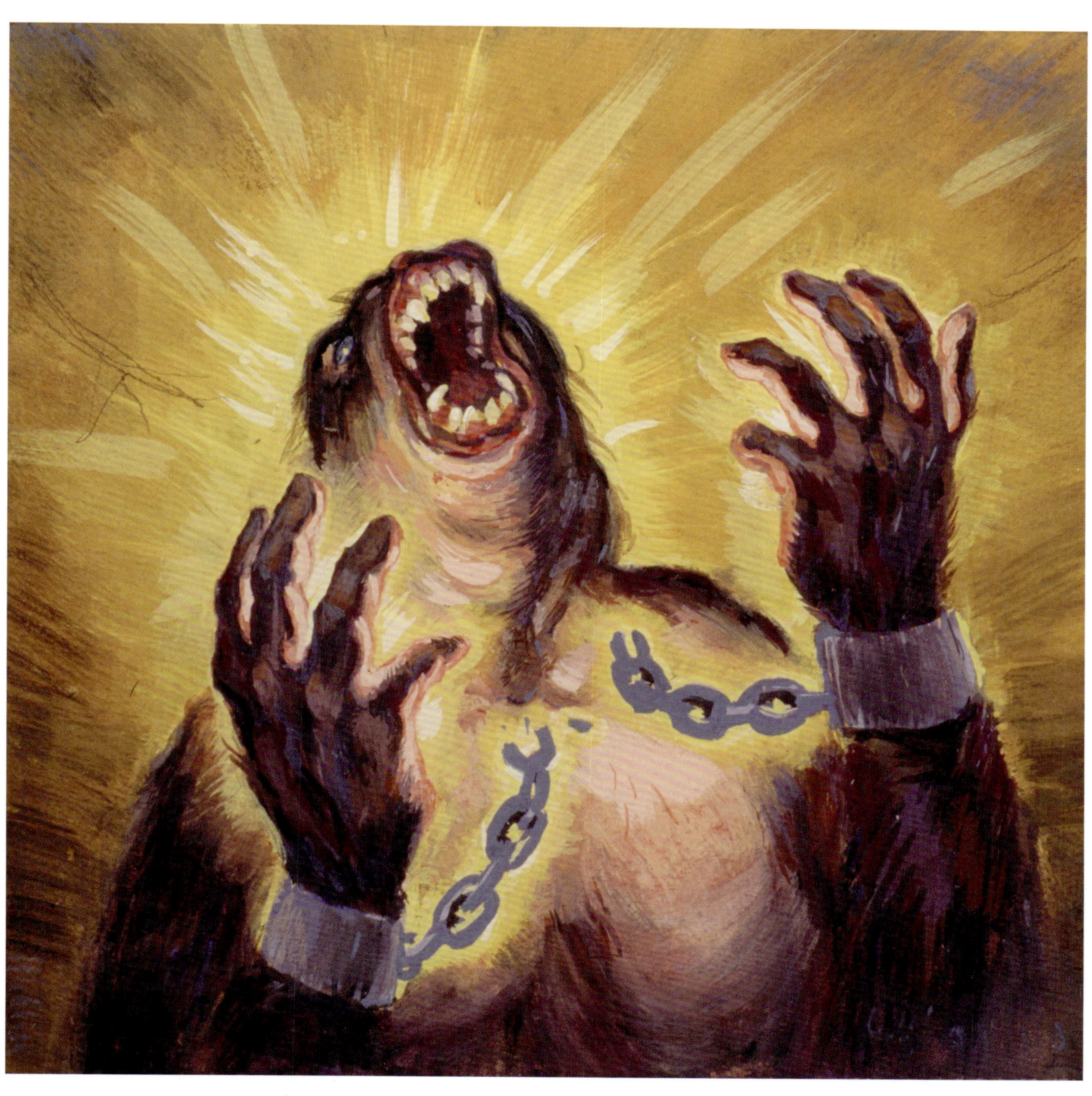

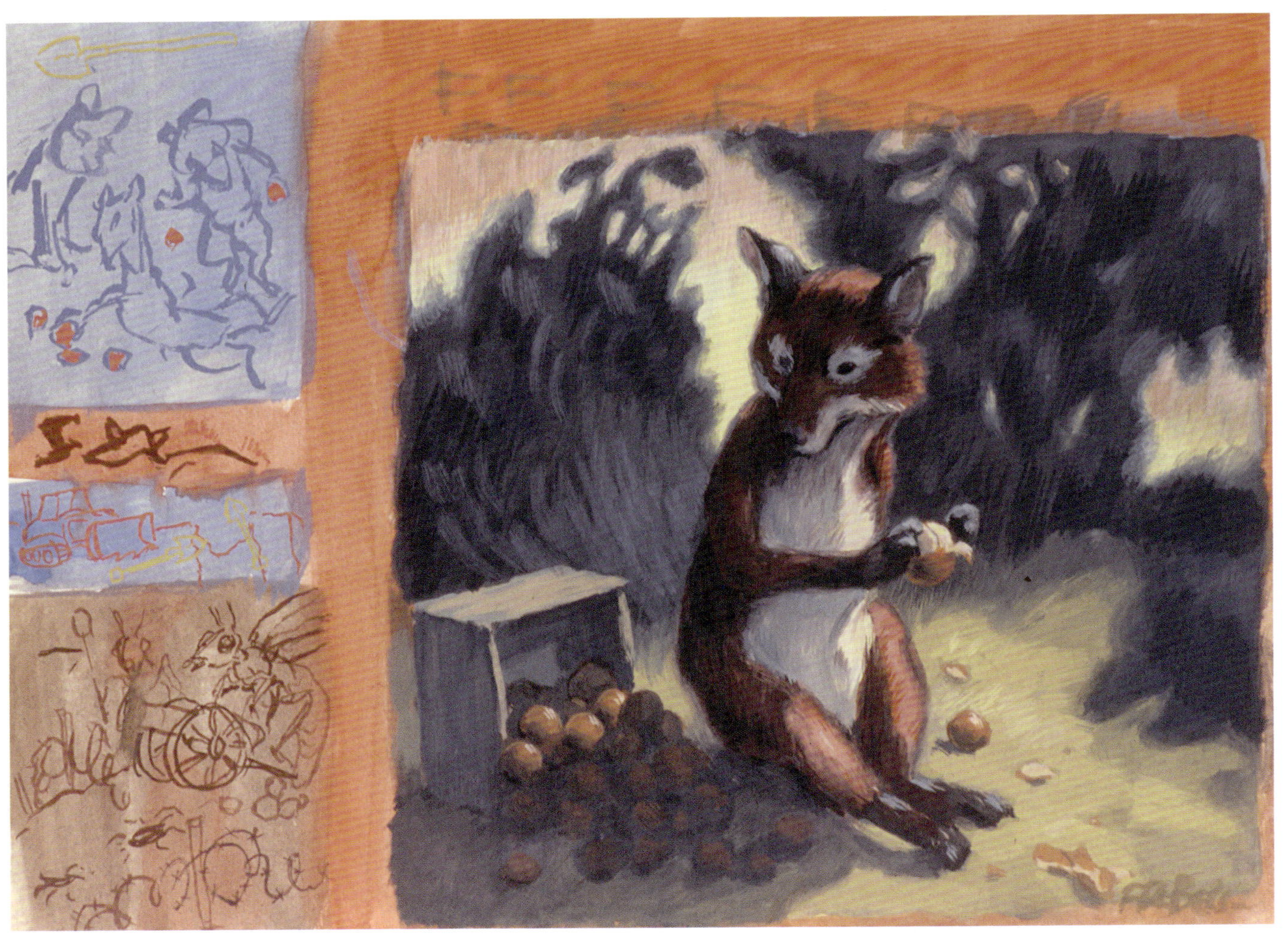

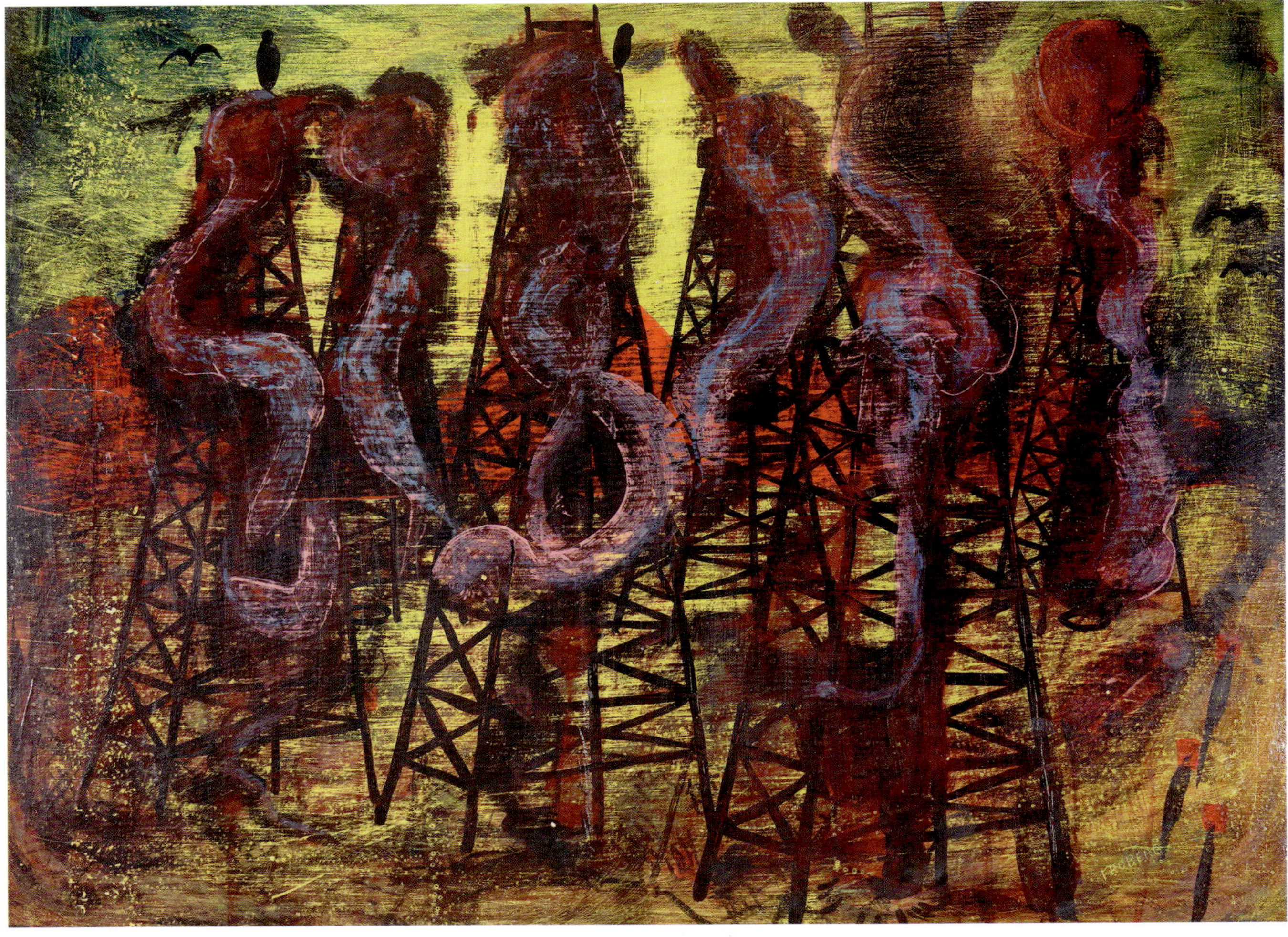

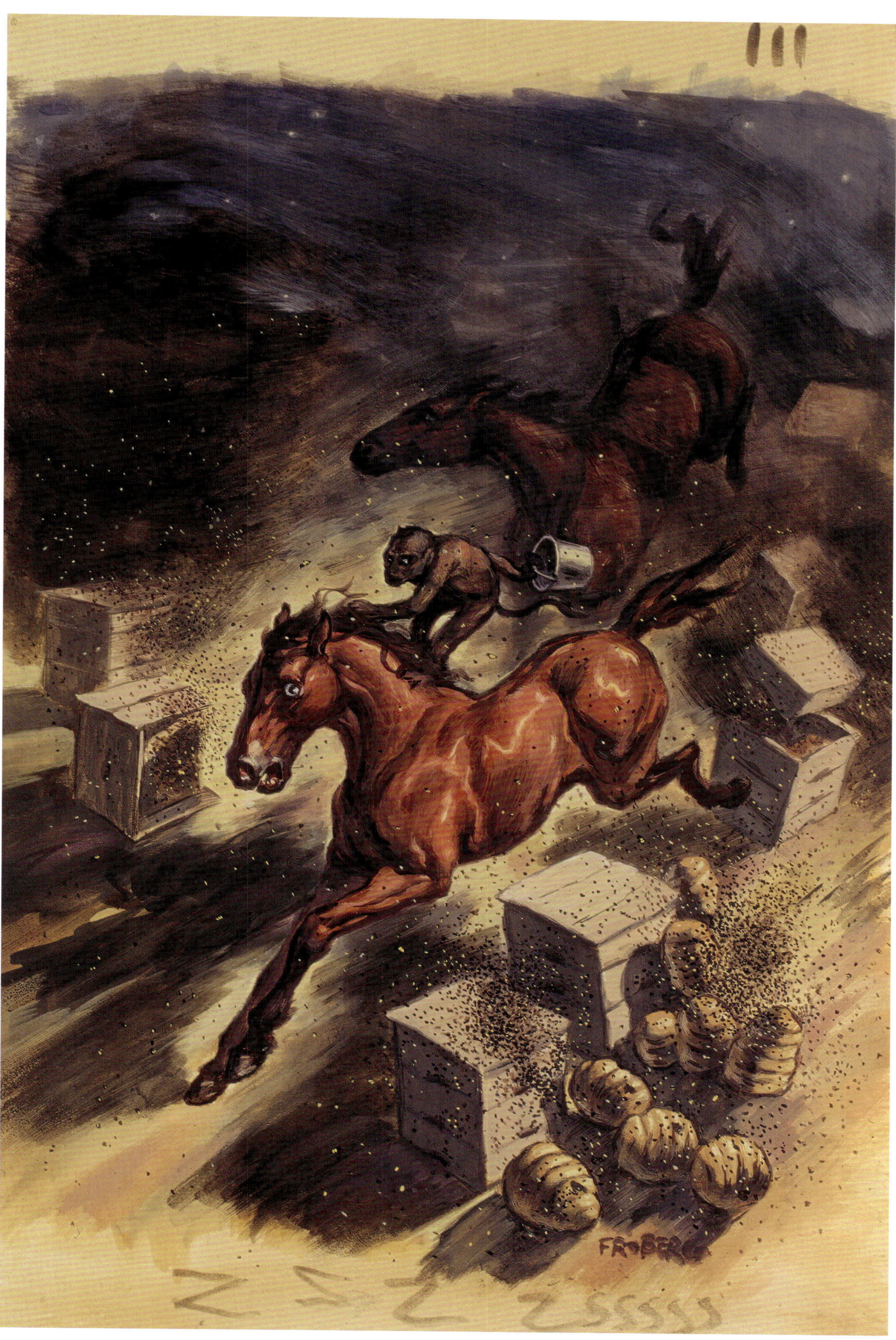

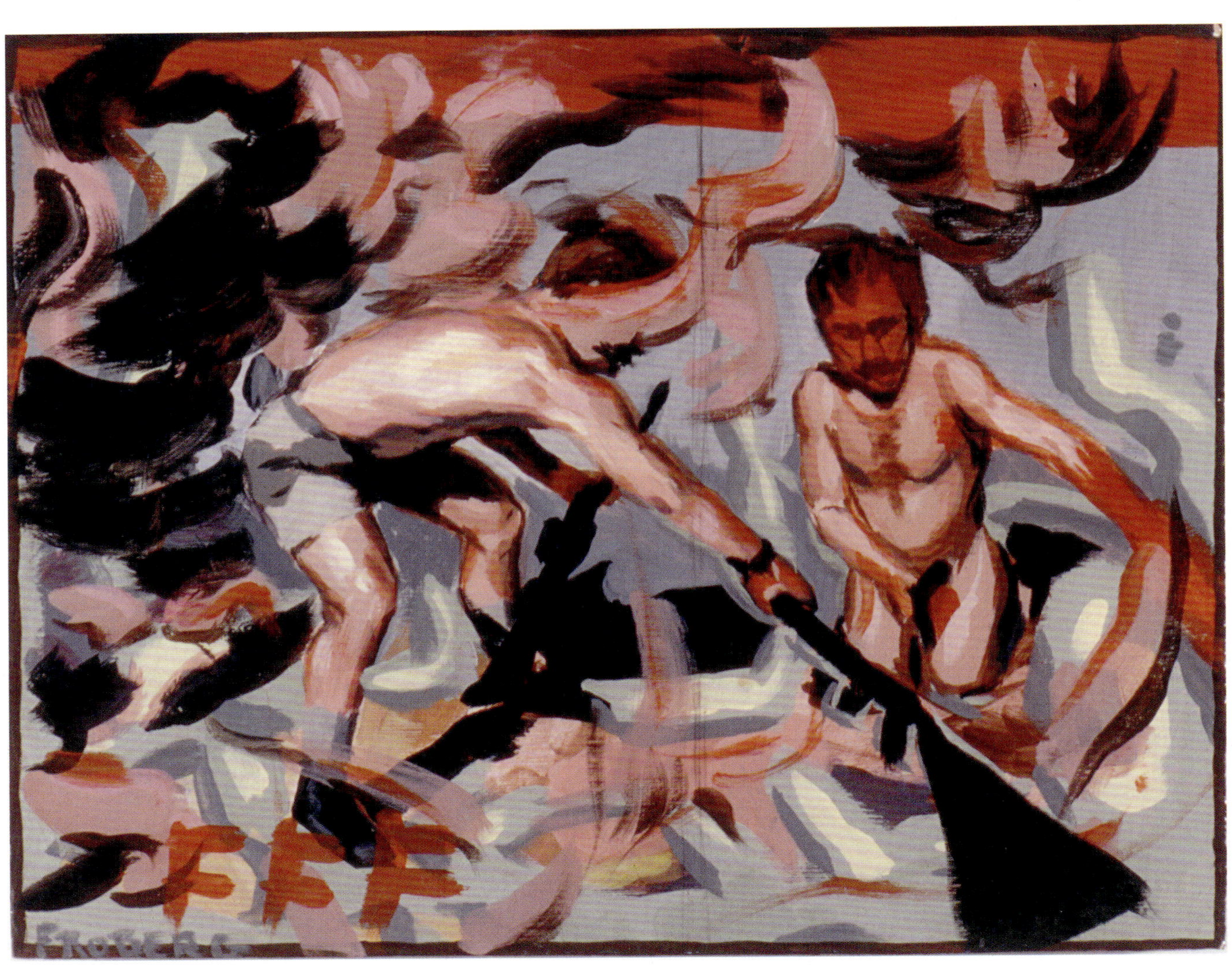

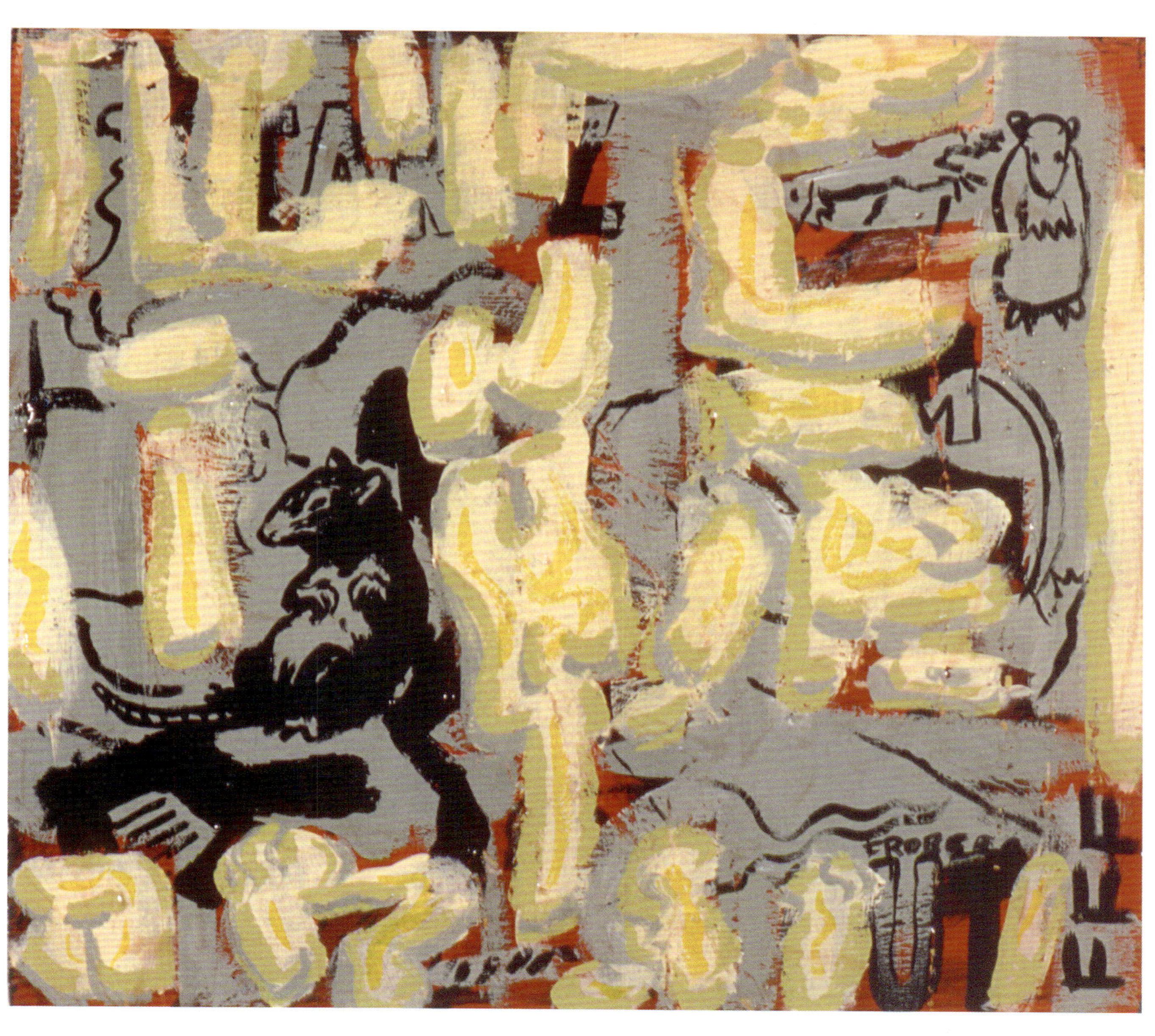

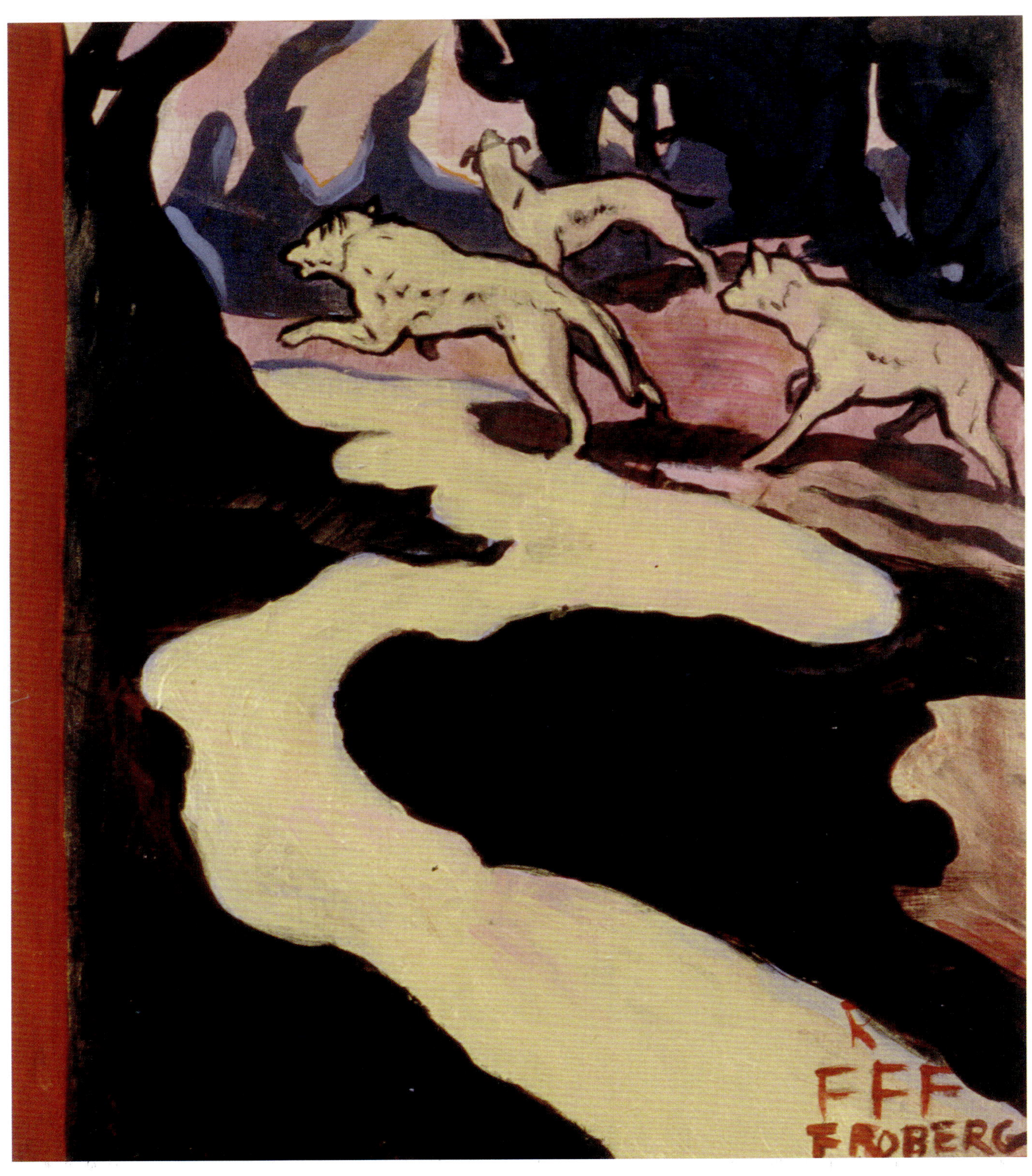

FFF
FROBERG

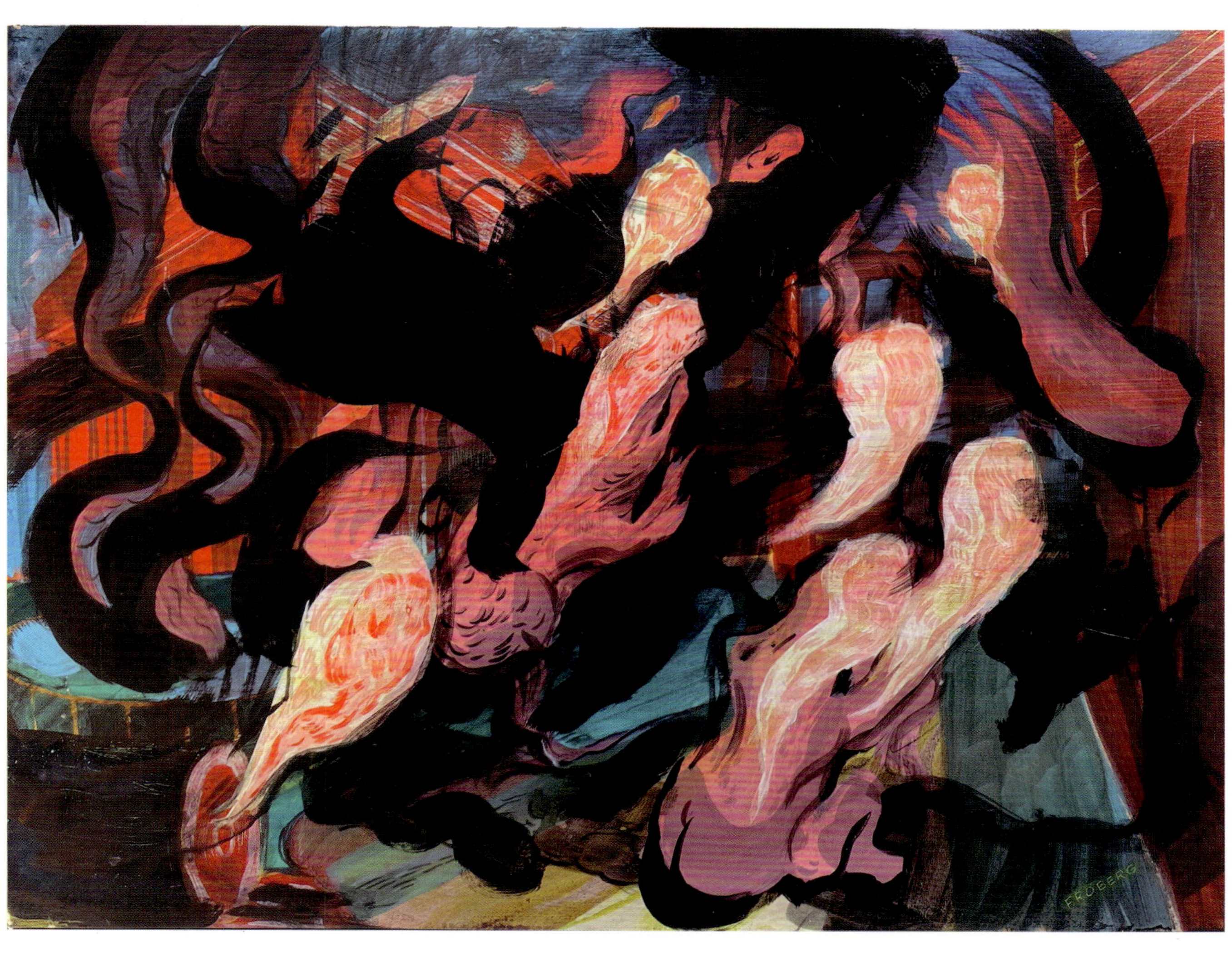

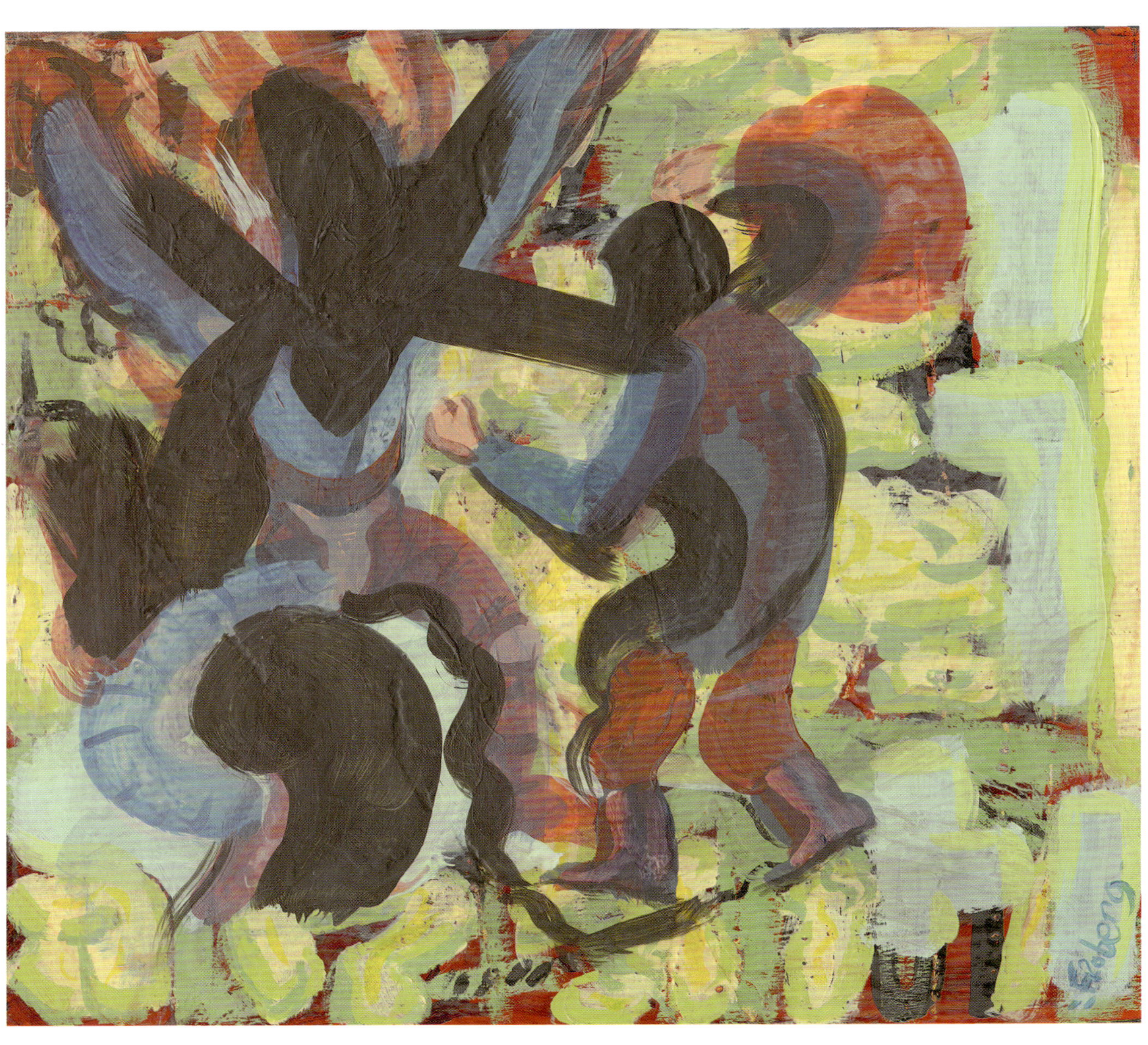

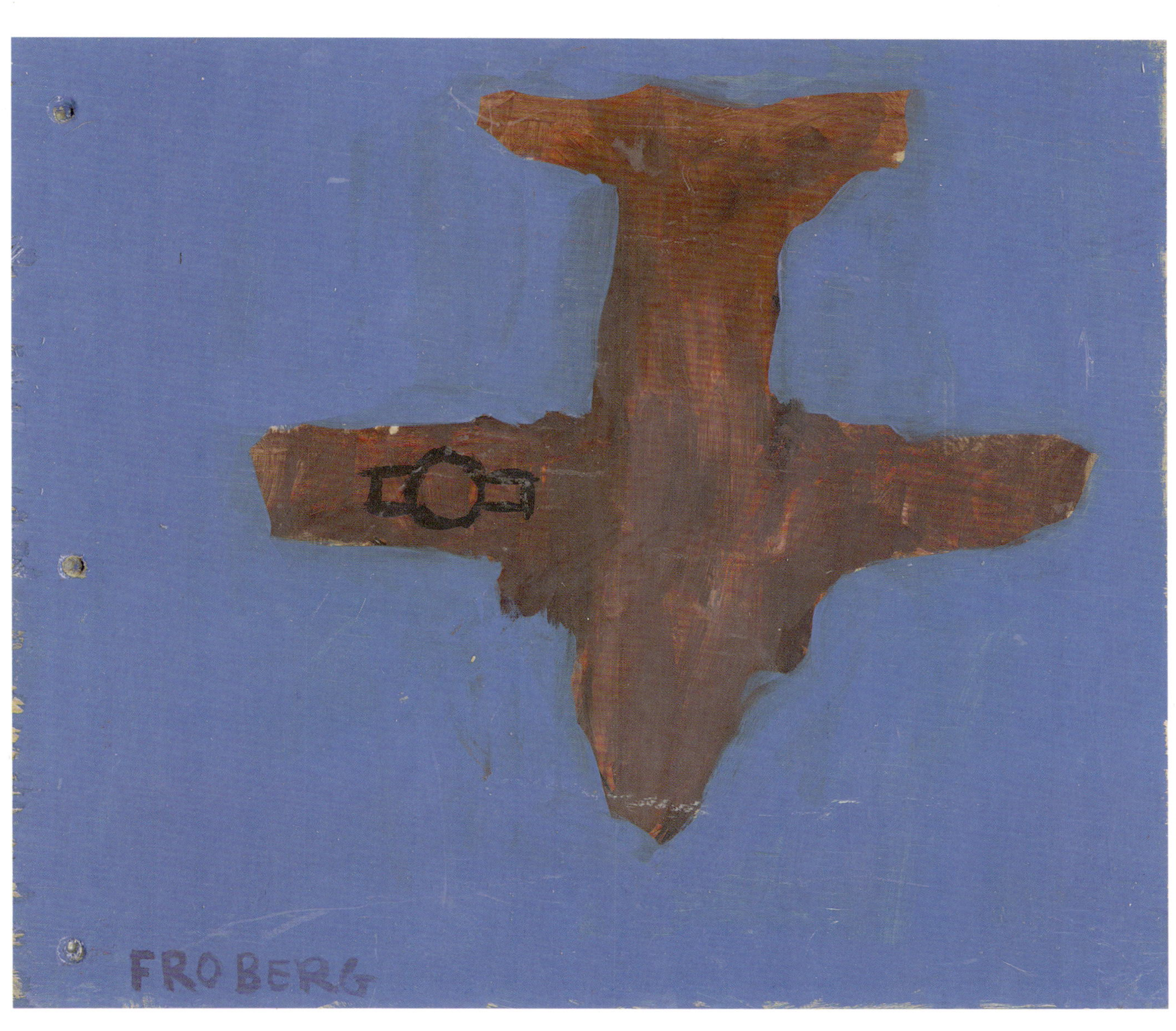

FROBERG

SIX

Ink Drawings

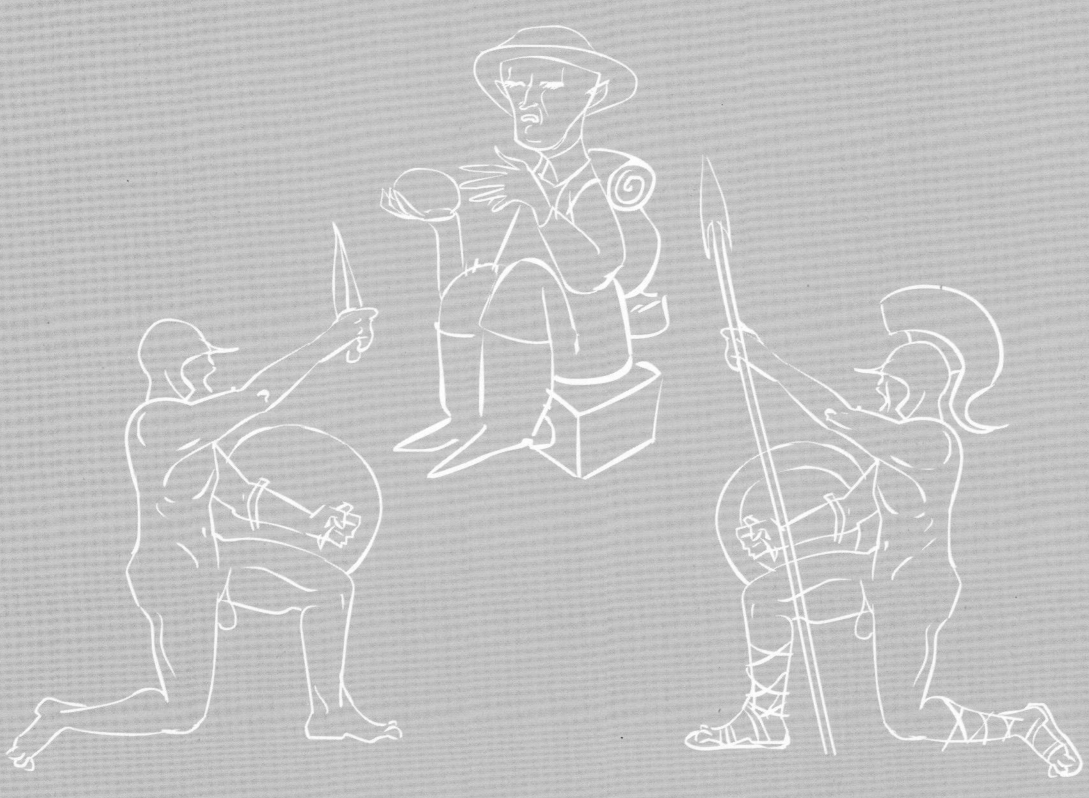

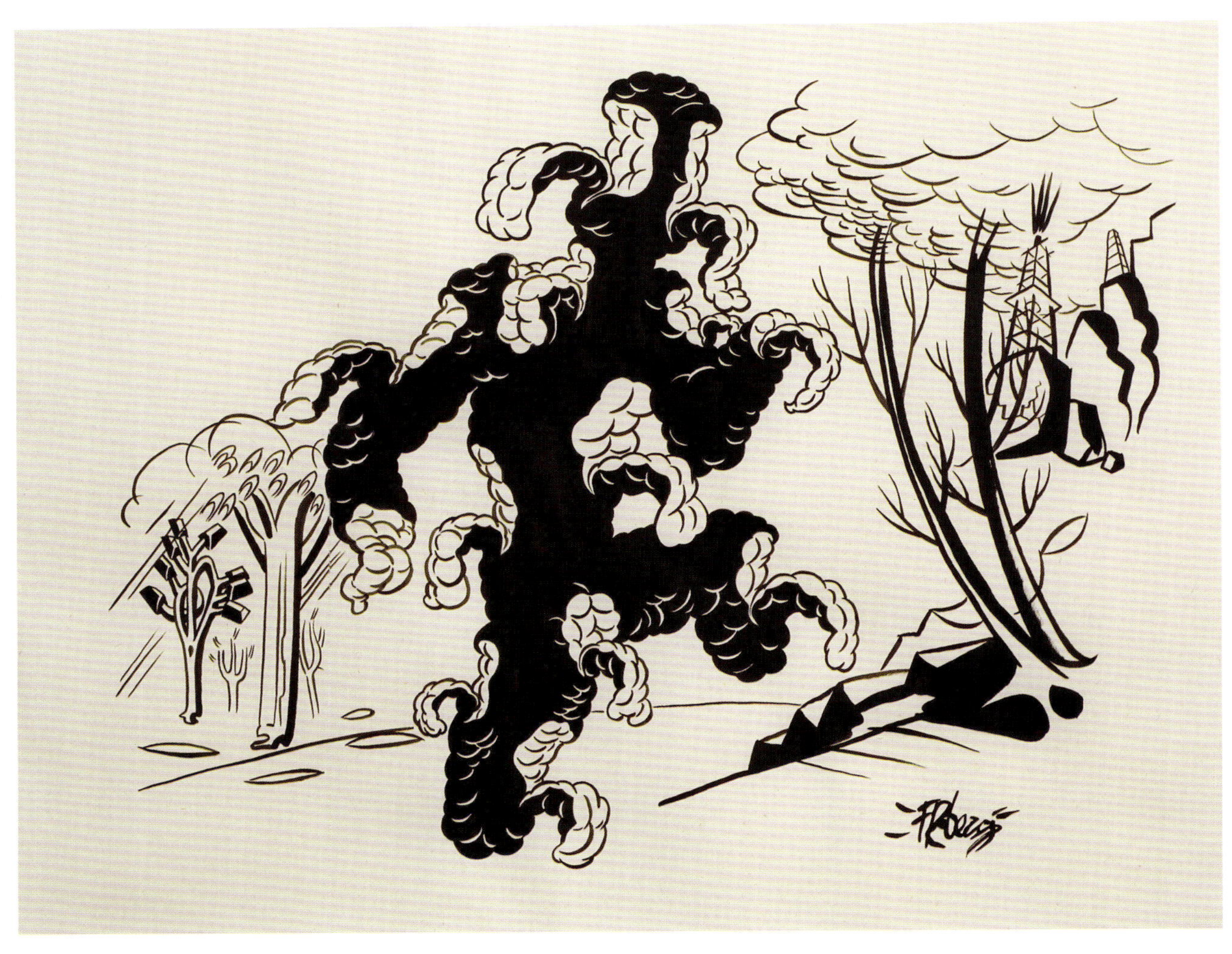

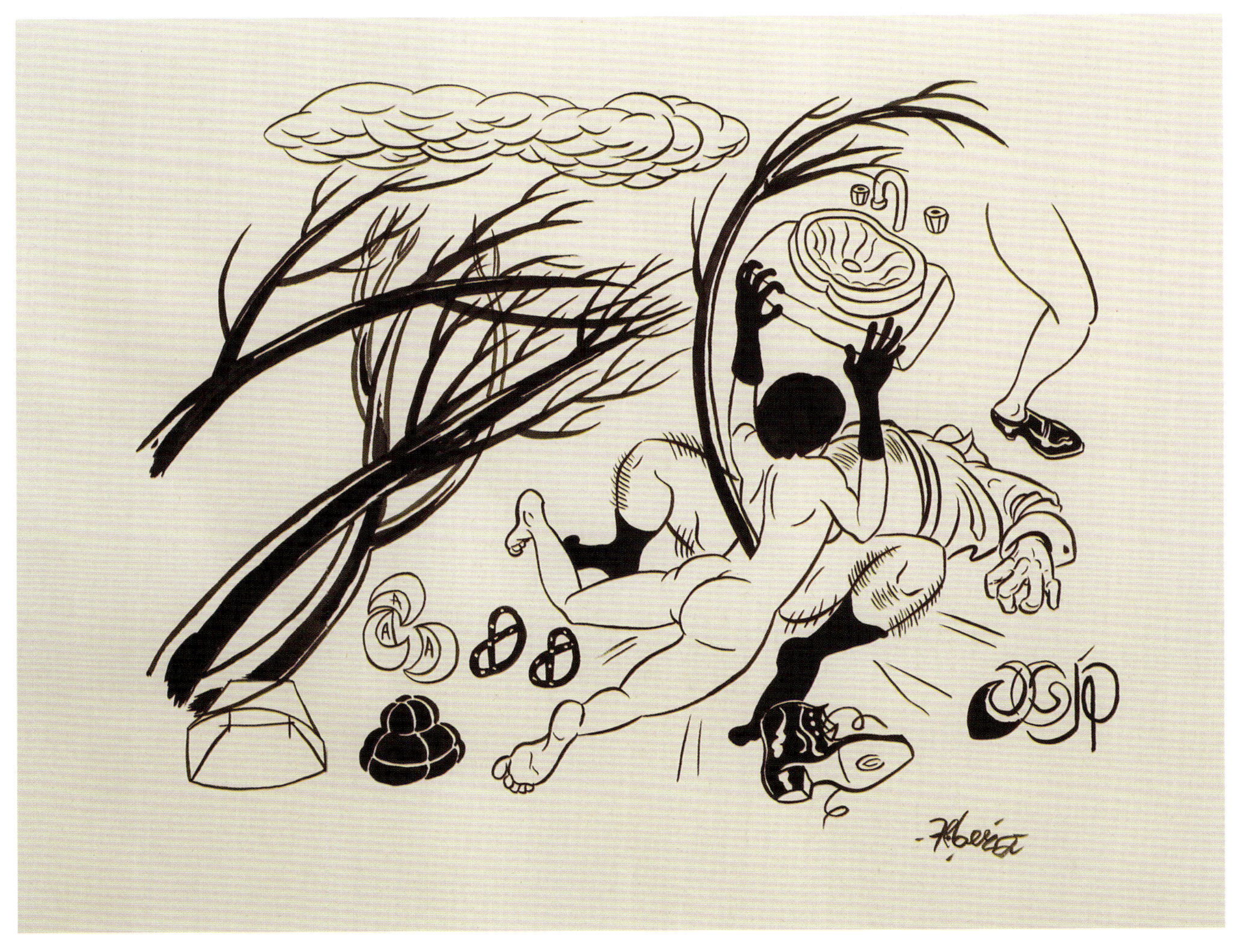

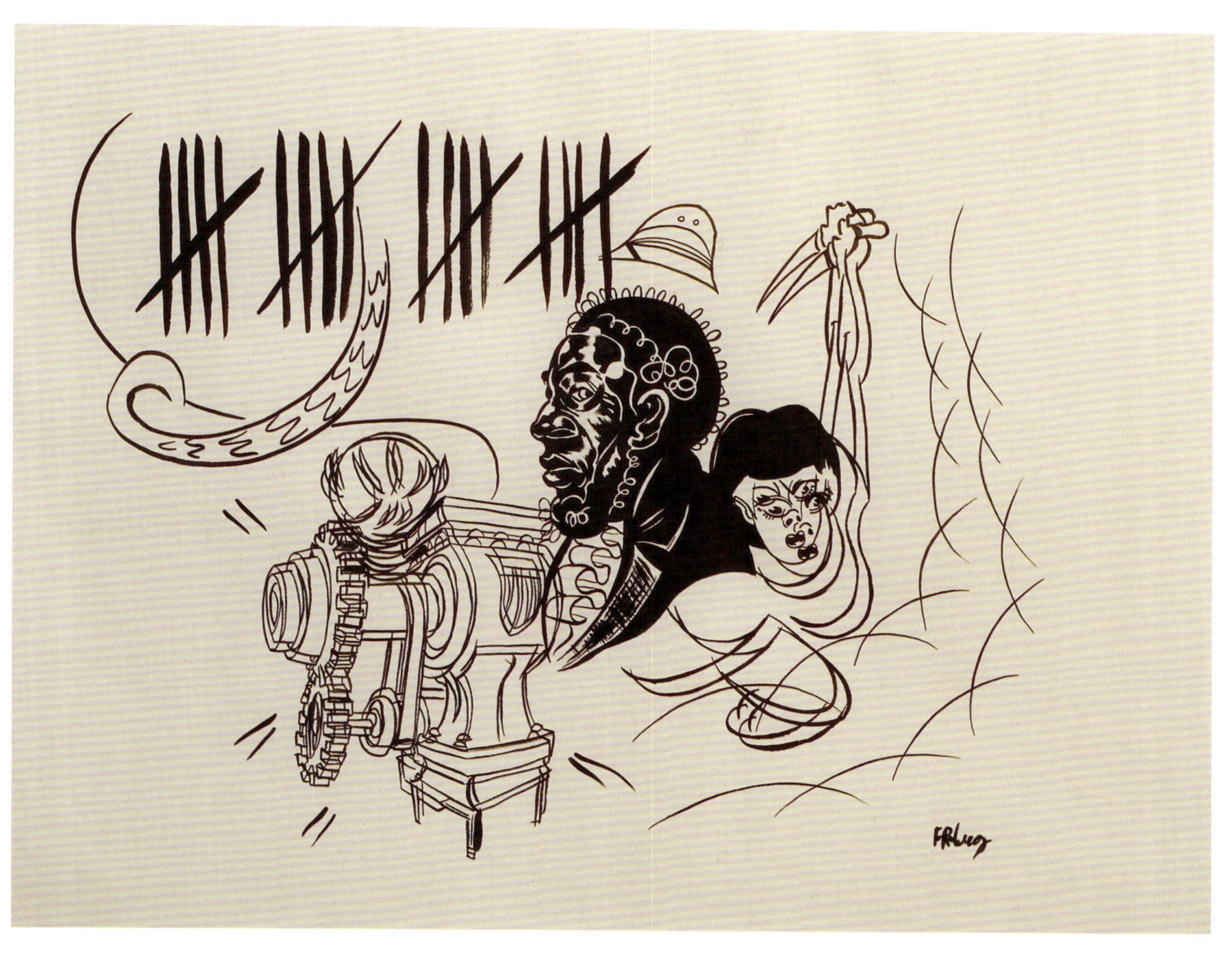

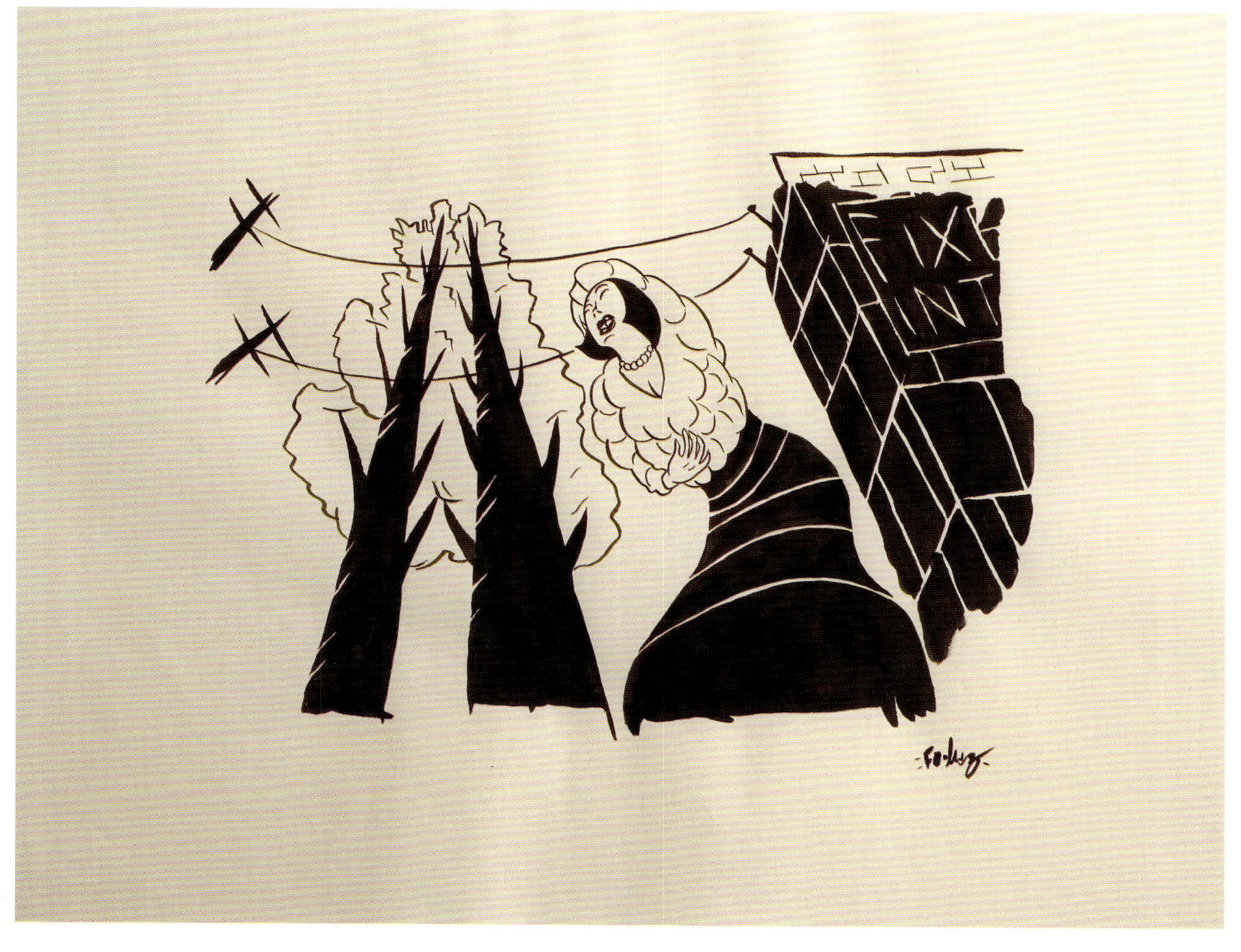

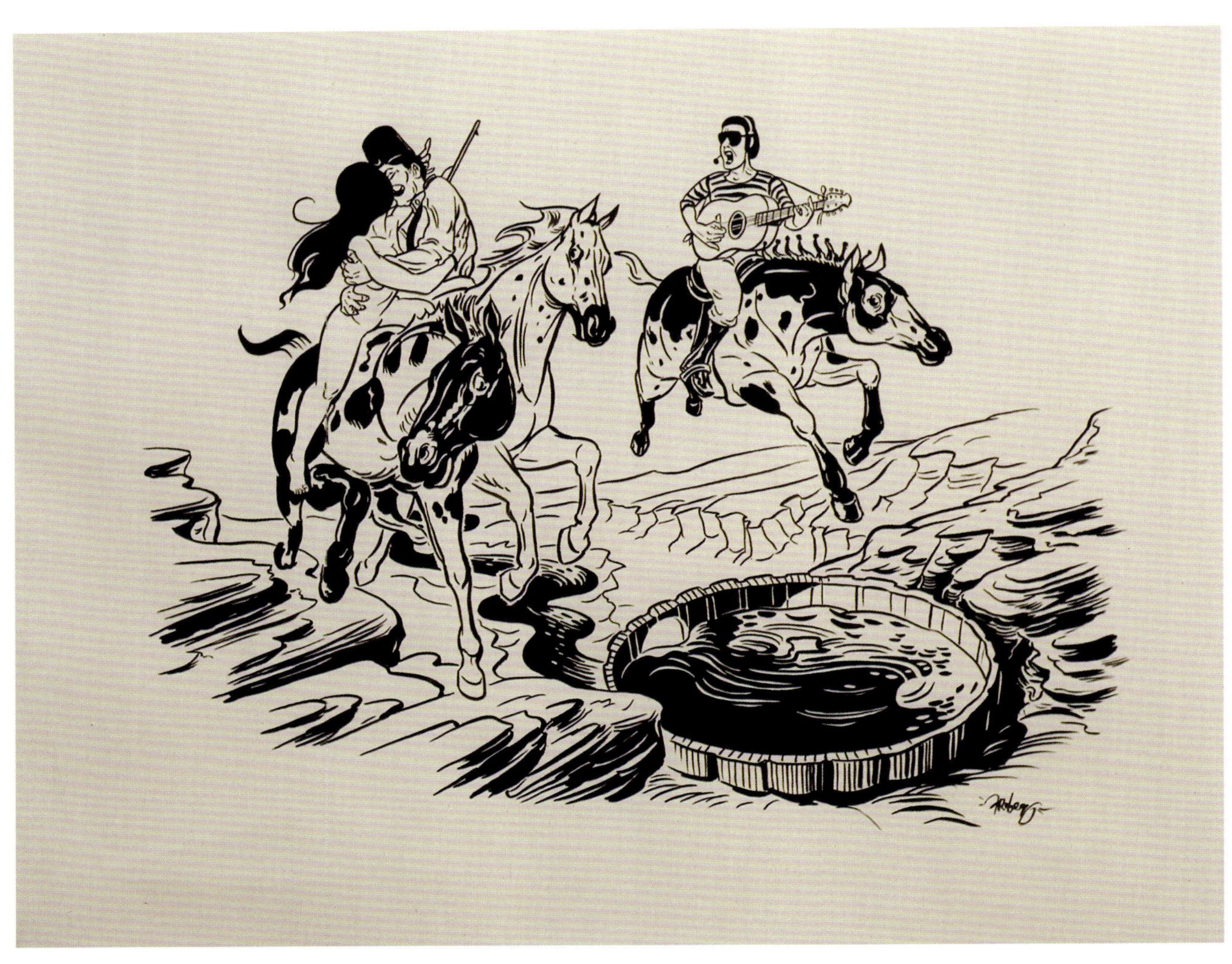

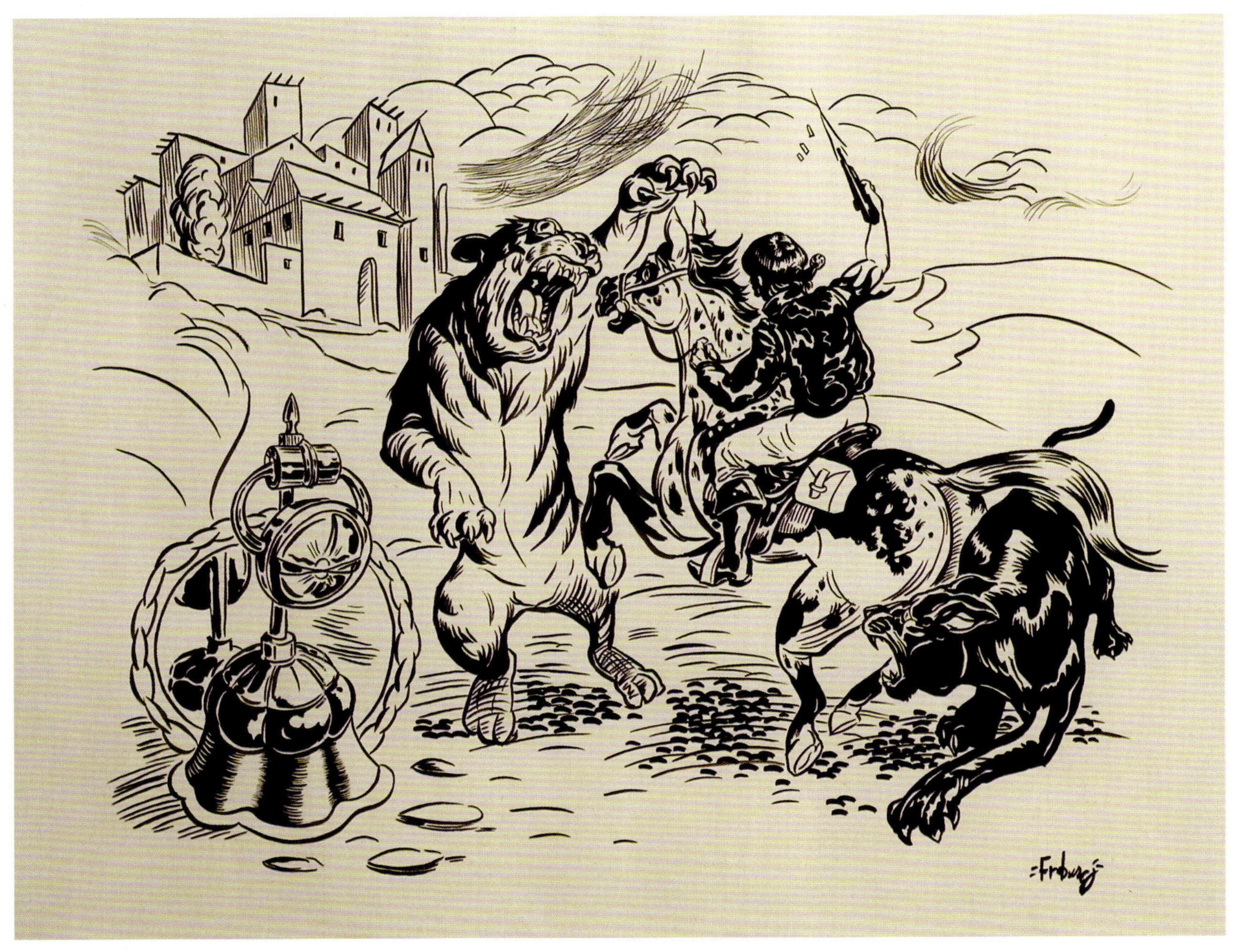

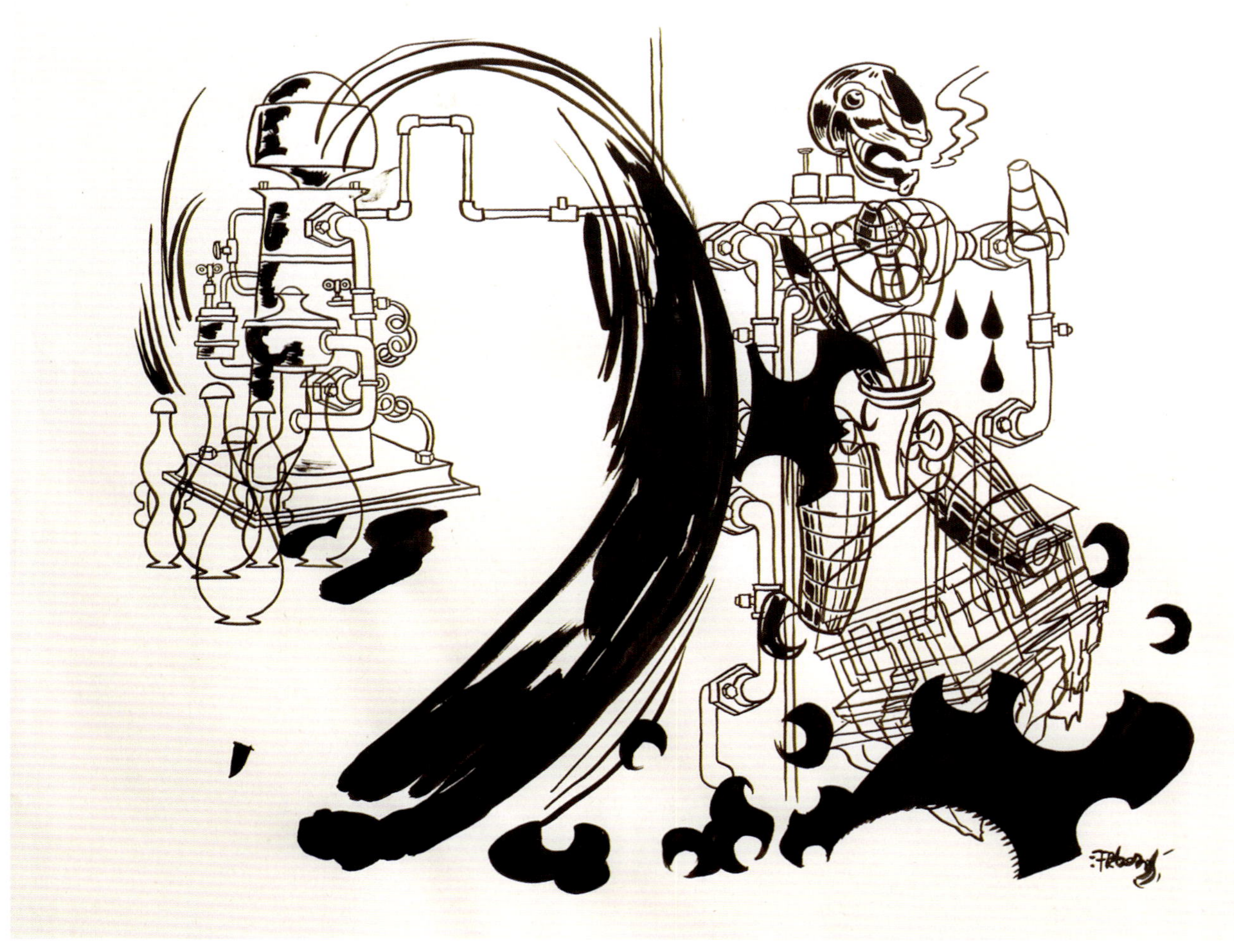

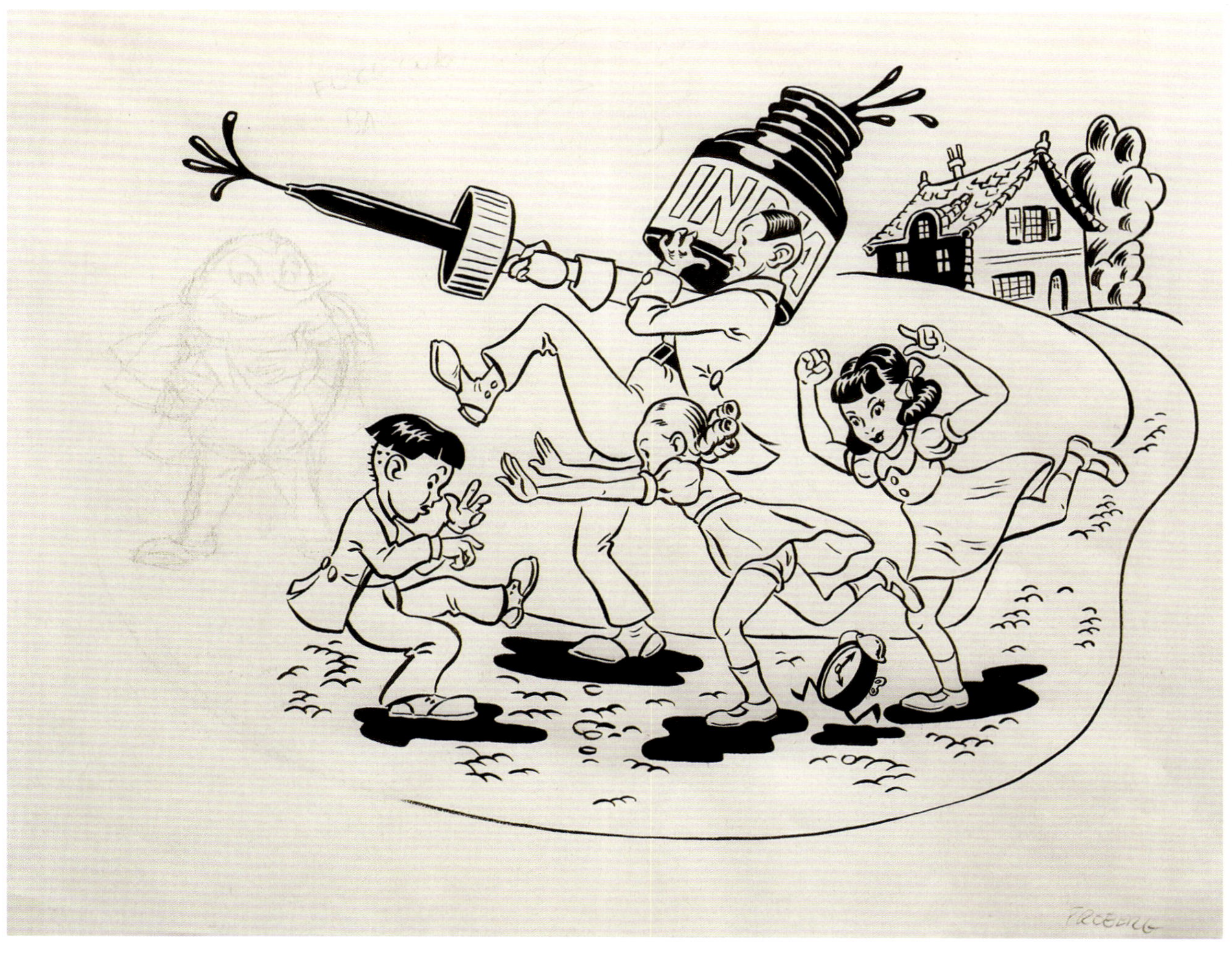

INDIA

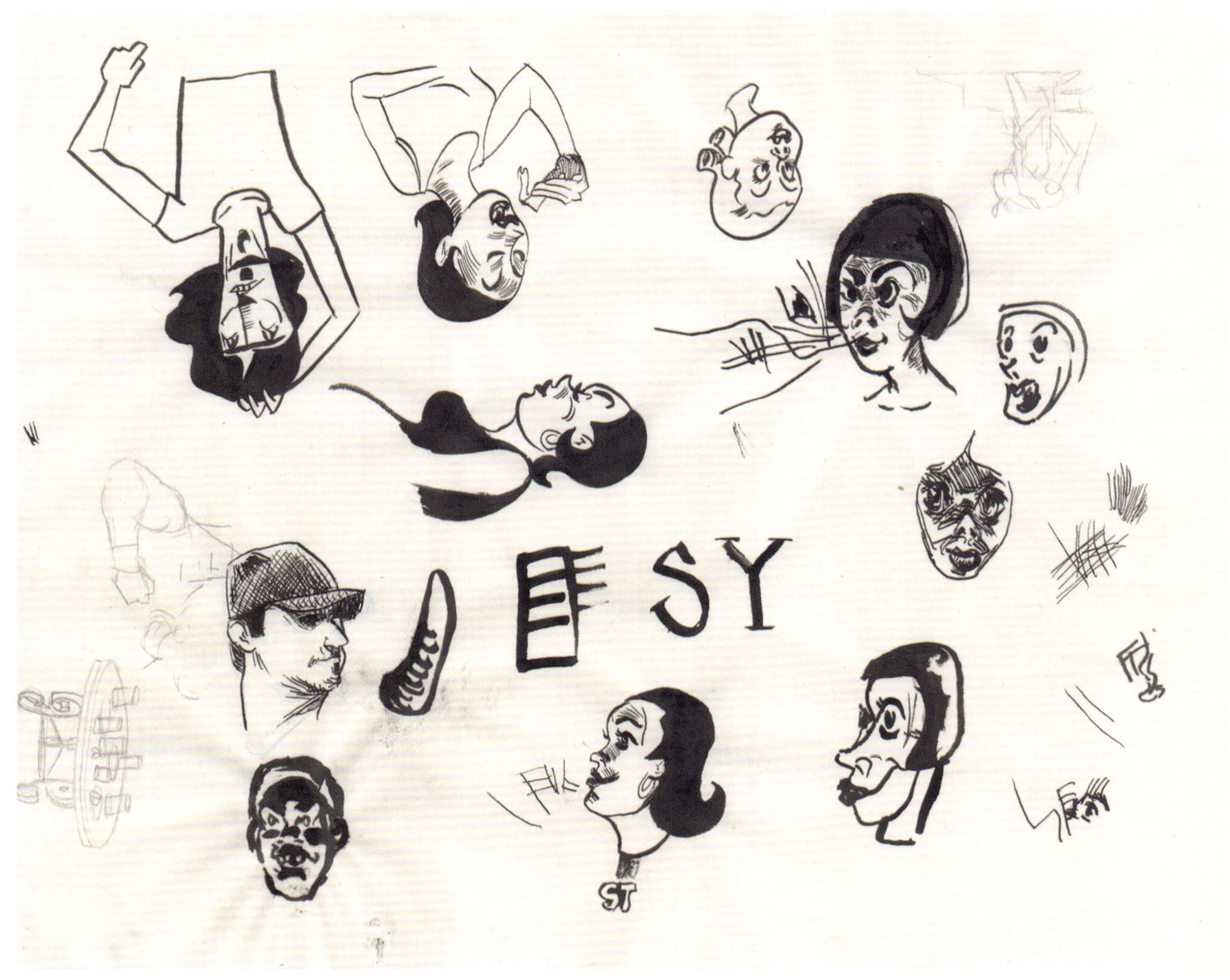

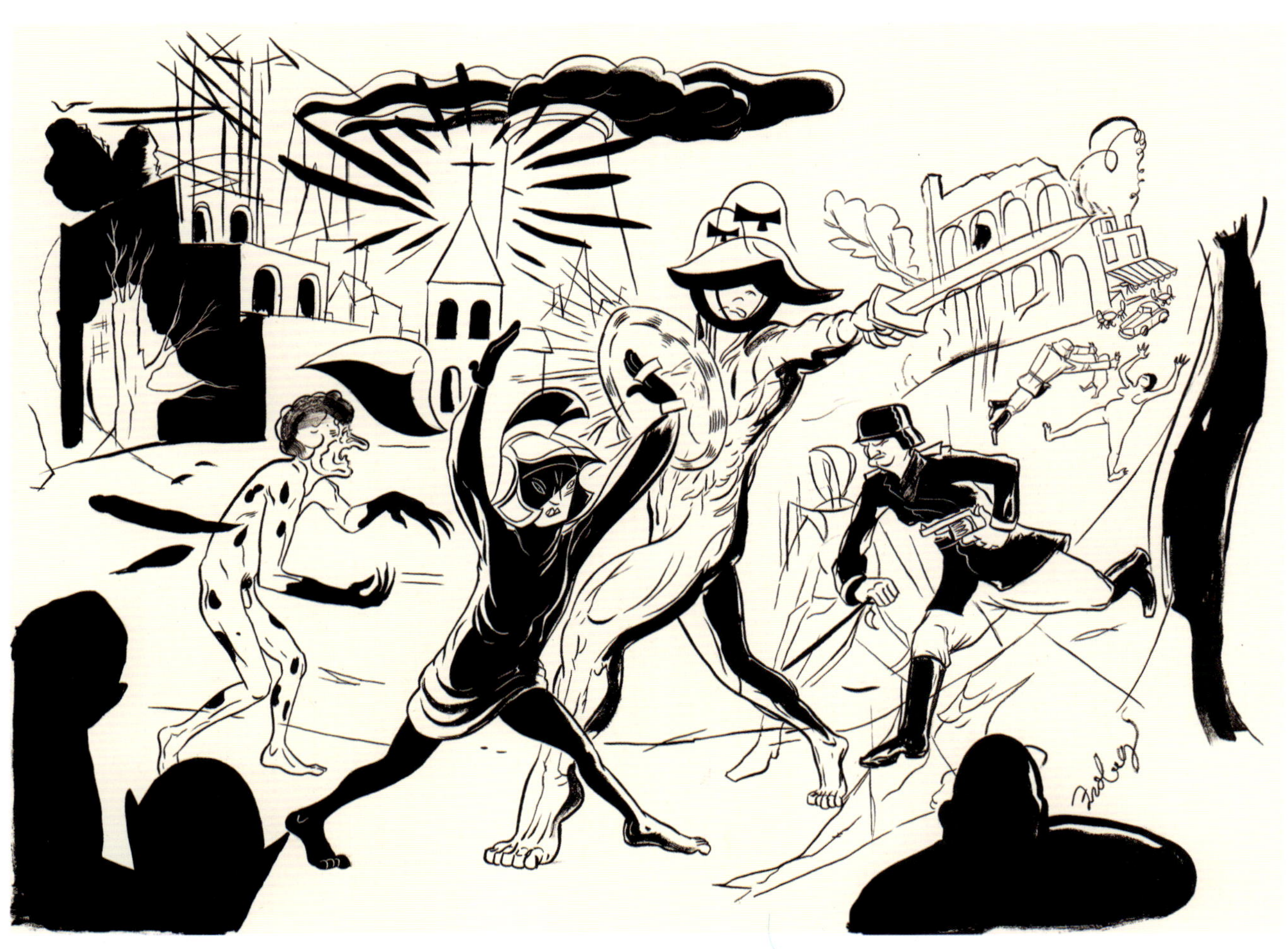

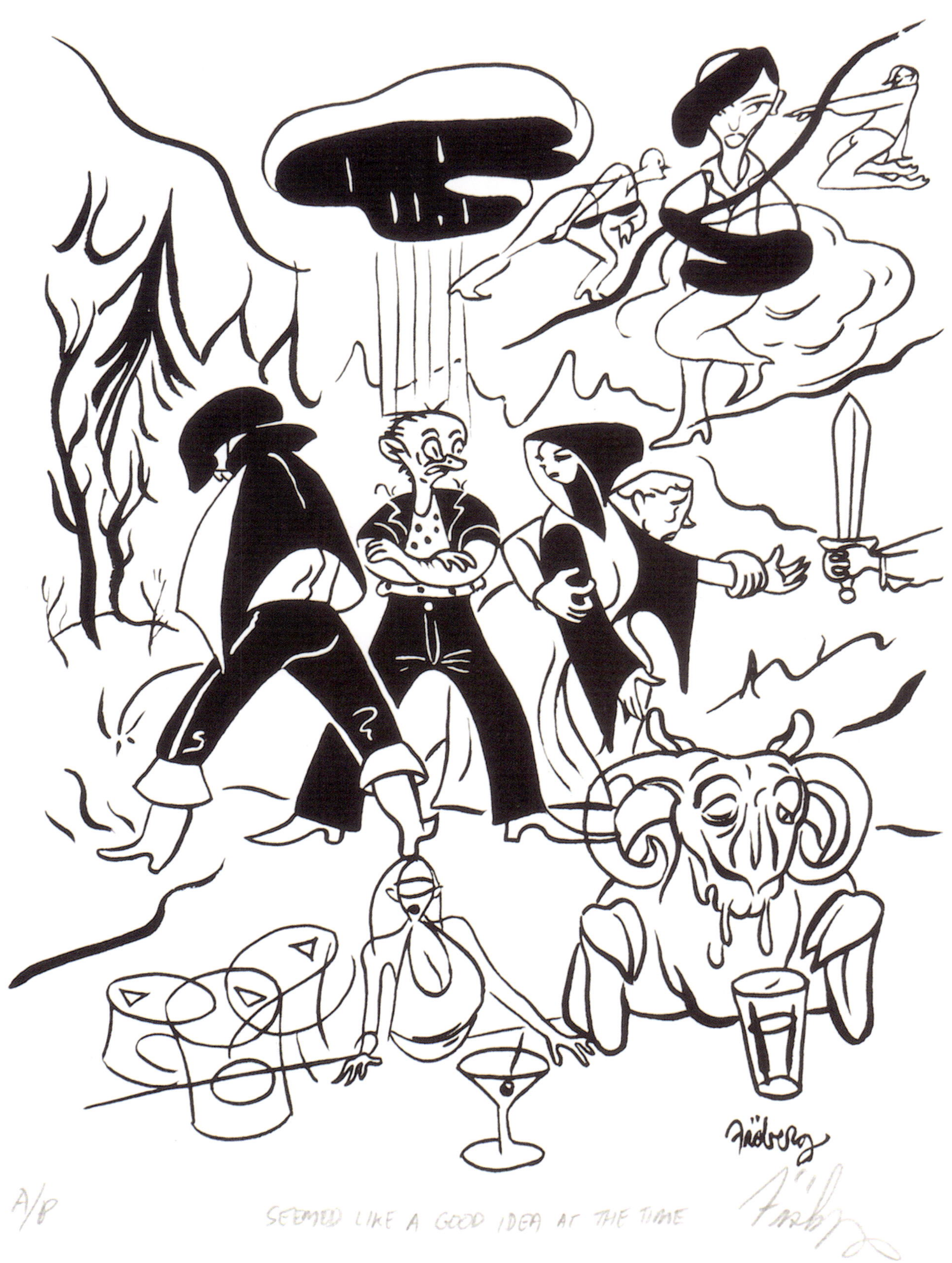

A/P   SEEMED LIKE A GOOD IDEA AT THE TIME

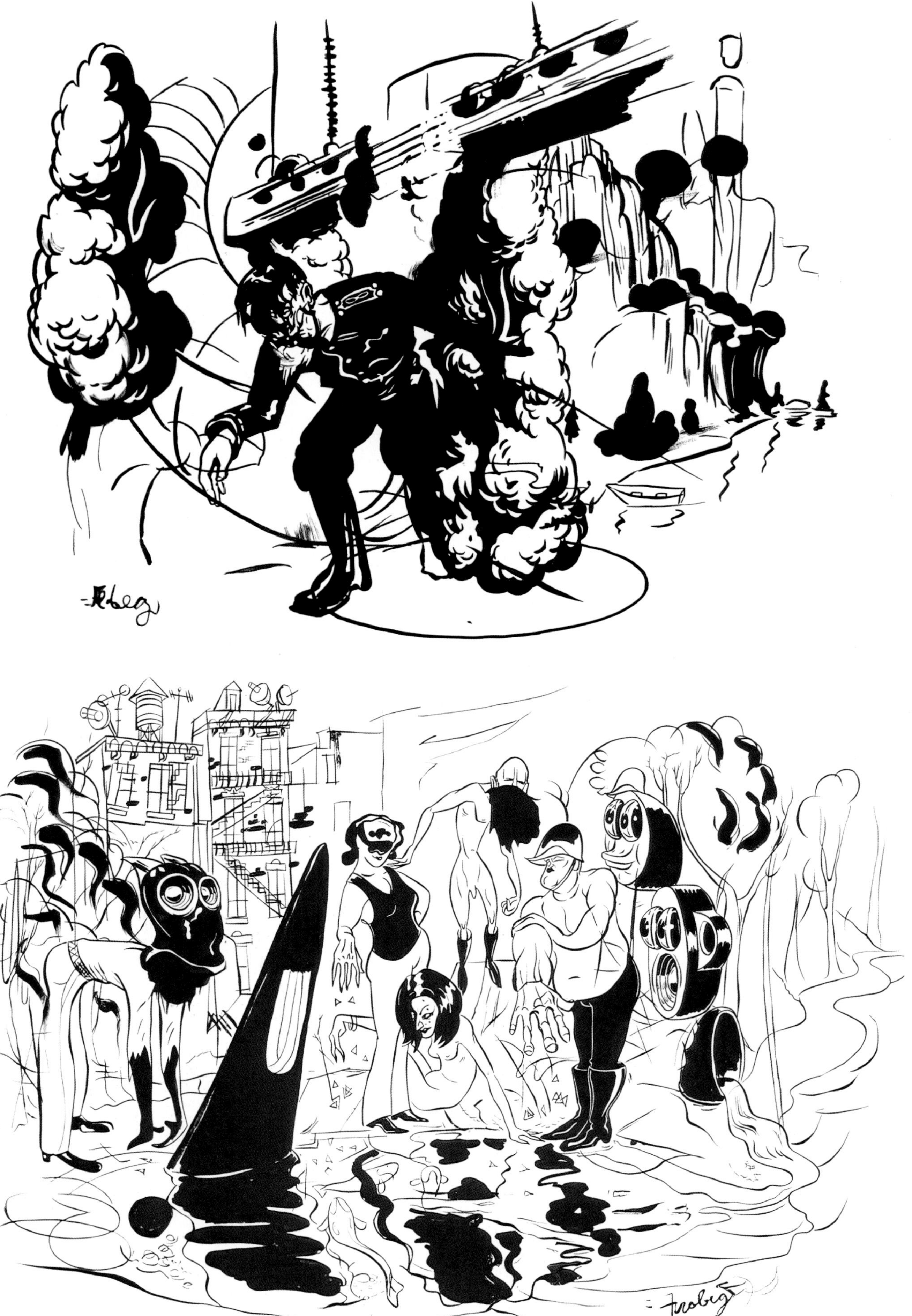

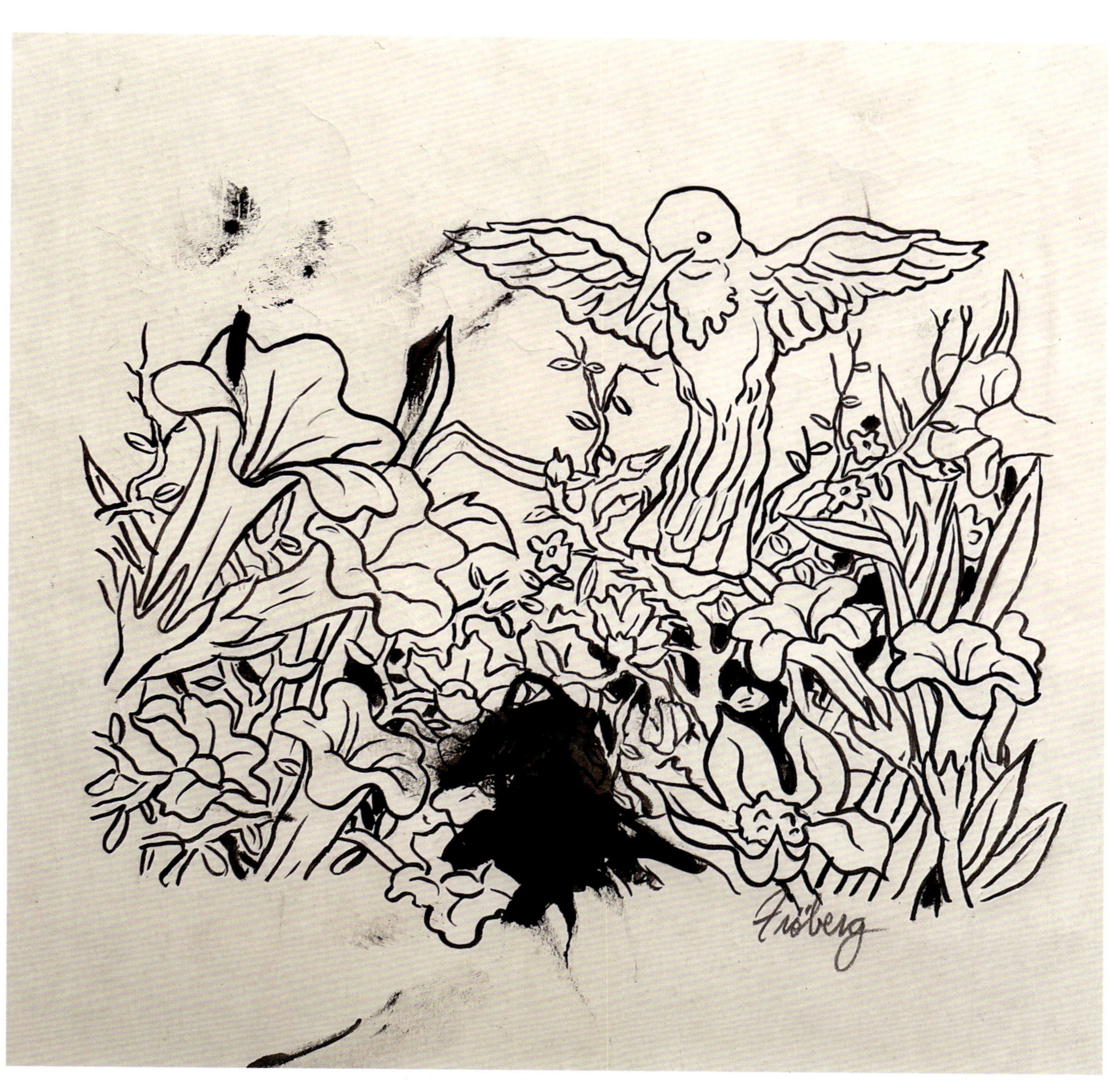

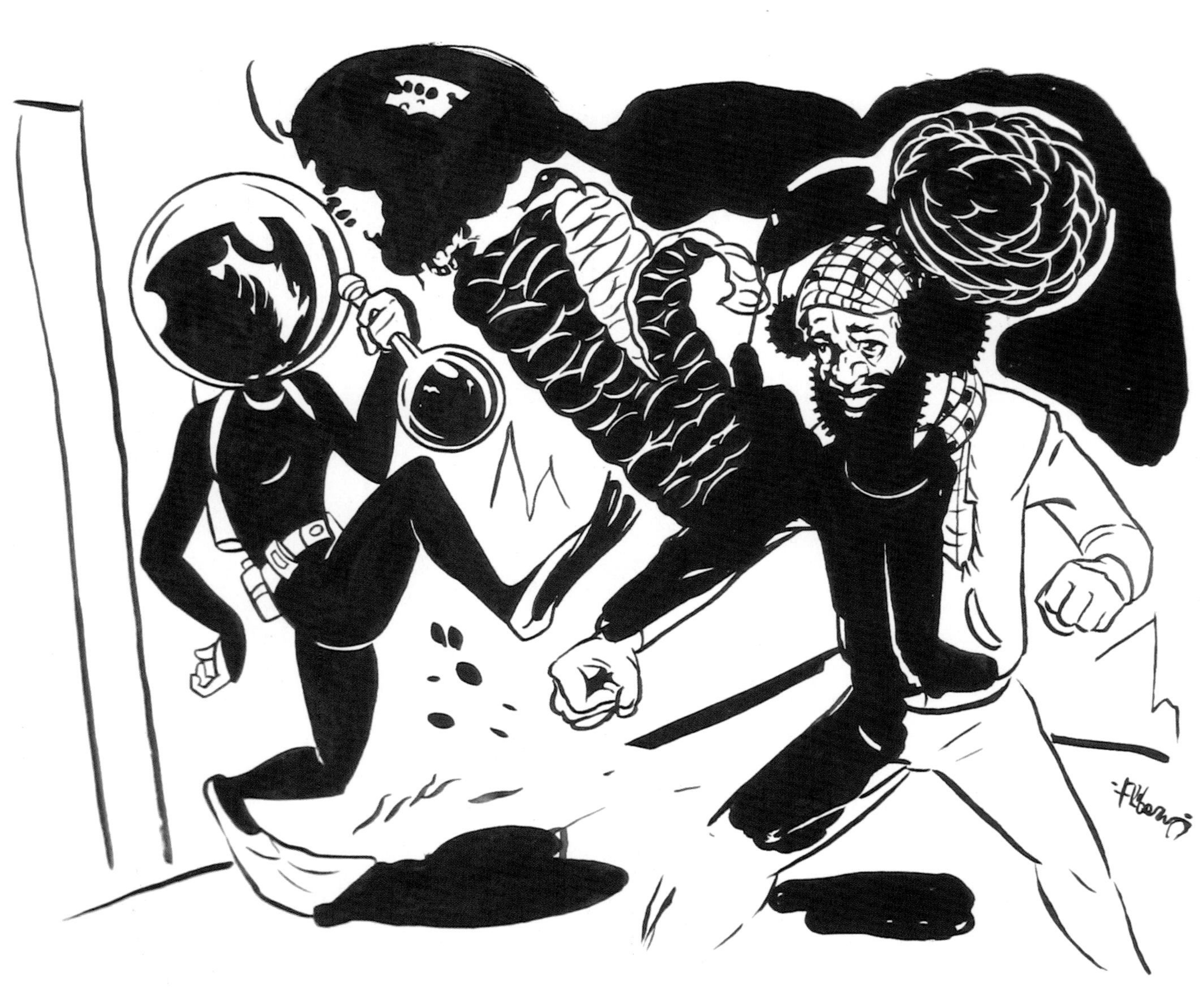

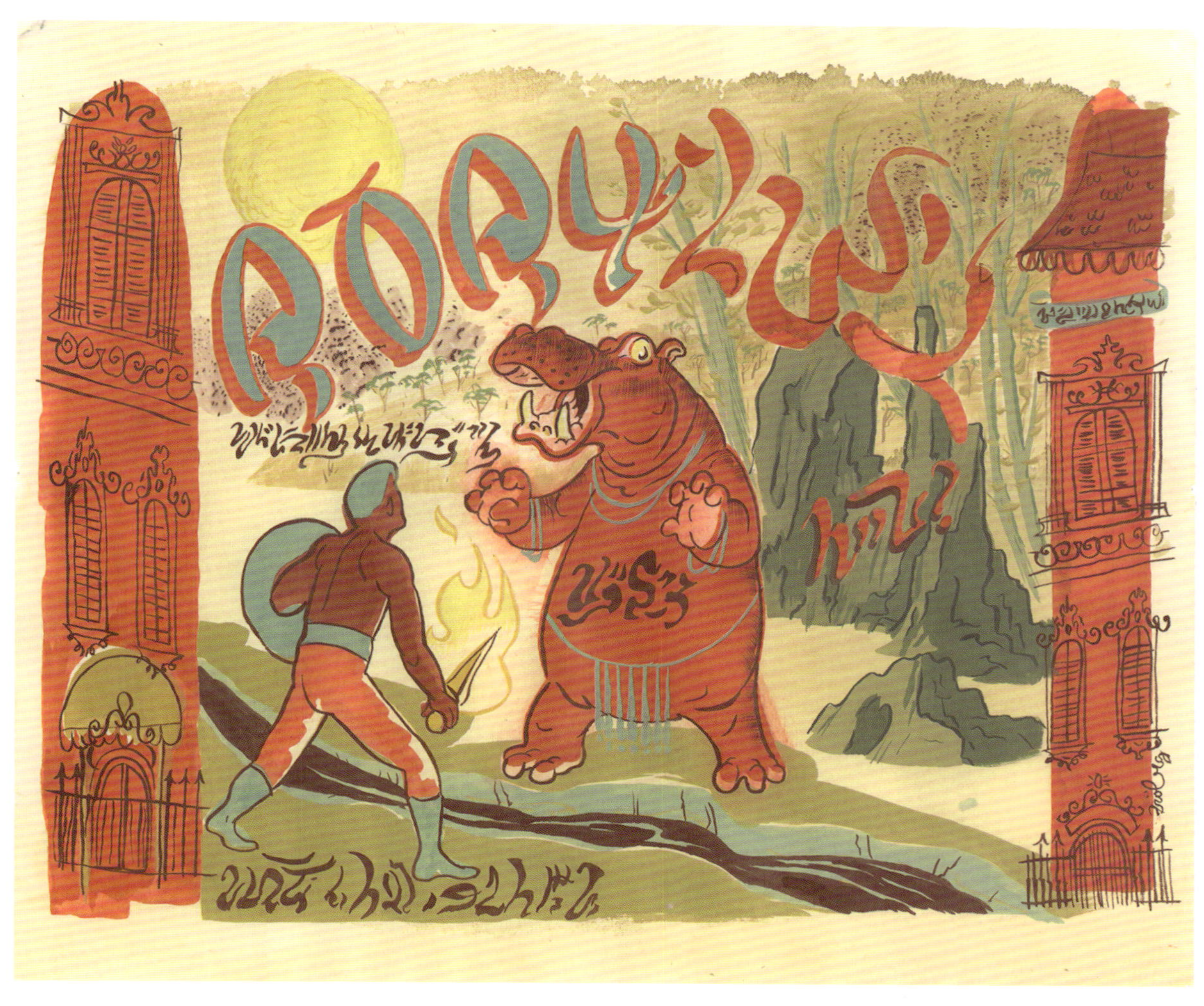

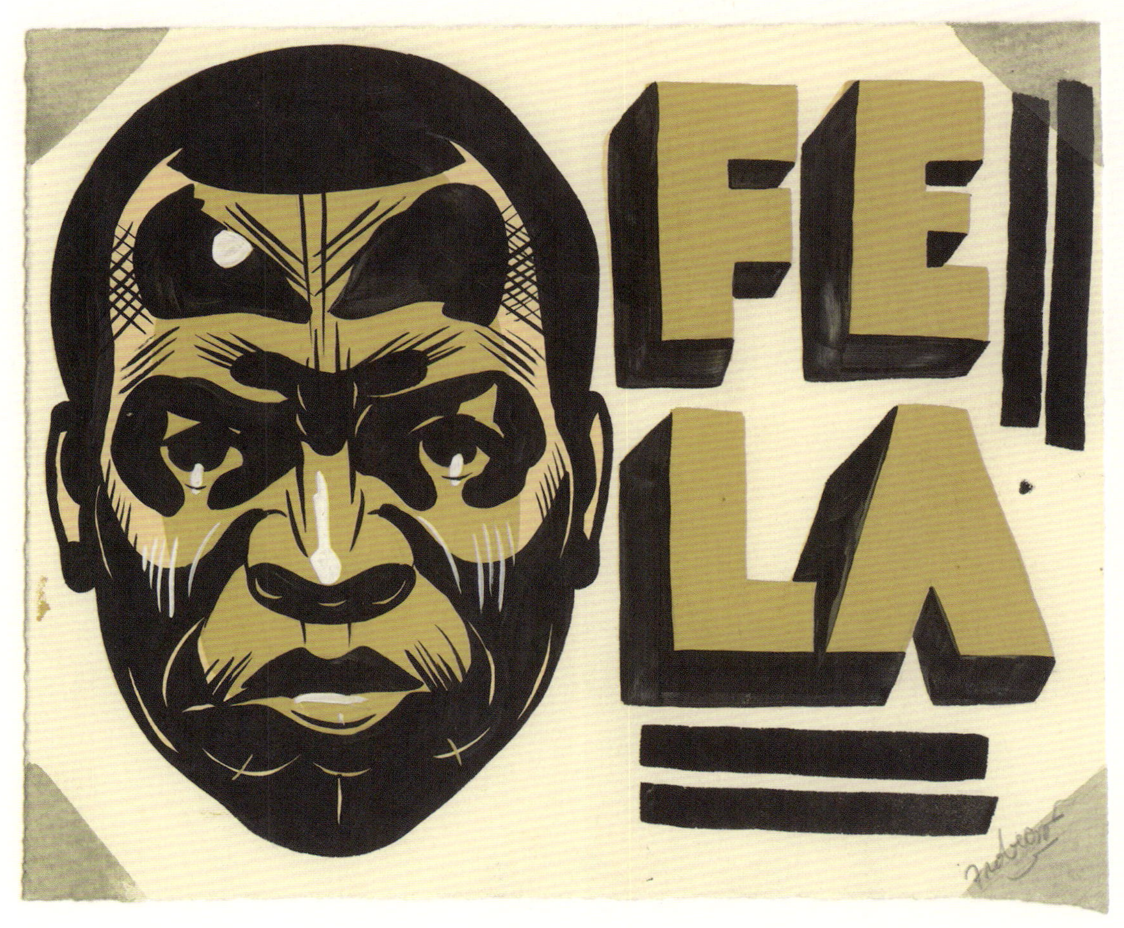
FE
LA

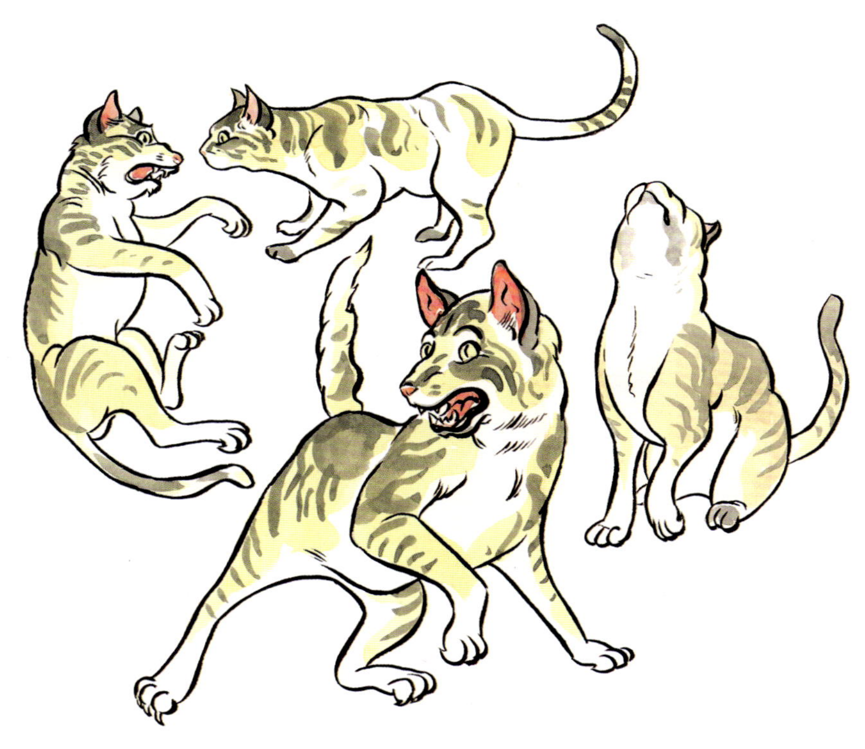

Cat That attacks mine   FROBERG

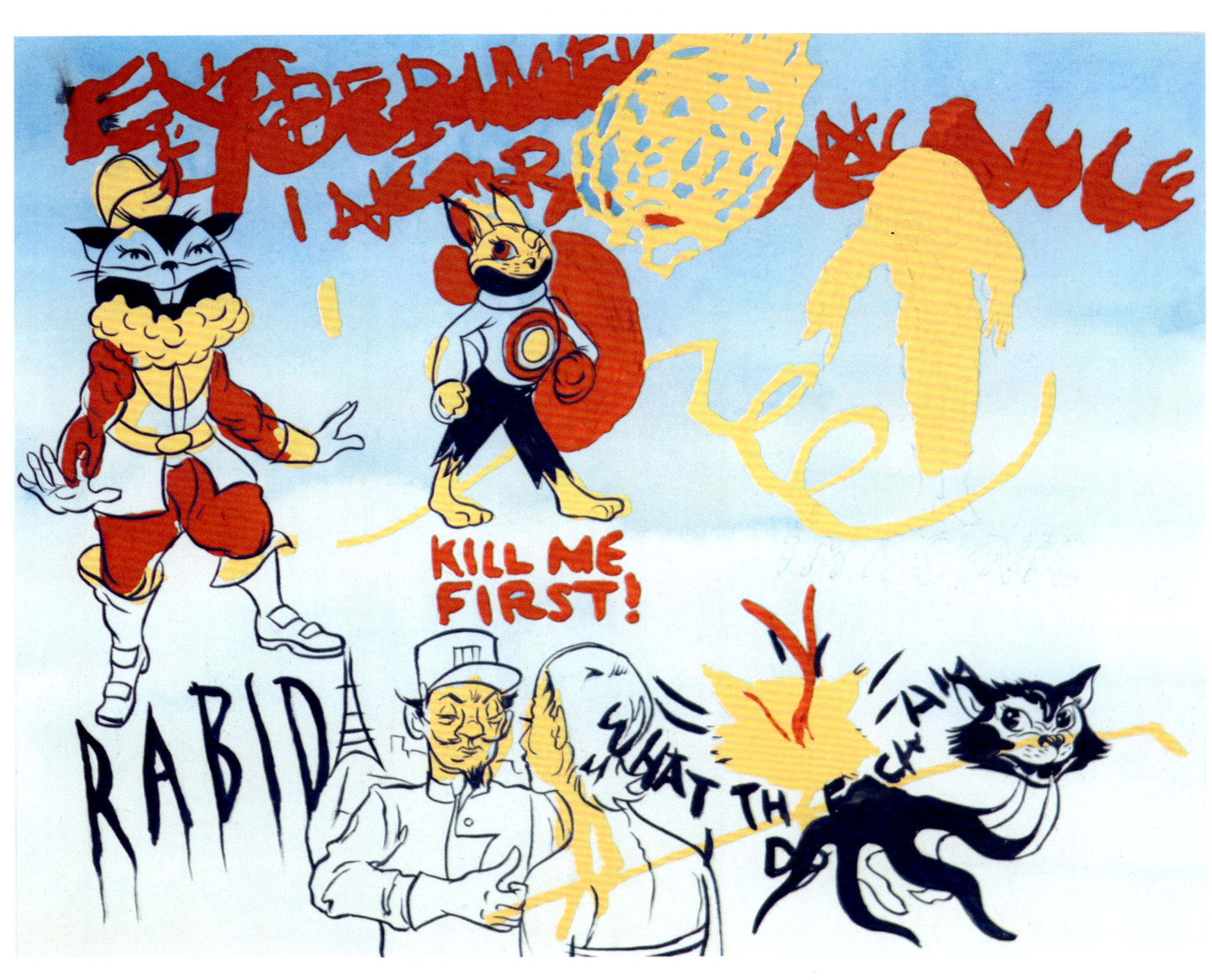

CLUBBED · SEAL
ARABS RAVISHING
WHITE WOMEN (CAMEL LAUGHS)
JACK O'LANTERN
MAN
INK MAN

MIT
NSA
IIII

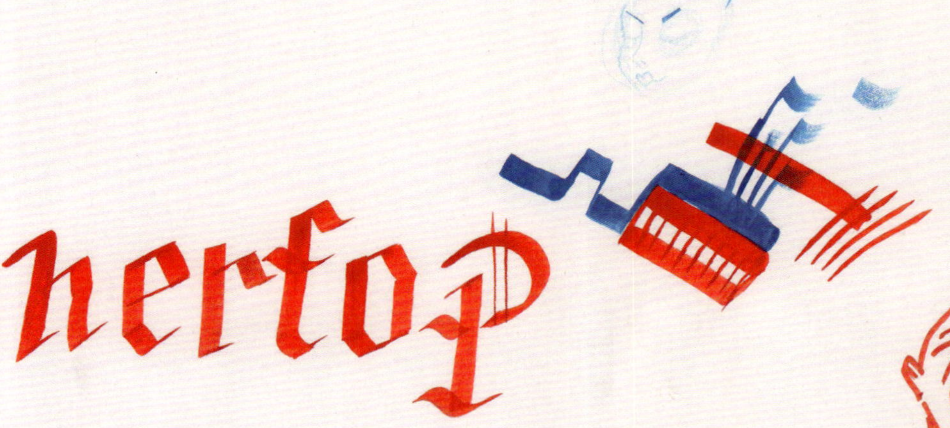
nerfop
Poop hole gang

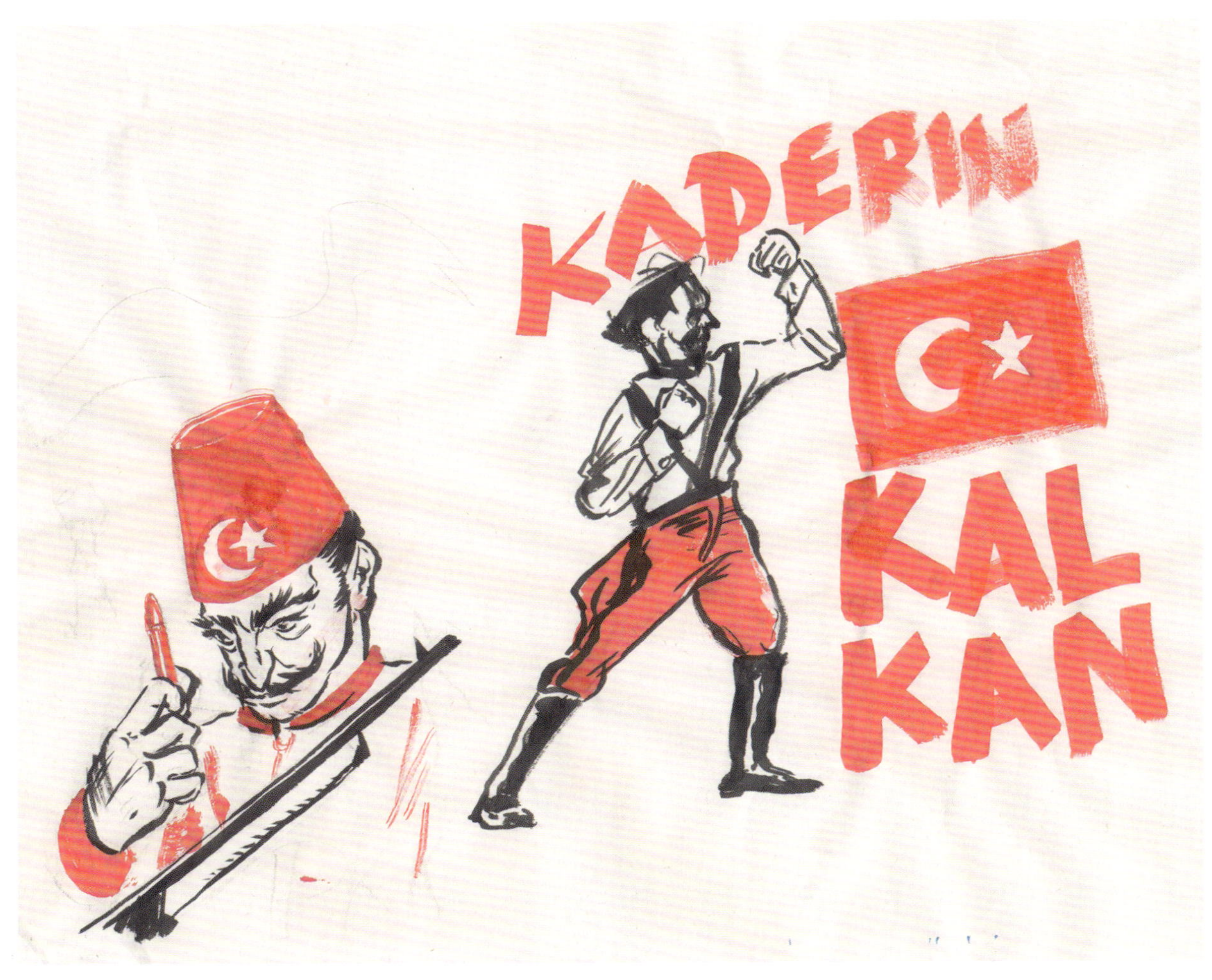
KAPERIN
KAL
KAN

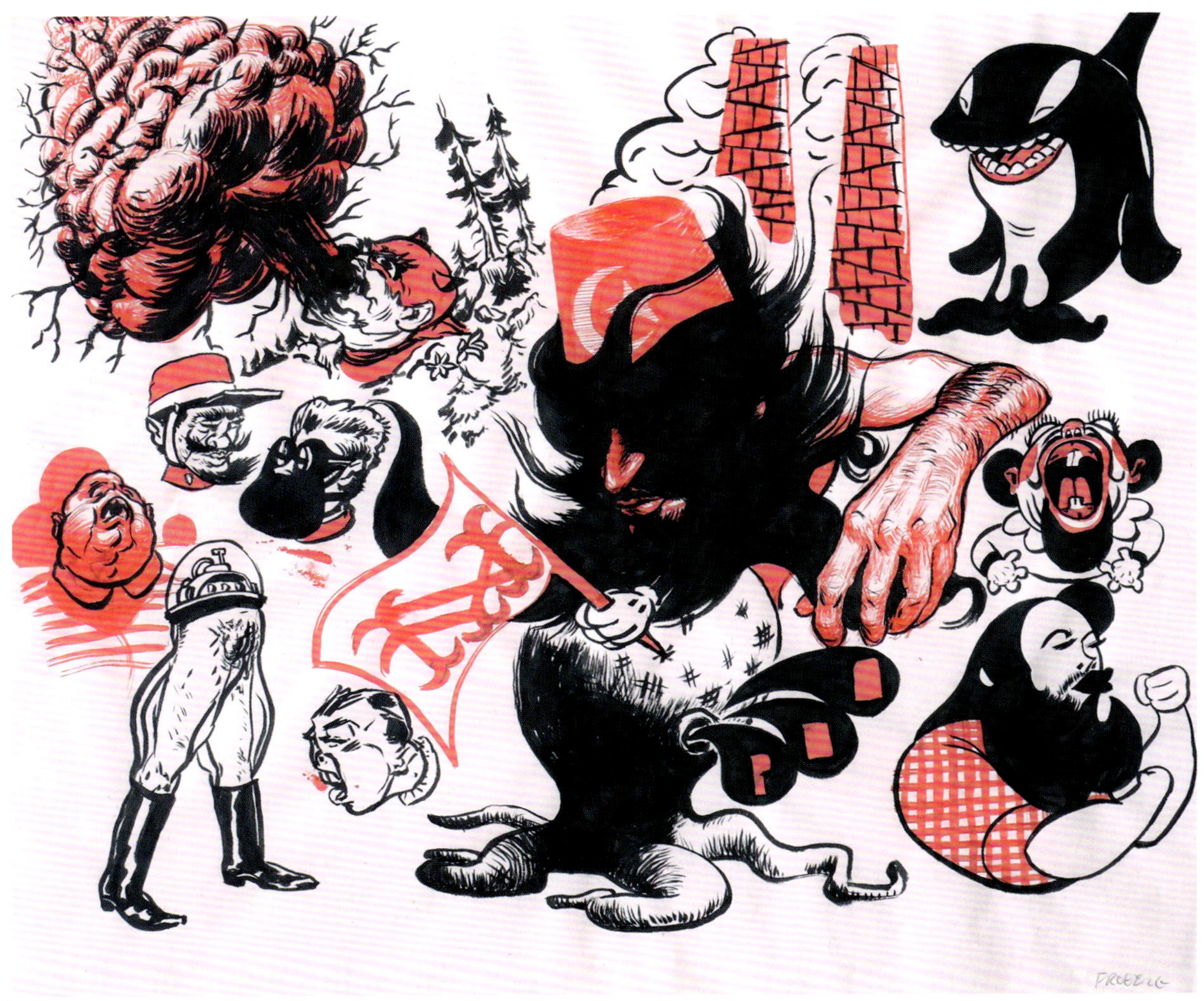
FREEDG

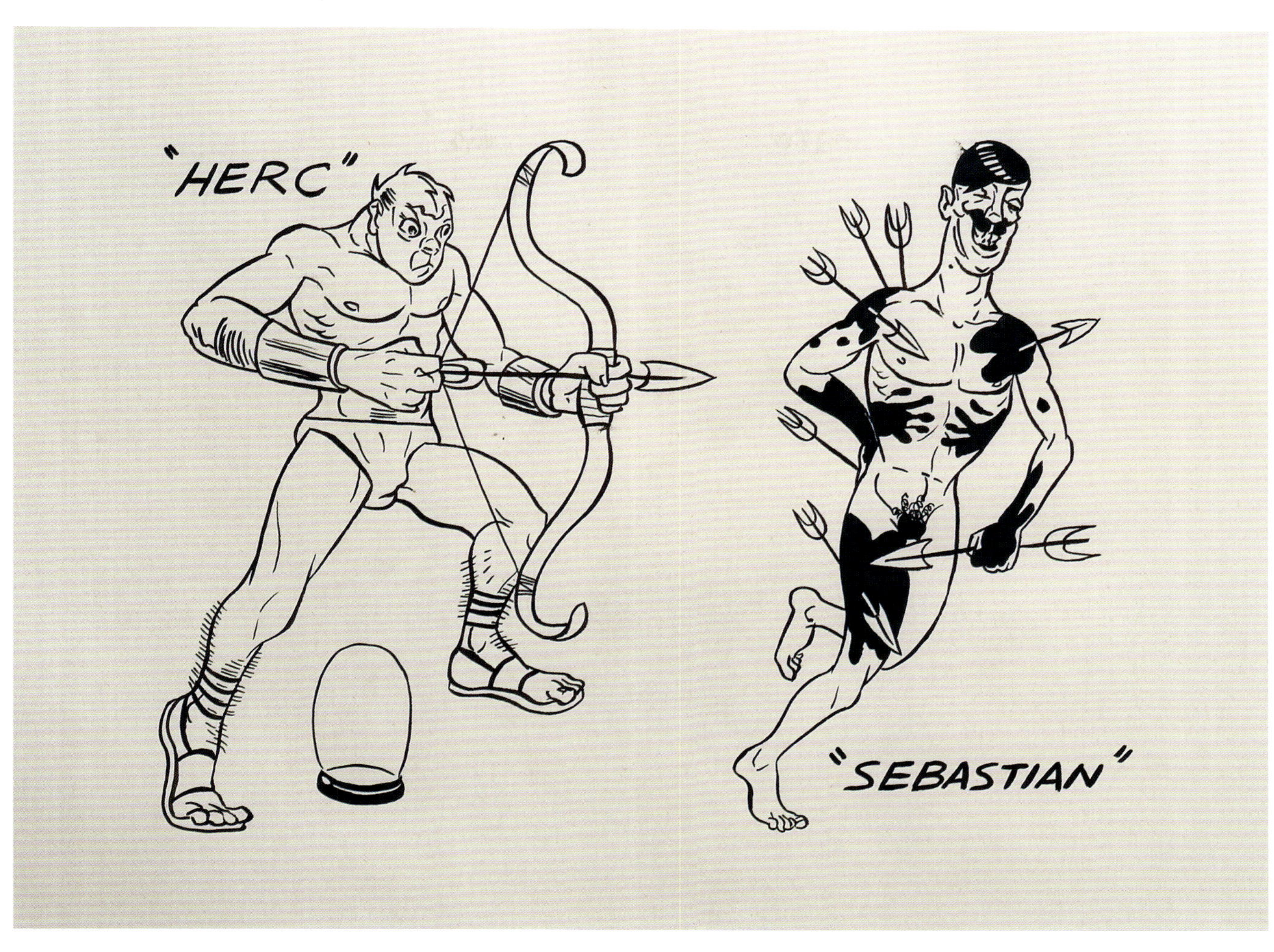

"HERC"
"SEBASTIAN"

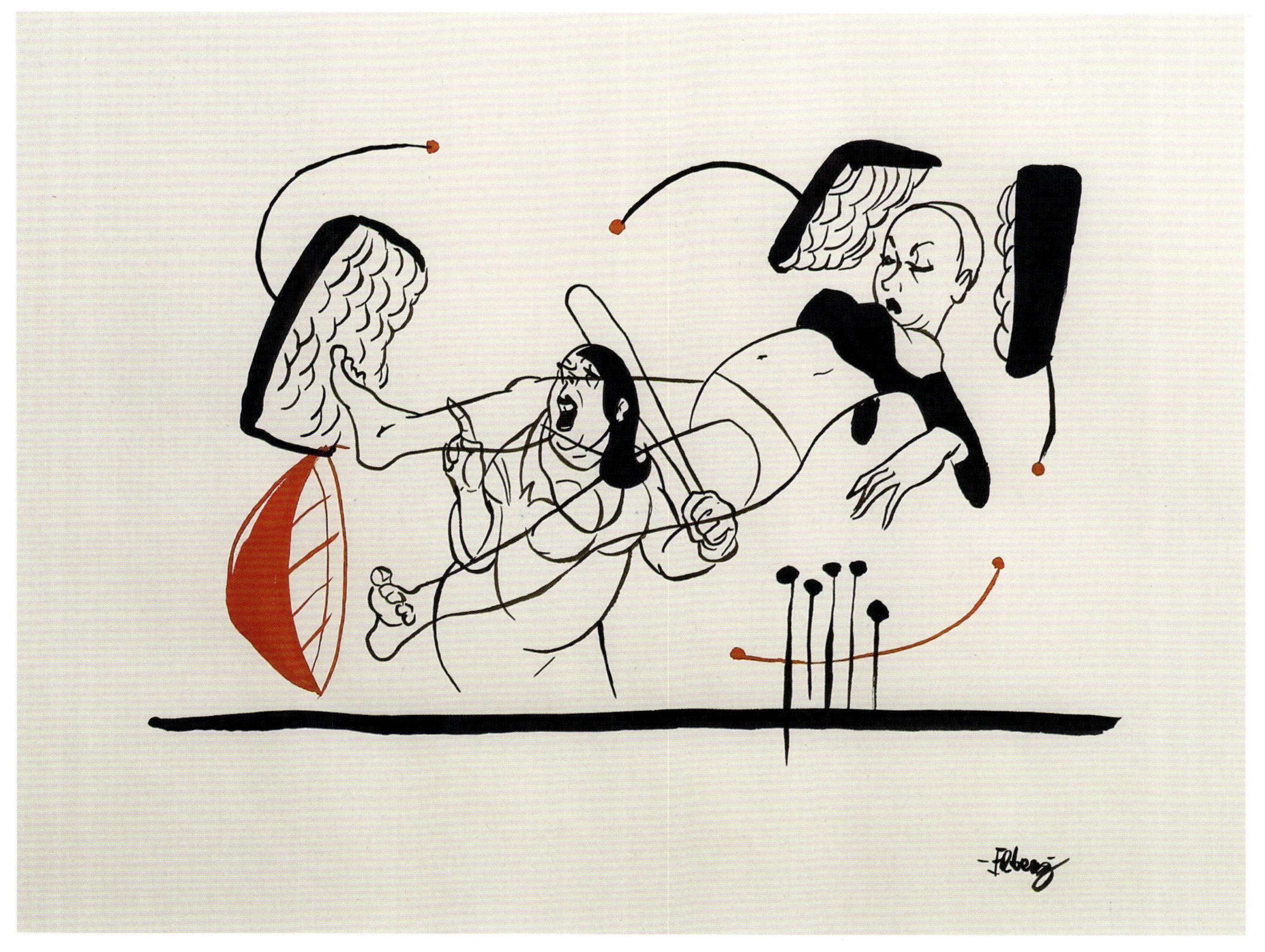

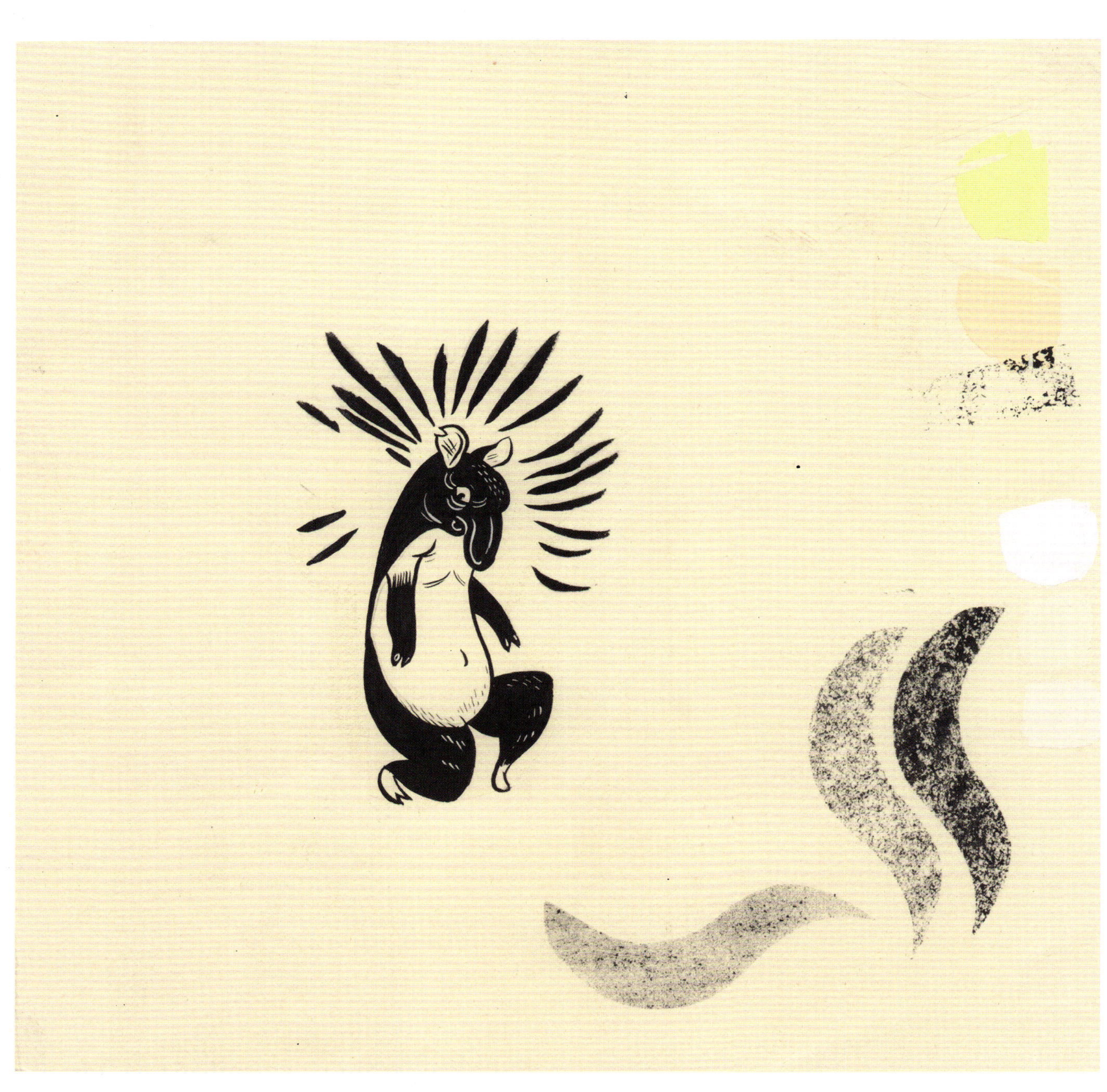

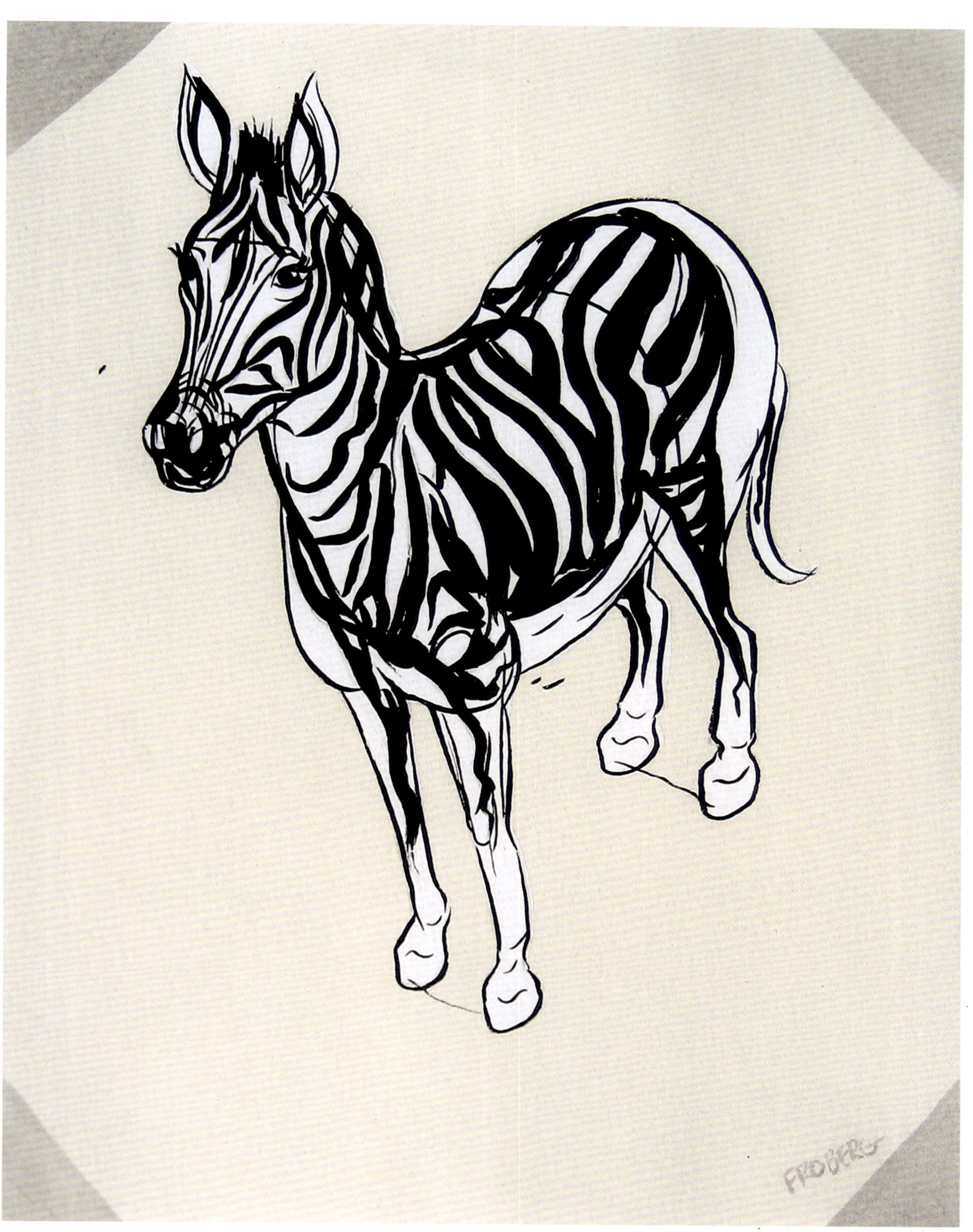

FROBERG

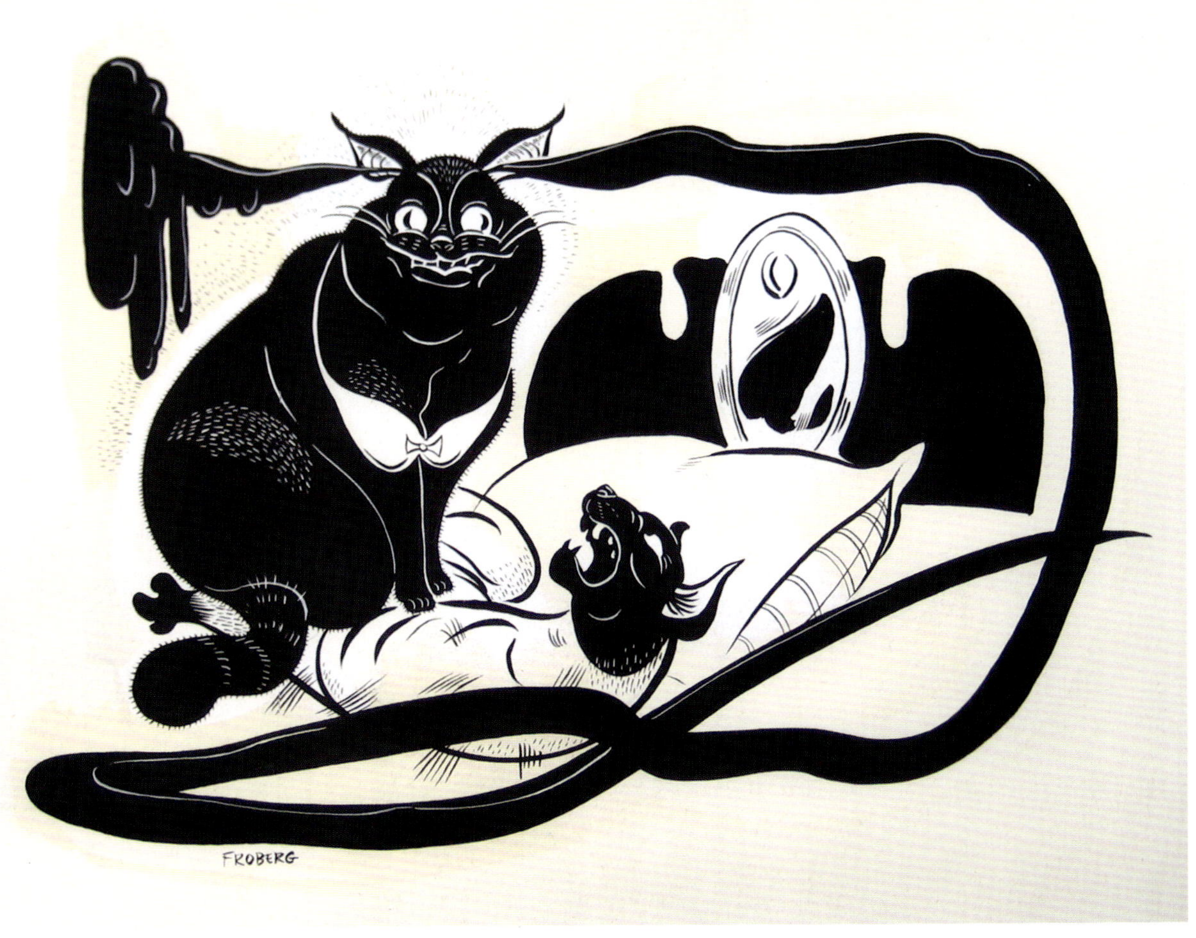
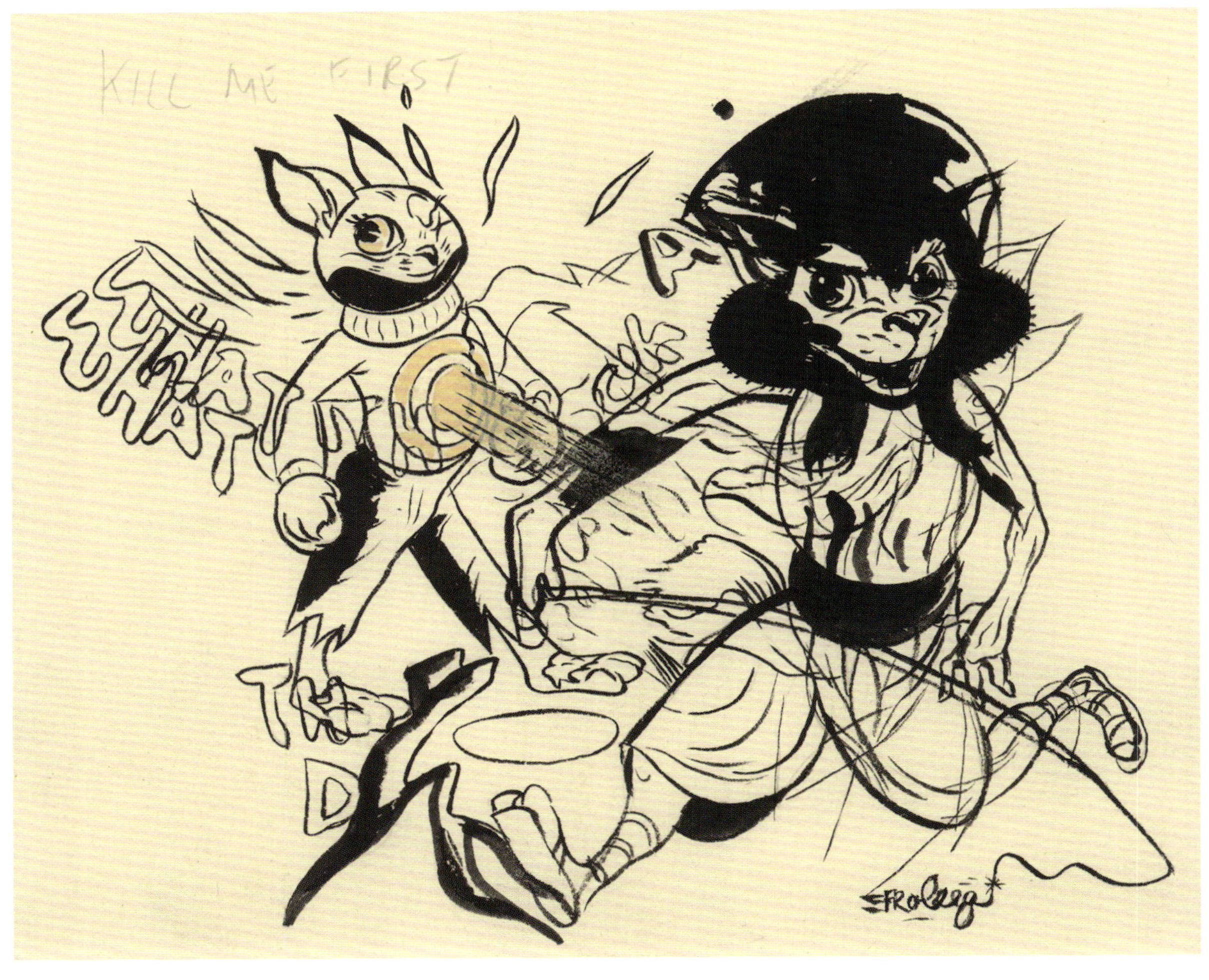
KILL ME FIRST

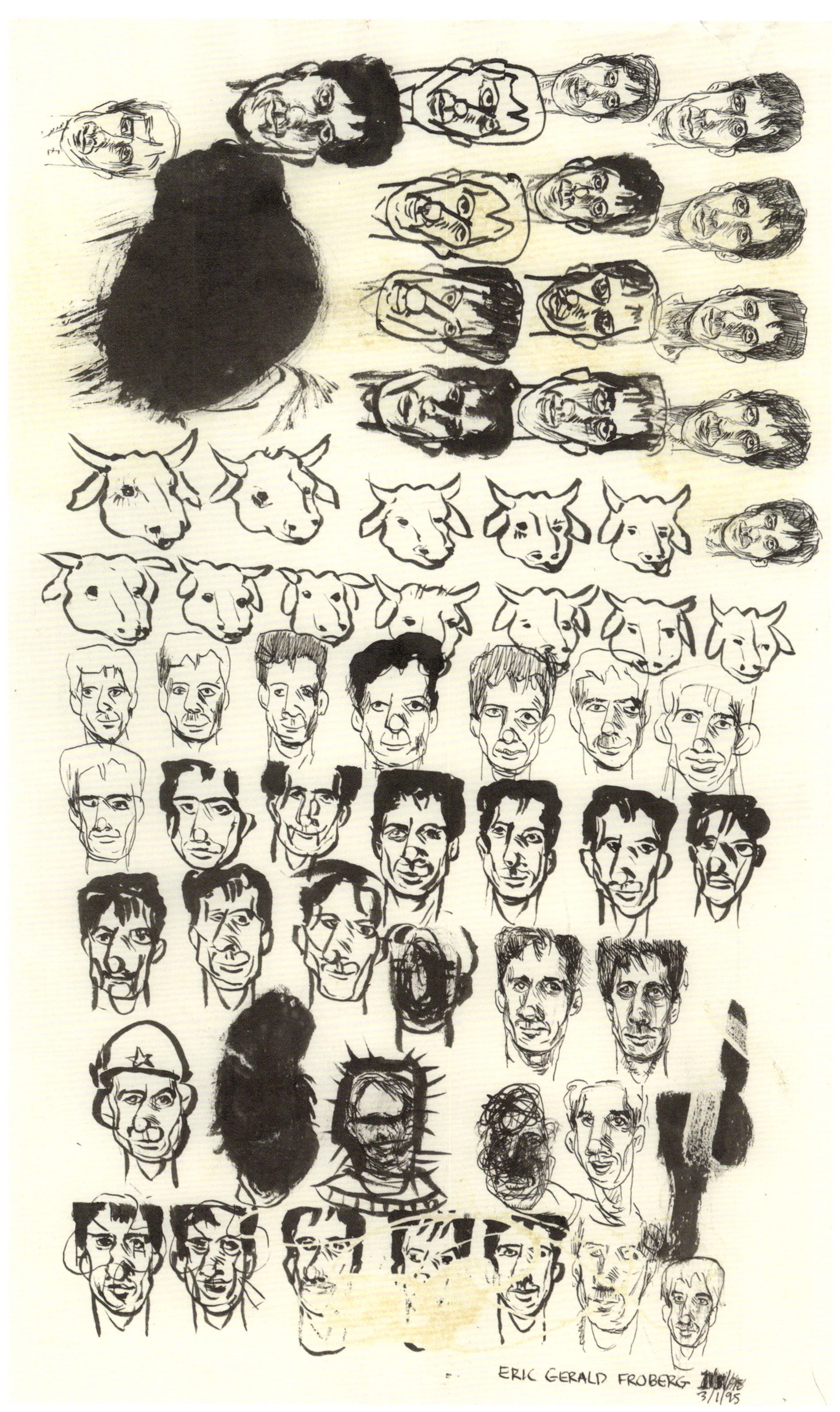

ERIC GERALD FROBERG
3/1/95

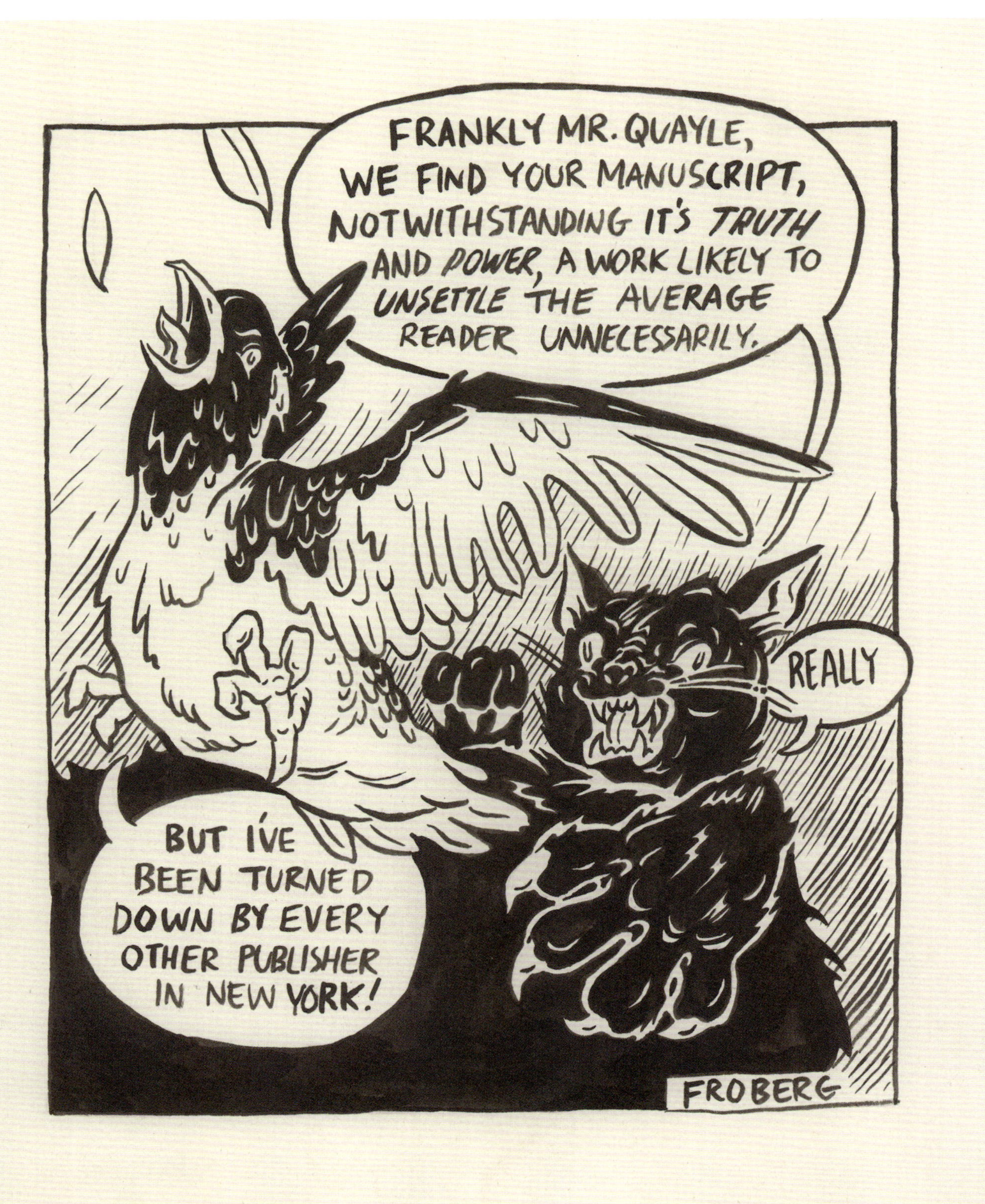

FRANKLY MR. QUAYLE, WE FIND YOUR MANUSCRIPT, NOTWITHSTANDING IT'S TRUTH AND POWER, A WORK LIKELY TO UNSETTLE THE AVERAGE READER UNNECESSARILY.
REALLY
BUT I'VE BEEN TURNED DOWN BY EVERY OTHER PUBLISHER IN NEW YORK!
FROBERG

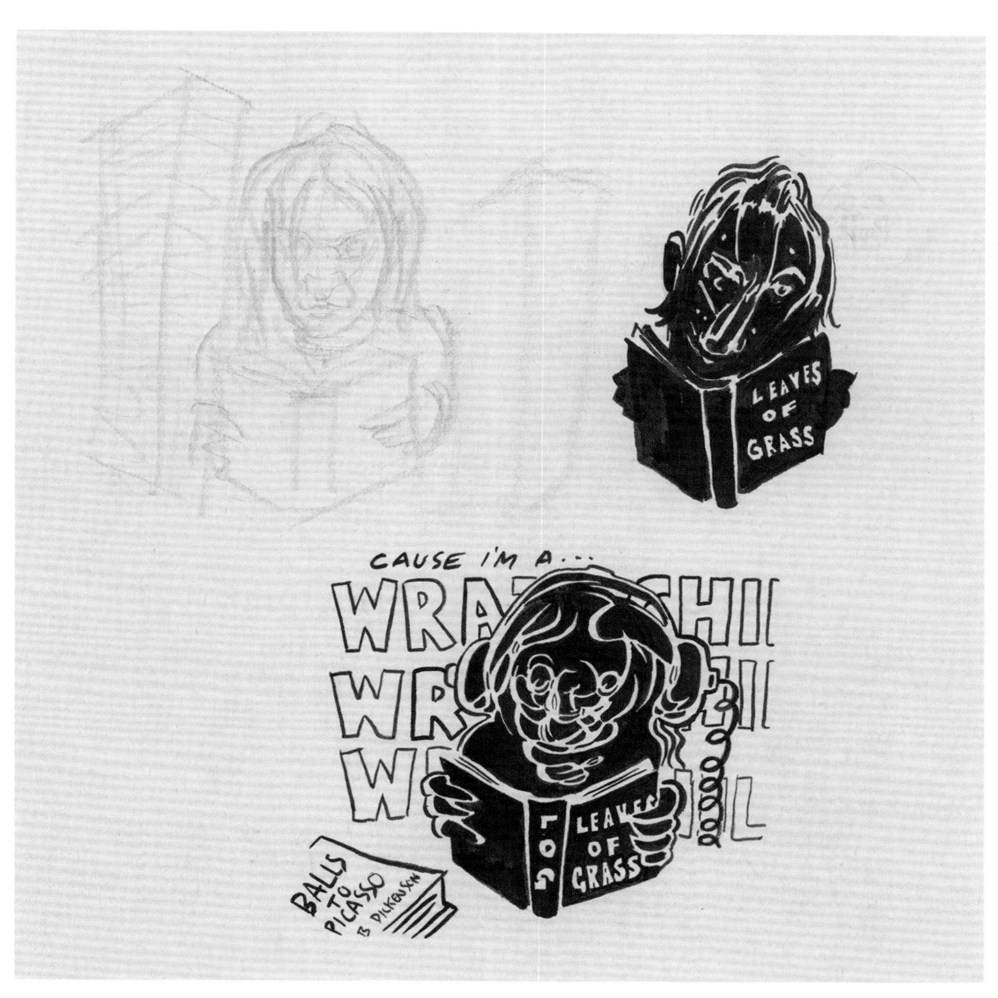

LEAVES OF GRASS
CAUSE I'M A...
WRAAACHII
WRAAACHII
WRAAACHII
LOG
LEAVES OF GRASS
BALLS TO PICASSO
B. DICKINSON

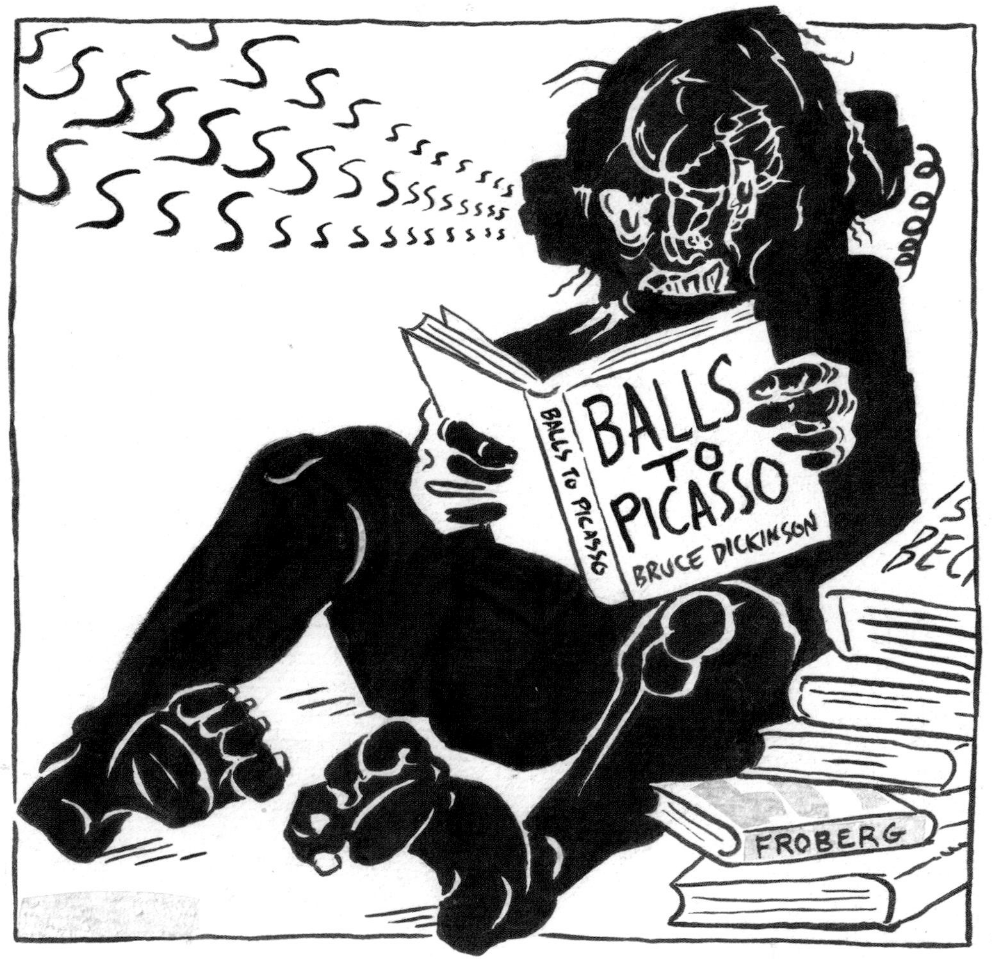

SSSSSSSSSSS
BALLS TO PICASSO
BALLS TO PICASSO
BRUCE DICKINSON
IS BEC
FROBERG

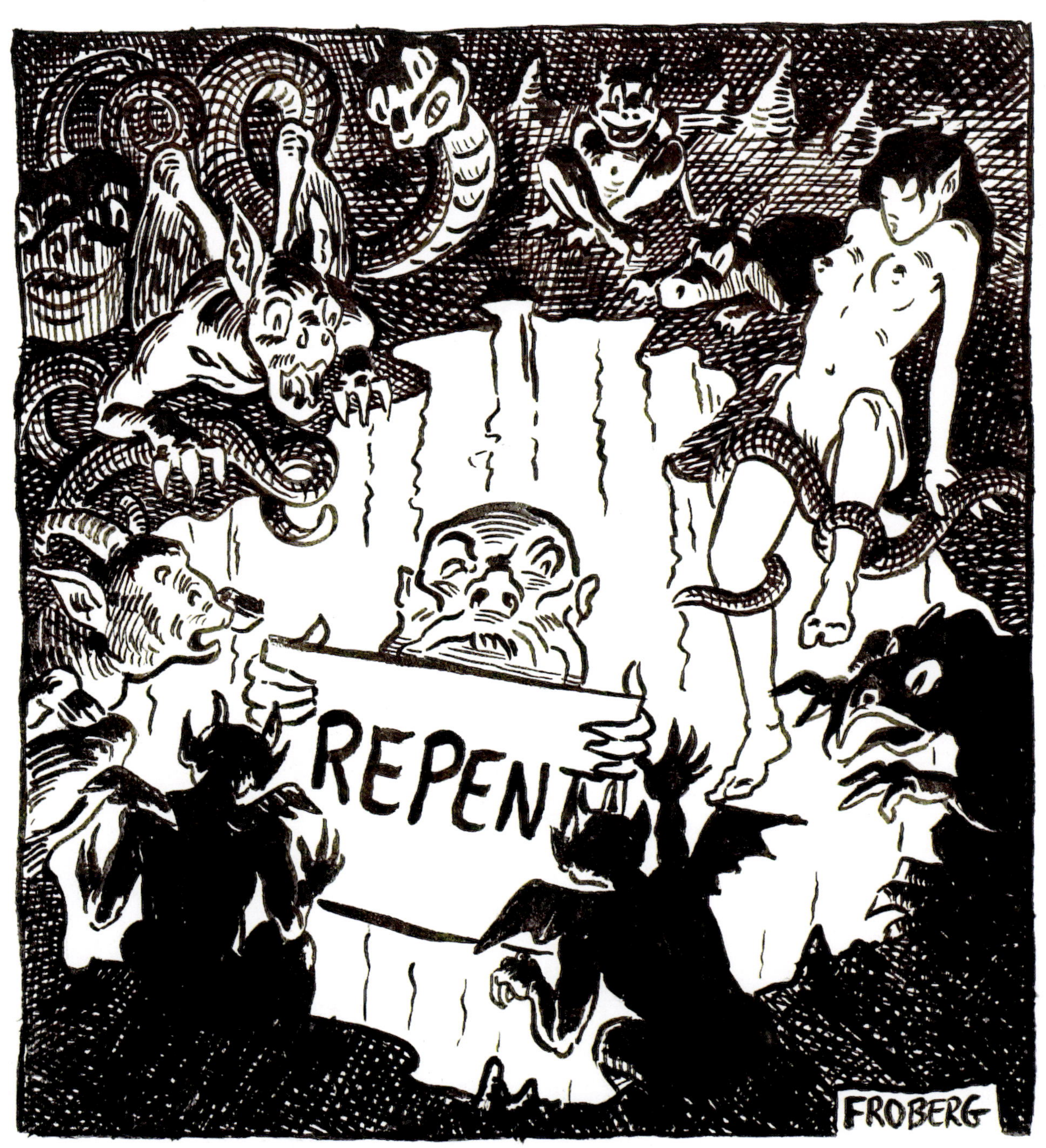

REPENT
FROBERG

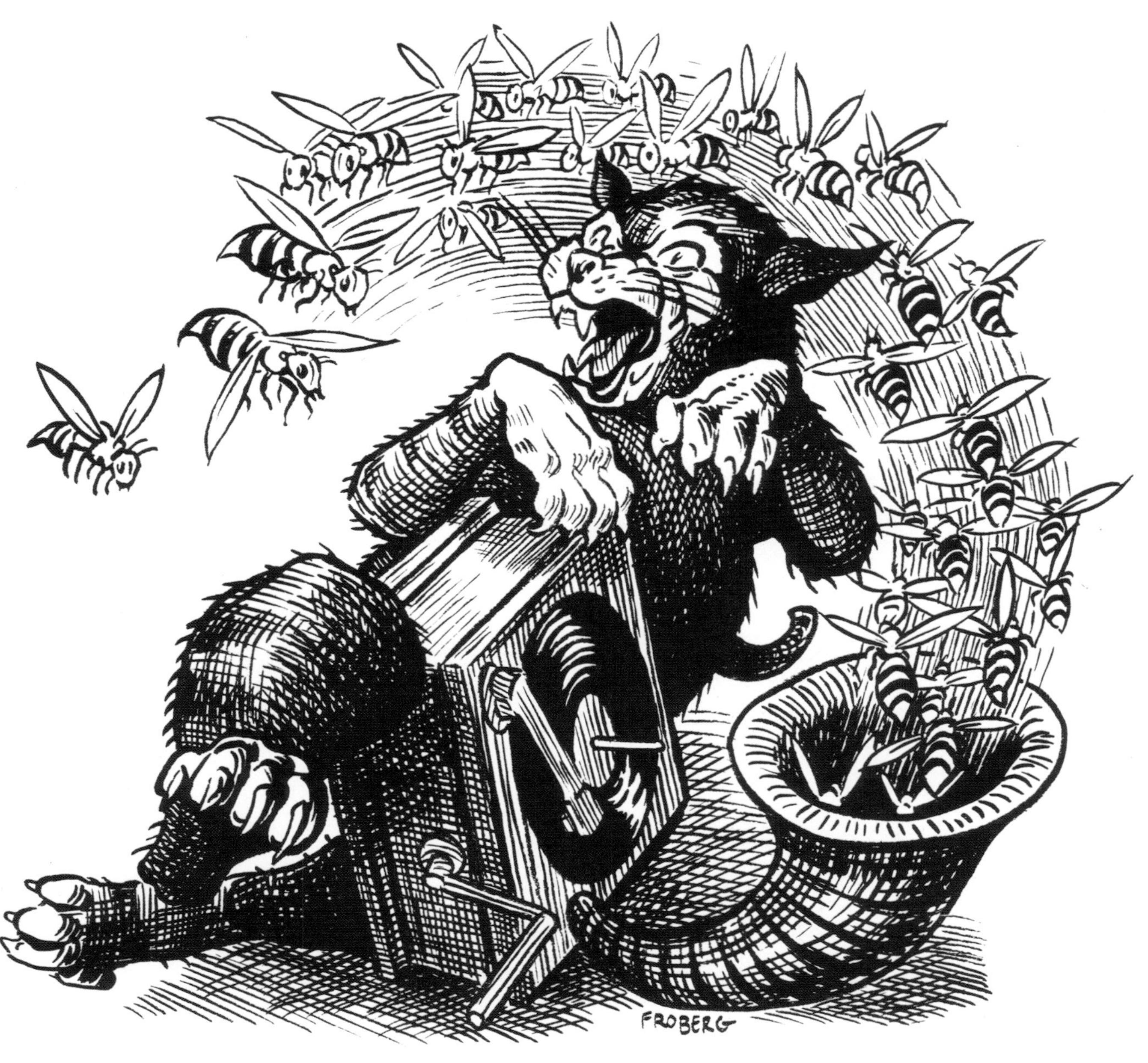

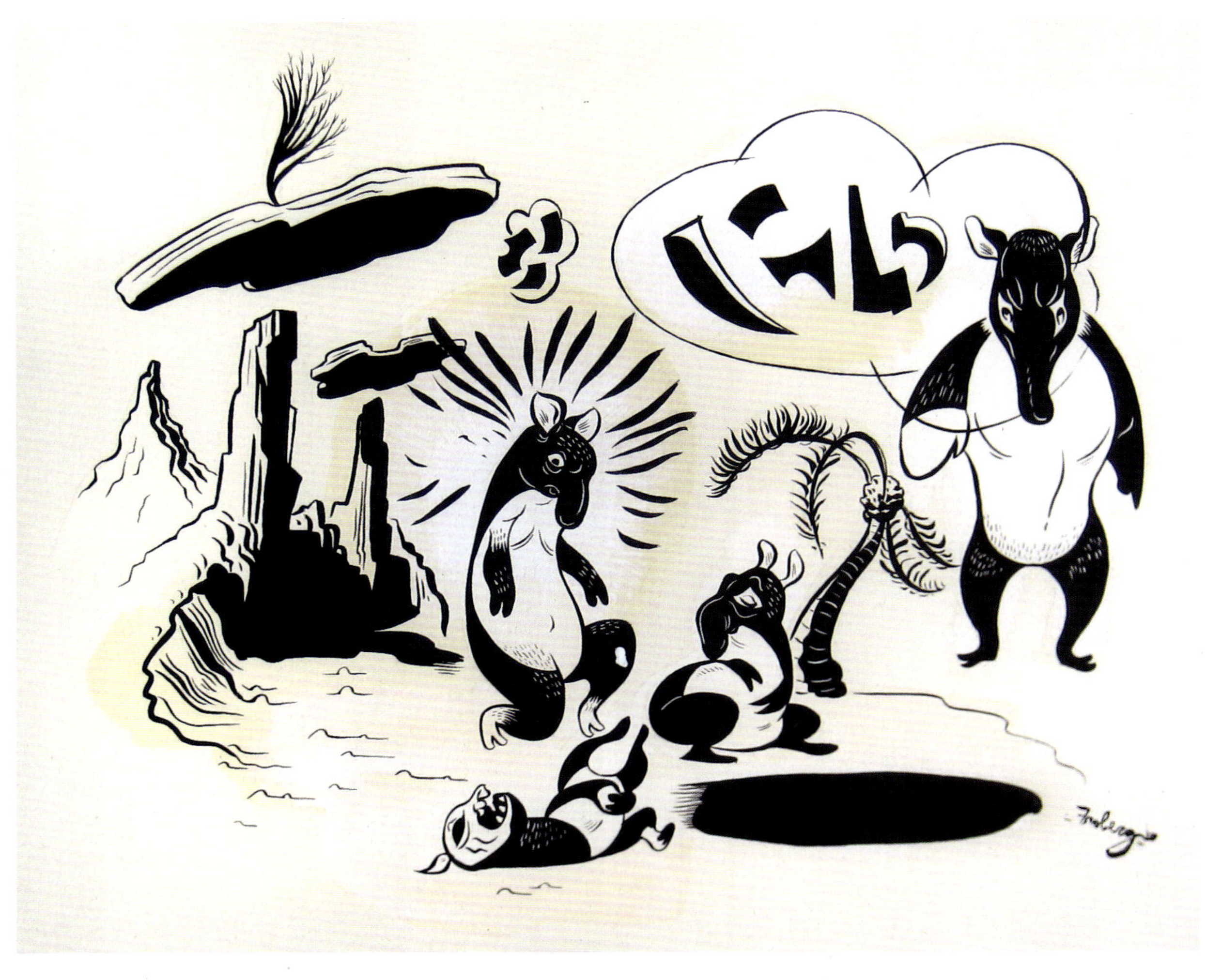

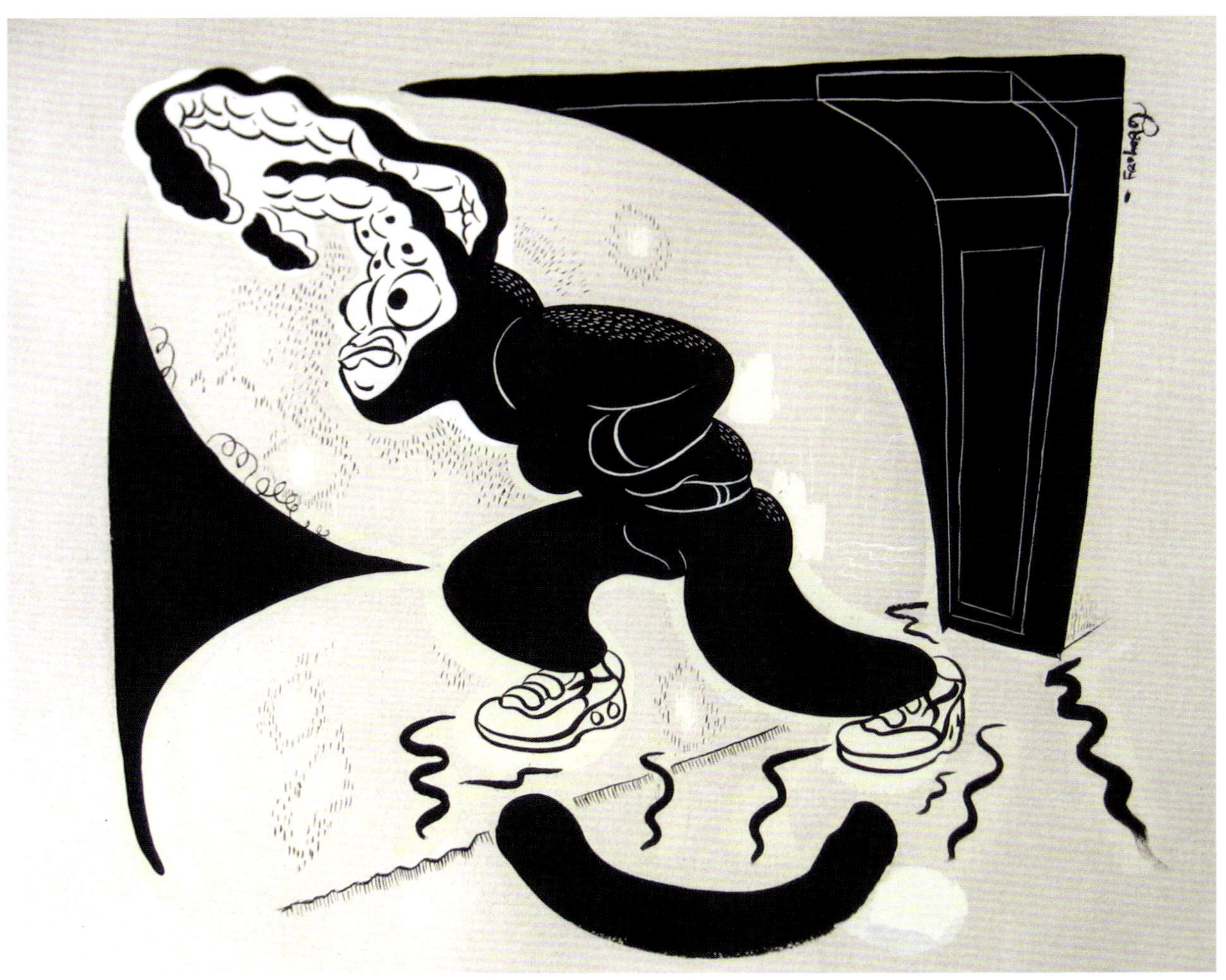

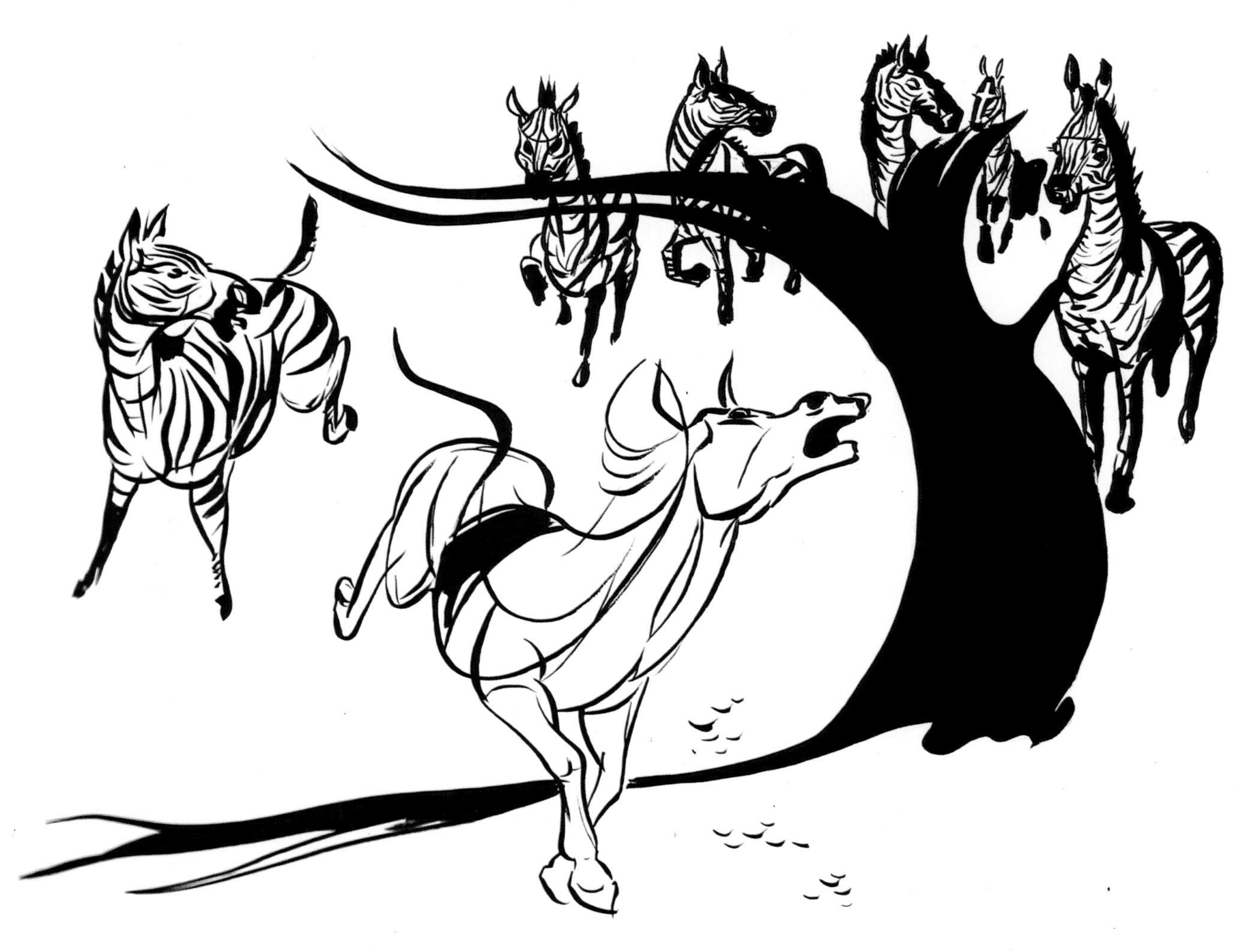

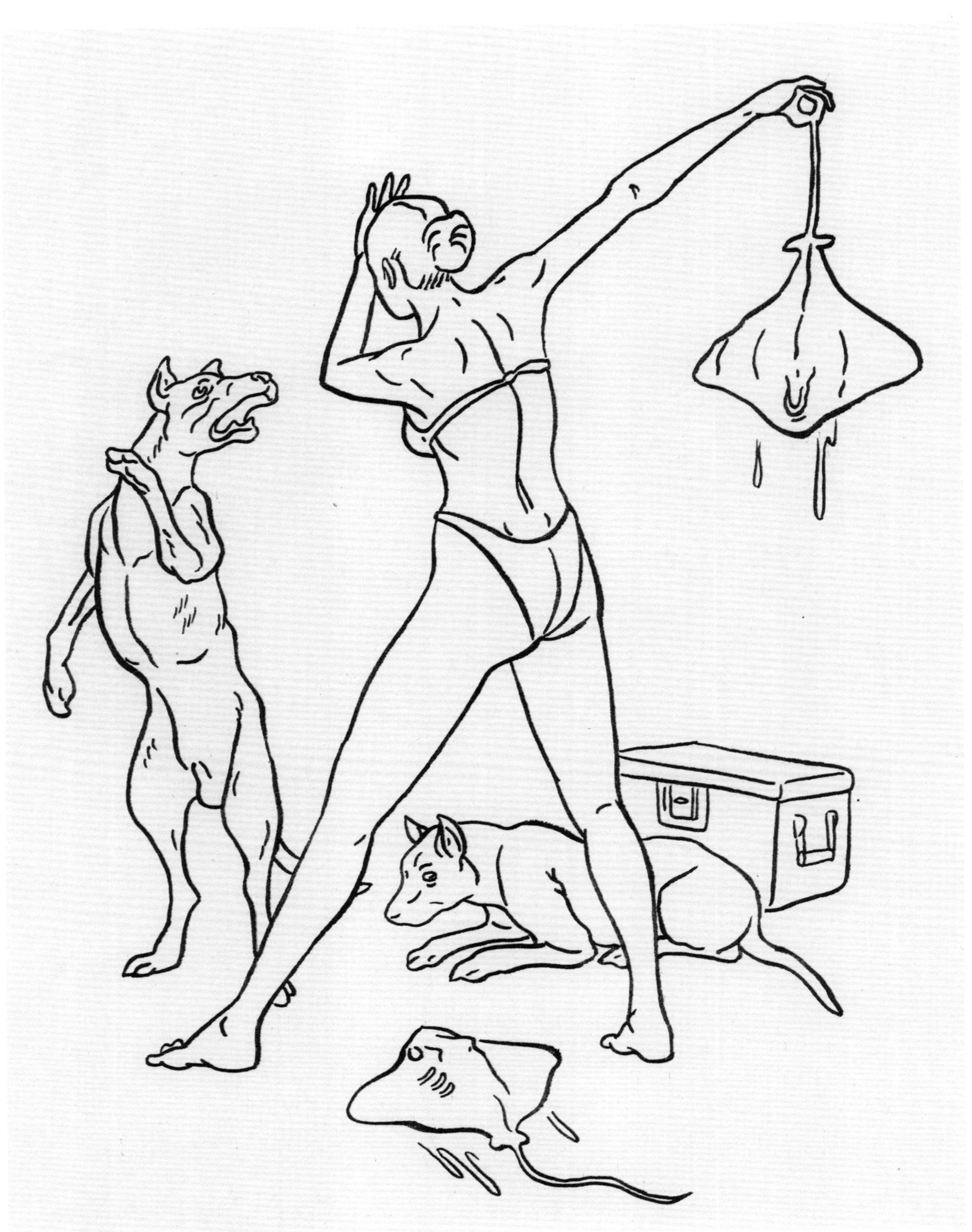

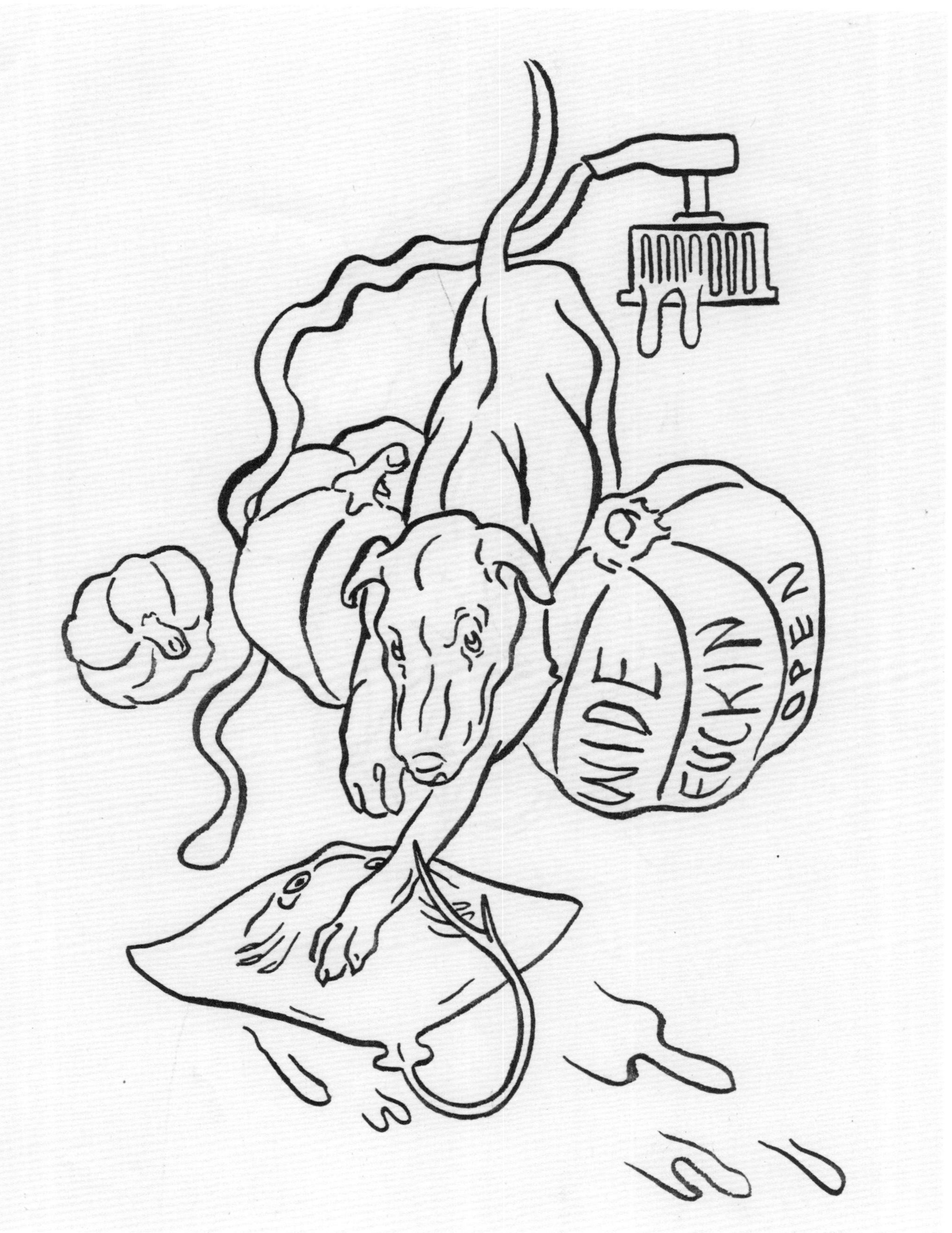

WIDE
FUCKIN
OPEN

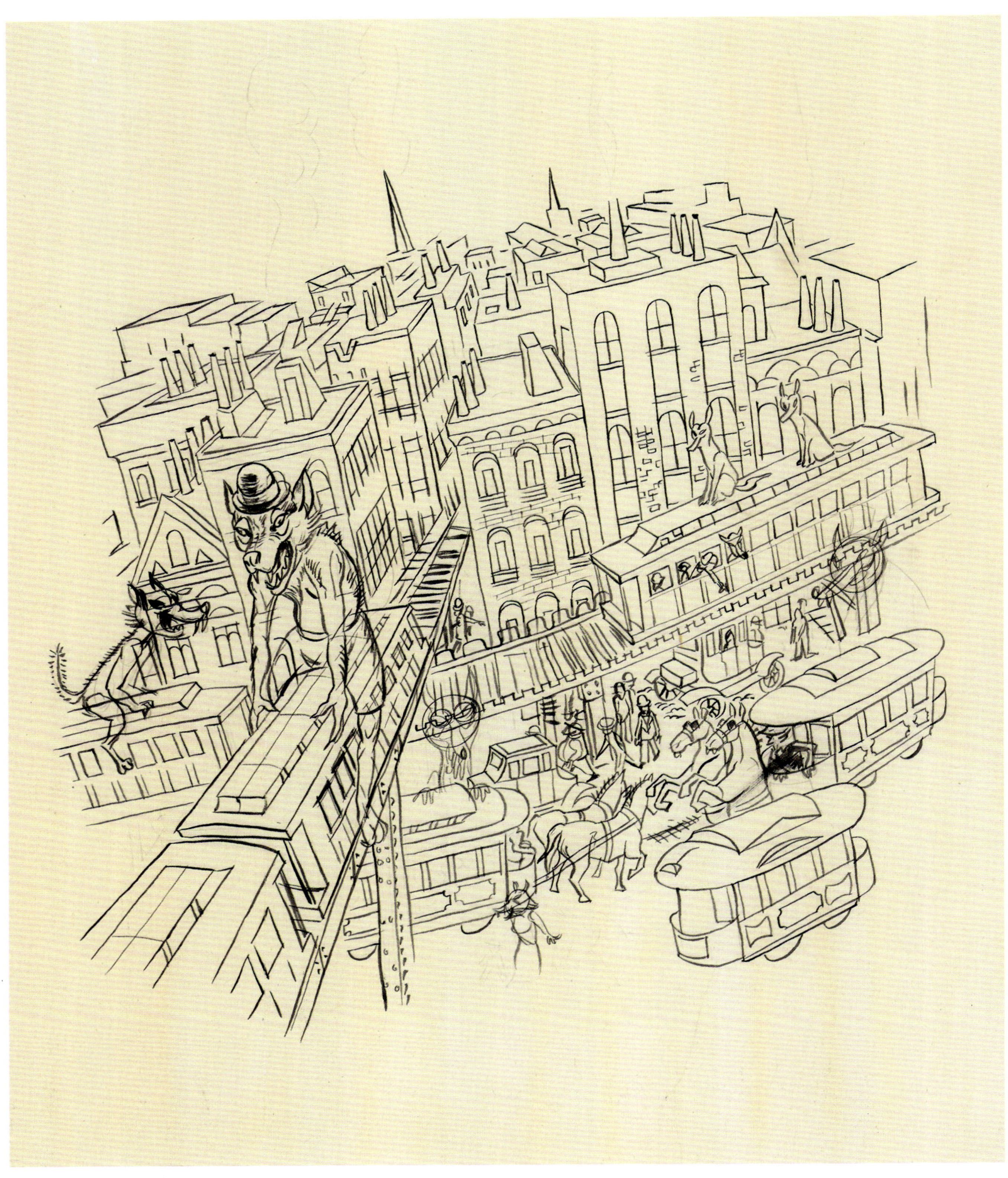

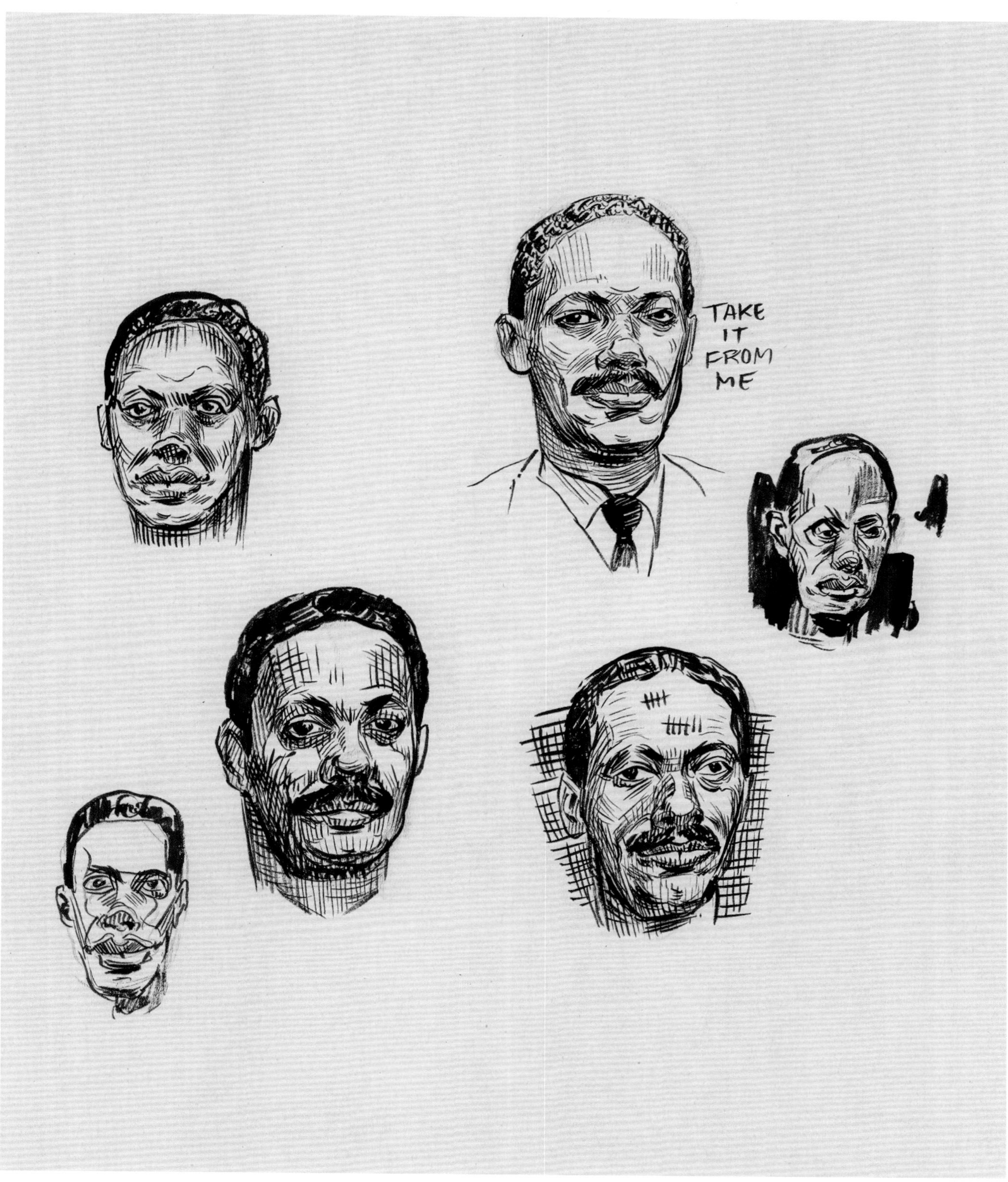
TAKE
IT
FROM
ME

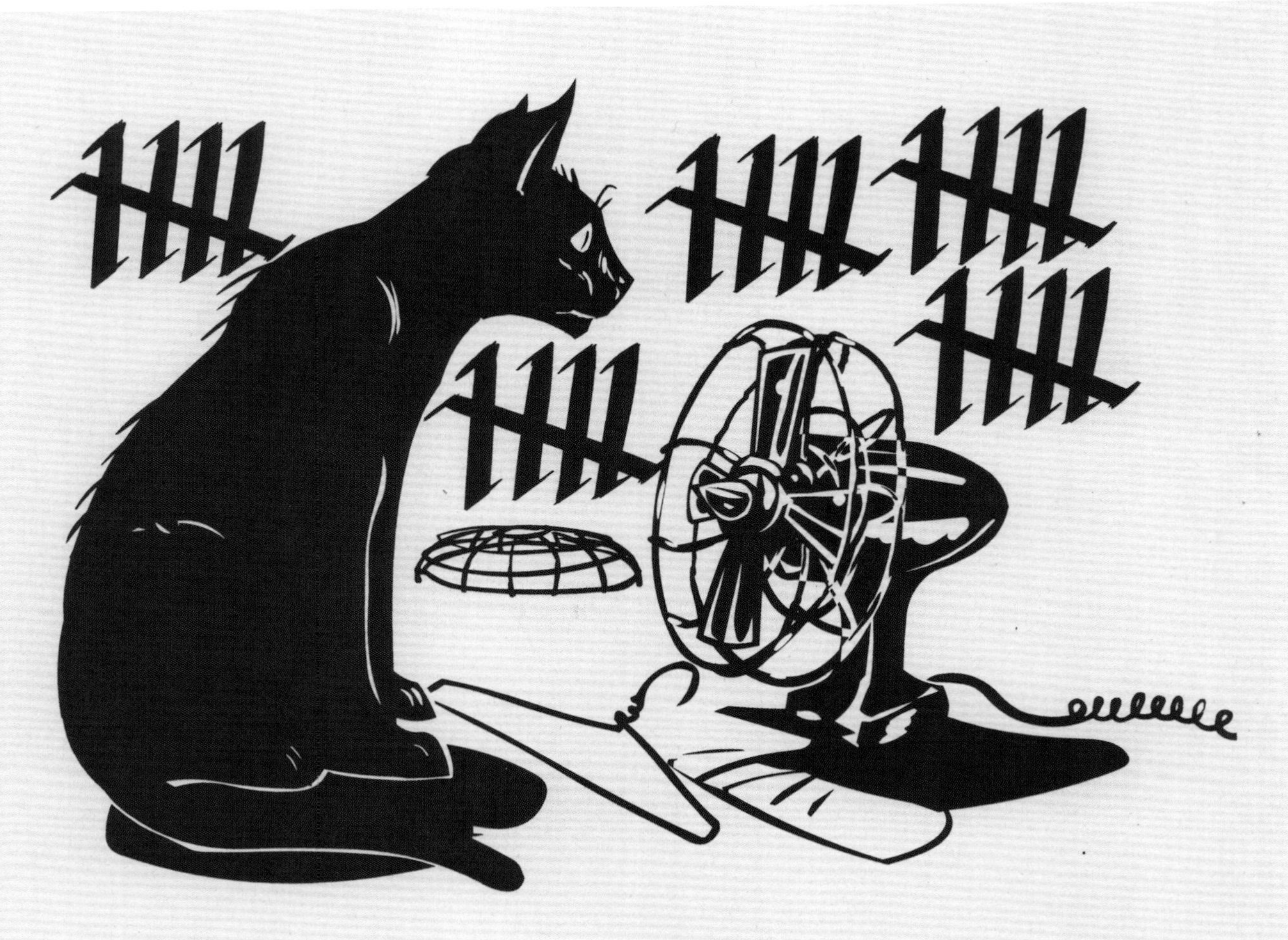

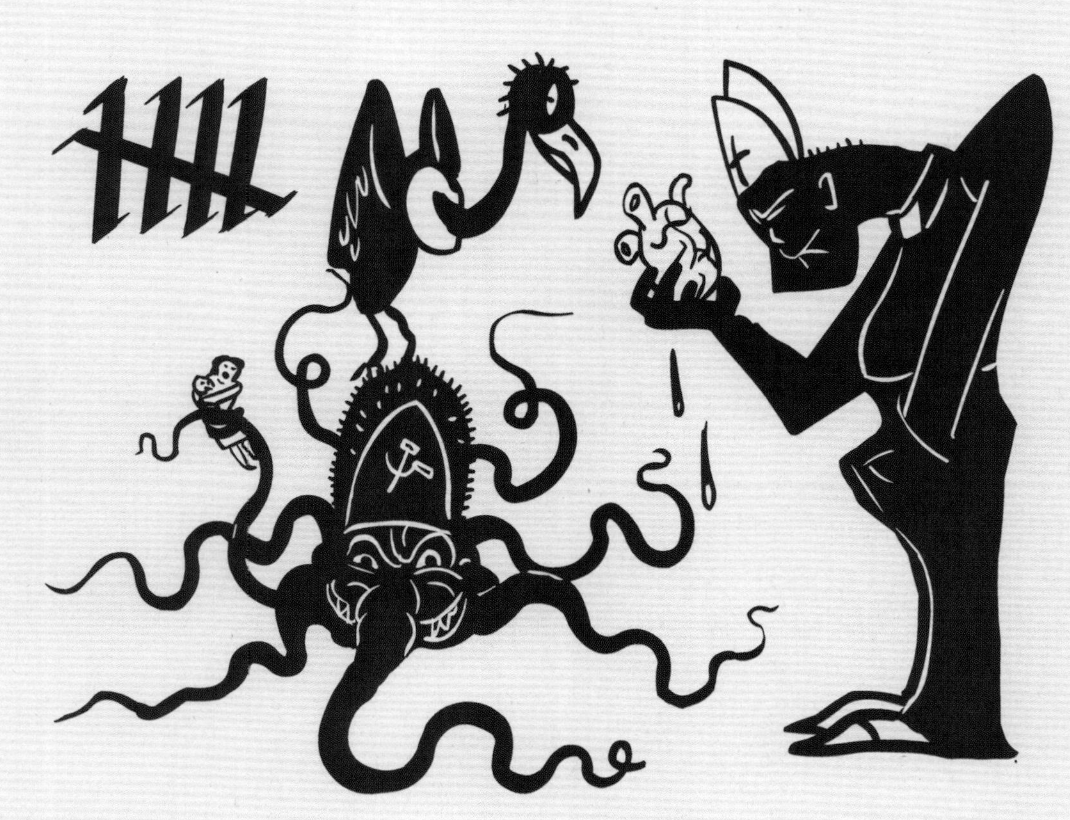

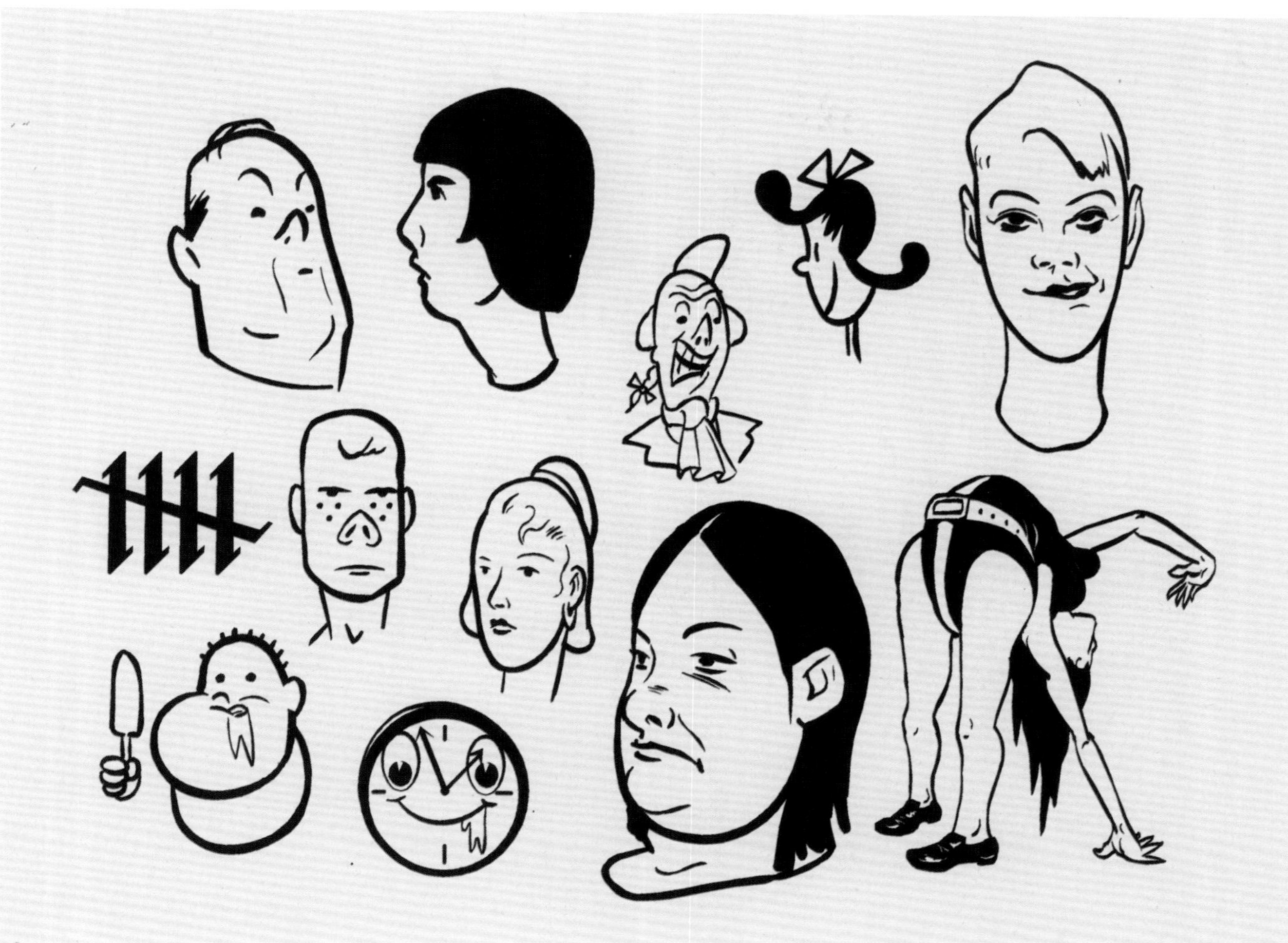

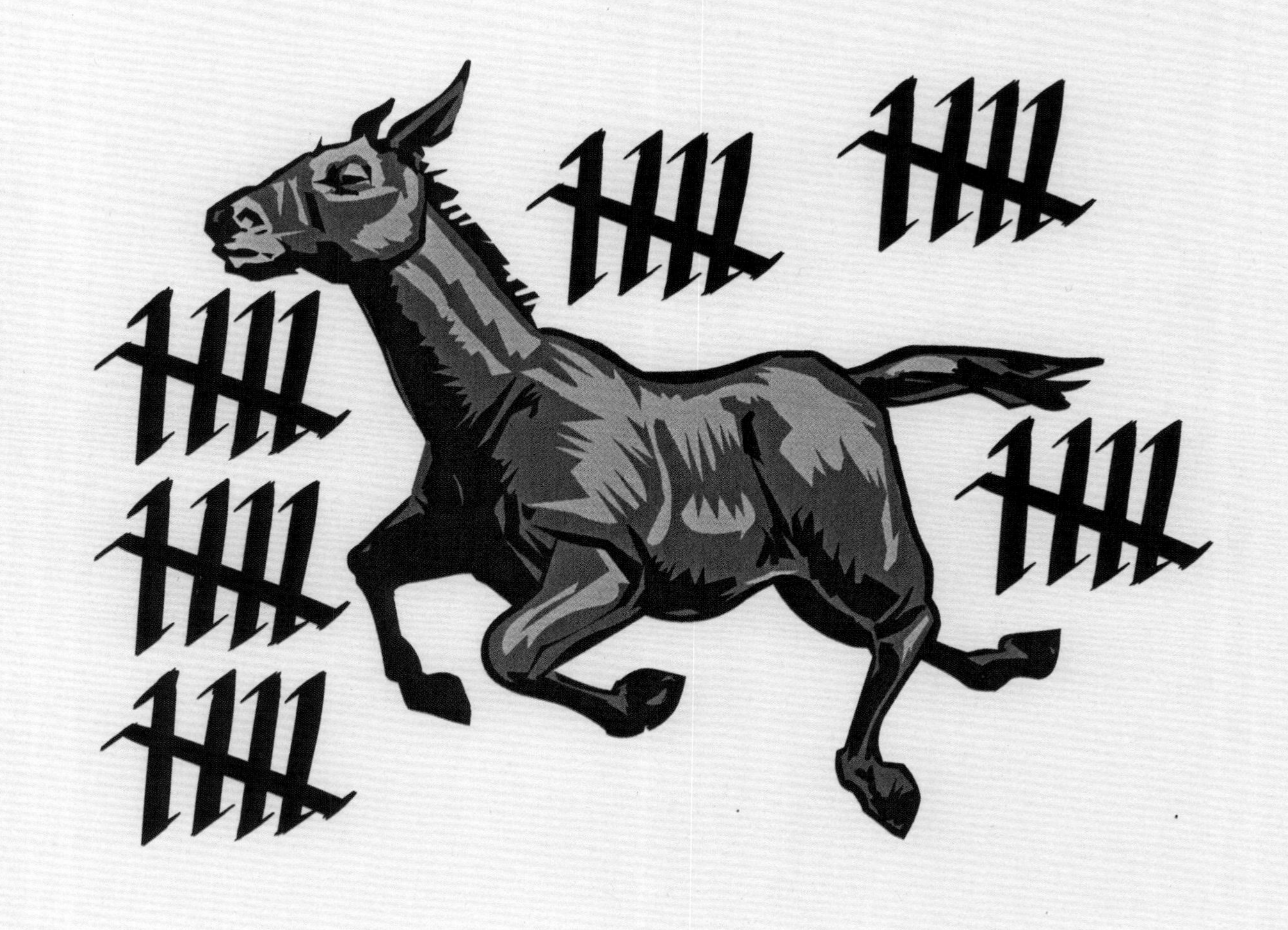

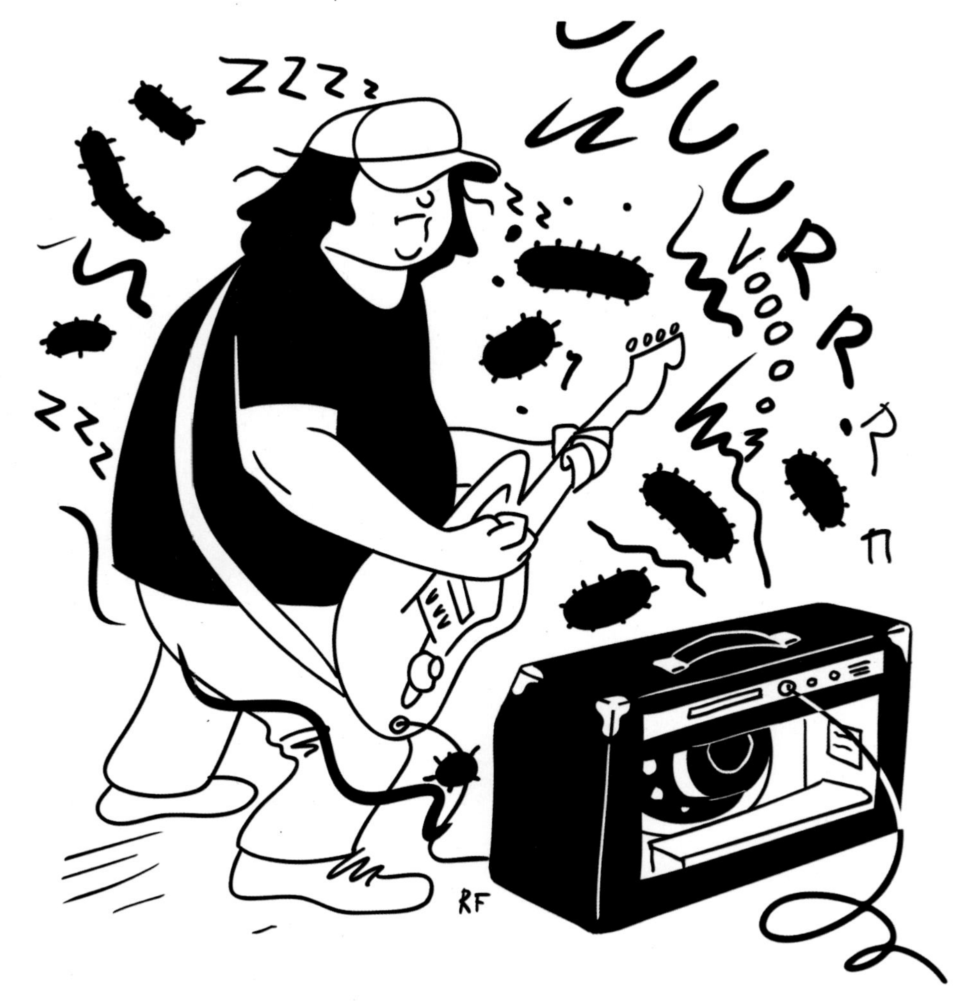

ZZZz
ZZz
ZZz
UUURR
W
VOOOO
RF

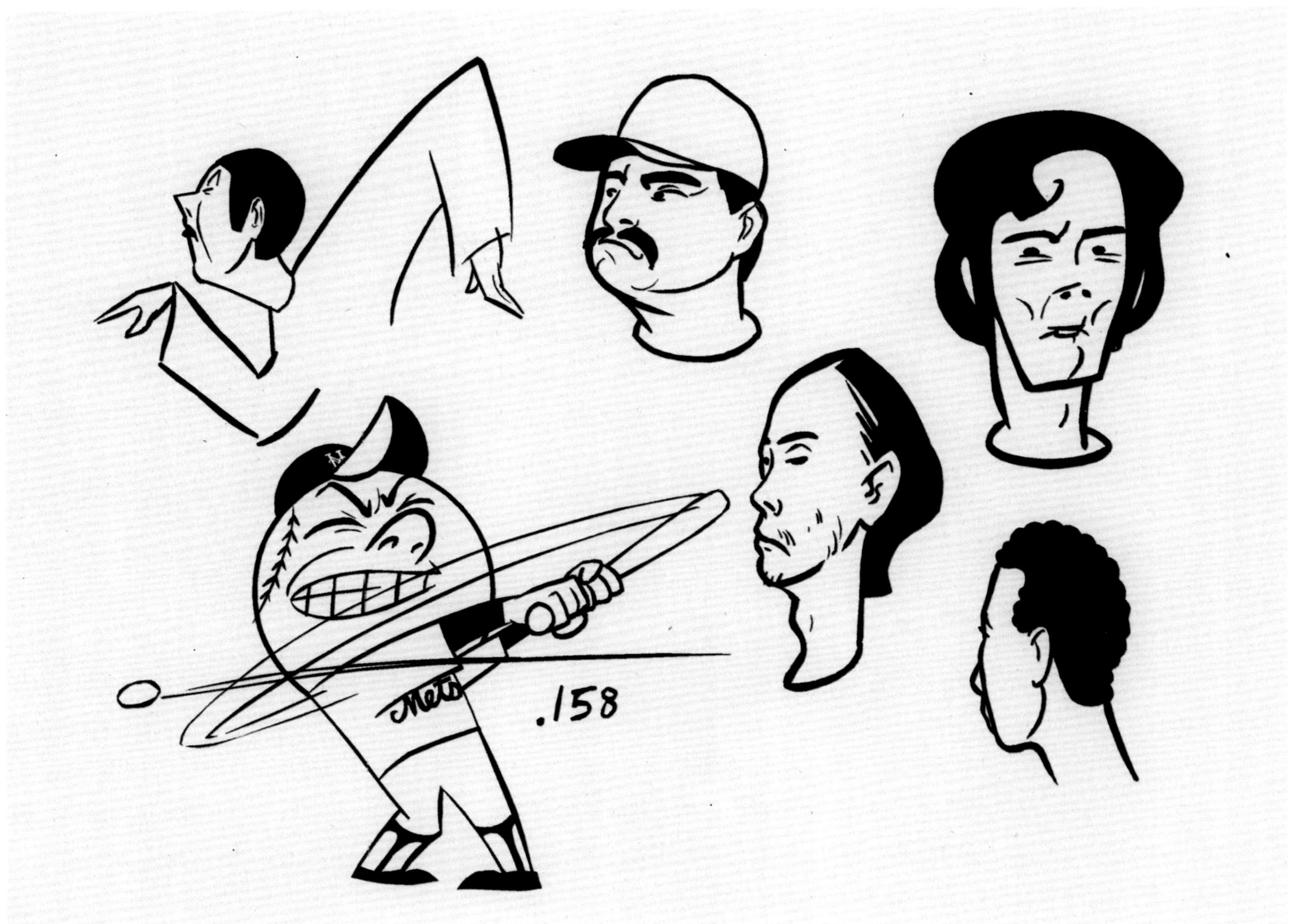

Mets
.158

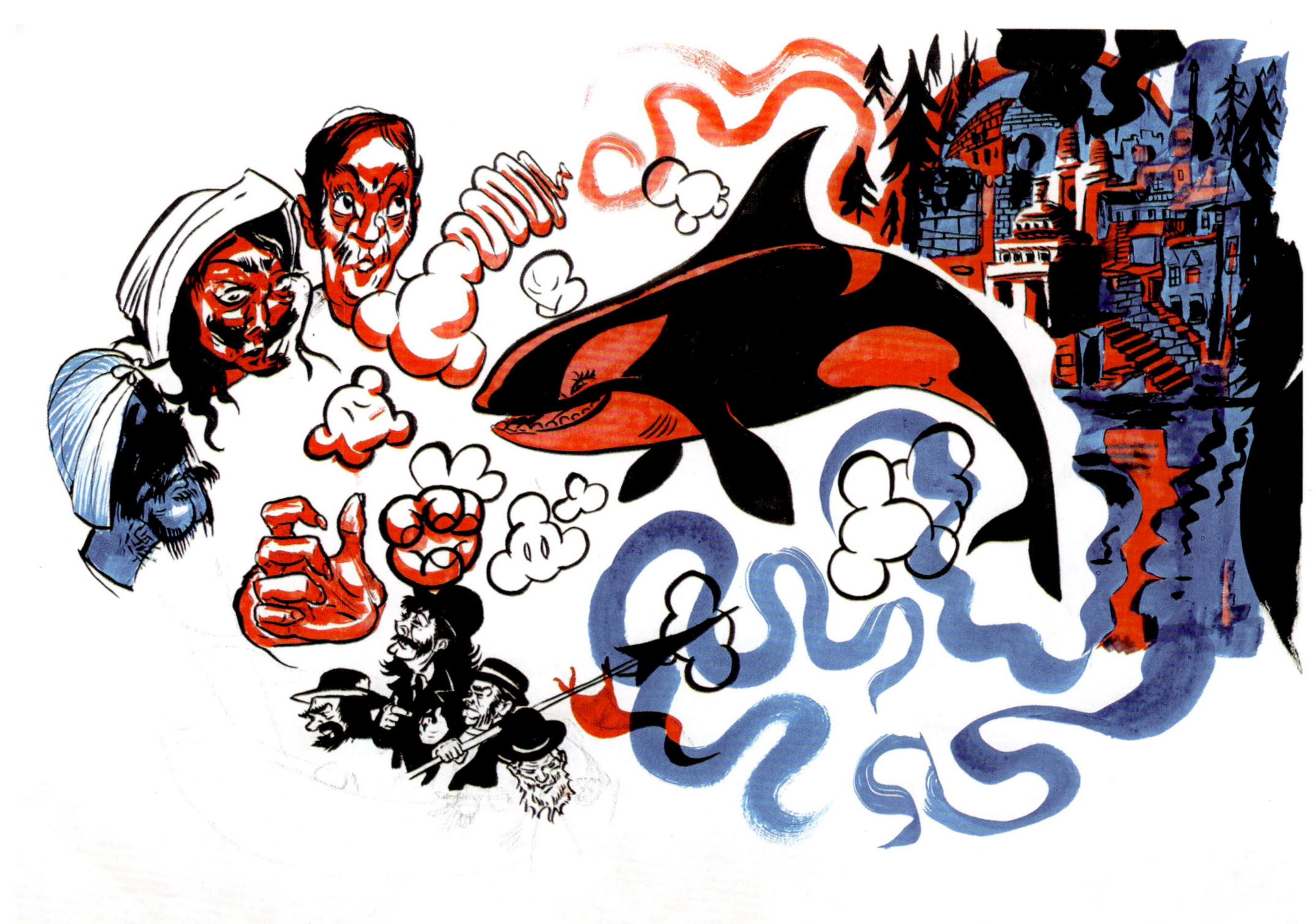

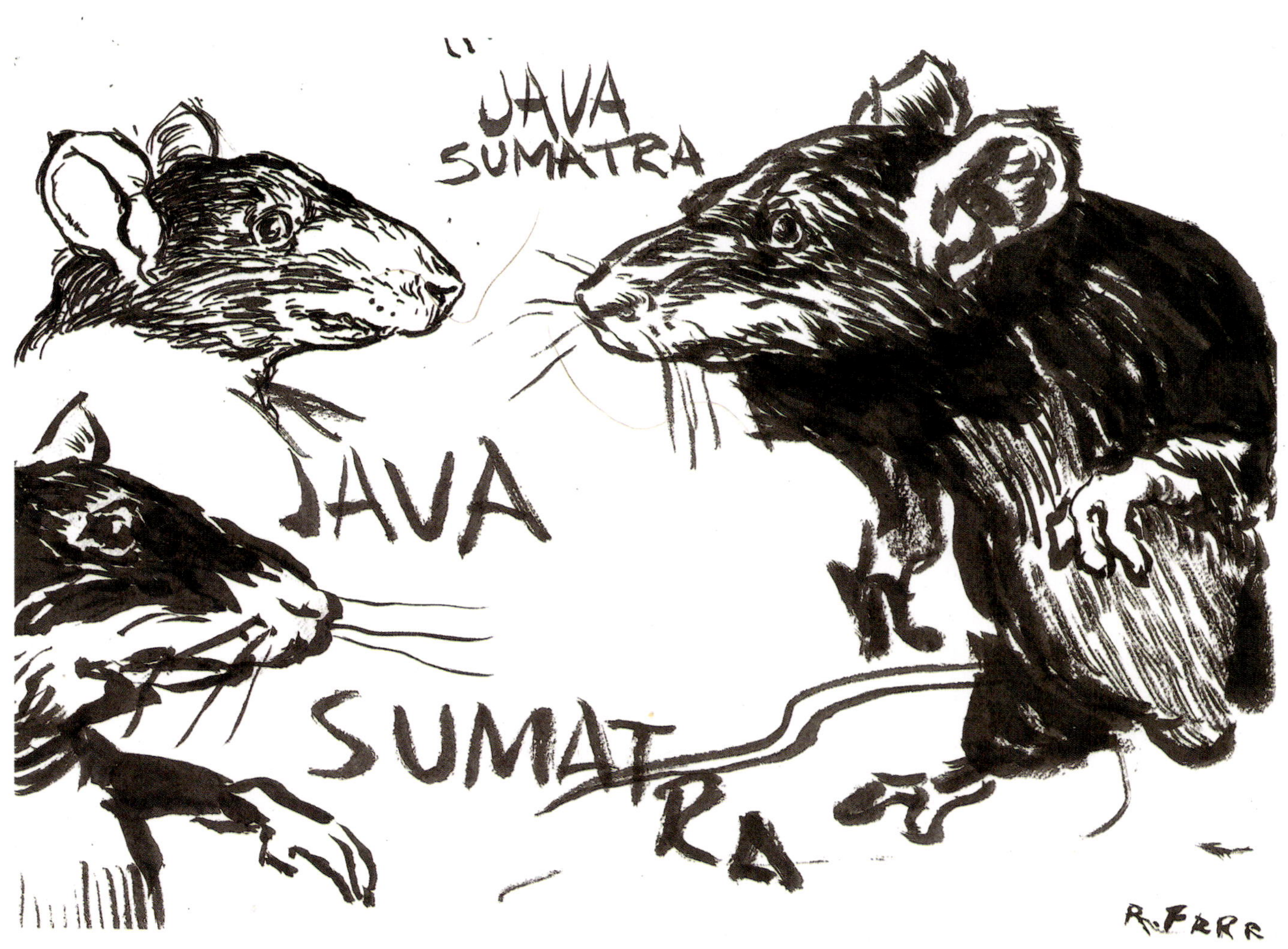

JAVA
SUMATRA
JAVA
SUMATRA
R·FRRR

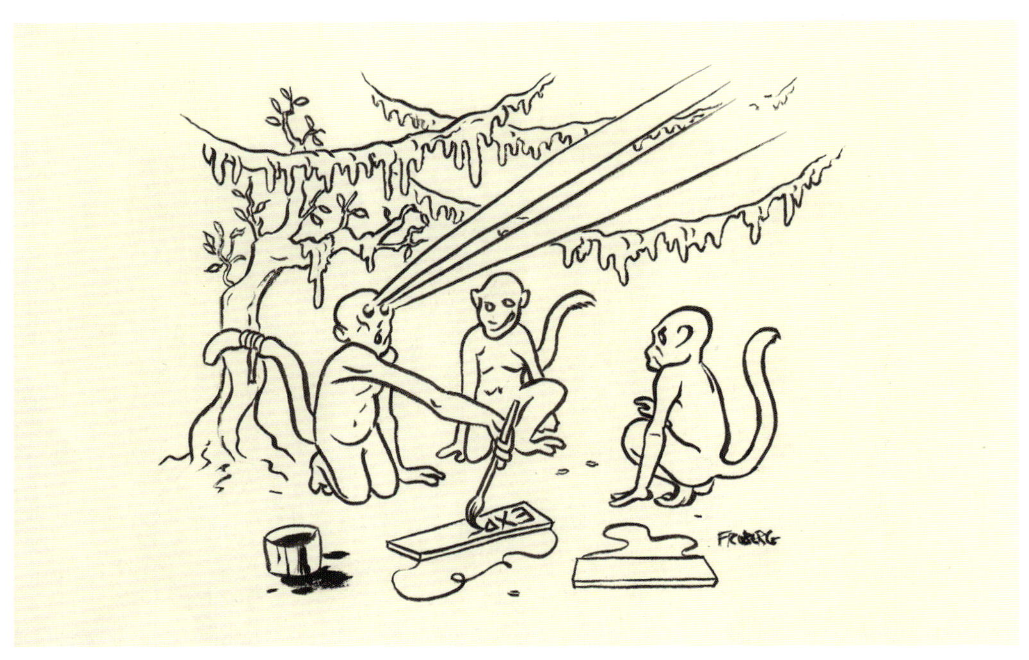
AXE

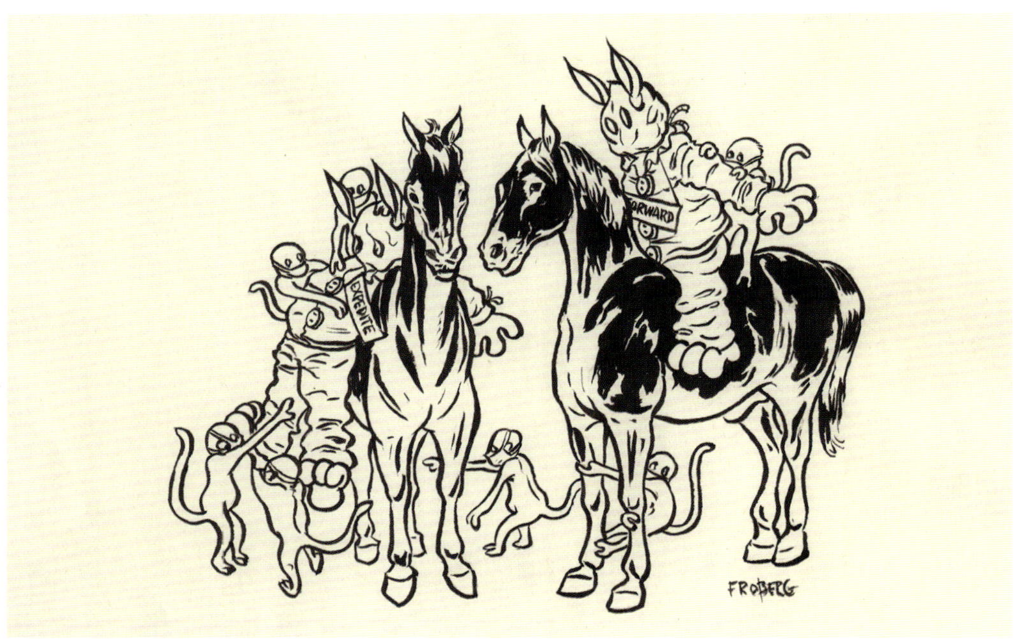
FORWARD
DYNAMITE

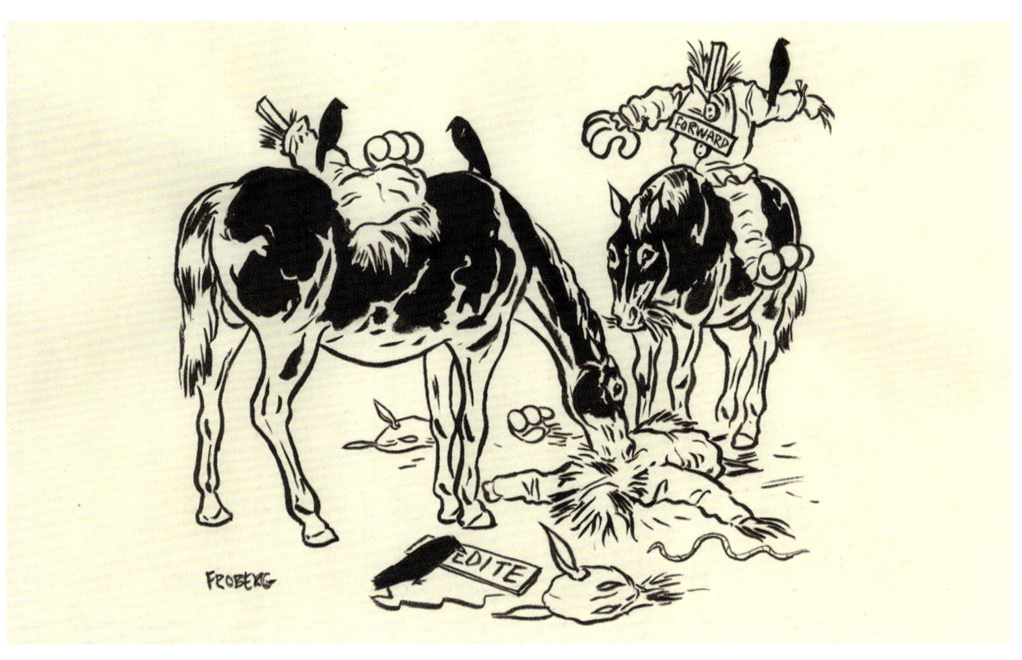
FORWARD
EDITE

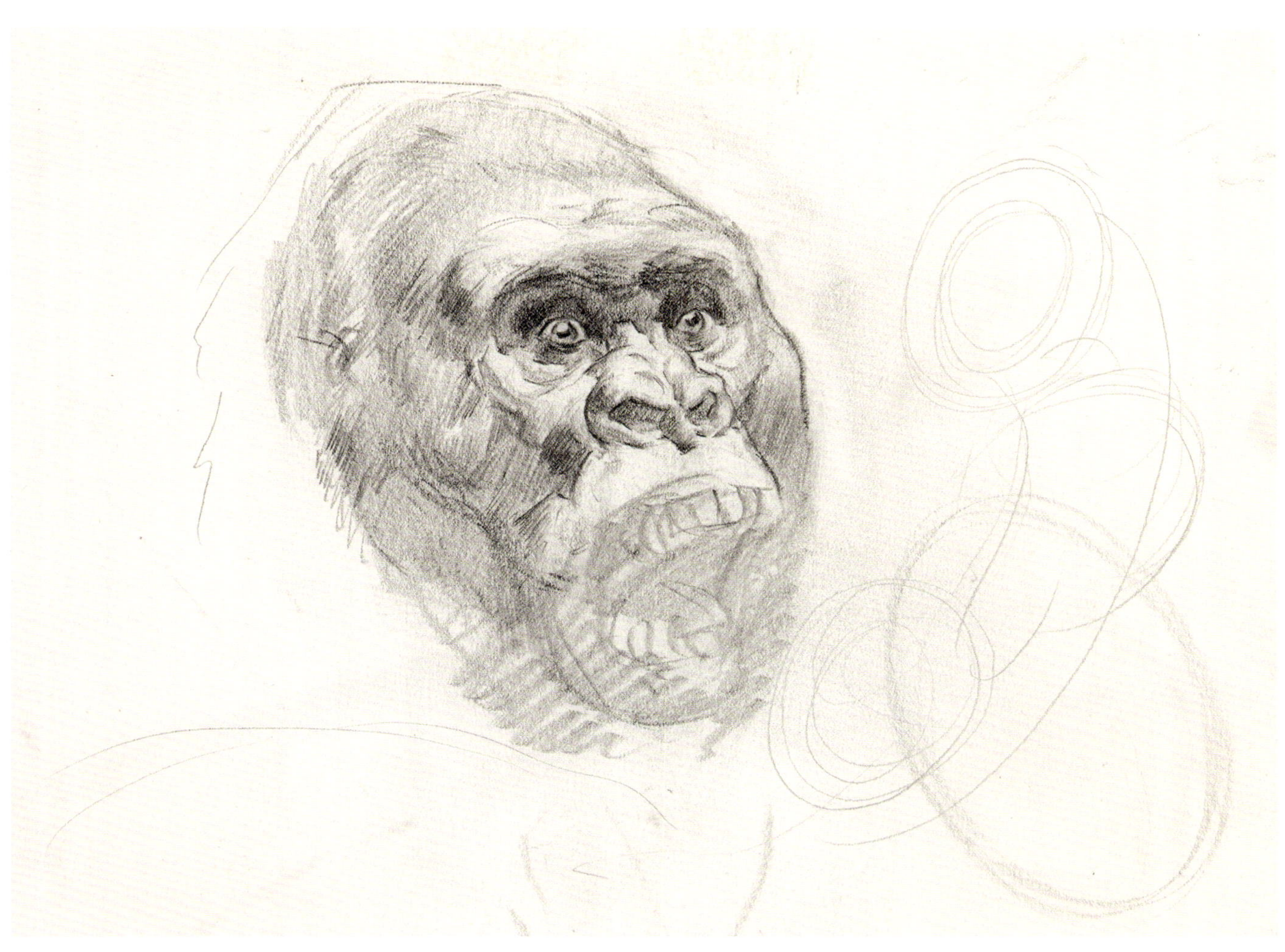

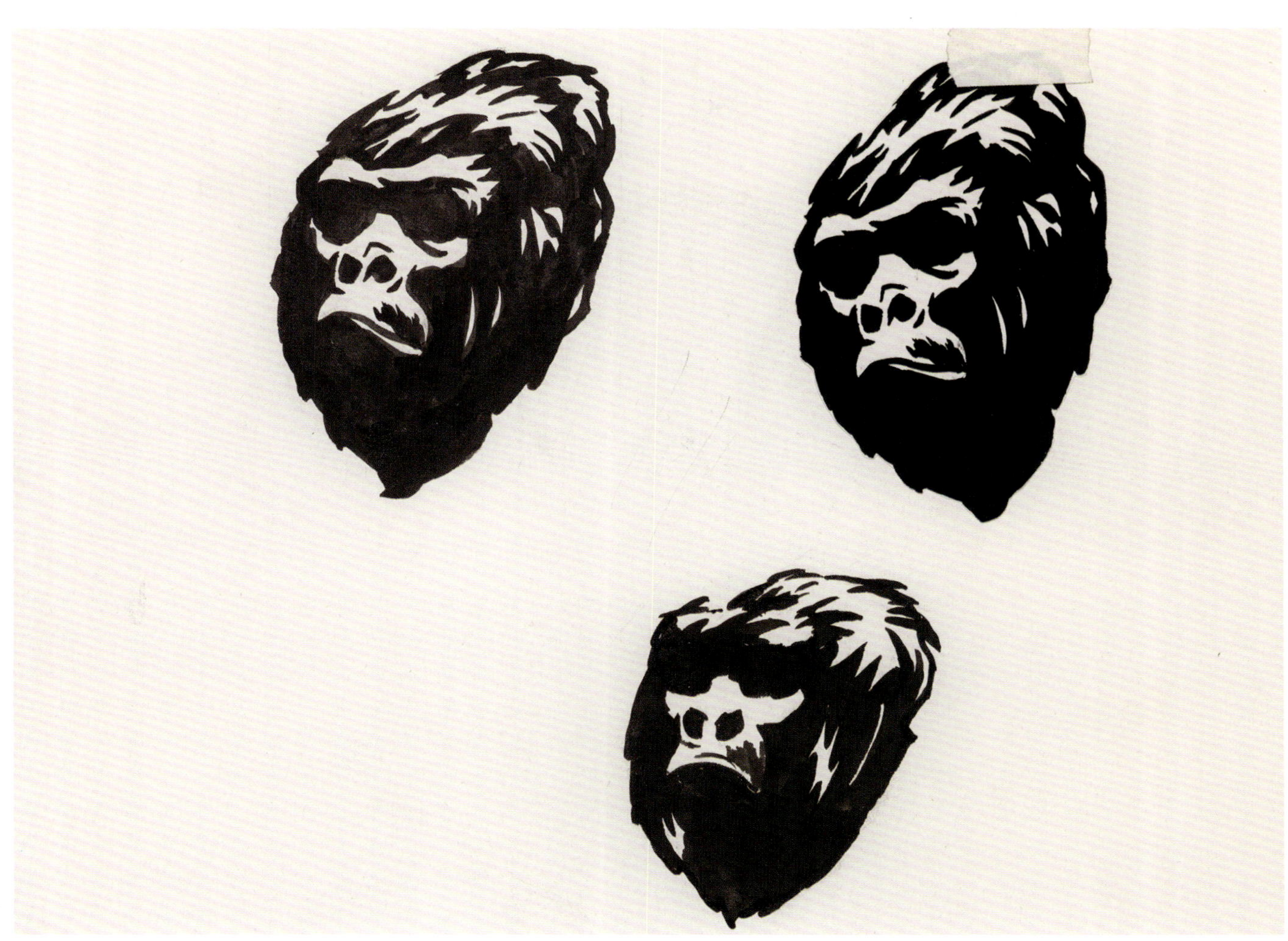

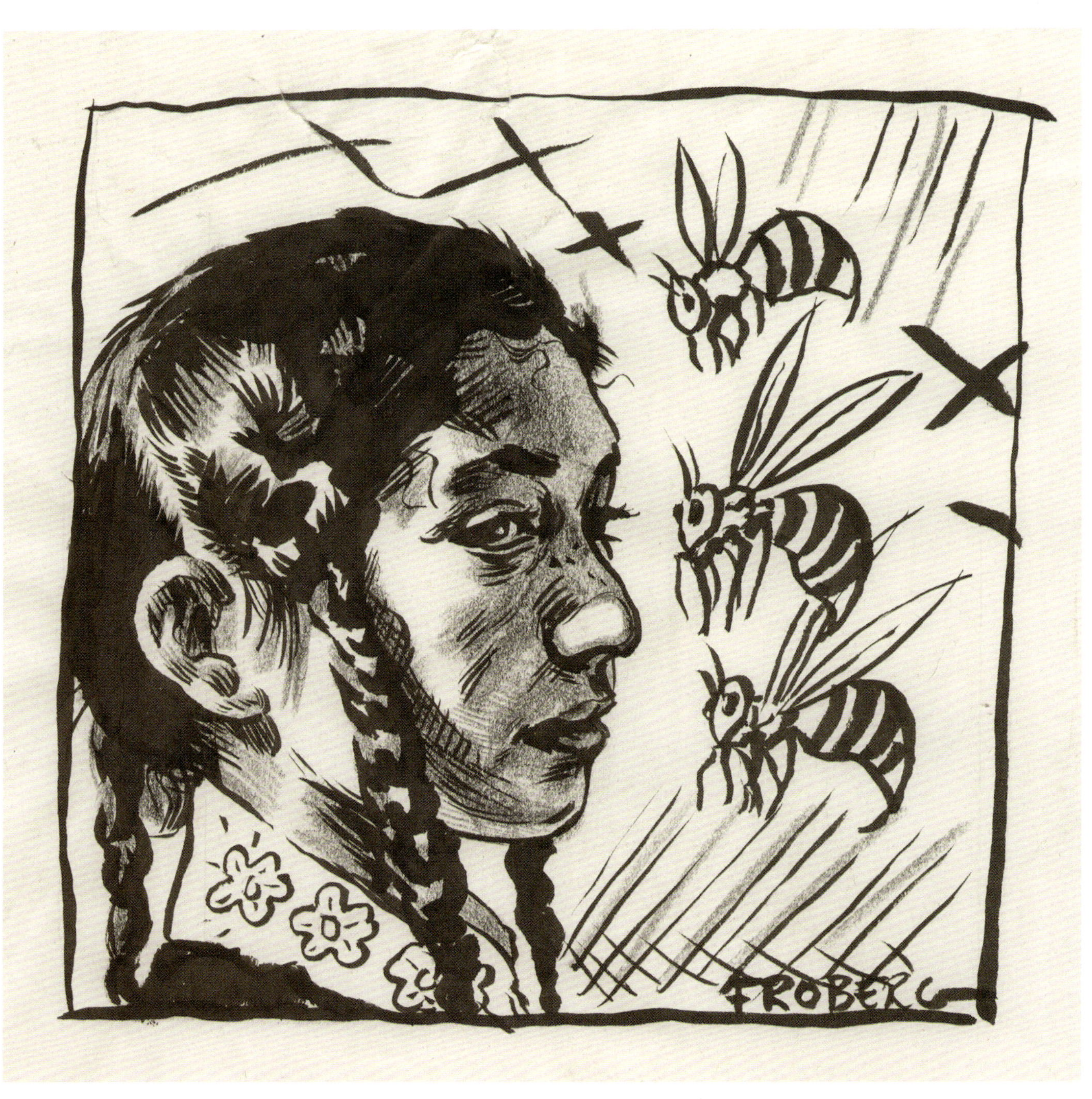
FROBERG

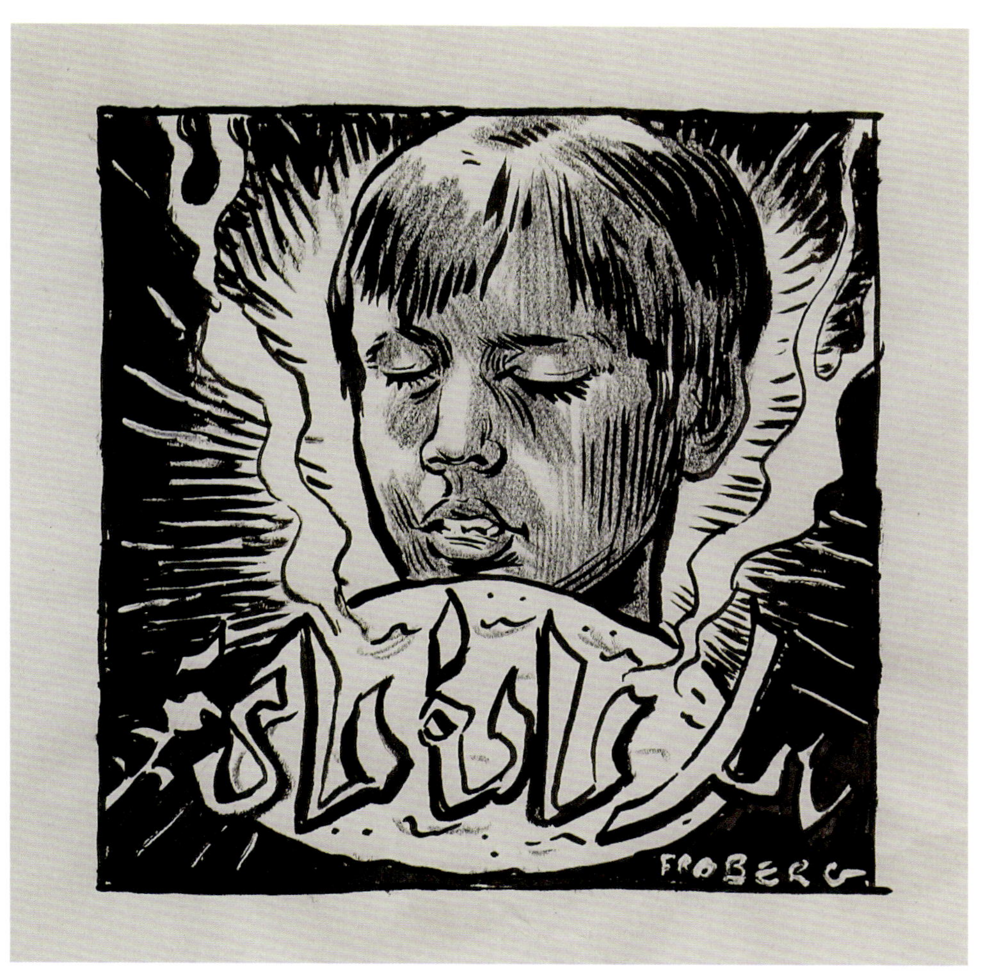

FROBERG.

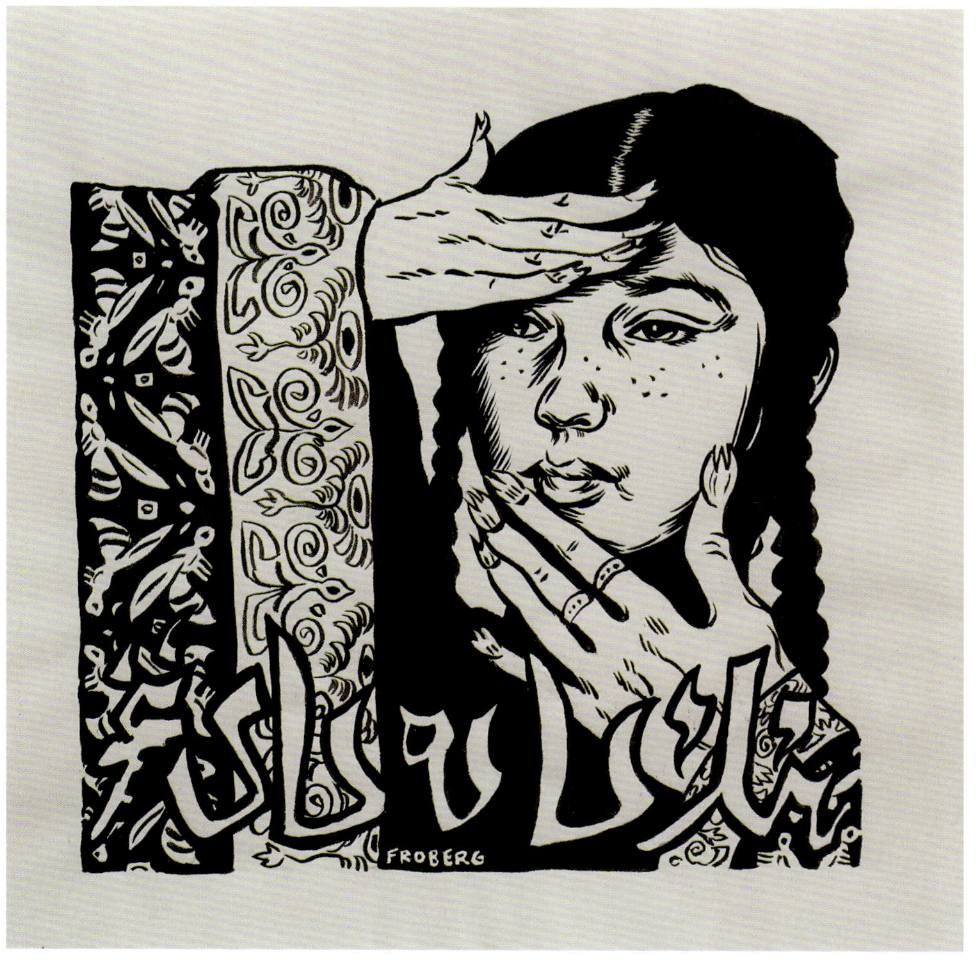

FROBERG

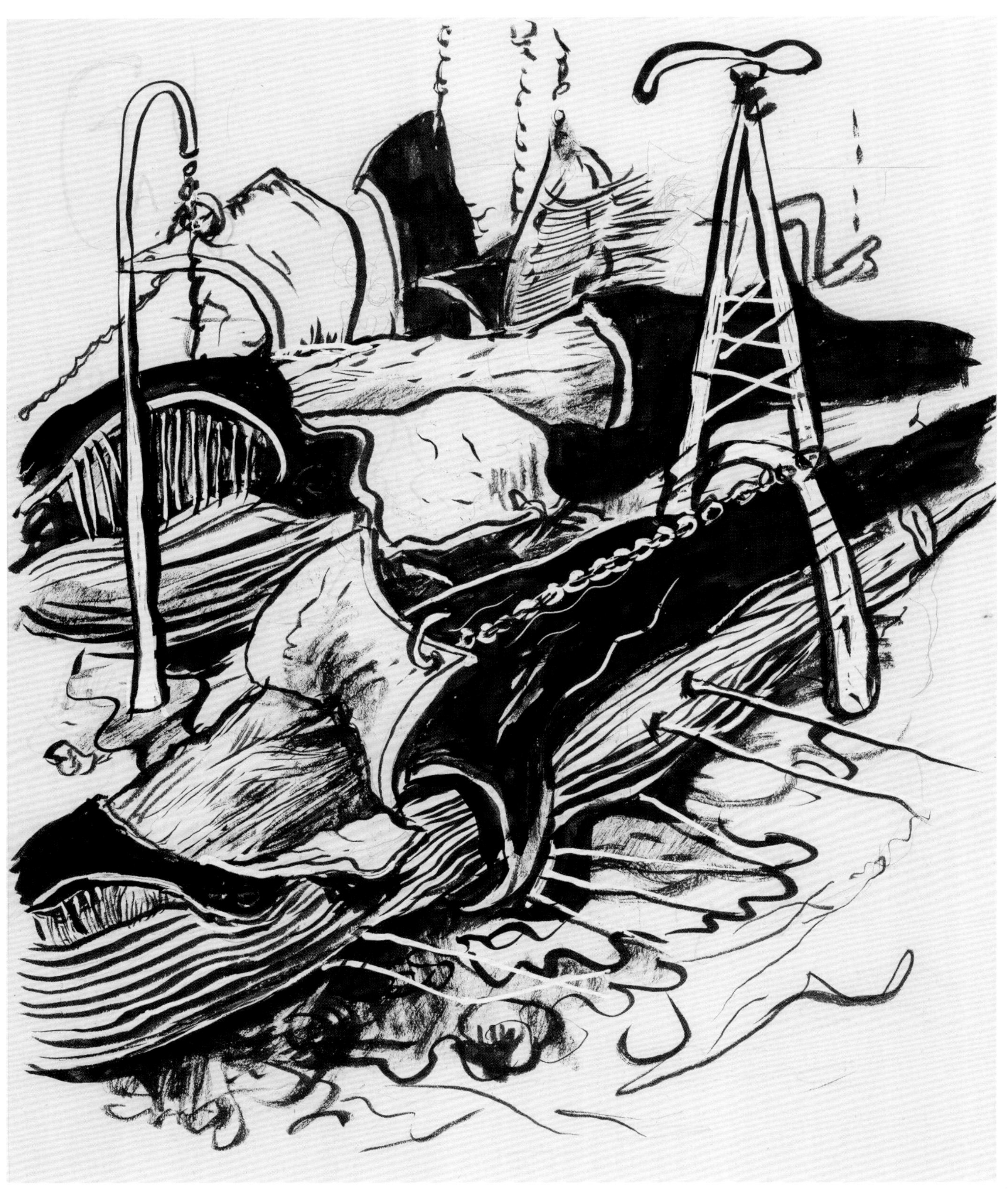

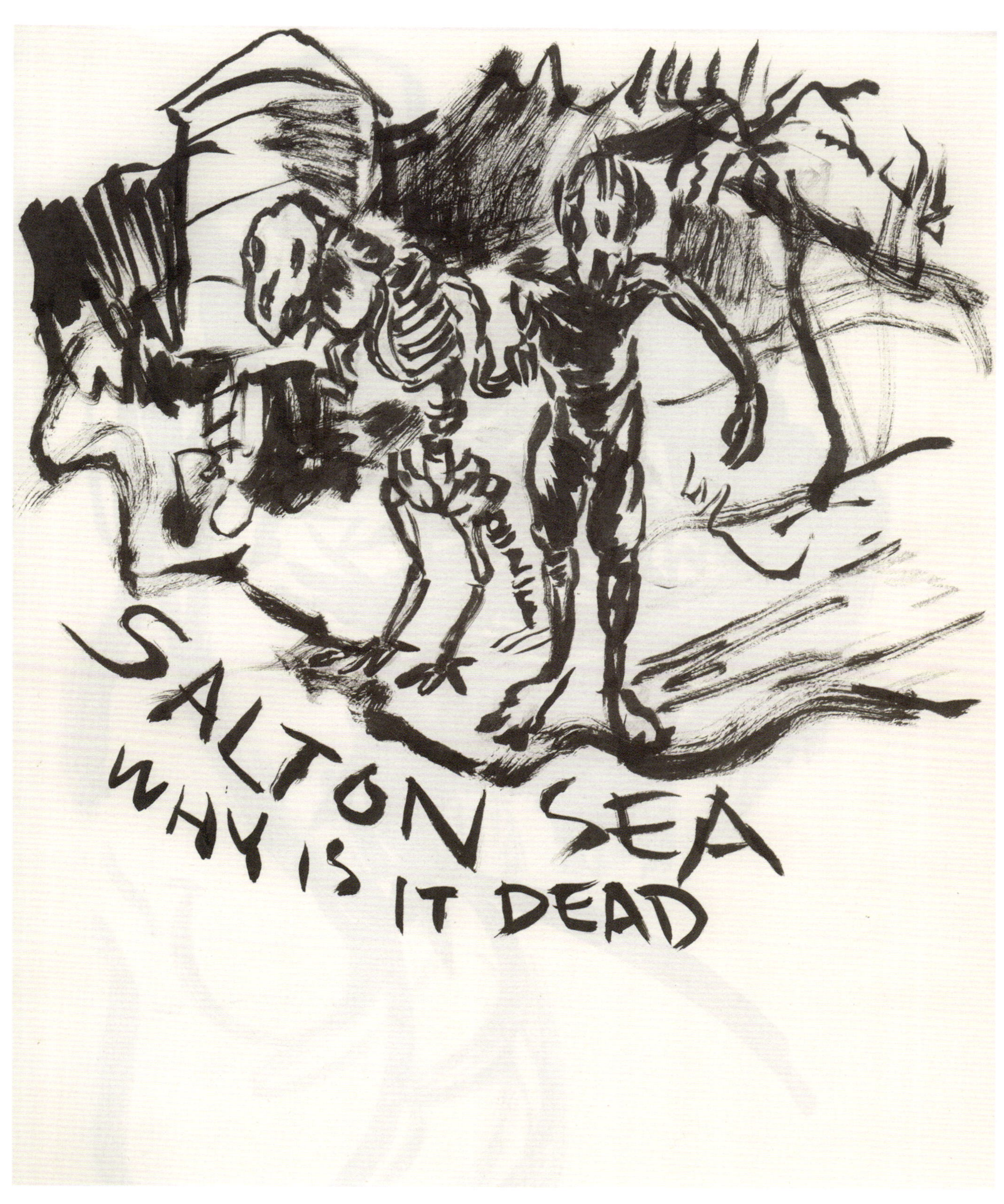
SALTON SEA
WHY IS IT DEAD

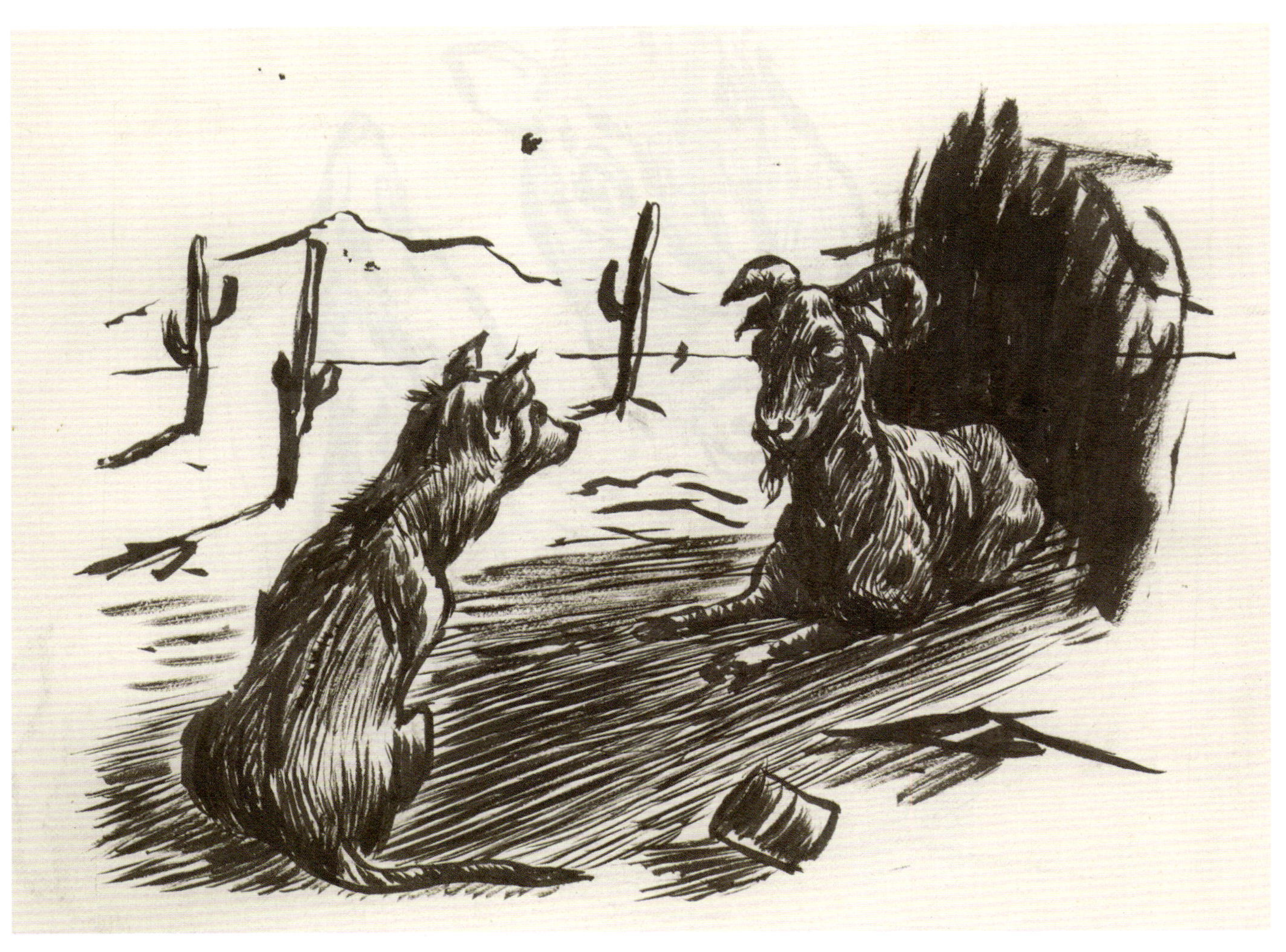

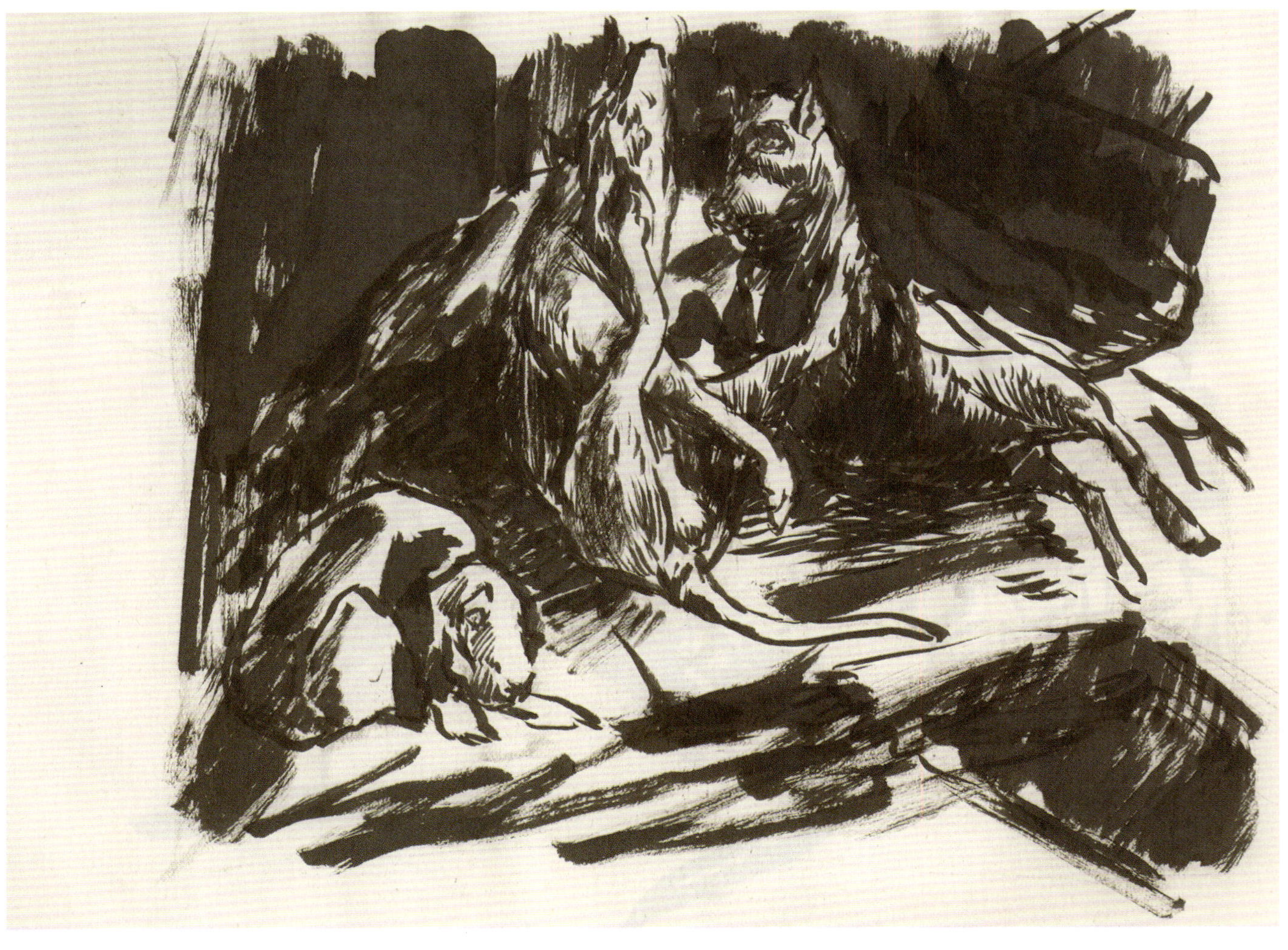

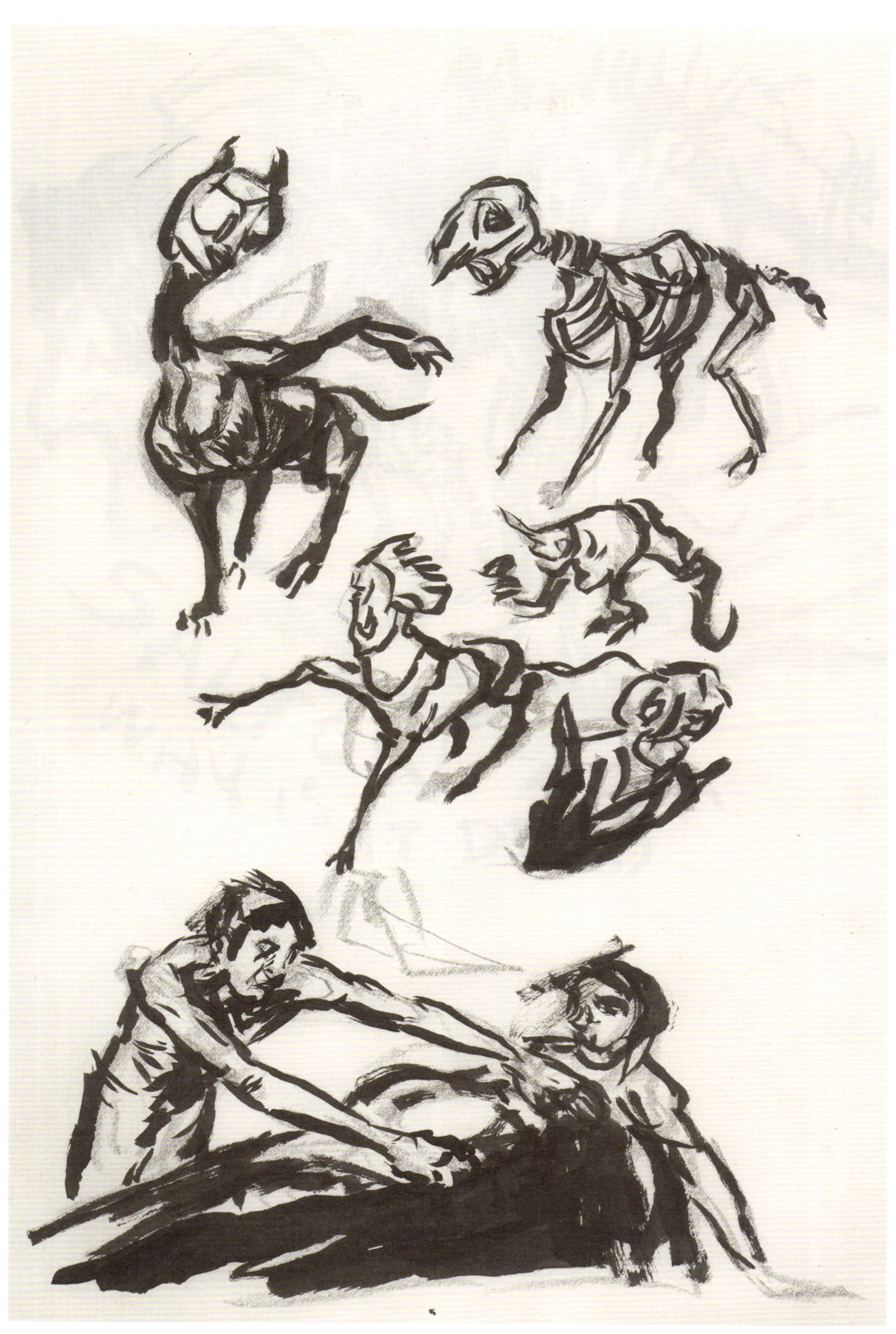

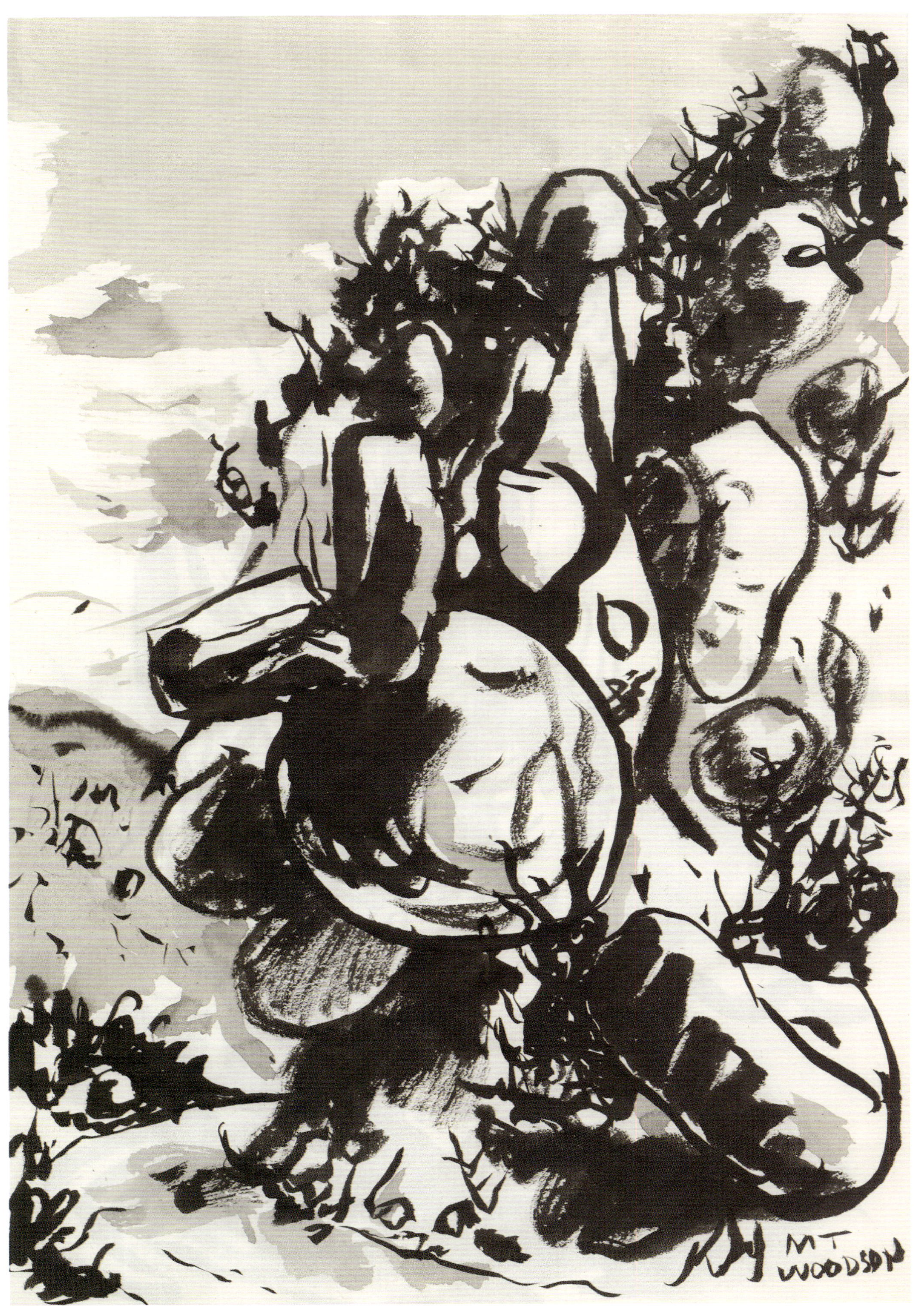
MT
WOODSON

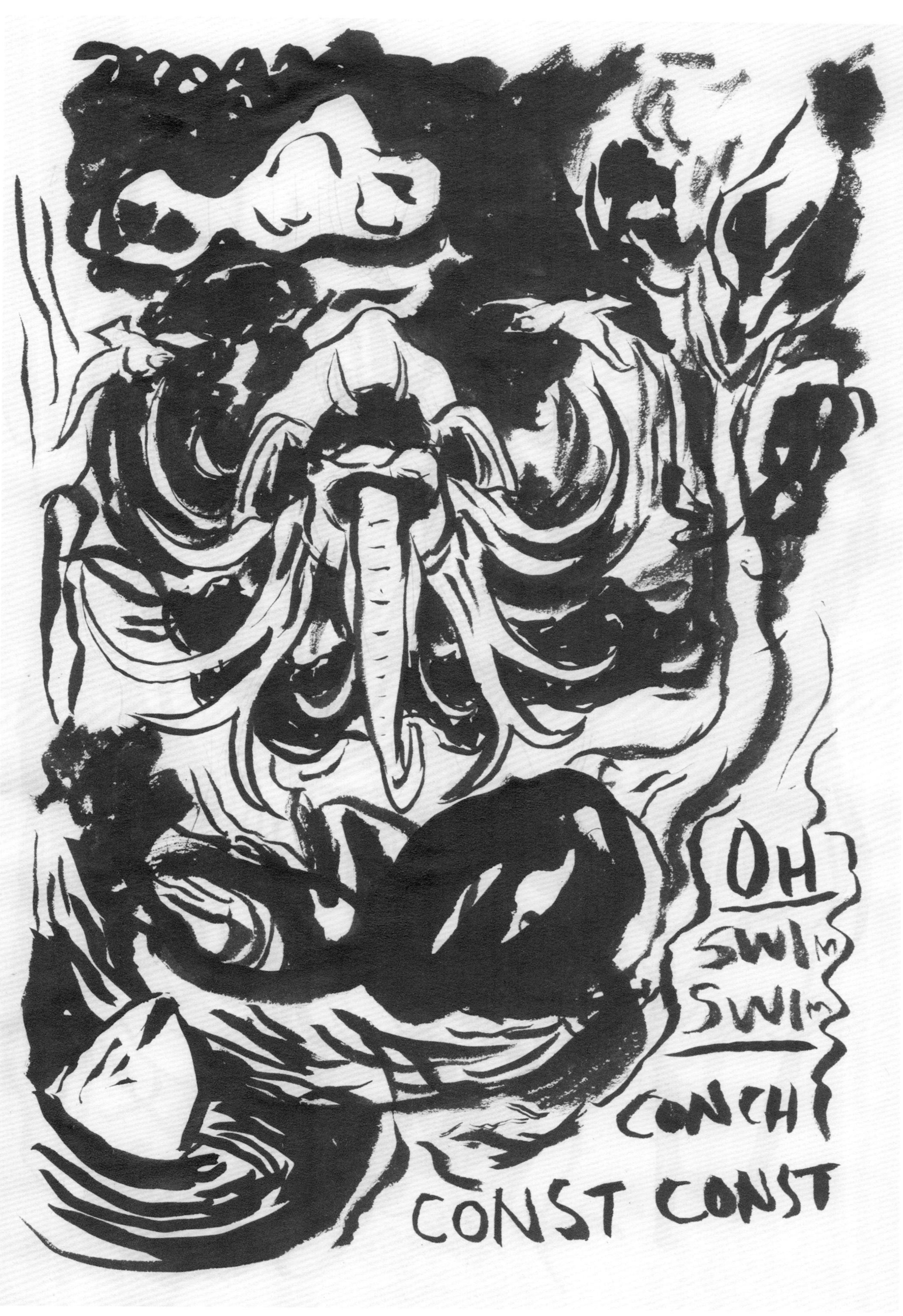

OH
SWIM
SWIM
CONCH
CONST CONST

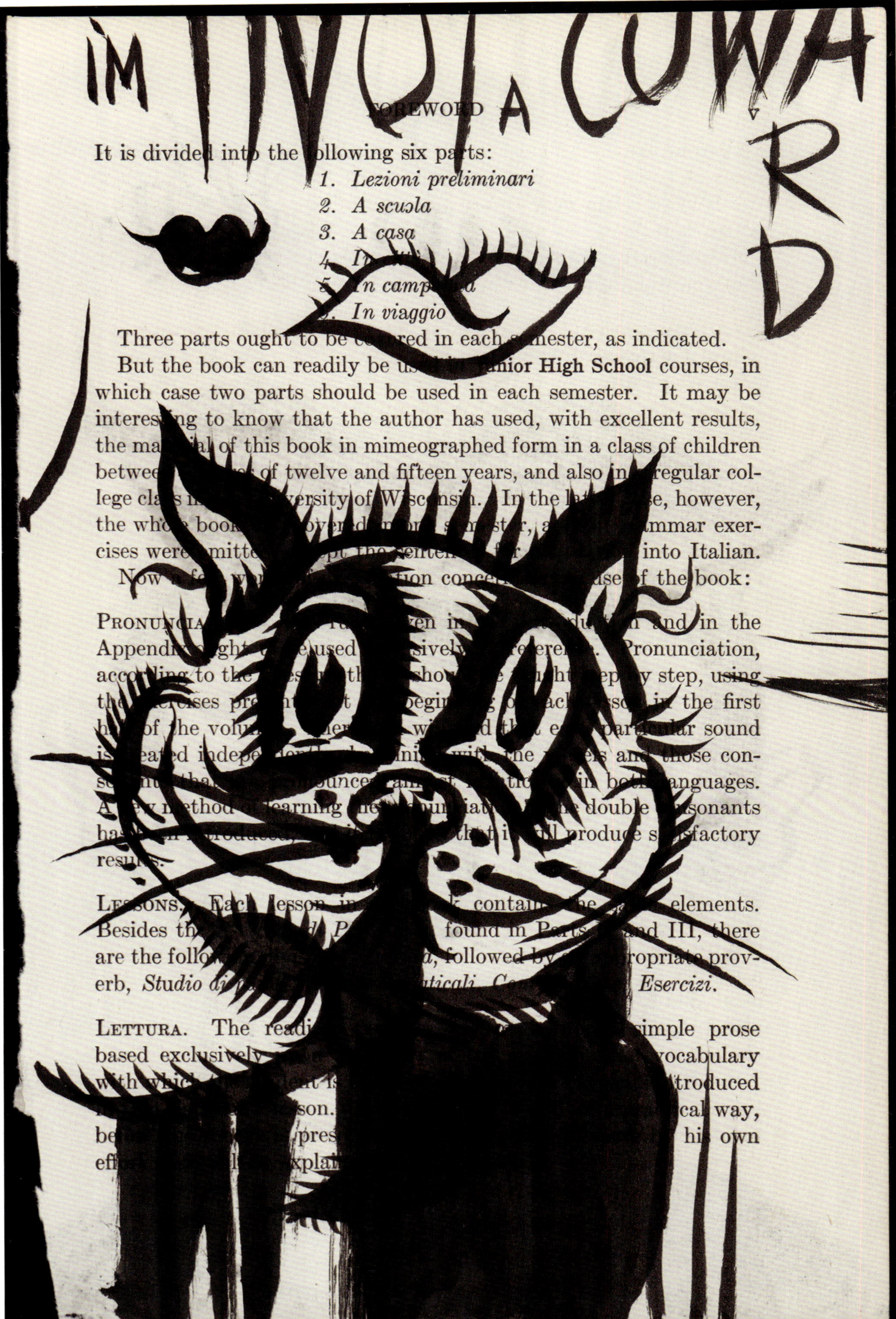

IM NOT A COWARD
FOREWORD
It is divided into the following six parts:
1. Lezioni preliminari
2. A scuola
3. A casa
4. In città
5. In campagna
6. In viaggio
Three parts ought to be covered in each semester, as indicated.
But the book can readily be used in Junior High School courses, in which case two parts should be used in each semester. It may be interesting to know that the author has used, with excellent results, the material of this book in mimeographed form in a class of children between the ages of twelve and fifteen years, and also in a regular college class in the University of Wisconsin. In the latter case, however, the whole book was covered in one semester, and the grammar exercises were omitted except the sentences for translation into Italian.
Now a few words of direction concerning the use of the book:
PRONUNCIATION is given in the Introduction and in the Appendix, and ought to be used extensively for reference. Pronunciation, according to the rules in this book, should be taught step by step, using the exercises provided at the beginning of each lesson in the first half of the volume. There it will be found that each particular sound is treated independently, beginning with the vowels and those consonants that are pronounced almost identically in both languages. A key method of learning the pronunciation of the double consonants has been introduced, one that it is felt will produce satisfactory results.
LESSONS. Each lesson in this book contains the same elements. Besides the Grammar and Pronunciation found in Parts II and III, there are the following: a Lettura, followed by an appropriate proverb, Studio di parole, Note grammaticali, Conversazione, and Esercizi.
LETTURA. The reading lessons are simple prose based exclusively on the vocabulary with which the student is already acquainted or which is introduced in the same lesson. They are arranged in a practical way, beginning with the presentation of his own efforts and explanations.

STUDIO DI PAROLE. The choice of the words included in the vocabu-laries is based on several published word lists. A few additional words and certain very common idiomatic expressions were added. Altogether, the active vocabulary which the student has to learn (fifteen or sixteen words for each lesson, as an average) suffices for the expression of thoughts in a large variety of fields.

NOTE GRAMMATICALI. The guiding principle which the author has followed is that of giving as few grammar rules as possible, presented in the simplest form. Only the essential points are given as required by the Minim... most important sch... Americ... Only the ... active ... studi...

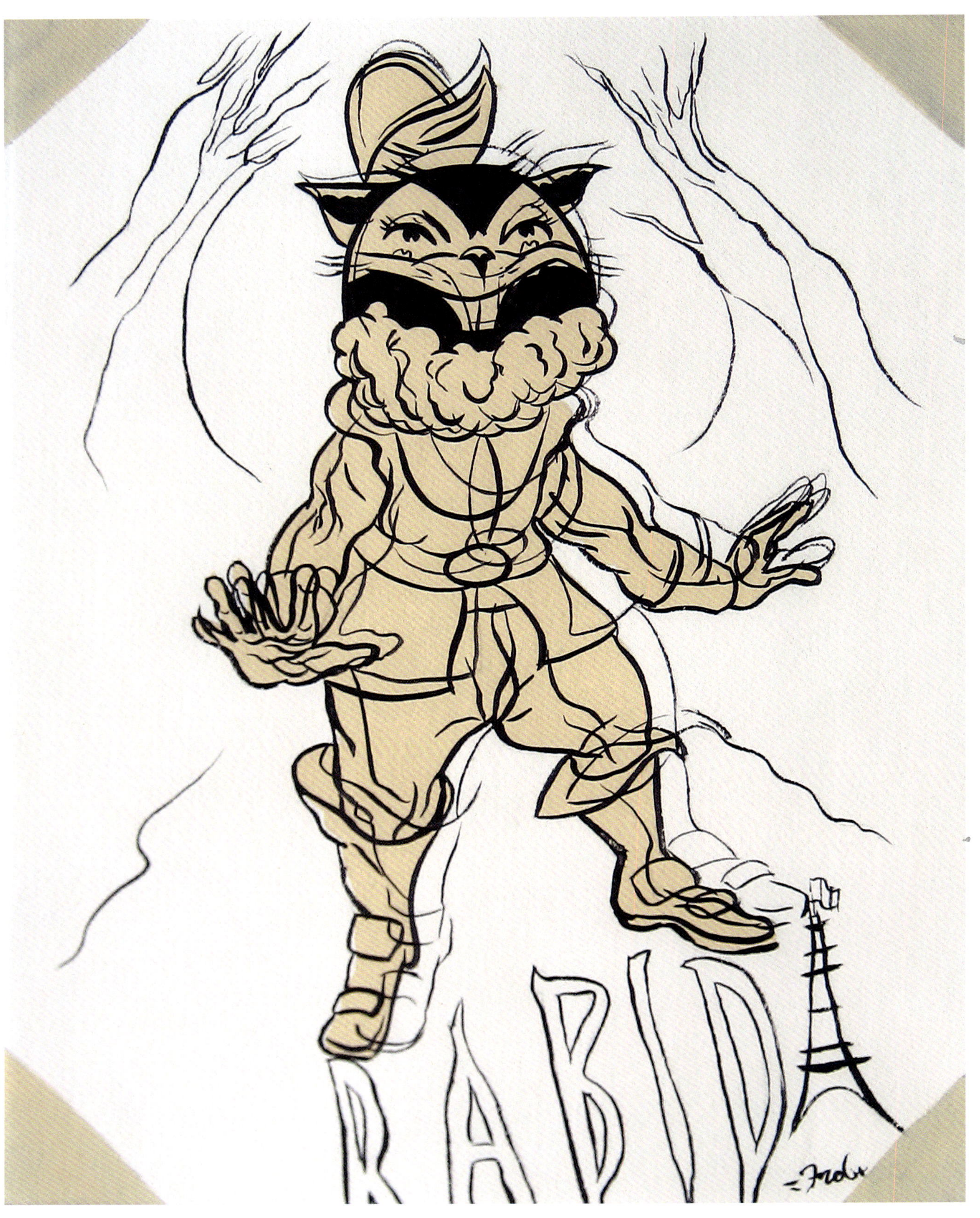

RABIDA

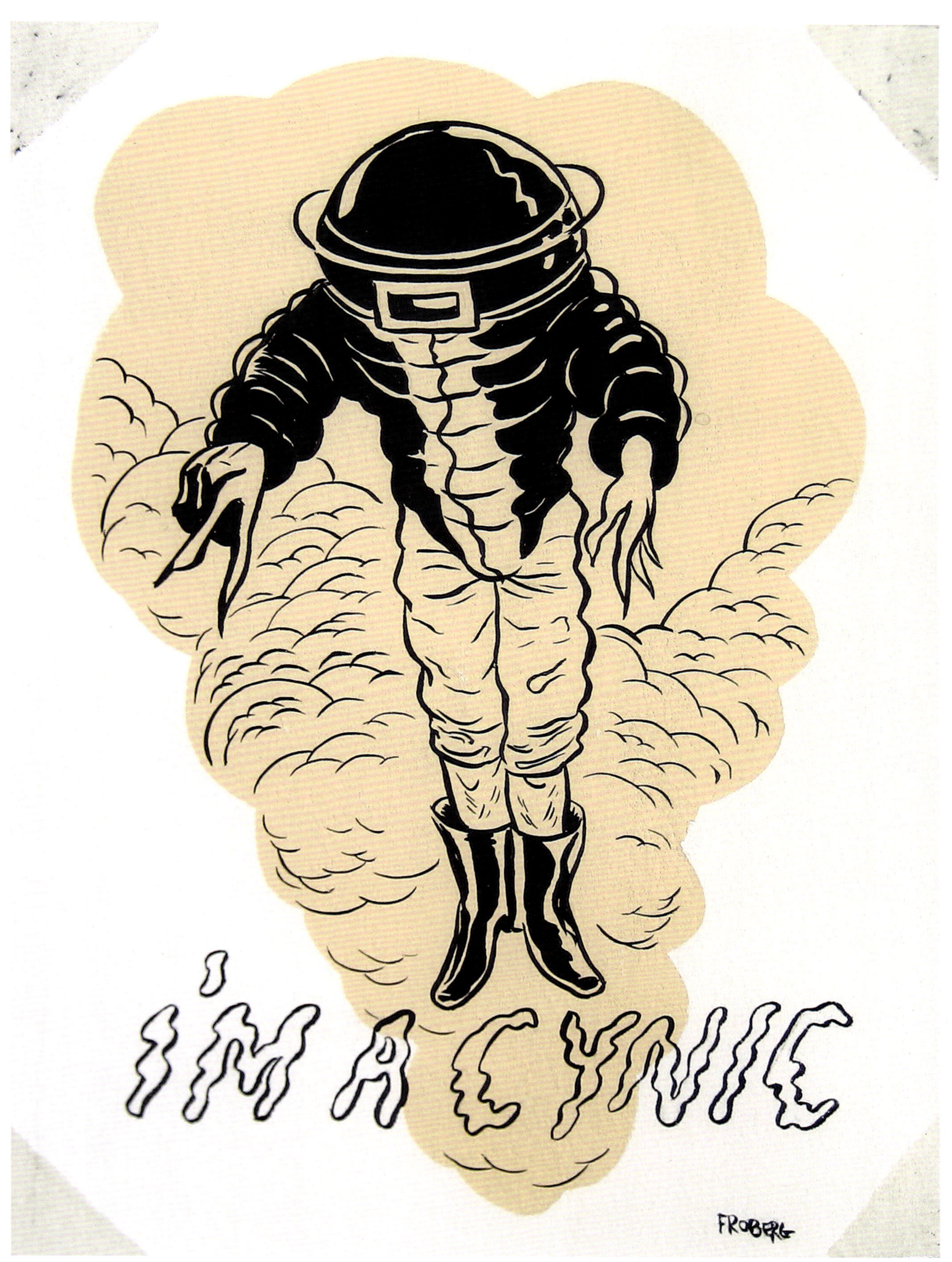
I'M A CYNIC
FROBERG

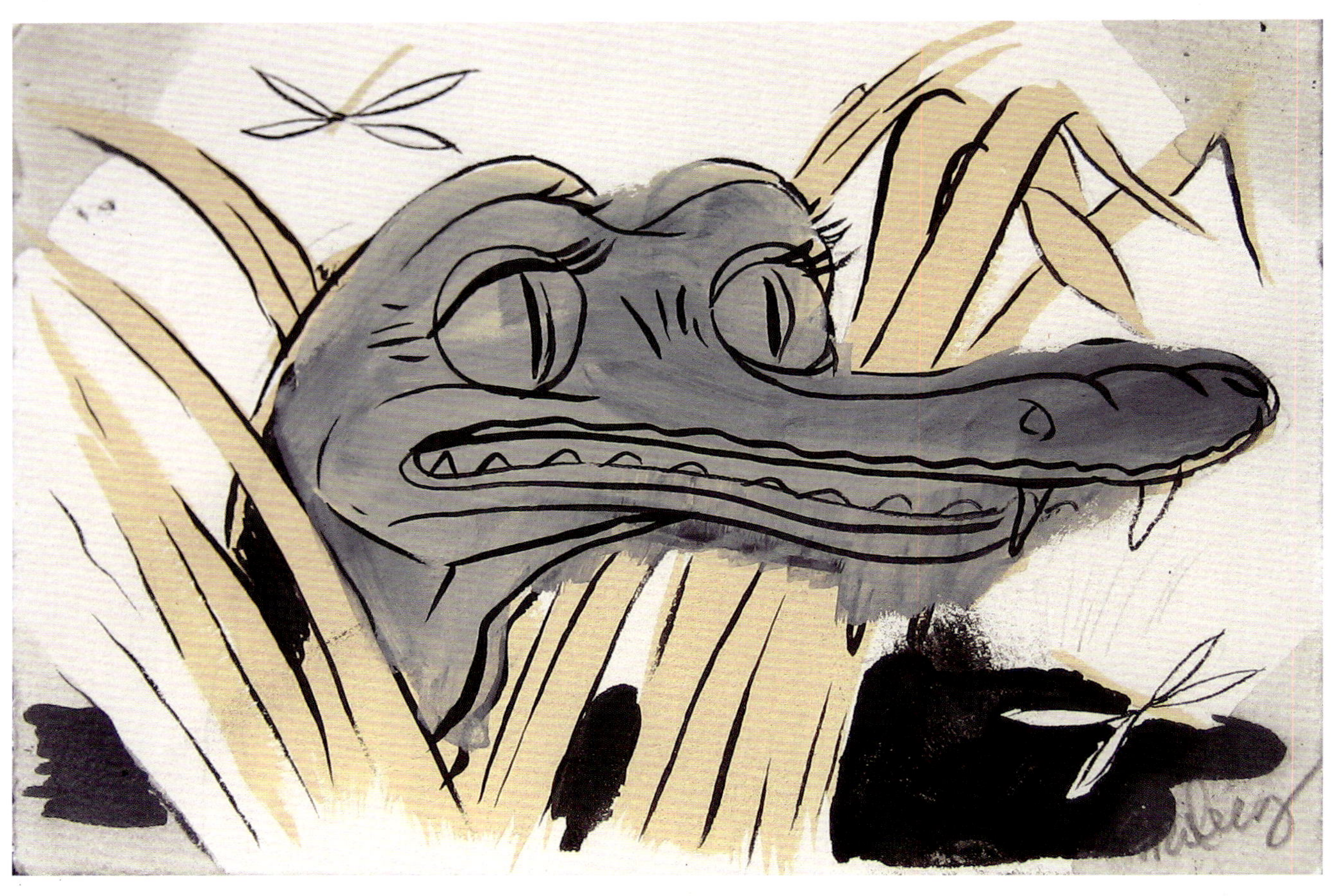

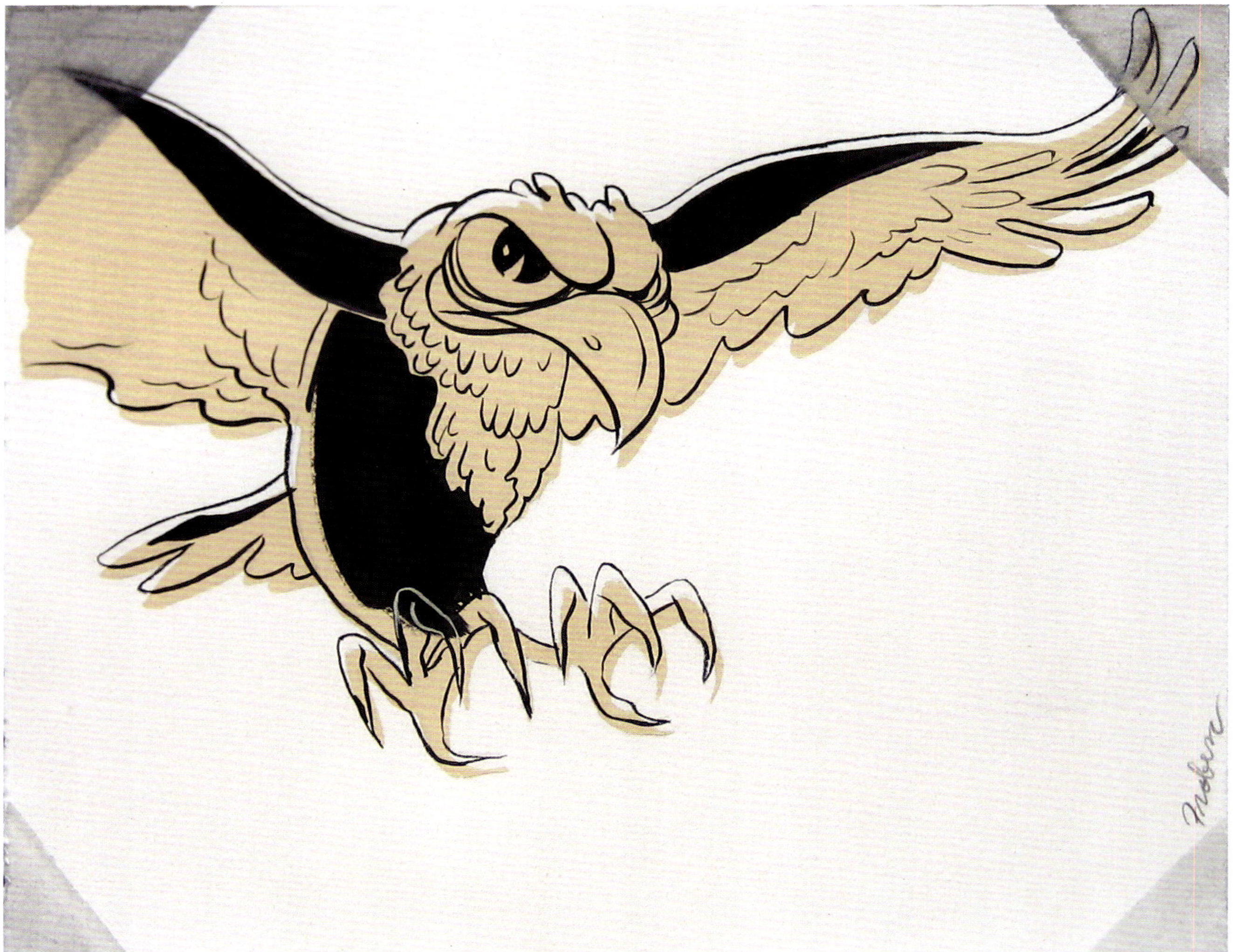

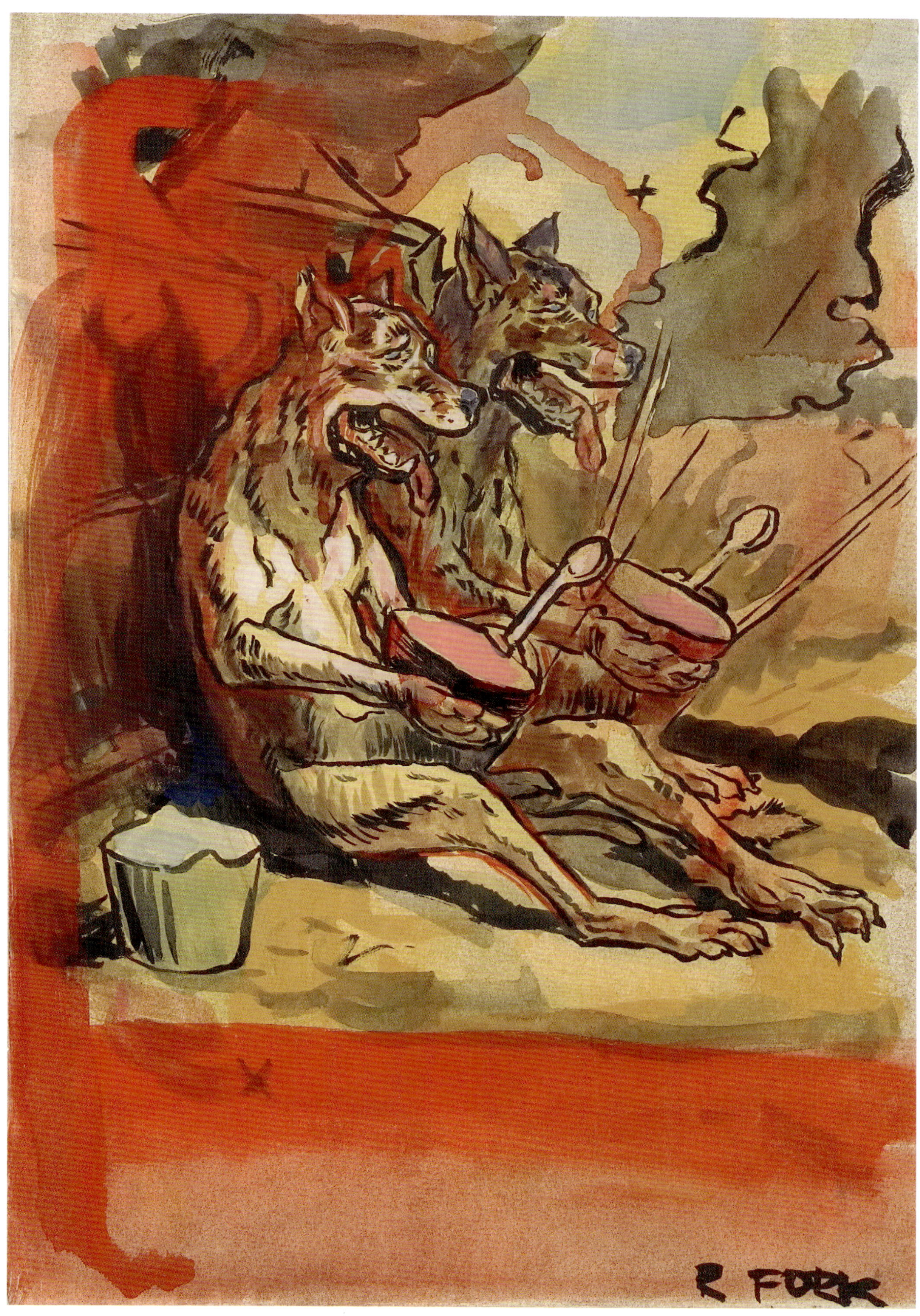

R FORK

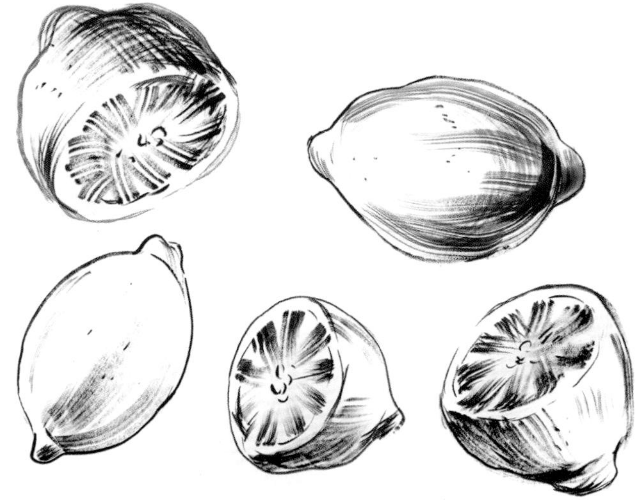

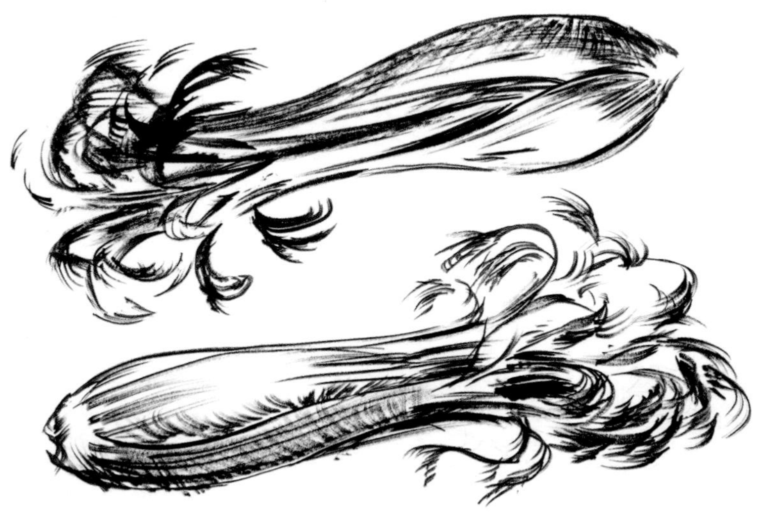

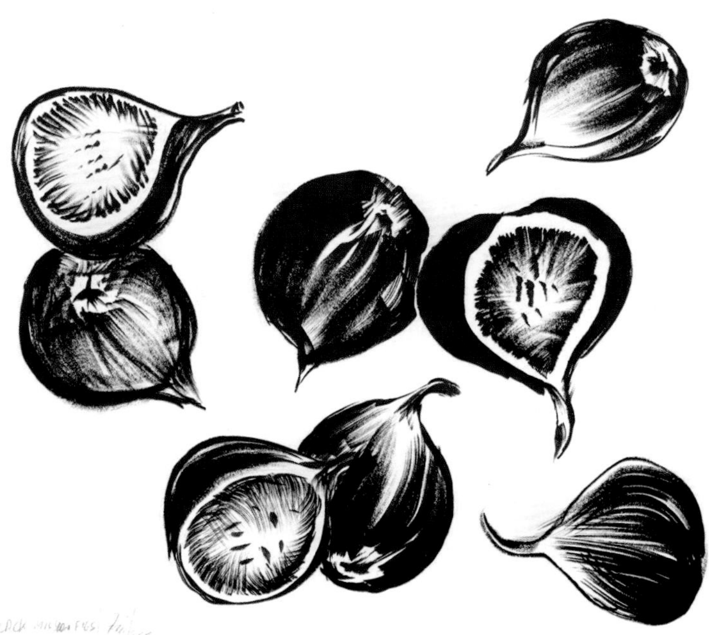

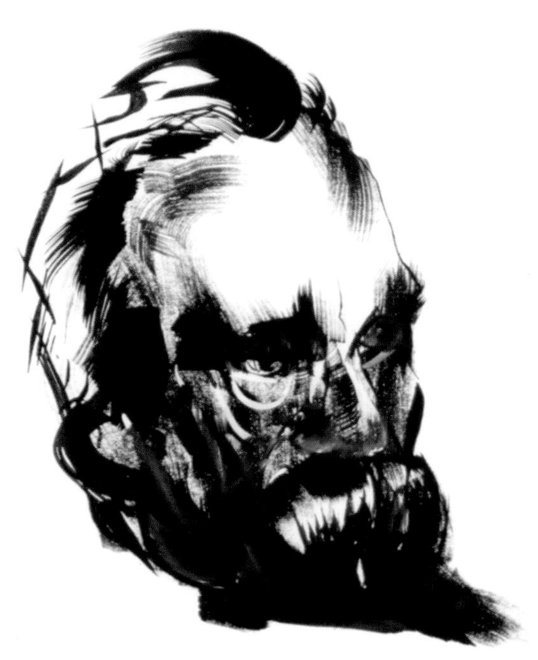
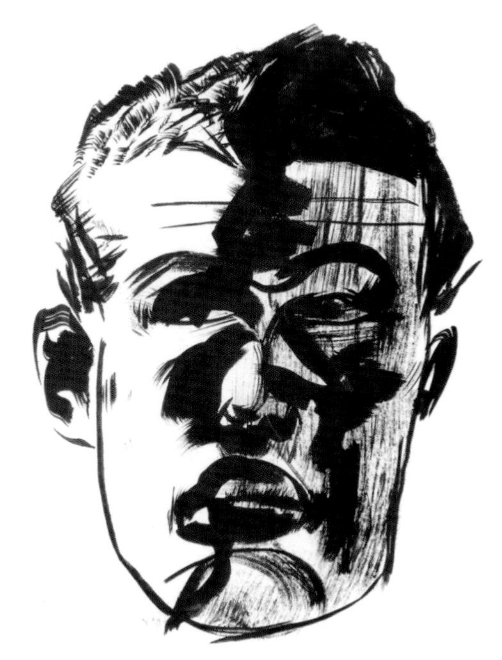
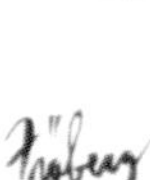
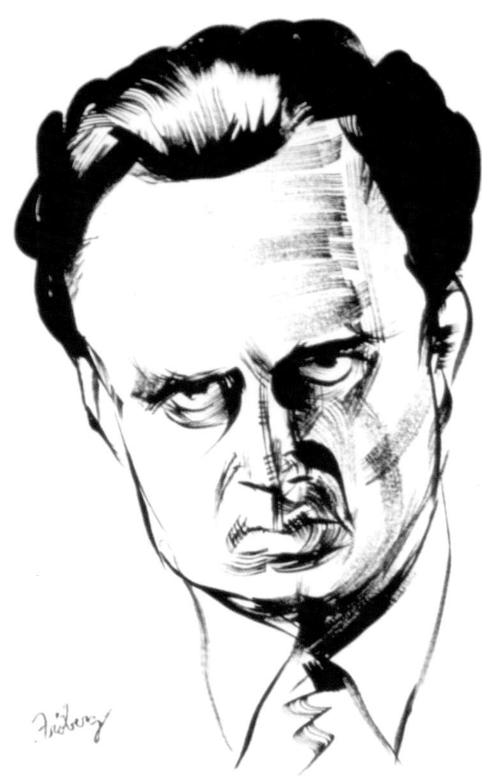
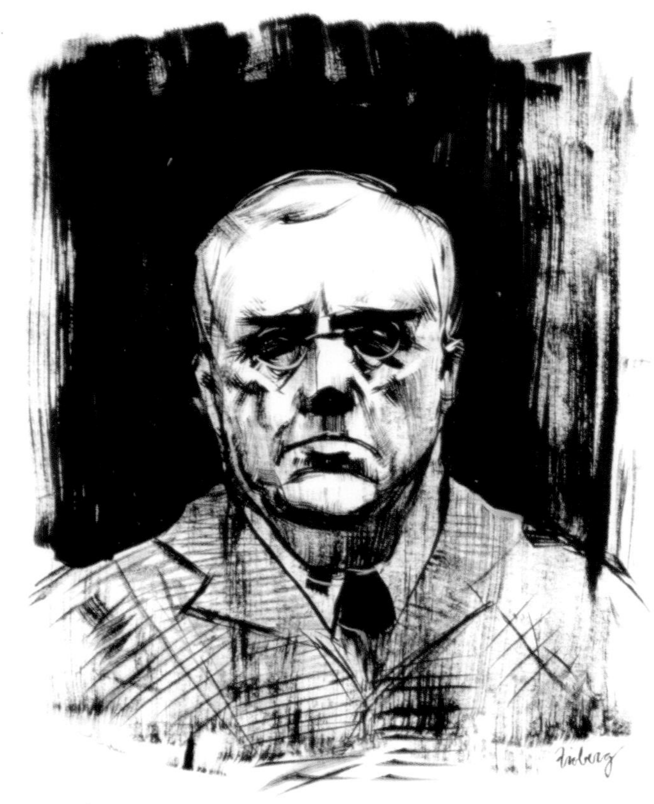

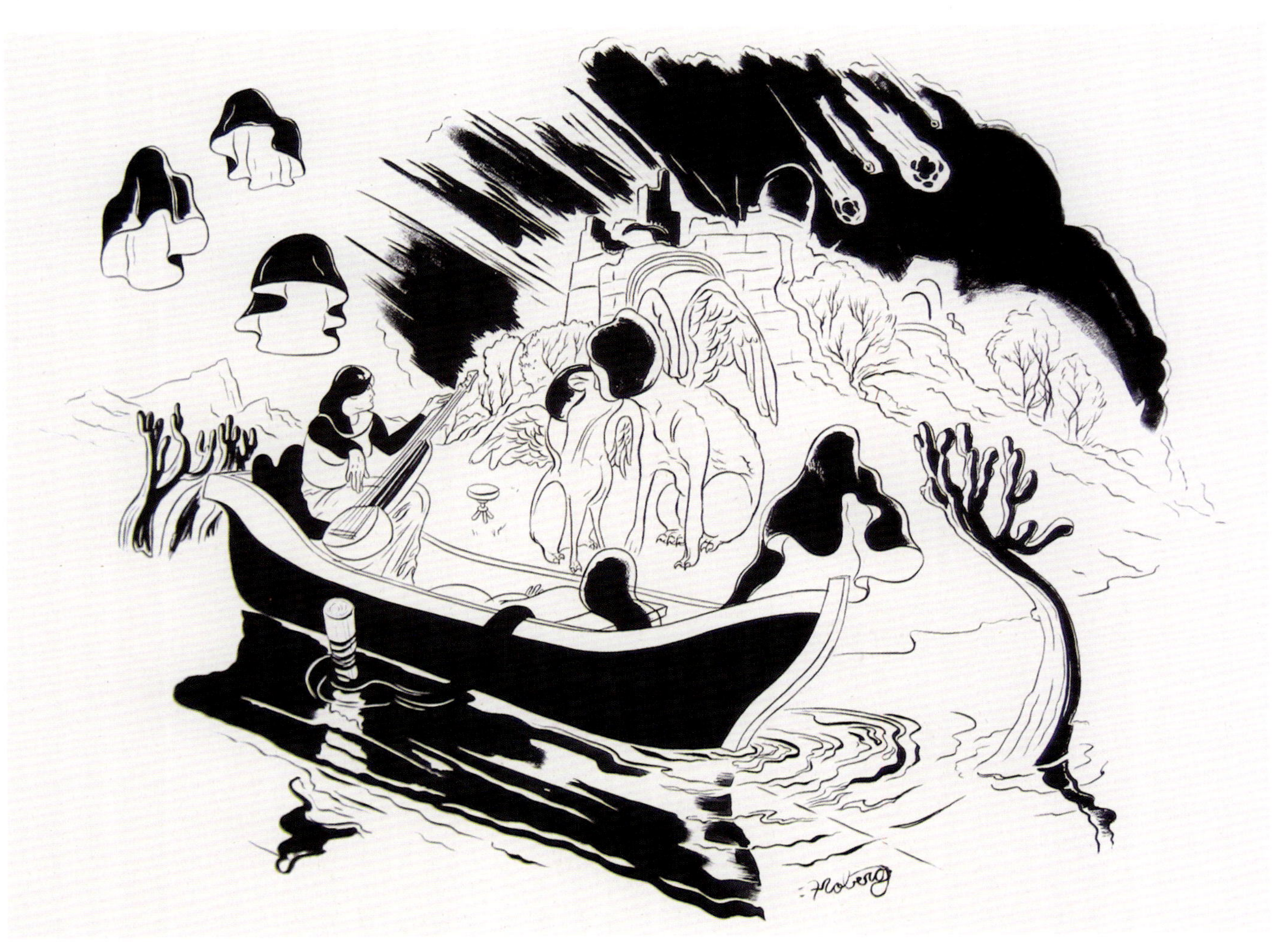

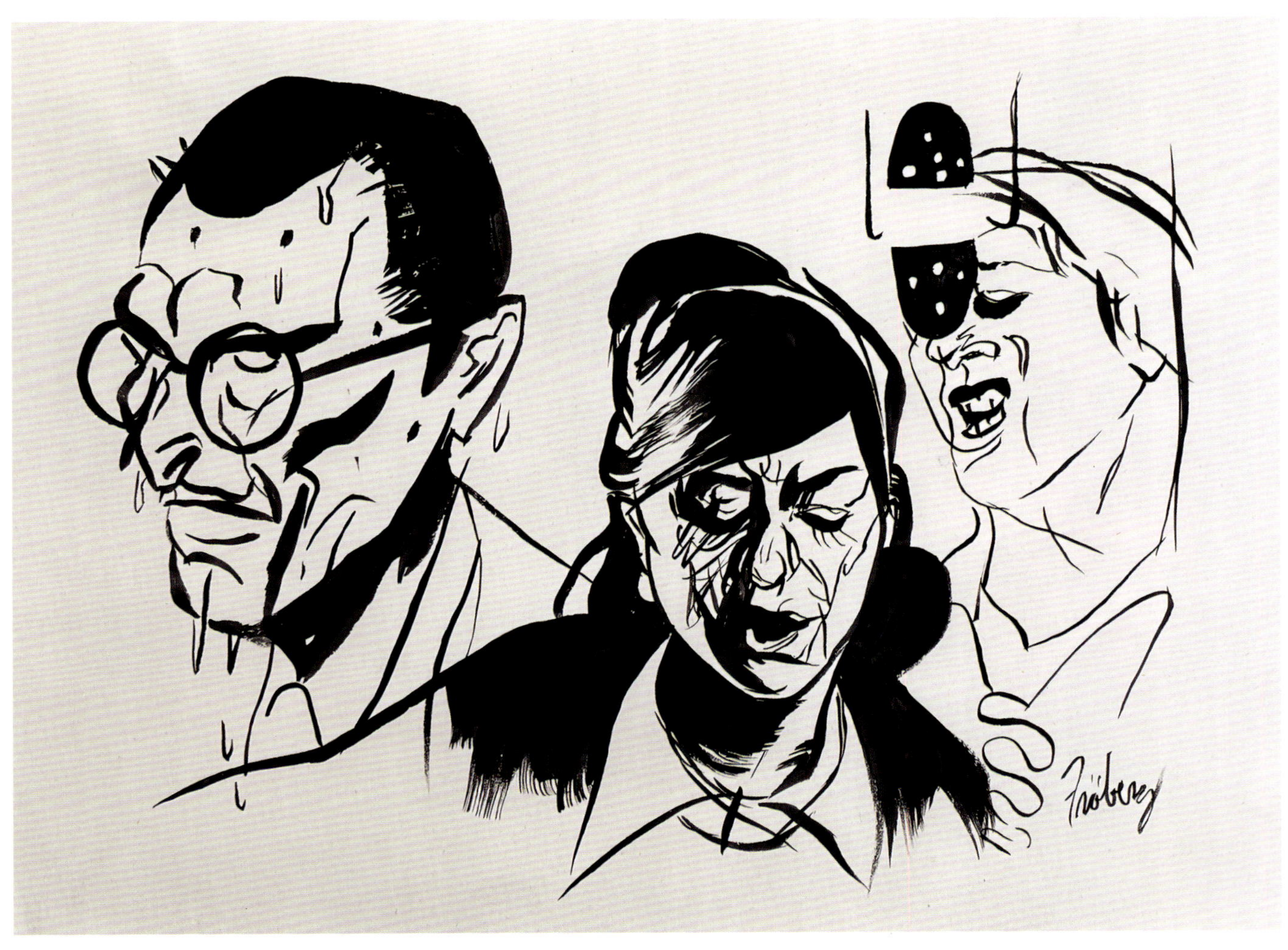

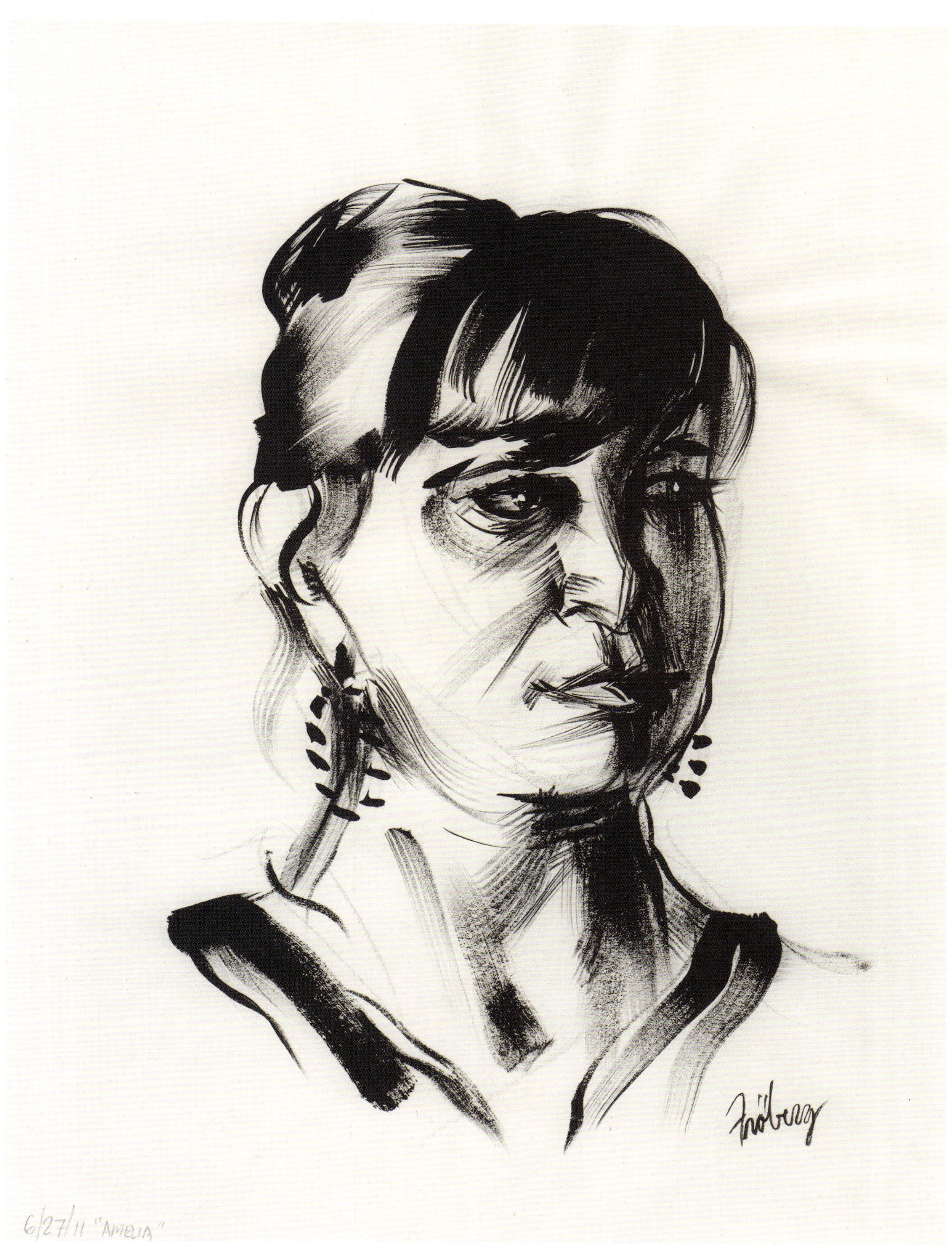

6/27/11 "Amelia"

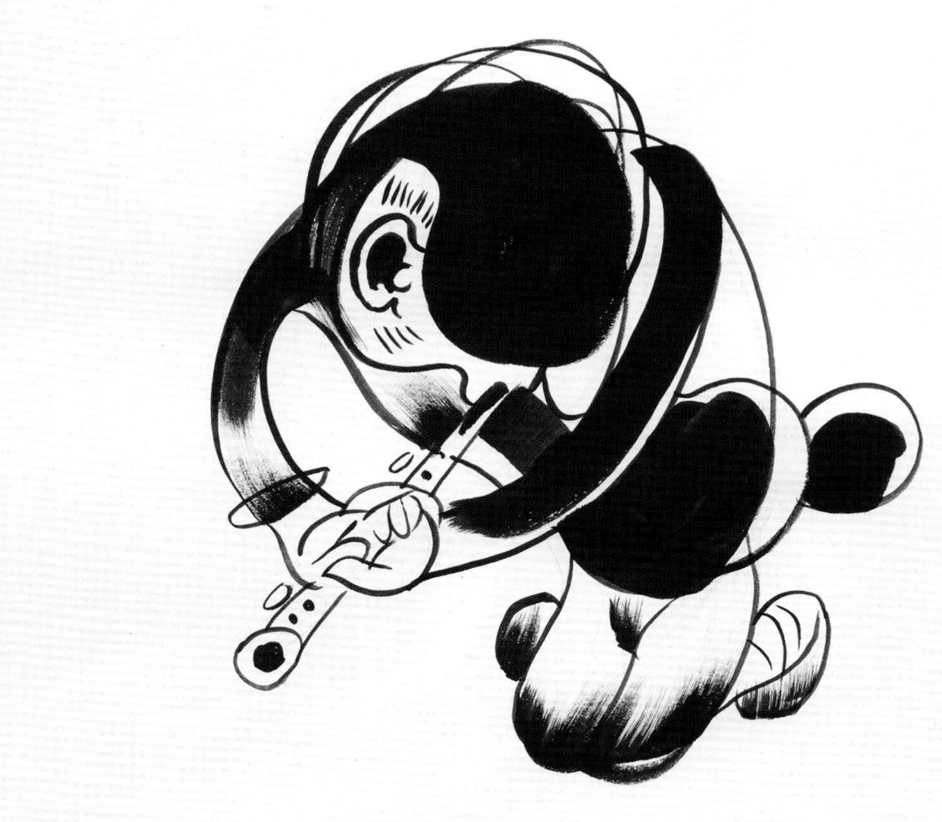

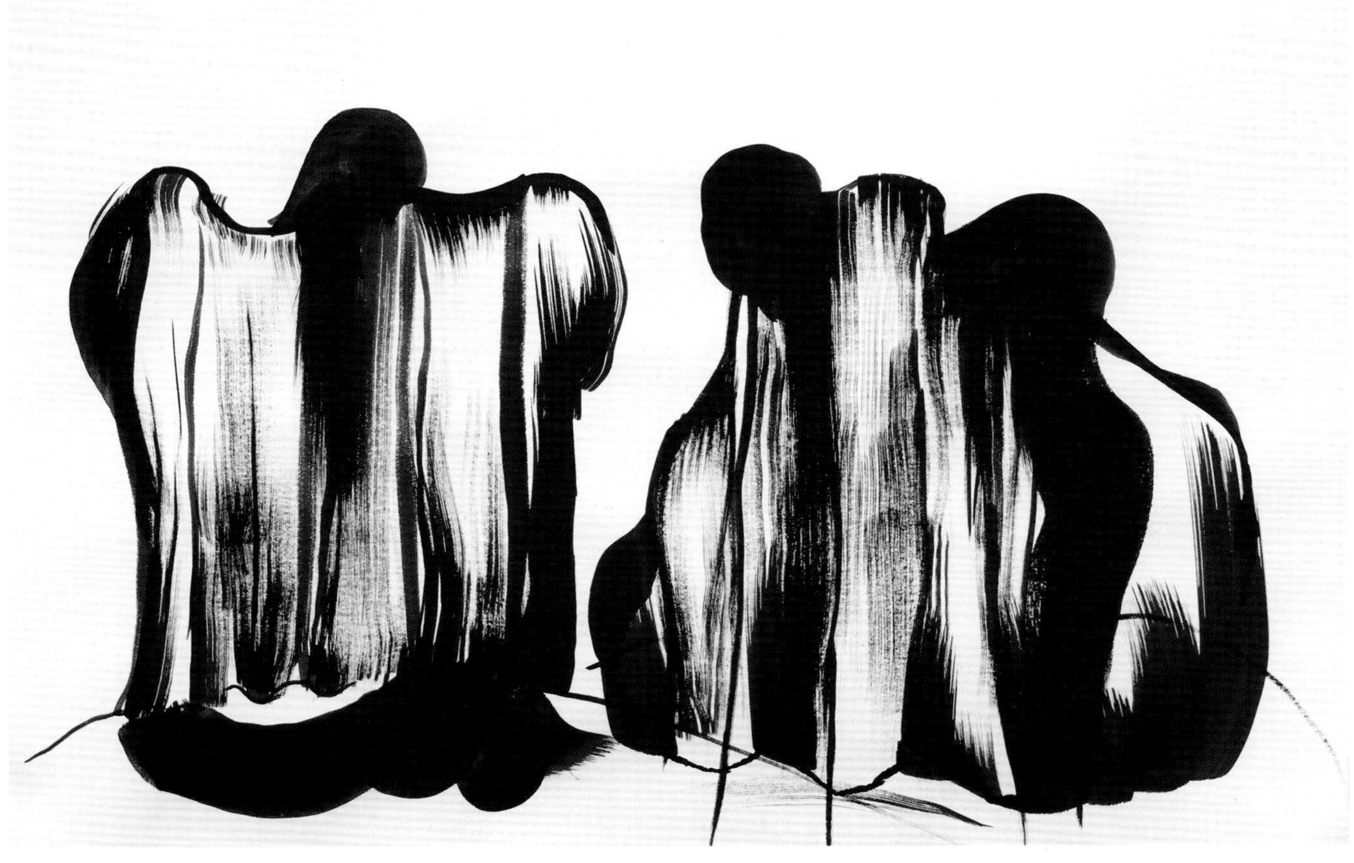

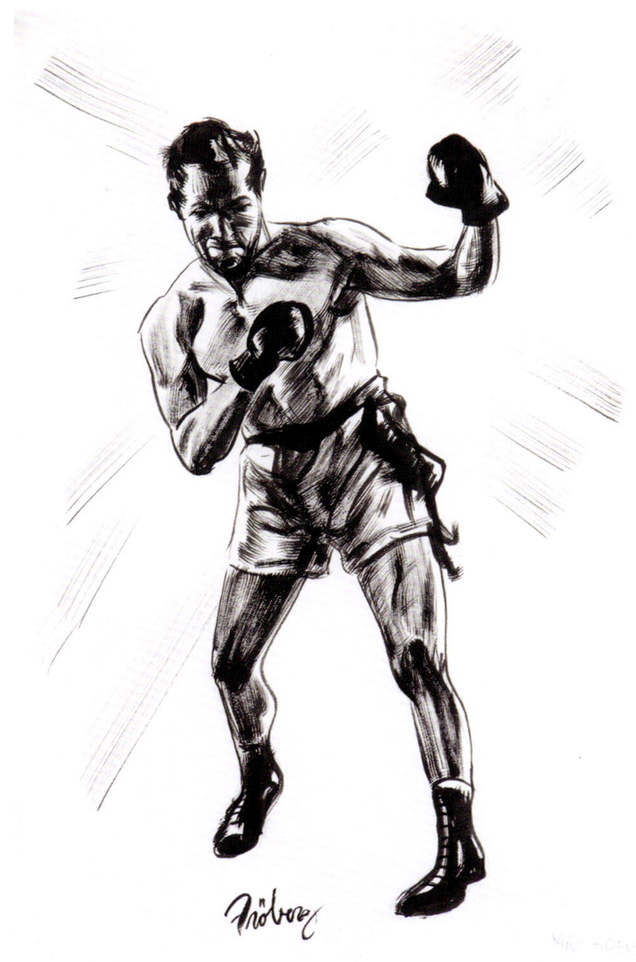

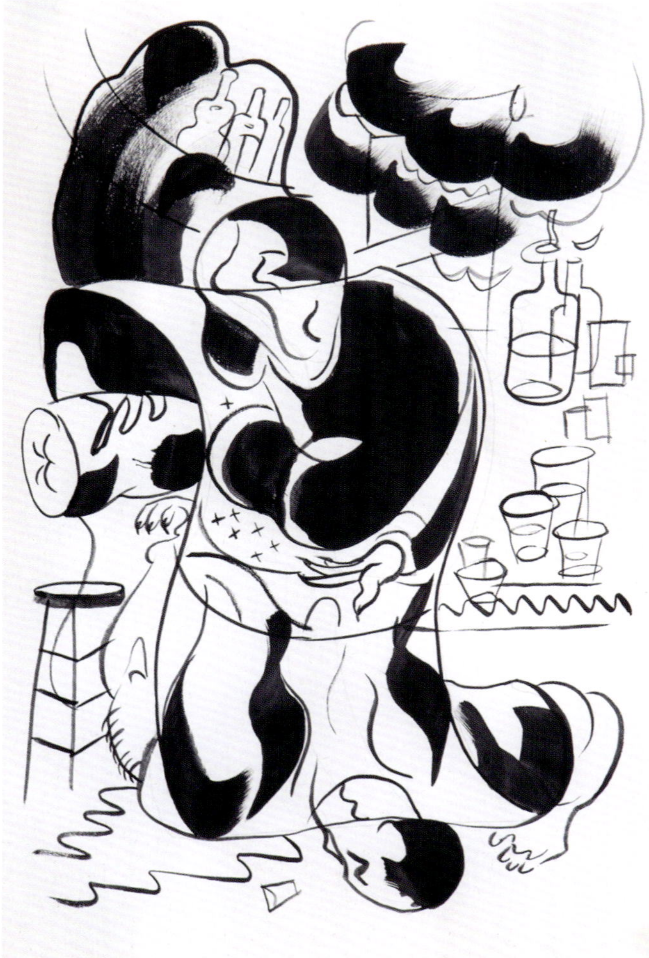

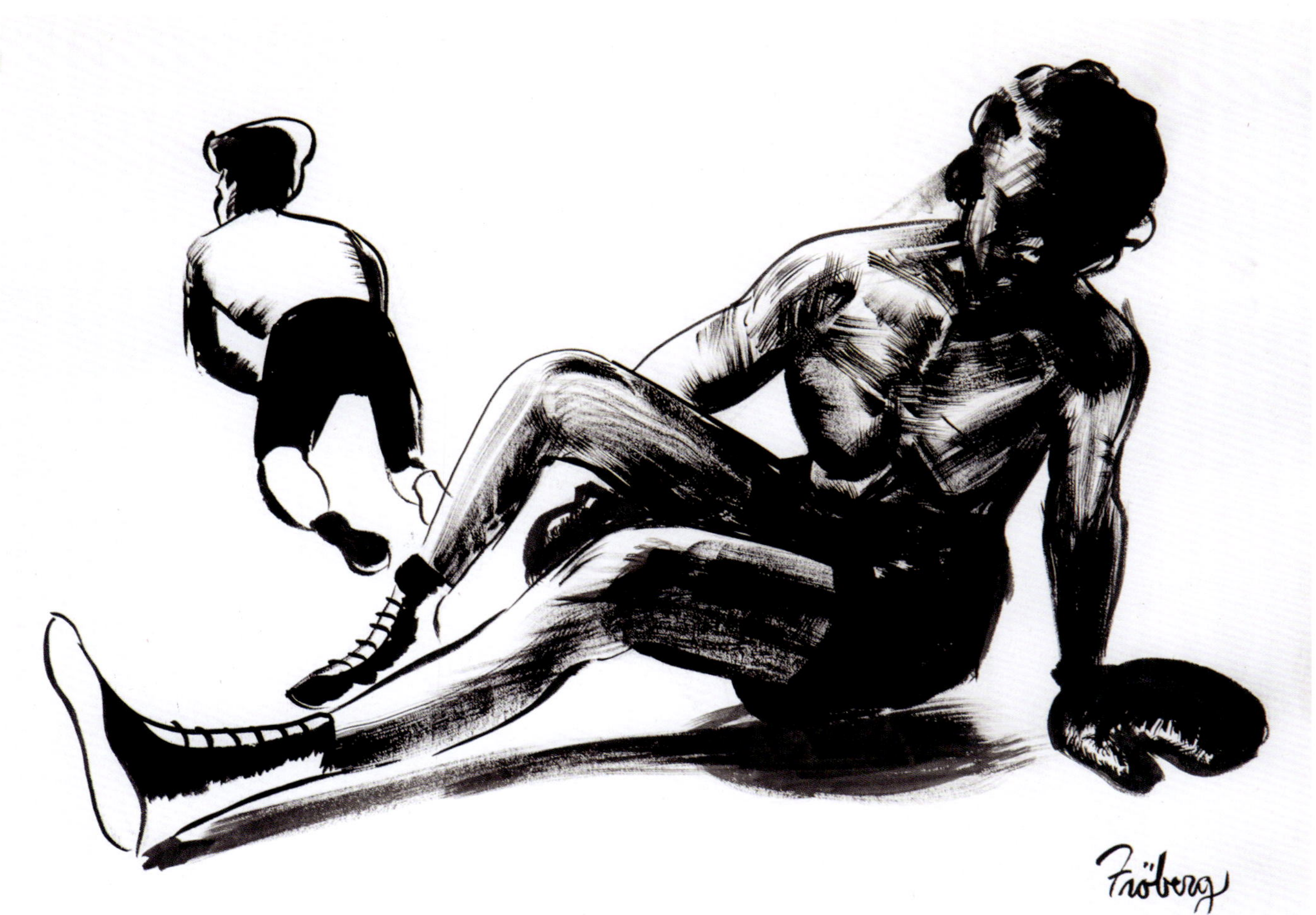

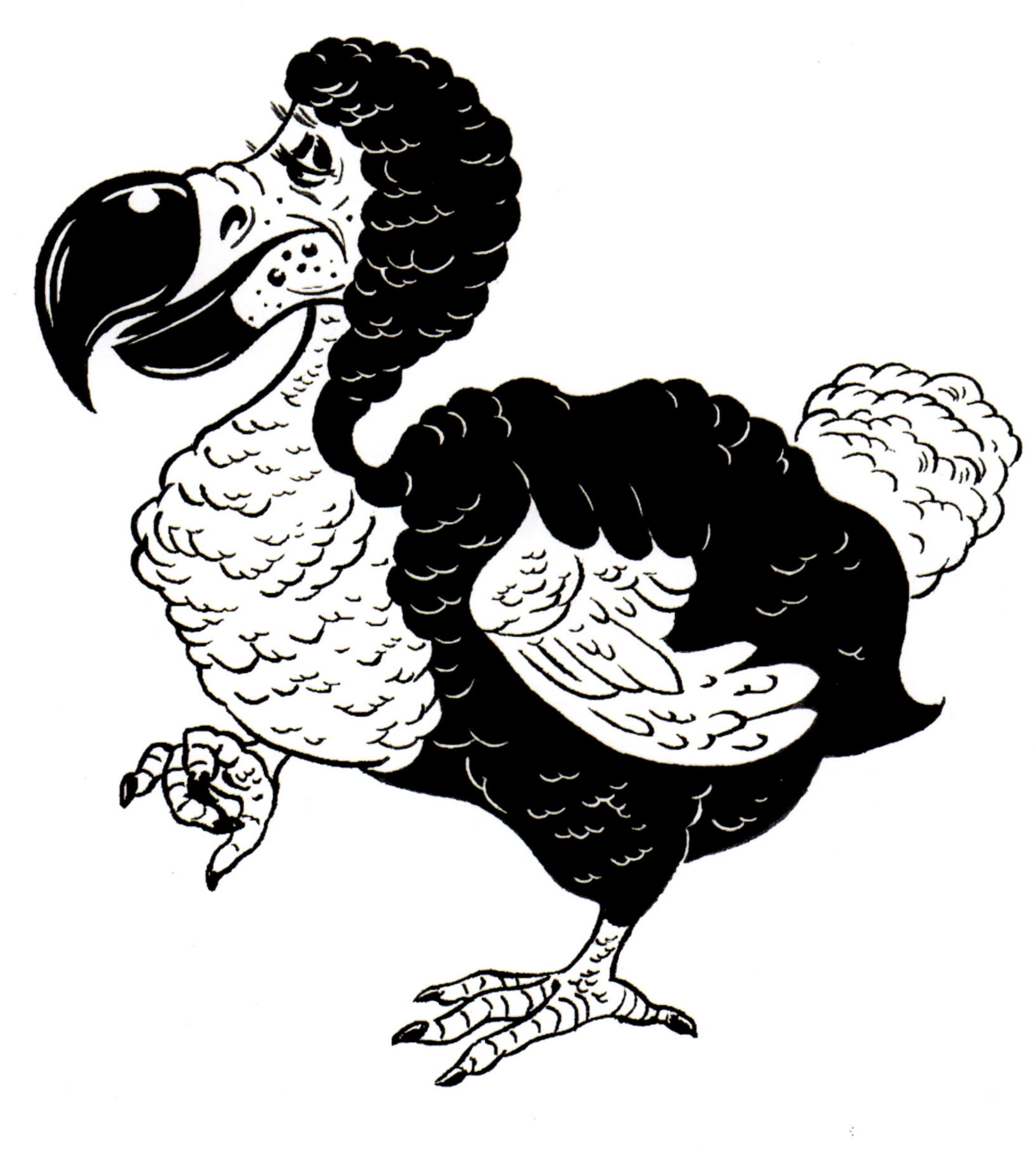

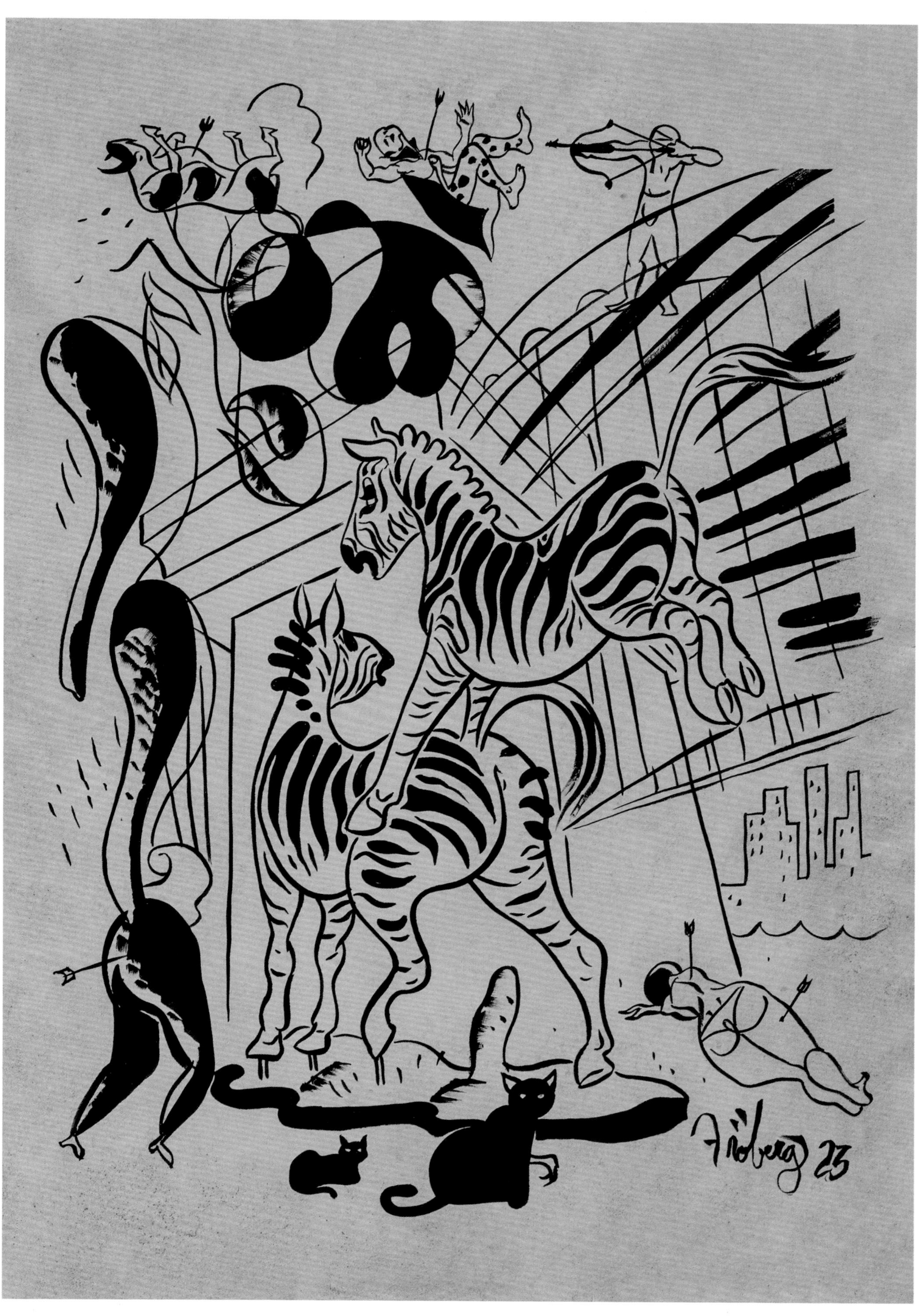

SEVEN
Digital Art, Sketches, and Animation

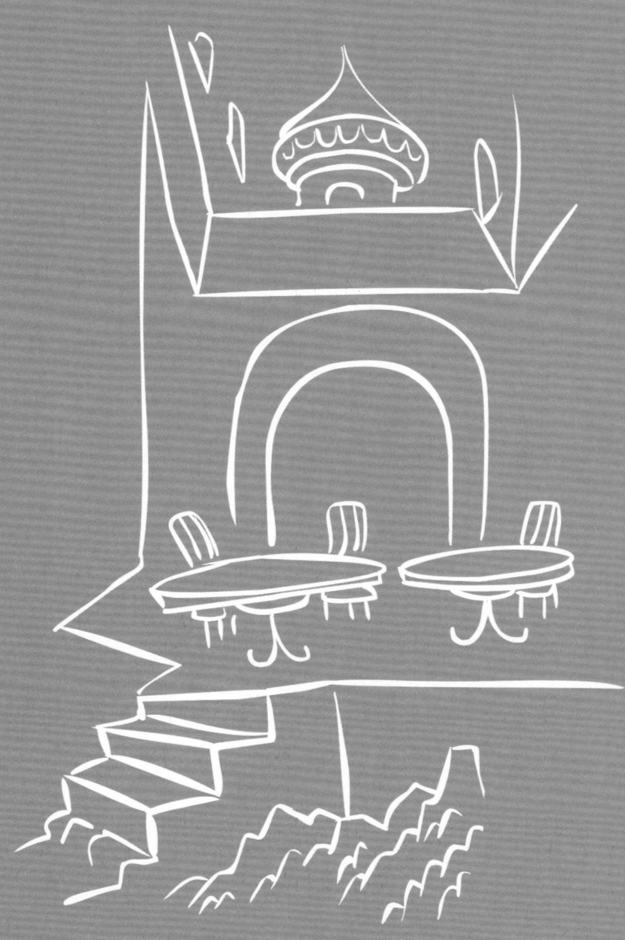

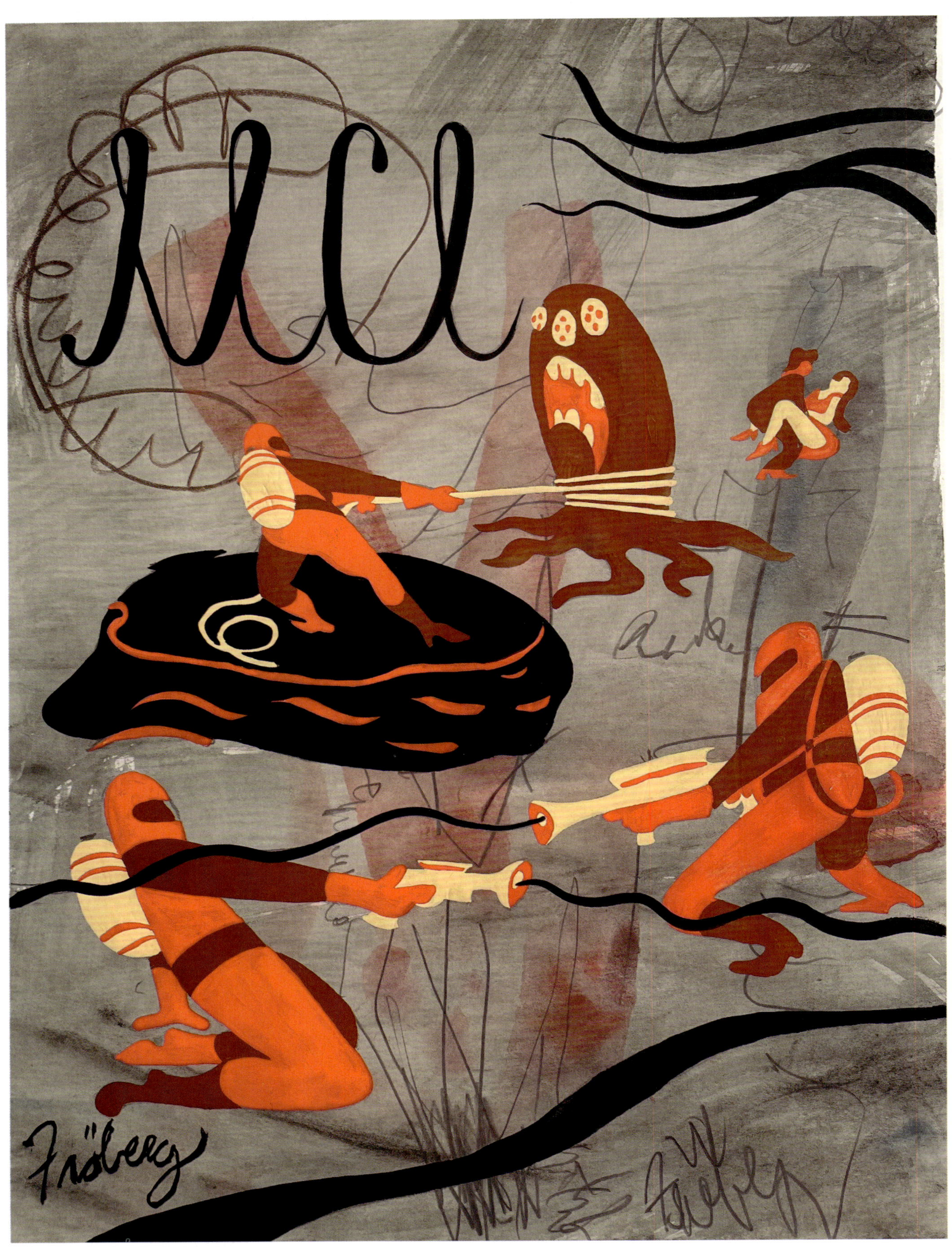
Fröberg

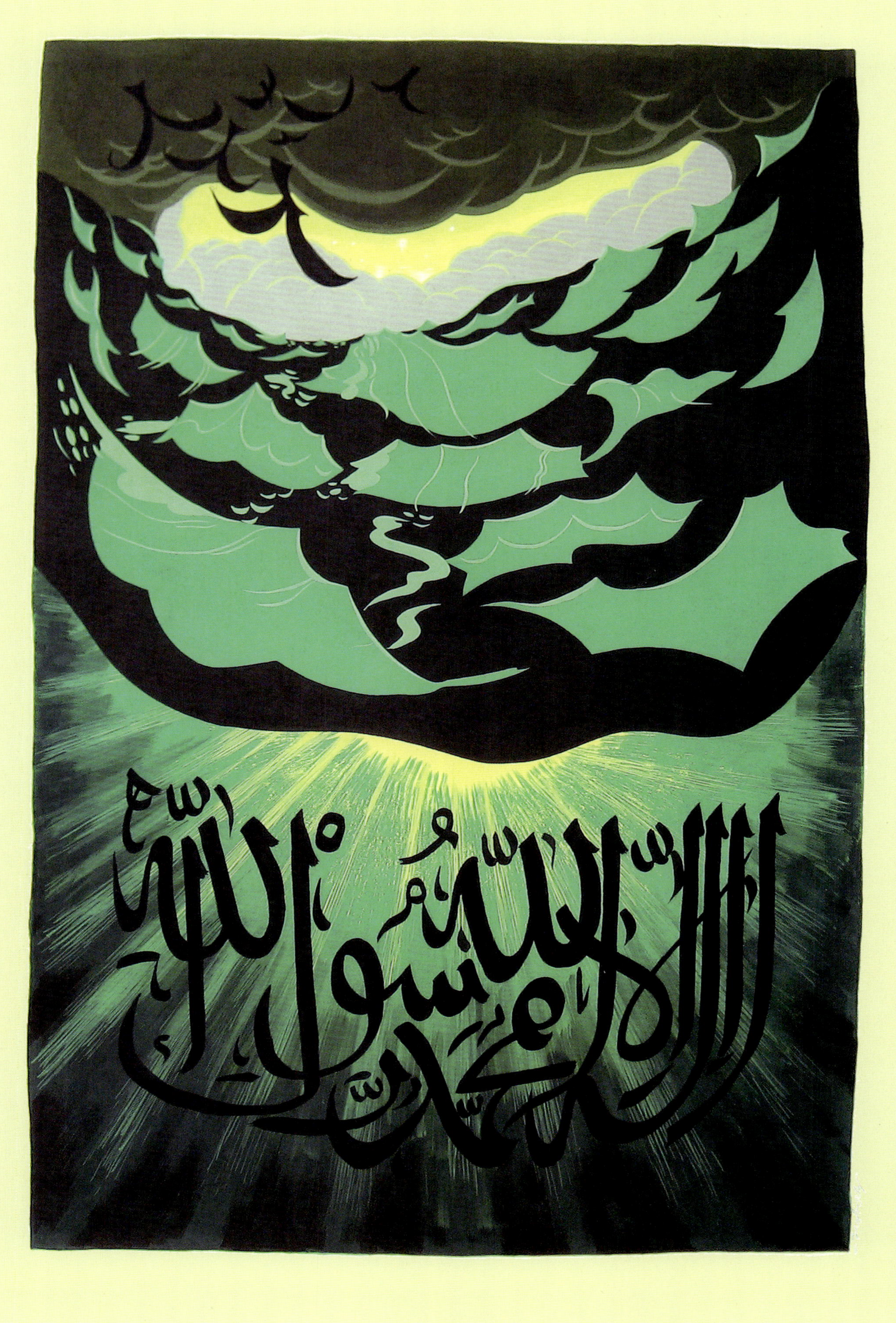

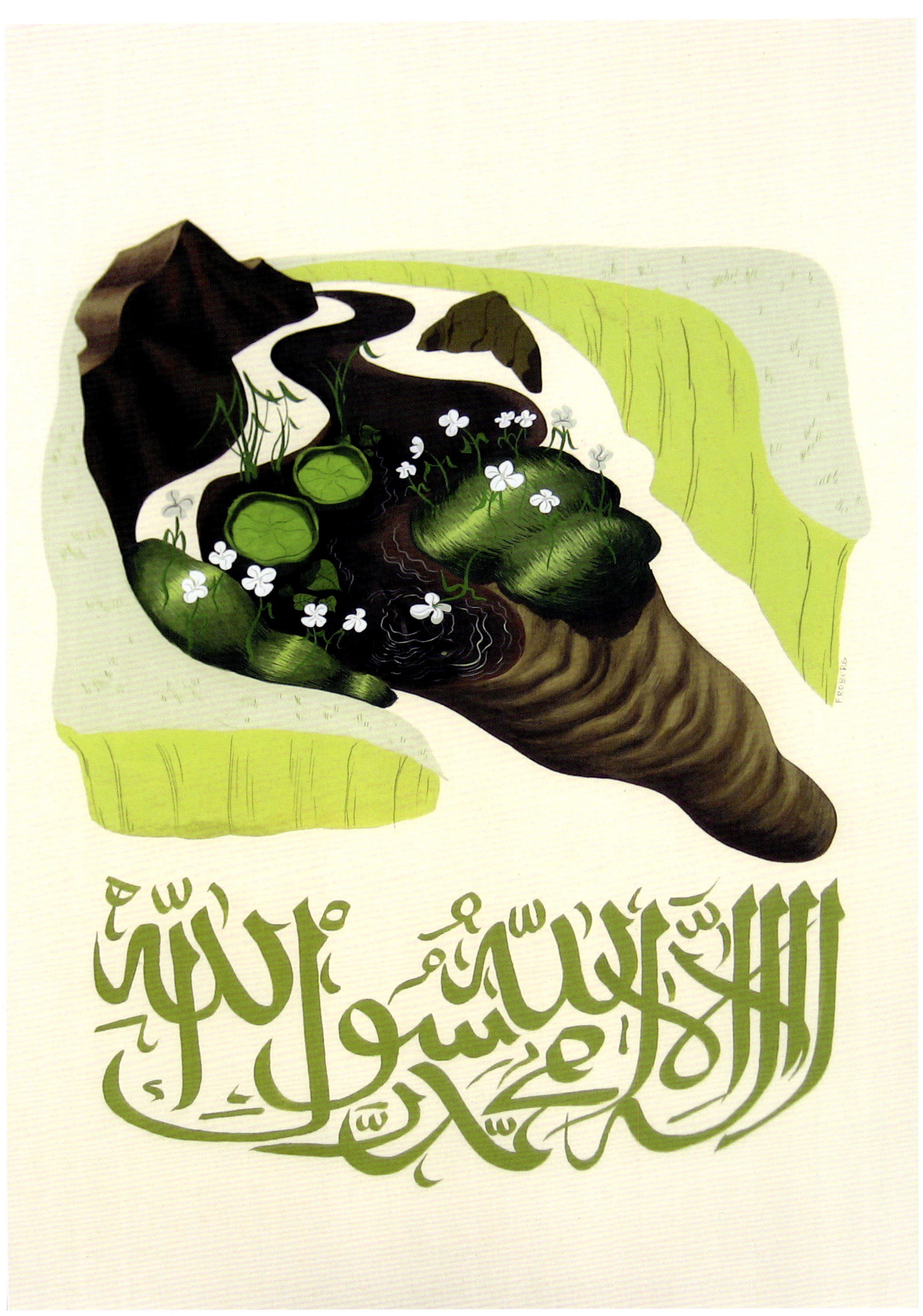

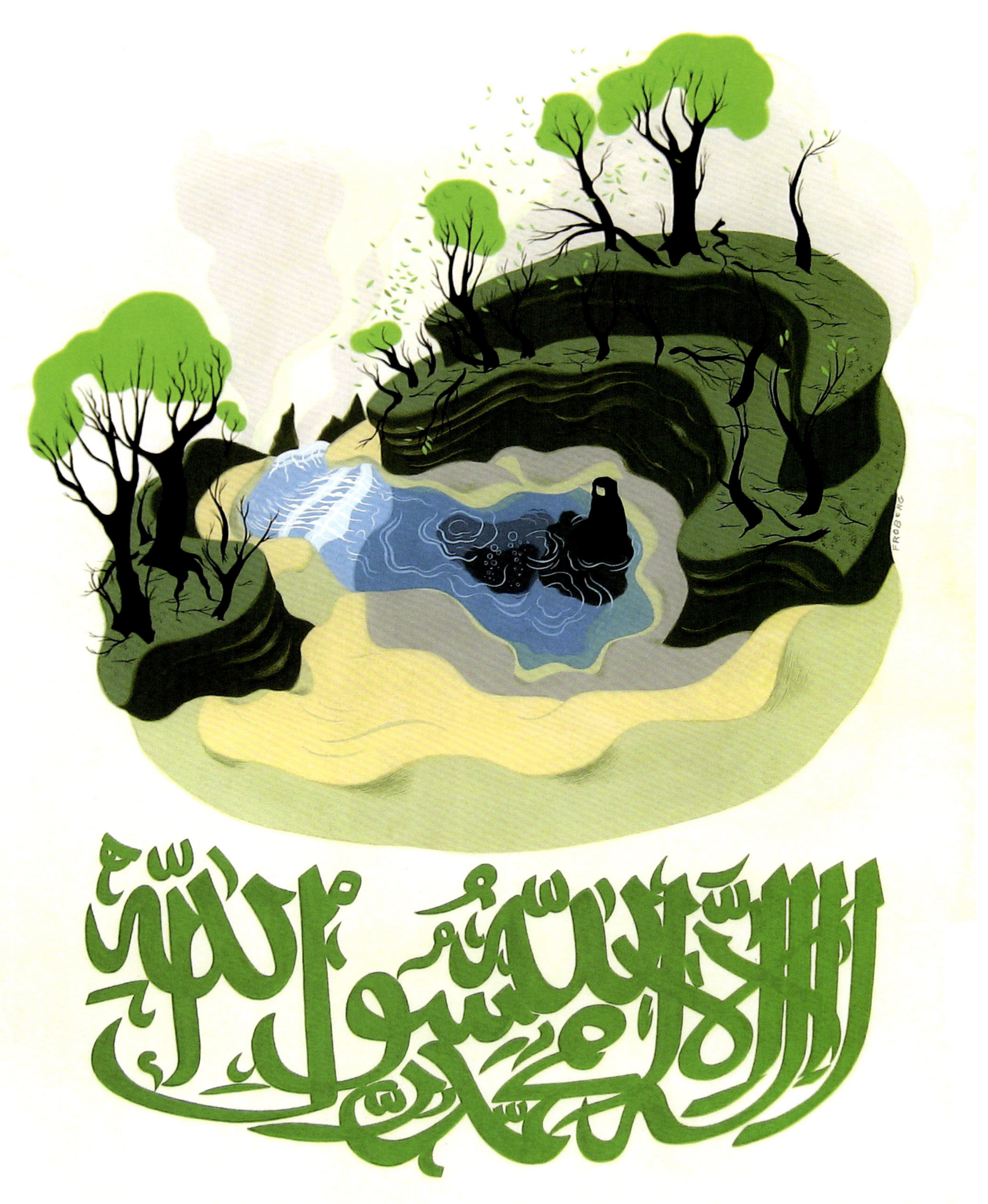

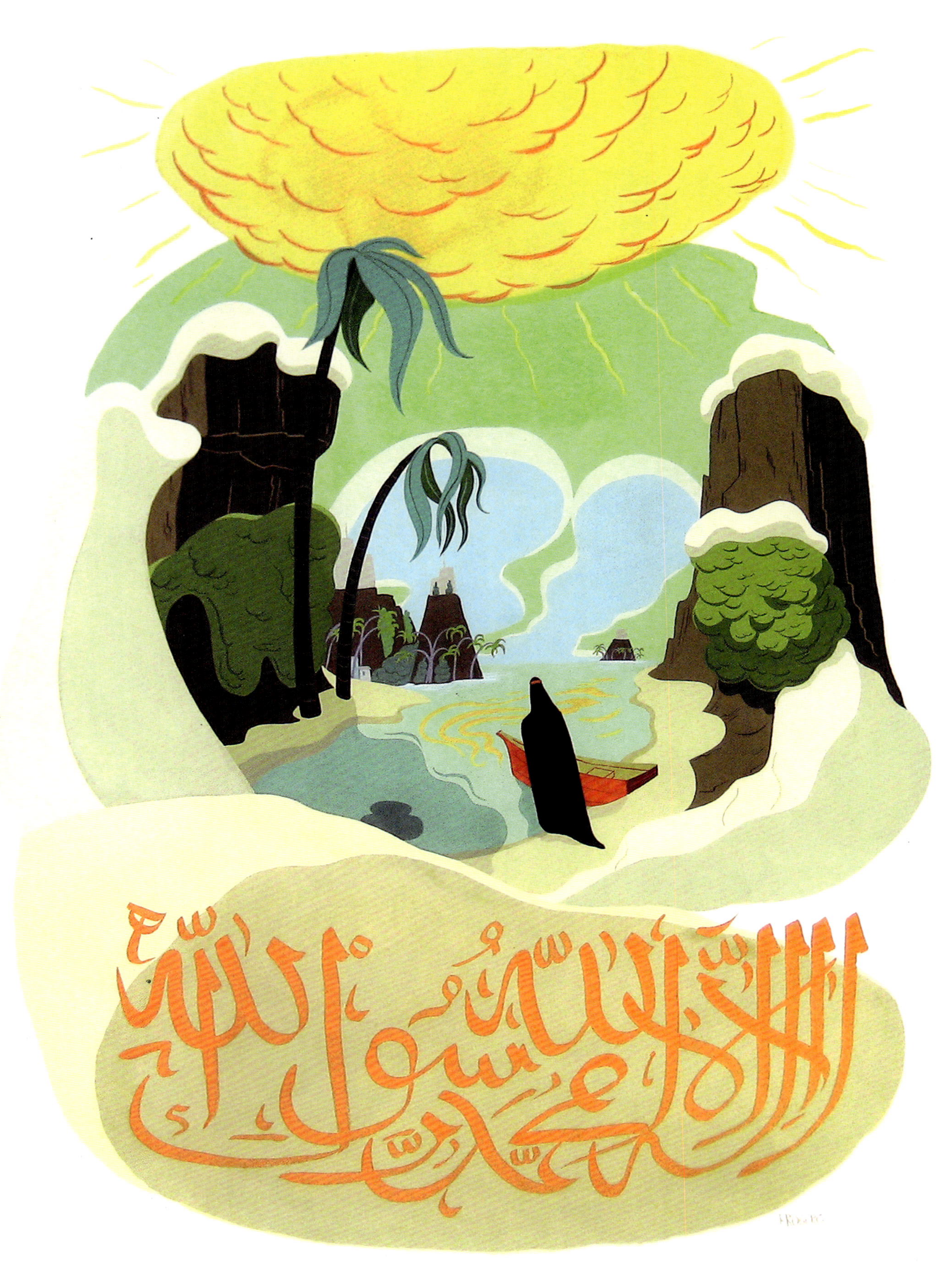

لا إله إلا الله محمد رسول الله

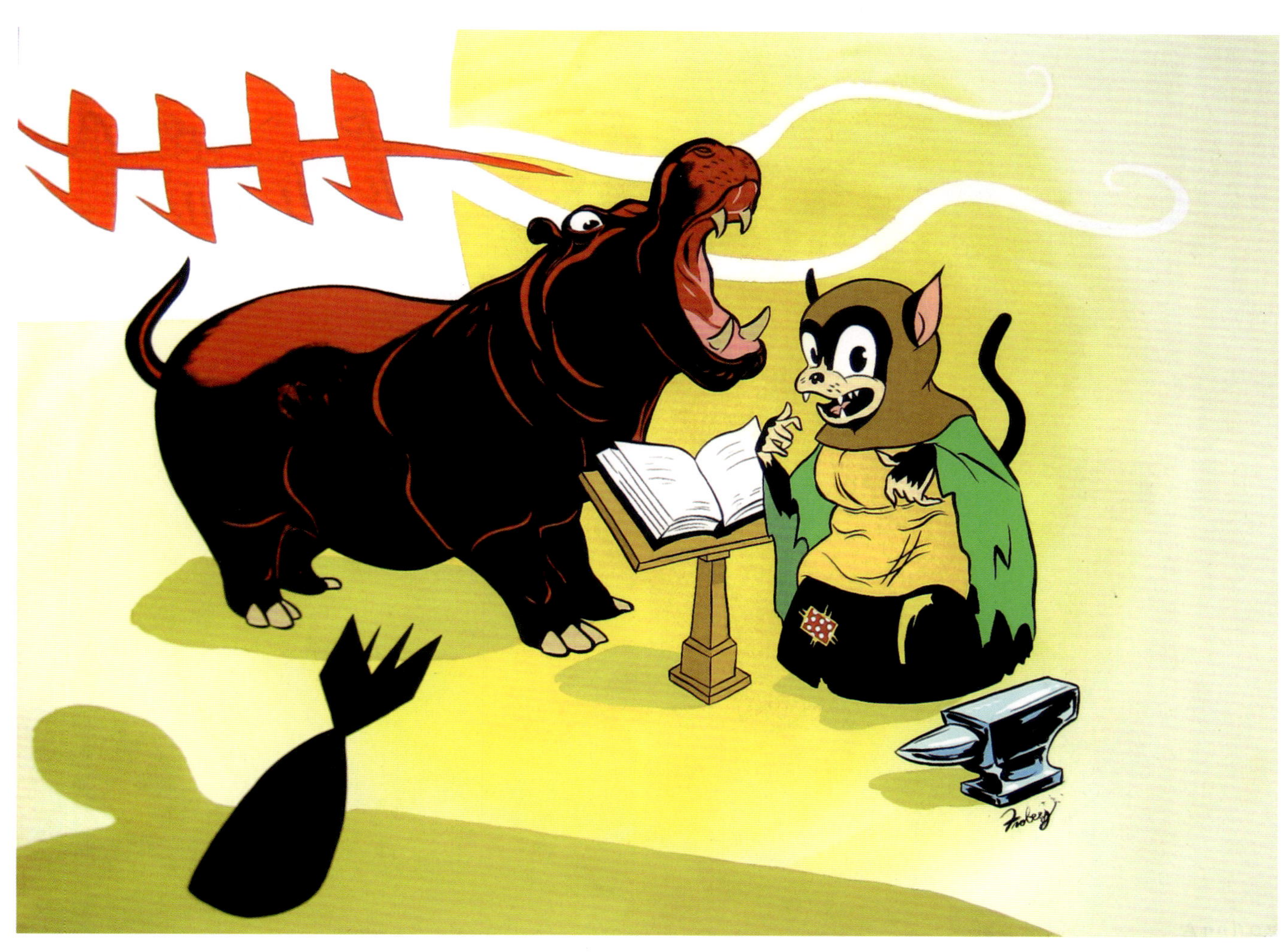

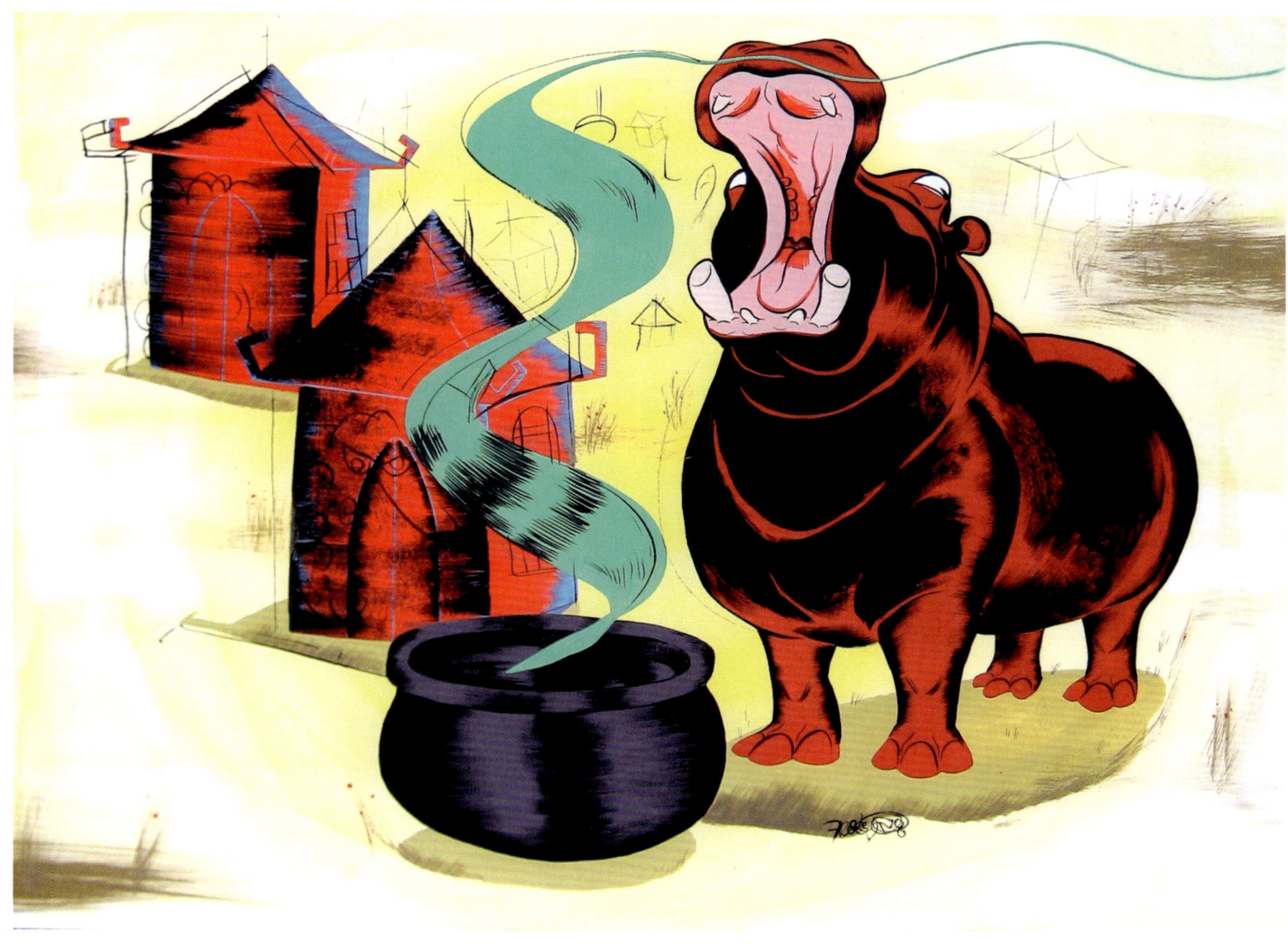

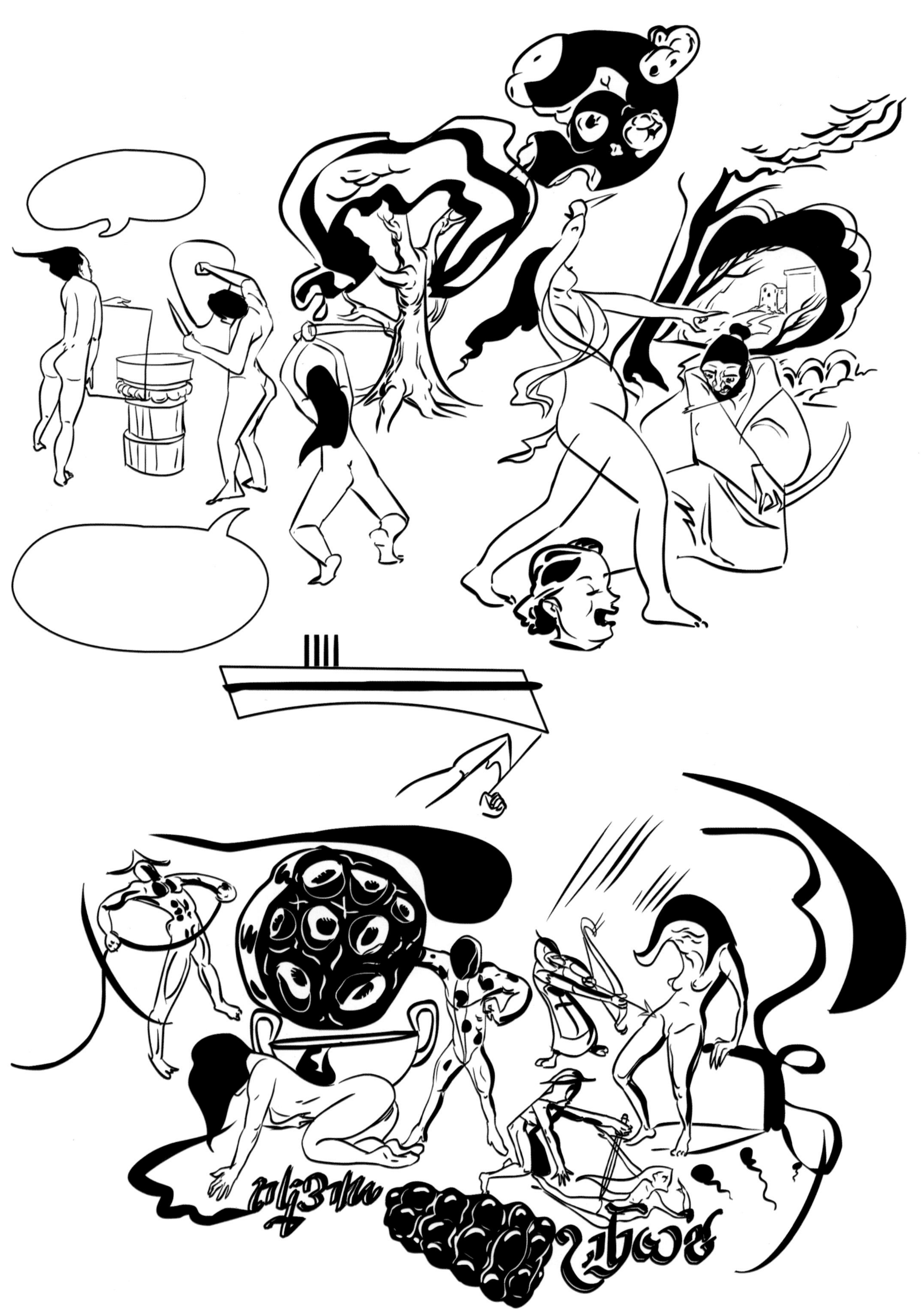

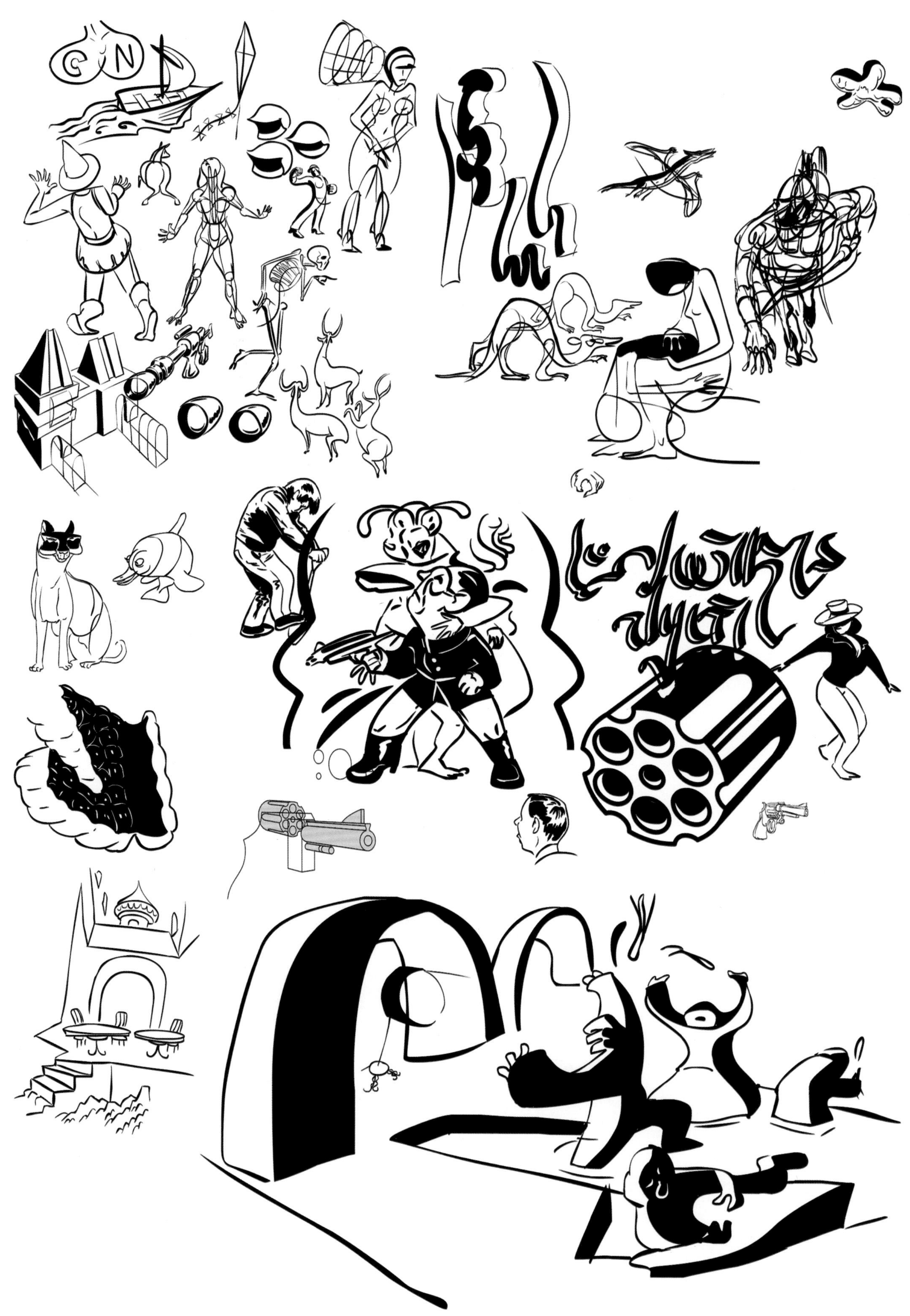

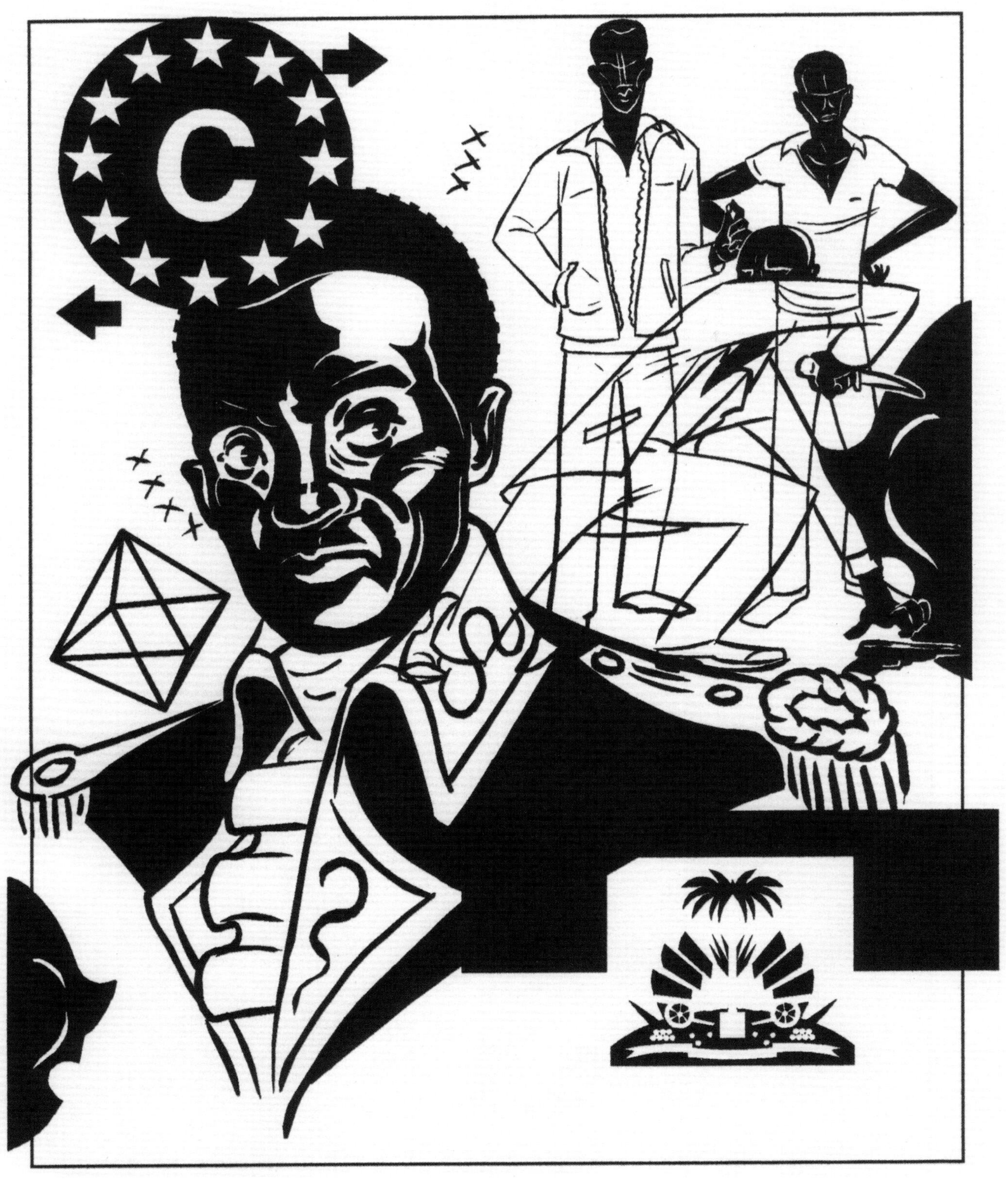

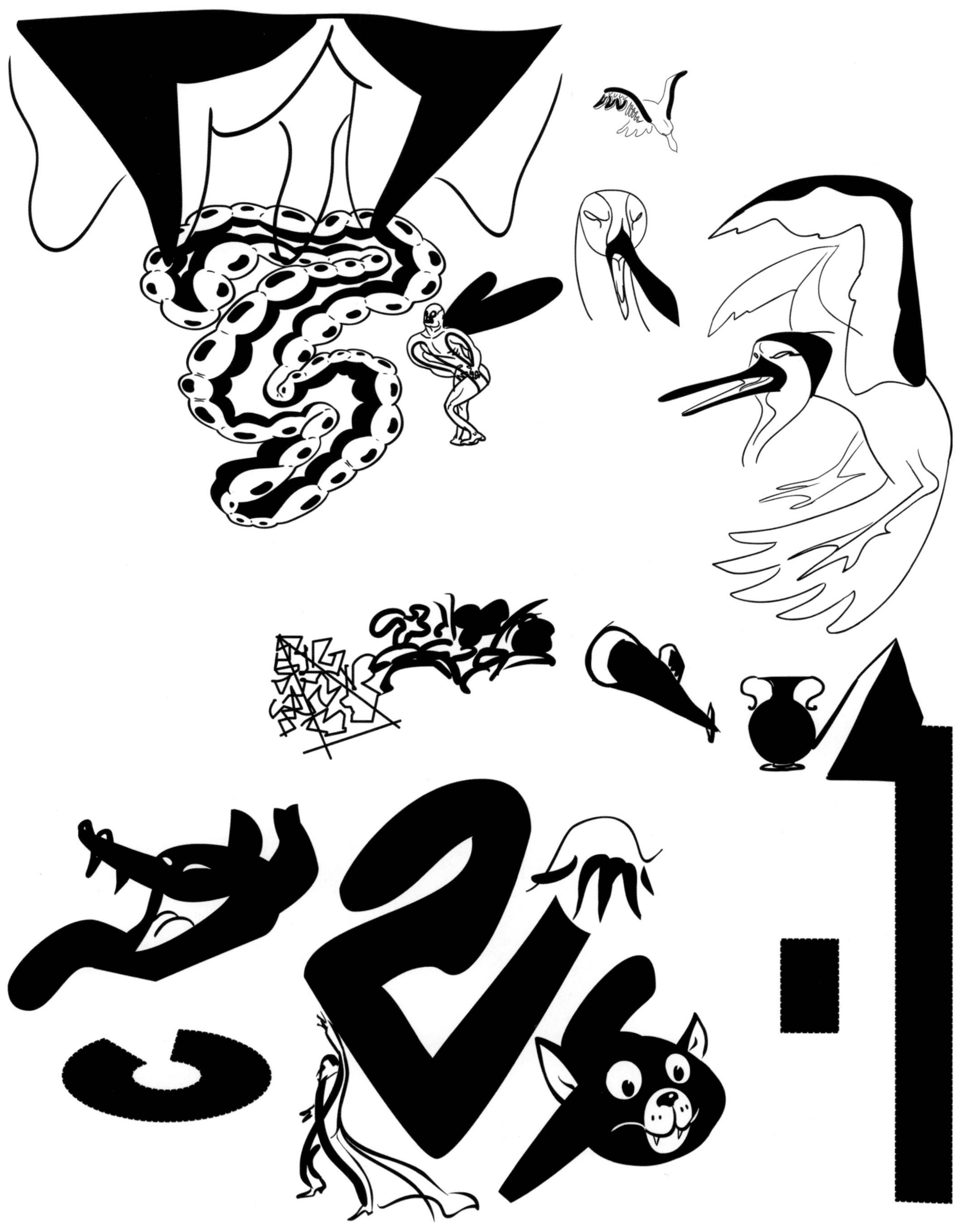

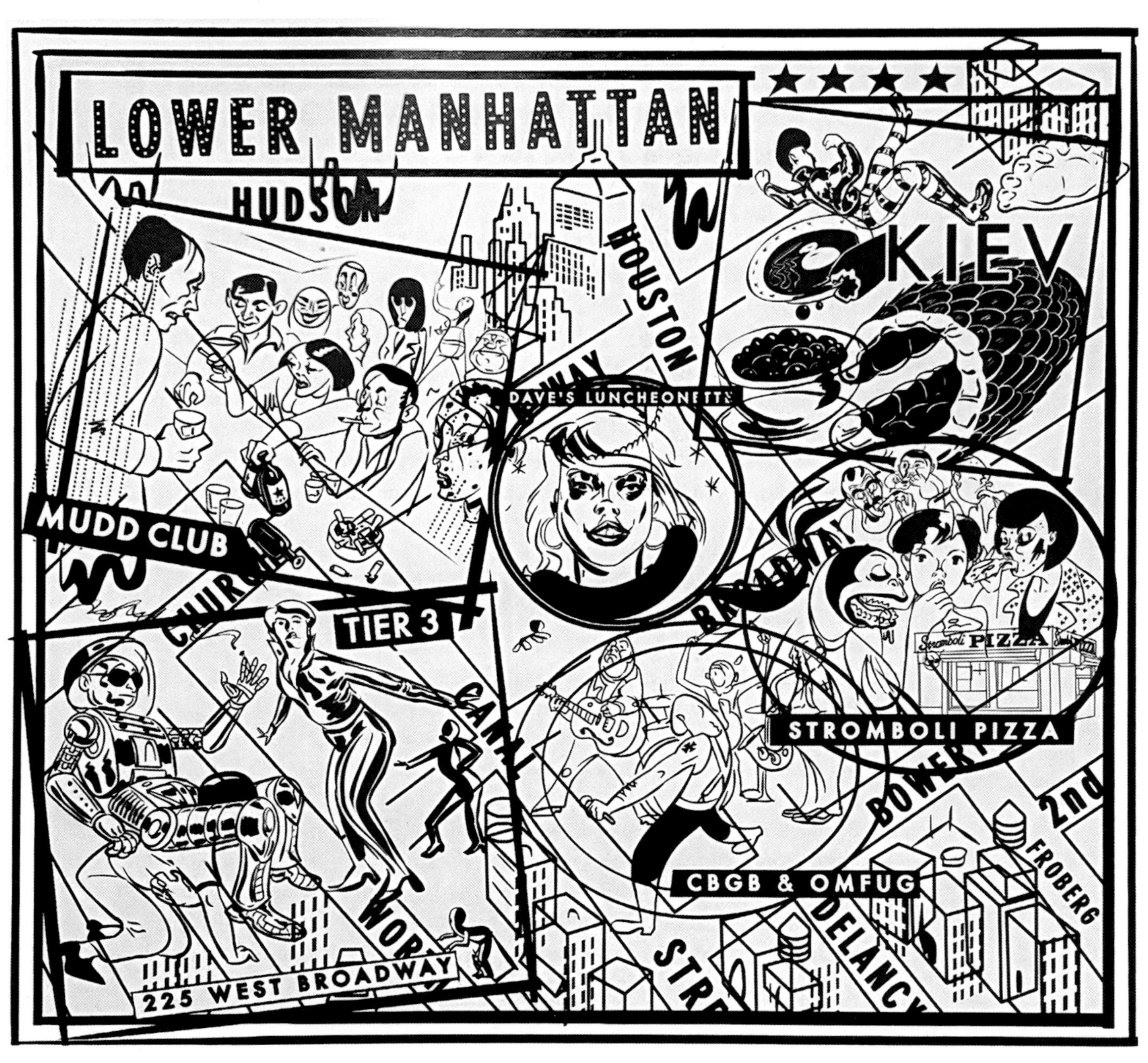

LOWER MANHATTAN
HUDSON
HOUSTON
KIEV
MUDD CLUB
DAVE'S LUNCHEONETTE
TIER 3
STROMBOLI PIZZA
Stromboli PIZZA
BOWERY
2nd
FROBERG
CBGB & OMFUG
DELANC
STR
225 WEST BROADWAY

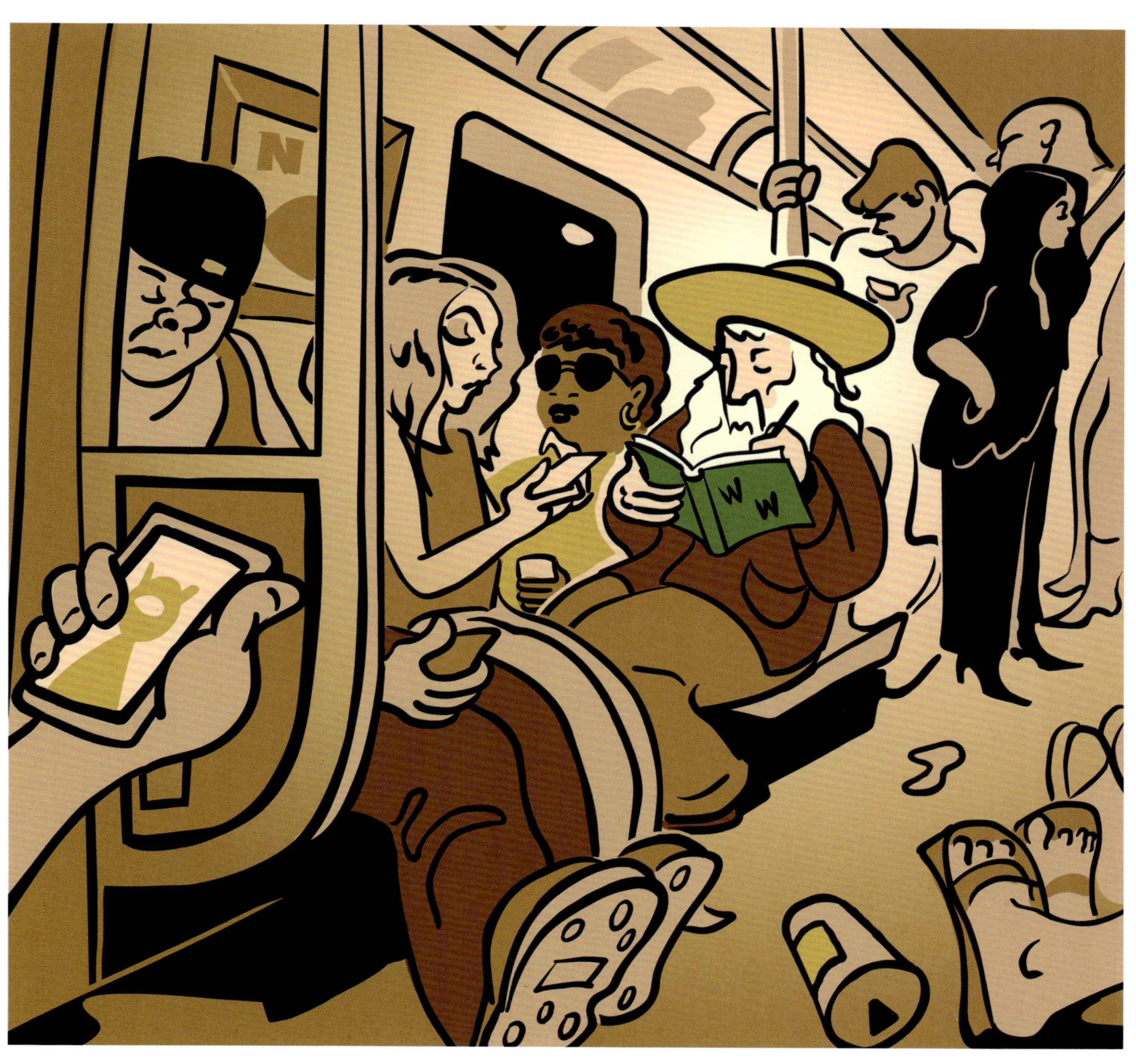
N
W
W

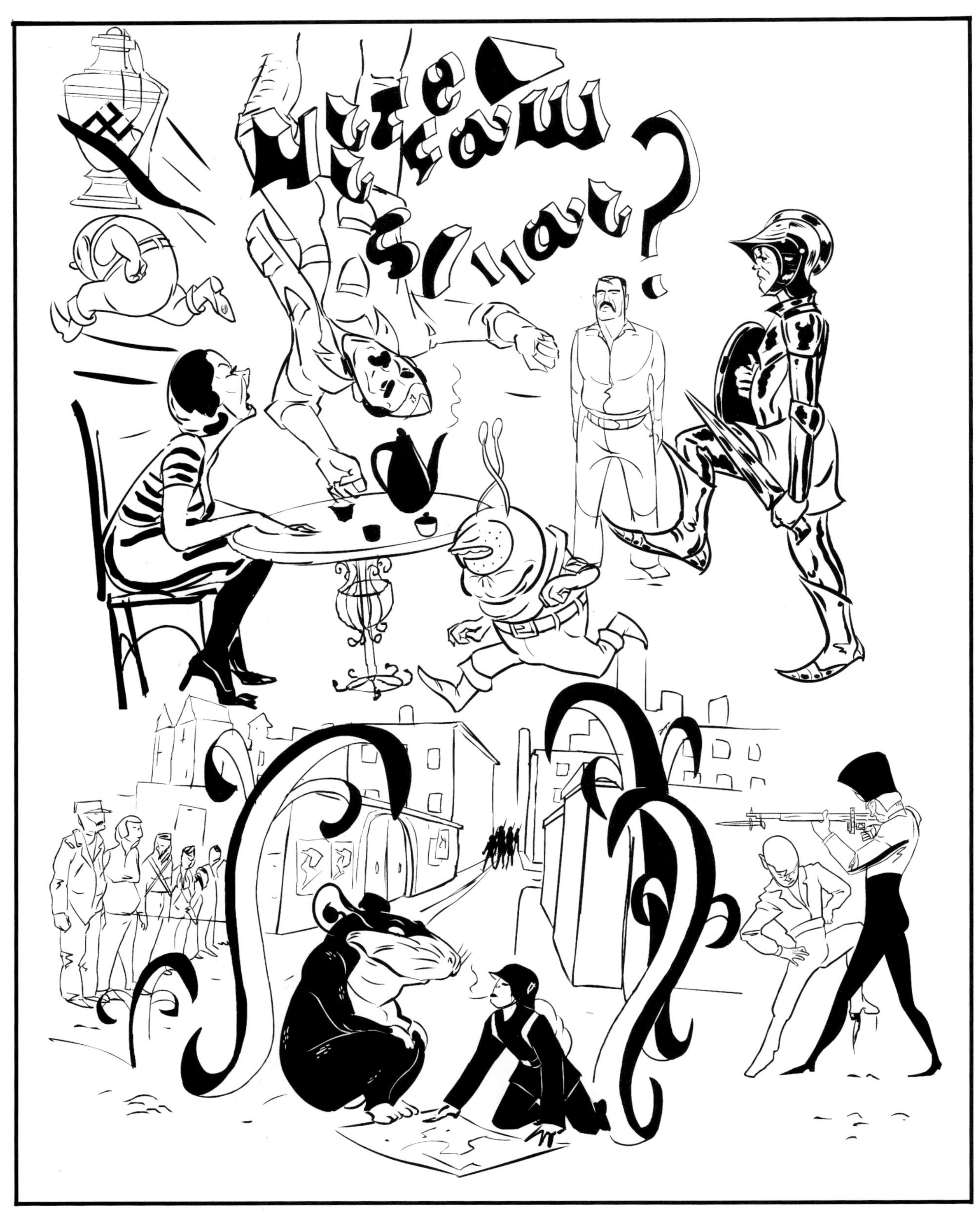

Foresight

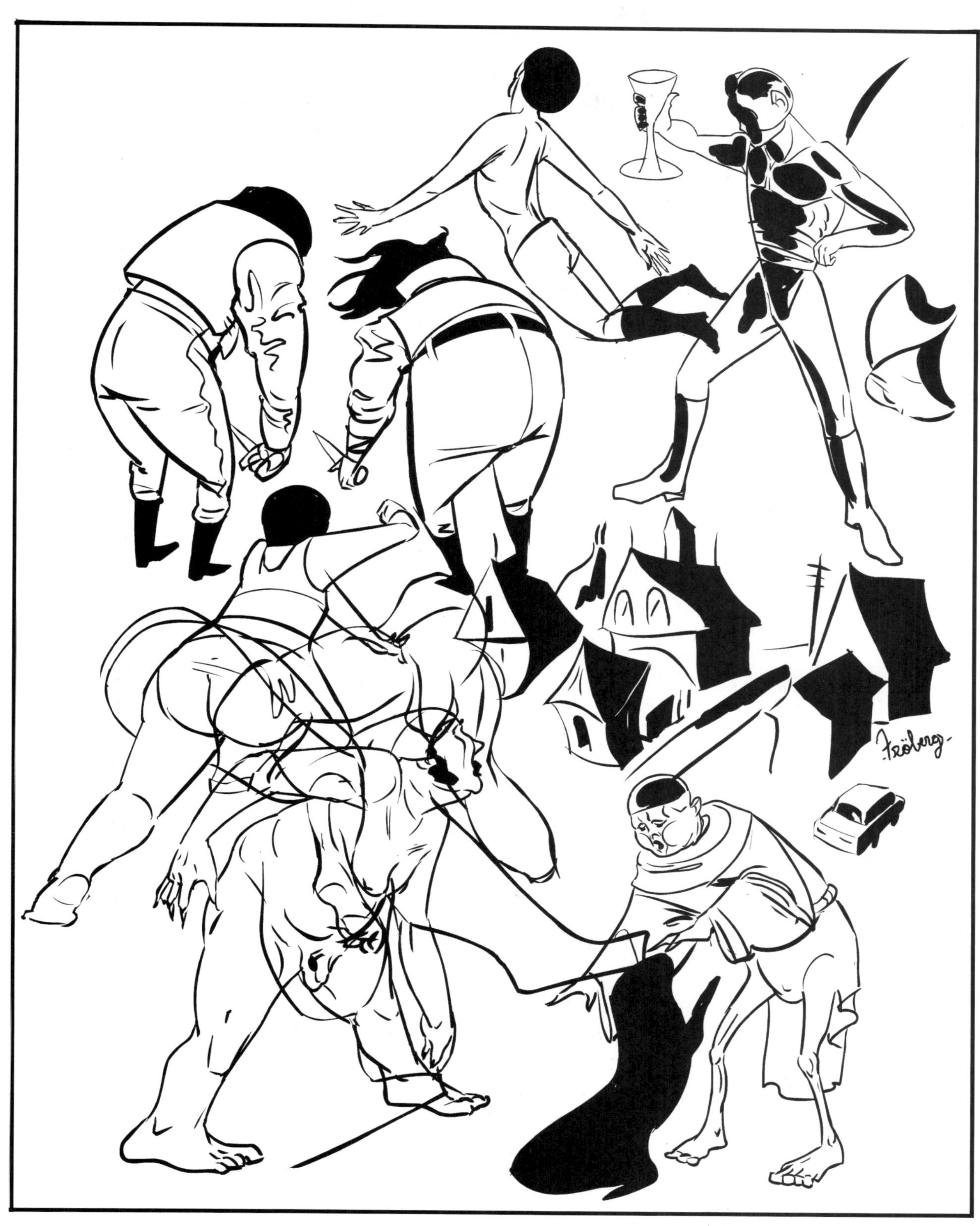

Solidarity

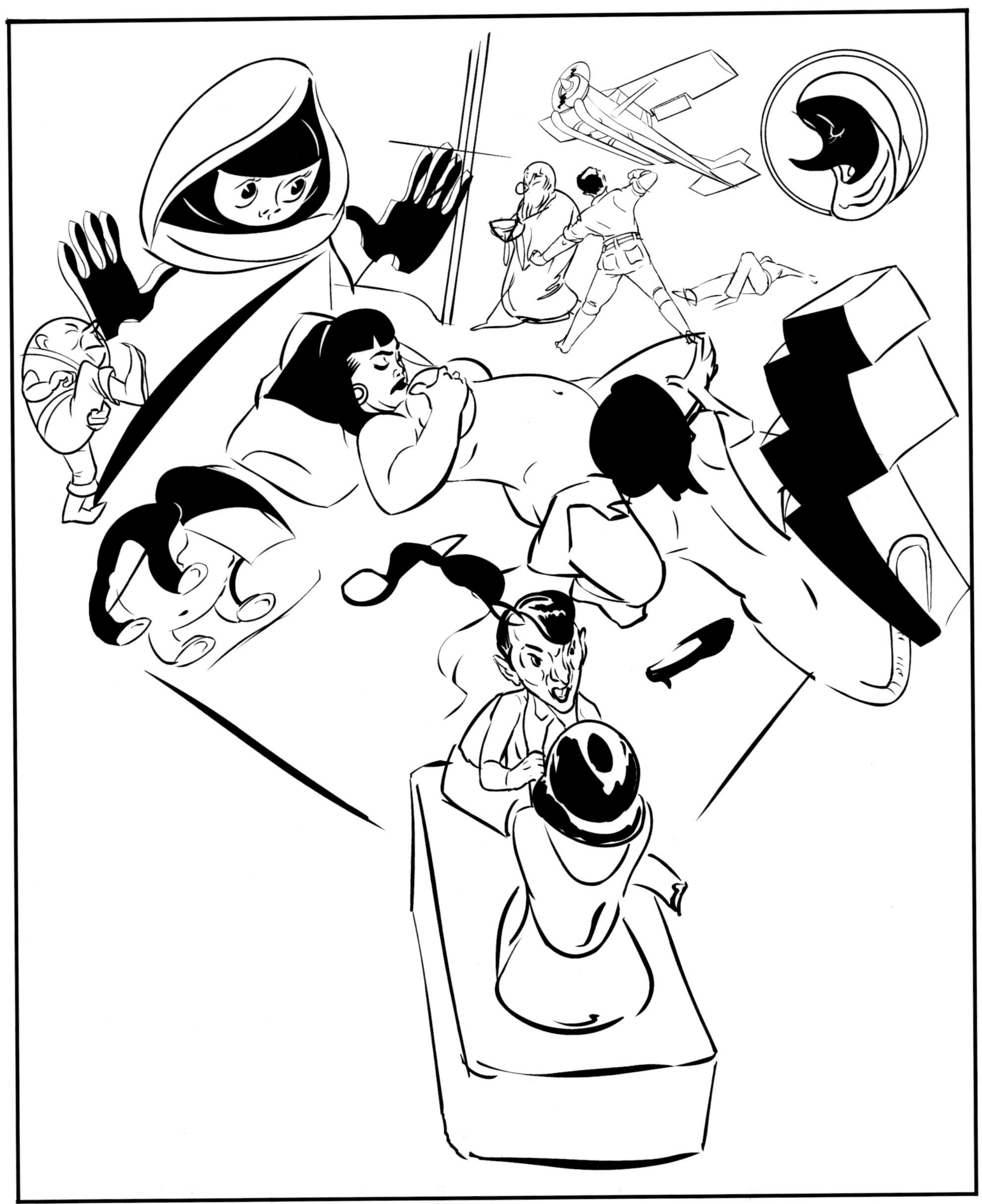

Privacy

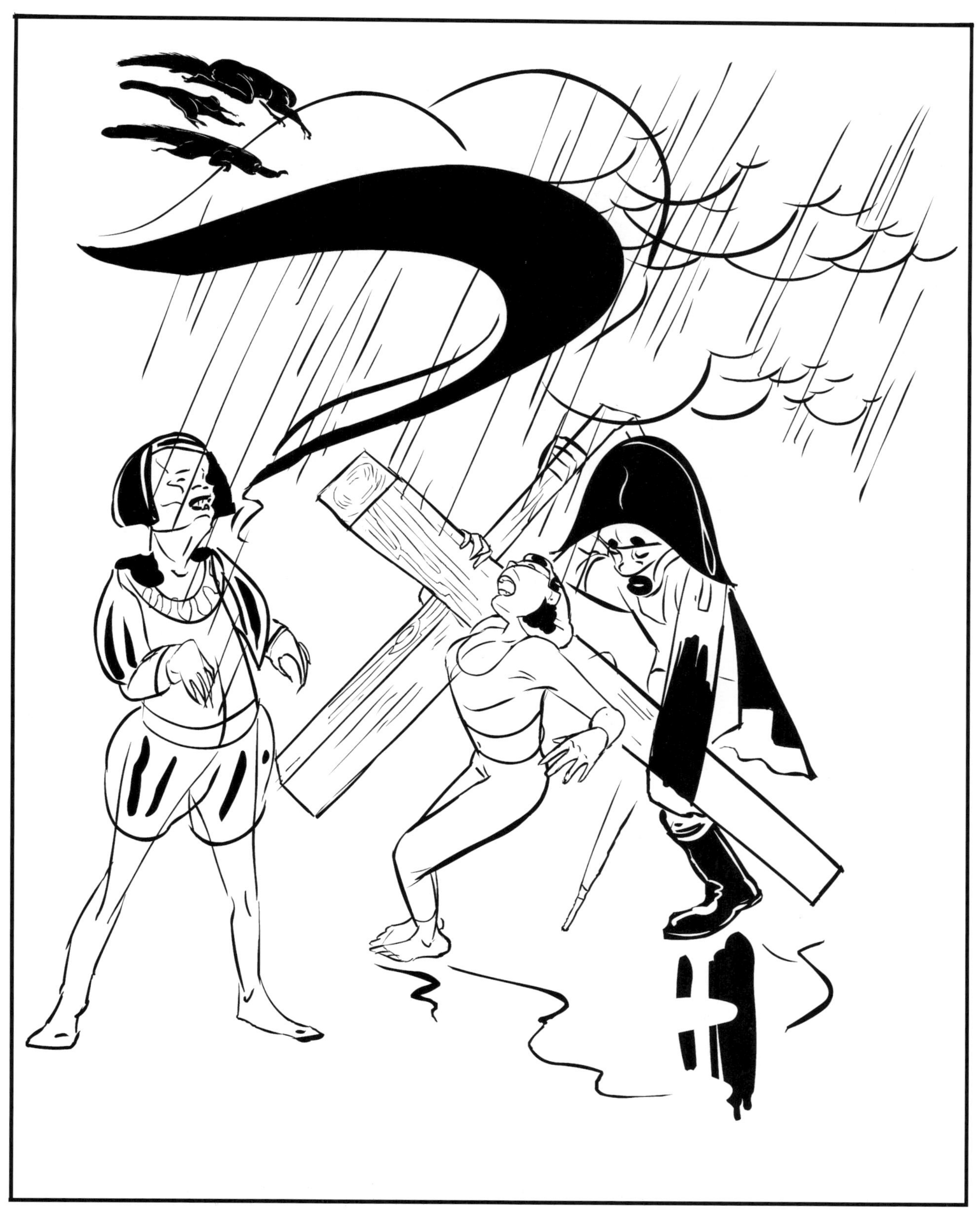

Altruism

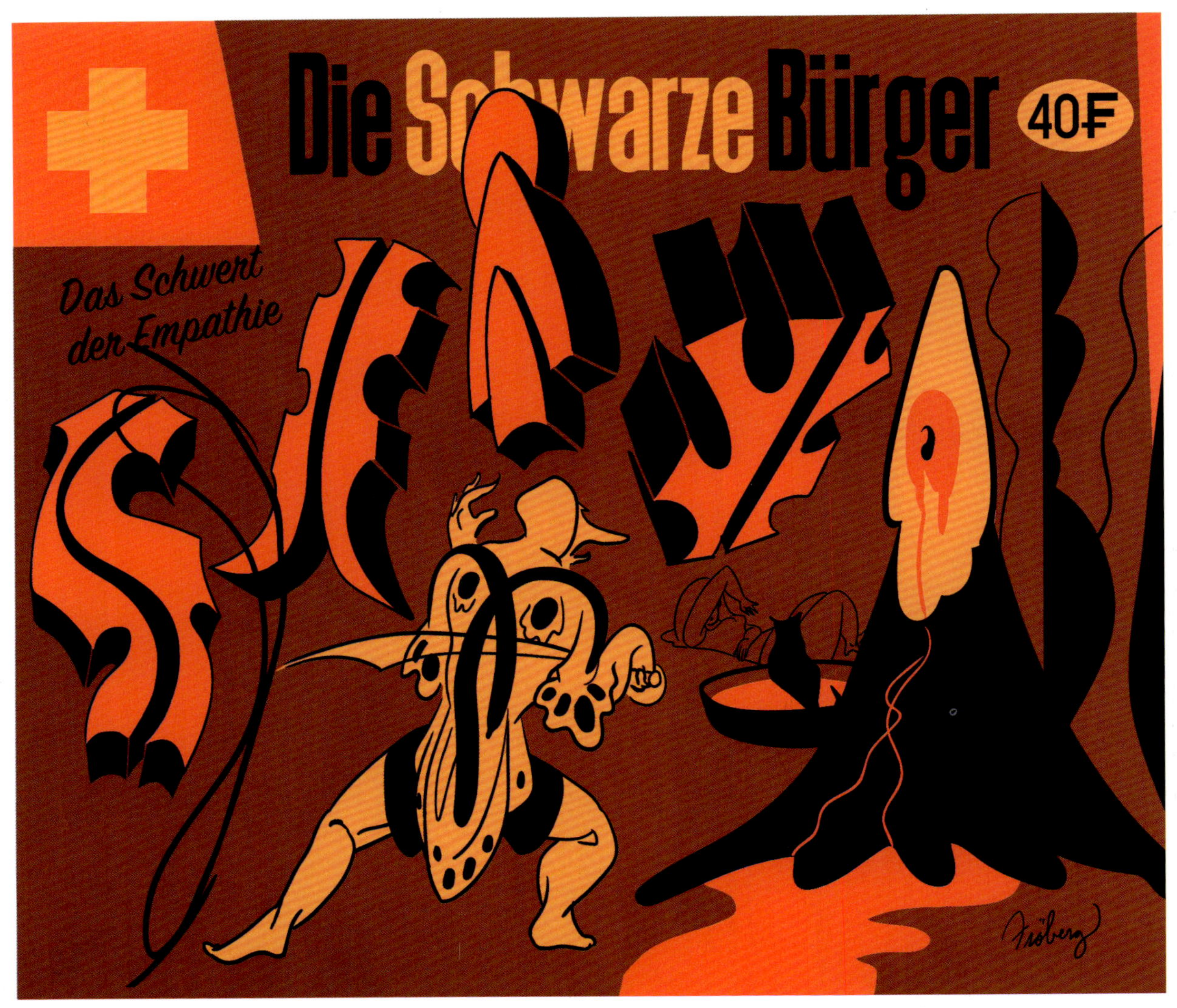

Die Schwarze Bürger
40F
Das Schwert
der Empathie
Fröberg

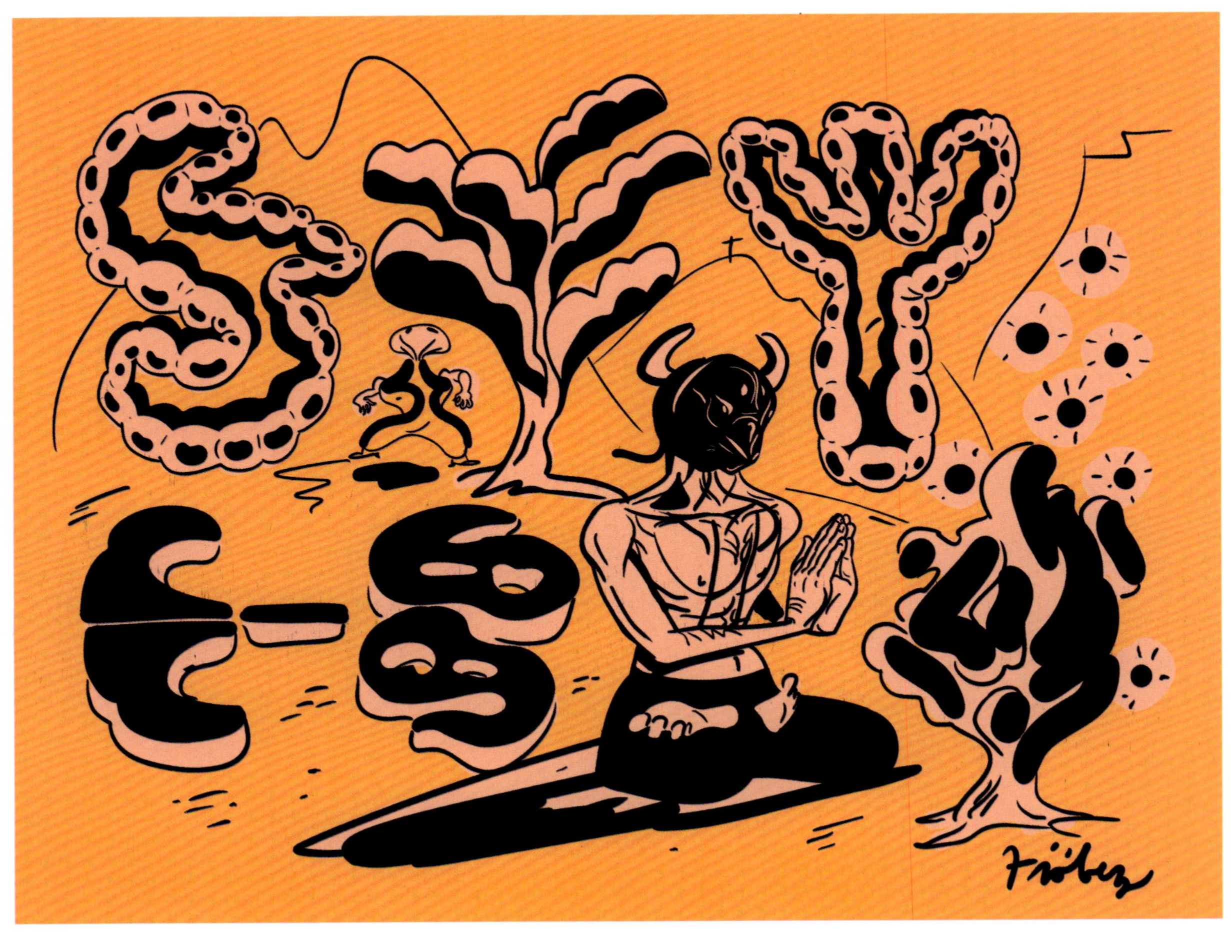

Fröberg

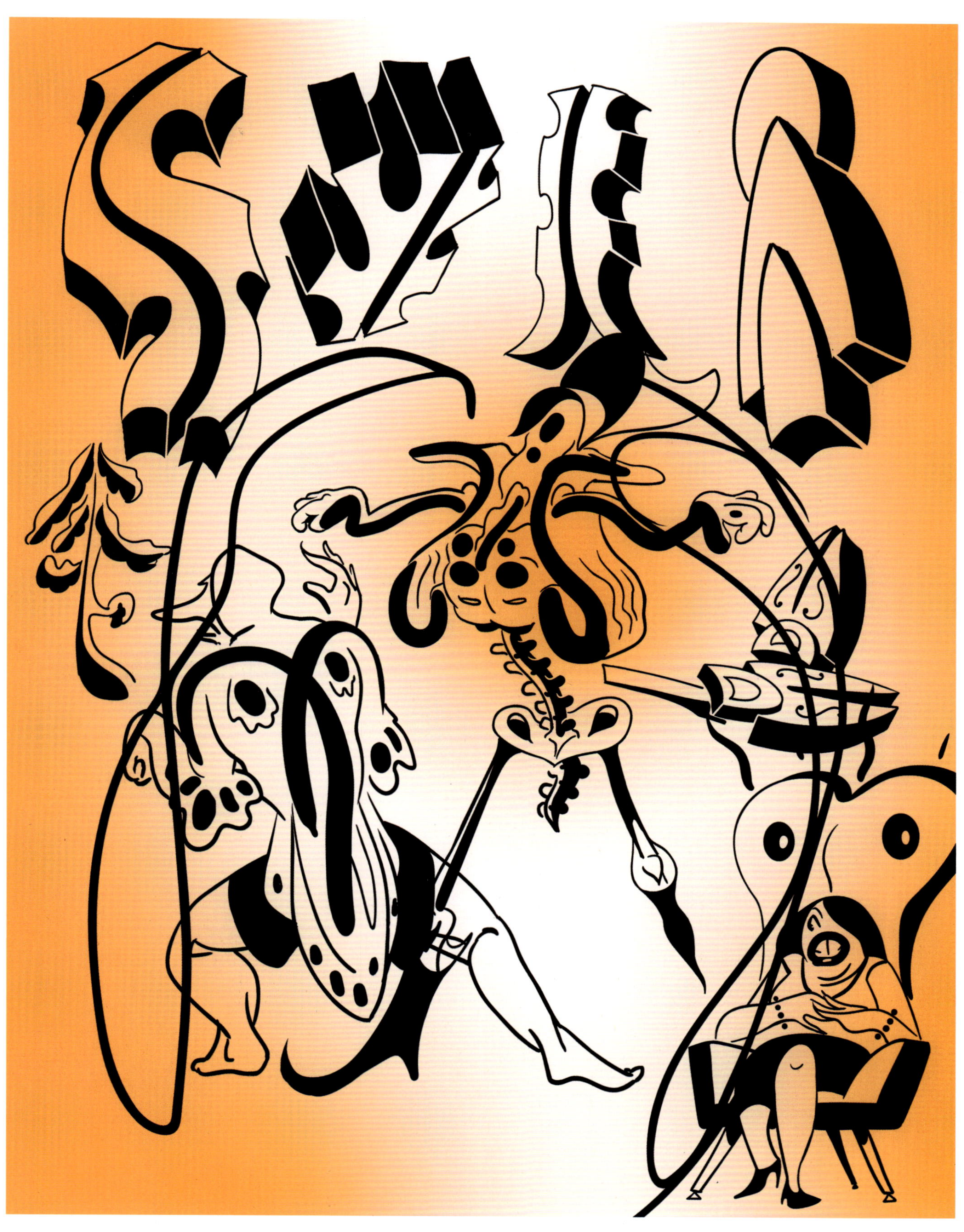

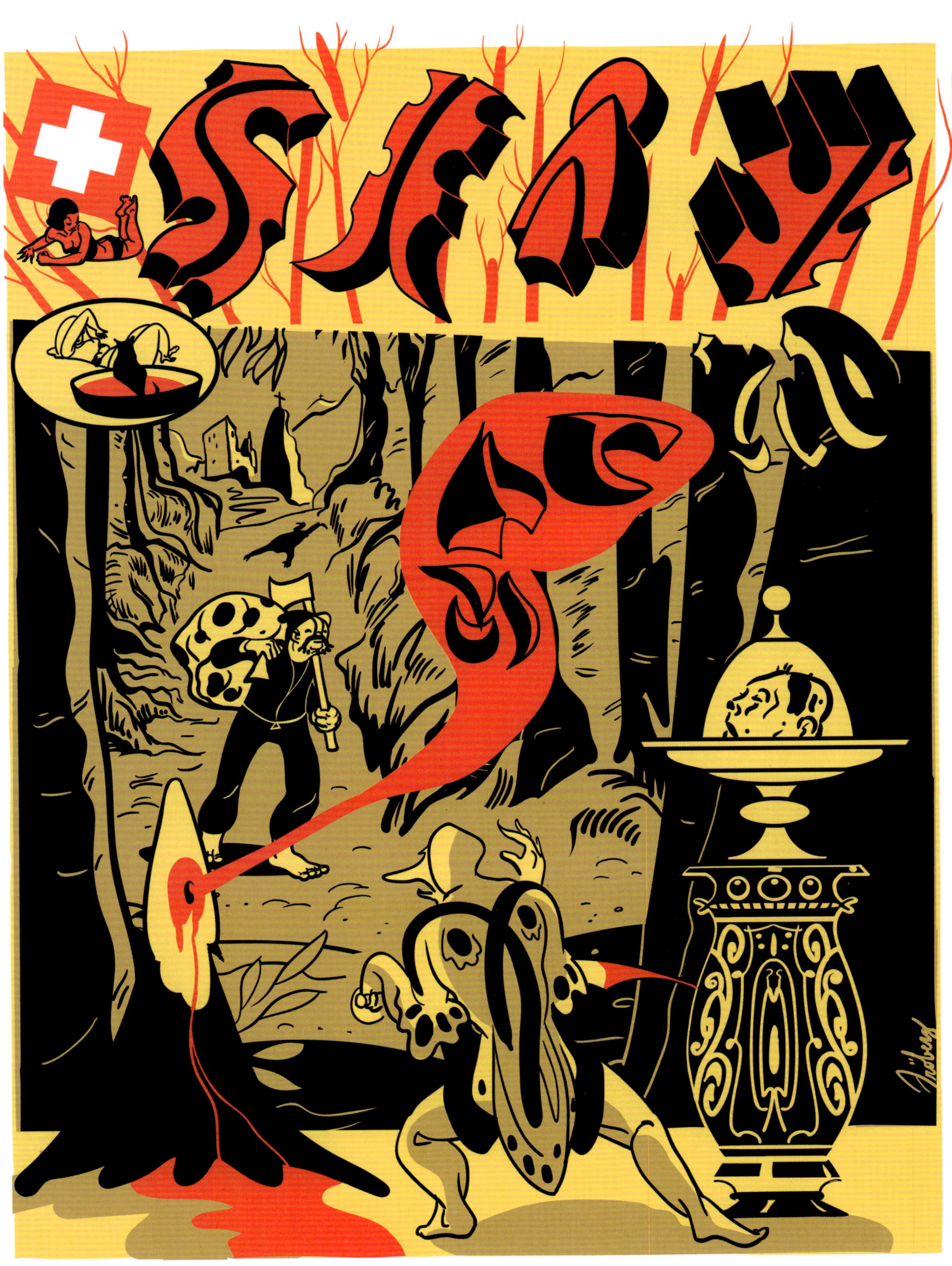

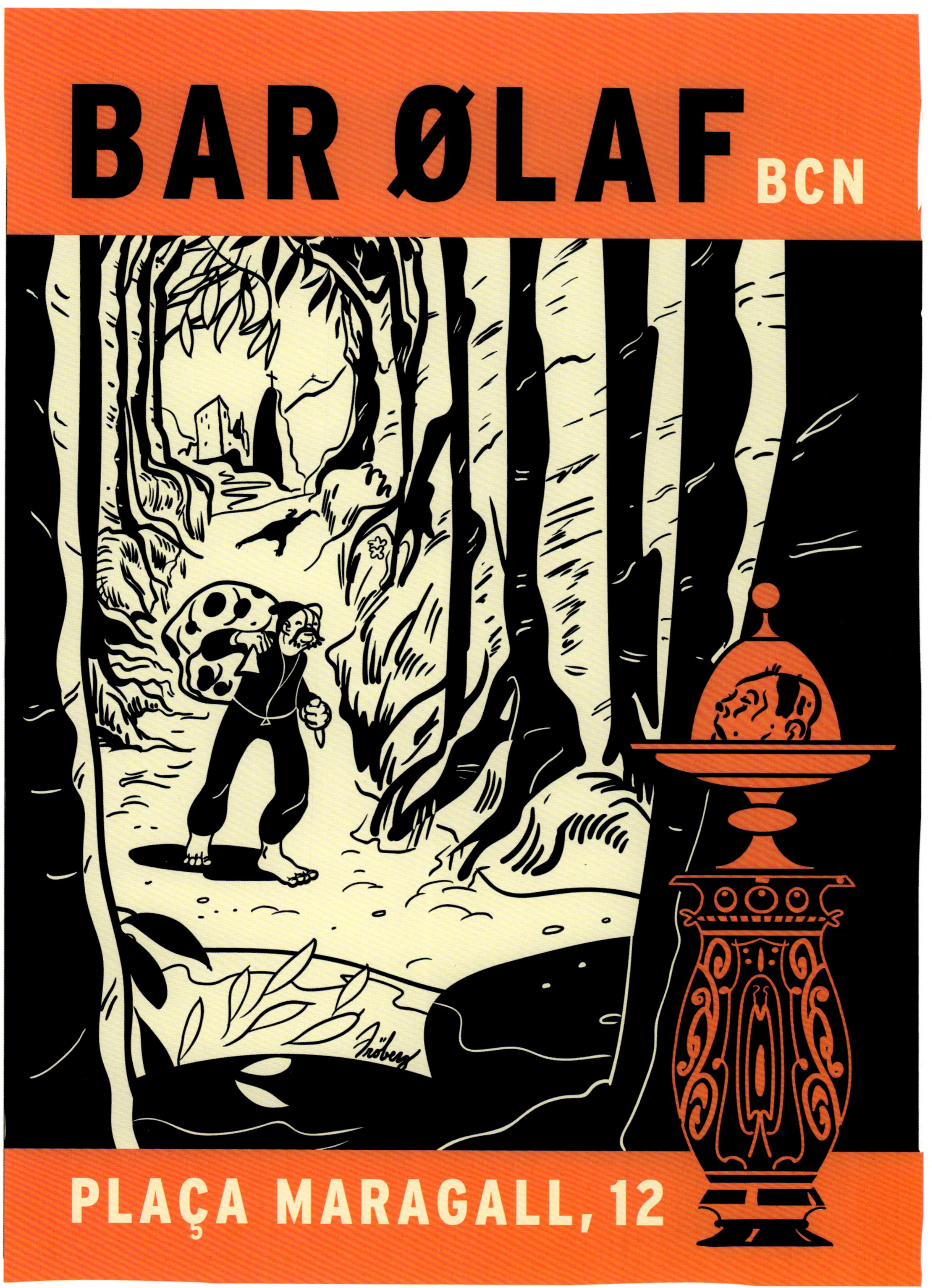

BAR ØLAF
BCN
PLAÇA MARAGALL, 12

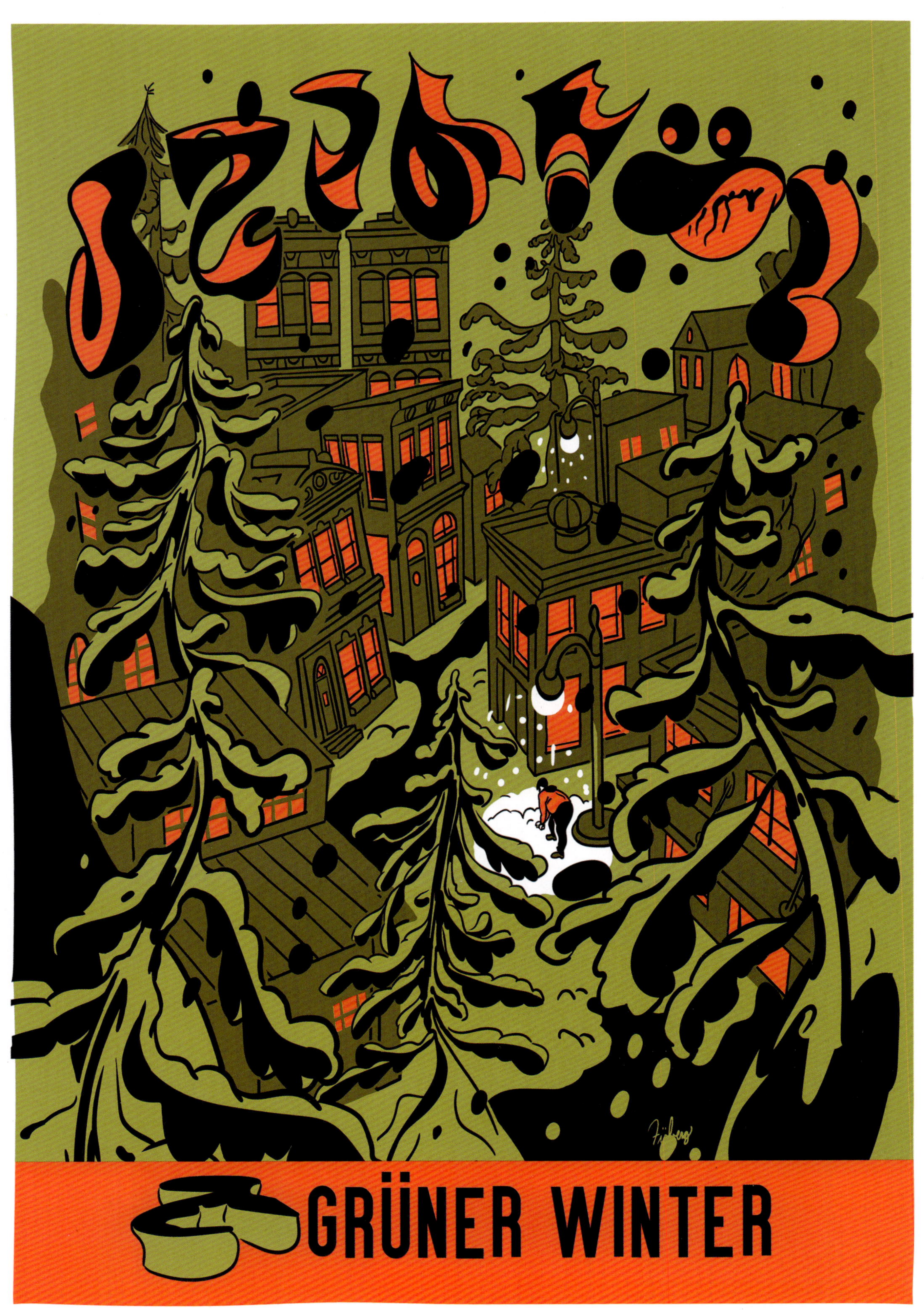

GRÜNER WINTER

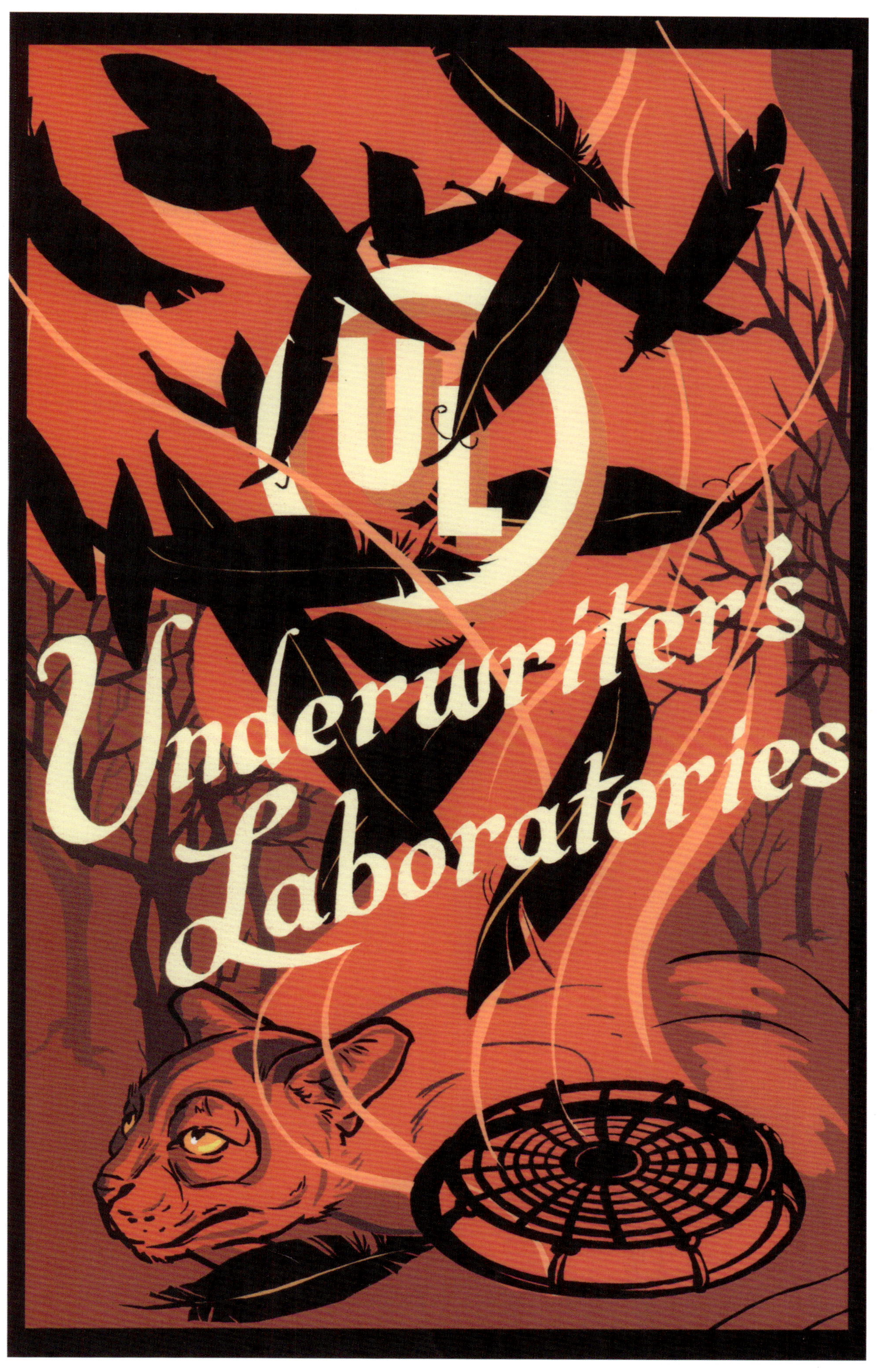

UL
Underwriter's
Laboratories

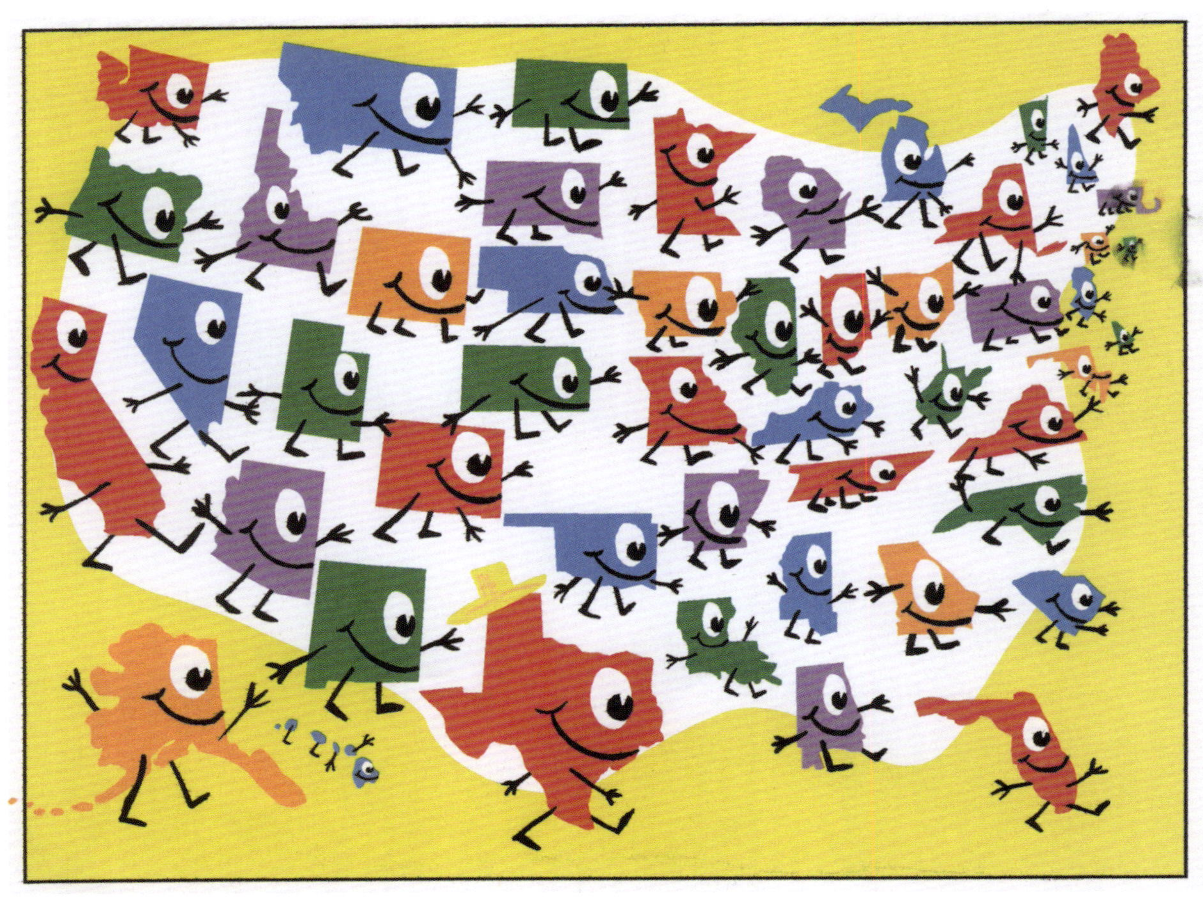

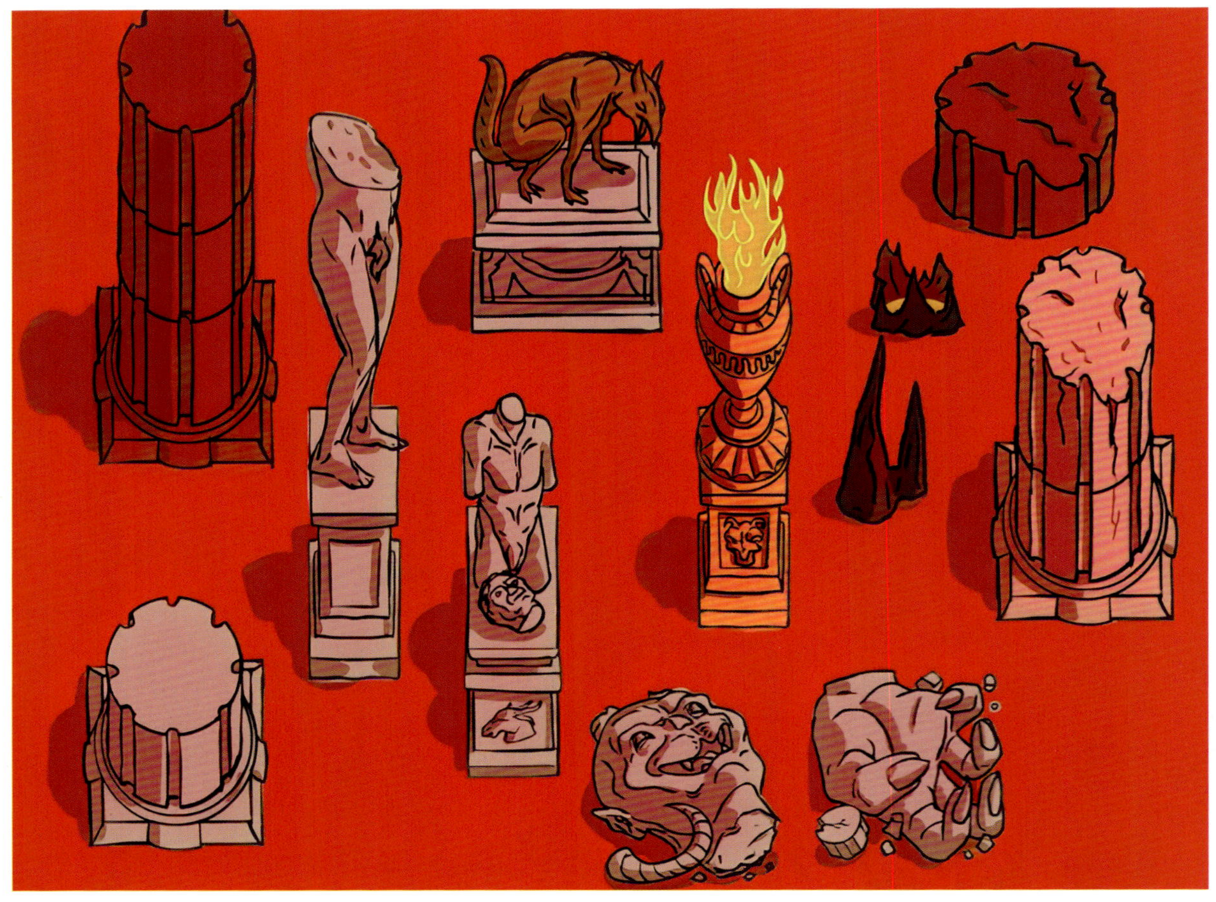

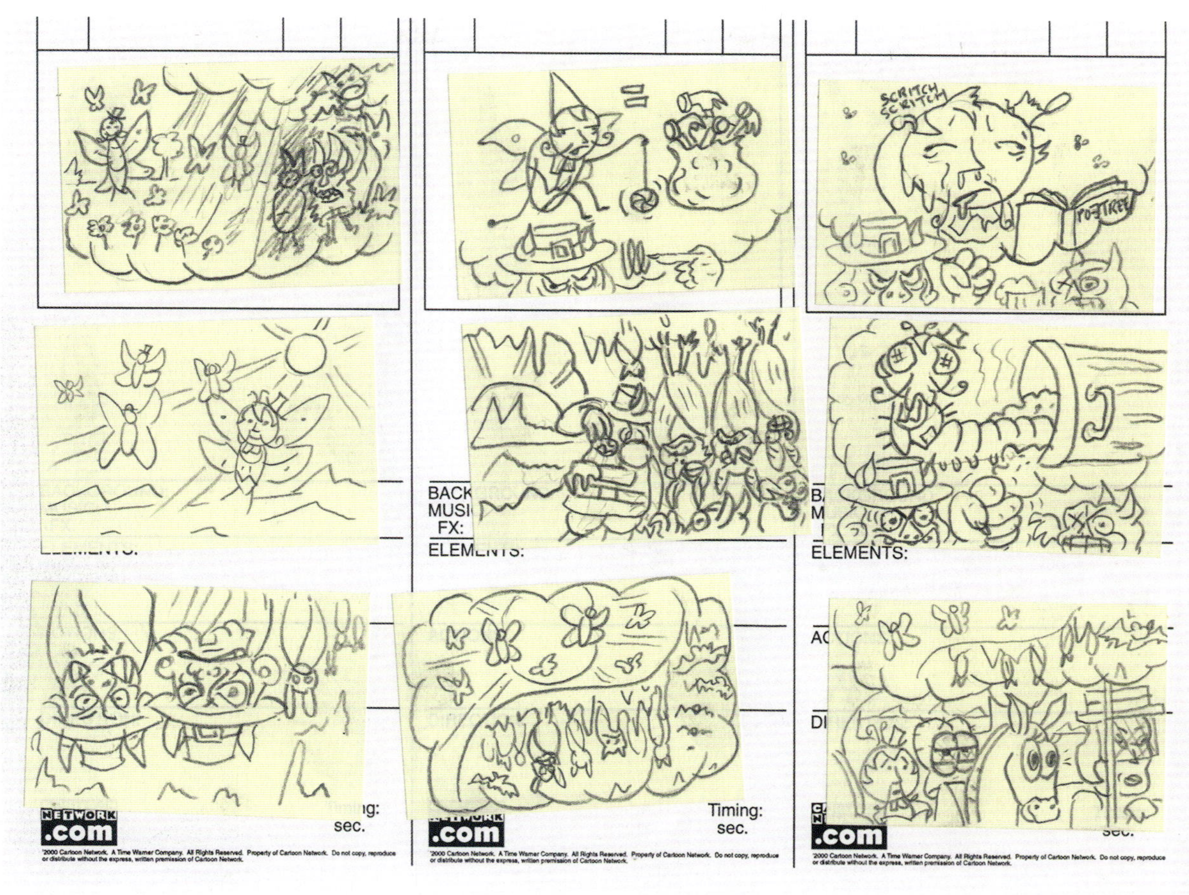
BACK
MUSI
FX:
ELEMENTS:
ELEMENTS:
Timing:
sec.
Timing:
sec.
.com
.com
.com
2000 Cartoon Network. A Time Warner Company. All Rights Reserved. Property of Cartoon Network. Do not copy, reproduce or distribute without the express, written permission of Cartoon Network.

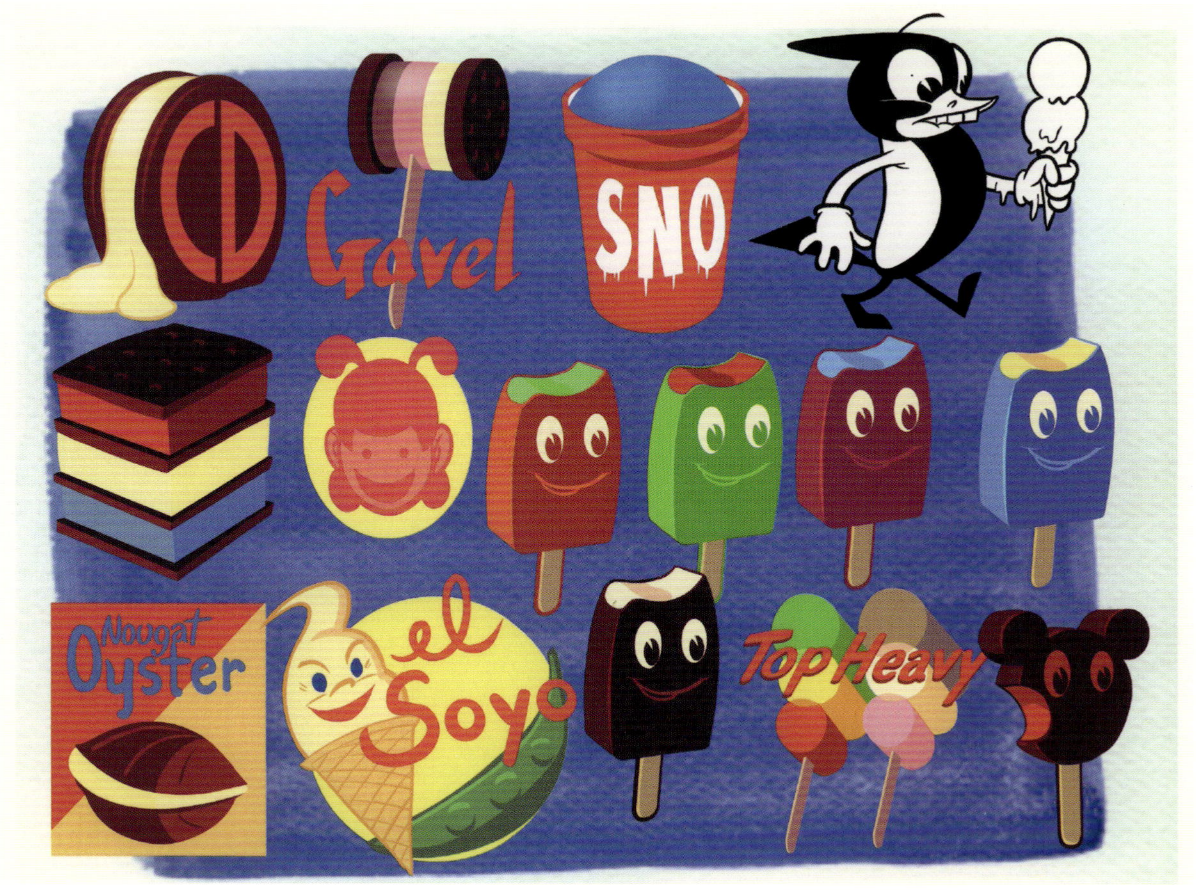
Gavel
SNO
Nougat
Oyster
el
Soyo
Top Heavy

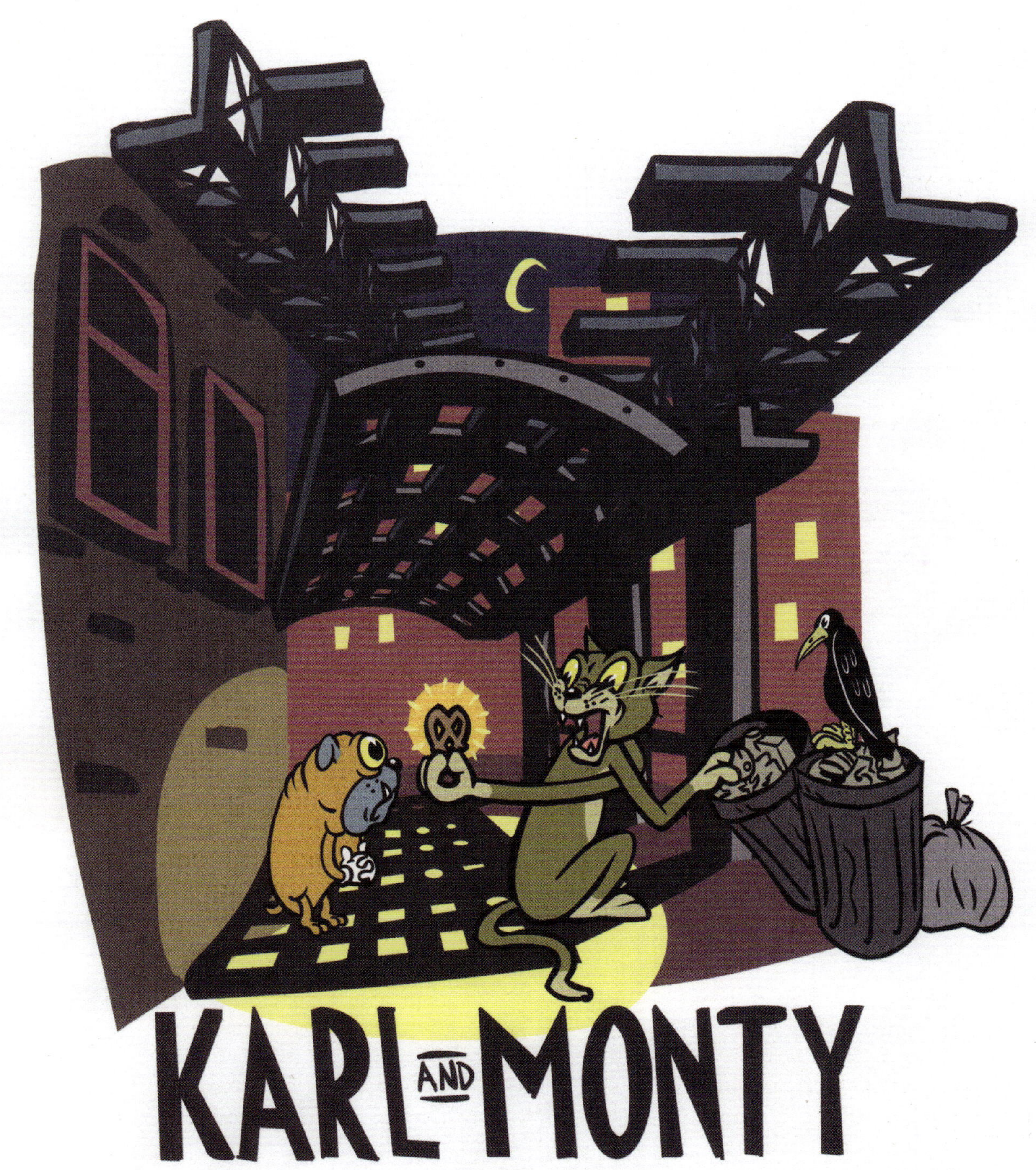

KARL AND MONTY

Karl is a runty apartment pug, presumably lost or abandoned, wandering the dark city streets. Monty the cat tends to overestimate his abilities as Karl's newly (self)appointed mentor, usually at his own bodily expense. Monty's schemes are often poorly thought through, and since Karl is incapable of speech (his communications are limited to grunts, whimpers, and various watery-eyed stares), he cannot object.

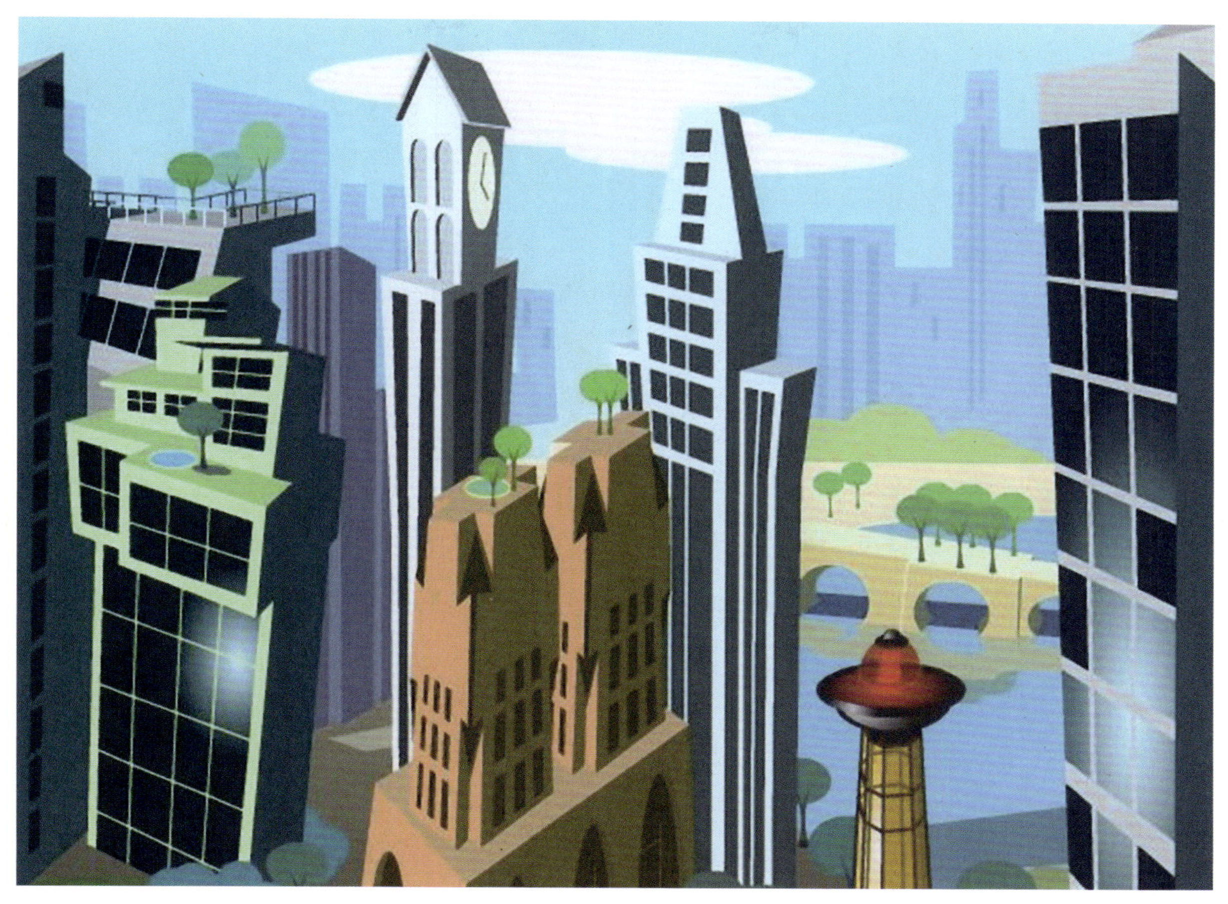

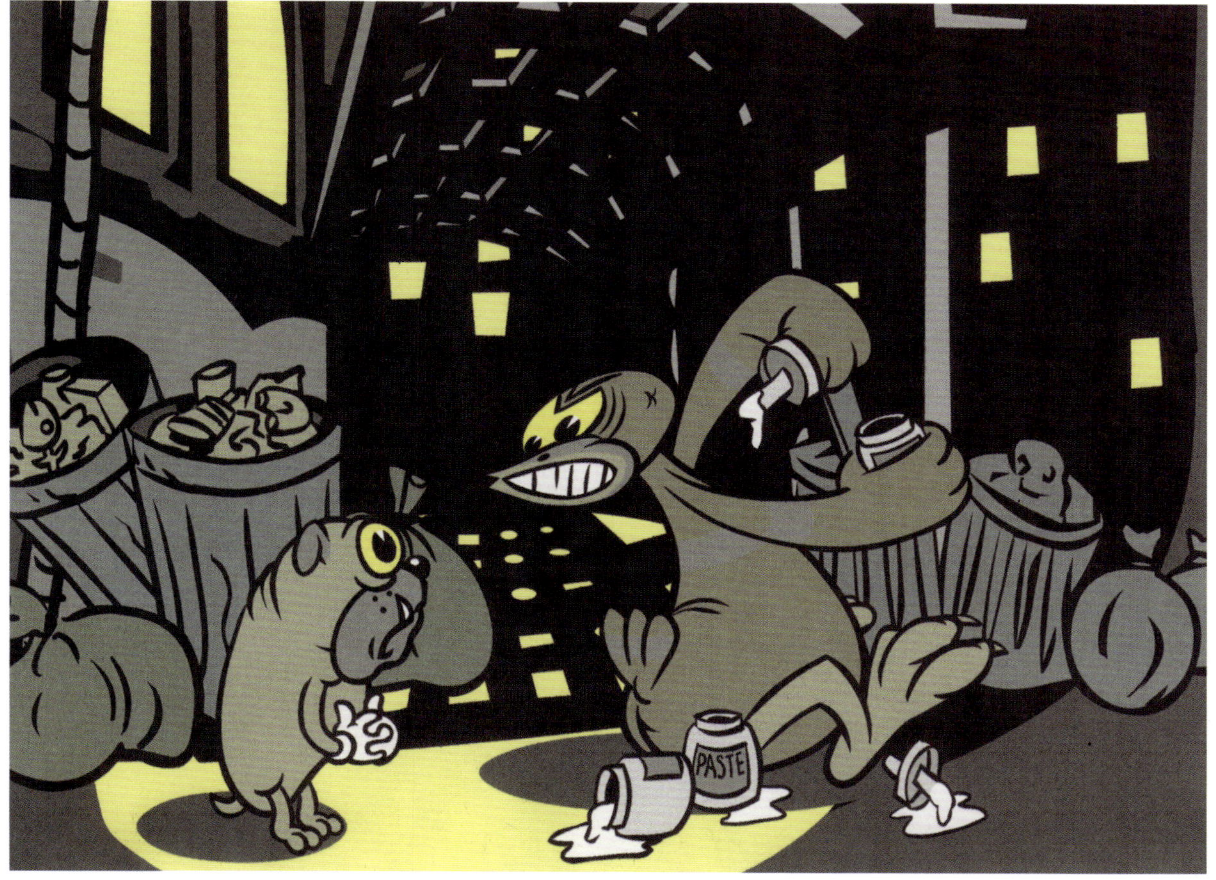
PASTE

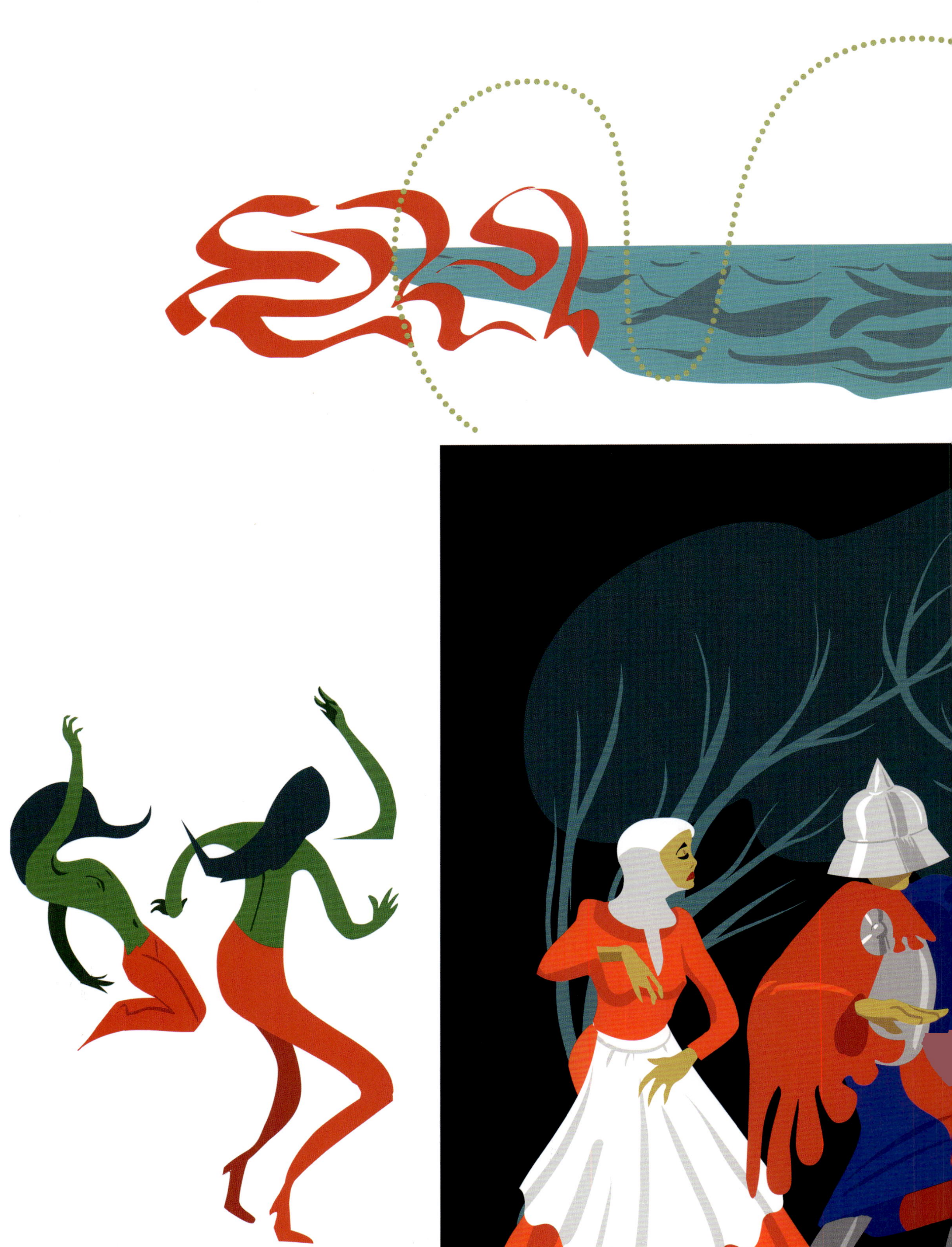

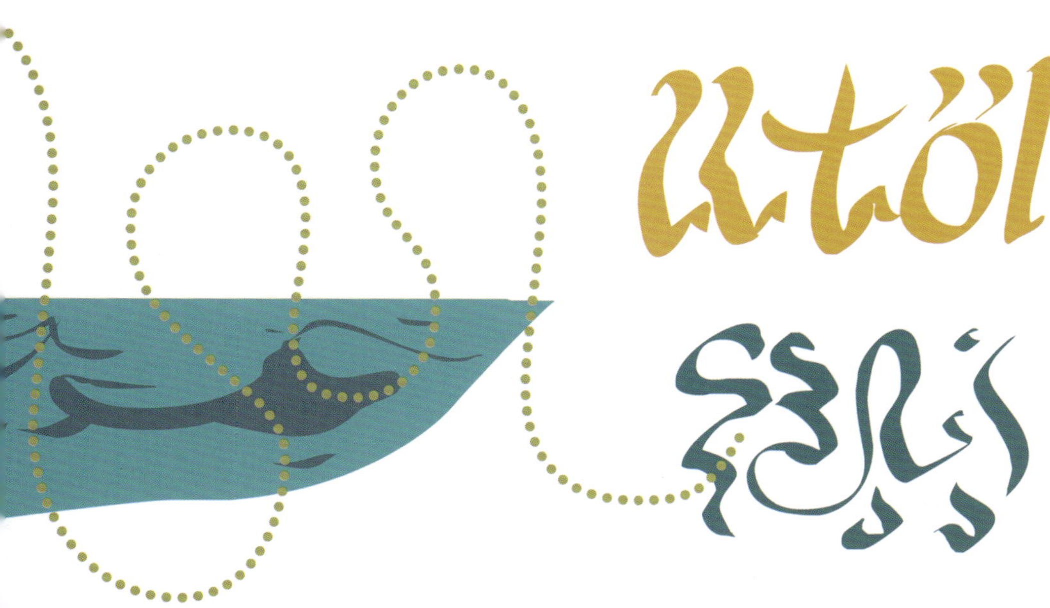

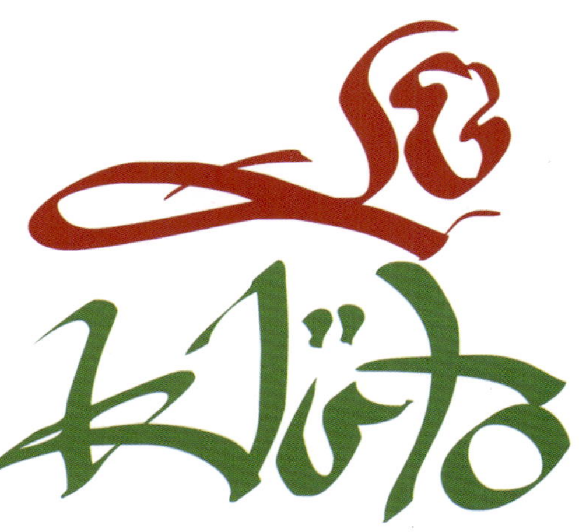

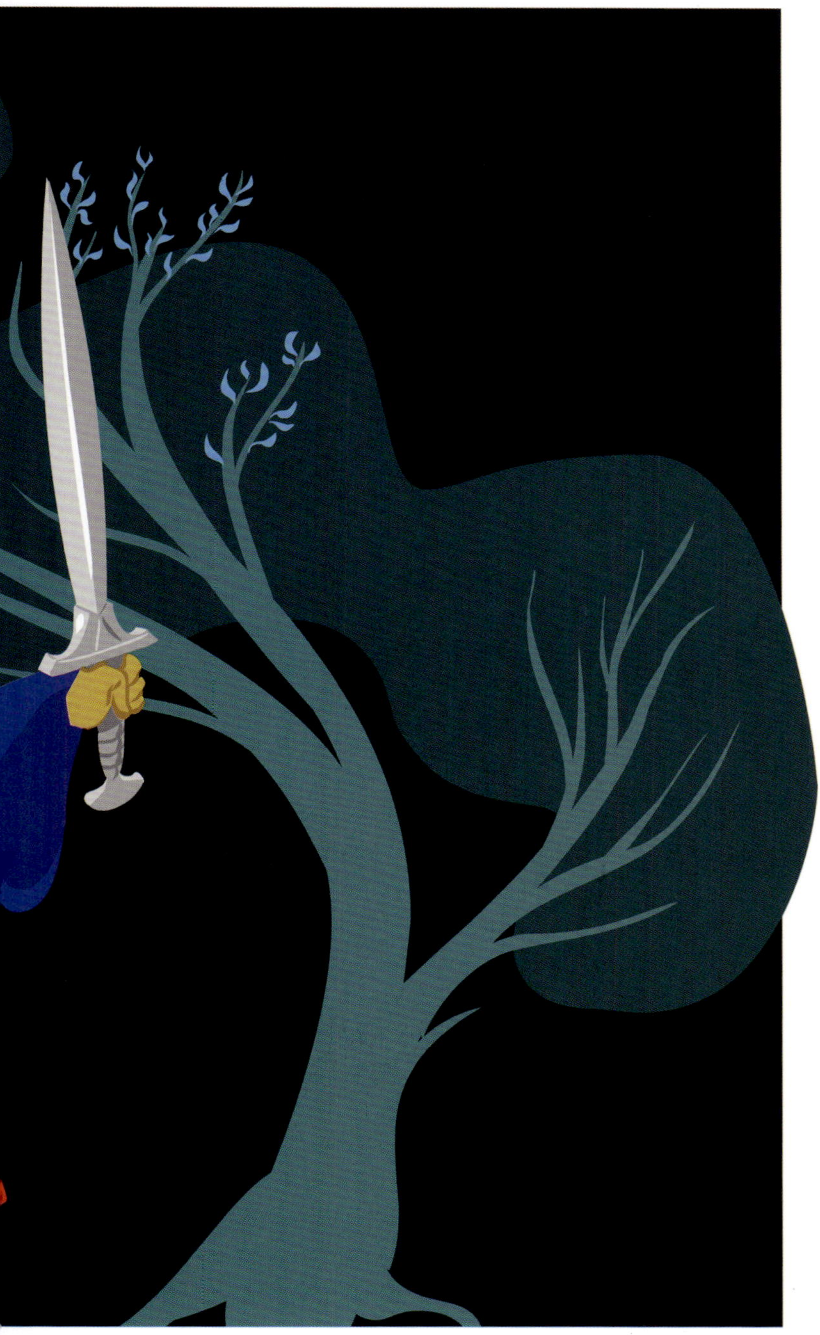

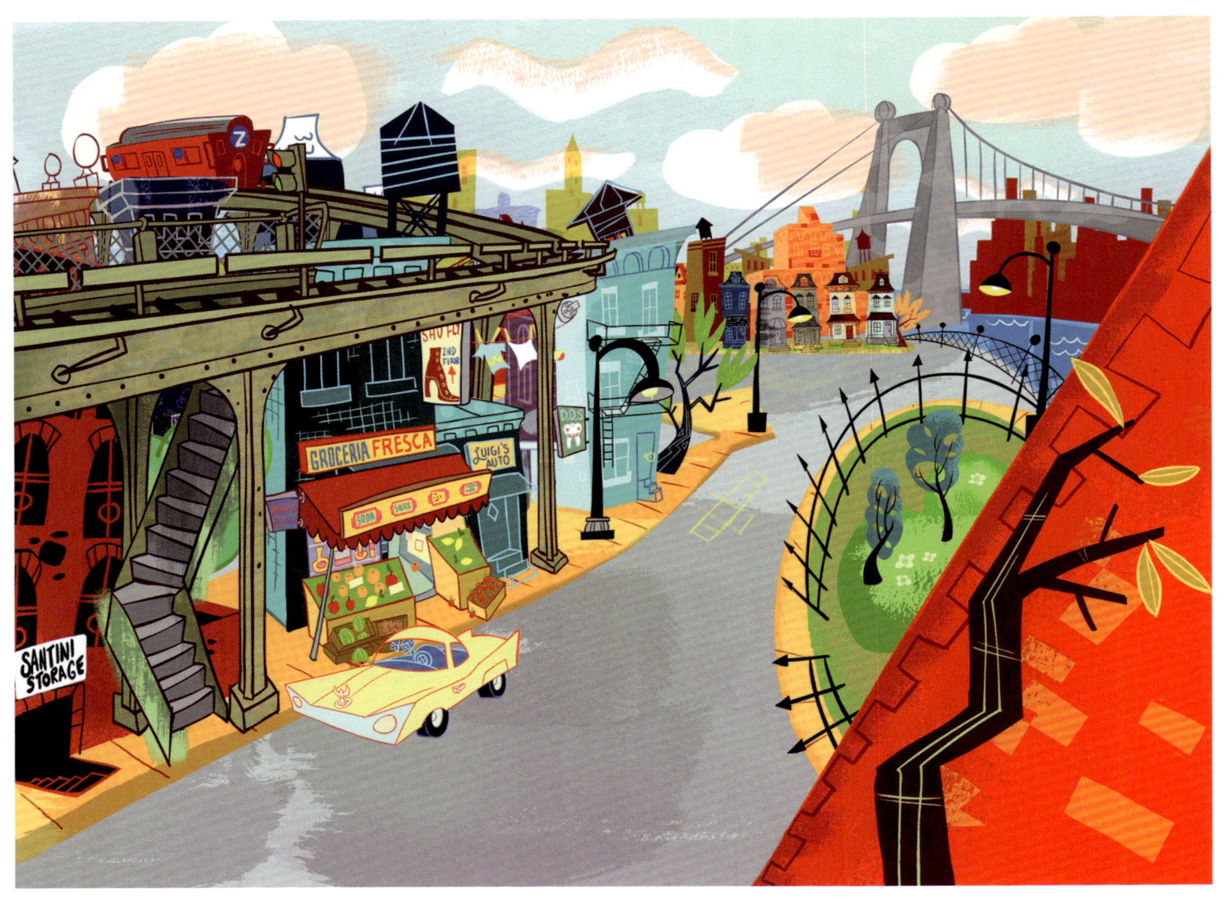

Z
SANTINI STORAGE
GROCERIA FRESCA
SODA
LUIGI'S AUTO

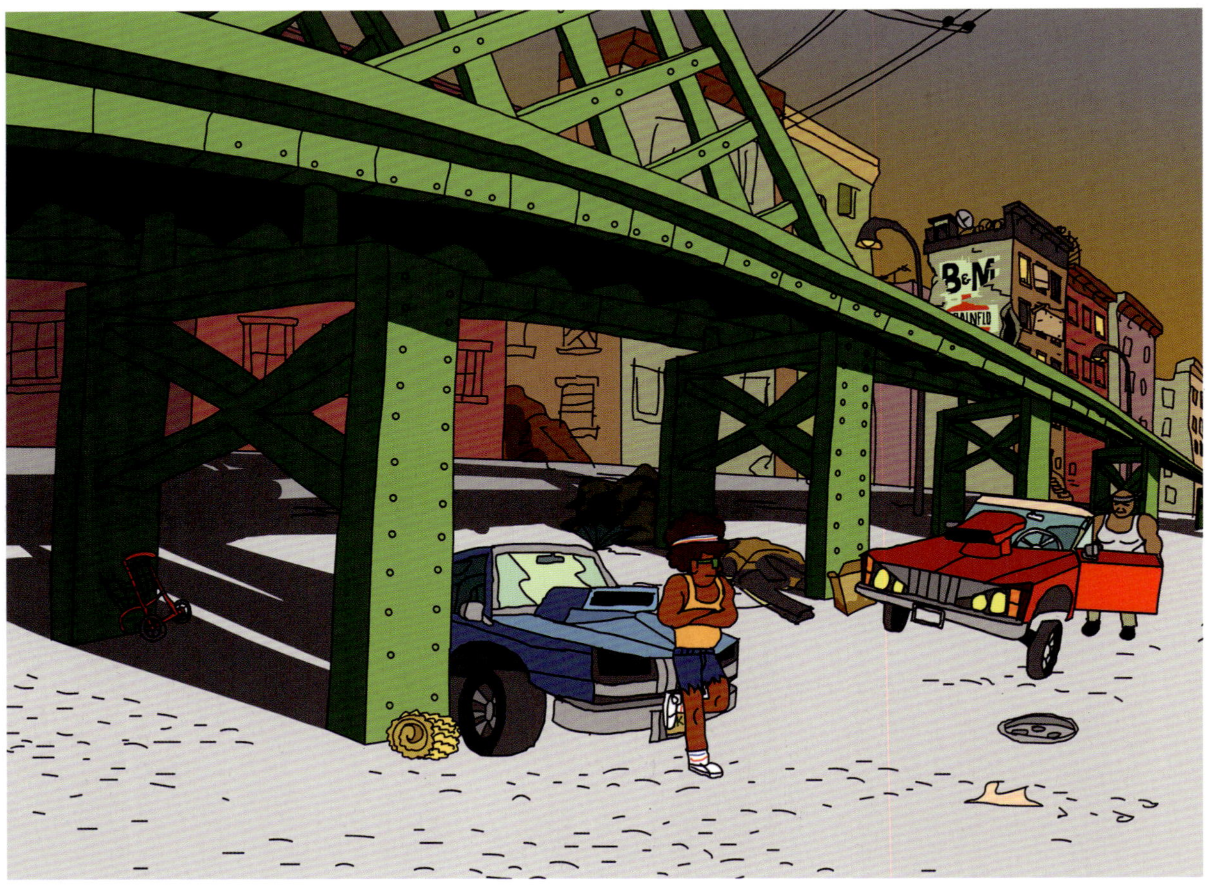

B&M

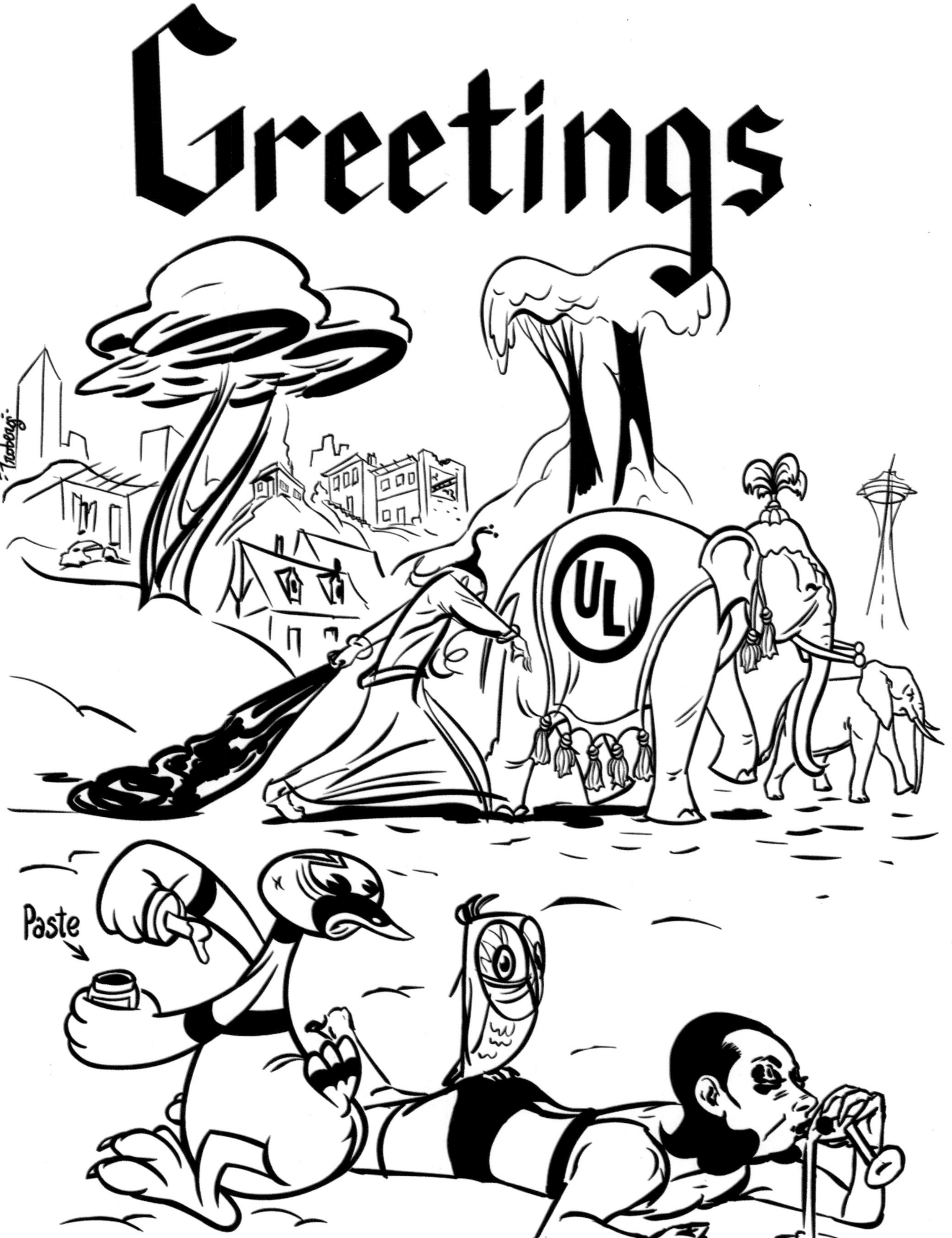

Greetings